THE STORY OF LAW

The Story of Law

SECOND EDITION

John Maxcy Zane

INTRODUCTION BY

JAMES M. BECK

NEW FOREWORD, ANNOTATIONS,

AND BIBLIOGRAPHIES BY

CHARLES J. REID, JR.

Liberty Fund

INDIANAPOLIS

This book is published by Liberty Fund, Inc., a foundation established
to encourage study of the ideal of a society of free and responsible individuals.

〖✳〗𒍢𒀀𒈦

The cuneiform inscription that serves as our logo and as the design motif
for our endpapers is the earliest-known written appearance of the word
"freedom" *(amagi)*, or "liberty." It is taken from a clay document written
about 2300 B.C. in the Sumerian city-state of Lagash.

Originally published in 1927 by Ives Washburn, Inc., New York

Illustrations from Corbis-Bettmann.

02 01 00 99 98 C 5 4 3 2 1
02 01 00 99 98 P 5 4 3 2 1

Library of Congress Cataloging-in-Publication Data

Zane, John Maxcy, 1863–1937.
The story of law / by John Maxcy Zane ; new foreword, annotations, and
bibliographies by Charles J. Reid, Jr.—2nd ed
p. cm.
Includes bibliographical references (p.) and index
ISBN 0-86597-190-0 (hardcover : alk. paper).—ISBN 0-86597-191-9
(pbk. : alk. paper)
1. Law—History. I. Title.
K150.Z36 1998
340´ .09—dc21   97-41097

Liberty Fund, Inc.,
8335 Allison Pointe Trail, Suite 300
Indianapolis, IN 46250-1687

CONTENTS

ILLUSTRATIONS

"It is the most original book in the English language on comparative law since Sir Henry Maine's great work sixty years ago. It is the richest canvas, if not the only one of its kind, yet produced." So wrote Dean John Henry Wigmore of the Northwestern University School of Law in his review of John M. Zane's *The Story of Law* when it first appeared in 1927. Wigmore, one of the most distinguished legal scholars of his time, appreciated Zane's unique contribution to legal history; for here was the first complete outline story of how law came into existence, developed, and changed through the ages, and why it plays such a prominent part in our lives today.

John Zane was not, however, an isolated genius. He was, rather, part of an age that treasured legal history in a way that the present age does not. *The Story of Law* appeared near the close of a period of enormous creativity. The nineteenth century had witnessed the flowering of two new ways of understanding legal history. The first was associated with a relatively new school of jurisprudence, historical jurisprudence, founded by Carl Friedrich von Savigny, which challenged the premises of natural lawyers and positivists alike. Historical jurisprudes argued that the law was neither the concrete expression of transcendent norms, as the natural lawyers contended, nor the product of sovereign command or toleration, as the positivists asserted. Rather, they claimed, law must be understood as the unique product of particular nations' backgrounds and cultures. It was the lawyer's task, according to this school of thought, to look to the past to identify principles consistent with a given nation's culture which could be used to resolve contemporary problems. The lawgiver who failed to understand his nation's tradition and relied upon reason or political will alone to promulgate laws was inevitably doomed to failure.

The roots of this new jurisprudence are traceable to such great seventeenth-century English lawyers as Sir Edward Coke, Sir John Selden, and Sir Matthew Hale, who deployed historical arguments both to restrict monarchical powers by appeal to a historically rooted constitution and to explain the paradox of a legal system that changed over the centuries yet remained the same system. But Coke, Selden, and Hale wrote against the backdrop of a unified and transnational European legal culture—called by many contemporary legal historians the *ius commune* —and in the context of a larger European jurisprudence that had successfully integrated natural law, positivism, and historical reasoning. The late eighteenth and early nineteenth centuries, nevertheless, witnessed the destruction of the *ius commune* and the severe weakening of an integrated understanding of the law under the assault of the nationalist impulse to exalt the law-making power of the state and the rationalist desire to reform traditional practices and institutions.[1]

Historical jurisprudence, as it developed during the course of the nineteenth century, rejected the rationalism of the reformers, substituting for it the history of the nation and the proper understanding of its "spirit" *(Volksgeist)*. Large numbers of historians, moved by the desire to trace the growth of their national legal systems, scoured the past to identify uniquely French or German or Italian or English elements, thereby shredding the wholeness of the old *ius commune.*

The second approach to the writing of legal history that blossomed in the nineteenth century was an offshoot of a particular kind of belief in the progress of humankind. In the eighteenth and nineteenth centuries, this faith came to acquire a peculiarly scientific cast: It came to be presumed that all of human development must have followed the same trajectory and that the organization and structure of primitive societies

1. See Harold J. Berman, "The Origins of Historical Jurisprudence: Coke, Selden, Hale," *Yale Law Journal* 103 (1994): 1651–1738.

might therefore be taken as evidence of the ways in which all persons must at one time have lived. The belief that societies grew in stages which could be labelled as more or less advanced led in turn to an effort to employ all of the skills of the scientist to classify and categorize and thereby discover the basic rules by which those stages developed. This basic concern also moved many of the leading legal historians of the time to look to non-Western societies in an attempt to discern within them the stages of legal development and the rules that governed their emergence, their flourishing, and their inevitable senescence.[2]

The great historians of the age, naturally, were able to draw on these twin tendencies for insights but were not limited by them. In the English tradition, Sir Frederic Maitland, Sir Frederick Pollock, and Sir William Holdsworth sought to describe the development of English legal institutions, although they were all mindful that English law was not the product of purely insular forces but shared in a much deeper Western legal tradition. Other historians proposed an evolutionary understanding of the whole of legal development. Thus, Sir Henry Sumner Maine argued that all legal development in the progressive societies of the West should be understood as a movement from status to contract—from collectivism, in other words, to individualism—while Sir Paul Vinogradoff set out to describe the development of law as the gradual elaboration and systematization of popular customary practices. Other scholars—whose names and works can be found in the annotated bibliography—wrote general outlines of the history of law, tracing its growth from the first stone tablets of Mesopotamia to the sophisticated efforts of contemporary lawyers to subject human life on a global scale to the rule of law.

The Story of Law was published as this outpouring of scholarship was drawing to a close. In a sense, this work stands as a sort of late summer harvest, collecting and winnowing the best of that which had gone before. Layer by layer, Zane re-creates the gradual growth and elaboration of the law from the first attempts of neolithic man to regulate his

---

2. See John W. Burrow, *Evolution and Society: A Study in Victorian Social Theory* (Cambridge: Cambridge University Press, 1966), especially pp. 137–78 (discussing the application of this new method to legal history); see also Krishan Kumar, "Maine and the Theory of Progress," in Alan Diamond, ed., *Sir Henry Maine: A Centennial Reappraisal* (Cambridge: Cambridge University Press, 1991), pp. 76–87.

living arrangements to recent times. Widely and deeply read, he drew judiciously upon his predecessors. One can detect the influence of Maine, Maitland, Vinogradoff, and others in the pages of this work.

But this work also stands as a monument to a now lost heroic age of lawyering. In the second half of the twentieth century, the kind of panoramic vision Zane's contemporaries took for granted has been kept alive by only a few historians. In the United States, Harold Berman has boldly defended the integrity of the Western legal tradition, contending that it has had a continuous existence from the eleventh century to the present, although its continued survival is grievously threatened.[3] Judge John Noonan, for his part, has examined the elaboration of the belief that justice should be uncorrupted by special favor or partisanship from Mesopotamian beginnings,[4] while Brian Tierney has identified a Western constitutional order with deep roots in the eleventh and twelfth centuries.[5] Alan Watson, whose career has bridged both the United States and Great Britain, has written systematically on Roman law and a number of other important questions.[6] In England, John H. Baker, S. F. C. Milsom, and the late T. F. T. Plucknett have examined comprehensively the growth of English law,[7] while on the Continent, Manlio Bellomo, Helmut Coing, and Jean Gaudemet have explored the essential unity of European—and by extension Western—legal history.[8]

John Zane has much to offer a new generation of readers. Unlike the legal positivists, he believed passionately in the transcendent importance

3. See Harold J. Berman, *Law and Revolution: The Formation of the Western Legal Tradition* (Cambridge: Harvard University Press, 1983).

4. See John T. Noonan, Jr., *Bribes* (New York: Macmillan, 1984).

5. See Brian Tierney, *Religion, Law, and the Growth of Constitutional Thought, 1150–1650* (Cambridge: Cambridge University Press, 1982).

6. Watson's contributions to legal history are reviewed in the bibliography.

7. See John H. Baker, *An Introduction to English Legal History*, 3d ed. (London: Butterworths, 1990); S. F. C. Milsom, *Historical Foundations of the Common Law*, 2d ed. (London: Butterworths, 1980); and T. F. T. Plucknett, *A Concise History of the Common Law*, 5th ed. (Boston: Little, Brown, 1956).

8. See Manlio Bellomo, *The Common Legal Past of Europe, 1000–1800* (Washington, D.C.: Catholic University of America Press, 1995); Helmut Coing, *Europäisches Rechtsgeschichte*, 2 vols. (Munich: C. H. Beck, 1985–89); and Jean Gaudemet, *Église et cité: Histoire du droit canonique* (Paris: Montchrestien, 1994).

that legal history has for the practice of law. Only by knowing the history and principles of the law could one become a truly great lawyer. That was because the law was, for Zane, a much deeper phenomenon than simply the particular pronouncements of a court or legislature. Indeed, the sovereign instruments of government were themselves bound to obey the law. The most these bodies could hope to achieve was to discover the law through a deep search of the past and a sympathetic understanding of present needs.

Zane's Legal Career

John Zane was born on March 26, 1863, in Springfield, Illinois, into a family with deep affinities for law and politics. His father, Charles Schuster Zane, had been active in Republican Party circles beginning in the late 1850s and had replaced Abraham Lincoln in the law firm of Lincoln and Herndon in March 1861, when Lincoln left Illinois to take the oath of office as the newly elected President of the United States. Charles Zane's wife, Margaret Maxcy Zane, was a niece of William Herndon, the other named partner in the Lincoln and Herndon firm and an important early Lincoln biographer.

The younger John Zane was a precocious student who mastered Latin and law French even before his adolescence. It seems as well that he had developed an abiding interest in the history of law at an early age. Thus the memorial to Zane in the *Chicago Bar Record* declares:

> It is related that when [Zane] was a boy at Springfield he used to delight in reading in the Supreme Court Library the old English Year Books; this extraordinary linguistic proficiency attracted the attention of Justice John Scholfield who, regretting his own inability to read the strange language of those tomes, asked the boy why he read them, and the answer was that he wanted to know the story of the law.[9]

Zane completed his undergraduate education at the University of Michigan in 1884, and, like his father, chose to take up the study of the law. Earlier that same year, the elder Zane had been appointed chief justice of the Federal Territorial Court in Utah, and John chose to relocate

9. "John M. Zane," *Chicago Bar Record* 19 (1938): 165.

to Salt Lake City to be with his family. John received an appointment as a clerk in the territorial court and commenced to read the law with his father. Reading the law with an established practitioner was then a common means of legal education.

John was admitted to the bar in 1888 and spent a total of eleven years, from 1888 to 1899, engaged in the practice of law in Utah. He distinguished himself especially as an appellate advocate, arguing, among other cases, a leading mining case, an early women's suffrage case, and an important anti-polygamy case.[10]

By the late 1890s, John Zane had established himself as one of the most important lawyers in Utah. He took a leading role in what was first the territorial and subsequently became the State Bar Association, and published his first academic article, a careful analysis of the language of the state constitution as finally ratified.[11] But already John Zane's Utah days were drawing to a close. He was preparing to move back to his native Illinois—not to Springfield, however, but to Chicago.

Chicago in 1900 was Carl Sandburg's "city with broad shoulders," full of swagger and promise. The Columbian Exposition of 1893 was still fresh in people's minds, and Chicago had already acquired for itself the nickname "the Windy City"—not for any meteorological phenomena but rather for the outspoken boosterism of its political classes. John Zane had affiliated himself with what became the firm of Shope, Mathis,

---

10. The mining case was *Wasatch Mining Company v. Crescent Mining Company,* 7 Utah 8 (1890). This case was heard twice by the United States Supreme Court, although John Zane took no part in its appeal. See *Wasatch Mining Company v. Crescent Mining Company,* 148 U.S. 293 (1893); *Crescent Mining Company v. Wasatch Mining Company,* 151 U.S. 317 (1894). The women's suffrage case was *Anderson v. Tyree,* 12 Utah 129 (1895). Zane took the position in this case that the Utah Enabling Act, which established the ground rules by which Utah was to be admitted to the Union, had abrogated prior territorial law conferring a broad suffrage on women. The anti-polygamy case was *Cope v. Cope,* 7 Utah 63 (1890), in which Zane argued that federal law prohibited children born of wives other than the first in polygamous unions from taking under territorial inheritance laws. This case was also appealed to the United States Supreme Court, which agreed with Zane's position, although Zane did not argue the appeal. See *Cope v. Cope,* 137 U.S. 682 (1891).

11. See John Maxcy Zane, "The Constitution of Utah," *Report of the Third Annual Meeting of the State Bar Association of Utah* 18–39 (1896).

Zane, and Weber,[12] and, in a Chicago sort of way, he announced his
arrival with the publication of a major treatise on banking law, a book the
compendious title to which—*The Law of Banks and Banking, Including
Acceptance, Demand, and Notice of Dishonor Upon Commercial Paper*—
was quickly abbreviated to *Zane on Banks and Banking*.[13]

The book evidences both Zane's enthusiasm for history and his technical mastery of the law of banking. In his prefatory note, he expressed
the wish that his book "be of use not only to lawyers, but also to bankers."[14] The introduction reveals Zane at his most magisterial, deftly tracing the origin of Anglo-American banking law to English theories of
bailment, trusteeship, and agency, and proposing to criticize courts that
failed to understand the historical roots of the concepts they all too
clumsily deployed. Bracton, Thomas More, and Francis Bacon, among
others, felicitously adorn these pages. Zane then proceeded to set out the
substantive law of banking in 852 densely written pages.

The treatise was unevenly received by reviewers, although this may
have been more the product of the author's difficult personality than of
a fair assessment of the book's strengths and weaknesses.[15] In any event,
the book was well received by bench and bar. It appears in the reported
arguments of counsel before the United States Supreme Court and was

12. Simeon P. Shope, one of the named partners, had formerly served as a justice of the
Illinois Supreme Court. Zane would eventually leave the Shope firm and practice as the lead
partner of several firms: Zane, Busby, and Weber; Zane, Morse, McKinney, and McIlvaine;
and Zane and Norman. Harold Norman, Zane's final law partner, practised with him from
1920 to 1937 and remained a fixture on the Chicago legal scene until the late 1970s.

13. See John Maxcy Zane, *The Law of Banks and Banking, Including Demand and
Notice of Dishonor Upon Commercial Paper* (Chicago: T. H. Flood, 1900).

14. Ibid., p. 3.

15. The reviewer for the *American Law Register* declared: "This work, we can safely
assert, is more than a restatement of the law of banking. It is a very thorough treatise
upon the theory underlying that law. The author is a forceful and original thinker; and,
while he admits that not all his doctrines are in accord with authority, they are well
defended in the text." See "Book Review: Banks and Banking," *American Law Register*
48 (1900): 563. The reviewer for the *American Law Review*, on the other hand, took Zane
to task for attempting to do too much in one book, and, in an ironic passage, stated that
despite a literary style that the reviewer found obscure and disagreeable in the extreme,
Zane "generally succeeds in setting the courts right." See "Book Review: Zane on Banks
and Banking," *American Law Review* 34 (1900): 638, 639.

frequently cited as authority for over four decades by both federal and state courts.[16]

Zane would spend the remainder of his career in Chicago, engaged for the most part in the practice of law, teaching only briefly at the Northwestern University School of Law and the University of Chicago. The heart of Zane's legal work was patent, trademark, and commercial law, and, indeed, one can trace the history of industrializing America in some of the patent and trademark cases which Zane litigated.[17] But Zane handled other types of cases as well, including actions under the antitrust laws, eminent-domain proceedings, and constitutional challenges to the authority of government to regulate industry.[18] Over the course of twenty-four years, beginning in 1912, Zane argued a total of six cases before the United States Supreme Court.[19]

But Zane did not neglect scholarship. He maintained the sort of life

16. The last reported citation of Zane's treatise occurs in 1943. See *Bromberg v. Bank of America National Trust and Savings Association*, 58 Cal.App. 2d 1, 135 P.2d. 689 (1943).

17. See, for example, *Carson Investment Company v. Anaconda Copper Mining*, 26 F.2d 651 (9th Cir., 1928) (involving patents on furnaces for the smelting of copper and other ore); *General Motors Corporation v. Swan Carburetor Company*, 88 F.2d 876 (6th Cir., 1937), cert. den., 302 U.S. 691 (1937) (involving patents on automotive manifolds and carburetors); *Motor Improvements, Inc. v. A.C. Sparkplug Company*, 80 F.2d 385 (1935), cert. den., *A.C. Sparkplug Company v. Motor Improvements, Inc.*, 298 U.S. 671 (1936) (involving patents on automotive oil filters); *Bell and Howell Company v. Bliss*, 262 F. 131 (7th Cir., 1919) (involving patents on film production equipment); *General Motors Corporation v. Blackmore*, 52 F.2d 725 (6th Cir., 1931) (involving patents on curtain rods for automobile touring cars); *Bird v. Elaborated Roofing of Buffalo*, 256 F. 366 (2d Cir., 1919) (involving patents on chemically treated roofing materials); *Keystone Driller Company v. Byers Machinery Company*, 4 F.Supp. 548 (N.D., Ohio, 1929) (involving patents on an excavating shovel capable of breaking through shale and sandstone); and *Chicago Flexible Shaft Company v. Katz Drug Company*, 72 F.2d 548 (3d Cir., 1934) (involving the "Mixmaster" kitchen appliance trademark).

18. See *Tilden v. Quaker Oats Company*, 1 F.2d. 160 (7th Cir., 1924) (antitrust); *Burke v. Sanitary District of Chicago*, 32 F.2d 27 (7th Cir., 1929), cert. den., *Burke v. Sanitary District of Chicago*, 280 U.S. 585 (1929) (eminent domain); *Parker, Webb, and Company v. Austin*, 156 Mich. 573, 121 N.W. 322 (1909) (constitutional challenge to administrative power).

19. See *Swanson v. Sears*, 224 U.S. 180 (1912) (a mining case); *Wabash Railroad Company v. Hayes*, 234 U.S. 86 (1914) (a workers' compensation case); *Board of Com-*

that has become seemingly impossible in today's age of specialization: that of advocate scholar. Beginning with an article on mining law that appeared in the *Harvard Law Review* in 1902, he published important articles in leading journals for the next three decades. He also published works on classical Rome and Roman law and Abraham Lincoln's constitutional theory, in addition to *The Story of Law* and his treatise on banking law. With Carl Zollmann, he also prepared in 1923 the ninth edition of *Bishop on Criminal Law*, a basic legal treatise that had been in print since the 1850s.[20]

In his later years, Zane threw himself passionately into the Chicago literary scene. He had been a member of the Caxton Club since 1916, and in 1928 he was elected its president.[21] Zane's election occurred at a particularly fateful time. The stock market crash of 1929 devastated the membership, and Zane was called upon to keep the club alive. The Caxton Club's history records that he performed this task with admirable success. He convinced many members to rescind their resignations and devised a variety of expedients to keep the club active despite its desperate financial state, such as luncheon gatherings that featured outstanding public speakers on important issues of the day. Correspondence in the club's archives indicates the extent of Zane's efforts to keep

---

missioners of the City and County of Denver v. Home Savings Bank, 236 U.S. 101 (1915) (a municipal bond case); *Toledo Scale Company v. Computing Scale Company*, 261 U.S. 399 (1923) (patent case over rights to a new type of scale); *Reinecke v. Spalding*, 280 U.S. 227 (1930) (taxability of income derived from mining activity); *Pick Manufacturing v. General Motors Corporation*, 299 U.S. 3 (1936) (challenge under the Clayton Act to the relationship between automobile manufacturers and dealers).

20. Joel Bishop, the author of *Bishop on Criminal Law*, was one of the most important of the nineteenth-century treatise writers, although he is barely remembered today. The foundations of his scholarship are reviewed in Stephen A. Siegel, "Joel Bishop's Orthodoxy," *Law and History Review* 13 (1995) 215–59. Carl Zollmann was one of the more prolific treatise writers of the first half of the twentieth century, producing major works on banking law and aviation law.

21. Named for William Caxton, who in 1475 produced the first printed books in England, the Caxton Club is a Chicago-based club of bibliophiles that has served both as a gathering place for book lovers and as a publisher of limited edition books of especially high quality. On the Caxton Club, see Frank J. Piehl, *The Caxton Club, 1895–1995: Celebrating a Century of the Book in Chicago* (Chicago: Caxton Club, 1995).

the club solvent. When the club published his work on Lincoln's constitutional thought, Zane felt it necessary to indemnify the club against any risk of financial loss.[22]

Zane remained active until the very end of his life. He continued to litigate and was reelected president of the Caxton Club in 1937, at the age of seventy-four. His final paper, "Oratory Is No More," delivered before the Chicago Literary Club in April 1937, is a stirring reminiscence, drawn from classical sources such as Cicero and Quintilian, and more recent sources such as Edmund Burke, of the qualities of good oratory and a lament that mass democratic movements and new technologies such as the radio have destroyed the orator and replaced him with the demagogue.[23] John Zane died unexpectedly on December 6, 1937, while visiting Pasadena, California.

An Appreciation

To appreciate *The Story of Law,* it is important to bear in mind that this work is not—and indeed cannot be—a comprehensive history, and that Zane was forced to employ principles of selection in determining what was to be included within his story. To say this is not to detract from the significance of Zane's accomplishment. *The Story of Law* remains uniquely valuable as a learned and highly readable account of the shaping of Western law from the Neolithic age to the dawn of the twentieth century.

We are fortunate in having Zane's own statement on the principles he used in selecting what went into the telling of *The Story of Law.* In a letter to John Wigmore in January 1928, Zane stated:

> I do not claim that it is a history of law in general, but it is an attempt to show the great formative elements that determined why law *is what it is among us* [emphasis in original]. To compress the matter within reasonable

22. Memorandum of agreement by John M. Zane, dated April 21, 1932. I am grateful to Frank J. Piehl and Brother Michael Grace, S.J., both of the Caxton Club, for information concerning this aspect of John Zane's career.

23. "Oratory Is No More" remains unpublished. A manuscript can be found in the Newberry Library of Chicago.

limits, it was necessary to disregard all the systems of law that do not belong in this direct development. I took the original primeval man, followed him through the great formative institutions that make the great heads of law, then took the Aryan with his developments among the Celts and Gauls and the Hindus, then passed to the contributions of the Semites, Babylonian and Jewish, then showed the original Aryan, Greek, then the Roman, and thence by the mediaeval feudal system to the English. Necessarily I left out the Egyptian, and the Hellenistic law after Justinian, where I could have done much with the Basilicata, but this system was too late. I also left out the Spanish, French, and German developments, because I was sticking to the trunk of the genealogical tree and then following the English limb. But what I kept in mind was private law as between man and man and the legal rules and institutions through which one citizen obtains his rights against another citizen. So when I reached the English law I did not pay much attention to the genesis of the political institutions except as they were purely conceived with the production, the modification, and the application of private law. When I reached our legal development I changed to constitutional law, for the reason that we have the unique development by which in a private lawsuit, a machinery is furnished which makes constitutional law binding in private litigation. This I say is the Reign of an Absolute Law. Perhaps I should have explained this for the benefit of the ordinary reader, but I felt sure that he would catch the drift of the book on its general lines.[24]

Chapter by chapter, Zane unravels the evolution of law in Western civilization. He stresses that the historian must always bear in mind that the development of law is necessarily related to fundamental "social facts."[25] Philosophers especially tend to forget the relationship between law and society, with disastrous consequences.

To a degree unusual but welcome among legal historians, Zane emphasizes the development of commerce as an integral part of the story of the law. The contributions of Babylon, Greece, and Rome to the

---

24. Letter of John M. Zane to John H. Wigmore, January 14, 1928, Wigmore Papers, Northwestern University School of Law.

25. For Zane's theory of law generally and the role that social facts play in his legal thinking, see his essay "German Legal Philosophy," *Michigan Law Review* 16 (1918): 287–375.

early history of commercial law are all reviewed here. Commerce is the main source of peace and progress in the world, and lawyers who promote its steady development are performing a public service. The English are especially praised for their integrity in dealing honestly even with their enemies: "[We are reminded] that during our Revolutionary War certain shares of Bank of England stock stood in the name of Washington, who was in arms against the English government, yet all through that war the dividends upon that bank stock were regularly paid to the commander of the army of rebellious Americans. Washington was a rebel in arms against England but the Bank of England was a commercial institution and here as always the honesty instituted by trade is far superior to any other conception of honest conduct."

It is to be regretted, however, that Zane placed little emphasis on the role religious thought played in shaping Western legal principles and institutions. His story is for the most part a secular one, its heroes consisting of urbane Roman lawyers and largely secularized Englishmen and Americans. As recent scholarship has shown, however, the canon lawyers of the twelfth through fifteenth centuries made an enormous contribution to the history of Western law.[26] Indeed, it has been convincingly argued that a distinctively Western law was only born in 1075 in the course of a "Papal Revolution" led by Pope Gregory VII against the domination of the Church by the Emperor Henry IV.[27] It was at that time that lawyers in attendance at the papal and imperial courts began to rework older sources into coherent claims of legal right on behalf of their patrons.

Similarly, Zane ignores the contributions of Protestant lawyers, whether in Lutheran Germany or in England in the mid-seventeenth century. But the Lutherans gave to the West a new emphasis on the Ten Commandments as a source of natural-law reasoning as well as new methods for organizing the law, while deeply devout Protestant lawyers such as Sir Matthew Hale (1609–76)—whom Zane dismisses in a few lines because of his participation in witch trials—contributed to the shaping of a new English legal philosophy that stressed continuity with

---

26. See James A. Brundage, *Medieval Canon Law* (London: Longman, 1995).
27. See Berman, *Law and Revolution, supra,* note 3.

the past, an adversary system of presenting evidence, and new standards of proof drawn from the scientific methods of Robert Boyle and other members of the Royal Society.[28]

It has now been seventy years since John Zane published his *Story of Law*. Notwithstanding the passage of time, additional research, and newly discovered documents, his account remains in general a highly accurate picture of the development of the law. Of course, every specialist can think of certain matters important to the development of a particular line of inquiry that were omitted, underemphasized, or perhaps given too much weight. But in the light of his bold and far-reaching commission, Zane executed his assignment admirably.

28. See Harold J. Berman and John Witte, Jr., "The Transformation of Western Legal Philosophy in Lutheran Germany," *Southern California Law Review* 62 (1989): 1575–1660 (discussing the development of a new type of natural-law reasoning); Harold J. Berman and Charles J. Reid, Jr., "Roman Law in Europe and the Jus Commune: A Historical Overview with an Emphasis on the New Legal Science of the Sixteenth Century," *Syracuse Journal of Law and Commerce* 20 (1994): 1–31 (discussing the Lutheran development of a topical method by which to organize the law); Harold J. Berman and Charles J. Reid, Jr., "The Transformation of English Legal Science: From Hale to Blackstone," *Emory Law Journal* 45 (1996): 437–522 (examining the various components of the new English science in the seventeenth and eighteenth centuries). See also Berman, "Origins of Historical Jurisprudence," *supra*, note 1.

INTRODUCTION

If "GOOD WINE NEEDS NO BUSH" and a good play, no prologue —and both assertions have the high authority of Shakespeare—then a good book is also its own justification. Hence my hesitation in writing an introduction for "The Story of Law." It needs none, and any attempt to interest the thoughtful reader in a work which will grip his fascinated interest from its initial chapter runs the danger of being "wasteful and ridiculous excess."

The subject matter is of enthralling interest, and it seems strange that so few attempts have hitherto been made to tell the story of law for the benefit of the general reader. The book is opportune, for one of the gratifying signs of recent times has been the reaction in the field of literature from the trivial and ephemeral to the serious and permanent. A few years ago it had seemed to some of us—paradoxical as such a conclusion was —that the age of expanding science and wider vision had resulted, with the average man, in an unprecedented dulling of the imagination and an unusual preference for the trivial and unimportant. I devoted the last four chapters of my book on the Constitution of the United States to the thesis that the evil of our generation was the loss of any true sense of the values of human life, and until recent years I had little occasion to modify this pessimistic conclusion. A few years ago it would have seemed improbable that books like Wells' "Outline of History" or Durant's "Story of Philosophy" could ever be among the season's best sellers. On the contrary, the book of which one could safely make such a prophecy would be the latest literary garbage. The age of the "moving picture" brain apparently asked nothing to satisfy its mental hunger than mental impressions as effervescent as a passing picture upon the cinema screen.

Then came a remarkable reaction, and the books that were among the best sellers were those which not only dealt with serious and difficult subjects, but attempted to cover the whole field of human development. How else can one explain the extraordinary success of Durant's "Story of Philosophy," which restates the mystical, and at times incomprehensible, speculations of great philosophers of all times?

If a book on philosophy can thus prove a best seller, how much more should a book on the history of the law, for the law is the concrete realization of philosophy. It is the synthesis of all the speculations of the ages as to the rules of human conduct, imposed in order to protect, not merely society as an organism, but the individual, from evil.

Moreover, the law is the microcosmic history of humanity. This book discloses the long wearisome climb of man through the ages to the heights which he now occupies, and from which he is ceaselessly pressing forward to even loftier summits of human achievement. The law concerns every human being. It is always with us, and directs the path of our destiny from the cradle to the grave. Even after we have joined the great majority, it is the law that determines what disposition shall be made of the property of one who no longer lives to protect his rights, and who, being dead, can have no rights.

Moreover, the law is identified with the whole history of human progress, and especially the progress of political society, as successive generations of man have walked with bleeding feet their *via dolorosa* from slavery to freedom. The dramatic episodes of history are generally connected with the law, and to every citizen who loves his country the events which have the greatest appeal are within the scope of this book. Our American epic struggle for independence was to vindicate an unwritten law as to the right of taxation, and no episode in our history is of greater dramatic interest and more creditable to the American people than the ability of the Fathers in a time of anarchy to meet in high convention, and, after discussing the fundamentals of human society for over four months, to draft a comprehensive charter of Government.

If this book is fortunate in its subject matter, it is doubly fortunate in its author, and here the writer of this introduction may justifiably indulge in a feeling of satisfaction. The publisher did me the compliment to ask me to suggest some American lawyer to write this book. I had some familiarity with the outstanding men of the American Bar. As Solicitor General of the United States for four years, I had occasion to meet distinguished living members of the American Bar from all sections of the country. To be asked to suggest the name of one of them was a task at once delicate and difficult. The difficulty lay in the curious fact that few lawyers are philosophers, and still fewer philosophers are lawyers. The reason is obvious. Philosophy deals with the abstract and law with the concrete, and while every lawyer ought to understand the philosophical basis of the law, he generally finds both his time and energies fully employed in determining what the law is, and he thus has little time for its philosophical justification. *"Sic ita Lex"* is the spirit in which he pursues his daily tasks, for he has little time or disposition to ask whether the law is a good one or a bad one. It is enough that it is the law, which the Courts will presumably enforce, and he must reckon with reality and not the abstract.

On the other hand, the philosopher, living in the rarefied atmosphere of abstract speculation, has little opportunity to study the practical problems of human laws in concrete application. It is for this reason, I suppose, that the most learned theorizers on the subject of the law, the learned professors in our law schools, neither have, nor have had, much practical experience in the administration of the law, and, on the other hand, the successful practitioner, who is confined to realities, has too often scant knowledge of the history of the law and its purely philosophical justification, and his attitude to it is a narrowly pragmatic one.

My task, therefore, was to suggest someone who was both a practical lawyer and a true philosopher, and if there be many such at the American Bar, the writer has yet to know them.

Even more was required, if this important book was to be worthy of its exalted subject. It required a lawyer who not only had a great gift of lucid expression, but that fine imagination which enables the deep thinker to convey his ideas to minds of a different caliber. Doubtless there were some philosophers at the Bar who could have written very learnedly on the subject, but whose treatment would have been obscure to the ordinary mind and of the dry-as-dust school of history. Others might have had the requisite clarity in expression, and yet they would lack that fine gift of imagination which makes the true teacher and enables him by charm of direction and telling analogy to hold the attention of readers to a subject which would not ordinarily attract their interest or enlist their sympathies.

The writer of this introduction happily recalled the reading of some legal essays of such unusual learning and clarity of diction that they had lingered in his memory. They were contributed to the Law Journals by a distinguished member of the Chicago Bar, who is the author of this book. I know of no one who so finely united the qualities to which I have referred, and I am sure that the readers of this book will confirm my estimate of its distinguished author's rare qualifications for a very difficult task. I believe I have done the thoughtful readers of this generation a real service in suggesting to the publisher that John M. Zane be invited to expound the history of law to the average man, and I am heartily glad that he consented to do so. Some great jurist once said that every lawyer owes a duty to his profession to write a book, and if so, Mr. Zane has now richly paid his debt, not only to his profession but to the reading public.

He has done so with surprising skill, and I know of no lawyer who could have done it better. Sympathy, imagination, varied knowledge, diction as crystalline clear as a mountain stream, and philosophical insight—all these great qualities are disclosed in these pages. The book is a real contribution to the literature of the day, and it will make its readers, whether lawyers or laymen, better citizens.

THE STORY OF LAW

CHAPTER I
The Physical Basis of Law

ALMOST EVERYONE of ordinary information understands very well what is meant by the word "law," but even the most learned jurists, when called upon to give an accurate definition of the term, find themselves at a loss. No jurist has yet achieved a definition of law that does not require the use of the idea of law, either implied or expressed, as a part of the definition. All will agree that the word in its meaning implies a set both of general principles and of particular rules. Upon law what we call rights are founded, and by it wrongs are forbidden; but if we ask the meaning of the terms "rights" and "wrongs" we simply move around a circle by saying that rights are what are legally recognized as rights and wrongs are what the law defines as wrongs. Thus we get back to the place whence we started.

A celebrated judge in this country has defined law as "a statement of the circumstances in which the public force will be brought to bear through the courts," but this definition makes an immaterial matter the substance of the definition and ignores altogether the idea that a law is a rule.[1] Law would exist without public force applied, for long before there were courts there was a great body of law that a man was bound not to

---

1. The judge is Oliver Wendell Holmes. See *American Banana Company v. United Fruit Company*, 213 U.S. 347, 356 (1909).—C. J. R., Jr.

violate and that was generally obeyed. The fact is that no one can go any further than to say that law is a part, and only a part, of the now large body of rules that govern men in their relations and conduct toward one another in the social organization to which they belong. Even here we must understand that we include rules which govern men in their relations to the social organization under which they live and that among civilized men law is considered to govern the relations of social organizations toward one another. For this latter kind of law we have the term "international law," and its enforcement is not made by any court. Rules of law at different times in the past have covered many more human relations than at other times. Generally speaking, the progress and development of law have been in differentiating rules of living that were of sufficient importance to the social organization to be regarded as law, from other rules, once as potent, that have gradually passed into mere social customs.

It is necessary at the outset to lay stress upon the dominating fact of men having always lived in social organizations. It is possibly conceivable that men might have lived as solitary animals, but if they had done so there would have been no laws. The existence of laws presupposes human beings living in a social complex. The science of law, if there is such a science, is but one of the several sciences that are concerned with men living in a social state. Sociology, ethics, politics, political economy, as well as history, biology and psychology, all have a common ground, for they are all social sciences or have social science aspects. They are all more or less related to each other, and all are necessary to a proper understanding of each science. This truth was happily expressed in the oration of the greatest of Roman advocates for the poet Archias—an oration which, as a whole, reached the highest ground ever attained by a lawyer in a forensic speech. There Cicero said that "all the sciences which pertain to human conduct have a sort of common bond and are related to one another by a kind of kinship in blood."

This fact of living in a social state is the fundamental fact for the history of law. The development of law has been merely one phase of the social development. This legal development has been a wholly natural social process and result, which man could no more have escaped than he could have avoided the compelling force of his physical frame. This truth as to human life having been always a social existence is the basis of Aristotle's famous deduction, "Man is a social animal."

So far as the sciences concerned with humanity give us light, men have always lived in society. This means not in the family, but in some social aggregate larger than the mere family of a male and female or females and children. The ordinary idea of human development has been that the family was the original unit, but, as will appear, the evidence to the contrary is so conclusive that it may be considered as settled that a family life was not developed by men until ages after their advent as animals truly and distinctly human beings, though of a low type of mental development as compared with civilized men. Human animals came out of some lower type of animal with the ways of living of creatures who lived in a herd. Man might have had some other kind of mind than he has, had he not been a social animal, but we must accept another fundamental proposition that man's mind is a social intelligence, and its processes are dictated by the fact that it has been made by the living in a social state and in no other condition. Law is, of course, the result of this socially formed mentality in adapting the race to its physical surroundings, and in striving to overcome those surroundings.

The time has long gone by when one should apologize for running counter to human conceptions that are founded upon human ignorance, inherited prejudice, or crass stupidity. If the purpose were to write a work upon geography, it would not be necessary to begin with an extended demonstration of the sphericity of the earth, although a few centuries ago a man could, with entire legality, have been burned at the stake for asserting such a proposition. Similarly in a work designed to explain the legal aspect of man's life, it must be assumed that human beings in their mental nature, and the laws as products of that nature, are the result of ages of evolutionary development, in spite of the fact that many honest and sincere people believe such teaching to be criminal and despite the fact, also, that in some parts of the United States such teaching has been made in fact a crime. Curiously enough, St. Isidore, who died A.D. 636, lays it down as undoubted truth that "at first men were naked and unarmed and helpless against wild beasts, without any protection against cold, without any way to preserve heat"; and Alcuin (A.D. 735–804), a great churchman, knew enough to say that "there was a time when men wandered like beasts here and there over the earth, without any power of reason whatever."

The story of the law must begin, then, with men as they first were in mind and body countless ages ago. Those original attributes of mind and body, inherited from age to age, practically rule men to–day, though generally in a subconscious or instinctive way. Through those many ages the physical frame of man has remained what it was in the beginning, but his mental development is entitled to be considered the most extraordinary phenomenon of organic life. A celebrated apothegm, originally stated in Latin, says that "in the world there is nothing great but man, and in man there is nothing great but mind." Yet it required many ages to create in man that greatness of intellect, and the expansion of the human intellect is still continuing.

The physical rules that govern our bodily frame are the same to–day that they were in the beginning of mankind, for that physical frame has suffered no change. The laws of generation, birth, nutrition, growth, decay, and death have the inevitability of natural law. Such physical laws are like all other rules which we call natural laws. They are fixed and unalterable by human effort. Violation of those physical laws produces physical results. But human laws have none of the inevitability of natural laws. They may be violated without any physical effect on the violator, for they attempt to make or are a standard of conduct of human beings toward one another. The scientific name given to the knowledge and the doctrine of human laws is "the science of jurisprudence." Law in this sense is commonly supposed to be the result of human reasoning and of conscious purpose. Yet there was a time, before man had developed the mental faculties necessary to produce consciously purposeful laws, when the rules that regulated human conduct in the social state had all the sureness and inevitability of natural law, for the laws existed merely as customary animal reactions to surrounding conditions.

If, to obtain a better perspective in looking at this matter, we should go back to a time preceding the existence of human beings on the earth, we should find ourselves toward the close of the vast geological age that is called the Tertiary. Nature had then completed her highest and most successful experiment, prior to the advent of human kind, in creating miniature animals suited to live upon this earth in a closely knit social community. In such social communities we shall find the analogies that are most suitable to describe men, who began as mere animals and have lived always in social communities of some kind, and have thus produced those rules of social conduct which we call "the laws."

There is an additional reason for beginning the history of the law with man's advent on the earth. Lawyers have never written legal history in a large way. The philosophical histories of the law have been the work of philosophers and metaphysicians, who have succeeded in rendering legal science unintelligible to lawyers and laymen alike. If we begin with man's beginning, we at once get rid of the wildness of metaphysics and the dreaming of philosophy, for that shadowy learning is purely a human mental construction. The world was the same practically that it is to-day just prior to man's coming. That coming added merely another kind of animal who knew neither philosophy nor metaphysics, but who had certain laws.

In the latter part of the Tertiary Age, just prior to man's coming, certain animals had already brought social existence to such a perfection that from a time over a million years ago until the present those animals have not been changed in their habits of life. They had then become, and they still remain, most successfully adapted to conditions. To these animals the Wise Man in Proverbs tells us to go for wisdom: "Go to the ant, thou sluggard, consider her ways and be wise." This is, of course, a commendation of the feverish and unremitting industry of the ant, that is to say, of the female ant. The less said about the male ant's industry, the better. But ants are more than a model for reclaiming the sluggard: Lessons of wisdom in the sphere of law, little dreamed of by the Wise Man, may also be obtained by going to these lowly insects.

It is not paradoxical even to speak of the jurisprudence of ants. They are, indeed, as the great Dramatist says:

> Creatures that by a rule in nature teach
> The act of order to a peopled kingdom.

They have a polity of their own through which their communes exist and prosper under a set of laws which provide for the perpetuation of the society, the care and rearing of the young, and the provision of food by artificial means for the support of the community—a set of laws so successful in operation that ants are by far the most numerous of all the animal inhabitants of the globe and are spread almost as widely as men in climates the most diverse. While not domesticated as are their cousins, the bees, they have been a source of perennial interest. The vast amount of writing upon them, recording in many volumes the results of observation and experiment, enables one to speak with certainty regarding these small creatures. The humor of Mark Twain upon the stupidity of ants cannot be considered valuable in a serious discussion.

I need not comment upon the well-known facts that ants are insects allied to the other Hymenoptera like the bees and wasps; that but one of the community, the queen, produces any progeny; that the community is divided into defined castes of wingless and aborted females, who are the workers, and winged males, who are an idle and worthless class, except as to the one which fertilizes the queen, whereupon the useless herd of drones is killed, submitting to this fate with resignation. The ants select places for building the communal dwelling with great care and judgment in reference to drainage and the nature of the soil. Rooms are provided in the general pueblo, so to speak, for use as nurseries in the rearing of the young as well as for the storage and preservation of food. Two of the notable advances of the human race toward civilization were the domestication of animals and the cultivation of plants, yet the leaf-cutting ants, in rooms provided by them in the communal dwelling, fertilize their darkened fields and cultivate minute plants that furnish a store of food. Likewise the honey ants, who live mainly upon the sweet juices of trees and plants, have their droves of aphides, which live upon and secrete for their ant-owners the sweet saps of trees. These droves are herded and regularly milked by the worker ants. They are in every sense the domesticated animals of the ants.

Then, too, these astonishing ants have learned the lesson of communal sanitation. Personal cleanliness and cleanliness of the dwelling are rigidly enforced among them. They are indefatigible in removing all sorts of litter and refuse of food from their homes. They even harbor beetles, it is said, in their nests, who are kept for the purpose of removing the communal garbage. The homes are regularly closed and sealed each day, and as regularly opened, and sentries are posted for guarding the gates.

Human maintenance of roads is a comparatively late development of civilization. The ants, however, have their made roads stretching from their homes in all directions, which seem to be laid out with care and which they follow in their food or predatory excursions. When, in making a road, they come to a rill of water, they tunnel it in true engineering fashion and maintain the tunnel. The building of a cylindrical arch is a great invention of our race, but the ants were doing it before the lowest type of humanity appeared on this planet. The leaf-cutting ants are ingenious enough to sew leaves together to suit their purposes.

The ants have their predatory instinct against strangers, just as our human race had and still has it. A column of driver ants on the march, devouring every creature they meet, is probably the fiercest carnivorous horde on this globe. A settled tribe of ants has its scouts who, like the scouts who spied out the Promised Land, go forth to look over the land and, when they find a commune of another tribe such as they desire to attack, rush back to the main body of the tribe and make some report; then the army, in a scene of frantic excitement, imitated in our cities when troops go forth to war, begins to form. The whole tribe, except the drones, rushes forth from its dwelling and takes up its march; it arrives at the place of attack, and a sudden savage onslaught is made. The tribe that is attacked fights gallantly for its homes and firesides. The assaulting army of female workers, like the standing army of women of Dahomey or the Amazon bands of Penthesilea on "the windy plain of Troy," fights as gallantly; at last all the warriors of the one tribe are killed, and the young and immature captives are carried away to be nurtured and brought up to increase the slave hordes of the conquerors. This is very like the Athenian conquest of the island of Melos, as related by Thucydides. It is very like the command to the Jews in Deuteronomy: "When the Lord thy God hath delivered it (a city) into thine hands, thou shalt smite every male thereof with the edge of the sword. But the

women, and the little ones and the cattle . . . shalt thou take unto thyself." And such is the primitive law of war everywhere among men.

The maintenance of slaves is probably the most curious anticipation
of the ants. The slave ants are obedient and hard-working; they seem to
be satisfied with their condition and are devoted to their masters. Certain
tribes of ants are perfectly helpless, and depend for their lives upon their
slaves. The ants, of course, instinctively are seeking more workers, and
the origin of slavery among men is precisely the same. Ants have no
weapons, but some of them develop better natural means of attack, for
among ants which have the soldier caste, who have larger heads and more
powerful jaws, there is shown an improved type of "shock troops" who
seem to be irresistible.

As a patriot devoted to her tribe and homeland, the ant is a wonderful creature. She knows no fear; she fights with devoted courage; she is
eager for battle; she hurls herself upon the foe; she never retreats; either
she dies on the field or she never leaves the field until the battle is won.
The ant knows no good for herself as separated from the good of the
community. If service be the test, she is entitled to the highest praise.
She is an indefatigable worker and carries, for her, immense burdens.
Her strength in proportion to her size is prodigious. If the burden is too
heavy for one, two or more unite in the work. Her readiness to sacrifice
herself for the public welfare is amazing.

With the altruistic civic service of the honey ants nothing in human
life can compare. Certain of these workers act as reservoirs for food.
They load themselves with sweet juices until their abdomens are for
their size enormously distended; then they laboriously make their way to
the home, and are helped by other ants up the wall of the room to the
ceiling, and there they cling day in and day out until their store of honey
is required by the society. Coöperation for the public good is the absolute
law of ant life, and this law is scrupulously obeyed. But at the same time
this intensity of communal life and feeling results among ants, as it often
has resulted among men, in a bitter hostility toward all stranger ants. We
have seen how remorseless they are in sacking the home of another community and in reducing its dwellers to slavery. Many an experiment has
shown that stranger ants introduced into an ant community are at once
set upon and killed.

It is a commonplace of observation of ants that the peculiarity of this organized community is that there is no apparent organization. Each individual seems to act on his own initiative, without directions or orders. There are no superiors or inferiors. The ideal of absolute equality reigns. There is no overlord, no standing army, no officers, no privates. There is a most effective government, but there are no governors. The varied and complicated facts of government in a great ant-city, its home-making, home-guarding, home-nurturing, its building of roads, storerooms, nurseries, and vast structures that, proportionately to the size of ants, are equal to great centers of human population, the gathering and distribution of supplies, the cultivation and storing of crops, the keeping of herds, waging of war, and utilizing of captives, are carried out with perfect regularity. The laws are self-enforced, are apparently never violated, and this work goes on with the regularity and precision of an automatic machine, "without guide, overseer or ruler." Ants have lived under their laws so long that they have become perfectly fitted to them, and even the time for closing the gates requires no warning sound of a curfew. Is it not plain that ants can live and work without direction or guide because, acting by instinct, they all act precisely alike?

It cannot be denied that this experiment of Nature is, to the extent that it has gone or can go, perfectly successful. The ants have certainly a considerable degree of what we usually call intelligence. And this is so with many other animals. A herd of musk-oxen in the frozen north, when it hears the hungry cry of a band of wolves, throws itself into battle array. The bulls face outward in a circle, standing shoulder to shoulder and presenting a ring of menacing horns to the foe. The cows and calves are all protected inside the barrier of menacing horns. It seems difficult to distinguish this conduct of musk-oxen from that of a wagon train of emigrants, let us say in 1850, crossing the western plains in the United States. When an Indian attack was impending, the wagons were arranged in a circle with the human beings, the horses and cattle inside the circle. These two performances differ little in intelligence. The musk-oxen are certainly acting with just as much intelligent coöperation as the human beings. The performances of the domesticated dog or the horse betray often the highest intelligence. The amazing communal life and engineering skill and discrimination of the beavers are reserved for later illustration. Similarly, the ant, when it decides to tunnel a stream or to select its home, acts with much intelligent judgment.

It is apparent that the laws of social organization of the ant are suited only to a natural condition where the young are produced by the one ant queen. The workers are all infertile, aborted females. The drones are killed at once after the queen has taken her nuptial flight. No possible dissensions in the community can arise like those of the bulls or stags or stallions fighting over the cows or does or mares. Nor can any question arise over property, for all the property connected with the community belongs to the whole community. This was the condition among primordial men. Every worker among the ants toils with all her might in obtaining the property, and all have equal access to it. Each ant acts as if its act could become a general rule of action, and this we shall see is true of all human primeval law. The natural condition of absolute equality results from each ant having full liberty to act like every other ant. The intense devotion to the community, the total ignoring of the individual, the innate passion for acquiring property for the community, are fundamental instincts that must be developed by any social animal that requires the storing of food in order that the community may survive.

Every ant community acts on the seeming principle, so popular among Socialists or incompetents, that the society owes a living to each of its members. No trouble, even, can arise over the young, for they belong to the whole community and are the cherished possession of the whole tribe. They have no parents, they are all orphans, and are brought up with the greatest care by the joint efforts of all the workers. Finally, the fact that these ants have continued in their habits of life without change through a million years indicates that the laws of social life that govern the ants have produced animals absolutely responsive and obedient to those laws. In other words, every ant is law-abiding. What, then, can be simpler to the reformer, than to turn humankind into ant-aping social communities and to make all men law-abiding?

Is it at all strange that the ideal commonwealths, which have been devised, borrow leaves from the book of the ants? All communal socialism is based upon the jurisprudence of the ants in an attempt to apply that polity to human beings. It is assumed that, like the life of the ants, all there is to human life is the problem of enough to eat and a roof to cover our heads. This is true of savage men. This is the Marxian assumption applied to civilized men. Almost every new religion begins with this fascinating dream of goods in common, no contentions, no degrees among men, all naturally working for the common end. The Socialists seem to look without disfavor even on predatory war, for this is the lesson of their exemplars, the ants. They find no place for the monogamous family life, for that is no part of the polity of the ants. Every ant society supports each individual ant. That is the theory of Socialism. The problem of socialistic communism is a very simple one on paper. Let each human being become as purely responsive to conditions as the ant, let him attain the perfect self-discipline and self-control, the self-abnegation and self-surrender of the ant, the devotion to the good of the community which is the controlling spring of emmet life—let each human being cease to be individual, and Socialism and Communism are very easy to attain. This means, of course, as we shall see, that the fundamental nature of the human mind as the ages have produced it, must be abolished. No one but an imbecile can hope for such a transformation or expect it.

If every act of the ant were not what, for want of a better word, we call instinctive, the mental constitution of the ant would have been certain to change in the course of a million of years. We content ourselves with saying that it is the nature of ants to act as they do. The laws of ant social life are inexorable and incapable of being changed unless they be changed by some new natural condition acting upon the ant. What we mean by this is probably the great generalization of Pascal, who was thinking of human beings: "What is nature? Perhaps a first custom, just as custom is a second nature."

The lesson we can learn from consulting the ants is that habits of acting or customary modes of acting of even intelligent animals become so fixed that it is impossible that they should be altered by mere animals, and so far as man as an animal has come out of his remote past, he has come stamped with this instinctive tendency to continue in customary habits of acting. But so far as he has become capable of altering his customary ways of acting, he has ceased to be a mere animal and has taken on, if you please, a Godlike attribute. But we may be certain that he will not alter his methods of life except to the extent that he is compelled to go. He will cling to as much of his ancestral robe of habit as he can retain.

Next, we may say that every social community of animals, by the very fact of its individuals living together, develops in each individual by nature or by habit or by customary mode of acting, an intense tendency in each individual to preserve that social community as an organization. In order to preserve the community there must be a store of food for the winter, requiring most intense labor. Hence come the ants' tribal property, the common home, the unified labor, and the practice of slavery. We shall find in primitive men these same instincts, the same tribal feeling, the utter lack of any conception of the individual. The individual counts for nothing in the preservation of the community. This is just as true as that in the animal, whether with or without a social organization, there existed the animal tendency to propagate its species, impressed upon every normal animal as a natural and ruling passion. These two tendencies, to propagate and to continue the herd, continued to exist in men from their stage of mere animality, and the two together make up what may be called the basis of human community life as it came from the hand of Nature.

Now at this point in the beginning of this history it is necessary to emphasize a fact as to ants and to make a distinction between their development and that of men. In the case of the ants, their mentality and their rules of life have become precisely equilibrated to their physical surroundings. Just as surely as the moon, the other planets, and the earth are held in their orbits by the balance that has been reached in the natural forces that govern their movements, so the ants, by the condition of equilibrium which they have reached with reference to their natural surroundings, are rendered incapable of escape from, or of changing, their rules of existence and of conduct toward one another. But with man it has not been so, for man's mentality in the long ages has suffered a great development.

Man began as an animal, responding merely to his surroundings, and the fact that he so began has led the Behaviorists to assert that such he has always remained. Their favorite thesis is that the individual man to-day is just what society has made him. This is true in a measure, but since man became civilized, the exact converse is shown to be true by the history of the law. Society now is what the individual man is making it. Somewhere in its development, by gradual and imperceptible degrees, the animal man passed from the stage of a brute wholly obedient to its circumstances and surroundings, to that of a being who, by his own purposeful mentality, could so alter the impact of his surroundings upon himself, that he could rise above the external world of the senses into the realm of the inner life of the spirit and could make it true that human society will become what the individual shall make it. To quote George Sand, the ideal life will become man's normal life as he shall one day know it. If it be said that this change of mentality is a mystery, the answer is that the change in mentality can be traced, that it is not nearly so great a mystery as the initial change from inorganic matter to organic life, that beginning of life in which all are compelled to believe. Human society has been altered and will continue to be altered and to be made still better as men continue to rise higher in the realm of that inner life of the spirit. The world of thought, the world of dream, and all the past and the future will become the possession of more and more men.

We can anticipate that man will never become like the ant, perfectly law-abiding and perfectly fixed in his obedience to the rules of his social life, for should that day come man would be incapable of improving his rules of life and incapable of progress. Yet this does not mean that progress lies in violating the law, but rather in the capacity to alter the law. It will always be true that the highest type of man will be the one who recognizes his duty to obey the laws, as witness Socrates who without compulsion or necessity, even probably against the desire of those who had condemned him, went confidently to his death rather than disobey the law.

Pope in his well-known lines asks a question and answers it:

> Why has not man a microscopic eye?
> For this plain reason, man is not a fly.

And if we ask why man has not developed a set of laws that all men instinctively obey, without question and without faltering, the answer is the plain reason that man has left that stage behind him. He has all of the intelligence of the ant but he has one infinitely higher attribute, that puts upon him certain evils, but at the same time opens to him an endless heritage of progress.

Every act of the ant is purely instinctive. She acts as she does because she cannot act otherwise. She has no choice. Human beings also have instincts. The great mass of our daily acts is purely instinctive, the experimental psychologists now tell us. Some of those instincts have improved and grown better with the improvement of the race. Our emotions of fear or bravery, of pity or harshness, of sympathy or ill will, of envy or generosity, of love or hatred, are not reasoned conclusions. When we are moved to tears or laughter, when our hearts glow and our eyes shine at hearing or reading of noble and heroic deeds, when we feel keenly the suffering of man or beast, when our minds are touched to generous compassion, we feel and act by instinct. Love for our parents or family, love of the home in which our eyes opened to the light, faithful affection for the streets over which our childish feet were led, and love for our country whose flag floating in the air is an inspiration and an undying hope, no less come to us by our instincts.

At the same time our self-assertion, our greed, envy, and covetousness, our feelings of self-interest and selfishness, our lowest attributes of sensuality or lust, all the influences of the body on the mind, are no less instinctive. Men mainly differ in the extent to which the intellect commands these instincts that have been inherited from the savage. Had men remained the creatures of merely instinctive intelligence they could doubtless have peopled the earth; they could have developed communities of a high order living under an absolute law reigning over individuals who would never violate the law. They would have developed a stability of institutions and thereby have become incapable of progress. But man has developed a higher type of mind capable of infinite expansion and of overcoming natural surroundings, and has thereby become able by his own purposeful exertions to keep constantly mounting to higher realms of existence.

While the communists have made an impossible application of the lesson of the ants, it seems possible that some philosopher, calling himself a jurist, as philosophers have the hardihood to do, thinking on the problems of social life as developing rules of law to govern the conduct of individuals toward one another, might have hit upon the inference that men must once have lived in a condition when they, too, would be as helpless in the grasp of their rules of social life as are the ants. If men had remained without any reasoning power whatever, they would have been helpless to change. The philosopher Hobbes, who claimed to be a jurist, once cast his eye upon these natural communities of ants, at a day before the evolutionary conception was at all understood. But Hobbes was definitely committed to the dogma that human law is a rule imposed by a superior ruler upon an inferior subject, and that not nature but authority creates law. This dogma long made jurisprudence a nightmare. Hobbes at once dismissed the ants as being wholly useless for a jurist's investigation. No doubt he saw that the polity of the ants entirely refuted his theory of law, and it was too much to ask of a philosopher that he should abandon his theory out of a regard for facts. The fact, however, remains that a large part of the law has always been dictated by natural causes and much of our jurisprudence is and must remain, however we disguise it, as inevitable as the jurisprudence of the ants.

How much more inspiring it is to believe, as the story of the law proves, that the creature man has achieved his own destiny! Grant that he is obedient to natural laws so far as he must be, yet as a docile echo of those laws, by the force of reasoning power alone, he has steadily rounded and continues to round the vast orb of his fate. No one can look at the story of the law and not be a firm believer in the future of the race. The informed lawyers, in spite of their often gloomy views, must be the true optimists. Legal history teaches that the science of jurisprudence, without which progress would have been impossible, is not the work of the few but of the many, not the work of lawgivers or of great men, but the steadily and silently built structure of voiceless millions, "who bravely led unrecorded lives and dwell in unvisited tombs."

It is a sound corrective to our thinking to remember, in the words of a great scientist, that "what we are is in part only of our own making; the greater part of ourselves has come down to us from the past. What we know and what we think is not a new fountain gushing fresh from the barren rock of the unknown at the stroke of the rod of our own intellect; it is a stream which flows by us and through us, fed by the far-off rivulets of long ago. As what we think and say to-day will mingle with and shape the thoughts of men in the years to come, so in the opinions and views which we are proud to hold to-day we may, by looking back, trace the influence of the thoughts of those who have gone before." It is in the history of the law, far more than in any other social science, that we catch from its very beginning the great corporate life of humanity which has made us what we are.

CHAPTER 2

Law Among Primordial Men

After the earth passed from the Tertiary Age into what has been called by some the Quaternary Age and by others the Pleistocene, there came upon the earth this new type of animal, *homo primigenius,* which was to have such a marvelous career. There were certain things about these new animals that gave promise. Their ancestors had passed their lives in the trees, a habitat retained by certain men in New Guinea to-day who are enough advanced to use the bow and arrow, but such life for men of the present is a reversion. The first human beings had definitely abandoned the trees and had come down to the earth. The hands of their hind members had been converted into feet, and this firm footing with the sigmoid flexure of the backbone enabled them to stand upright. It took, of course, ages to develop these physical changes, but at last there was a creature that (a happy omen) stood upright and could not only look the world in the face, but could turn his eyes upward to the stars.

In the gradual change into men, the possession of hands and a life in the trees had given to those prior creatures and to their descendants an unexampled development of brain resulting from the rapid correlation of eye and hand and intense muscular activity. Many eloquent pages have been written upon what the human hand has done for man and of its marvelous creations, but it is enough here to note this effect upon the brain. In tracing the legal story of these primeval men it is necessary to keep clearly in mind the general facts and not to become involved in a mass of irrelevant details.

A certain mentality, sufficient knowledge to obtain food, sufficient social instinct to keep them together in the group, sufficient animal cunning to avoid dangerous beasts, these primeval men, of course, possessed; but higher attributes they had none. Naked, without fire or shelter, without defensive weapons, condemned to live through long ages before they could acquire even the simplest artificial aids to life, these poor, naked, helpless wretches, amidst the laughter of the gods, as the ancients said, entered upon their career of the conquest of the world. All they had were their simple inherited animal instincts and their large brain structure. To speak of laws in connection with such beings is startling, but they had them—fixed, ineradicable customs that were written on their minds and which through our subconscious mentality often rule us to-day. But first it is necessary to get rid of an idea that has been of as much trouble to a true science of psychology as it has been to a true science of jurisprudence.

The poet Tennyson, thinking that he was stating the evolutionary conception of man's development, has the line: "The Lord let the house of a brute to the soul of a man." Nothing could be more characteristic of the old type of thought. Man, they say, was created with a soul, by which is meant the mentality that men have to-day. It may seem folly in this connection to quote Genesis, but if man as created in Adam "knew not good and evil," he was a complete brute. No one is prepared to admit that brutes have what these people call souls, and if the human frame once housed a brute, that brute could not have had the soul of a man. There has been no change in the housing, but the mentality that animated it is a mentality that has changed from that of a brute to the reasoning mind of a man. Since the human mind is a unity and since that mind was once the mind of a brute, and is to-day burdened with many brute inheritances, there must have been, on this theory, a time when the original brute's mind changed into a reasoning soul. So far as man's evolution is important in law, the mental development of the original brute is all that is of importance. The history of law can deal only with facts, mental or physical, and is not troubled by any inquiry as to exactly when the brute's mentality became what the poet calls a soul, for "soul" is a word of generalized indefiniteness.

But the science of law is concerned, as the sequel will show, with the time when the brute's wholly subconscious kind of mentality passed into a conscious mind. The change from primeval man to *homo sapiens* was a mental change. From that standpoint it is emphatically true that in the case of primordial men, "the house of a brute was let to the mind of a brute." This creature on coming into the world was so far from "trailing clouds of glory," as Wordsworth says, that he trailed with him brute instincts so imbedded in his mental nature that not yet and probably not for many ages will his descendant rid himself of that brutish mental inheritance that still debases and binds him down. All the so-called philosophies of law and practically all the theories of the development of the law of human personality and of property are befogged by this absurd assumption that men's laws have always been directed by men capable of reasoning. These people are always reasoning backward in a fuliginous misconception. Hence comes the futility of the so-called schools of legal philosophy. On the contrary, the laws as to personality and property had their beginnings among men who were ruled by instincts and even to-day man's instinctive subconscious mind brings to naught the hoped-for results of flawless and elaborated reasonings upon the law.

Considering this primeval man as he was, we must picture him as looking out upon a world of physical surroundings much what they are to-day. Earth, air and sky, sunshine and rain, hill and valley, all the works of Nature he saw. But to this brute, naked, without any storing of a food supply and without a fire, existence in any climate but a tropical one was impossible. One winter would have destroyed the race. The mere fact of the condition of the newborn child makes it plain that man originated and lived for uncounted ages in a tropical clime. It is also a necessary inference that these men were dark in color. It happened that in that Pleistocene time a tropical climate existed over Europe, Asia, and Africa almost to the North Pole. Such is the settled geological and zoölogical fact. Snow and ice were unknown to primordial man. This original seat of man may have been in Africa, Asia, or Europe. Europe was joined to

Africa by a land barrier through Sicily. The British Isles joined the main-land of Europe and there is no impossibility in either place of origin. Not only were these men black in color and hairy beasts, but they had the faces of the anthropoids. They had sufficient knowledge to keep them-selves alive, and hence they have survived. They lived a community life, that is to say, they lived the life of the herd, a condition inherited from some former existence; they had reached the human stage with the in-grained instincts of social animals.

The two basic instincts of course they had, first the instinct of all an-imals to propagate by the union of male and female, and the instinct to preserve the young. They had the instinct of all social animals to pre-serve the social organization, and this was an added tendency to pre-serving the young and protecting the females. Expressed in a more gen-eral way, it is true that all social animals have the instinct of common action for the common good of the particular aggregation of which they are a part. Practically we may say that all the laws or rules of acting that existed among them were ways of acting as mere animals to propagate their kind, to cling together as a community, and to preserve the young. Ages ago the Roman jurist Ulpian laid it down that the basis of natural law for human beings was the union of the male and female, the procre-ation of children, and the protection and bringing up of the children. The acquisitive instinct in these men was wanting, since they had no need for storing food. Being the creatures of instinct, they all acted alike, and, having no self-consciousness, knew not why they acted alike. The modes of conduct had all the inevitability of the customs of the ants, and like the ants they had no need for a guide or overseer or ruler. Kings, chiefs, headmen were unthinkable.

Like all other animals, they had not the slightest idea of how the off-spring of the females were generated. Hence it is easy to see that there was no family organization, no distinctly marked off family group. Nor is it likely that there was any possession by males of particular females, nor was there any such idea as that of fatherhood. Promiscuity was nec-essarily the rule. When the evidence is examined carefully it points to promiscuity, but a promiscuity of the animal, which pairs for the breed-ing season, not the promiscuity of the prostitute. The fact must be kept in mind that the offspring required nurture for some years until they became viable and the mother for years must know and nurture her own offspring. The herd knew by instinct, just as musk-oxen know, that the mothers with their children must be protected, otherwise the herd would not survive. They knew that on the children depended the future of the herd. Hence, by the working of natural laws, it is plain that the child for its early years at least would know its mother but it would have not the slightest conception of a father. The mother would know and nurture her child, and the social law was that the males protected the females and the young.

Language, except a few rude sounds, aided by signs or motions, was unknown among them, for the simple reason that language for its development requires a relatively higher type of intelligence. Language required not only memory but reasoning upon the products of memory. It was certain that when language should be developed there would be a word for a mother long before there was one for a father. In fact some savages, which to-day remain sunk in primeval brutishness, have words for mother and for child but have never had any word for father. The conception even yet does not exist among such degraded savages. We are at present in this story where all men were equally degraded.

Law as we have it has a division that may not be entirely logical but it is exceedingly convenient. It is the division into public law, which governs the relation of the individual to the social group, and private law, which governs the relations of individuals to other individuals in the group. Among these first men, the region of private law had no material upon which to exist. There was no property belonging to individuals or families, nor was there any opportunity for property, hence there was no stealing, no personal property law, no real property, no contract nor tort involving an injury to property, or a violation of a property right; there was no family law of domestic relations of husband and wife, parent and child, for the loose relations of men and women left no field for such law. There was no law either as to personality, since there was no such idea as personality.

But they had the social instinct and it dictated that every member of the community must not be guilty of conduct such that, in the inherited experience evidenced by customs of the members of the community, it would endanger the social existence. The certain result of this instinct would be that they would all act alike. One who did not act like his fellows must inevitably be forced out of the community. This, to a creature trained to live only as a social being, would be unendurable. If driven out of the community, where could he go? Even the drone ants, although they have wings to escape the wingless workers, who execute them, submit to certain death without hesitation and do this with entire willingness. Hence, from the social instinct, would come that deeply rooted tendency, which has never left man, to suit his conduct to that of his fellows, the desire to please and be pleasing to those with whom he lives in daily contact. This is a simple matter but it is necessarily the governing rule among all social animals. It lies at the basis of all law.

Translated into terms of law, this governing rule means that the conduct of each individual in general toward his fellow men must be in accordance with the general conduct and customary ways of the average man. Stated in another way, this means that every man should act so that his rule of action would be the general rule. We have seen that this rule applies to the social ants. The philosopher Kant thought that he had discovered the basis of all law in the proposition that one should so act that his rule of action could become a general law. This is precisely what primeval men were doing. This is precisely what all social animals have as a rule of conduct. Kant's discovery was the discovery that men have lived in a social condition. This standard of the conduct of the average man has in many respects never been improved upon.

When a judge to-day lays down the law to a jury by saying that if the defendant was guilty of a want of that care which would have been exercised by a man of ordinary care and prudence under the circumstances, he was guilty of negligence, the judge is charging in the exact terms of the workings of the mind of this ancestral animal. To-day the law is that one who acts to the injury of another contrary to the standard of care and prudence of an ordinary man, is doing something unlawful.

If it be said that this primeval law is wholly in the air because one must use the whole body of law to define an infraction of the law, the answer is plain out of our law to-day. The widest of all present offenses is that of conspiracy, which is defined to be an agreement between two or more to commit an unlawful act or to do a lawful act in an unlawful manner. This unlawful act need not be a criminal act. The whole body of law, civil and criminal, is used to define an infraction of it, for before a man can know that he is agreeing to do an unlawful act, he must know every act that the law declares to be unlawful. The law consoles the defendant by the cheerful words that a man is presumed to know the law, even if lawyers and judges are not so presumed. It is apparent that the principle that all men are presumed to know the law comes from a remote time.

Long ago in the Pleistocene Age, among these naked, helpless brutes, the one law, if expressed, would have covered public and private law, civil and penal law and would have read: Whoever is guilty of any act contrary to the customary ways of acting of the men of the community is guilty of an unlawful act and will be punished by banishment. This is more definite than our law of conspiracy. The poor civilized man can commit the offense of conspiracy by doing with others acts which would be perfectly lawful, if he did them by himself. The primitive man, however, could see in his daily life how others acted, and he had an instinct to act in the same way. But there was no enforcer of this rule of law except the opinion of the whole community. Those ancient forms of punishment, such as killing an offender by a shower of stones, point unmistakably to an enforcement of law by a mob embodying public opinion. Lynch law is merely a reversion to the ways of primeval men. It is more than a mere coincidence, as will later appear, that the general instinctive ways of acting that were produced by the rule of adaptation to surroundings remain still the basis of law. The words of the poet upon the law are strictly true:

> On the rock primeval hidden in the past its bases be,
> Block by block the endeavoring ages built it up to what we see.

The Behaviorist psychologists have noticed the primitive desires of social men and have tried to define them, but among them they have missed this rule of social conformity so important to a development of law and have not followed it out to where it produces law. Its fundamental effect was to produce in men what we now call shame, the sense or, if it be a better term, the reaction of shame. Shame arises purely from this commendation or disapproval of other beings. Long before he was capable of self-consciously knowing what he felt, the human being had this primitive feeling of shame, of being shamed in the presence of his fellows. Any deviation from the customary ways of his fellows would produce in him the sense of being below the standard of conduct, of having done something that those around him disapproved.

Whether we look at this feeling of shame from the subjective standpoint of the one who has the feeling of being shamed and humiliated, or from the objective standpoint of the rest of the community who look on the individual as being guilty of an act that ought to cause him to be ashamed, the result is the same. Each one of the community was driven to conform to customary ways of acting. This fundamental instinct is still as intense in us as in the original man. It is for law the most important instinct of the animal man, for upon it and not upon force or authority, has depended the growth and development of law. But it fixes, once for all, the important fact that law cannot be changed any faster than the mass of the community changes in opinion or belief. The most absolute despot that has ever lived, the force of legislation or the irrefutable arguments for change, cannot impose upon men a change in law until the mass of the community is ready to accept or has already accepted the change.

Since we are telling the story of law and adverting to general history only so far as necessary, we need say no more than that this primeval man from some tropical center, by the slow process of ages, became scattered over at least much of the then tropical parts of Africa, of Asia, and of Europe. We need not enter into the fierce battles of the anthropologists and ethnologists as to where this center was, nor as to what the original race or races were. It is certain that in the first half of the Pleistocene Age, at the very least two hundred and fifty thousand years ago, the human race became disseminated over various parts of Europe, Africa, and Asia. For probably more than one hundred and fifty thousand years primitive men in their tropical surroundings seem to have made little, if any progress; nor is it likely that they would have made much progress had not Nature forced a change.

To speak metaphorically, we may say that Nature, having seen the utter indolence of this latest animal, under the most favorable surroundings, where he was freed from all the necessities of laboring to preserve his life, began to despair of men as she had already despaired of the other tailless anthropoids, and decided that some change in surroundings was necessary to stir the indolent creature into effort toward self-improvement. At least, natural causes brought on what is called the Ice Age. Geologists tell us that at prior periods of geological history, ages of ice were prevalent. Various causes have been assigned for such a great climatic change, but with those causes we are not concerned. The fact is that the great field of ice began to form far in the north of Europe, not to speak of any other place, and in the ranges like the Alps, the Carpathians, the Caucasus.

Slowly, from year to year, from century to century, from age to age, the incredibly thick ice sheet from the north and the glaciers from the mountains, kept moving and pressing farther south and out of the mountains in all directions. At last far toward the south of Europe, an arctic climate prevailed, a short warm summer, and many long months of bitter cold. Take just one illustration: The Rhone glacier which now stops short at the opening to the valley at the Rhone Glacier Hotel, extended down the bottom of the valley, joined the tremendous glacier from Mont Blanc, filled with solid ice all the region of the Lake of Geneva, reached the Jura Mountains with an ice thickness of three thousand feet, topped the Jura range and extended onward until it joined the glaciers beyond Lyons from the mountains of Auvergne. All the tropical flora and fauna necessarily had been destroyed or driven southward with the hippos and the saurians. Probably the great mass of living men all over Europe had passed away. The original hairy, prognathous, anthropoidal brute had been wiped out, even if he had not been exterminated merely by the approach of arctic cold.

To form some conception of what a social community would do in the presence of such a profound calamity, we may take a lesson from the beavers. They, too, had been living in Europe since early in the Tertiary Age. Conditions were so favorable that, at one time in that age, a giant beaver was developed of proportions as large as those of a grizzly bear.

In a tropical climate they had no reason to develop their present peculiar genius. But with the advent of the Ice Age they found it necessary to bestir themselves if they intended to live. At least this is what they would have thought had they been capable of reflection. The beavers' food is the root of a water plant and the bark of certain trees. They live in a gregarious way and dwell in permanent societies. Such a colony has survived, according to actual observation, for two hundred years.

The beaver in this Ice Age developed extraordinary engineering and building skill in order to overcome the wintry climate that threatened his existence. First he must have a home, and a home that was comparatively safe. He, although a rodent, lived much in the water and he had his rodent teeth with which to cut down trees and he had his digging front paws. He took a place in the bank and below the surface of lowest water in the stream and ran a tunnel into the bank, first horizontally and then upward, what miners call a "raise" or "upraise," and at the top of the "raise" he excavated a large chamber, high enough to remain always above the level of high water in the stream. But at the same time this tunnel must be so placed that the water would not freeze down below the entrance to the tunnel, and thus cut off the beaver from his access to his food supply sunk to the bottom of the stream. In using engineering judgment he never failed in selection. He ran an opening for air from this room to the surface of the ground and covered the hole with sticks plastered together. This was a safe home in winter for most purposes. But later he learned to build an actual hut on top of the ground and plastered it together of sticks and mud. Access to this hut was through the tunnel. This dwelling, however, was not safe from a diving animal like the otter, which is one of the most voracious and predacious creatures known. If an otter entered the tunnel he could at leisure eat up the whole community. The beavers built a second tunnel giving another exit for the chamber, precisely as the miners have a main shaft and then another called the escape shaft.

The beavers must maintain a more or less fixed level of water in the stream. To do this they build a dam, starting it in the center of the stream, with a bunch of logs laid lengthwise in the stream and anchored to the bottom by means of stones and plastered clay. Gradually they build up their dam across the stream, plastered with mud on the upstream side and with a curve upstream. The curve toward the current is an astounding deduction. It gives strength to the dam. In course of time they exhaust the trees immediately adjacent to the stream, which furnish the bark they eat, so in the Ice Age they became hydraulic engineers, running canals back from the pond formed by their dam. These canals were run as truly as if done by a surveyor's level, so that they always remained full of water. Thus the beavers could tap a fresh supply of bark by felling trees, and the canals furnished their means of transport. They carefully kept the canals free from weeds.

Most ingenious of all their acts is their felling of trees so as to make them fall at the precise place they should fall alongside the stream or canal. They stored their food supply at the bottom of the stream by sticking it into the mud or loading it down with rocks. How many unsuccessful experiments went to the development of these various instinctive habits, no one can say, but thus the beavers prepared themselves to defy the arctic winters. Like the ants, every beaver works like a beaver and their communities have "no guide, overseer or ruler"; and thus they have continued through the ages, although in a warm climate they have abandoned most of the labor imposed on them by a long winter. This instinct to avoid work seems to be ingrained even in the subconscious mind of men.

Man, who had a much better brain than the beaver, was certainly capable of just as much. Perhaps he was not entirely unprepared. The approach of the Ice Age was gradual, lasting over many thousands of years. The first advent of chilly weather must have taught men the necessity of preserving fire. There was no necessity for inventing fire. It was there to use. Certainly they had felt no need of its uses in a tropical climate. Then and there, at the advent of the cold, began man's worship of fire and the cult of the sacred flame which must never be allowed to expire. True to his nature, man continued to worship the sacred flame, long after he had lost all necessity for maintaining a fire. At this time of the long approach of cold some one of humankind had found that a cutting edge, an actual weapon, could be fashioned by chipping flint. Slowly the flint knife, the flint-headed spear or javelin, and the flint axe came into use. These inventions made invincible weapons; they passed from tribe to tribe until all men were living in what is called the Old Stone Age, consisting of the Eolithic and Paleolithic ages. Still later, when men lived in swamps or beside lakes, came the bone harpoon for spearing fish or other animals. The bow and arrow was an invention of a much later time, for that invention required a complicated sort of ingenuity.

Man had now gained the beginning of his mastery over the wild beast and had begun to alter the course of nature. Just what is the connection between the Ice Age and the development of flint weapons archaeology has not certainly told us, but we know that the two phenomena are parallel. How far men had been carnivorous animals from the beginning we cannot say, but the human dentition, which is a compromise between that of a herbivore and that of a carnivore, had not changed since man's advent. Nor can we say whether human beings were originally fighting animals; but the proof points to their peaceful character. From the beginning they were both flesh-eating and plant-eating animals. But as soon as they became hunters of the wild beast, they would rapidly develop a fighting propensity. The general effect would be to strengthen the race with a better food supply, to give men courage and skill, and also would enable them to endure a harsher climate by reason of the covering of the body with the skins of their game. The naked brutes had begun to wear some kind of clothing.

Another change was not at first of so much importance, but it was to become so. Men naturally crept under available shelter and became cave dwellers. They were incapable of creating an artificial kind of dwelling. The use of fire enabled them to fight off the cold while sheltered in the cave, but it took men ages to learn the lesson that ants had acquired, of keeping their dwellings clean. The dwelling in caves threw men closer together. There was more communion among them and a common place to resort as a fixed abode. The development of an esthetic instinct will be noticed later. In this hunting stage language was developed, and was steadily improved. The development of spoken speech continued for countless years before a written speech was devised.

The Glacial Age gave mankind a thorough training before it relaxed its stern discipline. The ice sheets of tremendous thickness continued to advance and recede. A tropical climate would return to Europe and then the ice would again advance. Four times at least this change took place. And always came the cold and cruel winters, the failure of the food supply, the coming of famine, the dying women and children. A vivid picture of such a life is drawn in Longfellow's *Hiawatha*. Farther and farther to the south the mass of men were driven. During these changes new races appeared. Many causes may have contributed to this result in the long ages. Mixing of tribes or absorption of one tribe in another, cold and want, failure of food, inability to endure the severe climate, must all have been contributing causes. Fierce fighting must have gone on among these various tribes as they were constantly driven upon each other, for the acquisitive instinct, as we shall see, came into play. If the tropical fauna and flora perished in Europe, it is likely that countless human beings perished in the same way. The important thing for history of the law is that the constant struggle for life developed a much higher mentality in man. The improvement in weapons went on until gradually the human race, having passed into the nomad and then into the agricultural stage, was, long after the Ice Age ceased, in the New Stone Age with finely polished weapons of stone. Men probably lived in the Old Stone Age more than ten times the period from the beginning of the New Stone Age until the present. The advent of the Neolithic is placed at about 10,000 B.C.

As soon as the Glacial Ages began, the necessity for some sort of food supply developed, and a result was the hunting stage. Thus began tribal property. A tribe would locate itself with reference to a hunting ground, and then and there would be born the desire to keep that ground—an incipient patriotism. Any encroachment by another tribe would be repelled by force, and thus every tribe would be hostile to every other tribe. The instinct to hold the tribal property would arise simply from the desire to keep the food supply and the developed acquisitive instinct. Pedantic philosophers have sought the origin of ideas of tribal property in tangled metaphysics and in varied speculations, all involving elaborate reasoning in the then human beings. The primeval brute did not reason.

When another tribe was encroaching on his food supply, he simply re-
sisted. This is the simple explanation. Any animal will fight for its bone.
In the same way men sought to keep their cave dwellings. Thus it happened that the cave and the hunting ground were open to every one of
the tribe but to no one else. The game killed by any one of the tribe went
to support the tribe, but if it were killed by some one of another tribe, it
was taken away from the tribe, so to speak, in possession. Thus grew up
the bitter hostility between tribes, and the instinct that it was right to
take anything one could from another tribe or any member of it. No possible quarrel over property could arise between members of the same
tribe. Savages will despoil another tribe or its members. They will not
steal from their own tribe.

Thus, it is necessary to note, in this long development into the hunting stage, fixed elementary ideas of tribal property would develop. While
the hunter retained, of course, his weapons as his own, the game he
killed and the hunting fields would naturally be regarded as the possession of the tribe. This institution of tribal property was to be retained by
savage men for untold ages before the usage or law of property went further. After another long period the institution of tribal property was to
develop into family property, from which the passage to individual property would take place almost imperceptibly. But it all goes back to the instinct branded upon men to obtain and keep a food supply. The necessity for storing a supply of food would develop in men, as in all other
social creatures, not only the property but the acquisitive instinct, which
would become as deeply rooted as the sexual instinct. It was a mere development of that primeval social sense of preserving the herd, and was
of just as much compelling power as the instinct to conform one's own
conduct to that of others.

But, after all, the most important effect of the use of weapons and of
the hunting stage for producing law was in developing the fighting instinct. The fighting that went on through the migrations of tribes
caused by the ebb and flow of the Ice Ages, forced man to become a
fiercely predatory animal. Traceable to this hunting state are the two institutions of the capture of females, which would develop long afterwards into marriage by capture, and the capture of other tribesmen and

children, resulting in the institution of slavery. Slavery was produced for men just as it was produced for the ants. These developments were important, but not more so than the fact that the fighting instinct and its unrestrained savage passions would lead to fighting and killing within the tribe itself. To the development of law this was a matter of prime importance, since it was opposed to the instinct to protect and perpetuate the tribe. Fighting and killing within the tribe would lead to private war as soon as a notion of the kindred had been developed. The notion of kindred is necessary to the blood feud. From this time forth a new body of law that dealt with differences within the tribe was bound to develop.

To get the full effect of such changes, we must consider other advances. In the long ages men had accomplished more than the mere discovery of the use of weapons and of fire. Clay, when baked, would resist the action of fire. Such vessels of clay would be used for heating water and cooking food. This led to the making of pottery. The cooking of food by broiling over the open fire was well enough when meat was cooked, but the supply of meat was often precarious. With the opportunity resulting from the cooking of plant food, men could pass on to further steps in civilization. This discovery of the uses of pottery seems to have been made in the hunting stage of the cave dwellers. This development led directly to the cultivation of various kinds of wild plants.

Considerable knowledge has been gained of these hunter types, Chellean, Mousterian, Aurignacian, Magdalenian, Cro-Magnon, Azilian, and Solutrian, so called from the localities where the remains have been found. Some of them produced an exceedingly vivid and realistic representation of animals on pieces of bone, or on the walls of their caves. The use of color is striking, but the savage early began to paint himself, and his present female descendants still cling to those primitive means of embellishing, if not improving the countenance. But the story after a long time passes from these ancient hunters to men who had found the secret of domesticating animals: the sheep, supplying wool and warm skins; the cattle, supplying leather; the goat; the camel; even the elephant, and at last the horse. Men had long been wearing some sort of clothing as a protection against cold. It is idle to speak of any developing sense of modesty. Modesty is a result of the forced wearing of clothing to overcome the cold. After the wearing of clothing began and had become a fixed habit, it developed modesty. The weaving of cloth from linen, from wool, from camel's hair and goat's hair, began in this age.

Now began the great races of nomads driving their flocks and herds from one pasturage to another. These were the tent dwellers. Whether the domesticating of animals anticipated the family, we cannot tell, but as to the institution of property, the flock and herds stood upon precisely the same ground of a food supply and that property is a part of the self-preserving instinct of the tribal, social community. Just as the tribe had protected its hunting ground, so the tribe would preserve as tribal property its grazing ground. But the nomad stage lends itself to a family development, certainly a development of a kindred, the separation into kindreds, and to property as naturally belonging to the kindred.

Finally came what we may call the discovery of domesticating and improving the wild plants by cultivation of the soil. Men had already advanced to houses in the lake dwelling stage. They now could come together in villages and, with their cultivated fields, and protected by their houses, could attain a much higher stage of civilization. Each tribe would occupy its own village and farming lands. The fields for cultivation among primitive men appear first as tribal property parceled out to families, and so they remained for ages. The fields, of course, are an extension of the food supply and of the instinct in the community to preserve itself. But it is to be kept in mind that some men remained in the nomad stage while others passed on to the agricultural condition. The bases of civilization had thus been laid, and no part of them has ever been lost, except among those present savages who have degenerated from a higher stage.

All these steps would have been entirely useless had man not attained the conception of his own and of another's personality. This came about through language, and was necessarily predicated upon the living of men in a social state, for language belongs only to the associated state. All other inventions of men pale before the invention of language. Until that invention came, men were indeed, as the Roman poet sings, "a dumb and brutal herd"; but with language all things were opened unto them.

Language remained for ages merely spoken, and men reached comparatively high stages of civilization without any written speech. The effect of language cannot be overestimated.

By means of language men share the minds of others, and are enabled after long training to examine their own minds. Without language the realization of personality is psychologically impossible. Reasoning power arises solely from self-consciousness, and as soon as men became conscious of themselves and formed the idea of their own and others' personalities, they developed a conscience. This all results from the interaction of individual minds. But conscience, after all, is but another phase of the tendency of primeval men to conform their conduct to the general standards. With the advent of the first glimmerings of conscience we have reached the development of the moral instincts, and in after ages law would come to depend upon the moral sentiments.

The two moral sentiments with which law is closely associated and upon which all law depends, are the conceptions of the right and of the just. As we have seen, the social creature developed these customary ways of acting which correspond with his ingrained instinct of preserving his associated community. It is useless to speculate on the aeons required to develop the general conception of right. It was of an infinitely slow and gradual growth. The idea represented numberless individual and herd inductions of the social mind slowly developing into a reasoning mind. These inductions were necessarily judgments upon numberless concrete states of fact. At last a rule of conduct instinctively but consciously felt to be right was evolved, because every one acted in that way, and it must be right. That these judgments were the result of social experience goes without saying, and conduct was said to be right, when language reached the stage capable of expressing the idea, because the social experience showed that such conduct advanced the interests of the social community. What was right was that which accorded with customary ways of acting. The mental processes by which this moral idea of the rightful had been arrived at were not remembered, and they became "the broken potsherds of the past." The first custom had become a second nature, and each normal social mind of the individuals was furnished with these conceptions of the rightful.

Henceforth the idea of the rightful was instinctive, and it was not furnished by any process of reasoning, as the Socratic dialogues show. The idea of the rightful was solidly buttressed on the sense of shame. Thereupon these instinctive ideas of the rightful became in the mind the directing factors for deliberate reasoning in producing a moral judgment. Since law for primitive man, as we have seen, is simply the generalized conception of the customs acted upon for ages, it must be apparent that the customs result in the moral ideas of what is rightful. Thus it is that Cicero could say that "the mind, the foresight, the deliberate opinion of the community is placed in the laws." Since law always has been and always will be made by the general opinion and acceptance of the community, it is idle to say that there is no necessary and organic connection between the sentiment of right and the laws.

There is, however, another moral concept that enters into law, for it determines that a law must be a rule for all alike. Every man of ordinary intelligence knows that there is a difference between right and justice. Just what the difference is, he would have no little difficulty in explaining, but he knows that there is a difference, and if he should analyze the conception of justice to the heart of it, he would be compelled to say that justice is the putting of all men on the same basis, in other words, justice requires a rule to be applied to all alike. Going back to the primeval man in the social state, we have found that the natural condition is equality, and the fundamental notion at the basis of justice is, although primordial men were incapable of formulating it, that it is necessary for men living in a social state in a homogeneous condition of society to be granted and to have the same recognition, that is to say an equal right to an equal recognition. Every man has the right to act as others act. Hence each man has the right to do and to act in the customary way in which the other men are acting. It is a truism that customary ways of acting would never develop unless each man was at liberty to act in that way. This is all that liberty means. Yet profound philosophers like Kant and Hegel have thought that they made a discovery when they found the basis of law in liberty and equality. This is simply the assertion that law is based upon customary ways of acting. This thought simply spells equality, or, looked at from the standpoint that the law permits such conduct, it means an equal liberty. But why the philosophers should trumpet over this discovery of liberty and equality as the basis of law passeth all human comprehension. The short answer is that if members of a social community are to develop a custom by all of them acting in a certain way, they must have an equal liberty to act in that way. Without such liberty and equality there could be no custom and hence no law.

When, therefore, primeval men began to fight within the tribe and inflict personal injuries upon each other (and we speak of personal injuries, for injuries as to property were as yet improbable) a custom would develop consonant with justice and right, first, that for a man to injure another was wrong, because it was out of the customary ways of acting and it interfered with the social body and its peace and preservation; and secondly, if an injury was inflicted, justice and equality required that the injured—or, if he was killed, his kindred—had the right to be placed back upon an equality with the injurer. We are before a time when the idea of a compensation for an injury was conceived by humankind. Therefore the only conceivable right was the one to exact the very same injury, that is, the right to be put back upon an equality. We are as yet in the infancy of the law of damages, where no other recompense could be conceived. There was no possible recompense except the exact equivalent given by the *lex talionis;* an eye for an eye and a tooth for a tooth, or "whosoever sheddeth man's blood, by man shall his blood be shed." When it came to be applied, it was not only right and just, but no other remuneration or equivalent could be found. The application of these primitive conceptions will be later shown, but it is here to be said that it ought to go without saying that the idea of justice must have developed long before there were any introspective questionings as to the rightful. Right became a much more generalized conception than justice, for it carried, when fully developed, all the notions involved in proper and correct conduct, when justice was not at all concerned. Righteousness can be applied to conditions of mind, where conduct toward a fellow being is not necessarily involved.

In later ages in the highly developed Roman law of the jurisconsults which thirteen hundred years ago the Emperor Justinian caused to be compiled in the Roman Digest or Pandects, there was prefaced to the great mass of particular rules a general sketch of the law, patterned after the manual of a great law teacher called Gaius. This manual, both as the manual of Gaius and as that of Justinian's compilation, was called the Institutes of the law. At the very head of the Institutes is a definition of justice which is borrowed from a much earlier Roman definition. Justice is there said to be "the constant and perpetual willingness to render to each one his right." Among primeval men, among the Roman jurists, and among us to-day is the prevailing idea that what is due to each man, all men have the right to demand, and this demand can be answered only by a general rule which applies alike to all in the community.

Adverting for a moment to the customary ways of acting in the social state and the long ages required to develop them, it is plain that customs as a second nature would be clung to with the greatest stubbornness, for it is easier to act in the habitual way. Even among highly cultivated men "to act is easy, but to think is hard." We should expect to find customs in full force long after they should have been changed, and this is the history of law. That history may be summed up by saying that men cling to their customs. It is here that ideas of right among reasoning men begin to diverge from ideas of justice. To be just, men must act in the accustomed way, else liberty and equality are lost and men who are barred from the custom stand in a condition of unendurable shame. But to be suited to the newly conceived idea of the rightful in conduct men must develop a new custom; and this takes a long time. Yet, given time enough, the customs and habits tend to follow slowly and hesitatingly toward the rightful in the changing circumstances of a new life. So by the new custom, when properly developed and had a value, all sorts of injuries came to be compensated for in property. This will fully appear in the further history of the law.

We turn now to other factors causing the development of law. For a length of time of which we can form little conception, all kinship was traced only through the mother, and relationship through the father was unknown. But somewhere on the road the initial institution of a marital union developed, and in the nature of things this must have resulted from the knowledge obtained by human beings that children are born of the

conjugation of the male and the female. It dawned on the animal beginning to think that some part of the child belonged to the father. But the
fact which seems well attested, that relationship was traced only in the female line for many ages, points to the further fact that a family based on
the relationship of children through the apparent and proven fact of the
mother, was created before the mother became tied to a particular man.
So the family kinship was a kinship wholly through the mother. Whether
the first type of family consisted of a woman with several husbands or
several women and several men promiscuously united in one family, or
whether the family consisted simply of a mother and children will probably never be determined. It should be apparent that the development of
the idea of the kindred was a great step in itself. Its tendency to create
sentiments of sympathy and affection could not but make it a strong civilizing element. Especially strong would be the effect of the idea of the
kindred, along with increasing the number of objects of acquisition, in
spreading the idea that property belongs to the kindred; and thus advancing mankind found the tribes dividing into matriarchal families with
well defined rights of ownership in particular objects of property.

If we keep in mind that the ineradicable tendency of human beings is
to continue social habits long after reasons for a change have arisen, and
also that the ideas of chastity, fidelity, and jealousy took long ages to
come into existence, we should conclude that probably promiscuity, as
we have defined it above, continued long after the family of a kindred
came into existence. This would account for the long ages of the prevalence of the matriarchal family where the mother rules the family and a
father has no part. There is no question as to this fact. Basques in northern Spain and southern France, a very primitive race, show strong traces
of this ancient mother-headed and mother-ruled family. The legal rule
that relationship and succession to the family estate belonged wholly to
relatives through the mother and that any relationship through the father was not recognized settles the question.

In the end, however, the instinct to propagate uniting with the instinct which was just as strong, to protect the children, joined to the acquired knowledge of paternity, would lead to some form of permanent

union of man and woman. In no other way could the father's right in the
children be preserved. The curious fact is that the family of the woman,
of which her brothers formed a part, was clearly established before any
fixed marital union existed. And long after permanent marriages existed,
the husband was a mere skulker on the outside of the family, with no authority and no place in the family, and with little if any right in the family property. It is apparent that as soon as the idea of a kindred developed
and the tribe became made up of different kindreds, a more complicated
stage of human existence had been reached. It is probable that this stage
was reached when men were hunters. A woman or several women who
were sisters with their brothers would form a natural unit, and the property ownership of such a family would be extended to the game, as a
means of support for the family.

In the passage to the nomad stage the flocks and herds would thus become family property. But the idea that men fought for their women
with club and nail in their caves seems rank nonsense when applied to a
stage of human life where no such sentiments as chastity or fidelity in
the woman, or jealousy in the man, existed and the customs or laws were
based on a matriarchal family.

There is another reason for the development of the patriarchal family
than the one of acquired knowledge of paternity. Women were captured
in tribal fighting, and the captive necessarily belonged to the one who
took her. Or women were stolen from another tribe from a cause that
should here be stated. Property in women and their children would arise.
Without speculating on reasons, it is enough to state the fact that among
the tribes who passed on their laws to civilized men a custom arose that
men must not marry within their own kindred. In the matriarchal stage
it seems plain why such a custom might arise, since all the children were
brothers, all the uncles were fathers, and all the aunts were mothers. The
old and feeble, of course, caused no trouble; they were brutally abandoned and, if not killed, were left to die. This original type of marriage
is the so-called marriage outside the kindred or tribe, called exogamous,
which probably began with the development of kindreds. On the other
hand, the effects of capturing women with the resultant fighting would

at least compel the weaker tribes to interdict the capture, and to insist that marriage should take place only with other kindreds in the tribe, and thus would arise the marriage within the tribe, called endogamous marriage. This would lead directly to the marriage by purchase.

In this stage of society, three forms of customary law had their beginnings. As a habit arising from doubtful fatherhood, the children were required, at some stage of development, to be acknowledged by the father, and in consequence the newborn child was at his disposal to kill or to let live. The hideous practice of infanticide has been given other origins, but they do not seem to be as reasonable as the one that the newborn child was at the father's disposal. The direct inherited connection of such a right with a former stage of promiscuity is apparent. Whatever the explanation may be, the practice is fully established, and among the dark shadows cast in that former brutish life of man, none are so dark as those arising from infanticide, especially of the female children. Men continued it into the half-civilized stage and it passed into human sacrifice. In the pastoral age, male children were more valuable. But the father's power of life and death over his children is a fixed fact of the patriarchal family.

With the institution of marriage came the development of a large body of custom as to different kinds of marriage. Marriage by capture and marriage by purchase, with all the other regular and irregular unions, need not delay the story. We may remark in passing that trial marriages, which certain childishly minded persons now advocate, were tried in the savage state among the Scotch, the Scandinavians, the Celts, and the Germans.

Gradually the change into the form of family where the husband was the head of the family led to the right to participate in and succeed to the family property being confined to the male line. This passage to the type of family where the male was the head and only relationship through males was recognized by the laws, probably belongs to the nomad or pastoral stage, for the nomadic life would necessarily lead to separations into families, and the natural physical superiority of the male would come into play. It is a curious fact that in Latin the general term for blood-kindred, *cognati,* originally indicated relationship through the female, although it came to mean any blood relationship, while the later word, *agnati,* denoted relationship purely in the male line. How this patriarchal family, with the father as the head of the family, further developed, will be more properly noticed later on, but to the savage stage of doubtful paternity belongs the curious custom of the *couvade,* where the husband took to his bed and simulated the process of his giving birth to the newborn child. He felt that he must make some proof that the child was his own by public proclamation of his labor. Legal fictions come down from a very remote past.

When marital unions became fixed, the physical superiority of the male, uniting with his other instincts, would sometimes lead to the condition of a man with several mates. But it is always to be borne in mind that a polygamous family would be the exception, not the rule, on account of the inability of the average man to support more than one household. The working of this rule was seen among the Mormons in late years, where only a small proportion of the heads of families were polygamists. As soon as this possession of the female happened there was an opportunity to develop the ideas of chastity and fidelity, with a feeling of jealousy on the part of the male. The reaction of these new phases of life on the law are apparent, and into the law enters the institution of the male's exclusive possession of the female with her enforced fidelity. The woman now could become guilty, along with her paramour, of the capital crime of adultery.

The clan or tribe thus had become divided into numbers of families, first matriarchal and later patriarchal families. But these men who had always lived in social communities had become accustomed to the fact that one tribe was responsible as a whole to another tribe for any injury by a member of one tribe to a member of the other tribe. Hence in the development of the family, however it was developed, the one kindred or family was responsible to another kindred or family for any injury by a member of the one family to a member of the other family. It resulted from the social life that these primeval men could not think in terms of the individual. They clung to their ancestral ways and habits of thought. All law was drawn in the form of responsibility of one kindred for all its members to another kindred for injuries to members of the latter kindred. So it was in the case of property, first as tent dwellers with flocks and herds, later as village dwellers with plots of ground, as between tribes the property was recognized only as the property of a tribe, but within the tribe property, except the real estate and afterwards the property conception in real estate, was recognized only as the property of the family. The same responsibility of kindred to kindred applied to injuries to property. To Plato, who like most philosophers thought that he was intended for a lawgiver, although he had little comprehension of the fact that men cannot be molded by laws to a philosopher's model, it seemed that undifferentiated family property and the responsibility of the whole family were the ideals to be attained by law, even though the Greeks in his time had passed beyond this primitive condition.

Another element of this primeval life must be taken into account for the effect which it had upon the development of law. This creature found himself in a world of life and death, as well as of great natural forces, earthquake, storm, thunder, lightning, and flood. We can form little conception of what Europe was in the periods of the Ice Ages, with enormous rivers, vast lakes, and endless morasses. The inundations from melting snow and ice can hardly be imagined. These natural phenomena were terrifying. Magic, animism, and shamanism resulting from the terrors and fears of this poor savage need not detain us. A vast mass of different customs as to death, burial, and sacrifice were a natural result. The prevalent savage notions of things tabooed or forbidden are also of much importance in the law. Whatever may have been at the basis of the belief in spirits both good and evil, it is apparent that the conception of a spirit could not have been formed until men through language had gained the idea of personality.

The human race has never entirely recovered from the stage of fear. Every natural force and phenomenon was a spirit or a god. Devils and angels, spirits of the wood and stream, the lightning, the storm, the tempest, and the flood, the gentle and benign rulers of the spring and the harvest, the fell deities of danger and death, all were required to be propitiated by precious offerings. Every natural object became endowed with a spirit as a god. The gloomy history of human sacrifice and the widely disseminated practice of immolating the widow on the funeral pyre, we need not dwell upon. The frightful religious orgies where the savage returned to the original condition of promiscuity need not be considered. Just where in this sequence of savage thinking came in the worship of ancestors, we need not stop to inquire. It was a stage of savage belief that came to later men, and it created the law of adoption and of wills applied to family property. These practices and beliefs may have produced some temporary good, but they have left stains on the human mind that have been slowly eradicated.

One feature of this gloomy chronicle deserves notice. No doubt in these ages mental irregularities and insanity were more common than they are to-day, but it would be strange if an insane person should not be thought far more capable than an ordinary being. It long remained the practice for the prophets and sibyls and dispensers of oracles to imitate the ravings of the maniac. The original practices of wizards and magicians were probably based upon imitations of maniacal excitement. Persons who could go into a trance and afterwards relate extraordinary things seen or heard, had a far more valuable vein of exploitation than they have even to-day. There seems to be some connection between these kinds of men and the priests as they were developed. The priest gained his power by pretending to intervene between the savage and some god. The subject is shrouded in mystery, but we can reach the point that is required for the development of law by noticing that religions generally speaking developed into two kinds, one where there were many gods and goddesses identified with all sorts of objects and natural processes, and another where there was one god as the god of a particular tribe, who was at times in opposition to other gods of various kinds, and at other times in opposition to some particular malign deity. This fact and the production of the particular caste of priests is sufficient for our purposes here.

The connection of the matter with the law is that the law came to be the particular possession of the priests, who were considered as being able to intervene between men and their gods, and a mass of law was produced requiring particular conduct toward the gods. By a natural process the laws came to be ascribed by the priests to the god or gods. It is apparent that when the laws came to be ascribed to the god, they would still more tend to crystallize and become unalterable. The laws had now become divine. This belief belongs both to Aryans and to Semites and long formed a working influence in medieval and modern law.

This history has now proceeded to the point where the raw material, so to speak, of law has been ascertained. The fundamental physical factors, the raw human animal, the social community, the deep-seated, ingrained social instincts, the gradually expanding factors of civilization, the matriarchal family, the fixed domestic relations, the patriarchal family, the invention of a weapon, the expanding social type of mind, the development of the fighting instinct, the deep-seated acquisitive instinct for gathering and holding property, all modified by the slowly developing moral ideas of right and justice, constitute the raw material. It will next be in order to consider the races from which the development of law as we have it has proceeded, and to set forth first the primitive and then the ancient law, with the social basis that produced them.

But at this point it is necessary to make an observation, that should be axiomatic. There is, and in the nature of things there can be, no law before a condition arises to which it can be applied. Such law is unthinkable, yet John Chipman Gray in his book on *The Nature and Sources of Law* thought that he was proving something when he inquired, "What was the law in the time of Richard Coeur de Lion on the liability of a telegraph company to the person to whom a message was sent?" Could anything be more absurd? He was demonstrating merely that he did not know what law was. He might just as well inquire: "What debt did France owe the United States when Alexander the Great ruled in Babylon?" A rule of law is a fact as impalpable as a debt, arising out of human relations. It cannot exist where the relations on which it is founded do not exist.

Before leaving this subject of the law among primordial men we may dismiss once for all the schemes of socialistic communism. Never again can the human race or the human mind approach a condition where such an order of life is possible. With language and reasoning self-consciousness became possible, and a conscience developed in men the need for striving for consciously moral ends. The polity of the ants became from that period of development absolutely impossible among even barbarians. Then and there was founded "the one great society alone on earth, the noble living and the noble dead." It became a truth that man doth not live by bread alone; his truer and higher life slowly developing came more and more to rest upon those higher attributes of personality that doom forever a mere mechanical adaptation of men to Nature's decrees. The thinking, reasoning individual had emerged and step by step, even in sorrow, want, or obloquy, he was to rise above his surroundings. No longer was it possible for the individual to be swallowed up in the mass. No longer could all individuals be alike endowed with instincts acting precisely in the same way. The customary ways of acting, the law itself, must become a changing set of rules. New situations, wider mental horizons would create new duties. Time would make "ancient good uncouth." Those very scientists who call conscience a delusion are compelled to act in their own lives upon a power in themselves to choose good instead of evil. The laws became constructed first upon the responsibility of the kindred and then upon the individual's responsibility for his own acts, and without this responsibility social order is impossible among men.

But the very basis of legal responsibility and hence all basis in justice of law is denied by certain scientists and criminologists. They deny this freedom of choice. They maintain that free will is a delusion. They assert that man cannot rise to the realm of choice, that his choice is dictated by natural causes. The theological predestinarians substitute for natural causes the will of God. But the answer to all this is plain. When one speaks of freedom of choice, he means choice in that conduct which is possible to men, not choice in the things that are impossible. This freedom of choice is a condition of mind and results in an act of the mind. It is not a material thing. If a man believes that he has this freedom of choice—and all men believe it, for all act upon that belief—each man is as a demonstrated fact enjoying the condition of freedom of the will. But not all men are alike capable of choice in all things where a choice is possible. Few men can die as did Socrates for an abstract belief in his duty to obey the laws. The great mass of men are imperfectly capable of choice. The highest are capable, the lowest are not at all. A poet has set forth this truth in beautifully simple words:

> To every man there openeth,
> A way, and ways and a way,
> And the high soul climbs the high way
> And the low soul gropes the low;
> And in between on the misty flats,
> The rest drift to and fro.
> And to every man there openeth
> A high way and a low,
> And every man decideth
> The way his soul shall go.

CHAPTER 3

The Aryan Law

It is a commonplace among ethnologists that they can discern three primary races, the Negro, the Mongolian, and the Caucasic. This may be proven by cross sections of human hair, if in no other way. There was a Nilotic race, so called because in its original form it is still found along the Nile and because it came probably from that region. This undifferentiated race many ages ago furnished probably the basis for the Caucasic races. Its main developments correspond to the descendants of the three sons of Noah, the Hamites, the Semites, and the sons of Japhet. The ethnologist of Genesis was sound on the main fact of the single origin of the Caucasic races, even if the exploits of the temporary mariner Noah strain our credulity. There seems no reason to doubt that the original Nilotic race was approximately as dark as were the ancient Egyptians and Berbers. A great mass of this race passed to the north, and in the lapse of ages for apparent reasons became bleached into whiteness and in the farther north into blondness. One great spreading migration of this race peopled the shores of the Mediterranean. It is called the Mediterranean race. A part of the ancient inhabitants of Italy, Greece, France, Spain, and the British Isles belonged to this race. They found as their northern neighbors another Caucasic white race who are called the Alpines, and with them the northern portions of the Mediterranean race became mixed. The Alpines may have been tinged with Mongolian blood. Almost all of western Asia belonged to the Semitic portion of this Caucasic race.

Still farther to the north dwelt the part of the Caucasics that was afterwards to figure in ethnology as the Indo-European, or Aryan race, and this became probably the most mixed of all the races. The blond portion of this race has in late years been called the Nordics. Their descendants or supposed descendants have considered these Nordics a superior race, but this is a delusion of vanity and self-satisfaction. The mixed so-called Aryan race by migrations was to occupy Persia, northern India, as well as almost the whole of Europe. Some may differ from these classifications. Regardless of other considerations, the fact that this Caucasic race and the Aryan and Semitic portions of it are the only peoples of importance in the development of law among civilized men cannot be controverted. The migrations of the Aryan began apparently before those of the Semite, but the Semite earliest flowered, along with the Egyptian Hamite, into a very high civilization, while the Aryan was yet a wandering savage. The Aryan probably owed the civilization which he afterwards obtained to the Semite and to the Mediterranean race. In historical times we know that the so-called Nordics were civilized through their contacts with the Mediterranean race.

It may seem strange that omission is made of the Egyptians. The fact is that they, with all their talent, do not belong in the line of development. Nor can any sound idea of their law be obtained, until they passed under the Macedonian sway and borrowed much from the Greek law. But they had a very fine sense of justice and a powerful rhetorical appeal to justice, if we may trust the literature. A curious instance of a demand for legal redress against a grafting official remains to prove it. A peasant going from his oasis with his donkeys laden with produce is robbed by an official. He appeals for justice to a superior officer, who reports the matter to the king. The latter is so impressed by the peasant's eloquence that he prolongs the case until the peasant has made nine different speeches upon the high standard of even-handed justice. The king was evidently entranced with the peasant's eloquent eulogy. The translation given runs like this: "For thou art the father of the orphan, the husband of the widow, the brother of the forsaken maid, the apron of the motherless. Grant that I may set thy name in this land higher than all good laws, thou leader free from covetousness, great one free from pettiness, who bringest to naught the lie and causest right to be." He reaches still higher in this strain: "Thou rudder of heaven, thou prop of earth, thou measuring tape! Rudder, fail not. Prop, fall not. Measuring tape, make no error." He certainly deserved to win, as he did. His suit was granted, and the official punished.

Of the races in the true line of legal development we will notice the Aryans first, because the Semites at this same point of time represent a much higher culture. This Aryan race had the patriarchal household estate belonging to the family, the sacred fire and the worship of their ancestors in the male or agnatic line, and the forms of legal customs that go with such a development. At the same time, the aged and decrepit parents were thrust aside. Aryans had yet to learn a lesson in that respect from their Semitic relations. The power of the male head of the family over the family estate and over the conduct and the lives of those of the family was practically absolute. This was necessary in order to keep the family property together and in order to answer for the members of the family. It was a fairly reasonable rule for the condition of human life. The marriage custom was settled and the mass of people was monogamous. The chiefs and the rich, however, customarily had more than one wife. It has been said that monogamy was an evidence of the higher culture of the Aryans, and eulogies of their ancestors on this point have been offered by English and Germans; but the origin of monogamy was probably due wholly to economic factors. The prosaic consideration that Aryans were constantly sending off migratory bands makes it likely that they acted precisely as the beaver acts. When beavers migrate from their fixed home to establish a new one, it is always a pair that departs, and for the same reasons human beings were likely to enter upon their migrations in numbers of pairs. We may safely assume that the primitive man had as much social sense as the beaver. Instances like that of Abraham or the colonizing of the Greeks could be quoted to prove it.

These Aryans had developed, from their living in a constant state of movement, an unequal condition, due to the necessity for leaders and a crude sort of military discipline. The priestly function was well developed and they were ancestor worshipers. Among some of them the head of the family embodied this worship and was a priest as to its rites. They had also developed a system of serfdom or slavery. But it seems true that the Aryans were not cultivators of the soil.

The slaves and serfs represented generally captives in war or a conquered race. Whenever the rapacious Aryans came upon tribes cultivating the soil, serfdom took the form of a conquered race bound to the soil, rendering labor and services and grain or some kind of live stock to the master: but the slaves, at least, migrated with the tribe. Generally these serfs bound to the soil lived in a village community which represented, no doubt, the assembled dwellings of a kindred or large family of a subject tribe. This first form of slavery was not an oppressive system. The slaves belonged to the familia or household. The fact that the slaves or serfs were of the same race and color made ancient slavery a very different institution from the modern negro slavery. The institution was suited to the Aryan primitive cultivation. Social arrangements were simple. There was practically no division of labor, and of necessity the dependent classes were used as cultivators of the soil. The simple fact was that slave labor was unpaid labor. Payment for labor when no means of payment exist is legally unthinkable. Industrial organization of this kind can be traced in England from the Briton to the Anglo-Saxon and on to the English manor. Its development is no less clear in France.

It has been noted that slavery was a natural development among men just as it was among ants. This fact renders absurd the contention between two men considered jurists, Kohler and Stammler, as to whether slavery was right.[1] We may as well ask, is slavery among the ants right? It is idle to put the question as to primitive men, because they had no doubts on the subject. To them it was natural. Even to Plato or Aristotle it had no moral aspect. It took long ages to develop among men any conception of the rightfulness or wrongfulness of slavery. The fallacy of

---

1. Josef Kohler (1849–1919) and Rudolf Stammler (1856–1938), two leading German legal philosophers. Zane discusses Kohler at length in "German Legal Philosophy," *Michigan Law Review* 16 (1918): 287, 364–73.—C. J. R., Jr.

ascribing to primitive men our ideas of right and wrong ought to be apparent to any thinking man.

The joint family property still continued among these Aryans. The same form of patriarchal family or household is found among the Semites, the Indian Aryans, the Slavonic tribes, the Celts, and the Germans. It received its highest development among the Romans. Yet each male member of the family could for himself attain property of his own, except possibly among the early Latins. This family estate in land at first was inalienable by the head of the family, and upon his death it still remained to the family. It was considered as granted by the tribe to each family. The personal estate also was not alienable, but upon the death of the head of the family one-third was reserved to the family and one-third went to the deceased's funeral equipment, while the other third was spent in carousing when the corpse was cremated. It is needless to say that in later times the reservation of a third to the dead man went to the church. This early distinction between the inalienable land property and the personal property was of immense influence in later law. It led directly to the substitution of the eldest son for the father as inheriting the family estate in land, with the duty of providing the common home and endowing the daughters, who were excluded from succession to any interest in the landed property. The making of a will was, of course, unknown, for it could not be conceived of until language came to be written. But this supposed necessity and the custom of preserving the family property led to various legal rules that were later developed.

There remain various collections of law of different Aryan tribes after the great Aryan migrations, which are not yet properly classified and arranged. Developments, hundreds—it may be thousands—of years apart, are found side by side. Primitive collections of such laws are the Hindu collections in their sacred writings, and the Brehon law of the Celts, and the Germanic laws that are in some respects more primitive. The Teutonic customs will be reserved for the story of English law, in order to show its beginnings with the Anglo-Saxon customs grafted on the Briton or Celtic older organization of the conquered Celtic tribes. Although these Hindu and Brehon laws of certain Aryan tribes are in point of time later than the Babylonian law, we can use them here as illustrating the more primitive condition out of which the civilized systems of law arose. The Hindu laws are called the Laws of Manu. While the collection of these laws is, historically speaking, late, they embody much information on the ancient primitive customs of the Aryan race. The religious and legal customs are all grouped together, just as we find them in the laws of the Hebrews. Many customs appear to be obsolete, but the customary law is older than the sacred law. All the laws are given a divine origin and are not subject to change. The caste of the religious men, the priests, as the highest, next the caste of the warriors, next those of commerce and agriculture, are plain, while the servile classes, at least, represent the subdued and subject race. The patriarchal system, with the power of the head of the family, is well developed and the joint family property is in the family ownership. It is a sort of corporate ownership. There is the family home where all the agnates (relatives in the male line) and the unmarried females are entitled to a home. This is generally a collection of houses. This home and property is enjoyed in common and no account is kept of expenditures for each of the family, although the expenditures are by no means equal. The duty is added to discharge the debts of the dead, for the dead man with debts unpaid will suffer tortures and the duty is recognized to deliver him from torture, much as in later times the ignorant belief of belated primitives was and is that the soul of the deceased must by pious offices be ransomed from purgatory. This family system of owning property, with the added provision of the right of any male member of the family to acquire property for himself, provided he made no use of the family property, is recognized. The presumption is, however, that all acquisitions by members of the family are family property until they are shown to be otherwise. At the time of the Laws of Manu and ever since, a partition can be required by any of the agnate (male) members of the family clan, but this, of course, is a comparatively late development.

The Hindu system of law is of no particular value in an account of legal development, beyond the fact that it represents the stage of tribal organization suited to a conquering race which the Aryans developed. The priestly caste is exceedingly powerful. The patriarchal family with great power in the head of the family and with property segregated to the family is apparent. The exigencies of war had developed a warrior caste, held next in honor to the priestly class. The conquered community living in its small tribe village communities is a prominent feature of Indo-Aryan life. These Aryans came into India from the Persian uplands, whence, in after ages, other conquering hordes were to come and to reduce the Hindu Aryans to a servile condition in many parts of India. At some time these Aryans, however, developed the idea of individual responsibility, for in the Institutes of Manu is the deduction as a theory of human life, which is a great advance upon the primitive non-recognition of individual responsibility: "Singly each man cometh into the world, singly he departeth, singly he receiveth the reward of his good deeds, singly the punishment of his evil deeds." But this idea was not carried into the law of property.

Another migrating Aryan horde, called the Celts, moved in successive waves westward through Europe from some center whose location is hotly disputed. In their conquering career, they overran most of France, Spain, northern Italy, and the British Isles. They found a race, probably Alpine, in possession and subjugated and reduced it to a condition of serfdom, and in some instances amalgamated with it. It must be kept in mind that the conquering Celts were at a much lower stage of civilization than the dwellers in France and the British Isles whom they conquered. The subject race, as is usual, gradually civilized the conquerors. A collection of Celtic laws remains, but they are a mosaic of laws, centuries apart; some very archaic and others much later. Many of these laws are decisions of judges called Brehons. These laws have not been edited with sufficient discrimination to enable absolutely certain conclusions to be made, and in some instances it is difficult to determine whether we are dealing with fiction or fact. Perhaps there was imported into these laws some remnants of the Roman occupation of Britain.

These Celts had the regular Aryan tribal or clan organization, divided into patriarchal families, but they had developed a confederation of tribes, each clan claiming to be descended from a common ancestor; but in its later form, a clan could open to let in others not descended from the ancestor. The families were patriarchal and the family owned personal property at least. The older laws seem to come from the nomad stage.

The son succeeded the father as head of the family, but the family was becoming more fluid in that the older sons separated themselves from the family estate, taking some part of the property, while the youngest son stayed at home and succeeded to the estate that remained. In later English law this rule was called Borough English. This feature of the younger taking the hearth was the mark of the Kentish estate of gavelkind, and it was recognized in the English law as a customary local rule of law. The real property was considered as belonging to the clan. At the head of the confederated tribes, the chief had become a king, and under him were tribal kings. Below them were the heads of the clans. The priestly class was called the Druids and, like the Brahmins, they had no little power. It is now fairly well determined that the Druid priests were not Celtic in origin but belonged to the older Alpine conquered race.

The Druids seem to have been originally the judges of the laws, but they had been succeeded by a class of professional judges called Brehons. Each king had his advisers who may be called statesmen, and there was a well developed class of nobles, originally leaders in war, who became statesmen, and their sons, with the king's advisers and the Brehons, were considered the nobles. The clan property was set apart, so much of it to the head of the clan or sub-king, so much to the warriors, and to the advisers, and to the Brehons. Below the nobles was the large class of free clansmen, and below them was the servile class. The public organization seems about that which would be developed by any Aryan race engaged in fighting and overrunning territory under some sort of discipline.

A tendency to further differentiation requiring further laws was the land organization. The lands were parceled out to be occupied by individuals or by families and were inalienable, but lands that were occupied in this way were leased. There were two kinds of occupation under the possessors of land. The occupation by free farmers was by those who hired cattle to be run on a rental of one in seven. These contracts were solemnly and publicly made. This legal development belongs clearly to the pastoral stage. There was also the occupation of lands which the unfree were allowed to occupy, for which they made payments in produce. There was, of course, little law as to contracts. Trade was carried on by way of barter and payments were made in kind. Great stress was laid upon written contracts, but this must have been very late in Celtic law, and after they had gained a written language.

These tribes showed a distinct advance in some respects, although this condition did not exist until they had long been settled. Public assemblies of the tribe are ordinary among the Aryans. Among the Celts this custom developed until regular assemblies were periodically held. These assemblies had possibly been originally religious, or rather they were held on occasions of religious festivals. They were composed of the king and sub-kings, the heads of the clans, Brehons, other distinguished men, and the bards. At these assemblies the laws were recited. Some of the laws were in rhythmical form, showing extreme antiquity. No doubt such laws had been long in use. At the great assemblies modifications of the laws could be proclaimed, a new law announced by the king, with the approval and assent of those attending the assembly, which is the exact form of legislation in use under the early Norman kings in England. How far back in Aryan history this power of initiating legislation goes, there seems to be no means of ascertaining, but it certainly means that these Aryans had ceased to regard their laws as of divine origin, and it probably was the result of the laws ceasing to be in the custody of the priests.

The means by which disputes were determined present a unique development. These social aggregates called clans were attempting to develop customs that would cope with the disintegrating effects resulting from quarreling, fighting, injuries, and killings within the clan. It has already been explained that there were no tribunals, officers, prisons, or means of giving judgments or of executing them. The only method of redress for violations of the customary laws resulting in injury to others was self-help, backed by public opinion, and by making the kindred of the injurer responsible as a whole to the kindred of the injured. The individual in such a situation was helpless and the primitive mind did not comprehend the conception of an individual. In such a condition where self-help was necessary, private war would certainly result. Curiously enough, in Chicago to-day we see this same principle at work in a reversion to the savage state. By law the trade in intoxicating liquors is put beyond the pale of the law. The traders in intoxicants, called bootleggers, treating this lawless occupation as an open field for profitable exploiting, seize upon a certain district as their own, either by a right of occupancy or by the strong hand. This district is invaded by other purveyors of unlawful goods. The occupants respond with self-help in the form of killing the invaders and retaliatory killings go on. The result is private war in a community supposed to be fully policed. In other places the police, being engaged in the unlawful traffic, can preserve peace.

Among savage men where the feeling of kindred was strongly developed, the natural result of an injury would be that the kinsmen of the injured would seek redress and would immediately harry the kindred of the injurer. Probably the first appeal by the injured would be made to the whole clan. If the fact were plain, the public opinion of the assembly of the tribe might be enough to afford peaceable giving of redress, but since the only redress for a death was another death, it was certain that some other method of compensation would be sought; so there grew up a compensation system or tariffs for injuries, where the kindred of the injurer became bound to pay the compensation to the kindred of the injured. It must be noted that these injuries to person or property are merely private injuries. There was no law of crimes. This development seems to have been common to all the Caucasic tribes. There being no way of making new law, except as it should grow up in the customary way, it must be apparent that many ages of arbitrations and peaceful settlements were required to produce a set of customs upon this subject of compensation in property. Money was a late invention, and the tariffs were originally in some other kind and gradually became changed into money. But it is fairly certain that this sort of peaceful settlement, if the facts were in dispute, would not be acquiesced in. There was no way of making the settlement compulsory. Before the assembly of the tribe some kind of proceeding would take place to ascertain what the facts were. When the town meeting decided what the matter was, the injured could exert the right of self-help.

Then, as now, difficult cases would be the ones that would arise. Special knowledge of the customs would be required to decide them. Either the priests or the older and wiser men would be called upon to say what the laws were. Among the Celtic tribes the Druids were originally the custodians of the laws, but the Irish laws show that the Druids had been supplanted by a trained body of men called the Brehons, or judges. The haphazard legal knowledge of the priests was insufficient.

The Brehons were originally any of the learned men, and such a Brehon was attached to the court of every king or sub-king. If this be not romance, the Brehons did not hold a judicial office, but like the Roman jurisconsult belonged to a profession. They came to be legally trained men who had long studied the laws, but they had no compulsory jurisdiction. All their judgments were given in cases where the parties submitted a controversy to a particular Brehon. The party complaining could select any Brehon he pleased, and there seem to have been at last developed regular sittings of Brehons in courts. The Brehon received a customary fee of one-twelfth of the matter in dispute.

All acts against the person or the property were private injuries, and the redress was sought by the injured, if he was living, or by his family. The Brehon selected considered the case, but he seemingly did not settle the facts. They were settled by some local assembly in the regular Aryan public fashion. This settlement of facts having been submitted to the Brehon, he made his judgment and declared the compensation. This compensation was based upon rank. Where the injured was subjected to disgracing or humiliating acts, the compensation was increased, or, as we say, punitive damages were given. For the taking of human life, the compensation was the regular fixed price by law, if the killing was unintentional. If premeditated, the compensation was doubled. It was still heavier, according to the wealth of the injurer. This is the simon-pure law of punitive damages, at the common law, for a wilful injury. The damages for death went to the kindred. If the redress were for an injury to property, the restitution was in kind, double the amount of the injury. Here appears the *lex talionis* with a penalty added.

The Brehon procedure was made as compulsory as possible by the customs of distraining and of fasting. In the custom of fasting appears the old primitive idea of a violator of the custom being put to shame. The creditor whose debt was unpaid proceeded to the door of the debtor, just as in India the creditor is now accustomed to do, and at the door the creditor sat fasting. If the debtor submitted to the fasting, he was considered guilty of a most disgraceful act. He could stop the fasting by an offer to pay, or, as we say, by a tender of the debt. Fasting also could be stopped by the supposed debtor demanding a hearing before a Brehon. The claimant could proceed in the first instance by a distress, by seizing the property of the obligee by way of self-help, just as the landlord could distress at common law upon his demand for rent. The defendant in the distress could stop the distress by an offer to submit the case to a Brehon, just as the distress at the common law was stopped by a replevin, which was in fact the invoking of the judgment of a court as to the lawfulness of the distress. When the Brehon had given his judgment, a distress or distraint could be used to enforce it, and if there were no property, the person of the debtor could be seized.

This development in the Brehon laws is important as showing among primitive Aryans an attempt to reach an agreed tribunal, whose judgment could be enforced. It is characteristic of every primitive system, that before a tribunal can possess a power of decision in a controversy, or as we say, jurisdiction to decide it, the power or jurisdiction must be given by agreement of the parties to the dispute. It is also of importance because it is recognized that the tribunal must be endowed with special and expert knowledge of the laws. This means in modern phrase that lawyers are a necessity. The sequel in the history of law will show that the main difficulty in the law has not been in the law itself, or what the rule of law is, but rather, first, in devising an adequate tribunal to decide fairly the controversy in accordance with law, so that a rule of law applicable to all alike may be applied to all alike, and secondly, in so ordering procedure in applying the law that a right given by the law may always meet with proper redress. No little part of the difficulty has arisen in keeping the learned class of lawyers capable.

Before passing from this law of the Irish Celts, it may be said that substantially the same general organization of clan property existed among the Scottish clans in the Highlands, and this clan system of property passed on for many centuries until the exigencies of supposed statesmanship required the reduction of the clans to the sway of orderly English government. The legislators, being totally ignorant, apparently, of the kind of ownership of real property in the clans, and having no apparent knowledge of the fact that a part of the land of the clans belonged to each member of the clan, vested the whole real property of the clan in the chief. Ownership that had existed for many ages was ruthlessly destroyed in this way. Very few of the chiefs were worthy of such a responsibility, or were enlightened enough to deal fairly with their kinsmen in the clans. The consequences were no less deplorable in Scotland than in Ireland. The great body of each clan became mere renters, cotters, and tenants at will. The time came when it suited the chief to dispossess the helpless occupants whose titles ran back over thousands of years. The remorseless evictions were, as a matter of fact, based upon later laws which, let us hope unwittingly, simply confiscated rights in property that had been accepted and recognized for ages.

Before leaving the subject of Aryan laws, it will be proper to make some general observations on the Celts. If we may accept the Brehon law, the Celts in Ireland were further advanced in many ways than the Celtic tribes on the continent. The general organization on the continent was the same as that indicated in the Brehon law. The clan was divided into families, and the clans formed a tribe, and several tribes coalesced into a nation. Over each tribe was a chief and the chiefs of the clans made a sort of nobility. The Romans called, after their own analogy, these nobles the Senate. There had been in Gaul a king of federated tribes but those kings had been abolished, and there had been substituted an elective vergobret who had kingly functions. These human societies were in many respects feudal, made up of patrons and clients, to use the Roman terms. Below these classes were the serfs and slaves. In many places the lord lived in his larger timber mansion with the houses of his dependents surrounding.

When Caesar came into Gaul in 59 B.C. he found the Druids a powerful class. They were still in the old savage way performing human sacrifices. Either the Druids or the chiefs dispensed justice, settling disputes not only between individuals, but between the tribes. There was a peculiar anticipation of Romanism. If obedience was refused to the edicts of the Druids, the disobedient were excommunicated and denied religious observances, nor could they ask for justice before the tribunals.

These Celts were exceedingly advanced in certain ways just as were the Britons in England an advanced race at that time. The Gauls carried on commerce by means of their two-wheeled carts, so common in rural France to-day. They had manufactures of iron and pottery. One-half of the black and red ware in museums to-day that passes for Greek, came out of the great pottery factories in the Auvergne. They were experienced miners and they had among them large amounts of gold and silver. As cultivators of the soil they had taken on the skill of the Iberians submerged among them. They used a coultered plough and a reaper for wheat which Pliny the Elder asserts was a trough with dented edges made into teeth. It was mounted on two wheels drawn by two horses and the ears of wheat were cut off by the teeth and fell into the trough.

In southern Gaul the Greek city of Marseilles antedated the Gallic coming into Gaul. The Greeks there had introduced the olive and the vine and the cultivation of the vine had covered southern France and penetrated to Alsace. The Gallic methods of cultivation were superior to those of the early Romans. Italian Gaul was highly cultivated. When Hannibal's soldiers from the top of the Alps looked down into the valley of the Po, they thought they had found the garden of the world. These Gauls knew the use of fertilizers and produced very superior wheat, or as they called it, corn.

The cattle, horses and swine were noted and superior to anything in Italy. When Caesar conquered Gaul, he found so much wealth that he paid immense debts and became the richest man in Rome and had the means of rewarding all of his followers. These people wore trousers with a sort of smock coat and a cloak with a hood. Their taste for bright colors converted the Italians from the sober togas which they wore to the bright colors that are characteristic of Italy to-day. Thus early the French began to set the fashions for the world. Yet, so far as legal institutions were concerned, the Gauls were living on the plane of the barbarous customs of the Aryans. A comparison with what is told of the Germans at that time shows that the Germans as yet had not reached even the plane of cultivators of the soil.

The Roman conquest of Gaul was followed by a few abortive rebellions. Then the Gauls settled down to take on the culture of the Romans. Their acquisition was rapid. In a comparatively short time, fine cities, splendid mansions, great estates, productive factories of pottery and arms, made Gaul a very rich province. The Germans across the Rhine looked with wolfish eyes on this wealthy province. At last they gradually edged their way into Gaul and rapidly destroyed the greater part of its civilization. The situation that then arose will be portrayed in the chapter on medieval law.

CHAPTER 4

Babylonian Law

FROM THE LAWS OF THE CELTIC ARYANS it is necessary to go back in time some thousands of years in order to find the original line of legal development and a much higher condition of law. Leaving on one side the Egyptians, for the reason stated that they are not in that main line, the story of the law of civilized men begins with the Semites in Babylonia, thence it passes to Palestine, thence to the Greeks, the Romans, to continental Europe and to the English. It will appear that this legal evolution proceeds in an unbroken and continuous development with each race passing on something of achievement to its successors. It will be found, as already indicated, that the law continued to be made by the general average opinion of the social aggregate, with different ways of expressing this opinion, while the search still went on to devise a tribunal adequate and competent to ascertain the law in an authoritative way in the form of general rules, yet flexible enough to reconcile the rigidity of a general rule with particular circumstances of peculiar hardship. This search for a competent tribunal is the main problem of law.

The Semitic races are a part of the great Caucasic race. One part of the Semites flowered into a civilization, of the highest order till then attained, in that part of the world where Hebrew legend placed the original birthplace of man. This country was formed by the deposits of the Tigris and Euphrates rivers that flow from the highlands, and the fluviatile lands were constantly expanding into the great alluvial plain which lies at the head of the Persian Gulf. Prior to this time the most advanced portion of the human race in Egypt and in Asia had begun the use of the highly polished stone weapons which marked the beginning of the Neolithic Age. This could not have been subsequent to 10,000 B.C. An Aryan or Semitic race called the Sumerians (for the theory of the Mongolian character of the Sumerians is now exploded) was found in possession of this alluvial plain. They first developed to some extent this land. They had their villages, the cultivated lands, irrigating canals and a growing population. Their highest attainment was their development of written language. As in after ages "the Assyrian came down like a wolf on the fold," so the Semites came down on the Sumerians. Then first began that long series of conquests, whereby the more savage barbarian, seeing a rich land which has reached wealth and the comforts of civilization, true to his bandit and robbing nature which urges him to take what he can from others not of his tribe, moves with overwhelming force upon peace-loving, hard-working communities, and conquers them with fire and sword. Until the last few centuries this has been an easy task.

There has been much foolish talk to the effect that there is something weakening, enervating, and corrupting in honest work, in steady labor, and in the accumulation of wealth, whereby men are enabled to expand their minds and advance the march of civilization. Modern Europeans as well as the Romans and the Greeks used this language because they were descended from such covetous savages, but civilization is not corrupting nor enervating. The simple fact is that men who have work to do, who have learned the lesson of fruitful toil, who delight in seeing around them the works of peace and civilization, cannot always be ready for war, cannot be continually training themselves for battle as can the tribes of savages who are always ready to move in a compact mass on any unprepared community. An Alaric, an Attila, a Theodoric or a Clovis, a Gaulish Brennus, a Vandal Genseric, a Saracenic Othman, or Omar, or a Mongol Tamerlane deserves no credit for having overrun regions full of peaceful civilization. Their weapons were as good and their forces larger. On anything like equal terms the civilized man has always defeated the savage. But the nonsense about the corruptions of civilization is probably the most wearisome stuff in our histories.

As early as perhaps 5000 B.C. a Semitic tribe called Akkad, or Highlanders, moved down upon the Sumerians, and the union of these two races produced the most talented race that had yet appeared on the earth. The conquest was apparently an easy absorption of the invaders. The Semites appropriated as well as they could the Sumerian customs and established themselves in the Sumerian cities. There was developed in the course of a few thousand years by this Babylonian race a perfected system of irrigating canals applied to cultivated lands. The fertility of the country seemed afterwards to the Hebrews to make a veritable Garden of Eden. This race developed for western Asia, at least, the art of writing. The writing was by cuneiform characters upon clay plates that were then hardened and preserved. This method was older than and far superior to the cumbrous hieroglyphics of the Egyptians. The characters stood for syllables. The Semites expanded this writing into a most expressive language. The use of language in writing at once added great divisions to the law.

This race also probably invented the art of making weapons and other articles out of bronze, at first a natural alloy of copper. It is the first sign of metal-working in the history of the human race, and the bronze probably came from the Armenian country. As early as 5000 B.C. bronze articles are found in Babylonia. The working in bronze was probably the result of an accidental discovery, arising from the fact that bronze can easily be made malleable and then hardened. Bronze weapons were made in imitation of the cumbrous polished Neolithic stone weapons that had been in use over four thousand years; but so slow is man to change his ways that the use of bronze in Babylon did not become general until about 3000 B.C. The working in bronze passed to Egypt after a long interval, but the Bronze Age in Egypt did not begin until about 1600 B.C., and it passed to the Greeks about the same time.

The effect of the use of bronze became very soon apparent, as the bronze weapons were gradually made lighter, for they gave superior weapons and bronze tools made possible the dressing of stone and the building of stone structures.

The Babylonian cities with their growing manufactures and wealth formed the greatest center of trade in that age of the world. The main trade route from the Orient, with caravans continually setting out for Asia Minor and the Syrian cities, furnished a very large commerce. Manufacturing of various kinds in these cities made a division of labor possible. It is impossible to overestimate the change that had come. Suddenly, comparatively speaking, we are taken from the pastoral age of the Aryans and the Semites and put into a civilization of cultivated lands, an elaborate system of irrigation, permanent houses, large dwellings made of unbaked bricks or of stone, and of great temples. In fact it is apparent that the system of laws among the Babylonians must be adapted to a very high and complicated civilization of a great commercial community. Outlanders, being of some use, ceased to be enemies. Commerce cultivated good relations. Men in this complicated civilization owed duties to many more different people. A law of contract, of an easy and flexible kind, must develop to suit a commercial and banking stage, with cities engaged in manufacturing and in all kinds of commercial transactions, and a surrounding country engaged in very productive agriculture. Settled forms of agriculture add a new body of law. Yet necessarily their laws show many characteristics inherited from a primitive culture, for men will long cherish their used and accustomed ways.

The original form of government in the cities had been theocratic, following the common original development among Aryans and Semites, which originally lodged power in the priests and then passed the duty of leadership in war to kings and chiefs as a part of the discipline needed for conquering hordes. These Semites had passed far beyond the point of the polytheism of the Aryans. Each city had its own god, or in some instances a blend of more than one god, but the Semitic tendency was toward the one deity, although the Semites readily acknowledged that there were other gods presiding over other cities. Each city was ruled by a chief priest, and he gradually took on the proportions of a petty king but retained his character of a priest. This priest-king originally sat at the gate dispensing justice, as in other Semitic tribes like the Hebrews, hearing the complaints of suitors, adjusting their disputes, and laying down the law. But the Babylonians developed a trial court and an appellate court system.

At last one great king, Sargon, about 2500 B.C. subdued the whole of Babylonia and ruled a united kingdom. Two hundred years later came the greatest of these Babylonian rulers. He founded the city of Babylon, which was to remain for over seventeen hundred years the great city of the world. He kept his governor in each city, but the prevailing god in Babylonia came to be a blend of the two gods Baal and Marduk, whose great temple rose in Babylon. This king was Hammurabi and he was, no doubt, a very enlightened ruler. The kings of Babylon, for the protection of their trade route, gradually extended their empire toward the west until the Babylonian Empire stretched to the Syrian coast. They conquered by means of better weapons and a better discipline.

But these people were far from being entirely civilized. One curious survival is seen that must have been based upon some primitive belief that went back to a time when a wife, if she had no children, lost all right to share in the family estate, and lost her status as a wife. The reason for the legal custom was plain enough, and one result of this condition was that a wife could give her husband a slave or maidservant and claim the slave's children as her own. This practice is clear enough in the story of Abraham, Sarai, and Hagar. A different result of the legal situation as to a wife without children, inherited from a time of an utter lack of any idea of chastity, was a practice of virgins at the temple of Babylon. It is said that the original practice was for the virgin to stand at the temple and sell her favor for money to any casual passer in order to give the money to the temple as an offering to the great goddess Ishtar. Thus her fertility was assured. This form of the practice seems to be doubtful. The established practice was for the virgin to pay the priest for his embrace, and this is probably the original religious ceremony. It seems far more likely as a primitive priestly belief gradually becoming an imposition. It was widespread among the Aryans, and in India to-day the practice as a regular proceeding from a remote past is for the bride to cohabit first with a Brahmin priest. In Europe either the Celts or the prior inhabitants had the same ceremonial. It came down even to medieval times as the *jus primae noctis* or *le droit du seigneur,* but among the Semitic Hebrews the practice never existed, for among them, as among us, a lack of chastity in the bride that has been concealed is sufficient ground for annulling a marriage. But it is likely that the chastity idea is not a primitive belief.

A final invention that came out of these lands or Egypt was the discovery of the working of iron about 1400 B.C. It rapidly supplanted bronze, and as the Stone Age yielded to the Bronze, so the Bronze yielded to the Iron Age, and in the Iron Age with its modification of steel the world has always remained.

Owing to a wide use of writing among the Babylonians they committed all transactions to writing. Their legal custom (which is called a statute of frauds among us) that required practically every transaction to be evidenced by a writing, and the preservation in the ruins of cities of clay plates on which are written deeds, bills of sale, bonds, receipts, accounts, drafts drawn at a distance, promissory notes, and many judicial decisions constituting the oldest law reports, give us much more certainty as to Babylonian law than we have regarding any other ancient system except the Roman.

At the head of the government stands the king. He respects the rights of the different cities under his sway, but his kingdom is a city-state ruling other cities, as was the wide sway of Athens, of Rome, of Florence, of Milan, or of Venice in later ages. The king does not profess to be a lawgiver or a legislator, but he has the custody of the laws and he assumes the duty of saying what they are; and for the first time it appears that the state has assumed the duty of doing justice to its citizens. This point had slowly been reached through the ages and was a further development of the instinct, now a reasoned process, of protecting the social state. The laws are delivered to the king as divine by the god of the city, and the oldest collection of laws in existence is the so-called code of Hammurabi. It dates from between 2250 and 2000 B.C., and the older date is probably nearer the true time. These laws were first discovered from their inscription upon a diorite stone, but other older copies in clay have remained. This is the origin of the practice of the laws of various races being inscribed on stone. But in every instance such laws are merely the old, settled customs reduced to writing.

At the head of the stone is the figure of King Hammurabi receiving the laws from the seated figure of the god. The laws open with Hammurabi's words: "Law and justice I established in the land, I made happy the human race in those days." Thus early we get a picture of a great king who felt that his highest claim was that he made his people happy. The first part of the laws has been erased by some subsequent king, but the far greater part and all the important part of the laws inscribed remains. This code can be supplemented by a vast number of clay documents of various kinds mentioned above.

As time passed on, the Babylonian kingdom suffered many reverses. Gradually higher up on the rivers arose the state of Assyria with its god Ashur. The Assyrians had the same system of laws, generally speaking, and they had received from the Babylonians the art of writing documents. By this time a language called Aramaic and coming from Syria became widely diffused through all of Mesopotamia and many of the Assyrian documents are in this language, which seems to have been used indiscriminately with the Assyrian tongue. The Aramaic was afterwards to become the language of the Hebrews. In process of time the Assyrians absorbed much of the civilization of Babylon, but they were never the talented race that had made the first great civilization. As time went on the Assyrians, through their better disciplined army of bowmen—another instance of a better weapon and better discipline—became the conquerors of the world from 900 B.C. They disputed the control of the East with the Egyptians and after the great Egyptian conquerors overran the territory reaching from Egypt as far as Mesopotamia, the Assyrians conquered the Egyptians and ruled all of western Asia and Asia Minor in one great empire. A single people in their mountain fastnesses repelled the Assyrian conquest. They were a part of the Hebrews, although the greater part of Palestine passed to the Assyrian rule.

The Assyrian Empire exhausted itself by its continuous war and another Semitic race, the Chaldeans, resuscitated the great empire of Babylon. They finally conquered even the remnant of the Jews, destroyed Jerusalem and transported a large part of the population to Babylon, where it remained during the Captivity until the Babylonian

King Hammurabi receiving the laws from the seated figure of the god

Empire was finally destroyed by Cyrus, an Aryan conqueror from the uplands of Persia. But the laws of Hammurabi endured for thousands of years through all these changes; and even in after ages when Seleucia was the capital of the Seleucid successors of Alexander of Macedon, and still later when Bagdad was the city of the Caliphs, the successors of Mahomet, Omar, Othman, and Ali, the same laws continued to govern a fairly flourishing land. It was reserved for the Turk to turn Mesopotamia into a desert, but perhaps under another rule Babylonia may regain something of her ancient fertility.

As will later appear, many of these Babylonian laws, especially the commercial laws, passed to Palestine and Syria and to Asia Minor and its Greek cities, then to Greece itself and formed the basis of the commercial code at Athens. From Athens and Rhodes the same laws passed to Rome, and from Rome were diffused through continental Europe, and they exist to-day. One point to note is that the law among the Semites, being the expression of divine and errorless wisdom, must necessarily be unchangeable. The only way in which the law could be ameliorated was by a delivery of new law from the god to the priests or to the king. The connection between the law and the priest was plain in Babylon, but the secular judges and the civil courts gradually supplanted the judges and the priestly courts. This was the process in Palestine and long afterwards in England. From Palestine the connection between law and priest passed to Rome after the advent of Christianity, and out of the Hebrew law and the Roman law was created the canon law. This situation was dominant in Europe all through the Middle Ages, and from its results we are not yet entirely freed. These developments will be noted later in the proper connection.

In considering these laws of Babylonia we may consider first the public law. The king is the head of the state, the guarantor of the laws and of justice to his people, the high priest and representatives of the god. He rules by divine authority. The institutions were the work of the god. As St. Paul was afterwards to say, "The powers that be are ordained of God." The Babylonians agreed with the divine right of kings, which was afterwards to be developed by the philosophers of absolutism from Hobbes to Hegel. The king was deified just as afterwards were the

Roman emperors. Under the king were the nobles, the freemen, and the slaves. The word for a noble became also the word for a freeman, and this change showed a growing tendency to political equality. One distinction was that a freeman must accept compensation for an injury, while a noble could exact a retaliation for a corporal injury. The nobles were probably the conquering race and kept their own customs like the Franks in Gaul or the Normans in England. The noble for injuries inflicted by him paid a heavier compensation. The analogy of the situation to that of the Normans in England is plain. The freemen constituted the bulk of the community that was free. Below them were the slaves and serfs. The slave belonged to his master, but he could buy his freedom or could be manumitted. If a slave married a free woman, her children were free and half of the property was free to her. The slaves on the estates were generally of a subject race and were bound to the soil and had rights in the land they possessed. They were probably no worse off than the original English copyholder on the manorial estate.

Strangers and aliens were numerous in the cities. No question seems to have been made that they should have the benefit of the laws. It was a general rule among Semitic commercial communities that, to quote the Bible, "There shall be one law for the homeborn and for the stranger that sojourneth among you." Even in our Constitution the jurisdiction given to federal courts to protect the foreigner or the citizen out of his own state can be traced directly back to the Babylonian law. Generally speaking, there was one uniform system of law in Babylon, all received from the god and all in fact customary law. Much of the old savage law was gone. There was no tribal law. This had all passed into the state and city law. The practices of the blood feud, self-help except distress, and marriage by capture were gone, but the family solidarity and the district responsibility were substituted for the kindred. The law of exact retaliation remained as a rule of damages. There was private property in the head of the family as representing the whole family.

The king had his own estates. The different cities had the duties they levied on goods in transit and ferry dues. The ferry dues would indicate one public utility owned by the city. The land in private ownership had its fixed charges, like the knights' fees under the Norman kings. A definite area furnished for the army a bowman and a pikeman. The latter carried the shield for the bowman and for himself. Royal authorities commandeered property and gave a receipt for it. The land was bound to furnish the men for the army but the conscripts were often, it would seem, of the condition of serfs. The nobles went to war and no doubt furnished the officers for the army. The law was that a man was bound to serve but six times in the army.

Certain estates were held of the king, like the grand and petty sergeanties under the English kings, on personal services to be rendered to the king. All estates that were ancestral were tied to the family, but the holder could alienate them subject to the family right to redeem, which was not limited in time. This law among the Hebrews is vividly pictured in the book of Ruth. Much land was rented, especially by the temples, which held great possessions in land. This was to be repeated in the great possessions of the medieval church in Europe. The temple estates furnished many leases and many burdens were imposed on the temples. They must preserve certain hereditary rights in a portion of the temple of a character approaching the English advowson, or right to appoint the incumbent of a church. The temples were required to make advances to the poor and to furnish seed and corn and implements, and they were required to redeem certain prisoners who had been captured in war. It should be remembered that there were no poor laws in England until after the confiscation of the great estates of the abbeys and monasteries.

The law of landlord and tenant seems fairly enlightened. The rent was as contracted for, but if there was a failure of crop a moratorium or delay as to payment took place. If the rent was fixed, an accidental loss fell on the tenant; the tenant was bound to cultivate the land in a proper manner, or, as we should say, in a husbandlike manner, and he might leave the land if he left it in good condition. The tenant had power to sublet the land, but if the lease was one on profit-sharing, as where a temple was landlord, and the tenant was supplied with implements and cattle, there were harsh penalties on the tenant for selling the implements or mistreating or subletting the cattle. One very advanced sort of law was a building lease. The tenant put up the building which at the end of eight or ten years belonged to the landlord, just as we have our ninety-nine-year building leases. There were contracts of hiring cattle. The lessee was an insurer against loss, that is to say, he took the risk. He was required to keep the cattle properly bred and was responsible for any trespass on private property by the herd. Since there was an elaborate system of irrigation, that organization took the form which it has generally preserved. There was a general ditch from which the water was taken out into private ditches. It is probable that there was a public superintendence of the taking out of the water and of its use. The user was responsible for all damages resulting from the escape of the water after he had taken it. This law remains until the present day.

There was much employment of hired labor and in the case of all sorts of hired workmen the rate of wages was fixed by law. This is the original of the English Statutes of Laborers. There was a relation, therefore, of master and servant distinct from that of owner and slave or serf, just as that condition afterwards arose in England. In regard to other domestic relations, the law as to husband and wife provided for a marriage by purchase, arranged between the fathers. It must have been a curious sight throughout Babylonia, when the day came when all the unmarried girls of proper age were publicly put up for marriage by purchase. But it should be remembered that when in the early settlement of Virginia unmarried girls and women were brought over from England, they were put up for sale in the same way that fathers offered their daughters for sale in Babylonia. There was no marriage without a written contract, and it provided whether or not the husband became liable for his wife's debts before marriage. If the contract was silent, he became responsible, but by contract he could repel this liability. He was liable for his wife's debts after marriage. A divorce was optional with the husband, but if there were children their support and the wife's support must be provided for upon a divorce. This is our law of alimony. The wife had her action against the husband for cruelty and neglect, and if the husband died leaving children, the wife could not marry unless the interests of the children of her former husband were fully protected. In this early civilization a wife could be a sole trader, for there was a penalty directed against those who led married women into improvident mercantile ventures.

All deeds were drawn up by an officer corresponding to a notary. These men were called scribes or scriveners. The deeds were confirmed by oath as to the warranty and publicly sealed and witnessed by witnesses. The greatest freedom of contract by agreement existed, and it is probable that there was no formal character of contract. It was all a matter of intention and agreement as evidenced by a written document. The Babylonian law as to written agreements was about what our law is today. A contract put into writing cannot be contradicted by oral evidence to the effect that the parties made some other agreement. All were what we call consensual contracts and each contract provided that any dispute arising thereon should be submitted to the decision of the king, and the parties were bound to abide by that decision. This shows that the king's assumption of the readiness to do justice was not compulsory on the parties but was an arbitration to be agreed to, just as among the Celts the submission to the decision of a Brehon was not compulsory but the result of agreement. This was the original rule in English law as to a jury trial, when the jury was originally instituted. This is shown by our pleadings in the fact of what is called the similiter, where the one party puts himself upon the country, that is to say a jury, and the other party pleads that he doth the like. This is, in fact, an agreement to submit to a jury trial. All men know of the contracts among us to submit disputes arising under contracts or under wills to some kind of arbitration; but the conception of the jurisdiction of courts is so changed among us, that no agreement to arbitrate can oust the compulsory jurisdiction of courts.

All the different transactions of sale, lease, barter, gift, dedication, deposit, loan, and pledge were matters of contract. These legal transactions have never changed their character. The promissory note for money loaned took the form of a bond to pay. Lands or goods were delivered by means of the symbolical delivery of a staff or key, as in medieval English law of livery of seisin. The agreement to pay the purchase money was sometimes in the deed and sometimes put in the form of a bond. The seller sold the goods on the basis of *caveat emptor*. The correctness of this rule was debated in Roman law, but it was firmly imbedded in the common law of England. It means that the seller does not warrant the goods unless he agrees to warrant.

If a man bought or received goods on deposit from a minor or a slave without power of attorney, he must produce the seller and the bill of sale or the witnesses, or he died as a thief. A man was required to give up stolen property, but he had a five-fold remedy against one who had sold him stolen property. The purchase of goods abroad was subject to the true ownership, if the goods came to Babylonia. On a sale there was a warranty as to slaves which was generally against a particular kind of sickness for one hundred days. The female slave was delivered on a three days' approval. A Mann Act was certainly foreign to the ideas of these people.

Payment in commercial transactions was usually in money, stating the place of payment, but payments in produce were provided for with a statutory equivalence. In extensive trade transactions speculative contracts were made where money or goods were delivered to an agent to travel and sell and to reinvest the proceeds, and this sort of transaction is continued until the present day, as will appear later. By these commercial adventurings a large commerce was carried on. Caravans were public carriers and a written receipt for all goods was necessary, like our bill of lading. No other claim for goods could be made except for those in the receipt. This is the present law of carriers. If an agent to travel and sell or buy made no profit he was required to return double what was confided to him, and if a small profit was made he made up the deficiency. In other cases, and they were the normal rule, profits were shared, and, singularly enough, neither the carrier nor the agent to sell was responsible for an act of the public enemy.

On consignments to caravans the freight was paid in advance and the carrier was responsible at all events, except for acts of the public enemy. Warehouse receipts were issued for goods. Ships were hired for water carriage. On a contract for building a ship a warranty was made of seaworthiness for a certain period. In cases of collision of ships the moving ship was always at fault.

The liquor trade came in for its regulation. The keeper of a tavern must prevent disorderly conduct on the premises under pain of death. In commercial transactions payment through bankers or by written draft against deposit was common, and bonds to pay were negotiable. There was always a marriage contract, and if a wife had no written marriage contract she was not a wife in fact. Ignorant people still show an almost fanatical zeal over their marriage lines. But a curious survival was that the wife remained part of her father's family. Among the early Romans the wife passed to the husband's family. The wife forfeited her right as wife by misconduct, but upon her divorce she kept her dower property. If the wife failed in her action against her husband or was proven a bad wife, she was drowned. If a husband left his wife without maintenance she could take up with another man, but she must take her husband back when he returned, and her children went to the husband; otherwise she was treated as guilty of adultery. This would have been a pleasant land for Enoch Arden.

Monogamy was the rule. There were at the temples vestal virgins who married but were not supposed to have children. They furnished a substitute in the person of a handmaiden. The father had power over his daughter, but the brothers managed the sister's property until she married, and then her husband had control. The son became emancipated on his marriage if he was of age, and he obtained his share of the property. In other words the patriarchal family and its estate had ceased to exist except as a thing to be constantly divided.

Adoption of a child was common with childless people, but if an adopted child, on the discovery of his true parents, desired to return to them, his eye or tongue was torn out. It may be assumed, therefore, that an adoption generally stood. The adopted child shared in the family property as a child and all children shared equally in the father's estate. There was no right of the firstborn as among the Hebrews. A child could be disinherited only by a judicial decision.

The crime of adultery in the wife was recognized, but she was entitled to a kind of proof that survived for ages as the trial by ordeal. If when thrown into the river she sank, she was proven guilty, but if she floated her proof of innocence was complete. Babylonian women who intended to indulge a vagrant fancy were, no doubt, trained swimmers. In later ages William Rufus, the second Norman King of England, scoffed at the ordeal. It certainly would have been a sounder method of proof, if guilt had been shown by floating. All would have been guilty or drowned.

The law as to damages was strongly tinged by the primitive law of exact retaliation. If a builder built a house so that it fell and killed the owner, the builder was put to death, but if it killed the eldest son of the owner, the eldest son of the builder was put to death. It remained for the Jews to advance the law beyond this primitive stage and rescue the son. In any event, the builder rebuilt the fallen house. The law was that if any one destroyed another's eye, his own eye should be destroyed. If a bone was broken, his own bone was broken. If a tooth was knocked out, his own tooth was knocked out.

There were penalties of different amounts of savagery for theft, for illegal buying or selling, or receiving stolen goods. A false claim, kidnapping, harboring of fugitive slaves, and brigandage were offenses. If a debtor's son in the custody of the creditor suffered death caused by the creditor, the creditor's son was put to death, and in the case of a bad builder, the penalty was exact, owner for owner, son for son, daughter for daughter. Banishment and the lash were other methods of punishment, but there was no imprisonment, it is needless to say, because prisons were far in the future.

A curious fact was that the law as to dangerous animals at large was precisely the law of negligence. The responsibility of the owner depended upon his knowledge of the character of the animal. This, it will be seen, is the Hebrew law in Exodus and in Deuteronomy, and from the Hebrews it passed to the Romans and to England. Carelessness or neglect was punished and the standard of negligence seems to have approached our standard of reasonable care. A surgeon was held to strict accountability. If he caused loss of life or limb he lost his hands, if a veterinary, he paid for his malpractice. It has taken long ages for doctors to achieve the comfort of burying their mistakes.

It would seem that witnesses appeared before the judge and a curious analogy to our separation of witnesses at the trial was the injunction when witnesses were summoned that they must not come together. In later Hebrew law witnesses were examined separately. In certain cases where witnesses would have been of no particular value or could not be ascertained, the ordeal was resorted to as a method of proof. For instance, the law provided that if a man had placed a charm upon another, and had not justified himself, the supposed wizard could make his proof of innocence by going to the holy river and by plunging in. If he drowned the accuser took his house, but if he was saved and thus proven innocent, the accuser lost his life and his house. This should have discouraged prosecution for wizardry. The same ordeal was applied to a wife for unfaithfulness, but in that case when the wife passed safely through the ordeal, the husband did not lose his life. If men are of such a mentality that they believe in spells and witchcraft, there would seem to be no better proof in such a case than the ordeal. Even in England before Sir Matthew Hale in the last half of the seventeenth century, the question of guilt of witchcraft was submitted to a jury, and among us the witchcraft proceedings at Salem convince us that the primeval savage terrified by the dark fears cast by his own ignorance still had power in fixing the law.

Women devoted to a religious life suffered death for going into a wineshop, and the slanderer of a nun or of another's wife who could not justify was branded on the forehead. If a wife went insane she was required to be supported, but the husband could marry again. Such a law would have been a comfort to George Eliot. Whenever a contract was annulled it was canceled by being broken to pieces. Every decision of a court was given in writing. The deputy of the king in the various cities rendered decisions in the first instance and an appeal lay from his decision to a bench of judges who represented the king.

This is but a very abridged sketch of Babylonian law, but it shows what extraordinary advances had been made by this talented race. Many of the cumbrous practices of the earlier Aryans and Semites had been cast off, and the social organization was far on the highroad to the conditions afterwards attained at Rome. But it is here to be noticed that private personal property had at last emerged as the possession of the individual. Individual responsibility was beginning to dawn in the law. A law of crime as a public offense was dawning. The relaxing effects of a widely extended commerce on the primitive law are very plain. The law has now become complicated. No longer is the casual knowledge of the elders or the priests sufficient in the law. A learned class of judges is manning the king's courts, and justice has become something that the king owes to all his land. Had it not been for the destructive effects of a conquering race like the warrior tribe of Assyrians with their new disciplined army of bowmen, and for great conquerors like the Assyrian Esarhaddon, Sennacherib, and Shalmaneser, this splendid civilization might have gone on to the finest issues. Even as it was, civilization is such a priceless possession that Assyrian, Chaldean, Persian, Macedonian, and Saracen conquerors left this garden of the world with its law practically unharmed until the unspeakable Turk reduced it to beggary and barbarism.

CHAPTER 5

The Jewish Law

THE SEMITIC LAMP OF LEGAL CULTURE was passed on to another race whose genius lay in gradually ameliorating conditions in the law by elevating the ideas of the Deity, and by advancing the conceptions of rightful conduct. After Babylonia had long been a flourishing empire the Hebrew race emerged from a barbarous condition of life. They, by their very position, lay in a critical place. The marching and counter-marching armies of Semites and Egyptians, contending for the mastery of the world, passed over the land. The reëditing of the Hebrew documents after the Babylonian captivity renders it difficult to separate different stages of the Hebrew laws. But since those laws have exerted their great influence on the medieval and modern law of Europe in their form, as shown in the Bible, it is not necessary to do more than to take the laws as they now exist in what we consider the sacred Scriptures. Accuracies of translation are of no importance, for the Latin Vulgate version and the English translation of the Scriptures have been the form through which the Jewish influence on European law has been exerted. It makes no difference whether the translation was exact or not. We must accept the laws as they are in the Bible as translated, and they must be considered for legal purposes as correctly translated, for in that form they entered into the development of the law.

It goes without saying that the Hebrew laws are the product of a long development. They begin as primitive customs, which are gradually ameliorated with the progress of time. After the captivity at Babylon, many things from the Babylonian law were incorporated into the Jewish law. The Diaspora, or dispersion of the Jews, resulted in great Jewish communities in many lands. But the following sketch of Hebrew law will be confined to that part of the Jewish law which was passed on to the Romans and by means of the Scriptures and medieval priestly judges exerted so great an influence on modern law. The religious ceremonial law lies outside of this line of influence. We are not here concerned with the fact that critical study of the Scriptures would find much to criticize in the medieval lawyer's beliefs as to the original source of Hebrew law, and as to the validity of any assumption that those laws are properly called divine.

The first glimpse we obtain of the Jewish tribes shows a patriarchal form of family and a tribal organization where the priest is the ruler and leader of his people. The priest is the actual ruler and he alone was able to convey to his followers the commands of their god. He was the custodian of the laws, and was the judge of the disputes in the tribe. Thus would speak a medieval lawyer, using the Bible to ascertain its legal commands as the words of revealed truth. To him every text was the undoubted wisdom of Omnipotence and all the texts were to him of equal force and all came from the period and from the authorship that was claimed for them. The laws emanated from God and were divine, and the priest alone administered them.

The story of Jethro, the Midianite, the father-in-law of Moses, although very late and showing some Hebrew scribe rationalizing the ancient writings, indicates the condition and gives us our first example of a reformer of legal procedure. The tale indicates that Moses, with his duties as leader and ruler, mouthpiece of the God, recipient of the laws, and judge of all disputes, was an exceedingly busy man, wearing himself out in attending to his multiform duties. Jethro had come to visit his son-in-law and to congratulate him not only on having escaped out of Egypt, but on having so thoroughly "spoiled" the Egyptians just before starting. Moses in hospitable fashion had a dinner for his guest and invited to meet him Aaron and the elders. This has a modern sound. Aaron, a great talker, highly entertained the Midianite at the dinner, though he, no doubt, was discreetly silent regarding the golden calf episode. The next day Jethro, in wandering about, came upon the curious sight of Moses as he sat to judge the people "from the morning unto the evening." Jethro is the first on record of those curious animals who can sit patiently in a court room all day hoping for something to happen which may be interesting. It was, to use an anachronism, all Greek to Jethro, and he inquired of his son-in-law what he was doing, sitting alone all day with the people standing by. Moses replied that they came with a dispute "to enquire of God" and he judged "between one and another" and made them "know the statutes of God and his laws."

Jethro, who apparently had never seen such a performance before, replied at once with preternatural wisdom: "The thing that thou doest is not good." It wears you away and is too heavy for you and you cannot do it well all alone. "I will give thee counsel." Continue to intervene between the people and their God, teach them the ordinances and the laws, but "provide out of all the people able men" and let them judge the small disputes, but "every great matter they shall bring unto thee." Moses took the advice of this first and eminently sane reformer of procedure, and did choose able men who judged the people at all seasons and "the hard causes they brought unto Moses, but every small matter they judged themselves."

This is a belated priestly explanation of the institution of various kinds of courts and the general idea of an appellate court. Perhaps the Midianite nomad was a traveled man, and had seen such institutions in Babylon, where they had been in use for a thousand years or more. The story is clear as to the judicial function belonging to the priest.

It is of no importance to us that the exodus of six hundred thousand people, with flocks and herds, as Genesis represents it, would have required a train of march about two hundred miles long, that a forty years' sojourn in the desert of such an array is out of all question, that the function of manna to feed the array seems problematical with great flocks and herds available, for these supposed historical facts have nothing to do with the legal situation, except to show that the tribe was living in the pastoral or nomad stage.

Moses showing the tablets to the Israelites

The divine command, as the priestly scribes represented it, had been given expressly for a kingdom ruled by priests without a king, "a holy nation." This theocratic idea of government, advanced in the Scriptures, has never been given up by the religious, as witness the Puritans in England and New England and the Scotch Presbyterians. The system was a failure in Palestine as it will be everywhere. After an experience that left the Jews in subjection to the Philistines with their arms taken away from them, they demanded a king competent to lead. Samuel, the judge, is related to have painted for them a frightful picture of what kings would do to them, but the people "refused to obey the voice of Samuel" and very sensibly said: "We will have a king over us; that we also may be like all the nations; and that our king may judge us, and go out before us, and fight our battles." They were evidently weary of poor generals and poor judges, in spite of the startling performances of Samson, who was a judge of Israel. Singularly enough the account, which is, of course, by a priest, states that Samuel sought advice of the Lord and was told to let the people have their own way, that they would pay heavily for it. Thus happened in Palestine what had happened more than a thousand years before in Babylonia; the king became the fountain head of justice until, after Israel passed under the Assyrian and Judah under the Chaldean, the priestly rule was restored for a time.

The change to a kingly rule was immediately successful. The Jews grew in prosperity and wealth. They penetrated along the great trade routes and became active in commerce. They took their alphabet and the art of writing from the Phenicians. They produced a large amount of religious writing that was unparalleled in its elevation, although some of the Egyptian and the Babylonian literature of this kind is very beautiful. The state suffered dissensions in its exposed situation. The Kingdom became divided. These misfortunes were constantly treated by the priests as due to a departure from the worship of the Hebrew god and the rule of the kings was tempered by priestly rebukers, just as long afterwards St. Ambrose rebuked the Emperor Theodosius.[1] Underneath

---

1. St. Ambrose's rebuke of the Emperor Theodosius is discussed further at *infra*, p. 188.—C. J. R., Jr.

this history lies a legal development which began with the usual primitive practices of the Semites.

Among inherited primitive institutions the patriarchal family stands out very clearly, and as a consequence the custom of monogamy was prevalent. The head of the family seems to have had absolute power over his children, so much so that Abraham could prepare to offer his son as a sacrifice. This is the salient fact, a father had the power of life and death over his son. Marriage had become a matter of contract, and the husband had control over the wife. The forbidden degrees of marriage were all within the kindred, except that the Hebrews were commanded to marry within the tribe. This exclusiveness was fed by a jealousy of their God toward other gods, but this injunction to marry within the tribe was continually violated. The daughters of Heth that wearied Rebecca continued to be attractive. Property was originally family property and was kept within the family by the usual expedients. There were certain customs calculated to preserve the family and its property. The widow could call upon her deceased husband's nearest male relative to marry her. The original statement is that the widow could conscript her husband's brothers. The story of Ruth, a very late book in the Old Testament dating from a time after the Captivity, illustrates the situation and is interesting because it turns on a point of law.

A Hebrew, Elimelech, from Beth-lehem-judah, at a time of famine, in the period of the Judges and before Saul or David, went into the land of Moab, taking with him his wife Naomi and their two sons. The husband died, and the sons married in Moab, one marrying Ruth and the other Orpah, both Moabitesses. The sons died, and Naomi started to return to Judea. She advised her daughters-in-law to return to their own people, for Naomi said, "I have no other sons to marry you," meaning, of course, that if she had other sons the law would compel them to marry the widows. Orpah went back to her family, but Ruth "clave" to this pearl among mothers-in-law. The two women came back to Bethlehem in the beginning of the barley harvest. Naomi now looked for some one out of her husband's family to marry Ruth (the agnatic relation is emphasized; there was no duty to marry laid upon Naomi's own family). The law suddenly becomes wide enough to entrap as a husband for the widow any male kinsman of the dead husband of Ruth, but the law gave the preference to the nearest male kinsman. The law, however, meant nothing to this lady. She selected the wealthy Boaz, a kinsman of her husband's, but not the nearest; and Ruth, who had some confidence in her own good looks, suggested that she go to glean corn in the field in the hope she might "find grace" in some one's sight. The harvest field as a place to look for a husband sounds primitive. Naomi, no doubt, took care that Ruth went to the right place to find Boaz. The detail of the tale is too prolonged for quotation, but Boaz was helpless in the hands of the two women, and they schemed it so that Ruth was, as we should say, thoroughly compromised.

Boaz seemed much taken by Ruth's beauty, and by the fact, so flattering to an elderly man, that Ruth "followed not young men." There was, however, a kinsman nearer to Ruth's dead husband than was Boaz. This kinsman had the right or, perhaps we should say, the duty to marry her, but if the nearest kinsman would not exercise his privilege, Boaz announced himself an eager candidate as the next kinsman in line. Naomi, evidently instigated by Boaz, now called upon the kinsman to redeem a tract of land of her dead husband, or perhaps she put the land up for sale; and Boaz brought the nearer kinsman before the elders of the city and offered him the chance to buy or redeem, saying, "You buy also of Ruth and you must take her with the land"; but the kinsman said that he would be compelled to go into debt for the land, and he said to Boaz, "Buy it yourself." The beauty of Ruth had no effect upon this clod. Thereupon Boaz said unto the elders, "Ye are witnesses that I have bought the land of Elimelech and his two sons, and have bought Ruth, the Moabitess," wife of one of the sons. So Boaz married Ruth and the story ends with Naomi holding in her arms her first grandson, whose grandson was King David. He probably inherited his ability from his great-great-grandmother. Boaz was a doomed man as soon as Naomi selected him as a husband for Ruth.

When we look through this story to the legal conceptions behind, it shows the marriage by purchase, the fact that the land inheritance must be sold to, or, if sold, redeemed by, the nearest kinsman that wished to own it, and that it was the duty of the purchaser to take the widow of his kinsman along with the land. This tale has a plot founded upon a good law-point, the first of such plots on record. It is a curious mixture of primitive law, female perspicacity, love at first sight, and sound ideas of business.

In the earlier law a vein of unconscious humor is introduced by the provision that if the brother or kinsman of the dead husband was so ungallant as to refuse to marry the widow, he could be haled before the old men by the slighted widow, who was permitted to address him in exceedingly contemptuous terms, and then she was given the inestimable privilege of "spitting in his face." This also seems to be quite primitive; and yet the legend among the feminists is that the primitive laws were made by men for their own advantage.

Another primitive element in Jewish law is the *lex talionis*, the age-old expedient of an exact retaliation. It is said to the law-breaker, "If any mischief follow, then thou shalt give life for life, eye for eye, tooth for tooth, hand for hand, foot for foot, burning for burning, wound for wound, stripe for stripe." There crop out here and there the old taboos of defilement by the touching of any creeping thing, the eating of certain kinds of food, the eating of meat unless it have the proper butchering. All these taboos are most pronounced in the priestly code of law: "a blind man, or a lame, or he that hath a flat nose, or any thing superfluous, or a man that is brokenfooted, or brokenhanded, or crookbackt, or a dwarf, or that hath a blemish in his eye, or be scurvy, or scabbed . . . shall not come nigh" the altar. In the list of things forbidden to be eaten are the camel, hare, coney, horse, swine, eagle or osprey, the kite, vulture, raven, owl, hawk, cuckoo, swan, pelican, stork, cormorant, heron, lapwing, bat, every creeping thing that flieth and anything in the water without fins and scales. The reasons given for tabooing swine, "that it parteth the hoof but cheweth not the cud," points to some sort of prehistoric judgment that came out as a taboo. The camel's hump is said to be good eating, horseflesh is an excellent viand, and the swan for centuries graced the royal table. There is no reason for proscribing the eel, and locusts are said to be good food by those who enjoy them. What would become of crabs and lobsters under this divine command? Only a priest could object to ham or bacon. The injunction against eating anything that dieth of itself was sound from a sanitary standpoint. Other taboos are curious. The prohibition of a team made up of an ox and an ass, the command that a bastard's progeny shall not enter the congregation until the tenth generation, the injunctions to keep cattle of unmixed breed, not to sow mixed seed, not to wear any garment of mixed wool and linen, have some basis in primitive beliefs. Perhaps the injunction that a man shall not wear a woman's clothes, nor a woman a man's, belongs in the same category. But it would seem that the Jews had never heard of a mixed team of dog and woman, such as can be seen in some European countries.

The law considered peculiarly divine was the Ten Commandments which were delivered engraven on a stone "by the finger of God." Moses, in his disgust at the golden calf performance of his followers, broke up the first copy, but he was furnished with a second. These laws are of a legal, a religious, or a moral character. It is worthy of note that there is no sanction to those laws as delivered; that is to say, no punishment is prescribed; but the people are plainly told what evils will fall upon them if they violate these laws. Yet the evil is not to fall upon the wrongdoer, it is to involve both innocent and guilty in one common destruction. In other words, here in its baldest form is the old primitive idea of no individual responsibility, but the general liability of the tribe or the city or the kindred for the wrongdoing of any one of the tribe or city or kindred. This is a belief grounded in human nature, and few today who read and believe in the righteousness of the punishment foretold, feel any repugnance to the injustice of the penalty. But as will appear, the Jews themselves prescribed punishments upon individual breakers of these laws. In fact, the Bible itself shows that there was a customary law much older than the law delivered to Moses.

The first command is the injunction that is wholly religious: "I am the Lord, thy God . . . Thou shalt have no other gods before me." In the law that was said to be spoken by Moses, the injunction is given to kill any one, a brother, a son, a wife, or a friend, who enticeth to go and serve other gods. Such a one is to be stoned to death. The prophet Elijah smote or caused to be smitten many who longed after the worship of Baal. In another place there is an injunction to make no mention of the name of other gods, "neither let it be heard out of thy mouth." As soon as those of Christian faith obtained control of the government of the Roman Empire, the harsh laws against unbelievers that remained throughout the Middle Ages began. The offense at first was called apostasy. The term "atheist" had already been appropriated by the pagans as an opprobrious epithet to describe the Christians. A noted Christian martyr was hurled to the beasts in the Alexandrian Theater with the cry, "Away with the atheist." In the Middle Ages the denial of the formulated creed of the theologians was punishable by burning at the stake, and the melancholy instance of the learned Servetus at Geneva among the Calvinists rivals the folly of the death penalty imposed on Socrates. Savonarola's death at Florence by burning seems to have been compounded of a penalty for poor prophecy, a hot resentment against a priestly rule, and a general offensiveness to the ecclesiastical authorities.

The second command supports the first by forbidding the worship of idols in any form. The prohibition is directed against any image or likeness, not apparently against the worshipping of natural objects, such as the sun or the moon; but the law spoken by Moses is that worshipers of the sun or moon or other gods are to be stoned to death. The images and idols are ordered to be burned and destroyed. A prophet speaking in the name of other gods shall be put to death. In this connection is a sound legal test for true prophecy, where it is said that if the thing follow not nor come to pass, the Lord hath not spoken but it is the prophet's own presumptuous speech. This is equal to Jeremiah's statement: "When the word of the prophet shall come to pass, then shall the prophet be known, that the Lord hath truly sent him." If this was the sole test of prophecy, there was no reason why any one might not attempt it. If one by accident stumbled on a true prediction, he at once became a prophet. The commandment against idols itself imposes by way of punishment, after the Lord states that he is a jealous God, that the sins of the fathers shall be visited upon the third and fourth generation. This is the family responsibility substituted in the primitive way for an individual punishment, and it bore no appearance of harshness or injustice to those who were incapable of conceiving of individual responsibility.

The third command has been thought by some as intended to cover the case of one sworn on the name of God, who does not respect the oath. In the law is the command: "Ye shall not swear by my name falsely." This commandment has for ages dictated the form of the oath in court and the crime of perjury. At other times—and this is the common meaning ascribed to it—it has been considered as a command against profanity and blasphemy, because it was readily perceived that a law that forbade false statements merely when an oath was taken in the name of the Lord left much to be desired as a command to speak the truth. Yet this idea has had its effect. There are countless people who do not hesitate to prevaricate, but if they are put under oath the old commandment has its effect.

The fourth commandment enjoins one day of rest during the week. For the Jews this day was the Sabbath. A thousand years before that time the day of rest during the week was observed in Babylonia. In the commandment as edited, the day of rest is given as a resemblance of the creation of the world in six days, and the Lord's rest upon the seventh. To us this seems little short of irreverence. The later rationalists laid stress upon the value of the Sabbath as a day of rest. It was not only for believers, but for servants, slaves, and strangers, and the work cattle. It evidently belongs long after the nomadic days of Moses. It was a religious observance among the star-gazing Babylonians, celebrating the change in the phases of the moon, as the week is merely a quarter of the lunar month of twenty-eight days, each quarter corresponding to a phase of the moon. The last word in the Jewish law on the subject is that the day of rest exists "so that thine ox and ass" may rest and that "the son of thine handmaid" and the stranger may be refreshed. There is a case recorded of a poor wretch who went out gathering sticks on the Sabbath day and was stoned to death. This injunction carried into law in Christian countries not only has furnished material for the criminal law, but, in the civil law as to contracts made on Sunday, or a bill or note presented on Sunday, or any of the other varied circumstances in which the question arises, has produced some quite extraordinary law. The long insistence of the gloom of the Puritan Sunday among us has caused the strong reaction against it, which by very religious persons is ascribed to the machinations of the Evil One, whoever he or it may be.

The fifth commandment, to honor father and mother, shows that at last ancestor worship, so plain in the Hebrew writing, is having its effect. It is an immediate outgrowth of the patriarchal family. "Ye shall fear every man his mother and his father" is another form. He that smiteth his father or his mother or that curseth his father or his mother shall be put to death, is the legal form. Another provision of law was that a rebellious, incorrigible son, who refused to obey his parents, might be brought before the judges and by them he should be sentenced to be stoned to death. When King Herod desired to put his two sons to death, he quoted to the court which he assembled at Berytus this ancient law, as Josephus tells us in his *Antiquities of the Jews*. But if any one supposed that a mother would take part in this unique proceeding for putting to death a son, he must certainly have had little experience with the ways of mothers toward erring sons. This commandment is the basis in our law of what control parents can legally exercise over their children of maturer years. As a part of this law came the Jewish respect shown to the old. In the law they were commanded to rise up before the old, and this is to-day our custom of good manners, which only the uncouth or the ignorant disobey, although it is no longer law.

The sixth commandment is the prohibition against the killing of human beings. The Prayer Book translation attempts to rationalize this command by the translation: "Thou shalt do no murder"; but this is simply importing it into the later law. In primitive law every killing, accidental or otherwise, was an offense against the kindred. Men of that epoch were incapable of weighing the impalpable matter of intention. The original form of the law was, "He that smiteth a man so that he die shall be surely put to death," but it was later recognized that there was a difference in killing. Then it was said that if the killing was not premeditated, the slayer might flee to a city of refuge. The cities of refuge were in charge of the Levites. They were for the manslayer, that he "may flee thither which killeth any person at unawares"; that is to say, accidentally. There were three cities beyond the Jordan and three in the land of Canaan. The case is put of two men felling trees and the axe flying off the helve; in such case the killer shall flee to the city of refuge and live.

In this connection the avenger of blood appears. He is the one in primitive law who is acting for the kindred and carrying out the blood feud or law of self-help. By the custom he can kill the slayer wherever he finds him. The law was later rationalized by a consideration of intention and by the nature of the weapon, if iron or a stone or a hand weapon of wood. The killer, in case of the use of a deadly weapon, was a murderer and should be put to death. This in our law is a presumption of malice from the use of a deadly weapon. If the slayer kill out of malice or by lying in wait he is a murderer, but if he kill suddenly without malice (our manslaughter) or cast anything upon the deceased without seeing him, or accidentally, and was not his enemy, nor sought his harm, the congregation of the city of refuge shall deliver the accused out of the hand of the avenger of blood and there in the city of refuge he shall stay until the death of the high priest. But he must stay in the city of refuge. If he comes out he can be killed. After the death of the high priest, the slayer can return to his own land—a curious statute of limitations, but the event of a high priest's death was one that the whole public would know.

It appears that the Jews once had the old system of the composition or satisfaction given by the slayer for the killing, but murder had now become rationalized into, first, our murder or premeditated malicious killing; second, our manslaughter upon a sudden quarrel without malice; and, third, accidental killing. It became recognized that this offense of murder was no longer a private wrong to be settled by a composition or customary payment, for it was provided that the murderer must be put to death. No composition or satisfaction could be made for it, nor could there be any composition allowing a slayer to come out of a city of refuge. It need not be pointed out that the law of sanctuary in English law and all our present distinctions in the law of homicide trace directly back to the Semitic law. Connected with the law of homicide was that of assault and battery, but this injury was to be compensated for by paying for loss of time and by causing the injured to be thoroughly healed.

The seventh command shows the fully developed right in the head of the family to the fidelity of his wife. Adultery as an offense, however it may be rationalized, is really in the paramour an invasion of the husband's assumed right to exclude others, which is the legal definition of property. It was an offense in which then and now a married woman must be concerned. The Jews had none of the looseness in sexual ideas of the early Babylonians. If a woman married who was not a virgin, she should be stoned to death. The offense of adultery was one committed by a wife. It was not an offense in the married man unless he was the accomplice of a married woman; but modern law has given the wife a reciprocal right of exclusive possession. The law was that if a man committed adultery with another's wife, he should be put to death along with the erring wife. Fornication with an unbetrothed and unmarried woman required the offender to marry her, but if the father of the maid refused to allow the marriage, the offender was bound to pay money to the father of the damsel. The amount was the ordinary dowry of a virgin. This is our common law of the father recovering damages for seduction, given by the legal fiction of loss of service. Fornication with a betrothed maiden was treated as adultery. Fornication with a betrothed bondmaiden—i.e., a slave—was not punished by death but by scourging. The priests were certainly sound on the subject of conjugal fidelity in the wife.

The eighth command, against stealing, recognized the fully developed idea of property. The command was carried further in the injunction which is much less primitive in tone: "Ye shall not steal, neither deal falsely" with one another. "Thou shall not defraud thy neighbor." The idea of stealing is carried into fraud and deception. All stealing could be compensated at the rate of five oxen for an ox, and four sheep for a sheep. Stealing was as elsewhere a private injury. If the thief were found with the property, he paid double. There was no question that there was a clear right to kill the burglar, as to which some doubt has been made under our law.

The ninth command is one of mingled law and morality. It may be either an injunction to be honest in social relations or an injunction to speak the truth as a witness. The law in Exodus enjoins against raising a false report, or being an unrighteous witness, and in another place it is said: "Keep thee far from a false matter."

The tenth commandment is an injunction of morality against a state of mind. It is not a workable law, just as the injunction to "love thy neighbor as thyself," found in the Mosaic law, is not a workable law. Except where a belief is made a crime, the law deals only with acts.

The Ten Commandments do not cover, except inferentially, certain well-known subjects in law. In those other matters there appears in Jewish law a spirit of great liberality. If we take the condition of slavery, the master who caused a loss of an eye or a tooth to his servant thereby made the servant free. If a Jew was sold as a slave to another Jew, such a slave, man or woman, must be released at the end of the sixth year. The law proclaimed that the escaped slave should not be delivered to the owner. This divine law could have been quoted against our Fugitive Slave Law. Kidnapping to sell into slavery was visited with the death penalty. Perhaps the release to be given to debtors at the end of every seventh year was only a counsel of perfection, as was no doubt the general injunction to lend to the poor. Both injunctions affected only Jews as the recipients of bounty. Charity was strongly enjoined as a duty. In spite of the jealousy toward other gods and the endogamous practice of never marrying with any other tribe, the liberal Semitic law as to strangers was enjoined. The provision as to the one law for homeborn and stranger sojourning, supplemented by the extension of the right to claim a city of refuge, was given to the stranger. The stranger should not be vexed, but he "shall be unto you as one born among you, and thou shalt love him as thyself."

Just weights, just balances and just measures were enforced by the law. Fields should not be gleaned but should be left for the poor and for the cattle. "Thou shalt not muzzle the ox when he treadeth out the corn" is an oft-quoted duty. "Do not remove thy neighbor's landmark" became a curse in the minatory law. In the vineyard the passer-by might eat as he pleased, but he could not carry anything away. Land must lie fallow every seventh year, so the beasts could eat therein, and in the vineyard and oliveyard the crop was not to be gathered every seventh year. The employer was commanded to pay his laborer at the end of every day. The man who had a new wife was not to go out to war.

Witnesses were used in legal disputes. There was none of the old primitive methods of proof. The original rule which passed into the canon law and into our law of overcoming the effect of a sworn answer in equity, and into the law of treason, was that two or more witnesses were necessary to make the proof. This meant two eyewitnesses. The provision has caused endless trouble, but did something to ameliorate the English law of treason.

Certain changes were made in the law in progress of time. One was that the firstborn son should have a double portion. The case of the man who died leaving no son, but five daughters, produced the famous judgment that decided the law to be that if a man died leaving no son, his inheritance should pass to his daughters; if no daughters, to the deceased's brothers; if no brothers, then to the brothers of the deceased's father; and if these heirs fail, then unto his kinsmen that are next to him of his family. This was afterwards the pure Roman law of agnatic inheritance, except that in that law as it originally was, the daughters would not take a part. It is necessarily the law where kinship was traced only in the father's line. It is noticeable in Deuteronomy that there is no commercial or mercantile law, no provision as to all the varied contractual situations, which had appeared in the Babylonian law. For the most part there is no hint of a commercial community. Everything provided for suits the situation of a nomad tribe passing into a settled agricultural community.

But the greatest and most distinct triumph of the Jewish law was the final emergence of the individual. Quoted above is the much later Hindu statement. As we have seen, all the law of liability had been based upon the liability of the family or kindred. The innocent son was put to death for his father's fault; but at last came the law: "The fathers shall not be put to death for the children, neither shall the children be put to death for the fathers: every man shall be put to death for his own sin." No one can imagine how great an advance this was in all the criminal law or in private law where the *lex talionis* could be applied. At last, clearly and fully, the individual emerged as having rights of his own. No longer was the family treated as a whole in questions of responsibility.

There were defects like superstitious provisions of the law as to putting witches and wizards to death, or the stoning of a man or woman that hath a familiar spirit; but the English burned Joan of Arc at the stake, and all the excuse which they had was something of this character. The law of the Jews was entirely reasonable for their condition. Thus the general rule as to liability of an owner for an injury caused by a domestic animal was based upon the owner's knowledge of the dangerous character of the animal. In this connection appears too what became in English law the deodand; that is to say, the thing animate or inanimate which became forfeited because it had caused a death. In an English tin mine in the time of Richard II (1377–99 A.D.), a piece of rock fell from the roof and killed a man. The King, treating the whole mine as forfeited, granted it away to a third party. The King's grant caused a lawsuit where some fine distinctions were made.

The Hebrew law of general liability for animals ran in these terms: "If an ox gore a man or woman that they die, then the ox shall be surely stoned, and his flesh shall not be eaten [this is a taboo]; but the owner of the ox shall be quit." But if the ox was known to the owner to be dangerous and it was not kept in, the penalty was that the ox should be stoned and the owner put to death; but if a sum of money was imposed (here appears the money composition) he shall pay it, and likewise for a son or daughter. Should it be a servant killed, the payment was thirty shekels of silver and the ox to be stoned to death. The law as to a pit was that the owner of the pit must make good any loss, ox for ox, ass for ass, and the owner also retained the right to keep the injured animal. If an ox injured another ox, the owners of the two oxen were to divide the money arising from the sale of the wrongdoing ox and from the sale of the dead ox; but if the ox pushed in time past and was not kept in, the owner of the pushing ox must pay ox for ox. If a fire was kindled and it spread, the kindler of the fire must pay all the damage.

If goods were stolen from a bailee in possession of them, the judges were required to decide the matter, if the thief was not found. That is to say, each case depended upon its own circumstances. The law for mercantile transactions developed when the Jews became traders, as they did through all the cities of the Levant. But aside from the law, the peculiar value of the Hebrew Scriptures was that they taught an elevated system of morals, improving from remote times until the late period of the apocryphal book of Ecclesiasticus, or the Wisdom of Sirach. In future ages the Scriptures were to prove of incalculable value by producing

higher conceptions of morality, and by inculcating obedience to the
commands of righteousness. With the triumph of Christianity in the
Roman Empire every rule of the Scriptures that was legal passed over
into the later Roman law and then on to the English law as the divine revealed law of God, while the late and fully developed Jewish monothe-
ism and the abhorrence of idols have molded the Protestant religions
since the days of Luther. When that great ruler Ptolemy Philadelphus
was increasing his library at Alexandria, he brought from Palestine
seventy-two learned men to furnish him with a translation of the
Hebrew law into Greek. He and his scholars were much impressed by
the contents of these laws. From that time much knowledge of the
Hebrew law became current in the Hellenic world.

It is perhaps needless to say that the later developments of Hebrew
law and further illustrations of that law, growing more and more enlightened, making up a new and greater body of law, with the commentaries both upon the texts of the Mosaic law and upon the customary law,
not considered Mosaic or divine, are not noticed here because those
parts of the Jewish law-writing did not have any appreciable effect upon
the main stream of legal development. The insistence upon the Deity,
the one God, so powerful an influence in other systems of law, is the part
of the Jewish law to which the later reviser, uttering a final eloquent injunction, put into the mouth of Moses, is referring, when he says: "What
nation is there so great that hath statutes and judgments so righteous as
all this law which I set before you this day? . . . Keep therefore and do
them; for this is your wisdom and your understanding in the sight of the
nations, which shall hear all these statutes and say, Surely this great nation is a wise and understanding people."

As long ago as Josephus's book on the *Antiquities of the Jews* and his
Reply to Apion, and the sketch of his own Life, it was pointed out that
the ideas of the Jewish law were having their effect upon the Greek and
Roman law. Certainly the greatest single principle developed by the
Jewish priests in the realm of law was that each individual shall stand before the law responsible only for his own acts and the acts of those for
whom he has voluntarily made himself responsible. Both morality and
law were transformed when they cast off the primitive inheritance of a

solid kindred liability and substituted the reasoned and rational basis of individual liability. This, from the legal standpoint, deserves to be called the highest contribution of the Hebrew law.

For the general history of ideas, and especially of ideas in the realms of religion, the Jewish race produced that conception of immediate contact between man and the Deity, which no longer required the intervention of a priest to placate the Deity. The insistence in the New Testament upon the fatherhood of God and the brotherhood of man has in it nothing new or original. The Hebrew people had been passed through the fire and had come out of that purifying experience with enlarged ideas of mankind. The doctrines and writings of the Stoic philosophers would have furnished the world with the conception of the one God, but their cold and austere ideals lacked that touch of profound emotion toward God, with which the Psalms and the last part of the book called Isaiah, supplemented by the New Testament, were to enrich and elevate the spiritual experiences of the race, and to feed that growing conception of individual responsibility that has done so much to ameliorate the harshness of inherited rules of law.

CHAPTER 6

Law Among the Greeks

WHEN LAW AMONG THE GREEKS is reached we are at a period where jurisprudence is first begun to be studied. In some respects Grecian law (if it can be said in any true sense that law governed among them) from about 500 B.C. begins to take on in outward appearance a modern dress. To the talented portion of this race, with its intense brilliancy of intellect, so much is owed that it is possible to feel indulgence even for their mistakes in regard to matters in which they should not have failed. The tone of the great Roman advocate, the younger Pliny, toward the Greeks is admirable. He is writing to his friend Maximus, who is about to go to Greece as governor under the Emperor Trajan at the beginning of the second century of the Christian era. Pliny exhorts him:

> Remember that you are sent to that real and genuine Greece, where politeness and learning took their rise. You are sent to regulate the condition of her cities, to a society of men who breathe the spirit of true manhood and liberty, who have maintained their natural rights by courage, virtue, civil and religious faith. Revere their ancient glory and their very antiquity which, venerable in men, is sacred in states. Give to every one his full privileges and dignity. Even indulge his vanity. Remember that *they gave us laws*. Remember you are going to Athens and Sparta, and to deprive such a people of the declining shadow of liberty would be cruel, inhuman and barbarous.

But just as impressive is the colloquy upon Athens at the opening of the fifth book in Cicero's *De Finibus,* a none too lively work. It is almost a duty to quote the words of that greatest of all the men who have ever given themselves to the practice of law. He is speaking at a time when Athens had declined from her great estate to become a part of a Roman province, but was still the school and university of the civilized world. Cicero and his brother Quintus, his cousin Lucius Cicero, his lifelong friend Pomponius, better known as Atticus, and Marcus Piso, of a great Roman family, are studying at Athens. They had walked out of the city one afternoon from the Dipylon Gate to the Academy, to that

> olive grove of Academe,
> Plato's retirement, where the Attic bird
> Trills her thick-warbled notes the summer long.

These young college students, as we should say, are talking of their surroundings. One points to the chair whence once had come the golden voice of Plato; another says that he has just been looking at the village of Colonus near Athens and thinking of the noble choral ode of Sophocles and the lovely lines where the blind Oedipus, led by his daughter, comes to that hamlet, shadowed under the gray-green foliage of its olive trees. The youngest of them had visited the Bay of Phalerum and had walked on the shore, where Demosthenes had declaimed amidst the roll of the waves, and trained his voice to stem the clamor and uproar of the Athenian Assembly. Coming back he had turned out of his way to stand at the tomb of Pericles. Another had been in the gardens of Epicurus. Cicero himself speaks of the breadth of vision that comes from travel, and he points to the Hall of Carneades and muses on how it seems to be grieving for that mighty intellect and the sound of the voice now still. They talk of how endless are the scenes in Athens, where one can hardly go to a place where he does not feel that he is treading on historic ground. Piso adds that, whether it arises from a natural instinct or from an illusion, we are more touched when we see the places associated with great men or noble deeds than when we are told of them or read about them. To-day our students in the American School at Athens must often speak in much the same sense. This is all the more reason why one should feel indulgence for those to whom civilization owes so much, and should never seem to minimize the glory of this "mother of arts and eloquence."

The achievements of the Greeks in the fine arts of sculpture, painting, and architecture and in the beauty and richness of their literature still are in many ways unrivaled. Their attainments in science, considering that they were without the telescope, the microscope, and other instruments of precision, were remarkable. They ascertained that the earth was round, that it revolved upon its axis, that it moved around the sun, and that the axis of the earth was inclined to the plane in which it revolved around the sun. Both Aristotle and Plato, however, denied this fact and taught that the sun revolved around the earth. Eratosthenes, after their time, by a brilliant geometrical demonstration approached quite nearly to the true circumference and diameter of the earth. The fact that the moon revolved around the earth was known. The diameter of the moon, the fact that it shone by reflecting the light of the sun, and its distance from the earth were fairly well determined. Anaxagoras taught that the sun was a molten mass, but the ignorant were then as impervious to ideas as they are now, and he was saved from an Athenian indictment for impiety only by the exertions of the great Pericles. Aristarchus, a little later than Eratosthenes, approximated the size of the sun and its distance from the earth. The atomic theory of matter was suggested by Democritus, and the fact of gravitation was well known. Archimedes at Syracuse multiplied the uses of the screw and the lever, and showed what a practical mathematician could do in the siege of Syracuse by the Romans. The scientific writings of Aristotle were, for that age, a marvelous collection of knowledge, some of it much mistaken, but through Aristotle the Middle Ages obtained what it had for a scientific basis of thought. The world still teaches rules of grammar as the Greeks first classified and arranged the elements of language.

Once it was a received opinion that Greek development was comparatively short before it suddenly expanded into the splendid Periclean age at Athens. It was supposed that the race rapidly passed from a half-barbarous condition to a high civilization. But later investigation has proven that the Grecian, like other civilizations, represents a long sequence

where the barbarism of a conquering race is grafted upon a much older
and higher culture. Before Hammurabi ruled at Babylon, and perhaps a
thousand years before the Hebrew tribes possessed Palestine, a portion
of the Mediterranean race, closely allied to the Phenicians and
Philistines of later times, had in the island of Crete attained much civilization and was carrying on a large trade with Egypt and Asia. This civilization, called Minoan, after hundreds of years, penetrated to, and became diffused on, the mainland of Greece and northward as far as
Thessaly. Successive invasions of semi-civilized Achaeans and after a
few centuries Ionians and Aeolians, and still later Dorians, wrecked this
older civilization in the usual manner of Aryan barbarian invasions. But
the preceding civilization enabled the barbarians to absorb some of that
high culture and a portion of the Greeks was on the highroad toward the
later accomplishment.

So far as the history of law is concerned, we need not notice the
Dorians, whose leading state was Lacedaemon with its capital Sparta.
They, ruling a conquered subject race reduced to serfdom, were organized in military form and maintained, in a hostile population, the
barrack-room discipline of soldiers encamped amid a subject population. Their legendary lawgiver, Lycurgus, was a myth. Their customary
laws and institutions are of no importance, except that they explain some
of Plato's curious reactionary tendencies in his legal writing. The
Dorians who took possession of Crete had laws similar to Sparta's.
Those laws have been found engraven upon a wall at Gortyn. At Sparta
was first noticed the tendency of property to accumulate in the possession of women and the looseness of female morals that seems to go with
this development. The Greeks were indefatigable colonizers in almost
every direction, and their various city-states in southern Italy and in
Sicily, in northern Africa and as far away as Spain and southern France
at Massilia, now Marseilles, had their collections of Greek laws. These
laws may all be disregarded.

The story must be confined substantially to the single collection of
four Ionic tribes living in villages, inhabiting the hilltops around Athens
and the small surrounding territory of Attica. These people arrived from
the north with the ordinary barbarian Aryan institutions and customary

laws, and became a ruling class among the native inhabitants. While these invading Ionians were coalescing with the indigenous people, the Ionian and Aeolic cities on the Aegean Islands and the mainland of Asia were carrying on a great commerce as subjects of Asiatic rulers in lands that at last had come under the sway of the Great Kings, successors of the Persian Cyrus. As soon as authentic history begins, the confederacy of patriarchal kindreds forming the usual monogamous agnatic clans of Ionians in a natural course of events, absorbing an older and superior civilization at Athens, had a written language, borrowing the Phenician alphabet, and had gotten rid of a large part of the primitive Aryan conditions. The one savage trait which the Greeks never lost, and which makes Grecian history such a nightmare of wasted opportunity, is the intense zeal of the tribesman for his own tribe and his natural ingrained hatred for every other tribe. Plato in his ideal state pictured in the *Laws* could conceive of no other situation than a city-state under arms awaiting a treacherous attack from some neighboring city.

Passing over the legends of Theseus and succeeding kings at Athens, we come to an oligarchy of well-born (eupatrid) families who control the state. The Athenian political development took the course first of an overthrow of the oligarchs, followed by a popular government, which, as usual, reacted to a rule of tyrants, who were Pisistratus and his sons; then came an expulsion of the tyrants, after they had made Athens a leading state of Greece. The Persian wars soon afterward, with the glory of Marathon and Salamis, placed Athens at the head of Greece. The great commerce of the Ionian cities soon passed to Athens. This city, then, for over a hundred years, in spite of its misfortunes, was the chief depot of eastern commerce.

The legal development at Athens took a way hitherto untried. The Aryan Ionians, with laws unwritten and with those laws in the custody of the priests, who were represented by the patriarchal heads of the families of the well-born nobles, decided that a change in their laws was necessary. As we have seen, there were as yet but two methods of creating new law to suit changed conditions. One was by the slow way of developing new customs, the other by the announcement of laws given by some god. The Greeks had no idea of promulgating laws by means of a god, but they had accounted for their laws by mythical lawgivers who had given the laws, and they also had some general idea that the laws were of divine origin, since they were in the custody of the priestly class.

The customary laws handed down by spoken speech were in the hands of the eupatrid oligarchs, as was also the administration of the laws. This situation met the demand of the lower classes, gaining in strength, that these laws should be put into written forms so that they should be no longer the sole possession of the well-born. It was a widespread notion among the Greeks that the laws, if put into writing, became the aid and possession of the many.

> With written laws, the humblest in the state
> Is sure of equal justice with the great.

This same idea appeared later among the Romans. The demand was met by the Code of Draco. It also was demanded that the nobles should no longer monopolize the administration of the laws and sit in judgment in the courts. To insure this result, the obvious thing was to use what they had. This is the instinctive course of all men to patch and use the ancestral robe of custom.

The Athenians had kept the Aryan conception of the general power of the tribal assembly. In fact, the popular belief that all political power came from this assembly resulted in a general political theory that the public assembly was the source of all legislative, executive, and judicial functions. Hence it was an easy step, when it seemed necessary to revise the laws, to constitute, in accordance with the method of tradition, by the vote of the assembly, an actual lawgiver in the person of Solon. But here it should be noted that this conception of undivided political power was destined for almost two thousand years to rule enlightened mankind. That length of time was required for men to recover from this mingling in the one popular assembly, or in the one ruling force such as a king, of powers radically distinct.

In an age incapable of thoroughly sound legal analysis—and this is true of the Greeks because the race had not yet the experience necessary to find a basis for such reasoning—men had not analyzed far enough to deduce that the legislative function consists in announcing a rule of law to govern future happenings, that the judicial function, on the other hand, consists in applying to a happening that becomes the subject of litigation a rule of law existing when the happening took place. If a new rule is announced by legislative power to govern a completed transaction, the power exerted is not a legislative power, but an arbitrary edict abrogating the applicable rule of law as to a past transaction and withdrawing from the party whose conduct is in question the equal application of the laws. For his particular case the party has been made an outlaw. As we have seen, the idea and concept of justice demand as the very essence of justice, preëxisting rules of law applicable to all alike and impartially applied. If this is not the situation, justice does not exist, nor do laws exist.

"Law is something more than mere will exerted as an act of power." Such is the weighty language of the Supreme Court of the United States.[1] Hence, when the legal system is so instituted that the legislative body can decide a lawsuit by an edict for a particular case, it is neither legislating nor adjudicating, but is simply exerting arbitrary and uncontrolled power, than which nothing is more contrary to the fundamental basis of justice. But this was not understood at Athens, nor was it understood at Rome during the days of the Roman Republic, nor is it understood to-day by those who talk of free judicial decision, meaning a decision where the judge freely disregards the law, because he thinks that for the particular case he can make a better law.

It is true that Aristotle pointed out from Athenian history the evil of government by edicts, but he did not go far enough to find that his fundamental ideas of the law were, as we shall show, unsound. He was merely dreaming on the subject of a state ruled by law. Cicero, with truer insight, in his *Topica* stated: "Justice requires that in the same cases there shall be the same laws." Or, as it has been stated in modern law, "The equal protection of the laws means the protection of equal laws."[2] Rome never truly developed this idea of justice, and of equal laws, until the

1. In *Hurtado v. California*, 110 U.S. 516, 535 (1884).—C. J. R., Jr.
2. *Michigan Central Railroad Company v. Powers*, 201 U.S. 245 (1906) (argument of counsel).—C. J. R., Jr.

Republic was no more. In order to insure equal laws it was found, long ages after the Greeks and Romans, that the judicial power must be separately and independently exercised. If a man cannot to-day see that it is in reason impossible to govern a completed transaction by a rule of law invented after the transaction happened, he is not a reasonable human being. Even in trivial matters like a game of cards, the none too intellectual devotees of that pursuit recognize at once the nonsense of inventing a rule to govern a play after the play has been made. To card players it is an axiom that the rule existing when the play was made must govern the play, and that has been the actual demand of justice as to important matters in all the ages since the idea of justice was first comprehended by men. The groping of the ages has been toward an administration of equal laws. It will now be explained why it was that under the Athenian system there never could result a government of laws.

Why it is that different races should receive an inclination in certain directions, we shall probably never have knowledge enough to ascertain. The Hebrew with his genius for speculating upon the righteousness of life inspired by God, the Greek with his genius for speculating on the nature of all the sciences and his passion for a democratic form of government, the Roman with his genius for institutions of government and laws, are instances of certain ingrained racial characteristics for which we find no explanation.

First of races to develop what we call the democratic form was the Athenian. Under Solon's legislation about 592 B.C., as supplemented by later legislation of 507 B.C., the popular assembly of all the citizens of Athens became the final depositary of all executive, legislative, and judicial power. This government was on its face democratic, but as a matter of fact it was merely a democracy of a ruling class. Athens was ruled by a close body of citizens limited to men of Athenian birth and descent. This body never exceeded thirty thousand and generally did not exceed twenty thousand men. It is likely that an assembly was rarely convened with six thousand. The homogeneity of the citizen body could not be disturbed by the admission of new kinds of citizens. The far greater number of free residents at Athens could never be granted citizenship by any process analogous to our naturalization procedure; they must always remain resident aliens. Yet this class owned by far the larger part of the wealth of Athens. Below the citizens and the free aliens was the still more numerous class of slaves. The resident aliens and the slaves carried on almost all the handicrafts, the manufacturing, the buying and selling, the occupations of a laboring and a middle class. It became a mark of inferiority for an Athenian citizen to engage in most of such occupations, except that in the larger transactions of foreign trade moneyed citizens took a part, as soon as the commercial supremacy of Athens was secured. Plato in his *Laws* interdicts all commercial occupations to free citizens, and in this he is reflecting more or less current ideas among the Athenians.

The farming people of Attica, who were all citizens, had in process of time so exceeded their means of living that on their primitive inalienable holdings they were practically serfs bound for debts to the wealthy among the citizens, who, by a natural process, were the oligarchs. Even if "money has never cared who owns it," wealth has always made its holders influential. Solon's primary step was to cancel by an act of confiscation the indebtedness of the landholding citizens and to render the farming class, temporarily at least, independent of the moneyed class. At the same time land was rendered alienable and each son was emancipated from the father's patriarchal rule as soon as the son reached the age of eighteen and was enrolled in the military force of the state. Thus was abolished the age-old inalienable Aryan family estate and the patriarchal family, but the fact remained that the father could not disinherit his children. This idea in the law that the father has family property and ought not to disinherit his children is a living power in law to-day.

Another feature of Athenian polity was the confirmation in the assembly of citizens of all the legislative, executive, and judicial power. Solon's division of the citizens into four classes, according to income, had little, if any, effect upon government. The legislative body was uncontrolled. The courts were in fact popular courts made up of citizens, and the numbers of the judges in them were so large that they were considered as branches of the assembly. Jurors were in fact judges, for these so-called dicasts or jurors made the judgment. Numbers of two hundred, five hundred, a thousand, and for certain matters a much larger number were provided. The jury list to supply the courts to the number

of six thousand was made up from the body of the citizens and was constituted anew every year. These jurors came to be paid officers. The
dogma of democracy was that each citizen was competent to perform
any function of government, and the public officers were selected by lot,
except the generals to command the army or the fleet. They were elected
by the assembly. By a natural process almost every citizen who needed
the money was put upon the public pay-roll. The Greeks were brushed
by the wings of representative government, for representative delegates
from Greek city-states formed the Amphictyonic League as well as the
Delian League of Athens, but the conception of a representative government never produced any result, just as their knowledge of the ex-
pansive power of steam never produced a steam motor.

It is a strange thing that Plato could see the folly of selecting for public officials wholly incompetent men, and yet saw nothing absurd in the
election of generals or admirals. He has a dialogue where he represents
Pericles, the son of the great Pericles, as coming up to Socrates and complaining that the Athenians had just selected as general a man without
military or naval training, simply a very successful man of business.
Socrates, in the dialogue, begins his process of questioning and shows by
Pericles' own admissions that many of the qualities of a successful business man would be needed in a general; and thereupon the assumption
is that the Athenians have made a wise choice. Young Pericles departs
apparently much befogged and is seemingly incapable of pointing out
the crass fallacy in the reasoning. Such reasoning probably was the cause
of the fact that Athenian armies usually but not always fled from the field
of battle. In our democracy the process is reversed. A successful general
is selected to some high office that he is incapable of filling, and in it he
makes himself a spectacle of utter failure as a civil magistrate.

But there was some saving sense among conservative men regarding
this power of the popular assembly to change the laws at will. There was
a feeling that the laws ought not to be lightly changed. To guard against
this evil the old Council of the Areopagus was left with a function of
guarding the laws. Later, wardens or guardians of the law were provided.
A proceeding was provided for putting a law upon trial with appointed
accusers and defenders who argued the question before the assembly.

Still later a regular action before the popular court was authorized to be brought by any one. The proposer of the law was treated as responsible for its failure or success, and the lawsuit was against him. The whole question of the legality of the manner in which a law was proposed or passed and its goodness as compared with some prior existing law or some other possible law, was tried before the assembly in a prosecution or indictment of a private citizen.

To us, such expedients seem childish, for the question of the constitutionality of the law, as we say, was confused with its expediency; but, if we assume the state of political development at Athens to be what it was, and the fact that the whole body of the people were legislating and that this whole body could not condemn itself, the expedient seems the only thing possible, if the sins of the people were to be shifted. When a bad law is passed to-day, we still cling to this primal belief that the stupid public is not at fault, that it has been misled or deceived. Aristophanes, in one of his comedies, brought the people on the stage as Demos, where it was led around by the nose, cajoled and flattered and deceived and made a fool of by artful demagogues. No doubt the play was highly applauded by the Athenians, who could not comprehend that the fable was narrated of themselves. The fact taught by the law is that any political society has the laws that it deserves.

There was provided also a council, originally the old Council of the Areopagus, and it was succeeded by Solon's Council of Five Hundred, who were chosen by lot. This body carried on the administrative business by a division into committees. To this Council was given the duty of preparing the legislation to be proposed before the Assembly, and originally a proper bill coming to the Assembly from the Council was necessary to legislation, but this safeguard was swept away. Certain executive officers, called archons, presided over the Assembly and the courts. One of them, the archon king, was so called because he succeeded to the priestly functions of the ancient kings in respect of religious observances and the domestic relations of husband and wife, guardian and ward, and the estates and wills of deceased persons. In later times, in medieval England, the ecclesiastical courts performed much the same functions as did the archon king's court at Athens.

Another important feature of the Athenian legal system was Solon's legislation giving to any citizen the right to take up the cause of any fellow citizen and to help him to obtain justice. This right was one both of accusing and of defending, but it was never expanded into the hiring of a lawyer, for there was no such class in Greece. Every kind of magistrate was compelled to render an account of his service to the assembly and was subject to a suit of some kind brought by any informer or accuser impeaching his action. Even generals of armies or fleets were subject to this kind of attack.

But the most curious production in a legal way of this jealous insistence upon the rights of democracy was the proceeding before the Assembly called ostracism. By a vote of the Assembly any citizen could be banished without a hearing, without a trial. It amounted to a legislative judgment of condemnation of a person accused. It is precisely the vicious and brutal bill of attainder used so long by the English Parliament with melancholy results. In England a legislative proceeding was used to put a political opponent to death when he could not be convicted by the regular processes of a court. Legislators can always be relied upon to have less conscience than judges. The bill of attainder is forbidden by our national constitution and our state constitutions. The Assembly also had a proceeding whereby a charge was brought in the Assembly and a prosecution directed to be made in a popular court, in the general manner of our impeachment, but the proceeding was not confined to public officers. This sort of proceeding was copied by the English and it remains with us as a prosecution of a public officer for high crimes and misdemeanors before a legislative body. Under our institution of a Congress of two chambers, the lower house prefers the accusation against a public officer and its truth is tried by the upper chamber. This is the English impeachment by the Commons, tried by the House of Lords. Each of our states has the same form of prosecution. In Athens any citizen brought an impeachment, and it was authorized in the popular Assembly and the matter tried in one of the town-meeting courts.

Under the English system prevalent in this country, the judge or judges of the court exercise a control over the verdicts of juries in three ways. Preliminarily to the trial the court settles the issues, that is to say, it determines the question that is to be submitted to the jury; next, upon the trial it instructs the jury as to what the law is, bearing upon their deliberations; finally, the court, if it is not satisfied with the verdict of the jury, will set the verdict aside. But at Athens, while there may have been some supervision over the questions to be submitted to the jury through the presiding archon (and as to this matter there is grave doubt), the whole case, matter of law and matter of fact, was submitted to the uncontrolled jury. Even if there had been control, the archon chosen by lot had no special knowledge of the law and was an ordinary uninstructed citizen holding his office but a short term. His supervision would have been of no advantage in any way in settling what was to be tried or in supervising the trial. He was no more than the foreman of the jury. At the trial he had no control over the jury; it made its finding as it pleased and there was no way of revising a palpably erroneous finding. The demos never would have submitted to the spectacle of an official overruling the action of the popular assembly or of any popular court. If the jury decided any suit in accordance with the actual law, it would be an accident. Hence under the Athenian system, according to what is stated above as to justice, there was practically no provision for compelling a court to decide in accordance with law, and as a necessary result there was little, if any, justice; there was no government of laws, no security that a litigant would get his rights as the law defined them. Every case was likely to be decided according to a special rule made for the occasion. There were courts for the districts into which Attica was divided, but the appeals from those courts went to the popular courts at Athens, where the same evil met appeals.

Aristotle deceived himself by the assumption that in any popular gathering like the Athenian legislative assembly or in a popular court like an Athenian dicasterium, the result arrived at would always reflect a higher wisdom than the average wisdom of the members of the assembly or jury. This is a wholly gratuitous assumption. It might be a result of deliberations and discussions of the members among themselves, but in the case of the courts any communication among jurors was forbidden or at least was impossible. The jury simply voted without any deliberation among its members. There was no opportunity for the jurors to discuss the matter and to let the better intelligence among them have its influence.

Aristotle in his writings could not throw any clear light upon the anomalous situation at Athens. He classified justice as being of two kinds: (1) general justice, which is a complex of all the rules of law formulated by the state to be legally obligatory upon all members of the community; and (2) the specific virtue of justice, which consists of all the rules of fairness which should govern relations between all members of the community. No one has ever solved the principle of this classification. Aristotle gives no logical definition of general justice except that it included what we call public law and rights of property and possession. Specific justice he divided into distributive justice, which defines all the rights and duties which are apportioned to one person against or in favor of others, and into what he called corrective justice, which covers all the functions of justice for the enforcement of rights or the redress of wrongs. Perhaps in a hazy way this latter distinction between distributive and corrective justice is the distinction now made between substantive law, which defines actual rights and wrongs, and adjective law, which defines the methods and procedure by which rights are enforced and wrongs redressed by courts.

Another defect in the law was its rigid formalistic character under which the party suing must recover what he sued for, neither more nor less. Proposals were made to change the method of trial so that a verdict of less than the amount sued for could be recovered, but Aristotle argues strenuously against such a proposition, and in a court composed of so many members without any chance for discussion among them, it is difficult to conceive how such a result could be attained.

But even if there had been under the Athenian system any chance for a rule of law or for an adequate tribunal to apply the law, that chance was wholly destroyed by a principle for making up a new law or of avoiding the rule of law, by abrogating the applicable law altogether. Aristotle adds another kind of justice to his absurd classification and division, which he calls fairness or reasonableness. The Greek word is *epieikeia*, which came later to mean, appropriately enough, "idle chatter." It is in short the principle that a rule of law must be of general application but that if in a particular concrete case the law may seem to produce a result deemed unfair or unjust or inequitable by the jurors or judges, the law will not be applied. This principle covered by verbiage has been defined to be a correction of the law in some particular of justice, wherein the law by reason of its universality is deficient. In other words, it is a power in a court to suspend the law because it is conceived that in a particular case the rule will produce an unjust result. What could be simpler? Although justice requires a general rule applied to all alike, if there is to be either liberty or equality under the law, yet justice also requires the exact converse of this rule—a suspension or repeal of the law in a particular instance—in order to provide that justice according to law shall not be injustice. It is true that in a later body of law there was a common law and an equitable system, but the latter system had its own settled. rules, and those rules were applied to all alike. The equitable rules actually governed and hence they were the law, whatever the common law might say.

Aristotle seems to have provided for the sphere of public law, but he does not in fact suggest, and a Greek in a city-state was incapable of conceiving, that the individual citizen could have any rights that would be protected from the state. While the Athenian judges were required to take an oath that they would not allow the repudiation of debts or a redivision of the land, confiscations and expropriations of the property of the rich were common. No title that came from the state could be disputed, and the state was left to compensate the robbed citizen. This is our law to-day as to certain taxes. Every one must pay the income tax assessed, even though it be a public stealing and robbery, and must after paying sue to recover the payment. All democracies are alike in their methods.

The Greeks had an arbitrary system of imposing a public service, called a liturgy, upon a particular citizen. Such public services were fitting out ships, equipping embassies, providing dramatic choruses, or contributing to the expenses of religious celebrations. For this condition a remedy was provided whereby a citizen upon whom such a charge was imposed could bring an action against another citizen claiming that the other was better able to respond to the tax. This is much as if one citizen could sue another on the ground that a particular tax imposed was unfair as between them. The imposition of these public burdens was really a form of taxation, and thus early began the system of making a tax unequal by the attempt to make the richer men pay proportionately a much higher tax. It is characteristic of all democracies to attempt this taxation. The best instance we know of is the increase in percentage of taxation with reference to a man's income. Nothing could be balder than this, but, at least, all men falling under the classification must respond; while at Athens a particular individual was selected to pay an onerous tax. It is idle to speak of law or equality or uniformity under such a system.

It must be evident why it was that Athens had no particular profession or order of men who were learned in the law. Every citizen was competent to know and judge the law. Hence there was no such practice as that of a citizen appearing by attorney or advocate. The citizen must manage his own case and make his own plea. A legal profession was banned, as Plato makes plain in his *Laws*. All the litigant could do was to hire some orator to write out a speech for him to deliver. The Attic orators wrote many such speeches and it is to those speeches that we are indebted for most of our knowledge of the Athenian law. Judges who knew little of the law, and probably cared less about it, were not a tribunal where a trained lawyer would be of any use. If a man had a contract, the contract when broken was likely to be abrogated if a situation developed where a town-meeting jury would consider an enforcement unjust. If a man had left a will there was no certainty that it would stand, and so it was of every other legal relation. It is no wonder that Aristotle, in his muddy way, sighed for a constitutional system, where laws and not personal caprice would rule; and yet he had a conception of law that prevented any rule of law from prevailing.

The Greeks devised a way of getting certain cases to arbitration. In fact it was a common expedient to agree upon an arbitrator. The arbitrator's finding, however, could come before a court for enforcement, and when it did it would seem that the record made before the arbitrator was all that could be considered by the court. The attempt to avoid the courts by means of an arbitration was to the Greeks a method of escaping not from the law, but from the trammels of legal procedure. But, of course, it would result then, as often it results now, in the rule of law not being applied to the controversy.

The acute minds of these Athenian Greeks developed a very considerable body of law. Personal security was protected by the usual private remedies for assault, or for slander in public places. There was a well-developed division of law as to artificial persons, such as religious societies approaching our churches, clubs, burial societies, trading societies, privateering or piratical societies, and the like. The by-laws of such organizations were treated as lawful and binding. The modern law of corporations can be traced through Roman law to the Greeks. In the family relations, marriage and divorce had their body of law. Marriage at the order of the parents was the usual rule. The wife became a part of the husband's family. The relation of guardian and ward was looked after as was the devolution of the property of an intestate. The orator Demosthenes was left by his father, another Demosthenes, an estate of about thirty thousand dollars. His cousin Aphobus became his guardian and squandered most of the estate. Demosthenes, when he came of age, sued him for the property lost. Guardians or conservators could be appointed for spendthrifts squandering their own estate. In the family law the patriarchal household was abolished by the law that the son became emancipated on his enrolment for military service at the age of eighteen.

The laws of Solon gave to every childless citizen the right to make a will, but, of course, the law had not progressed so far as to allow a man to leave all his property away from his children. There was an action at law to set aside a will if made in extreme old age, or when the testator was of unsound mind, or was acting under undue influence, at least under female influence.

The law as to possession and ownership of property was sufficient to protect it, if applied. Damages to property, real or personal, were provided. Damages for acts of one's animals, or slaves, were given. Leases of land were common. Actions for rent were given. Forcible entry upon possession was forbidden. Even the right to the use of a name could be litigated, and one of Demosthenes's speeches is about the exclusive right to a name. Such law would protect the exclusive enjoyment of trade names and might prevent unfair trading.

Private international law and the right of citizens in another state were secured by conventions between such cities. These conventions gave to citizens of either state the benefit of the laws of the state where they were sojourning. In many respects the Greeks developed a public international law and some private international law.

There was, of course, the usual confusion between crime and private wrong. Homicide was a private wrong and its prosecution was left to the kindred. A bargain could be made with the slayer. The distinction was made between murder and manslaughter, between an intentional premeditated killing and a killing in sudden passion. There was no law of sanctuary as among the Jews. The law gave the kindred the right to declare a feud against the slayer and the kindred could compromise the matter, unless it were a premeditated killing. In actual murder the only way of avoiding capital punishment was perpetual exile. As we have seen, among the Jews a true murder could not be compromised by a money payment. This sort of law came into our system of law as the legal prohibition against compounding a felony. Justifiable homicide was recognized in Greek law. If the wounded man pardoned his assailant before dying, the kindred could not prosecute for the killing. According to their ideas, the injured man could release the cause of action before his death by a forgiveness. The law is otherwise among us, for the theory of the law seems to be that the deceased has nothing to do with the cause of action. It is given to those who are declared to be entitled to the cause of action.

In the penal law there was a mixture of public law and private law. Assault, false imprisonment, homicide, rape, theft, maiming, slander, and contumelious treatment were treated as private injuries, yet a part of the recovery went to the state. In a number of cases the law inflicted punishment without any private recovery. Adultery was a subject for public prosecution. Personal revenge by a husband for adultery or by the lover of a concubine for poaching on the preserve was justifiable as a part of the primitive law of self-help, and a killing for that reason was justifiable.

The law developed many different kinds of actions—indictments, public prosecutions or impeachments, actions for impiety, for violence, for the recovery of real and personal property. There were various different forms of lawsuits with particular names. There was no developed

preventive remedy by injunction. A different remedy was provided for
the recovery of personal property from that for the recovery of real
property. The laws provided in certain commercial cases a summary
remedy and trial within thirty days.

It is apparent that this is a very highly advanced system of law. But it
is in the realm of contractual relations, pledges, mortgages, trading ventures, banking operations that we reach the highest development. Such
business was done by written contract, and the written contract precluded proof of any other contract made. As is well known, after the
Battle of Salamis and the defeat of the Persian fleet, Athens founded the
Delian League, and by a natural process made herself the great entrepôt
of commerce. She, by her laws, so regulated her commerce that it must
all pass to Athens, much in the manner that the English made and used
their Navigation Laws. To conduct such a commerce, advances of
money by capitalists were necessary. Athens found such a commercial
system ready to her hand in the Babylonian system of merchant adven-
turing, which had been adopted in the Ionic cities in Asia. Thence it
found its way to Athens, when, after the Persian wars, she acquired her
great commerce.

As an illustration of the written contract being the sole contract, we
may instance the case of a woman banker, Nicarete, at Thespiae. She had
made loans to the City of Orchomenos in Boeotia. Borrowings by municipalities were common. These loans of Nicarete had been made at
various times and, as usual, the city was unable to pay upon the maturity
of the loan. A contract was thereupon drawn up whereby a loan to the
amount of the advances to the city was recited to have been made to
named officials of the city and ten citizens selected by the banker. This
was, of course, contrary to the fact. The pretended loan gave power to
the banker to proceed to collect by execution against the property of
these persons. The new loan was made payable to bearer. Thus it appears
that an agreement to pay money took the form of a negotiable promissory note or its equivalent, deliverable from bearer to bearer. What was
desired to be done was for the city to obtain an extension of the loan,
which the banker was willing to grant upon further parties becoming
makers of the paper, and making themselves personally and primarily

liable along with the city. The transaction was in fact a renewal of the loan, by the taking up of the outstanding paper, by a new note with new makers. It is certain that the substituted agreement would never have been made if it had lain in the power of the parties to defeat the contract by proof that the substituted contract did not express the real transaction. There seems to be no reason to doubt that the Greek law was at all different from the Babylonian or from our own to the effect that what the parties put into writing to be the contract they cannot deny by oral evidence. The rule, by a strange misnomer, in our law is called the parol evidence rule.

Upon the maturity of this fictitious loan another delay in payment took place. A new agreement was made that the city itself would pay the loan in two months, and when that time came the city paid. Whether this new paper released the makers of the second note does not appear. The practice of making a loan to a city, enforcible by execution against citizens, seems to have been a common device. It was evident that whenever an execution was provided for in the contract itself, the Greek law was providing a means, just as our contracts often provide a means, of obtaining the remedy as a matter of course. The Greeks had judgment notes also, just as we have.

Personal arrest on debt was abolished by Solon, but the remedy of distress by self-help remained. Contracts of surety-ship were common, but the surety became bound not secondarily to his principal but primarily. Almost every contract was buttressed by sureties, such as loans and leases. Where sureties became liable for the appearance of a criminal, if the criminal absconded, they might be subjected to the punishment. Our device of a bail bond in a penal sum of money was not reached by the Grecian law.

The provisions of law as to leases were peculiar in that a conveyance prevailed over a lease existing on the land. Our rule is to the contrary in that possession of the land by the tenant is notice of his rights. Special clauses as to the method of cultivation were common. Temple lands were often leased in perpetuity upon a rent reserved. A lease in perpetuity upon a rent reserved presents some very curious questions in our law. The law as to sales of goods was clear, and sales were generally publicly made before witnesses or in the open market. A close supervision was exercised over the quality of the goods and honest weights. Sales could be made upon credit, and one of the changes in the law proposed in Plato's *Laws* was that all sales upon credit should be abolished. Title in the goods passed upon payment, either in cash or by credit; but in our law title passes upon the bargain as to goods in existence and ascertained.

It will be seen that all the great heads of the law are well represented in Athenian law, and that so far as general rules are concerned Greek law would in its main lines be found to differ little from our own. The difficulty with it as a system was its failure to develop a competent tribunal to apply the law. That the state owed the duty of doing justice between its citizens would not have been questioned by Greeks, and the Greek law had lost the primitive element of an agreed submission to the tribunal provided by the law, before the tribunal could force the attendance of the defendant.

When through the conquests of Alexander the Great and the existence of the kingdoms of the Hellenic successors of Alexander, Greek rule became distributed over the eastern world, this system of Hellenic law became almost a world system, and through the Romans and their praetorian law, called the law of nations, its principles continued to survive. So much was this the case that when the Corpus Juris of Justinian was compiled, it would have been difficult to separate Roman from Greek elements; for as Pliny the Younger said, the Greeks gave to the Romans their laws.

CHAPTER 7

A Greek Lawsuit

In order to see the Athenian law in action, it will not be out of place to give some life and reality to a particular lawsuit. We know something of it because one of the parties hired Demosthenes to write a speech for him to deliver to the Athenian court where the case was tried. It arose under a law which in effect provided that merchandising loans at Athens must be made on merchandising to or from Athens. A law read: "It shall not be lawful for any Athenian or any alien residing at Athens or any person under their control to lend out money on a ship which is not commissioned to bring goods to Athens." Another law prohibited any person resident in the Athenian State from transporting grain direct to any harbor but the Piraeus. These laws governed the whole Delian League under the Athenian supremacy and the Athenian colonies and dependencies long afterwards, though sometimes Athens allowed the contrary to be done. Wardens were kept at Sestos in the Dardanelles to enforce this law against all passing ships.

The Greek trader was generally a merchant adventurer who was advanced money—or financed, as we say—by some man of means at Athens. The contract generally described what the voyage should be, and determined the goods that were to be the subject of the speculation. This commerce made Athens, city-state as it was, a great cosmopolitan center. It is needless to say that the harbor at Athens was thronged with vessels and the returns upon this commerce enriched all classes at

Athens. In those days an Athenian named Demon, who was an uncle of the orator Demosthenes, was a man of property at Athens, and he had a lawsuit in regard to goods purchased on such a loan. The circumstances that were disclosed were sensational enough to satisfy the yearnings of a yellow sheet. The case is remarkable for showing that the active trading Greek was then, as he is to-day, often more or less of a rascal. Surroundings may change, but human nature is the one unchangeable thing in this hoary old world. It was true then, as now, of the Greeks:

> Still to the neighboring ports they waft
> Proverbial wiles and ancient craft.

The Romans, with their sound character, had little respect for Grecian honesty. Cicero, the unfailing eulogist of Greece, felt this want of moral stamina when he said: "I grant them all manner of literary and rhetorical skill, but that race never understood or cared for the sacred binding force of testimony given in a court of law." To the Roman, the hungry little Greek rascal became proverbial.

Even after Athens lost her primacy at sea, she yet had a large accumulated capital for merchandising and she took care by her laws, as has been stated, that all merchandising on Athenian money and of the cities that she controlled should subserve Athenian commerce, and that every lawful merchant venture at sea should favor Athens as a distributing point for the goods of the eastern and western Mediterranean and for those brought from the Black Sea, which they called the Euxine.

The support of the population of Attica required large importations, especially of grain from Sicily or other points, and such ventures were required to be financed. The capitalist with money to lend was not prepared to trust his body to the treacherous seas. The trader who was ready to risk his life in commerce had no money or capital. The foreign dealers with goods to sell would not extend credit to an Athenian, any more than to-day a foreigner would trust an American importer. The man who carried on trade by borrowing the capitalist's money and by paying the borrowed money as cash to the seller operated then much as he would operate to-day. Although, then as now, the importer was sometimes a rascal, we may call him by the dignified term of merchant adventurer.

Such a merchant adventurer was Protus at Athens. He applied to the capitalist Demon for a loan to finance a shipment of grain from Syracuse to Athens and obtained the money for that purpose. The amount of the loan Demosthenes does not betray in the speech he wrote for Demon, but we may suppose it to be large, for the shipment took the whole vessel. It does not appear that Protus took goods bought with Demon's money out to Syracuse and converted them there into cash with which to buy the grain. It would seem that he simply took out Demon's money on the empty vessel.

It must be noted, also, that in those days of small vessels a responsible carrier was not easy to find, and it would seem that there was at that time no such thing as a bill of lading. Under the Babylonian law, the carrier of the goods gave a bill of lading and was responsible for every loss except that arising from the public enemy. At Rhodes and at Alexandria, in the next centuries, the carriers gave bills of lading and from that day to this the carrier has always receipted by bill of lading for the merchandise to be carried. Among the Greeks the owner of goods or his representative accompanied the goods as a "super-cargo," because the Greek law had not developed a carrier's liability.

To make sure of a vessel to bring the grain from Syracuse to Athens, an impecunious Greek colonial from Marseilles, named Hegestratus, who was at Athens with a vessel, was engaged to bring the grain from Sicily. Hegestratus promptly mortgaged his vessel and, no doubt, the freight to be earned, in order to fit out his vessel with tackle and supplies and to obtain money to pay the crew. The crew appear to have been men from Marseilles.

We may picture Protus setting out from Athens on his voyage in the ship skippered by Hegestratus and arriving at Syracuse. There he bought a shipload of grain, paid the export duties and loaded his grain upon the ship. While Protus was waiting for the vessel to sail, and probably wine-bibbing at a convenient wineshop, boasting loudly, like a true Athenian, of the wonders of Athens and refreshing himself after the arduous labors of superintending the slaves in loading, Hegestratus, the unscrupulous colonial, tried to improve his time by looking for some personal gain from rascality. His vessel was mortgaged. All he could look for was the freight money. He did improve, or rather misemploy, his time by finding a person at Syracuse named Zenothemis, and represented to Zenothemis that he had a ship lying in the harbor laden with grain that he was about to take to Athens. Hegestratus asked Zenothemis to obtain for him a loan on the cargo, offering a commission. He, no doubt, took Zenothemis and showed him the ship with the grain in it.

In spite of the abuse of Zenothemis in the speech which Demosthenes wrote for Demon to deliver—a feature without which an Athenian oration would be unrecognizable—it seems probable that Zenothemis believed the grain on the ship to belong to Hegestratus. Zenothemis at any rate represented Hegestratus to Syracusan capitalists to be the owner of the load of grain and obtained for Hegestratus a loan from them upon the cargo. Hegestratus does not appear to have given a mortgage on the cargo of grain, and Zenothemis accompanied the cargo to protect his principals. Hegestratus promptly sent to Marseilles the money obtained by this fraudulent transaction. But it is evident from the speech that the cargo was at the risk of the Syracusan money lenders and that the payment of the loan was contingent upon the arrival of the cargo at Athens. Every man at this time was his own insurer, and the liability of Protus to Demon was likewise contingent upon the safe arrival.

It is impossible to suppose that the Zenothemis loan furnished the money to purchase the grain, for in that event Hegestratus would have had no money to send to Marseilles. He could not have made a single drachma if the loan bought the cargo. Protus, of course, paid the port dues on export, but the idea that he was given a receipt or document therefor which would prove the fact is not tenable. Such proof would probably mean nothing to such expert forgers as Greeks.

We should now state the character of the loan that Demon had made to Protus. The contract is not set forth in the speech but it was, *mutatis mutandis*, like the contract set forth in the speech against Lacritus, among Demosthenes's orations. That contract, regarding a trading venture to the Euxine, recites the loan made to the trader to be invested in casks of wine at Mende in Thrace, to be laden in the twenty-oared galley of Hyblesius. The goods to be purchased are by the contract hypothecated to the lender with a covenant by the borrower that no money should be owing on those goods at the time of purchase and that no further money would be borrowed on them by the trader. The goods were to be sold in Pontus on the southern shore of the Black Sea, and other goods were to be purchased with the avails for the return voyage to Athens. If the goods were brought safely to Athens, the borrower within twenty days of arrival (in which period doubtless there would be time to sell the goods) should reimburse the loan to the lender with twenty-two and one-half per cent interest, without any abatement except for jettison (i.e., goods thrown overboard to save the vessel). Upon the arrival of the goods they should be delivered to the lender until the money borrowed had been paid, and if the money should not be paid as provided, the lender might sell or pledge the goods, and if there should be any deficiency in the proceeds to pay the loan, should have execution for the deficiency against the borrower. This transaction means, of course, that Protus and Demon together would sell the grain at Athens.

Any one will note that the necessities of the commerce dictate the contract. Marine insurance was unknown until it was invented at Rhodes in the form of reciprocal insurance, which has become in late years so common among us. The risks of navigation could not be obviated by insurance and the lender took the risk of shipwreck or jettison. The lender thought nothing of the borrower's ability to pay but looked to the goods. As soon as the goods were purchased and ascertained they became at the risk of the lender, and the goods were dedicated to the loan. In the meantime the borrower, though in possession, is in possession as the representative of the lender, and the contract creates a *pro forma* hypothecation. The goods are in fact the goods of the lender, for as soon as it is possible they are delivered to him, but for twenty days or longer the borrower can sell them to realize the loan. They are sold apparently as the goods of the lender. The Greek law or any other intelligent system of law, except certain law of a "country town" type, would see no objection to the borrower having the power of sale as agent of the lender. Out of the proceeds the loan is to be paid, any excess of proceeds over the loan and interest goes to the borrower, and any deficiency is paid by the borrower.

The Protus contract with Demon differed from the Lacritus contract in that no purchase of goods and conversion thereof into other goods

was provided for. It will be seen that the Greek law recognized a mortgage of the vessel, a hypothecation or pledge of goods, and a special
contract of merchandising for the protection of the lender of money to
be used for the express purpose of investment in particular goods, on
the principle that the goods purchased shall realize the loan. It is the
same principle as the equitable one that he who pays the purchase
money owns the thing purchased, which comes out of the Roman law. It
is a common thing in modern business for a banker to buy a draft with
a bill of lading attached, and upon acceptance of the draft to deliver the
goods in the bill of lading to the drawee of the draft to dispose of as the
agent of the banker, but without any power to the drawee to store the
goods or to treat them as his own. As it was in Greek law, this title is
good in the banker.

It is apparent that when Hegestratus represented himself to be the
owner of the cargo and obtained a loan from Syracusan money lenders
upon the cargo, he probably had no criminal intention of casting the vessel away, but as with Tito in *Romola,* one rascality led to another. He intended to swindle the Syracusans and to get away from the vessel before
it reached Athens. Hegestratus could not appear with his ship at Athens,
for his fraud would be at once exposed. Probably he intended at some
point before arriving at Athens to decamp, leaving his vessel to the mortgagees, and the cargo to be fought over by Protus, representing Demon,
and Zenothemis, representing the Syracusans. Hegestratus's money was
safe at Marseilles, and he expected to reach there and enjoy his ill-gotten
gains. There being no extradition laws, he need not trouble himself
about pursuit. Possibly he could restore some dilapidated temple, repent
of his evil deeds and the priests would enable him to die in the odor of
sanctity at peace with the gods.

This was the situation when the vessel sailed from Syracuse. A cargo
of grain was on board and certain passengers were accommodated with
passage. Protus and Zenothemis were two of the passengers. They were
watching over the same cargo, but representing hostile interests. Hegestratus must have been a shallow-pated fool to suppose that two Greeks
could keep silent about their business. Zenothemis soon learned that
Protus owned the cargo, and at once Zenothemis compelled Hegestratus

to give him a writing. What it was, the speech does not say, but it was probably a conveyance outright of the cargo and it was lodged in Greek fashion with a passenger. This paper Hegestratus could very well give, because he never intended to dispute the cargo, or for that matter the vessel, with any one. When he obtained the Syracusan loan and dispatched the money to Marseilles he had exhausted his field of illicit profit.

It now dawned on Hegestratus that if he could sink the vessel he would be rid of his troubles. Probably he felt that Zenothemis and Protus would keep a strict watch on him so that he could not get away, unless in the confusion of a sinking. He imagined that if he could sink the vessel, the cargo would cease to exist and all contention would be at an end, because the loss of cargo would end the Protus property as well as the Syracusan loan. He was benevolently saving Protus and Zenothemis from the burden of a Greek lawsuit. Hegestratus waited until the ship was close enough to the island of Cephallenia to let all escape from a sinking vessel, and there he put his brilliant plan into execution.

One night he left the garlic-scented Greeks snoring on the deck, went below and proceeded to cut a hole in the bottom of the vessel. He seems to have been a clumsy imbecile, for the noise he made betrayed him and, when detected, he rushed on deck and, knowing a boat was being towed astern, jumped for the boat, intending to cut it adrift and thus get away. But in the darkness he missed the boat and was drowned. As the Greeks would say, the goddess Nemesis was dogging his footsteps. By the exertions of the passengers and the crew, stimulated by rewards offered by Protus, the ship was saved and brought into the harbor of Cephallenia. Here Zenothemis went into alliance with the crew who were from Marseilles, and insisted that the vessel should be navigated to Marseilles. Athens, of course, was the one place on the Mediterranean that Zenothemis did not desire the ship to reach, and he no doubt thought that on the voyage to Marseilles the ship would put into Syracuse, where an appropriation of the cargo to the Syracuse loan would be easily obtained.

It is likely that the repairs of the vessel took some time; perhaps it was necessary to unload it. In the meantime Protus appealed for help to Demon at Athens. Demon sent out a pettifogger named Aristophon, said to be of the Council. He had been paid by the side that hired him and sent him out, and was ready to earn another fee on the opposite side. Zenothemis appears to have bought him up at once; but in spite of all they could do, the Cephallenian authorities decided that the ship must proceed to Athens, whither she was bound. They enforced the decision. So we may suppose the vessel rounding the treacherous capes of the Peloponnesus and arriving at the Piraeus with the disputed cargo. The three precious rascals, Protus, Zenothemis and the pettifogger, were on board, but missing was the chief rascal Hegestratus, whose Nemesis had found him out.

Upon arrival the mortgagees of the vessel took possession of the vessel and Protus took possession of the grain. Thereupon Zenothemis claimed that he was in possession of the cargo. The archaic Greek procedure probably required self-help to the extent that Zenothemis could insist upon being removed by a fiction of force and that he could require that the actual owner, the one entitled to the possession, should remove him. He refused to recognize Protus as owner, and thereupon Demon took possession and removed him. Enough appears from the speech to show that the Athenian law treated Demon and not Protus as owner, and this would be the law to this day in a commercial country.

Demon and Protus proposed to Zenothemis that they should go before the authorities at Syracuse, and if it appeared that Protus had bought the corn and that the customs' duties were paid by him, Zenothemis should be punished as a rogue; but if it proved otherwise, he should receive the corn and his expenses and damages to the amount of a talent. Naturally Zenothemis refused this absurd offer, for he was no rogue in his own eyes, even if he had been deceived by Hegestratus. So Demon took possession and was sued. The curious thing is that Zenothemis, to be on the safe side, brought two actions, one against Protus and another against Demon. It is certain that the one against Demon was under a special statute giving jurisdiction as to merchandising to and from Athens. The other action against Protus was probably another kind of action, but what it was is problematical.

While these two actions were pending, the price of wheat fell at Athens so much that Protus no longer had any profit, but was confronted by an execution for a deficiency. Demon made this plain to him, as the speech confesses. Protus, being a Greek, thereupon naturally dealt with Zenothemis as his only chance for profit. It was made worth Protus's while to abscond and Zenothemis promptly took judgment against Protus by default. Demon was now without the evidence of Protus to show that Demon's money bought the grain at Syracuse, and this fact made Demon's case less certain. He would find trouble, too, in the consideration that by the default judgment against Protus, Demon's title was made questionable at least to a jury. So it became necessary for Demon to hunt for a technicality, unless he was prepared to go into court, relying upon truth and justice, and this would not occur to any Athenian save Socrates, who suffered death for his temerity.

The fact that the dead Hegestratus could not possibly have bought the shipload of corn was the controlling fact. Zenothemis claimed title solely through Hegestratus, who had no title and could give none. The controlling fact is not even referred to in the speech. It is urged in the speech that Zenothemis on shipboard obtained a writing from Hegestratus, that he tried to divert the ship to Marseilles, that he made some arrangement with Protus for the default, and did not detain Protus as he could have done, and such like trivial matters, but the one controlling fact of Hegestratus's inability to buy any corn or even to outfit his ship is not urged, nor is it shown that if Protus had not in fact bought the grain, Hegestratus could not have realized anything from the Syracusan loan. It is plain that if Hegestratus had not gotten a loan in Syracuse on corn of Protus already laden, he would have made no money and would have had no motive for casting away the vessel. This point seems to have evaded Demosthenes.

The action of Zenothemis against Demon, being under the statute, was required to be based on a merchandising venture to or from Athens or both, and it is difficult to see how a grain-loan made at Syracuse or a sale on the high seas fell under the terms of the law. This is what Demon pleaded as a technical defense. It was his only plea apparently, and perhaps a defendant could plead but one defense. This plea, where the difference between issues of fact and issues of law was not provided for in the procedure, went to the jury, who would decide upon the whole controversy.

Upon the trial the actual defense pleaded under the statute was merely stated in the speech for Demon and then the orator proceeded to argue that Zenothemis had no merits on the facts. It was, of course, utterly immaterial to the pure legal defense pleaded whether Zenothemis had the property right in the grain or not. The speech is confused and we have not all of it. Instead of relying upon the actual facts showing a plain, straightforward case, the orator attempts to show that from the beginning at Syracuse Zenothemis was in a scheme with Hegestratus to defraud Protus and Demon. But this was not tenable under the actual facts. The result is a case so muddy that it tends to show very clearly the confused, formless mode of a Greek trial. In the hands of a genuine pleader like Lysias, the case might have been much better and more strongly put. Demosthenes was essentially a politician, and after that a forensic speaker. He is never in any of his orations in law cases very clear as to his facts, probably because a politician looks at a law case in accordance with the prescription of Lear to the blind Gloster:

> "Get thee glass eyes,
> And, like a scurvy politician, seem to see
> The things thou dost not."

How the case turned out we do not know. Since Demon had a straightforward, honest case he was probably defeated before an Athenian jury. Zenothemis probably hired Aeschines to write a speech for him and thus obtained the services of one of the greatest oratorical prevaricators in history. Zenothemis appeared in rags, a pitiful object, a stranger in destitution. He said in his speech that his forbears were Athenians and that it was not his fault that he had not been born under the shadow of the Acropolis. He rapped out some fine phrases borrowed from Pericles upon the glorious City of the Violet Crown, and denounced the grasping money power personified in the respectable, if wealthy, Demon. Protus came in for a castigation. It is said that he had run away because he had been drunk all the time and had embezzled Demon's money. It was claimed probably that the Syracusans' money bought the corn to ship it to Athens and that the witnesses for Demon were all suborned. How he explained Hegestratus in accordance with

Demosthenes rehearsing an oration

this contention is a subject for a very vigorous imagination. Almost every Greek case seems to have a stale odor of rascality hanging around it.

As we have seen, this sort of transaction was originally provided for in Babylonia. Thence it passed to Asia Minor and on to Athens. The maritime loan *ad respondentia,* borrowed by the English from the older European commerce, is practically this contract. It appears in the Roman civil law, borrowed from the Greek. It passed with the commerce to the Genoese, the Pisans, the Florentines, and finally to Venice when she held "the gorgeous East in fee." Wool was imported from England to Bruges in the thirteen hundreds on this kind of contract, and on money supplied by the branch houses of Venetian bankers. An instance will be shown hereafter. As the *respondentia* loan, it has long been a feature of the English law and most sedulously protected first in admiralty and by the chancellor, then by the common law, after judges of enlightenment pulled out some new mercantile stops in that old, broken-winded instrument.

In the course of time an improvement has changed the rule of risk to the lender. Marine insurance has enabled the lender to exact from the borrower the taking out of insurance for the lender to the value of the goods. There was no longer any maritime risk. In another respect there has been an improvement. The great mass of marine carriage is now conducted by responsible carriers. Their bills of lading are marketable. The bill of lading, symbolical of the goods, by its transfer passes title. The holder of the bill of lading is completely protected while the goods are carried. The lender, by having the bill of lading made out to him, by exacting insurance payable to him, is protected until the goods bought with his advance come to the port of entry. In the simple commerce at Athens the lender, being present at the port, could take possession of the goods and sell them if the borrower did not. He could in any event be present at the sale by the borrower and protect his ownership.

But the plain fact that the straightforward case of Demon must be pleaded on a purely technical defense, that a rascally skipper would dare to sell goods confided to his carriage, and that the purchaser of the goods from the skipper without any title at all could make such a strong defense, shows the law in one of its stages of most glorious uncertainty. It is no wonder that the Greeks by their contracts sought to avoid the necessity for any recourse to their courts. Yet even to-day the lender is always in peril. The Supreme Court of the United States once made a stupid decision that enabled the assignees of a fraudulent importer to prevail over an honest lender.[1] The law was correctly held as to the lender's title, but the decision was ruined by the extraordinary holding that the document which provided that the importer could receive possession of the goods as agents for sale, thereby gave an implied authority to the agent to take out warehouse receipts in his own name. The holding was that a document which provided that the agent for sale could take out documents of title *for the account of the lender* impliedly authorized the agent to take out documents in his own name. Probably an Athenian jury could have done better than our Supreme Court on this question. That decision was written by a justice,[2] who is now practicing law, and it is to be hoped that in the practice he may have an opportunity to learn that a power of agency permitting the agent to take out a document of title for the account of his principal means, as it has, for almost a hundred years, been understood to mean, that the document is to be taken out in the name of the principal. One would think that a trade document in long use would have met inquiry as to the well-known usages of the trade.

1. The case is *Commercial National Bank of New Orleans v. Canal-Louisiana Bank and Trust Company*, 239 U.S. 520 (1916).
2. Chief Justice Charles Evans Hughes. Zane criticizes this opinion extensively in his article "A Modern Instance of *Zenothemis v. Demon*," *Michigan Law Review* 23 (1925): 339, 353–56.—C. J. R., Jr.

CHAPTER 8

Greek Philosophy of Law

Hᴵᵀʜᴇʀᴛᴏ ᴛʜᴇ ʟᴀᴡ has gone on in a course of orderly development from the days of the pristine savage, untroubled by any philosophical speculations. The savage had his ways of legal acting because he could not act otherwise. The primeval hunter has gone about developing further the primitive institutions according to the best light that he had, but his light is to this enlightened age mainly darkness. The pastoral nomad and the first agriculturists had carried the development still further, until at last civilization had slowly adapted primitive ways to enlightened conditions. To give the laws a greater binding force, they had been accounted for as being given from God. The Greeks in their high stage of civilization had gotten rid of almost all the primitive notions, individual property had been developed, a fixed and settled form of marriage, a monogamous family, the recognition of the citizen's duties to his country, to his family, to his fellow citizens, had all become clear. Individual liability for individual acts had been made plain. The laws, as providing for all these relations, were well recognized. They had been put into written form. The state had assumed the duty of deciding all legal controversies for the benefit of the citizens, and it had furnished tribunals, poor as they were, for deciding these controversies. The state had also furnished through the assemblage of the citizens a means for changing or adding to the laws. This made it possible, instead of the long wait for the development of a new or altered custom, to show by act of the legislative assembly the general acceptance of and acquiescence in a new custom or law. Now the laws, when so passed, disclosed that they were being enacted with a conscious purpose in the minds of the legislators. These are all undoubtedly great advances.

As we have noted before, the precepts of morality, due to the general sentiments of right, were changing from age to age as humankind was improving. The improvement in such moral ideas of the rightful could not but be accompanied by improvements in the law. It could be seen by many thinkers that they themselves were far above most of their fellow men in an improved moral outlook. To such individual men some of the laws seemed to be wrong both in apparent intention and in application. To be able to say that those laws were in fact wrong, it must be said that they were wrong according to some standard. What, then, was this standard? It would not do at all for the critic of the law to appeal to his own mind as the standard; he must create an artificial standard of some kind. It was apparent that it could no longer be said that the laws were divine, because it could be seen that they were being made by human agency, and it was also apparent that those laws were being passed with a conscious, purposeful intent in the citizens who voted for the laws. But there still remained the old idea, inculcated in the priests, that law came from a god or the gods.

By speculation on the nature and omnipotence and omniscience of the gods it was deduced that human laws ought to correspond to the laws decreed or that would have been decreed by the gods. This standard was simply what any one's mind would ascribe to the gods. This standard, so artificially created, was said to be the law or laws that were eternal and unchangeable, for they must be eternal and unchangeable if they were divine. As developed by the Stoics, this idea of law changed its name into natural law. This eternal and unchangeable law could be ascertained only by the power of individual reason, but what one man would think entitled to be called such law, another man might think not at all such.

In the application of this standard to human laws, there was necessarily created a distinction between human law actually in force and being obeyed, which was called the positive law, and that other kind of ideal, unchangeable, and eternal law, whenever the laws differed from what the mind of the observer would prescribe as eternally just and right. But mankind has always been dominated by phrases, and when it was said that the laws were not in accordance with natural law, the hearer accepted the statement. The hearer did not go further and say that what this man means is that the human laws do not correspond with what this man has in his mind as that which he has reasoned out and decided that his own reason would decree if it were making the laws. But it is plain that this natural law of reason was merely another human construction.

In the *Antigone* of Sophocles the lawmaker had decreed that any funeral rites paid to certain traitorous persons named would be unlawful acts. This was, of course, a bad law because it applied to particular persons; it was not general in its application. If the law had been that any funeral rites paid to any traitor should be unlawful, and had been in force when the traitor died, the law might have been good. As the matter stood in Greek law, the edict of the lawgiver was invalid as *ex post facto*. So there was no need for Sophocles to appeal to anything but human law. Antigone, recognizing as the law of nature or of god the age-old custom that the surviving relatives must bury the dead with appropriate ceremonies, wilfully disobeyed the human law of King Creon, who had made the law. When charged with the criminal act, Antigone pleaded the excuse, now considerably time-worn, of the higher law. She says of Creon's law: "It was not Zeus that proclaimed such a law nor does Justice that dwells with the gods below set such laws for the obedience of men; nor did I deem that your decree could be so strong that a mortal could overrule the unwritten and unfailing laws of the gods; for their life is not of to-day nor of yesterday but for eternity, and no one knows when they appeared." The fact here was that Sophocles did not know what the Greek law was.

Again in his *Oedipus Rex*, Sophocles returns to the thought of these higher laws. He there speaks of "laws that in the highest heaven had their birth, neither did the race of mortal men create them, nor shall oblivion ever put them to sleep, for the power of God is mighty in them and never groweth old." This law is ordained, according to the poet, by the divine power of reason. Since this thought has been of great force in Roman and in modern law, we may here quote Cicero in his speech for Milo, on this natural law: "The law which was never written and which we were never taught which we never learned by reading, but which was drawn from Nature herself, in which we have never been instructed, but for which we were made, which was never created by man's institutions, but with which we are all imbued." In another place he sets forth the whole idea: "True law is right reason pervading us all, constant and eternal. This law it is impious to abrogate or to derogate from; neither senate nor people can release us from it. It did not begin to be law when it was written but when it sprang coeval with the divine mind. It is derived from that most ancient and principal nature of all things, to which all law is directed." This law, the Stoics contended, was the production of the divine reason. But it is still plain that this divine law of reason is merely another human construction.

The German scholar Jellinek in modern times has taken this same old idea, dressed it up in a new set of words and boldly proclaimed that he has discovered the test of righteous law as contrasted with existing law and that if his test be applied to the existing law it can be converted into a righteous law.[1] But this is merely another human construction of an individual mind asserting that his deductions are ultimate wisdom. The law has relied and will always rely upon the collected wisdom of men in modifying the law.

Demosthenes in one of his speeches says of the laws: "They have for their intention and purpose the just, the noble, and the advantageous, and this common purpose embraces all equally and alike. They must be obeyed for many reasons and especially because every law is a gift of the gods, an institution of wise men, a common agreement according to which all in the city have agreed to live. It is the means of correction of wrongdoers, whether wilfully or unintentionally they violate the law." It is apparent that the distinction between natural or divine law and the actual law of the city was not present to the mind of the Greek orator. He said that the positive law was divine, which was the Hebrew doctrine. When the Roman jurists came to recast the Roman civil law into a world

1. Georg Jellinek, 1851–1911.—C. J. R., Jr.

system, so that it should be shorn of all its special features inherited from the Roman city-state and its primitive rules, the appeal was to a supposed general law of nations, afterwards called the law of nature. The Romans were wise enough to find the basis of legal principle for general application in those common conceptions of law and justice which they found in force in all the civilized systems, especially the Greek, with which they came into contact. Because they found those rules of law generally accepted, they called them the law of nations.

Certain general principles of law, necessary to justice, the Greeks recognized. They denied the validity of legislation, civil or criminal, passed after the act to which it is applied. This prohibition of *ex post facto* legislation in criminal matters is in all our American constitutions, although retrospective legislation has in some cases been upheld in regard to civil matters. The Greeks recognized clearly in theory that a law must be in fact a rule, it cannot be an edict for a particular case; but the difficulty was that while their theory was sound, their practice was continually the opposite. So it was with liberty. There is no end of rhetorical writing about liberty itself, but the writers are referring to the independence of the state. The citizen is unprotected from the state, and the individual counts for nothing.

A Greek writer is summing up the difference between nature and the law. He says that law is the result of an agreement, but nature is a growth and the growth is almost certain to be right. In this statement, of course, he is confused by an appearance, for if the law is anything, it is a natural growth. What confused him was the multitude of regulatory laws among the Greeks, for he says: "The law has laid down for the eyes what they ought and ought not to see, for the ears what they ought and ought not to hear, for the tongue what it ought and ought not to say, for the hands what they ought and ought not to do, for the feet whither they ought and ought not to go, and for the mind what it ought and ought not to desire." Then he goes on to say as to one's following the precepts of the law: "Now if those who adopted such courses as these had any protection from the laws, whereas those who did not follow them but opposed them incurred loss, obedience to the laws would not be without advantage; but as it happens, legal justice does not protect those who follow the rules of the law. For it does not prevent the injured from being injured nor the aggressor from making aggression. It merely holds him over until punishment is inflicted." But what this critic is looking for is a system of law where all will be law-abiding; and that, we saw in the opening chapter, is a stage of human existence to which man can never return.

Protagoras was adumbrating a fragment of truth when he explained by myth why men had laws. He said: "The first men were quite helpless and threatened with extermination by wild animals. Prometheus brought them intelligence enough to ward off this danger. They collected themselves into cities, but could not live in harmony, and they began to fight among themselves. Zeus then sent Hermes to men with a consciousness of shame and justice." If he had had any conception of the actual human development he could have said that most men are so constituted as to have a consciousness of shame when they deviate from the community standard, that justice requires that the community standard should be applied alike to all, and that this community standard is embodied in primitive laws.

In the natural course we come to Plato. He is so much a great literary artist that even a paucity of matter on law can be atoned for by the perfection of his style. He lived in the age of a worn-out and defeated democracy at Athens. An aristocrat by disposition and by birth, he was naturally wearied by what he saw around him. Satisfied of the incompetence of men to govern themselves, he sighed for a return to older things. He compared his situation to that of a man who has taken refuge from a high wind behind a wall. To him it was impossible to take part in public affairs. The ordinary citizen, even one who desired to know something of philosophy, he compared to a wretched little tinker who has married his master's daughter, attained some prosperity and is vastly intelligent in his own conceit. From the chaos which he saw around him he turned to nature, trying to connect the law which he saw with some background of natural justice.

With such ideas in mind Plato attempted to draw up a system of laws for an ideal state. It should have taught him something that he had gone to Syracuse at the request of Dion, and the Syracusan tyrant, the Elder Dionysius, had been so irritated by his legislative work that he had sold him into slavery, from which he was rescued by a ransom. How it was that under Greek law Dionysius could give to some slave dealer a good title to Plato is not explained, but it is accepted as a fact. Later in life he had gone on a second lawmaking venture to Syracuse for the Younger Dionysius and had created such a condition that he was glad to escape with his life.

Plato really had no conception of the practical circumstances that govern human life. He had never formed a general view of the vast influences of commerce in improving the destinies of mankind. "Trade," as Bulwer says in his play, is "the calm health of nations." It makes for honesty, fair dealing, mutual comprehension, sanity and soundness, toleration of others, peace among men, aggregations of capital, division of labor, the ease and comfort and grace of life, the leisure for study, and the amelioration of customs and manners that produces so large a part of civilization. Plato was attempting to turn society back to some little country town with primitive manners and institutions, where no money circulated, where no one worked but slaves, where the citizens would pass their days basking in the sunlight of Socratic discussions on the just, the virtuous, and the good, while a set of philosophers governed. The Greeks could well answer in the words of Omar:

> Myself when young did eagerly frequent
> Doctor and Saint, and heard great argument
>   About it and about: but evermore
> Came out by the same door wherein I went.

Plato did not even understand that the commercial law was the most important kind of law, and this was proven by the fact, as Demosthenes said, that commercial law was the same over all Greece. To Plato commerce and trade were great evils, and he placed his ideal state so far from the seashore that it could have no trade. Land commerce could not exist without roads, although, having no idea of the cost, Plato supposed that a large country village could build good roads in all directions. He had no understanding of the difficulties at the bottom of the Athenian organization. Its mass of unpaid labor, in the form of slaves, never occurred to him as standing in the way of progress. Slavery was to him so natural a thing that it never occurred to him to wonder what his law of nature would say to such a condition. Probably he would have answered that most men are fit only to be slaves. But the fact that he had been sold into slavery himself ought to have taught him some indulgence for undeserved misfortune.

Plato, with all these limitations, could still say that, "until philosophers become kings or kings become philosophers, the state will never cease from its evils." Of course, in saying "philosophers" he means Platos. This has almost the solid, rock-ribbed conceit of Goethe's exclamation when he reached Rome: "Here I adore my own genius." This calm assumption of Plato's that a philosopher could make good laws has in it something pathetic. He had learned nothing by his double experience at Syracuse. It takes the accumulated errors, mistakes, and concentrated effort of many ages to make a good law, and yet a philosopher or a legislator assumes that he can dash off a full system in a few hours. Locke, with far more knowledge than Plato, attempted a system of laws for a little American colony. The result was a farrago of impracticable nonsense. Bentham, the great lawgiver, was so deluded that he thought that he knew all the law in the world. He concocted a constitution which he professed would suit the Khedive of Egypt, the wild Indian rabble of a newly freed South American republic, a state of the United States, and every other political society. Many philosophers have thought with Plato that God and nature had designed them for lawgivers, but doubtless they have all been mistaken.

Plato had the courage of his convictions, and he outlined his first-class state in the *Republic* and his second-class state in the *Laws*. We need not delay on the *Republic*. Plato himself admits his fantastic state to be utterly impossible among any sort of human beings which he knew. From the *Republic* the socialists could have obtained their ideas of a community of wives, intense neighborliness in the conjugal relations, and children brought up as state orphans. The looseness of morals at Sparta exercised a sort of fascination upon him. The governing body of philosophers in his *Republic* would have made a government where every day would be an open season for killing philosophers, or selling them into slavery.

The *Laws* sets forth his second-rate state, which he recommended as a practical conception. It was composed in his old age, and has some of the garrulous signs of senescence. He is fair enough not to foist this dialogue upon Socrates. More people have written about Plato's *Laws* than have read the book. In that respect it is like that monstrous work, Hobbes's *Leviathan,* which Hobbes supposed to be a juristic work. Grammarians, classical commentators, and scholars, who had no practical sense in regard to law and no standpoint of experience from which to judge Plato's system, have been deeply impressed by the *Laws,* but there is really nothing of value in the book, although many simple souls with no understanding of the many sides to civilization have been impressed.

It is in the form of a dialogue in which a chattering Athenian holds forth to a chuckle-headed Spartan and a stupid Cretan. The Athenian is at no pains to conceal his contempt for the men he is talking to and lectures them like a school-teacher instructing a lower grade of children. The Spartan and Cretan drink in his words with absolute reverence. His state, of course, is a city-state. It is composed of 5,040 heads of families. The number 5,040 is, says Plato, full of magic, for it can be divided by every integer from one to ten. With five to every family, there would be 25,200 people. If the population shows signs of redundancy, it can be kept down by what is now called birth control, or the unfortunate redundants can be sent off as a colony. The land is to be allotted to the families in equal proportions, the number of households must never be decreased, and the land holdings are to be inalienable and never to be unoccupied. A widow could call upon her husband's nearest undisposed-of kinsman to marry her, after the manner of the Hebrew custom called the "levirate," which was noticed under Hebrew law in connection with the story of Ruth. All these provisions are copied from the original Aryan barbarism. The Athenians had long forgotten this system, and Plato was working off on them the lumber of discarded institutions, which Solon had abolished when he acted as lawgiver.

Over this sort of obsolete organization he places what he calls law wardens, an old disused sort of Athenian official. These law wardens are to be elected. Everything bad in the Athenian system he unerringly selects. He is so much a school-teacher, accustomed to instructing the young, that he has the naïve idea that if mature people are told by law to do something they will do it. There was never a greater error made by a philosopher. When the law meets the approval of the common sense of people generally, that law will be obeyed; but a law that a large minority thinks wrong and refuses to obey never will become actual law until the people come to a practically general agreement in its favor. Nothing is more absurd than continual and minute regulations. Plato has minute regulations for convivial intercourse. The music to be heard and the melodies to be used, he insisted, should be embodied in the law, after selection by qualified men. He would have had a censorship over the poets, whom he regarded as a dangerous class. Yet he had been a poet in his youth and had written much poetry. The public choruses were to be composed, one of children, another of young men, a third of older men from thirty to sixty. They were to sing that "the happiest are the holiest," in older to inculcate a moral lesson.

A prayer-meeting of evangelicals would be a lively gathering compared to one of these symposia. Even the relief of getting artificially elated, as a relief against the songs, was to be denied these poor wretches, singing "the happiest are the holiest." The drinking of wine was forbidden except on special occasions, and to young men not permitted at all. This prohibition, Plato sapiently remarks, would keep down the size of the vineyards. This might be so, but it would have taken an army of hired mercenaries to enforce the law.

His theory of human development was that after a great deluge there was a state of mankind where there were no poor nor rich, where men knew nothing of war and were more temperate and more just than they afterwards became. These men had no laws but dwelt in rocks or on mountains with no special intercourse, and every man was judge of his wife and children. To him, of course, the original unit was the family. He tells us that these separate families did not trouble about each other. As time went on, however, families, he said, came into union, and then they formed states by some sort of social compact, we may suppose, like Rousseau's *contrat social*. For almost two thousand years this beginning for society has been accepted by intelligent men. It belongs with the dream of an original Golden Age.

He announces as his first general principle that the citizen who does not know how to choose between good and evil must have no authority in the state. Curiously enough, at that very time in Athens this principle was the standard to determine whether a man was insane or not. So his first principle reduces to the proposition that no insane man ought to have any authority in the state. This seems eminently proper. According to the law then in force at Athens, this man who knew not good from evil was subject to having a curator appointed to look after him. The Athenian law was certainly sounder than Plato's conception, for it took care of the insane man, while Plato would have an examination merely to see if he could be elected to office.

Plato now proceeds to sketch the Spartan state with some respect and criticizes the Persians and the Athenians. Some of his minute regulations he takes from Sparta. Then he shows his prejudice against commerce and naval power, as noted above. He says that he is rid in his state of shipping and merchandise and peddling and innkeeping and customs and mines and loans and usury, and he is legislating for a community of farmers, shepherds, and bee-keepers. The law of marriage he regulates like a philosopher. He has no objection to easy divorce. A man must marry or pay a yearly fine. Celibacy he places among the heavily taxed luxuries.

His next proposal is that most laws should have a persuasive preamble, so as to make people believe them to be good laws. Persuasion, he wisely says, like a school-teacher renouncing the rod, is better than force. No one was to make a fortune in his state, for all the vocations of gain are denied to freemen. There seems to be no question about slavery in his ideal state, and the slaves are to carry on such menial work. There can be no silver or gold in his city-state. Money causes too many evils.

There are numerous provisions regarding the inalienable family properties and how to cultivate them. He probably never cultivated a farm in his life. He proposes a general election proceeding, where first the three hundred highest on the ballots are taken, then a second election for one hundred out of the three hundred, then a third election of thirty-seven out of the one hundred. These men so elected are to be guardians of the law (magistrates and judges), and thirty-seven is another magic number. Elective judges are intensely modern, and the worst institution in government. These men shall divide the citizens into four classes according to their property, like Solon's four classes, and enter them on the registers. Any man owning more than his share of property is to have his excess confiscated, and if he makes a false return, he shall lose his share in the public property and in distributions of money. But since he had no money in his state, he seems to be wandering. Generals are to be elected and the citizens are to be enrolled in the army. Priests and priestesses are to be elected.

He lays it down that there should be few judges, and those few good, and that causes should first be tried before a court of neighbors. From this court an appeal should be allowed, and if necessary a second appeal to a still higher court, whose decisions should be final. A proceeding is provided for suing a judge for having intentionally decided wrongfully. This is the most vicious of all his proposals in the *Laws*. A litigant loses his case, then he sues the judge. The guardians of the law shall try the judge and if the judge is found guilty, he shall pay one-half the damages, unless the law wardens assess a higher penalty. The borders of his state would need to be closely guarded to prevent the judges from fleeing the country.

After providing the forms and ceremonies of marriage, and incidentally making some very harsh remarks on the female sex, he comes to the children. The state regulates their education, even to the games they shall play, and these games are not to be changed or altered because that would tend to make them, when grown up, seek changes in the laws. This seems to be very philosophic. The girls are to be brought up to the use of arms. Religion, temples, cultivation of the soil, division of the produce of the soil, are all minutely regulated. He provides for the resident aliens and slaves.

He treats of the offense of temple robbery as the worst crime, and its punishment is by fine or imprisonment or death. Treason comes next, then larceny. A discussion follows as to how to compensate the injured and at the same time reform the injurer. Even a lawsuit is to be educational. A madman can be guilty of a tort and shall pay only the exact damage, Plato says, but he neglects to say how the madman shall be reformed. It is not necessary to go into his discussion of homicide. His law on that subject is the Athenian law. Plato has the primitive law that the nearest relation of the homicidal victim prosecutes. But Plato adds that if he does not prosecute, the relative shall suffer five years' banishment.

The old primitive notions crop out in Plato in regard to the trial of animals for killing a man or of a lifeless thing killing a man. The penalty for the animal is death, but the lifeless thing is to be taken to the border and cast into an adjacent country. This is the inherited taboo of the savage, who thinks the lifeless thing pollutes the land.

The killing of a thief entering the house is justifiable, but the killing of a footpad can be justifiably done only in self-defense. What would be self-defense against a footpad, he wisely leaves unexplained. The violator of a woman or a boy is to be killed by any male relative; and the killing in defending one's father who is doing no wrong, or of one's mother or child or brother, is justified. There are many other provisions, most of them evidently copied from the Athenian law.

Like most philosophers he dislikes lawyers. The Sophists had evidently been contending that Greece needed some sort of lawyers, or at least advocates. Upon them apparently he has the following passage: "To the many noble things in human life there clings a canker that poisons and corrupts them. No one would deny that justice between men is a noble thing and that it has civilized all human affairs. And if justice be noble, how can we deny that pleading is also a noble thing? But these noble things are in disrepute owing to a foul art cloaking itself under a fair name, which claims first that there is a device for dealing with lawsuits and that it is the one which is able, by pleading and helping another to plead, to win the victory, whether in a just or unjust case; and it also asserts that both this art itself and the arguments which proceed from it are a gift offered to any man who gives money in exchange. This art, if it be really an art or merely an artless trick got by habit and practice, must never if possible arise in our state." An indictment of such men is provided for and a punishment.

He gives us a new idea upon the subject of sworn pleadings. All pleadings ought to be unsworn because lawsuits are frequent and half the citizens are thereby made perjurers. He evidently despaired of the Greeks' ever becoming a truthful race. In a trial he believes that no expedients to excite sympathy should be allowed, but only what is just ought to be said, and in proper language, confined to the point. It must be said that the performances to excite sympathy at Athens have been paralleled in contemporary trials among us.

One curious regulation is that no man under forty is to be permitted to go abroad except on a public embassy. There seems to be in his mind the thought that there is something corrupting in travel, which a man cannot withstand until he is forty years of age. Plato also believed that no man should occupy public office after he is seventy years old.

It would appear that Plato's *Laws* have much fine writing upon the duty of the state to cultivate virtue in its citizens. He has one long passage justifying a belief in the gods. But it must be apparent to any one who has read much of Plato that he had no faith in the gods of the vulgar. He really believed in the one Deity, the Moral Governor of the universe. But in the inhabitants of Olympus, with their passions and crimes, he could not have had the slightest belief.

His ideal second-rate state and its laws are simply an impossibility. Such a regimen has never been possible upon this earth among any sort of men. His attitude is essentially that of the school-teacher dealing with immature minds. Grown men can never be governed on such a basis. The idea seems never to have occurred to him that his fixed ideas of right and wrong would not in the coming ages be accepted by enlightened men. The purely relative conception of the moral ideas changing with a changing world, improving with an improving world, was beyond his imagination. But his idea of a fixed and immutable system of legal principles, born coeval with the divine mind, an idea not his own, was to govern legal thinking for many generations. Greek thinkers were prolific in ideas upon the law, but these were mainly the product of inexperience. Yet the actual laws were really fairly reasonable for their condition. It was the incapacity of the Greek in administration of the law that prevented him from even approaching a government of men according to law.

The Athenians, however, had developed the legal fact of private property, a fact which has remained without question until modern times. In almost the whole of Greece outside of the great commercial centers of Athens and Corinth the property conceptions of primitive society remained. In the primitive society within the group of family or tribe, everything, even the work of every day, is thought of as a matter to be done in common. All the possessions are common property. The land, the flocks and the herds are common property. But as soon as commerce and trade, based upon money as a means of exchange, begin to develop, there comes a great increase in the wealth in movables. Individual ownership is necessary to exchange. It is impossible for group and group to deal with each other in the hurried movement of commerce. At Athens this great movement of commerce placed practically all wealth in the form of movables. In Athens in the course of centuries it was found that the land itself must become an article of trade. Land that could not be sold and dealt in would have no exchangeable value, just as a parcel of real estate to-day to which a good transferable title cannot be given, is of no exchangeable value. The group ownership would, under those circumstances, in a commercial community at once yield to an ownership that could be made available in commerce. We shall see that the same influences at Rome gave to the head of the family this private, single ownership in land. In the feudal ages the various limitations on ownership took land out of the avenues of commerce. Long after movables in England had been freely transferable, land became so. The disposition of land by will became as easy as the disposition of movables by will had been for centuries and private property became the rule.

In the last century the philosophers have entered upon the quest of a theory to account for and justify private property, including in that term everything which is now included. Property in a thing generally means the right to exclude others from it. There is sometimes added as a part of property the right to contract, as a valuable property right. The explanations of property have been various. It has been explained in this story how private property came about. It was a natural development and it needs no justification. All the justifications amount in ultimate analysis to the same thing, whether the justification given is metaphysical or actual. The real justification is a more prosaic matter. Private property in real and personal property exists because if not so owned, the property cannot be bought and sold and disposed of in the ordinary course of trade. If the world is prepared to go back to Plato's condition of a little town with inalienable family holdings and each holding self-supporting, with no trade or exchange of property in the town, with every householder owning enough forced and unpaid labor to cultivate the land and produce everything necessary for the family, it would be a very easy matter to get rid of individual private property. But this social organization is an idle dream, it could never be attained. On the other hand the history of law and the general history of the world teaches that the institution of private property is in accordance with a developed human mind, in accordance with developed human institutions. Nothing is more silly than to say that the law made private property. The fact is the exact opposite. Private property came to exist and it made the law. Until that human mind can be changed, it is idle to think of abolishing private property. If the law should attempt to prohibit the transactions of human life based upon private property, no one would obey the law. Therefore the search for a justification of the institution of private property is like a search for a justification of the constitution of the human mind.

CHAPTER 9

The Roman Creation of Modern Law

THE MODERN WORLD IS INDEBTED to Rome for its classification, general theory, and method of applying the law. It is impossible to conceive what our legal system would be had not the Roman jurists labored for centuries upon the general principles and particular rules that gradually created the finished law of Rome. When the Western Roman Empire was overthrown by hordes of savages, who were incapable of either applying the Roman law or comprehending the situations to which it was applicable, civilization went into an eclipse that did not pass from the earth until barbarous usages became slowly absorbed into the reviving Roman law. That law came back to Europe as the written law and furnished a common law for Italy, France, and Spain and at last for Germany. Just as the ancient temples and public buildings of Rome provided a storehouse of building material for later buildings, so the Roman law was an unfailing treasure house of legal reasoning and principles for the modern world. Modern European law and even the English law in its substance and deductive methods was built of Roman materials.

The Romans as a race had a special genius for law, but it required ages for that genius fully to develop, and almost a thousand years for Rome to acquire the wealth of legal experience that was needed to produce such jurists as Gaius, Pomponius, Scaevola, Papinian, Paul, Ulpian, and Modestinus, not to mention a host of others, some of whom are known and still more are unknown. If it be true, as one of our great publicists, Webster, has said, that whoever labors upon the Temple of Justice "with usefulness and distinction, whoever clears its foundations, strengthens its pillars, adorns its entablatures or contributes to raise its august dome still higher in the skies, connects himself in name and fame with that which is and must be as durable as the frame of human society"; it follows that the names of those who gave their lives to the fabric of Roman jurisprudence are entitled to a renown as enduring as our present civilization. To them the Romans of to-day in their Palace of Justice have given a proper and an artistic recognition by a collection of statues of the great makers of the civil law. It is related that the three greatest among them, Papinian, Paul, and Ulpian, once sat together as a court at Eboracum, now the city of York, when Britain was a happy and flourishing Roman province.

That court brings vividly to mind the vicissitudes of the law, for not a long period after that court was sitting at York, the refined and enlightened jurisprudence of a Roman province was replaced for seven hundred years by the uncouth customs of brutal Saxons and piratical Danes. When, in the twelfth century of this era, the Norman lawyers of Henry II began to rear again in England a structure of civilized law, they did not even know that ages before them the greatest jurists in the world had been dispensing justice from London to the Tweed.

When we seek the essential elements of the Roman contribution to the growth of jurisprudence, we find them not only in the discovery and recognition of improved rules of law, but still more in the development of a milieu or an atmosphere of legal reasoning, wherein civilized jurisprudence could expand and adapt its rules to the expansion and multiplying of relations and duties arising from a social life growing more and more complicated. Had it not been that Rome gained a governing position and became the center of the world's affairs, the development of Roman law would not have been possible.

We have seen in the past history of the law, that the knowledge of law was a possession of the priests, whether among the Celtic races, the Babylonians, or the Hebrews. The Greeks freed themselves from this bondage to the priests, but their political structure was such that they did not produce either an adequate tribunal for assuring a rule of law or a body of jurists who could create a general classification of the principles of law and of its particular rules. Nor did they have an order of advocates or practicing lawyers, who by the representation of clients in the courts, could do something toward the correct application of the law to actual controversies. Greece had its courts so modeled that a professional class of lawyers could not be developed, and the temper of the people and of the philosophers was, as we have seen, hostile to such a class.

The history of the law teaches that without a professional class of lawyers, a reign of law is impossible. With the priests the law is always secondary to what they esteem the interests of religion. But to lawyers the law comes first, and its interests are paramount. The reason is the same in each case. The priests live by religion, the lawyer lives by law. Each profession is characterized by its own peculiar type of thought and of mind, yet sometimes the same individual shows a talent in both lines, for, to name but one instance, it is plain that the *Institutes* of Calvin could not have been written by any one who had not received a legal training. As we shall see, the English law owes its beginnings to men who were educated as priests.

When we examine the legal development of Rome it is easy to find in her professional class the secret of the unexampled soundness of Roman law. But for such a class to have full scope it is necessary that there should be an adequate tribunal, and this sort of tribunal it was the greatness of the practical Roman genius to have developed. Acres of books constituting an enormous literature have been written in the Middle Ages and in modern times upon the ancient Roman law. Theoretical jurists, classical scholars, classical commentators, and glossators have done this work. The texts of the Roman law have been analyzed word by word with the utmost meticulosity, but to a modern lawyer, who is versed in the actual life of the law, who has been engaged in the application of the rules of law to the endlessly varying situations and changes in modern life, this vast literature of pedantic comment is repellent, for the practical spirit and genius of Roman law is not there. It was in all things a useful, everyday system. The lawyer who reads of it desires to see it in its daily operation as such a system. He can never hope to master the great mass of technical terms of the writers upon Roman law. The general reader would never feel that he had leisure or inclination to attempt to read even a summary of it, unless he should happen to be attracted by Gibbon's famous chapter in his *Decline and Fall,* which is an extraordinary performance for one not a lawyer, but yet is in parts very misleading. Ingenious inferences upon the doctrine of possession, fine-spun theories of the nexal contract, search for the secret of Quiritarian ownership, researches as to the meaning of real contracts, discussions over things *mancipi* or *nec mancipi* or over stipulations or literal contracts are all very well for the humor of the scholar, but what an actual lawyer desires is some sense of the effect upon human life of that law in operation.

A German writer, Ihering, has ventured the fanciful picture that once, pondering a problem of Roman law, he proceeded to exorcise in clouds of cigar smoke the spirit of the jurist Gaius.[1] Gaius, Ihering says, when summoned from "the vasty deep," appeared in his physical body, and, strange to say, did not object to the appalling stench of a German cigar. He is described "as a strange figure of a man, tall, shriveled, slightly bow-legged, with freckled brow and the general air of a schoolmaster." This is hopeless in its lack of insight. Gaius certainly was not, as Ihering pictures him, an underfed pedagogue, although he might have been a Syrian Greek. But this "strange figure" is all the learned German scholar got out of the interview. He was imposed upon by a false spirit. He should have seen no freckled pedant, but a fine, upstanding, eagle-faced leader in the law.

So it has been with the great law speeches of Roman advocates that remain. English legal history tells us how much of the value of the law depends upon the work of the advocate in the court room. But very noted classical scholars, commenting upon such speeches as Cicero's, weary us in their dry-as-dust way, with complaints that ideas are repeated, that adjectives are multiplied, that the speeches, as they say, are tumid, while they cannot catch the stirring life of the occasion, the emphasis of repetition, the glow of the oratory, the roll of the periods, the overwhelming rush and thunder of the eloquence. Mommsen's carping against Cicero is probably the most repulsive thing in historical

---

1. Rudolf von Ihering, more commonly spelled von Jhering (1818–92).—C. J. R., Jr.

writing.[2] The whole effect, meaning, and power of the speeches pass over the heads of such people, who cannot be conceived as capable of any sort of forensic oratory.

A trial of an important case in the great days of the Republic was a struggle of legal giants. When Cicero, by his mere opening of the case against Verres, defended by Hortensius, the leader of the Roman bar, drove Verres out of the court room into lifelong banishment, the occasion was a great legal drama. In the days of the Empire, in the age of the Antonines, Pliny the Younger gives us a picture as vivid as that of the arraignment of Warren Hastings. An African governor is being prosecuted before the Senate for trampling upon the rights of African subjects. The Emperor Trajan is presiding over a great concourse of the Senate. Pliny and the historian Tacitus, his bosom friend, were prosecuting. Pliny spoke for five hours and we get a touch of the courtesy of the Emperor, who expressed the fear that Pliny was exerting himself beyond what his delicate health would permit. After Pliny's opening speech the advocate for the defendant exerted all his talents in a very skillful and adroit defense. The prosecution was closed by Tacitus replying "in a strain of the most powerful eloquence and with a certain dignity, which distinguishes all of his speeches."

This scene just quoted comes from a period of the Roman law, when it had almost reached its zenith. The full development of Roman law required from 753 B.C., the assumed date of the founding of Rome, to about 250 A.D., a period of a thousand years. Then followed an era of compiling until the Corpus Juris of Justinian was put together, beginning just before 537 A.D. The innumerable books of Roman law were thrown aside, lost and forgotten, until, after centuries of futile glossators and commentators, a giant like Cujas could reconstruct some of those lost treatises.[3]

---

2. Theodor Mommsen (1817–1903).—C. J. R., Jr.

3. Jacques Cujas (1522–90), French jurist who sought to recover accurate readings of the Justinian texts, the Theodosian Code, and other leading Roman law documents. He was particularly known for placing the cause of scholarship above the sectarian politics of his day.—C. J. R., Jr.

Roman law arose in a modest way among a collection of village communities where small Aryan tribes which had wandered into Italy came together, about 750 B.C., for mutual protection and made a common religious center at Alba Longa and a common trading place where the Roman forum stands to-day. Upon the surrounding hills grew the city, and from them, as her throne of empire, Rome was to rule the world. These tribes had the usual Aryan primitive organization. They had the patriarchal family, tracing relationship solely in the male line. There was the usual inalienable land-holding of the family, which had grown out of the tribal holding. Each family was ruled by the father with despotic power of life and death over all the members of the household. This was the primitive institution that we saw among the Greeks and the Hebrews. These families were branches of larger kindreds uniting in still larger kindreds called *gentes* or clans, tracing back to a common ancestor. Each male member of the clan bore as his middle name that of the common ancestor.

When one looks at Roman patrician names, such as those of the two great commanders, Publius Cornelius Scipio and Lucius Cornelius Sulla, and that of the Catilinarian conspirator, Publius Cornelius Lentulus, he knows that they claim a common ancestor named Cornelius, who has given his name to the *gens Cornelia*, that that clan has at least three branches, one the kindred of the Scipiones, another the kindred of the Sullae, and a third the kindred of the Lentuli, and that each man is the head of a family or *domus* with some remnants of the father's power over the household. The Roman had developed to a marked degree the worship of his ancestors. He kept their images in his hall. On state occasions those effigies were carried in procession. They were the household gods of his hearthstone and to them he offered sacrifice. In the days of Rome's greatest power the Roman patrician patronized the sculptor's art mainly that he might look upon the portrait statues and busts before which he daily paid homage to his fathers.

These gentile clans were united into tribes and the heads of the clans formed the governing body of the united tribes. They were the patricians who formed the governing body called the Senate. In early times a man was a Senator because he was a patrician by birth; in later days he was a patrician because he or his father was a Senator. Each clan had its horde of dependents called clients. They were probably the remains of a conquered race. The clients and other freemen formed the body called plebeians, who were the Roman people. The full designation of the social organization required both patricians and plebeians. It was shown by those initial letters borne on the standards of the legions and in use in many ways to-day in Rome, S.P.Q.R. (*Senatus Populusque Romanus*). It is almost a shock to find those initials masquerading on a street sign in modern Rome warning of some municipal work.

The patricians at first absorbed all the governmental as well as priestly offices and powers in the city-state. The tribes came to be headed by an elective king, but in time rulers of the Etruscan race subdued and governed as hereditary kings these Latin tribes for a long period. This is all there is to the story of the Roman kings, for even Livy, who told the story, no more believed in his Romulus, Numa Pompilius, Tullus Hostilius, or Tarquinius Priscus, than Virgil believed in his tales of the Trojan Aeneas as the ancestor of the Julian *gens*. The end of the Etruscan rule came when the last Tarquin was driven out. Two elective consuls became head of the state with all the powers of a king, but each having a veto on the other. This double-headed executive was probably borrowed from Sparta. The ruling class of patricians was alone eligible to fill the consular office and the Senate could not act in legislation except upon a bill or law proposed by a consul. Rome had also the primitive assembly of the tribes, common among the Aryans, that appeared in the institution called the *comitia* or assembly.

The Roman race had certain characteristics, an intensely conservative character, a natural steadiness, steadfastness and dignity, a profound patriotism, and readiness to sacrifice for the common society. They had that natural social talent so marked in the Anglo-Norman, which enables one class to compromise with another. They had a sort of native instinct for uniting in the presence of a common danger. At bottom they were a just race with a developed sense for justice and a fear of arbitrary power, which gradually hedged around all departments of the government with checks and balances that prevented any class from having its own headstrong way. The tribes absorbed neighboring tribes.

When a Sabine family headed by Appius Claudius, or, to use the antique name, Attus Clausus, joined the Roman state, the Claudian family with its dependents numbered five thousand. These Claudii, especially the kindred of them called the Neros, became the very front of the patricians. The plebeian clients formed *gentes* or clans of their own. Thus the Marcelli, who afterwards were a great patrician family, were originally a plebeian family. The first emperor, Augustus, was in his paternal descent an Octavius of a plebeian gens, but through his grandmother, the sister of Caius Julius Caesar, and by the adoption of his granduncle Caesar, belonged to the *gens Julia*, which claimed the highest patrician descent.

The early history of Rome for legal purposes is the breaking up of the clan organization by the substitution of families and a struggle of the plebeians to obtain a share of the political power. Plebeians gained eligibility to the consulship and to the lower offices of quaestor and praetor through which a man must pass to become eligible to the consulship. They gained the concession that no citizen could be put to death without the vote of the general assembly, with the exception that dictatorial power removed this restriction. Plebeians gained officers of their own, called tribunes, and at last they obtained legislative power on the initiative of the tribunes. The tribunes were given a veto against senatorial action and each tribune had a veto on another tribune. There was, also, another sort of check. The Romans had a religious system of divination by augurs and soothsayers who declared the auspices favorable or unfavorable, and this sort of Mumbo Jumbo work in which no enlightened Roman believed, could stop political action. The general legislative body was the convocation of all citizens in the *comitia* to which the Senate could propose a law. The differences between the different forms of the *comitia* are not here important. There were decrees of the Senate called *senatus consulta*, resolutions of the *plebs* called *plebiscita*, and regularly passed laws of the assembly called *leges*. All of them created law, but, as will appear, the creation of the body of Roman law was by other means.

At first the laws were oral and knowledge of them until men learned to read and write was in the custody of the patricians; and, precisely as at Athens, the plebeians, as soon as they were able to read, demanded written laws so that all might know the law. The demand was for laws that were certain and definite, to which all had access. Decemvirs (ten men) were appointed to get together a body of law which was enacted in the Twelve Tables engraved on wood or brass and displayed in the Forum for all to read. There is a statement in Livy that commissioners were appointed to go to Greece and bring back the knowledge of their laws for the benefit of the state. Whether this be true or not, the Romans, long before they had any political clash with Greece, had a rather close knowledge of the Greek law through the Greeks of southern Italy. The parallels are too close to be the result of accident. The demand for written law was Greek in its origin. This is not at all strange. All social animals are necessarily very imitative, prone to follow as savages the customs of the tribe. Men, as they grew more enlightened, developed the tendency to imitate other peoples. This was pronounced among the Hebrews and according to their writings this failing brought endless woes upon the Jews. This imitative trait is shown no less in the way in which the use of polished stone weapons, of pottery, of bronze weapons, and at last of iron weapons spread among barbarians. It is just as marked in regard to institutions and laws. So powerful is it that one legal writer has found improvement in law to lie wholly in imitation. But the question is as to who instructed the race imitated. Progress and development were required to begin somewhere. The lever and fulcrum can accomplish wonders but the fulcrum must stand on something. Whatever the fact may be, the Roman was improving his primitive law as he was fighting his way to the headship of Italy.

Fortunately for Rome, the Gauls or Celts in their migrations descended upon Italy. They ruined the Etruscan state, so much so that all of northern Italy became Celtic and was called Cisalpine Gaul. The Gauls would have taken the Capitol itself, had not Rome been saved by the cackling of the sacred geese, which for once fulfilled a useful purpose. Rome, freed from the danger of Etruria, gradually fought its way to the control of all Italy. It was a lovely land. Even in her ruin Byron could sing of her "immaculate charm that cannot be defaced." The Greeks had given this land the name of the Hesperides, "the golden Italy." Cicero, Rome's greatest advocate, was born at Arpinum, which still

> Like an eagle's nest, hangs on the crest
> Of purple Apennine.

In his speech on his return from exile, he apostrophized his native land: "Our Fatherland, Immortal Gods, my tongue can hardly tell my love and delight in her. This Italy of ours, how lovely she is, how renowned are her cities, how beautiful her varied landscapes, her fertile fields, her harvests; how magnificent is this city and its civilization, the nobility of this commonwealth and your dignity and majesty!"

After gaining Italy the Romans were compelled to contest the western Mediterranean with the Carthaginians. They won the long struggle of many years, destroyed Carthage, and gained Spain, Sicily, and northern Africa. Here the conservative Senate would have stopped, but the Macedonian power took issue with Rome, and Macedonia with Greece became a Roman province. The assaults of Mithridates from Asia Minor and of the Seleucid successors of Alexander from Syria forced Rome into Asia Minor and Syria. Afterwards Caesar conquered Gaul and annexed Egypt. At last the Roman Empire was complete.

In the meantime Rome had become the capital of the world. No longer was commerce confined to the highways of the sea. The great system of Roman roads tied the empire together. We see a picture of safe and easy travel and a vast commerce moving across the seas, which had been swept clear of pirates, and along thoroughfares, kept in constant policing and repair by local effort. Superb bridges (some of them remain to-day) spanned the great rivers not only in Italy but far out in Spain, in Gaul, or on the Danube. A class of great capitalists of the Equestrian order had been developed, for commercial pursuits were interdicted to Senators. Partnerships and corporations were numerous. All the legal instruments of commerce and of its speculative ventures existed. Carriers by land and sea were plentiful. The days of barter had long passed away. Money was the medium of exchange. Bankers and money changers lined the Forum. Land had become private property fully alienable by the owner, as it was among the Greeks, and the utmost freedom in willing property existed.

So far as the ownership of all kinds of property is concerned, private property and its alienability, as complete as they are to-day, had resulted from this great commercial expansion.

To understand how Roman law became a world system, we must conceive the whole civilized world as under the Roman sway ruled by Roman governors. England and France were wealthy provinces, Spain enjoyed a prosperity she has never again attained. Southern Germany and Austria proper were as well off as they are to-day. The Illyrian province, now a part of Jugo-Slavia, recruited the legions; the Balkan states were a great Roman province; in material well-being Greece, Macedonia, and Thrace were never so prosperous; Asia Minor and Syria were full of wealthy cities; Egypt up to the falls of the Nile was the granary of the world and Northern Africa fringed the Mediterranean with cities whose ruins, covered with sand or surrounded by hovels, are all that remain of so much prosperity and splendor.

Over this vast domain descended the blessings of the Roman peace. Imagine a world where for two hundred years in all this area there was no war, and none of the losses and devastation of war. The fighting with the savages on the borders of the Empire, protected by the legions, was hardly more to the Romans than were our border fights with the Indians. Italy itself was glad to feel the repose and stability of the Empire. The individual cases of prosecution under a Nero or a Domitian were little more thought of among the mass of the people than the prosecutions of trust magnates among us. In this sort of world, made up of so many different kinds of races, was built the fabric of Roman law, in order that it might be a general law applicable throughout all the Roman world.

The two engines that created the law were the Roman court with an adequate procedure, and the profession of lawyers made up of jurists and advocates. It is easy to describe in a general way the advance in law which resulted from an adequate tribunal for deciding legal controversies under the assistance and supervision of the professional class. The result was that in almost all the departments of law, as a competent lawyer knows it at this time, a solution for legal controversies can be found by means of either the principles or the particular rules of Roman jurisprudence. That solution would not differ except in rare cases from the solution which our courts would offer, while the main elements in our procedure can be traced directly back to the civil law, as we call the Roman law in distinction from our common law. We shall now describe this advance to highly civilized law.

When the laws at the demand of the plebeians had been put into a written form, they were called the law of the Twelve Tables, although, of course, the Twelve Tables had behind them a mass of customary law. In kingly times the king had been high priest, leader in war, and judge. After the kings were gone, the consuls had these powers. To relieve the consuls of judicial work an elective officer, called a praetor, was provided. Custom and statute were among the Greeks methods of creating law, but in Rome the judicial magistrate had the peculiar power not only of deciding the law but in accordance with an early statute, of announcing on what principles he would grant justice and the forms that he would use. In this way the praetors substituted new methods of pleading in place of the old primitive rules. These announced rules were binding upon the praetor himself and they, being adopted and added to by one successor after another, became a collection of law showing the principles upon which relief would be granted or refused, the method of proceeding and the legal formulae necessary to be used. This collection came to be called the Edict, supplementing both custom and statute. It was of the same character but much wider in extent than our court rules.

The law, however, that was applied to Roman citizens could not be applied to strangers, and another praetor, called the Peregrine or the strangers' praetor, was provided for deciding causes arising between strangers, and between strangers and citizens.

At first among the Romans the priests gave guidance as to what were the customary laws and gave public consultations upon the law. These priests were patricians and belonged to the body presided over by the Pontifex Maximus, from whom the Pope in later times took his title. But after the Twelve Tables and the Edict had made the law public and secularized it, the patricians, who were not priests, still studied the law and men of learning in the law supplanted the priests, by giving consultations and drawing up the forms and by guiding and directing the legal formulae and the procedure. At first the patricians monopolized this legal profession. In course of time written expositions of the law began to appear and the professional class of legal advisers was in full operation. Almost all of the patricians felt it to be their duty to study the law on account of another peculiar situation at Rome which will now be explained.

Attached to every Roman clan, as we have seen, was a body of plebeians called the clients. It was the duty of the head of the clan as patron to represent these dependent clients. When the clans broke up and the family was substituted, the head of the family had his clients. By a natural process in the city with its intense political life, every man of character, birth, and standing gathered around him a body of clients. Persons of almost every condition became clients. People who sought the support of a powerful friend, the needy or ambitious, men who could be counted on at an election or mere parasites attached themselves to some patron. Sometimes aliens like Archias or subject cities or Italian municipalities sought a protector. The most powerful of all patrons came to be the skilled orator. A man like Cicero would have his close friends, others who were his companions or others who merely waited upon his public appearances. Thus grew up the order of advocates, whose services were gratuitously rendered to every friend and client. The services of the patron were not to be compensated. Laws existed against payment, but at last the laws against paying the advocates fell into disuse by a process which a cynic would pronounce the most natural thing in the world.

Theoretically the Roman advocate was a man of rank and property who, without reward, devoted his talents to the practice of advocacy in lawsuits for the benefit of his friends and clients. The career of an advocate was, outside of the army, the best road to honor and high office. This tradition of an unpaid advocacy continued until the days of the Empire. Pliny tells a tale of a certain advocate who had been hired as counsel for the city of Vicenza in its lawsuit over its right to maintain a public market.

The lawyer had made an appearance for which he had received two hundred and fifty dollars and he had also received one hundred and seventy-five dollars for a second appearance to be made. When the day of hearing came he was missing. He was cited before the Senate, and

Cicero attacking Catiline before the Roman Senate

asked for its clemency on the ground that his friends had persuaded him not to appear on account of a certain influential Senator. The Senate was about to absolve him when the tribune arose with his veto. Pliny says that it was an eloquent and impressive remonstrance. He said that the profession had become venal, that advocates took money, sometimes even to betray their clients, and that they made a shameful trade of their profession. Instead of honor being their reward, as it used to be, the tribune asserted, they even took large and annual salaries. Then the tribune read the laws against fees to advocates.

This remonstrance in the Senate stirred up the city. The judges began to enforce the law. The criminal judge announced that every party appearing in his court should take an oath that he had not paid or promised his advocate a fee. After the case was over a party was permitted to pay his advocate a gratuity not exceeding four hundred dollars. Many of the lawyers complained bitterly of these obsolete laws. But such is the effect of tradition and of the Roman law that to-day in France an advocate cannot sue for a fee nor in England can a barrister maintain such an action.

The jurisconsults, however, only advised and counseled. Finally under Augustus they became patented counsel and filled a public office. They, as Cicero said, practiced the art of the good and equal. The praetors simply took what the jurisconsults gave them as law. The greater part of the Roman law was wholly customary. It did not exist in the form of statutes and consequently the jurisconsults were left free to make the law so that it would become ready to meet the expanding life of Rome. Cicero's book "*On the Laws*" has not been preserved. The fourth book has been lost. It dealt with the judicial tribunals. If we could have Cicero's exposition of the Roman courts as they were in his day, we would see the Roman law at a time when it was first entering upon its period of great expansion, before the old and original form of the courts had been lost.

The praetor of Rome who judged cases for the citizens was supplanted, as stated above, by the praetor for the strangers (*praetor peregrinus*). To these strangers the Roman law had no application. It had a rigid, formalistic kind of procedure wholly inapplicable to cases arising among foreigners. The *praetor peregrinus* naturally tried to find those rules of law which would be suitable to foreigners and by the aid of the jurisconsults found those rules which were accepted among most of the nations under the Roman sway. This action of the foreign praetor reacted upon the praetor for the Romans and it was perceived that the narrow and rigid rules of the Roman city law must be remodeled to suit the sentiments of right and justice among civilized men generally. The Roman praetors were practical men; they had no more use for metaphysics than the modern English lawyer has had for that science. They were not muddled by any conception of a natural law of reason, but both praetors and jurisconsults saw that they must strive to make the law conform as nearly as possible to the developed ideas of right and justice among all classes of men growing more and more civilized.

As it has been stated in an earlier chapter, justice among men requires that the same rule shall be applied to all men in a similar situation. Justice is not primarily concerned with the rightness or wrongness of the actual rule. That is to be determined by right as found in general notions of public utility. The Greeks were continually getting befogged between justice and right and this is the fault of all the metaphysical cast of law. Men are satisfied generally with the justice of a rule if it applies to all alike. The rules of law, as Roman experience proves, are bound to respond sooner or later to the generally diffused ideas of rightfulness and especially the rules are expected to be consonant with ordinarily accepted ideas of public utility, for, as Horace says in his *Satires*, utility is almost the mother of law and equity and laws were devised through fear of injustice.

The jurisconsults, therefore, applied themselves to find the underlying principle that would make a general rule and at the same time be consonant with right. These general rules the jurisconsults applied by taking a particular case and making a careful analysis of it so as to bring it under a general rule of law by means of analogy, extending the rule on the grounds of utility and social expediency. This is the method of judges to-day, proceeding on the analogies of prior established rules as shown in published decisions. This method at Rome brought for the first time into the world what is called the legal cast of mind, the resolving of a particular case in accordance with a general rule that would thus sat-

isfy the demands of justice and at the same time be suited to the sentiments of the rightful and the ethical. When this sort of solution was
made it was called "elegant" and this is why in the first English law book,
called Glanville, the strange phrase occurs regarding an ordinance devised under Henry II that it was "elegantly" inserted into the law.

These solutions of the jurisconsults were collected and published as
responsa, or *sententiae* or *regulae*, being answers or decisions or rules in
particular cases. They were digested under proper heads and the law was
classified in regard to matters as they came up in the practice. The literature of this law, interpreting the customary law as well as the statutes,
grew continually from century to century, so that Pomponius could say
that the true civil law consisted wholly of the interpretation of the
learned lawyers. The only restriction was that no customary law could
derogate from a specific statute, just as in our law to-day it is settled that
no custom can be pleaded that is contrary to the law itself. Thus grew up
in Roman law the distinction between *jus* (law in general) and *lex*, which
was law that depended upon a statute.

At the same time the law laid down by the peregrine praetor for his
methods of trial was expanding. He applied the rules of law as between
foreigners, and between Romans and foreigners. The Hebrews' idea, as
we have seen, was to give the stranger the benefit of the home law. It did
not occur to them that it was not a great advance to let the stranger have
the benefit of the home law. The Roman, however, went further. He had
the good sense to see that his law was obsolete. He saw that for foreigners the rules to be applied must be those that were of general application,
and this law he called the *jus gentium*, the law of nations, far broader and
more liberal in its terms. At last these bodies of law all coalesced into a
set of rules where the *jus gentium* supplanted altogether the strict law of
the Romans and the Roman law had become a world system, applicable
throughout the Roman Empire, where Roman governors and officials
applied and enforced it.

The original system was simplified from its primitive character into a
plain, straightforward body of law. Its procedure was rationalized. The
litigant stated his case and asked the magistrate to authorize a suit. If
there was no formula in the books, the magistrate would devise one. The

defendant was called in and he must respond to the case stated by the plaintiff. If he could not deny the plaintiff's right the plaintiff took judgment. If he did deny it he made a defense by answer, but if he pleaded some countervailing right in himself the defense was called an exception. These matters are of importance because they dictated the English practice at the common law and they made the English system of pleading. Thereupon the praetor, in a written document, stated the issue, and upon that issue or points in dispute the matter went to a single judge or to arbiters, one or more, to be decided on the testimony of witnesses, documentary evidence, or admissions or other proof. The primitive device in Greek law that the plaintiff must recover what he claimed and no less was done away with and if it was a question of damages, the judge assessed them.

A sketch of the private law among the Romans will be given in the next chapter in connection with the compilation made under the Emperor Justinian. Here it is sufficient to say that in the time of the Republic the Roman private law had still far to go before it became a world system.

It was in criminal law that the Republic, like most democracies or attempts at democracy, fell short. In a criminal court there was a large body of jurors. The jurors were often bribed, just as the voters at an election of consuls or tribunes were bribed. Laws against bribery were multiplied but they did little good. One of Cicero's great speeches was in the case of Muraena, prosecuted for bribery at a consular election. Cicero was for the defendant and his defense is a curious conglomeration of very fine speaking but quite irrelevant matters. The jurors were intelligent enough, for otherwise ridicule of the Stoic doctrines of Cato, the prosecutor, would have been impossible. The famous prosecution of Clodius was notorious. The story that is told of this trial shows that the public was much incensed at the acquittal of Clodius. The jurors required an armed guard in order to get home in safety. Some one suggested that they were afraid of being held up and robbed of the bribe money that had been received. The use of bands of thugs at elections, such as officiated at Rome, is not unknown among us. Nor are instances wanting of bribed jurors or bribed electors in our highly advanced administration of justice.

One of these popular courts remained from a time that cannot be discovered. It was concerned with many civil matters, but its most important jurisdiction was in testamentary disputes. It was called the Centumviral or "Hundred Men Court." It was probably borrowed from the popular courts of the Greeks. It was a favorite court for the training of young advocates. Pliny, the lawyer, states that, when he was a young man, he appeared often in the Hundred Men Court.

> The business there [he says] is more fatiguing than pleasant. The cases are mostly trifling and inconsiderable. Rarely is there one worth speaking in, either from the importance of the question or from the rank of the parties. There are few advocates there I take any pleasure in working with. The rest, a lot of imprudent young fellows, many of whom we know nothing about, come here to gain practice in speaking and conduct themselves with such forwardness and such an utter want of deference, that my friend Attilius put it exactly when he said, "Boys set out at the bar with cases in the Hundred Court, just as they do at school with Homer," meaning that they begin with what they ought to end. But in former times, so my elders tell me, no youth even of the best families was allowed in court unless introduced by some person of consular dignity. As things are now all distinctions are leveled and the present young generation, instead of waiting to be introduced, break in of their own accord. The audience at their heels is worthy of such orators. It is a low rabble of hired mercenaries supplied by contract. They get together in the middle of the court, where the dole is dealt out openly to them. This dirty business increases every day. Only yesterday two of my household were paid fifty cents apiece to cheer somebody or other. This is what the higher eloquence goes for. The leader of the gang stands up and signals for applause; most of the thick-headed fellows know nothing about what is said and must have a signal. If you hear cheering in a court you know that the one who gets the most applause deserves it the least. Licinius began this by asking his friends to come and hear him. My tutor Quintilian told me that the great lawyer Domitius Afer was once speaking in his usual slow and impressive way, when he heard near him in another court a great applauding. He stopped until the noise ceased. He began again and was interrupted a second and a third time. He asked then, "Who is speaking." "Licinius," he was told, upon which he broke off his speech, saying, "Eloquence is no more." But then

it had simply begun to decline; now it is almost extinct. I stay in the court because of my years and the interests of my friends, as I fear they would think I stayed out to avoid work rather than these indecencies, but I am effecting a gradual retreat.

Pliny tells of one of his cases in the Hundred Court. To explain it let it be understood that a Roman could will his property as he pleased, but a proceeding could be brought to set aside the will in the Hundred Court on the ground of undue influence or on the ground that it was wanting in natural duty. The case gives one an insight into the art of advocacy at Rome.

Pliny's client was a daughter suing her stepmother for her patrimony. The father of Pliny's client, an old man, seized with "a love fit at fourscore," had brought home a stepmother. The love fit was fatal, for the old man was dead after eleven days of the malady, but the stepmother, like a modern "gold-digger," bade fair to make way with the old man's estate under a will which he had made. Pliny's client, "a lady ennobled not only by birth, but by marriage to a husband of praetorian rank," was compelled to sue the stepmother for her patrimony. Friends innumerable attended on both sides. The benches were thronged and even the galleries were filled. Around in all the available space stood spectators, men and women who could hear little, craning their necks to see—fathers, daughters, and stepmothers, all warmly interested.

The daughter won her case and we may pardon Pliny, flushed with victory, for writing to a friend in this strain: "I send you my speech. Take it up as the Cyclops took up the shining arms of Aeneas. I could not shorten it. Notice the abundance of the topics treated, the careful order in which the points are stated, and the little narratives interspersed to give it an air of novelty. I may say privately to you that there is a great warmth and a sublimity in parts of it, but I keep those parts woven in with close reasoning. I had to bring in dry computations, descending from the orator to the accountant. Sometimes I gave free rein to my indignation and my compassion and I was borne along like a vessel before every varying gust. In a word, my friends say that this is my Oration on the Crown." This comparison to the masterpiece of Demosthenes is rather strong, but there is to the most cold-blooded of lawyers a solid satisfaction in winning a difficult case that will excuse some excess of enthusiasm. But even after Pliny, a hundred years more was needed for Roman law to attain under Papinian and Ulpian its highest level in those great jurisconsults.

The finest speech of eulogy in the history of the bar is that which was made by Cicero upon his friend Sulpicius, "the Roman friend of Rome's least mortal mind." Sulpicius was an exceedingly learned jurisconsult. He died in the public service upon an embassy on behalf of the Senate to Mark Antony. In this speech, called Cicero's Ninth Philippic, is a sentence which describes exactly but in an almost untranslatable way the function of the Roman jurisconsult. Cicero says that Sulpicius was not less a master of law than of justice (*non minus juris consultus quam justitiae*). This is the true breed of lawyer, striving always to be in command of all the learning of the law, but striving no less earnestly to make the law fit the equality of justice and the ethical demand of righteousness. These Roman advocates and jurisconsults must always be to a lawyer a subject of intense interest. Two of them have left collections of letters. No one can read these letters of Cicero and Pliny without knowing that this was a world in which tolerant, kindly gentlemen abounded. It is the tone of men who are merciful, just, and humane in the exercise of power. Even that prodigious prevaricator or retailer of baseless scandal, Suetonius, cannot obscure the Roman gentlemen. The historian Merivale says of Pliny that no other of the ancients comes so near to our conception of a gentleman in mind, breeding, and position. Something regarding him may serve to bring before us the life of a Roman lawyer.[4]

Pliny's wealth gave him the setting for a life of cultivation. He enjoyed a great ancestral estate on Lake Como with two splendid villas. Men to-day can point out the peculiarly intermittent spring that Pliny describes. He had another large estate in Tuscany at the foot of the

---

4. Zane has more to say about Pliny the Younger (A.D. 61 or 62–113) in his essay, "A Roman Lawyer," *Illinois Law Review* 8 (1914): 575–93. The historian referred to is Charles Merivale (1808–93).—C. J. R., Jr.

Apennines with a lovely outlook described in one of his most charming letters. He had still another estate at Tifernum, "green Tifernum, the hill of vines," and suburban villas at Tivoli, at Praeneste, and at Tusculum, with a winter home on the ocean. Here Pliny had a splendid library. Libraries were common among the Romans, and Cicero tells of his visiting the villas of friends to consult books, when he was writing his treatises.

Pliny is defending his friend Bassus, who had been governor of Bithynia. Bessus instructs his lawyer to open the defense by representing the consideration due to illustrious birth and public services, how once before he had been wrongly prosecuted and triumphantly acquitted, how now his accusers were professional informers, making money by their trade; but on the main point to show that all his actions had been just and that he deserved not only an acquittal, but commendation. The real difficulty, says Pliny, was that, in the simplicity of his heart, Bassus, who had been there before as assistant governor and had many friends, was so indiscreet as to have exchanged presents with friends upon his birthday. The laws expressly forbade the receiving of presents by a governor. "Now what should I do?" says Pliny. "If I denied the fact, it was notorious, Bassus had openly stated it even to the Emperor. If I appealed to the clemency of the court, I would ruin my client at once by acknowledging that he had done wrong. If I justified an act knowing it to be illegal, I would injure my own character as a citizen and would not help him. So I hit upon the middle course of contending that the Senate in its plenary power as a court could hold that the acts, while within the rigid letter of the law, were not within its spirit, and such is the law." On this theory he made his defense.

Each side was given six hours, and Bassus asked Pliny to speak five hours and his associate to speak one. Pliny continues: "When I had spoken three hours and a half night came on. I had, it seemed to me, made a good impression and I did not want to resume next morning, for I was afraid I could not again arouse the interest. A speech is carried along by its continued flow, it keeps up its own fire, but a remission allows the audience to get cold. It is like a torch kept brightly glowing by continuous motion, but if it goes out it is hard to rekindle. But Bassus implored me

to go on in the morning, so I did and found the Senate fresh and lively."
Bassus was acquitted, and when, says Pliny, the fine old man, broken by
age and anxiety, came out of the Senate House, the crowd, remembering
how he had been banished by Domitian, a name never mentioned except
in connection with some undeserved misfortune, greeted him with
cheering and acclamations.

Pliny's life, like that of the other leading Roman advocates, was a laborious one of working hard at the profession because he loved it. When
he was a judge and minister of finance, his time was taken up by hearing
cases, passing upon pleadings, and making up the public accounts. While
practising law, his days were occupied with drawing wills, with consultations, or pleading in the courts. Little time had he to go to his villas in
the north; while at Rome he attends in the city all day and at evening sets
out for his villa on the sea or at Tusculum or Tivoli, returning in the
morning. He regrets that his time is so much taken up with trivial matters. He writes to a friend up at Como: "What are you doing? Reading,
hunting, fishing, I suppose, while I am restless and impatient at my not
being able as well to enjoy what I long for. Shall I ever break away from
these ties of business? Never, I fear; fresh employment keeps adding itself to the old. Such an endless train of business is daily pressing upon
me and riveting my chains tighter."

He loved the place where he was born. "How is that sweet Como of
ours looking? What of my most enticing of villas, the portico where it is
perpetual spring, that shadiest of plane-tree walks, the crystal canal that
winds along its flowery banks, and the Lake lying below so lovely to the
view?" Still that glittering Lake, lovely under the brilliance of the Italian
sky, spreads her enchantments. "What have you to tell me," he continues, "of that soft yet firm running track, the sunny bathroom, those large
dining rooms, and the small one, and all those elegant apartments for repose?" He gives us a lovely picture of a friend, a high-class Roman who
had retired, a man who had commanded armies and held great offices.
Everything about him was composed and dignified, a serene life full of
ease and repose. "You could imagine you were listening to some worthy
of the ancient days, what deeds, what men, what serene wisdom you hear
about. He composes most elegant lyrics, Greek and Latin, so wonder-

fully sweet and gay they are, and his own unsullied life lends them additional charm." His splendid entertainments, his grave politeness and ur-
banity are painted for us. "This is the sort of life," says Pliny, "I am
going to have when I arrive at those years which shall justify me in retiring from active life. Meanwhile I am worried with a thousand affairs,
but my old friend, too, for many years discharged his professional duties,
held magistracies, governed provinces, and by hard toil earned his repose." This time, alas, never came for Pliny, but he comforts himself
with the thought that to be engaged in the public service, to hear and determine cases, to explain the laws, and to administer justice, is a part and
the noblest part of philosophy, since it is reducing to practice what her
professors ought to teach in speculation.

But freedom to Pliny did not mean anything more than a government
regulated by law, and he was certainly not a leveler. The Romans of his
day were free men in his eyes and it is true that the goodness of the private law redeems many a defect in the government of the Empire.
Writing to a provincial governor, Pliny recommends him to so conduct
himself as to preserve the proper distinctions of rank and dignity; when
they are once confounded and all thrown upon a level, nothing can be
more unequal than that kind of equality. He tells of an old friend of his
who had suffered from his early years from rheumatic gout or arthritis
which, first attacking his feet, had in the passing years affected the whole
body. The old man was racked with pain and said: "I suppose you wonder why I endure all these miseries. I would not, if it were not that I have
the hope that I shall outlive, if only for one day, that villain Domitian."
The Emperor Domitian was assassinated and Pliny tells how then this
old Roman, who could now die a free and unenslaved man, rejecting the
prayers of his family and friends, calmly committed suicide. Even the
Emperor Nerva was not too much of a ruler to listen to the truth. There
is a story of Pliny dining with Nerva; placed next to the Emperor was
Veiento, who had been guilty of cruel and base conduct under Domitian.
The conversation turned on a certain blind but remorseless informer,
who was then dead. "Where," asked Nerva, "would he be at the present
time, if he were alive?" A Roman at the table, looking hard at Veiento,
replied: "He would probably be dining with us."

Pliny as an advocate would not be complete without a reference to the best letter in the whole collection, which describes the scene of terror at the great eruption of Vesuvius, when Pompeii and Herculaneum were overwhelmed. Pliny, then a boy of seventeen, and his mother were with his uncle, the Elder Pliny, who was in command of the Roman fleet at the great naval base at Misenum on the Bay of Naples. A strange black cloud appeared over the mountain. An imploring letter from the other side of the Bay came to the Admiral from a lady whose villa lay at the foot of Vesuvius. The brave old Roman manned his galleys and steered straight across the bay for the mountain, from which he never returned. The earthquake was rocking the land, the ocean was rushing back and forth on the shore, the air was filled with ashes and cinders. The darkness that had obscured the day was illumined only by the flames and flashes from the mountain. The boy was young and active, and his mother, who was too corpulent to flee, begged him to leave the house, but he would not go without her. Hand in hand he and his mother started along the road in that scene of confusion and terror— "the shrieking women, crying children, shouting men, some calling for their parents, others for their husbands, others for their children, some lifting up their hands to the gods, but the greater part convinced that there were now no gods at all, and that the final endless night had come upon the world."

But the gods had not ceased to exist. To quote the Christmas hymn, "Apollo, Pallas, Jove, and Mars held undisturbed their ancient reign" for centuries more. Pliny, in the latter part of his life, as governor of Bithynia, came in contact with the new sect of Christians, who seemed to him a strange sort of ignorant and superstitious people. Naturally he felt little sympathy with a religion that had arisen among the slaves and fishermen of the East. His friend Tacitus called it a depraved and ignorant superstition. But this new religion had a proselytizing power as great as that of Buddhism and it became the state religion of the Empire, and through that religion the ideas of the Hebrew law were to become, by means of the Christians, a determining factor in jurisprudence. The priests of the Church, as the only literate class, were to hold in their hands through the long darkness of the barbarian invasions and conquests, the destinies of the law in the western European world. With the advent of Christianity as the religion of the state, the seat of empire moved to the refounded Byzantium, called the City of Constantine. The language of the Roman law became Greek and it is now necessary to describe its fortunes when it passed into Grecian hands.

CHAPTER 10

The Greek Compilation of Roman Law

IN THE AGE OF THE ANTONINES the gradually accumulated praetorian law was enacted into the form of the Perpetual Edict by the
Emperor Hadrian. The theory of law applicable to the Emperor as the
legislative power that the Roman people had confided to the Emperor
the function of legislation, was now developed. Great lawyers were now
holding the posts of power and were utilized as administrators. Papinian
was praetorian prefect under Severus and Caracalla, the unworthy son of
Severus, put him to death. Ulpian had been the assistant of Papinian,
and became his successor as praetorian prefect. Ulpian lost his life in a
mutiny of the praetorian guard. From this time forward the Empire was
often rent among rival claimants to the imperium. After another such
struggle Constantine, who had become sole Emperor, definitely made
Christianity the state religion and transferred the capital of the Empire
to the Greek Byzantium, which he renamed Constantinople. The official
language of the law became Greek and naturally something had to be
done regarding the vast literature of the law. For a hundred years or
more attempts continued to reduce the law to less bulky form. It was a
movement among the lawyers themselves, just as when the language of
the English law was changed, as we shall see, there was an insistent demand, headed by Bacon, to get rid of the great bulk of the Anglo-
Norman books of law and the Anglo-Norman Year Book reports.

In the meantime practically all of the Latin part of the Empire, the most of Italy, Northern Africa, Spain, Gaul, and Britain had passed to the barbarians and the Emperor Justinian was sole Roman Emperor, reigning at Constantinople. He appointed a commission to reduce the bulk of legal literature. The head of the commission was Tribonian. In a succession of years the commission reported the result of their labors. Out of the great bulk of the juristic writing was formed in fifty books the Digest, which consists of extracts from writers on the law and responses of jurisconsults. The greater part of those extracts consisted of quotations from five great juristic writers, Gaius, Papinian, Ulpian, Paul, and Modestinus. Others are quoted but the quotations are not numerous. Extracts from Ulpian, who was a prolific writer, constitute almost a third of the Digest. The ablest of them all was Papinian.

The legislation of the emperors that was considered important was compiled in the form of the Code, which is nothing more than a collection of laws promulgated by different emperors. Much of the Code defines the status of the church and its institutions. Next was arranged the part of the compilation which is called the Institutes. Gaius had written a book called the Institutes. It was a general classification and arrangement of the principles of the Roman law, to serve the same purpose as any general book of instruction such as Blackstone's Commentaries. This book was taken for the Institutes of Justinian.

When this had been completed a series of laws was promulgated to supplement the Code and the Digest. These new laws of Justinian were called the Novels, or New Laws. Among them was the law, numbered one hundred and eighteen, which regulated descent of intestate property and wiped out the succession confined to males. It put into statutory form the long established custom. Every statute of descent in this land is modeled upon this novel of Justinian.

As soon as this compilation was made the Greek version was sent throughout the eastern dominions and the Latin version was sent to what remained to Justinian in Italy and North Africa of the former Western Roman Empire. But in the confusion resulting from the battles of Justinian's generals with the barbarians, and from the irruption of the Lombards, this Justinianean compilation was practically forgotten, if it had ever been generally known.

Justinian I, Roman Emperor (483–565) gives his codex to Tribonian,
who headed commission to collect imperial statutes

The changes made in the Roman law by the compilers under Justinian have been greatly exaggerated. To one who is comparing manuscripts of a writer like Virgil or Horace, the presence or absence of a word is of great importance, but when a legal text is in question the insertion of a word to make the matter clearer or a recasting of a sentence which does not alter the sense is of no importance whatever. Yet industrious men of the level of grammarians have published books containing conjectural changes made by Tribonian and his colleagues in the texts; but these supposed changes are generally of little, if any, importance.

Perhaps an illustration of this kind of work and of what a waste it is will not be out of place. In the Digest under the general subject of "Release" is quoted an extract from the fifth book of a jurisconsult, Cervidius Scaevola. It is his opinion upon a case put to him. The Digests of Scaevola were edited and published by a pupil, Claudius Tryphoninus, who sometimes adds corrections or comments of his own. The extract is this:

> A mother managed the estate of her daughter. The latter was the heiress of her father, who had died intestate. The mother delivered property of her daughter to bankers to be sold and a contract to that effect was made by the bankers with the mother. The bankers paid to the mother the whole price realized, and it was the price named in the contract; and for nine years thereafter whatever transactions there were regarding the daughter's estate were done by the mother in the name of her daughter. Then the mother married the daughter and delivered the estate of the daughter to the husband. The question asked was whether the daughter had any cause of action against the bankers, since not the daughter herself but the mother had stipulated the price for the goods that had been sold. Scaevola answered shortly that if the inquiry was whether by that payment the bankers had been legally released, they were legally released. He means, of course, released from their contract.

But Tryphoninus, not understanding the narrow limitation put on the question by Scaevola, makes a comment as follows:

> This question depends upon a matter of fact, whether the bankers would appear to have paid the price of the articles in good faith to the

mother, who had no right of administration. If they knew this they are not
released, provided the mother is insolvent.

There is a tremendous amount of writing over this passage. In the
matter of law Scaevola is right; but the two men are answering different
questions. The case put to Scaevola is based upon one single point of
complaint, namely, that the price was named by the mother and not by
the daughter. A trained lawyer can answer that question only as Scaevola
did. The case as put to him meant: if the daughter sued the bankers on
this contract with the mother, could she recover, or did she have a cause
of action against them by the single fact that her mother and not herself
named the price in the contract? If she sued on the contract she adopted
it. The price became binding upon her and the bankers had paid that
price, and so far as that contract was concerned the bankers were released. This is why Scaevola put the construction on the question "if the
inquiry was whether the bankers had been released," meaning released
from the contract.

But Tryphoninus puts a new construction on the question, which is
whether on the whole transaction the daughter had any cause of action
against the bankers under any circumstances, and whether the payment
by the bankers released them from any and all liability to the daughter.
On this view he makes the point that the mother having no right of administration—and such then was the law, for a woman could not be a
tutor or guardian of the estate of her daughter—the bankers were not
justified in dealing with the mother if they knew that she was selling her
daughter's property. Even so, the daughter could not repudiate the
transaction, if she had taken the price from her mother. The daughter
could not have both that price and another price for the goods. He assumes that she had not, and treats the mother as primarily liable to the
daughter for disposing of the goods, and makes the bankers liable only if
the mother cannot respond.

In our law to-day the transaction would be treated on the basis of the
act of an administrator *de son tort*. If the price realized was a reasonable
price and it passed into the daughter's estate and she got the benefit of
it, she suffered no damage.

Now this simple case is loaded down with acres of comment. It is contended that Tribonian changed the text of Scaevola. Attempts are made to reconstruct the actual extract, this one being assumed to be false; many conjectural emendations are made, all wholly unnecessary, for the opinion as it stands is good Roman law. Tribonian and his colleagues may safely be presumed to have known as much of their subject as these modern commentators. The compilers let the comment of Tryphoninus stand "for what it was worth," which was very little, for Tryphoninus had not gone far enough into the case to see that the daughter could not have over again the price of the goods, if she had already received in her estate a reasonable price. This illustration will show how useless is much of the comment on Roman law.

Hitherto the Roman law has been considered in the department of private law applicable between citizens, and the excellence of the Roman law was in its system of private law, governing rights and duties as between individuals. In the field of public law, while it is true that many valuable lessons may be drawn from the polity of Rome, it is also true that she missed a great opportunity. The conception of a city-state drawing its revenue from the provinces doomed the Romans, as it did the Greeks, to sterility in devising new forms of institutions for wide realms. It is useless to speculate upon what would have been the result if, in the dying years of the Republic, constructive statesmanship could have remodeled Roman institutions upon the basis of a general citizenship in the Empire and a federated government. There was, in Italy at least, a population habituated to freedom in government. But the differences in culture among the nations which made up the Empire were too great, and political experience was too narrow to attain a federated commonwealth. Only an emperor with supreme power of administration and legislation was considered competent to deal with such a complicated situation. The selection of the ruler depended on the army, or a part of it. Internecine struggles between rival claimants sapped the strength of the whole realm. Whenever the occupant of the throne was feeble, incompetent, or ungovernable, the whole system was thrown out of function. Doubtless a great system of administration was devised, but no sentiment of nationality was nurtured, so that attachment to the government could become a living force of patriotism. Yet the resistance offered by the Empire through a long succession of years was marvelous, even though the legions were distributed over too long a frontier, beset in every part by those whose strongest instinct was pillage and the savage tendency to steal from another tribe.

Many reasons have been assigned for the fall of the Western Empire, but those reasons are never causes but the results of weakness. The favorite theme of the corruptions of civilization is baseless. Increasing civilization is never a deterioration. It is an improvement in mental and physical well-being. It always represents a greater social cohesion and a better capacity for discipline. One element of weakness, and that the greatest, was the presence of hordes of slaves and serfs. To them one master was as good as another. They were always ready to assist any invader, and to take part in the overthrow of existing institutions. This is the true reason why wealthy and populous provinces so quickly reverted to a condition of barbarism, where so much of the Roman system of private law could find little to which it was applicable. To such people civilized institutions were as useless as the famous cooking stoves sent by Carl Schurz, then Secretary of the Interior, to adorn the tepees of the Indians.

Before leaving the subject of Roman law it may be well to give a general sketch of the private law as it had become in the latter days of the Empire. As we have seen the Greeks had developed the idea in law that a contract results from an agreement. All the old formalities were swept away and the contract is the result of intention. This idea the Roman jurists thoroughly formulated. All that part of the law which is concerned with business, trade, and commerce was fully developed. Contracts of sale, of mortgage, of pledge and all the legal implements of credit and banking and for the transfer of funds, contracts of various kinds pertaining to trading and business ventures, including insurance, the law of partnerships and corporations of almost every condition, all the law of what were called bailments and the law of loans and surety-ship and warranty, were fully developed, but were to pass away as soon as commerce was destroyed. The law of property in movables was adapted by the Romans to all the exigencies and demands of business, trade, and commerce. Without going into the history of the law of real property at Rome, it is enough to say here that the property of the clan passed into the property of the family and at last into private property in land freely alienable by individuals, a result that had been already reached among the Greeks. All the different methods of placing mortgages or liens upon land and of alienating land or the possession or use of it, all the various servitudes or rights in another's land, were recognized and defined in the law. It is not necessary to enter into the minutiae of the Roman doctrines of ownership or possession. In the domestic relations of husband and wife, with the accompanying law of marriage and divorce, the law applying to the relation of parent and child, of guardian and ward and the custody of incompetents is in essence and principle our law to-day. Slavery as a means of obtaining unpaid labor was still a natural condition, but it was recognized that slavery existed by reason of the existing law of practically all countries, although by the law of nature all men should be free. The condition of slaves was generally being greatly ameliorated and the Christian Church was setting its face steadily against the institution. Serfs attached to the soil had their onerous duties but the law protected their correlative rights of occupancy.

Infringements of the rights of personal security and of property were all legal wrongs, giving rise to all the various kinds of obligations to make redress, such as we know, and they were supported by the fact that many wrongs were public crimes. Public prosecutions were constantly supplanting private prosecutions. Legal inhibitions against fraud or duress or violence would well solve such questions arising in our law. Roman law in its injunction in favor of good faith went further than our common law. On a sale without a warranty, express or implied, our law puts all risk of the condition of the article upon the buyer, while in an insurance contract derived from the Roman law, the fullest disclosure is required in marine insurance and provisions therefor are inserted in an application for fire or life insurance. The duty to disclose on a sale facts affecting the price, a duty which the common law denied, was well settled in Roman law.

In the management of property, such as the use of water for irrigation, the Roman law would not differ from our own. But in the case of water being upon land from natural causes, the common law requires each landowner to protect himself against his neighbor, while the civil law did not go so far. A proprietor must avoid the precipitation from his own land of even natural waters upon his neighbor's land. The systems are in accord as to the law relating to a proprietor's being entitled to the right of support of his own land in its natural condition by his neighbor's land.

The Roman law as to intestacy and the devolution of property had gotten rid of all the primitive features, such as the succession confined to males. Wills could be freely made and set aside for sufficient grounds, but Justinian's law denied the right to a father or mother to wholly disinherit the child. Likewise in the Justinianean law the process of the praetor referring the issue to another for trial was supplanted by the praetor both settling the issue and deciding it. In English law all the tribunals that were governed by the ecclesiastical or canon law followed the procedure of Justinian, while the English common law, after a century of experiment and irresolution, adopted in a modified form the older procedure of the praetorian law. Other changes made by the Corpus Juris are not of sufficient importance to detain us. The differences are matters of detail, for the Institutes of Justinian, which formed a general outline of Roman law, are almost the same as the older Institutes of Gaius. One of the romances of the law was the discovery by the historian Niebuhr at Verona in 1816 of the lost Institutes of Gaius. He had in his hands a manuscript which was a palimpsest, that is to say, a manuscript in which the original writing had been taken off in order to write upon the pages again. Niebuhr saw some of the words, not entirely erased, of the former treatise. He brought out upon the pages the older writing and he had found the lost legal treasure of Gaius.

The fortunes of Roman law when its language became Greek, and its further history in the Eastern Roman Empire, are outside the scope of this history, for the future of civilized law was to be found in those lands which formed the nations of modern Europe, more especially Spain, France, the Netherlands, Germany, and England. The development of the English legal system will be separately treated, for it presents a connected story much like that of the Roman development.

It has been stated before that the failure of Greek law was in its inability to discover a tribunal competent to expand, administer, and apply the private law among even its own citizens. This failure arose both from the popular nature of the tribunals and from the want of a legal professional class. It remained in the evolution of law for the Roman to develop this competent tribunal and a powerful profession. The result was that among the Romans there was a rule of law. Among them it was not possible to have a condition where the tribunal openly avowed that it would apply to a controversy the unquestioned law applicable, only when it seemed proper to apply it. As long as litigants are represented in court by trained lawyers the insistence will be upon the rule of law. The difference will be as to what rule of law is applicable, and this will depend upon the facts and upon all those considerations arising from analogy and from logical reasoning, which are deemed of importance. This was the method of the jurisconsults in advising as to a rule. It is necessarily the method used wherever litigants are represented by trained lawyers.

The cheerful optimism of the Greeks in their revolt against the old system of the laws in the custody and knowledge of the priests and their successors, and their reliance upon the reasoning powers of the average individual citizen, carried them to the extreme that every citizen was a competent lawyer and judge without assistance from any class specially learned in the law. The Roman in his slow, sagacious, conservative way, reached a golden mean. The law ceased to be a system of priestly incantation or class imposture, and its destinies were put into the hands of a learned profession whose ranks were open to average citizens. From this conception of a proper milieu of the law, the civilized world has never departed, for the inherited experience of ages has taught the civilized man that in no other way can a citizen be made sure of his rights. This important cultural idea, with all the various applications of law to a condition of life which was essentially modern in its multiplied relations among men, is our heritage from Rome.

CHAPTER 11

Medieval Law in Europe

HADRIAN, WHO RULED THE ROMAN EMPIRE from 117 to 138 A.D., was a man of great cultivation and learning. He spent ten years of his reign in traveling from end to end of his wide realm, not only that he might become acquainted with the needs of the Empire, but that he might carefully investigate all governmental matters. His suite of jurists, secretaries and military staff put together the results. He penetrated lands even the most remote from Rome, such as Egypt and Britain. He built the fortified wall across Britain as a protection against the rude savages of the north. He corrected whatsoever he could find to correct, and to him more than any one else is due the perfected machinery of the Roman system.

The fine results of the long Roman peace were visible to Hadrian everywhere. Life was civilized, easy, and comfortable, prosperity abounded in all the different lands. Commerce and trade were safe and moved easily across land and sea. He found in the provinces humanity on as high a level as that of Italy. He found the courts functioning and the law well administered. Schools of law where thousands of students were trained in the Roman law existed in the various provinces. All classes and conditions of men dwelt secure under a system of equitable legality.

He did not forget to adorn the old cities with many handsome buildings. When he returned to Rome he caused the body of praetorian law to be arranged and reëdited by a great jurisconsult in the form of the Perpetual Edict. After a well spent life, when he felt that death was soon to be upon him, with the pagan fearless realization of death that was afterwards to be replaced by terror, he wrote to his own soul the graceful little elegy that has baffled so many gifted translators. It begins, translated literally, but without any approach to the beauty of the original:

> Charming little spirit, hastening away,
> Guest and companion of my body's clay,
> Whither art thou now departing?

Few men find charm in communion with their own souls.

But it would have been a bitter experience for that gracious and elevated spirit to revisit the earth seven hundred and fifty years after his death. Instead of the improvement that he would have hoped for, he would have been appalled at the ruin of the social order. Constant war and continuous barbarous inroads had destroyed the costly fabric of civilization in all the western lands of his former empire. Italy, Africa, Spain, Gaul, and Britain had become a pillage and a prey. The population was decimated, the cities depopulated. The arts of building were almost forgotten. Everywhere he would have found half-civilized men ruling the Roman lands as cruel and brutal overlords. He would have heard that for a few years a great Frankish empire of Charlemagne had promised some improvement, but it had been followed by an even worse condition. The offices of schools, arts, and letters were forgotten. Ignorance was dominant. Trade and commerce were gone. Travel was everywhere unsafe. Instead of the great orderly Roman administration, lawless counts and barons levied tribute on their weaker neighbors. The organization resulting from social cohesion had passed into the disorganization of the feudal condition.

Especially would he have been astonished at the eclipse of all forms of respectable legal administration. The general courts were not even a tradition. The fine structure of Roman law that had cost so many centuries of patient effort had fallen before the onslaughts of the barbarians. All kinds of law were debased and mixed up in hopeless confusion. In the same city or county the barbarian was governed by his law, the former Roman citizens by a bastard sort of Roman legal tradition. Written law was practically useless in populations where few knew how to write or to read. All the law was unsettled, and definiteness was lost in warring customs. Every little sway of a feudal lord had its own law administered by the lord's own court. The men of the Church alone had any knowledge of law or of letters. A black night of lawlessness and disorder seemed to have settled down in every one of these once prosperous lands.

Hadrian had departed from a world where the social virtues of kindliness, justice, charity, philanthropy, and mercy had tempered humanity, where there was ease and grace and comfort in life, where increasing division of labor and constant contact among men had taught the social classes toleration of one another. He would have returned to a world whose whole tone was that of cruelty. Even the Church, a wholly new organization to him, had become in the centuries disorganized and corrupt. Men of virtue and of any little learning had chosen the unsocial course of retiring into monasteries. He would have been required to go far out into Ireland to find remnants of classical learning. The Church in its canon law had kept alive some parts of the Roman law, but learned lawyers and jurisconsults had left the earth. The best kind of law can live only in the best conditions and must have material circumstances to which it may be applied.

The tone of society was not only one of deep ignorance, but of bitter, harsh intolerance. The religious idea that all the knowledge necessary to men was to be found in the revealed wisdom of the Bible and that all goodness in this world and all chance of inheriting the world to come were annexed to a particular faith had produced the usual results. The pagan world had cared little about beliefs. Every kind of religion and every sort of god had been welcome there. But the intolerance of the western Christians had cut them off from all communion with even the Christians of the East. Men were ready to butcher each other over mere words in the expression of a mystical creed. While the career of a churchman was the only career for those who desired knowledge, the bitter prejudice of the sixth and seventh century Christians against the pagan books and education had proscribed the masterpieces of Latin literature as heretical. This feeling was a living force. Intolerance in religion fed the fires of human cruelty and oppression, while the native savagery of the ruling barbarians found a congenial atmosphere in the savagery of a proscriptive creed.

The doctrine of revealed truth had had an unhappy effect upon scientific knowledge. Even the recognition of the spheroidal form of the earth, which is fundamental for any correct knowledge of the earth, was found to be contrary to revealed religion. Lactantius, one of the great early writers of the Church, discoursed in this fashion on the question: "Is it possible that men can be so absurd as to believe that there are crops and trees on the other side of the earth that hang downward, and that men have their feet higher than their heads? If you ask them how they defend these monstrosities, why things do not fall away from the earth on that side, they reply that the nature of things is such that heavy bodies tend toward the center like the spokes of a wheel, while light bodies, as clouds, smoke, and fire, tend from the center to the heavens on all sides. Now I am really at a loss what to say of those who, when they have once gone wrong, steadily persevere in their folly and defend one absurd opinion by another."

This extract shows, of course, that Lactantius knew the better teaching and that there were yet some men who had not yielded to the ignorance of superstition. If this Christian Father, an enlightened man for his age, with access to correct knowledge, was sunk in this self-satisfied stupidity, what must have been the Stygian darkness of the degraded and bigoted multitude? Historical knowledge had ceased. One absurd creature, seeing the Temple of Janus, asserted that Janus was a son of Noah and founded Rome. An English judge as late as the reign of Queen Mary, in an opinion from the bench, said that Janus was Noah himself, and was pictured with two heads (*bifrons*), one looking back to the flood and the other looking forward from the work of the flood. Lord Chief Justice Coke's prefaces to his Institutes, written under James I, show an ignorance of history almost as deep as his innate cruelty of disposition. Even to-day the world has not entirely recovered from the Dark Ages. In that medieval age the most imbecile credulity had replaced all scientific knowledge. A belief in evil spirits, good and bad angels, witchcraft, enchantments, all the old primitive machinery of fear, had returned to men.

Miracles were so numerous as to have become ordinary happenings. The Pope himself, quite an intelligent man for that age, had seen, after a successful defense of the papal part of Rome, the archangel Michael sheathing his flaming sword as the spirit stood upon Hadrian's tomb. From that day in remembrance of the archangel's appearance, the tomb, disfigured and debased, has remained the Castel Sant' Angelo, the Castle of the Holy Angel. The early Romans had their tale of the great Twin Brethren, Castor and Pollux, leading the Romans at Lake Regillus. The same kind of angels that the devout Pope saw led the Mormon prophet Joseph Smith to the hill of Cumorah and there discovered to him the golden plates of the Book of Mormon. Miracles of all sorts abounded and a saint who could not achieve the miraculous was no saint at all. Perhaps we should not wonder at that age, for there are yet people who read the *Lives of the Saints* with entire belief and edification.

But, ignorant, degraded, and superstitious as even the ablest men had become, the sentiment for law and justice is so ingrained in mankind that a constant demand had been voiced through these Dark Ages for a reign of law. St. Augustine, who had seen the devastating descent of the Vandals upon his native city in Africa, insisted in his book, *The City of God*, that "where there is not true justice, law cannot exist," and that "without justice an association of men in the bond of law cannot possibly continue." The Roman conception of a state bound and governed by the rules of law was a living belief. Augustine also said: "If justice be taken away, what are governments but great bands of robbers, and, if justice is not necessary to a state, a band of robbers is a small state." As to the temporal laws, he said, "Although men decided as to them, when they were made, yet when they are once made and published it is not permissible to judge otherwise than according to them."

When the Emperor Theodosius, in spite of a solemn engagement, put to the sword thousands of citizens when he took the revolted city of Salonica, the Bishop of Milan, St. Ambrose, as a rebuke to such cruelty, refused him communion, and said to him: "Have you not given laws, and is it permissible for any one to judge otherwise than by them? What you have commanded to others you have commanded even to yourself, for the Emperor makes the laws and he must be the first to observe them."

In the wreck of the Empire and during the invasions of the hordes from the north, law became more and more an institution of the past. The Church strove to convert the barbarians from their heathenish religions and savage, primitive notions, and it kept insisting that these barbarous rulers must observe the law. St. Isidore of Seville laid it down: "It is just that the prince should obey his own laws. For the authority of his voice is just only if he is not permitted to do what he has forbidden to the people." He added: "He does not rule who does not rule rightly; therefore the name of king is held on condition of doing right and is lost by wrongdoing." The great Archbishop of Rheims, Hincmar, relying upon St. Ambrose, said in one of his works: "Therefore the just laws promulgated either by the people or the prince are to be vindicated justly and reasonably in every case whatever." He repeats the idea: "Kings and ministers of the state have laws by which they ought to rule in every province; they have the laws of Christian kings, their ancestors, which have been promulgated by the general consent of their faithful subjects to bind all equally." Finally Charles the Bald of France, grandson of Charlemagne, was compelled to recognize that laws are made "by the consent of the people upon the institution of the king."

Out of the wreck of the ancient world had been saved the idea of the equality of the law and its naturalness. Cicero's famous saying, "Nothing certainly is more ennobling than for us to plainly understand that we are born to justice, and that law is instituted not by opinion but by nature," was supported by his words that are a commonplace with us: "If the fortunes of all cannot be equal, if the mental capacities of all cannot be the same, at least the legal rights of all those who are citizens of the same state ought to be equal." The great ecclesiastics insisted upon the Roman idea of natural law as a sort of divine law. The Roman Digest had asserted: "By natural law all men are born free," and "By natural law all men are equal," and "Liberty is the power given to every one to do whatsoever is not prohibited by law." St. Gregory the Great, a Pope who, in spite of his own bad Latin, and his distrust of good Latin, was ready to accept the Digest, lays it down that "by nature all men are equal," and

Ambrosiaster asserts it as divine law that "God did not make slaves and free men, but all of us are born free." St. Isidore, improving on Ulpian, says: "Things required by natural law are marriage, succession to property, bringing up of children, one common security for all, one liberty for all, and the right to acquire those things which are capable of possession in air, earth, and sea." This good old saint, the man of widest learning of his time, comes very near to stating the basis of all sound law.

But such utterances as these had little power to save. The laws at last reached a condition of inextricable confusion. The barbarians demanded their own savage and primitive customs for themselves. Certain rulers had caused to be compiled in a poor and inferior way the Roman laws as they could obtain them prior to the compilation of Justinian, of which they knew nothing. Charlemagne had reduced to writing the primitive laws of the barbarians, except the one paramount law of the barbarian not in writing, the good old barbarian rule, that they shall take who have the power, and they shall keep, who can. The conflicting laws side by side, governing different classes in the same community were an insuperable obstacle to any general rule of law. The great ecclesiastics had in mind a general, equal law, according to the Roman conception. The important maxim to them was controlling: "Justice is the constant and perpetual willingness to render to every one his right," and the further maxim that "the precepts of justice are to live uprightly, not to injure another, and to render to every one his right." The difficulty was, in the confused condition, to find any place for the maxims. One old law book asserted that "if anything is found in the laws that is useless, unobserved, or contrary to equity, we stamp it under our feet." Ivo of Chartres, an early and a very great canonist, said as to this difficulty of deciding whether a law applied: "A law must be honest, just, possible, according to nature and the custom of the country, convenient to the time and place, plain, written not for some private advantage but for the common benefit of the citizens." In the welter and wreck of the destruction of the Western Empire and of the consequent Dark Ages, it is worth while to notice that the idea of a rule of law was not lost.

But a rule of law was impossible except as the Church in her ecclesiastical tribunals could lay down one law to be observed everywhere for every one who sought the courts of the Church. In all the lay tribunals law was whatever superior force pronounced to be law in any particular case. This arose from the rapidly growing feudal system. Imagine a condition of society where every one in order to live must seek a protector and put himself wholly under his control, where every one must become the liegeman of another more powerful. Since all sorts of property that could be carried away were wholly in the power of the stronger, all that was left for the mass of men to cling to was the land. The land could not be stolen, carried, led or driven away. Whoever expected to live must live by means of the land. He needed no title if some one would protect his occupancy. The barbarian conquerors claimed to own all the land, but it was of little use to them unless there were men to work and cultivate it. All those who lived upon it, serf or free, must recognize the conqueror's title.

But it was not enough to be a conqueror. Some of the conquerors were more powerful than others, and the more powerful took property wherever they found it. It naturally turned out that every man became either willingly or unwillingly the man of some overlord. The world became composed wholly of lords and tenants. The tenant did homage to his lord for his land and the lord invested him with a title derived from himself. The serf took an oath of fealty to his superior and was allowed to occupy his little portion of land. Everywhere except where the old Roman law of ownership and title survived, the governing rule was "No land without a lord."

At the bottom were the serfs; they held their land from the immediate occupant above them. The serf was protected by local custom as long as he performed the services, often very onerous, due to his lord, such as working upon the lord's land so many days, or rendering to the lord certain produce of the land. But the serf, or *villanus*, was protected not from any recognition of justice but because his service and labor were valuable property. Next above the serfs were the free tenants. The lowest of them held by the rendition of service or rents of various kinds. Still higher were those who held their land on military service to be rendered to their immediate lord. And so the gradations went on up to the ruler of the state. Much of this situation arose from the voluntary act of the vassals seeking protection. On the other hand a lord desired followers and men. They were the source of his power. He would grant land upon all kinds of service: military service, menial service, the rendition of rent or provisions or anything else that he required. Sometimes the favored follower or vassal would be given an estate upon a merely nominal service, such as a rose or a glove.

The estate of the lord in the land was called a fief, and the one who held it from the king was called the tenant in chief; then came mesne (in between) tenants down to the terre tenants, who actually had possession. The terre tenant would grant or recognize rights of occupancy in his underlings. In feudal law the lord would hold the direct dominion or ownership of the land and the vassal would hold the right to use the land, the ownership in use. Various other incidental rights connected with fiefs such as wardship, marriage, reliefs, and aids can best be noticed under the law of England, where the feudal system was most symmetrical. It is not here necessary to consider how fiefs first granted for life became inheritable, nor is it necessary to point out the tendency of such an organization to split up the state into separate sovereignties.

The two elements of feudal law that are of especial importance are, first, the return to a state of private war between the holders of fiefs, who had no common judge or arbiter, and the right that came to be conceded to every lord of a fief to hold a court to judge all controversies between his tenants whether bond or free.

The general effect of the right to resort to private war, conceded by even so great a king as Louis IX of France, necessarily put an end to all law as between the holders of fiefs. In the Dark Ages the Church strove by every means in its power to put an end to this condition. The Truce of God was an agreement to abolish private war. The time from Thursday night to Monday morning was made a truce in memory of the Saviour's crucifixion and resurrection. But the peculiar outgrowth of this condition was the barbarous survival of the right of trial by battle, which by a sort of common-law imbecility survived in England and was claimed and conceded as a right in the year of our Lord, 1819. It must be plain that when rights can be decided by the event of a fight, law ceases to exist.

The other feature of feudality by which a lord had the right to judge his tenants and was the fountain of justice to them led directly to the destruction or, what is the same thing, caused the prevention of, any rule of general law. Each fief depended for justice on the will of the lord or upon the decision of some one to whom the lord confided the jurisdiction. Generally, however, the lord was interested only in the fees resulting and in the profits of justice. He left the court to his free tenants, who pronounced the judgment of the court. Wherever such courts exist, a rule of law is, of course, more impossible than it was in the Greek popular courts.

But these baronial or manorial jurisdictions could not decide controversies between the lords of fees. One of the parties could not in such disputes give law for himself. There were crimes also of such importance that they were considered the subject of general justice. As to them, in France the right to judge was confided to superior lords. Thus it came about in France that general courts for a province or county would be held, and thus it resulted in after times, that the law changed as often as a county border was passed. This result could be removed only by some enactment of general law for the whole of France. It was not reached until the Code Napoléon made one system of law for the whole French nation.

While the feudal system was growing and destroying all chance for a general law in France, events were happening elsewhere that were of advantage to the recreation of law. In Italy the Lombards had been unable to root out the Roman law, for they could not work out any system without using portions of the Roman law. These parvenus were like others. They tried to ape the manners of the established and better bred. After the barbarous Lombard rule had met its fate at the hands of the Franks, the Italian cities were growing up again to some position of power and influence. They were gradually uprooting the rule of the nobles who were generally an inheritance of barbarian overlords. Commerce and trade, which are the result simply of a widespread desire to accumulate property, and which are, practically speaking, the only active instruments for civilizing men, were springing into life, and manufacturing was again reviving in the Italian cities. Soon wealth was to accumulate, the banking interest was to revive, and the extension of trade was to carry the operations of Italian banking houses throughout northern Europe.

As a natural result of the dominance of the Goths and of the continuous fighting in Italy of Justinian's armies under Belisarius and Narses, and at last of the withdrawal of the armies of the Eastern Empire and the undisturbed rule of the Lombards, nothing was left of schools of law. The tradition of law was kept alive by notaries. It is not necessary to note any study of the Lombard law. It is ridiculous to call the legal study at Pavia anything approaching a liberal study of Roman law. But in some way manuscripts of the compilation of Justinian came into the hands of a teacher of law at Bologna. This teacher Irnerius dates from 1100 to 1150 A.D.[1] A great advance had been made since 850 A.D. Certainly the time was long enough to have accomplished something. Other teachers succeeded Irnerius and some of them went out to teach law in other lands. They had the full collection of Justinian's law: the Code, the Digest, the Institutes, and the Novels. Their method of exposition was by glossing or explanations on the side of the manuscript page. A practical reason, the cost of vellum, made this the usual course as to all manuscripts. The trouble with such a plan is that a teacher without his manuscript glossed is perfectly helpless. But gloss multiplied upon gloss with cross references to other passages in the Corpus Juris, until the mass of matter became unmanageable. Thereupon the elder Accursius compiled the glosses into the Great Gloss. Azo, the greatest of the school, devised a *summa*, or summary, which repeated and arranged the Institutes with some part of the Code. This Summa of Azo is of importance because Bracton, the first great writer in English law, obtained from Azo what equipment he had for writing the general theory and classification of law.

Any one who has read a part even of the work of these Glossators ought to be able to judge their jejune work. They had no sufficient equipment of knowledge. They knew nothing of history and could not locate themselves in the law. They fumbled their material so much that

---

1. Irnerius is now thought by many to have begun his career in the 1080s. He probably died by 1130.—C. J. R., Jr.

they could not use it. They had in their hands the finest products of the finest minds of the Roman world, and they could not use it for any purpose that was valuable. But, as usual, those who do not read these writings have exaggerated notions of their value. The Great Gloss of Accursius is inconceivably dreary reading. It is now of value only as indicating diverse readings of manuscripts. The Glossators did attempt to deduce now and then a general maxim, called a "brocard," but that work is accurately described by an old lawyer as "cartloads of brocards to obscure the holiness of knowledge and the sacrosanctitude of truth." Even Hallam says that Irnerius made the translation of the Novels called the Authenticum. There could be no greater error. Justinian's Novels were written and published as laws in Greek, not in Latin. Justinian sent to the western lands reconquered by his generals a Latin version of his New Laws called the Authenticum. It went to Ravenna and from there passed to Bologna. The fortune of time has placed a very fine copy of it that was made for the Emperor Frederick II in the library of the University of Chicago. Any one who cursorily reads it can know at once that Irnerius was incapable of making such a translation.

The Glossators did not revive the juristic method, an achievement with which they are credited. As a matter of fact they were teachers of the law, but they were at the same time practical lawyers open to employment. It ought not to be necessary to say that generally speaking the most competent lawyers are found employed where the most money is forthcoming. Hence one who has any practical sense would know that these men, who knew more law than others, were generally in the employ of the German emperors or of some royal personage. Philip the Fair of France in his contest with Pope Boniface VIII had accomplished Romanist lawyers in his pay. The chronicler tells us that Henry II of England kept in his pay a gang of "bellowing legists" (Roman civil lawyers) whom he turned loose whenever he desired any particular legal result. These Bologna lawyers produced the kind of law that was needed. Similar phenomena we have seen in our own times in the case of those who can afford to pay.

Probably the real reason that caused the revival of the study of the Roman Digest and the Code, was that parts of that law could be used primarily to support the emperors in their struggle for Italy. There was a demand for that kind of law. At any rate these men versed in the Roman law figured an imperial law presiding over all local law. The Pope had crowned and anointed Charlemagne as the Roman Emperor. This empire had descended to the Ottos of Germany and their successors. The Bologna lawyers supplied the legal conceptions and wrote the language of the medieval emperors, by which they claimed to be the successors of the divine Augustus, Trajan, Constantine, and Justinian. The lawyers had little historical knowledge to trouble them, and they were acquainted with Italian conditions. For Italy the Bologna lawyers and their successors almost produced in theory a federated empire. They showed that all the north Italian cities owed fealty to the emperors, and that the imperial law of Rome presided over the various local laws. The poet Dante, more of a poet than statesman, was a warm supporter of the imperial claim of an empire, where the Italian cities should be a portion of the subject lands. There can be no question that if these lawyers could have had their way, the great Roman empire would have been restored.

But the growing separate and distinct nationalities of France, Spain, and England were too strong. The real struggle was masked by the fact that the papacy claimed that it was the representative of God on earth and superior to all earthly rulers. This claim had always to meet the opposition of the medieval lawyers. Innocent II, Gregory VII, Boniface VIII, and Innocent III carried the pretensions of the papacy very far, for they, in an age of superstition and fear, held the weapons of interdict and excommunication, but they failed. Could the popes have forgotten that they were priests and put themselves at the head of a national movement for Italy, the result would have been otherwise. But this was practically impossible, for the revenues of the papacy came from many lands. Italy for centuries paid the penalty of the lesson taught by these Italian doctors of the law that Italy could have no separate nationality. Its lands were harried, its wealth sacrificed, its institutions destroyed by the marching and countermarching of German, French, Spanish, and Austrian armies, mingled with the mercenaries of small Italian states. In all that sad and dreary history but one Italian emerged who could have been, had he not died so early, a medieval Cavour for Italy.

These Italian lawyers, called the Glossators, were bound down by their historical ignorance. They assumed that the Roman pope was the lineal successor of the Pontifex Maximus, head of a college of pagan hierophants. They struggled hard to reconcile the Roman law with the local law. They, in some ways, spoke the language of independence. Azo, the greatest doctor of them all, "the master of all the masters of law," and Pope Gregory IX agreed that custom can make, abrogate, and interpret legislation. The whole school recognized that the function of making as well as of interpreting law belongs to the State. These legists asserted that as the people had given to the Emperor the power of legislation, they could resume it again. Irnerius, the first of them, was decided upon the question that the people had the duty of law-making in order to provide for individuals as members of society. Equality before the law was to them a necessity. They repeat the phrases of Cicero and expound in that sense the language of the Code and Digest. They are plainly hostile to any royal pretension that the ruler is not bound by the law. Irnerius had reached the conception of vested rights and due process of law. He asserts that the Emperor cannot annul a sale, a will, or a donation, he cannot confer a monopoly, he cannot do anything contrary to the written or the unwritten law, nor can he give judgment without hearing both sides. Azo asserts that the Emperor could not make laws without the consent of his chief officers and senate. These men understood what the Digest meant by the statement that whatever pleased the Emperor had the force of law. He had the power because he was given it by the people. They met trouble in the phrase that the Emperor is freed from the laws. This meant the ordinary police and private laws that could not apply to him. They quoted, however, the Code in the famous Digna Vox rescript:

> It is a saying worthy of the majesty of the ruler that the Emperor should acknowledge that he is bound by the laws, for upon the authority of the law his authority depends, and in truth it is more advantageous to the commonwealth that the principate should be subject to the laws.

But the search of the writings of the Glossators, their dry comments and mistaken applications of the literal sense while they missed the ju-

ristic method, will not produce much that is valuable. They were not able
to devise even a proper method of citation. The unilluminating matter
has no relief of any kind. There is a tendency to run out into fine-spun
distinctions, so general in that age, and much of the writing is rendered
worthless. Late writers seem to think that these Glossators performed a
great work in what it has become fashionable to call the legal renaissance
of the twelfth century. As a penalty for this remarkable statement they
should be compelled to read page after page of the Gloss in connection
with the text of the law, and they would soon have an ennuied sense of
the triviality, often departing into absurdity, of most of the Gloss. The
truth is that these people had no sufficient legal atmosphere, and the
curse laid upon them of utter sterility is the curse that afterwards made
the ruin of the English common law. They lacked information sufficient
to teach them the meaning of the things with which they were dealing.
The tendency of lawyers to degenerate into mere technicians, when they
have, as is often the case, no proper aid from general information, has always made the greater part of the profession lineal descendants of these
Glossators.

A man is talking pure rhetoric and not fact who can say that "the
works of these men are the only productions of medieval learning to
which one can turn with some possibility of finding a solution of the
doubts, difficulties, and problems which still beset the modern student."
Their main value to-day for a student is to teach him how far men can
go astray when they talk of a subject of which they know little. If he cannot see how far these Glossators fail adequately to explain the writers in
the Digest, he may be certain that to him apply Dryden's caustic lines:

> The midwife laid her hand on his thick skull,
> With this prophetic blessing, "Be thou dull."

The thirteenth century continues with the futilities of the Glossators.
The transition to the fourteenth century offers more relief. Civilians of
a new sort have come upon the scene, who are called the Commentators.
They gave up the gloss style of writing for actual comment and disqui-
sition. They certainly had more knowledge. Men were gradually growing away from conditions of barbarism. The greater knowledge from the

East was teaching many new things. Legal conditions were becoming more settled. The personal law that followed men had been as much a necessity as is to-day extraterritoriality of law in certain countries. But this personal law had given way to a territorial law. The territorial law was taking on more of the Roman law. The effects of the growing cities, expanding trade, and increasing wealth were having their effect in making conditions for the application of better law. But feudality and the lack of intercourse between men, the splitting up of the country into small jurisdictions, had created numberless bodies of local law. The Commentators threw themselves mainly upon propositions of the conflict of laws in trying to find rules to govern a particular transaction, where it was contended that different laws could be applied. This law has always continued to have a very great value, although the Commentators carried finespun distinctions to an inordinate thinness.

The conflict of laws is yet a great head in the law. Especially in the United States, composed of federated states, has this question of what law should govern had an immense importance. The courts of law of various states were open to all. A contract might be made in one state by citizens of another state to be performed in a third state, and might be sued upon in a fourth state. In the time of the Commentators the Medici bankers, Florentine subjects, at their branch house in the Netherlands might enter into a contract to be performed in Venice, and suit might be brought upon it in a court of the Visconti Duke at Milan. The laws of these different local divisions, states, cities, or provinces might differ greatly, and very troublesome questions might arise both in the application and in the proof of foreign law. In this particular subject the medieval law is the basis for the modern law, and this law may truly be said to have a value for the modern student. It does show a sense of juristic method and when we read it Astraea seems to be again on earth.

The great man of this school of Commentators was Bartolus of Sassoferrato. He was not only a teacher, but he had actual experience as a judge and as a jurisconsult giving *responsa*, or answers, upon legal questions. He wrote a number of legal tractates and in them we can find the general theory of the law in this conflicting condition. They still theorized the situation that the Roman law was the ruling law of the Empire,

Bartolus (1314–57)

that the Italian states were parts of the Empire, that each Italian state had its own body of customary laws and its own legislation over which presided the imperial law of the Digest and the Code. Thus the federated state was roughly prefigured. The rule applicable under the feudal system of private war between societies enjoying different laws and no common arbiter was applicable. Bartolus did not rise to the level of law that the Emperor could compel these subjects to implead each other in an imperial court, for no machinery existed, but he did hold that in such a contest neither of the contending parties could rely upon his own law, and in instituting private war each was governed by the power of a superior authority. He said: "All the doctors of the law incline to the opinion that against the man or people, who neglects to do justice and to render what is due, resort can be had to a superior who may permit reprisals to the two litigants. First is required the authority of a superior for it is not lawful for any one by his own authority to give law unto himself. Second, it is required that the authority of the superior should interpose itself upon just cause."

This law is applicable now to disputes between states of this Union. They may implead each other in the superior's court, the Supreme Court of the United States. The machinery exists, and the contest is not to be governed by the law of either litigant, but by the law of the superior. Our Supreme Court says that "it must follow and apply the rules of general law even if legislation of one or both of the States seems to stand in the way."[2] It is rather a pity that the judge writing this opinion did not cite Bartolus, especially when in another connection he had ascribed to a phrase of Bartolus, a meaning exactly contrary to the meaning of Bartolus.

The authority of Bartolus could also be cited for further adaptations of the idea of an imperial or federal law in this country of ours. One may take those many instances where our Federal Courts, under the authority of the Supreme Court, refuse to recognize a rule of state law where it conflicts with a general law considered to be better and more just.

2. *Missouri v. Illinois and the Sanitary District of Chicago*, 200 U.S. 496, 520 (1906).— C. J. R., Jr.

Doubtless the Supreme Court did not know that it was following the example of the Roman praetors in being guided by general rules of law rather than the local law of the Roman city-state, or that it was following Bartolus in his conception of an overruling imperial law.

These Commentators did very able work upon the law, but they were entirely eclipsed by the great Romanists of the Renaissance, the true Renaissance of the fifteenth and sixteenth centuries. The ablest of those scholars was Cujas, and it is worth a trip to the heart of the old, sleepy French province of Berry to find the place from which Cujas sent forth his flood of light upon the Corpus Juris of Justinian. Modern Romanist scholars like Savigny have simply quarried into the wealthy deposit of material left by Cujas.

It is necessary now to turn to a system of law which had been growing in the tribunals of the Church. As a matter of necessity the Church kept to the Roman law, for the legal rights of the Christians and the power of the Church and its officers were defined by the compiled rescripts of the Christian emperors. Matters of marriage and divorce and matters of intestate succession were naturally left to the Church tribunals. Marriage was a sacrament and not to be touched by unholy hands. The Church courts had in their hands all the matters affecting last wills and testaments. This may seem strange, but it is not. Land was for ages the only wealth. No will could be made of land. The feudal system had fixed its descent, and land had practically reverted to the condition of the inalienable holding under the primitive law. Even when the right to alienate land became recognized, after a requirement, for a time, that the lord's assent was necessary, no corresponding power to leave it by will was created. The small amount of property originally passing by will or upon an intestate's death gave no great opportunity for governmental fees and charges, and we may be very sure that if there had been such a chance, the officers of a ruler would never have omitted an opportunity for more revenue, any more than a modern taxing body or legislature would omit to take advantage of any new means of squeezing out of the taxpayer a greater governmental revenue.

In those days the ordinary ruler thought that his poor subject might gain a chance for heaven by letting the priests have a part of the little personal property that he had left. They let the priests have a sort of inheritance tax. Every one believed that prayers for the dead were efficacious, and should be paid for. So what could be done except to take the cost of the prayers out of the decedent's estate? This belief had come down, as we have seen, from primitive times. The Church very properly for that time taught that a deceased whose debts were not paid could never get out of purgatory. This is the reason why a testator in his will always begins with the injunction to pay all his just debts and liabilities. It is a wholly unnecessary clause. The debts must be paid under the law. But it is the irony of life that the most hardened atheistical lawyer when he comes to write a will slavishly inserts a clause dictated by the priests.

Naturally the Church claimed jurisdiction over all questions involving any of the clergy, even over crimes committed by them, and over all questions of Church property and Church discipline. Some unusually religious rulers were willing to leave to the Church tribunals a dispute between a layman and the Church as to whether land was ecclesiastical or not, but no English king was ever willing to do so. The Church was not permitted to obtain jurisdiction over private disputes of any other kind, although from very early days there are left descriptions of how the early Christians, taking a Biblical injunction literally, carried all their disputes to the bishop and how the bishop, assisted by elders, judged the various controversies. These decisions, it is needless to say, make an extraordinary travesty of the law. A contract was enforcible or not enforcible as the bishop's court would decide whether it would, in accordance with Christian charity, be equitable to enforce it.

The profits of private litigation were too great for any feudal ruler to allow them to the Church. Certain matters of contract, involving good faith, were allowed to the Church tribunals, for the civil courts refused to recognize such contracts. All the petty offenses like adultery, fornication or other sinful lapses including, of course, heretical utterances or blasphemy, were confided to the Church authorities. The jurisdiction over perjury was originally a matter for the Church tribunals.

The ecclesiastical courts were the bishop's courts, but the archdeacon of a diocese was given some jurisdiction mainly over petty offenses. He had his priestly summoners who pried into the private lives of the parishioners to enable the venerable archdeacon to levy fines on gay ladies and fast men. The minutiae of these courts are not important. Appeals lay, however, in ecclesiastical cases to the Pope at Rome, sitting in his curia. The practice, of course, in the ecclesiastical courts was in the hands of ecclesiastical lawyers, and the multiplication of cases and appeals made the profession of much importance in that law. The lawyers tended to make the practice uniform, while the one presiding appeal court made the substantive ecclesiastical law uniform. These tribunals produced a body of law culled from the decisions. The Pope promulgated additional matters by exercising the function of legislation. The Church Councils legislated. Finally came the elements of divine law introduced into the canon law. No churchman questioned that Moses had received the body of law in the first five books of the Old Testament directly from on high. All of it that seemed capable of incorporation in the canon law was inserted. The proof by two necessary witnesses came into the law in this way.

In the English chancery court this rule of the Hebrew law furnished the basis for the practice in chancery courts that the sworn answer must be overcome by the testimony of two witnesses or by one witness corroborated by other evidence. In the English law of treason the rule of the Hebrew law as to two witnesses was always recognized. The piety of chancellors caused them to refer in their opinions to the Scriptures. As late as decisions by Lord Chancellor Ellesmere under James I, his opinions will be found to be adorned by references to the Bible. Exodus was an unanswerable authority. Such references were notable during the Puritan domination, while the Anglican churchmen based their dogma of the divine character of the kingly office upon the text that "the powers that be are ordained of God." James I believed that such texts gave him the right to dispense justice in his courts.

This whole collection of decisions, legislation human and divine, with rules of practice was called the canon law, wholly Roman except in the Hebrew elements. This body of law was collected in various books whose names are of no importance here. The fact that is of importance is that these courts followed the rules and the practice of the Roman law. This was not a fact of so much importance on the Continent, but in

England, as we shall see, it became a matter of transcendent influence on the law. This situation explains why the practice of our chancery courts, the substance of our law of marriage and divorce, the law regarding wills, bequests, legacies, advancements, the practice and rules applied in our admiralty courts from the very beginning have all been openly dictated by the Roman law. The influence of Roman law on our common law has been more hidden.

The greatest effect of the canon law was to introduce into English law the conception of the Roman theory of contract, as being a question of agreement and intention. It will be seen that for centuries in England it was in the court of the chancellor that informal contracts were recognized and enforced. If a question of good faith were involved the ecclesiastical courts originally would take jurisdiction, but this jurisdiction was lost. The chancellor, however, retained his jurisdiction and it was from the chancery court that the general doctrines of the Roman law on the subject of contract gradually passed to the courts of common law.

This description of legal conditions on the continent of Europe has reached the point where the development of English law can be explained under the influence of the Roman and Canon law. For us the story of the law now turns to that English race to which we owe all our legal institutions. It would be far off the plan of this book to show how the Roman law finally supplanted every local system in the continental western lands that had been provinces of the Empire.

It is not a pleasant task to review the destruction of civilization in medieval times. Romances and tales of chivalry can never make that arid waste of cruelty and oppression other than what it was. We may whitewash our ancestors in all imaginable ways, but we cannot change the fact that they did their brutal worst to destroy all civilizing tendencies in the law. But there is some relief to the darkness. The ideal of kindness, compassion, and pity did not leave the earth. In the cloisters were many men of saintly lives. When Otto III of Germany tore out the tongue and blinded a priest at Rome who had opposed his course, an aged monk named Nilus, then over eighty years old, took a long journey to Rome to comfort the sufferer and rebuke the cruelty of the Emperor. It was just at the close of this darkened time that the founder of the Franciscan

Friars created a new order to alleviate the sufferings of mankind, just as the order of the Dominicans was being founded to disseminate knowledge by becoming the preachers and instructors of Europe. The finest devotional book in literature, the *Imitation of Christ*, followed in the fourteenth century.

Perhaps we ought not to be too censorious of an age which believed in the legal theory that in a trial by battle God would give the victory to the one in the right, and in a trial by the ordeal God would intervene to protect an innocent person from conviction, for probably the majority of men whom we call civilized still persist in such beliefs.[3] The fact that men can so quickly relapse to primitive notions under adverse conditions tends to prove, as many other human traits tend to prove, that the veneer with which civilization can cover the original animal is never so thick as our self-flattery would make us believe. It was in 1204 that the gang of pirates and freebooters calling themselves Crusaders for the Sepulcher of Christ captured and sacked the capital and ruined the empire of the Eastern Christians. The looting of Rome by pious sons of the Church far surpassed in its savagery the work of Alaric and Genseric. It was not many years ago that the troops of powers supposed to be civilized were looting, pillaging, and outraging helpless noncombatants in the city of Peking.

---

3. Zane here paints with too broad a brush. The judicial ordeal became the subject of consistent clerical attack in the twelfth century, and clerical participation in ordeals was outlawed in 1215, thus effectively putting an end to the practice. See John W. Baldwin, "The Intellectual Preparation for the Canon of 1215 Against Ordeals," *Speculum* 36 (1961): 613–36.—C. J. R., Jr.

CHAPTER 12

The Origins of English Law

THE ROMAN DIGEST in the words of Gaius, in his treatise on the Law of the Twelve Tables, has told us how important are the origins of any system of law. But the beginnings of English law have become entangled in the historical controversy concerning the nature of England's debt to the Anglo-Saxon element of her population. Many English historians have mistakenly attributed everything of importance in English institutions to that element. Their position has determined that of the legal historians. The foundation of this mistaken structure has been a crass misrepresentation of the Anglo-Saxon conquest of England. That conquest covered a long period. It began in Roman times with depredations along the coast of Britain. There was a special officer in the Roman administration called the Count of the Saxon shore, whose duty it was to ward off the thieving pirates from across the sea. Infiltration of barbarians occurred in Britain just as it took place in Gaul. About 450 A.D. the irruptions took on a much more formidable character, for the Roman legions had been withdrawn in 407 A.D. and quarreling had arisen among the British tribes. For almost two hundred years the aggressions from Germany continued until the conquest was complete, except for Wales and the northernmost part of England. The tribes of Angles, Saxons, and Jutes carved out their own territory and divided the conquered inhabitants among the tribes as they were located.

Historians like Freeman, Froude, and Stubbs, in order to maintain the thesis that everything which we call English is due to the Anglo-Saxons, have represented the invading Anglo-Saxon as far more savage, remorseless, and brutal than he actually was.[1] It was an article of the true faith with such historians that the invaders, with hideous and implacable cruelty, swept the face of England bare of all former inhabitants and thoroughly devastated the whole country. They have tried to ennoble the invaders by painting in the most lurid colors their innate ferocity. That the original Celtic conquest of either Gaul or Britain was not of this order was too plain for words, although it is true that the Celts imposed their language and tribal institutions upon the original inhabitants. That the later conquests of Gaul by the Franks, of Spain by the Visigoths, of Italy by the Lombards, were not of this savage description was admitted by all writers.

Common sense should have taught that in the nature of things conquests of settled and cultivated lands were never of this appalling description. The barbarians invaded settled lands because the inhabitants of them were richer and had more visible wealth. This course was due to the primitive instinct of one tribe to steal from and rob another tribe. But the robbers may be credited with sense enough to desire to retain something of value out of the robbery. Especially they desire to keep the unpaid labor of the existing population by reducing it to serfdom or slavery. No barbarian works if he can help it, and the best way for him to avoid work was to enslave some other persons to work for him. No doubt the fine Roman villas with the comforts of cultivated Roman life were destroyed or fell at once into ruin in Britain, for such conveniences and advantages were as much wasted on the invaders as would be porcelain bathtubs set up in tenements designed for Croatian immigrants. The cultivated lands worked by serfs, the invaders could utilize, although many of the male Britons were killed in the struggle.

Since this Anglo-Saxon myth was invented by Freeman and followed by Green and other writers, much work has been done in the archaeol-

---

1. Edward A. Freeman (1823–92), James Anthony Froude (1818–94), and Bishop William Stubbs (1825–1901).—C. J. R., Jr.

ogy and ethnology of England and of the English race. It is now reasonably plain that the original inhabitants of England were of that Iberian or Ligurian or Alpine race which, wherever it came from, originally is found in Italy, Spain, Gaul, and southern Germany some time after the close of the last Ice Age. This original population of Britain cultivated the soil and followed the calling of pastoral men as well. Like all the first agriculturists, they lived in village communities. They represented a stage of considerable culture, as their pottery alone would prove. Their fine cultivation of the soil, their superior methods of mining and their fishing for pearls in the rivers of Great Britain, cannot be disputed. They were certainly much more advanced in civilization than the Celts, when the latter overran western Europe. Temporarily submerged by the Celts, this Iberian race assimilated the Celtic invaders, and when Caesar landed in Britain he found a race of cultivators of the soil with droves of swine and cattle, using the horse and the horse-drawn vehicle. Had Britain been as worthless as Germany was with its morasses and forest and lack of agriculture, Caesar and his successors would have left it alone.

During the long Roman occupation this mixed population became much Romanized. Christianity penetrated among them and passed into Ireland and northern Britain. After the Romans withdrew their legions and the Anglo-Saxon invasions in great force began, it is not unlikely that some Britons passed into Ireland and gave to the Irish laws some of those curious touches of Roman law which seem so much out of place in the Brehon law and which have discredited it. It is certainly true that in Ireland was found an advanced Latin Christian culture, when England, France, and Spain were in the lowest depths of the Dark Ages. Many of these Britons crossed the Channel into Brittany in France, and made that province. But a large part of the existing population stayed upon the conquered land as serfs during the Anglo-Saxon invasions, and as all men do in the presence of a dominating lower culture, they rapidly deteriorated.

This original population after a time assimilated the Anglo-Saxons so well that to-day ethnology shows the prevailing type of head and feature in England to be still the ancient Iberian. In time the Anglo-Saxons became cultivators of the soil and swineherds, of whom the illustrious

Cedric in *Ivanhoe* is such a shining example. The native village communities persevered from Iberian through Celtic and Roman into Anglo-Saxon times. They furnished the foundation for the Roman country estate system, which existed in Roman Britain, and for that incipient manorial system which shows in the Anglo-Saxon period; and, mixed with Anglo-Saxons, they supplied the developed manorial system of serfs in Plantagenet times. These serfs became the villains of the earlier English law and the copyholders of the later law.

The Anglo-Saxon period of England lasted from 450 A.D. to the Norman Conquest in 1066, a period almost twice as long as it has taken to settle and develop the United States. During that long period great changes took place in the Anglo-Saxons. When they landed their institutions were of the most primitive description. They were wild and savage even for Germany. They parceled out the land among the leaders of tribes called kings; the noble class among them and the freemen obtained their share of the soil. The invaders, it is likely, brought few slaves, and they had the system of kindreds, the ordinary Aryan development. They had the general tribal assembly, which elected the leaders and passed upon disputes among the kindreds. They had the composition system for homicide and other wrongs, but they still were at the stage where if a dispute arose and composition was not accepted, the blood feud was the result. They were as yet in the stage where the loose organization of the tribe had not assumed the duty of adjudicating law for the kindreds or members of the kindreds, and where all submission to any tribunal was voluntary with the disputants.

As soon as the work of Anglo-Saxon conquest was complete, and in fact before it was complete, these various tribes of Angles and Saxons, whose only occupation was war, naturally began to fight among themselves. The ordinary freemen formed the fighting force under their nobles and kings. The result of tribal warfare was to consolidate aggregations of tribes on almost the lines of the present shires of England. The West Saxons, the East Saxons, the Kentishmen, the Mercians, and the Anglians were the main consolidations, but gradually the West Saxons fought their way to leadership. Before this had happened the Roman Church had converted these people to Christianity. At once came in the churchmen with the Church institutions, and the elevating influence of the Roman legal tradition was felt. The Church rapidly obtained property, bishops were appointed, monasteries were introduced. The churchmen brought in the written document and deeds for lands of the kind that prevailed upon the Continent.

From the constant state of warfare, the same effects resulted as upon the Continent: the feudal system began to develop, weaker men put themselves under the protection of stronger men, the kings granted lands to their followers upon services, but much of the land remained on the old holding of the conquerors. Land held on that original title was called *folcland,* or land held by the title given from the conquering tribe, or folk. The land held by deed, in Anglo-Saxon called book or writing, was called *bocland.* The kings, of course, granting land to their followers, used the book or deed. The Church took care that its lands were held by deed, or as the records show, if deeds were wanting, they had no difficulty in forging them.

By the aid of the churchmen a further step was made by transforming the county assembly into a regular court. The tribe was divided into hundreds, where the basis of the numbering was a hundred families. Distances were long and traveling difficult, so, as a natural convenience the hundred formed a court for their small disputes. A further subdivision was of the hundreds into tithings, or combinations of ten families, where the members of the tithings became responsible for order among themselves. This organization was called afterwards by the Normans the frankpledge. The large convocation of freemen was the county court, which was made up of representatives from the hundreds. It is likely that the county court was originally presided over by the bishop and the tribal leader who passed for a king. It formed a means of dispensing some sort of justice for the tribe. When consolidations of tribes took place the former tribal chieftains became ealdormen. Still later the head of the county was the earl, who took the place of the ealdorman. The kings in imitation of continental royalty had their immediate followers called the king's thanes.

The whole point is that all the change and improvement in the law came from the influence of the churchmen. They alone had the necessary knowledge; they knew how to draw the documents, they furnished the kings with royal clerks, and all their knowledge of law came to them from their clerical education as in the Canon law.

At last the West Saxons fought their way to the sole kingship. An additional set of rules and institutions was now needed to consolidate and support the general kingly office, which had become hereditary. Especially was needed a means of raising revenue and an army. These methods were borrowed through the churchmen directly from the Continent. It must be kept in mind that in that age a bishop was a prince and a ruler in his own diocese. He was generally the greatest landowner, and his ecclesiastical preëminence was supported by the power to damn or to save. Very often he was a fighting man leading his own troops. The court of the Church and the lay court were not separate. The bishop generally presided in the county court, and no doubt his influence was paramount. He or his priestly advisers could alone expound the law, and he naturally expounded the canon law, which was the Roman law. It was not, of course, the Roman law of the Corpus Juris of Justinian, but it was the Roman tradition that had persevered so far as there were conditions to which its rules could be applied. The men in the county court, the representatives of the hundreds, as matter of form, made the judgment or, in their phrase, spoke the doom, but it was the ecclesiastics who wrote the doom or who told the Anglo-Saxon doomsmen what to say.

The various institutions of the developing Anglo-Saxon age kept apparently in close touch with developments on the Continent. The feudal aids, the imposition of military service on the land, the granting of lands for particular services, the forms of the deeds, the organization of the royal power, all show this imitation of the continental condition. Anything that is written shows its priestly origin.

As this development was going on, the Anglo-Saxons were subjected to a series of raids by the Danes. A large part of England was lost to these Danish invaders. London was kept by the Saxons, but the Thames River was the boundary between Saxon and Dane. This boundary turned north on the Thames and ran up the middle of England. Almost half of England became Danish in the sense that the Danes ruled there. The basis of the population still remained what it had been. Compared with the original dwellers, the proportion of Anglo-Saxons or Danes was relatively small. At last Danish kings overran all England and Cnut and his sons ruled for a period. They ruled by means of the same kind of law as the Angles had. Then the Anglo-Saxon kingship was restored under Edward the Confessor. He had passed his early years as an exile in Normandy, had received all his education there, and while he sat upon the throne did all that was in his power to introduce the Norman institutions and manners. When he died, Harold, a mixed Saxon and Dane, seized the kingship; but William, the Duke of Normandy, claiming under the nomination of Edward the Confessor, descended upon England and in the one Battle of Hastings destroyed the Anglo-Saxon army and rapidly overran the country, which thenceforth was ruled by Normans.

From this time forward the two coalescing systems in the law were the Anglo-Saxon, largely formed on the Roman tradition, and the Norman, which was almost wholly the product of the Roman model. Not much change was needed in Anglo-Saxon institutions to adapt them to the Norman desires, while the body of substantive law was relatively small, owing to the simple condition of society. To make this plain it is necessary to show what the Anglo-Saxon legal system, ruled in all intellectual matters by the men of the Church, had become under the consolidated kingship.

In the first place, all tribal and family ownership of land had passed into individual ownership. The classes of people, the king, the nobles, the freemen, the serfs and slaves, were the common ingredients of the continental feudal state. The churchmen constituted a class of themselves, and in England ruled their own affairs, and taxed themselves if they were taxed. The population was arranged so that a certain number of men became responsible for the conduct of each one of them. The system of compensation for injuries was indicated by the terms *wer*, or compensation to the family for a death, *bot*, compensation to an individual for any other kind of injury, and *wite*, which was a sort of fine to the lord possessing jurisdiction (called in their words *sac* and *soc*) over the place where the injury happened. The human slave or servant, the non-human animal or the inanimate thing causing an injury became forfeitable as a deodand. This principle almost certainly was introduced by the priests out of their divine law taken from the Bible. While all offenses were considered private matters, there were certain acts that were offenses against the king. This was an idea evidently borrowed from the Continent, a relic of the Roman law. The Anglo-Saxon law did not enter into questions of intention as to responsibility. A man was liable for the conduct of himself or his slave or serf, or for one of his family, or for animals or things under his control. The medieval mind was not capable of the refined distinctions of the Roman law.

The land system was mainly one of dependence. The open-field system of husbandry existed. Dependent village communities with open fields were the rule. In addition to the *folcland* and *bocland* heretofore mentioned, there was the lease of land for one or more lives. This land was not usually alienable by the lessee. No distinction yet existed as to estates of freehold and less than freehold. The law as to marriage and divorce was wholly the churchman's Roman law. In regard to movable property, possession was property and sales were required to be made openly. There was practically no developed law of contract. The Anglo-Saxons had had no law as to wills, but the priests had introduced that law from the Roman law. If the churchmen expected to get lands or property of any kind, they must, when the sick man lay cowering in the fear of death, be able to offer him absolution and a safe journey to heaven, provided, of course, he showed his remorse and penitence by willing property and deeding land. Wills mean individual property. Such wills or deeds conveyed land directly to God and his church or to his Saint at a certain place.

The procedure of the courts was formalistic, but the churchmen had introduced a writ on the Roman model, which was the same for the recovery of both real and personal property. If a man kept real property from the owner, he deforced him, and this was true of a debt as well as all other personal property. Such a procedure could apply only to tangible property.

The churchmen recognized the value of the oath in legal proceedings and the county court applied the remedies. The man making the claim appeared and made oath to his claim stated according to a rigid form. He was supported by others as witnesses, called the *secta* (suit) by the churchmen. Thereupon the defendant was served with notice to appear and good summoners proved the service, if it was necessary to prove it. The defendant appeared and took a formalistic oath of denial of the claim and offered to produce his proof. All this must be done according to form or the party at fault lost the case. The usual and normal course was for the court to decide who should have the right to make proof. There was never any trial, never any rational weighing of contradictory evidence. It was all a formal affair. If, for instance, the question was as to a debt, the pleading of the plaintiff was that the defendant owed him money. The defendant denied that he owed money to the plaintiff. This performance leaves the whole question in the air. Does the defendant mean to say that there was once a debt and that he had paid it, or does he mean to say that there never was any debt? If he denies that any debt ever was created, then the plaintiff ought to prove the debt. But if he admits that a debt existed but that he has paid it, then he ought to prove the payment. No one is able to say what an Anglo-Saxon court would do in such a case.

In after times, in Henry I's reign, the course would be that the court would examine the plaintiff's suit or witnesses, and if the court thought that it was fairly plain that there was a debt and that the defendant meant that the debt had been paid, it would award the proof to the plaintiff, and if the plaintiff took his oath before God upon the holy Gospels that there was a debt and that the defendant had not paid it, and his witnesses swore that they believed him, he recovered and the defendant's proof was never heard at all. On the other hand, if the court thought that it was not plain that there was a debt, it would award the proof to the defendant. This meant that the defendant must take his oath supported by twice as many witnesses as the plaintiff had witnesses in his suit. This was called defending two-handed or four-handed or six-handed or twelve-handed, as the case might require. Thus, if the plaintiff had one witness, the defendant defended with two witnesses, thus giving effect to the biblical injunction of two for one. If the plaintiff had two witnesses or three or six, the defendant defended by four or six or twelve. There is some uncertainty as to whether the defendant counted as a witness. At any rate all that the supporting witnesses swore to was not any fact but merely that they believed the defendant or the plaintiff as the case might be. It is likely that in Anglo-Saxon times the whole proceeding was one where the defendant was always awarded the proof.

This proceeding was the one regarding every civil claim. In criminal cases the defendant made his defense by the aid of compurgators or witnesses, but if he was of bad character or the crime was a grave one, he was subjected to the ordeal, which was made by the churchmen a merciful proceeding. The Conqueror's son, William Rufus, openly hooted at this priestly ordeal as an effective mode of criminal trial. In a case involving a sale, or the recovery of specific goods, or land, the procedure of awarding proof applied. But wherever there was a document with witnesses or transaction witnesses the proof was called proof by witnesses, and it prevailed over wager of law. It is possible that the court might find some way to award the proof, so that the party palpably in the right might recover.

The normal form of trial under the Anglo-Saxons was a defense by means of an oath of the defendant and his fellow swearers. It was afterwards called wager of law, and the defendant, by demanding this defense, was said to wage his law. It is apparent that as a mode of rational trial it was an absurdity. In an early Anglo-Norman Year Book, Chief Justice Bereford said that by it any dishonest man with six rascals to aid him could swear any honest man out of his goods. The Norman judges refused to apply it except in a few actions. In the local courts manned by Anglo-Saxons it was continually used. Its evil results were probably the reason why for hundreds of years, in the English common-law procedure, trial by actual witnesses was unknown. No experienced man would believe witnesses whom a party brought to swear for him. In view of the moral development of the community, not yet made fairly honest by business or trade, the conclusion was sound. Even to-day any lawyer of experience knows that he hears more falsehood than truth in testimony given in court. A matter to be noted in regard to the exculpating witnesses is that they are measured by the ratio of two for one. It ought to be plain to every one that this practice was a churchman's invention based upon the Hebrew law requirement that two witnesses are required to prove a fact as against the denial of one. There was nothing Anglo-Saxon about this provision, except the childish belief in the value of the oaths.

It results from what has been said that practically everything in Anglo-Saxon law, so far as it was substantive law, and the most of the procedural law came from the churchmen who were trained in the canon law. The Saxons seem to have been a profoundly stupid race and they found it difficult to take on any semblance of culture. The wager of law was a primitive inheritance, but the churchmen had remolded it. Whether the ordeal was an inheritance from the Hebrew law through the churchmen or a part of the primitive law may be disputed. If it were not plain how in other instances the churchmen imported the Hebrew law, there would be more question. There is such proof; in an edict of Charles the Bald the process is shown:

A question arose as to what should be done in the case of a freeman who had sold himself as a slave. The Salic law and the laws of Frankish kings were consulted. They were silent. The churchmen proffered the Bible, which provided that a man who had delivered himself into servitude should be a slave for six years but should be declared free in the seventh year. This was accepted by the king as the period of servitude by contract of sale. The laws of the Roman Emperors stipulated that if a freeman under stress of circumstances had sold his children into slavery, they could regain their liberty by paying back the purchase price and five per centum thereon. So Charles decided that such was already the law as to children sold and he made the Roman law applicable also to one who had sold himself. His process was to amend the divine law which made the slave free in the seventh year as a part of the general Hebrew law of acquittance at every seventh year without any payment. He applied the period, but added the requirement that freedom must be paid for by reimbursing the purchaser.

All the feudal law and the private jurisdictions of the lords came from the Continent. The churchmen probably introduced it to give them control over their own lands and their own tenants. The very method of serving a summons at the residence upon the defendant, or if he be absent upon a member of his household, was a Norman importation from the Roman law. The devastation was so bad in France that there was added to the law the provision that service could be made by leaving a copy of the writ where the home formerly stood.

Into this condition of Anglo-Saxon law were suddenly introduced Norman rulers with their Norman organization. William the Conqueror dispossessed every Anglo-Saxon landholder who had been in arms with Harold. He left certain of the native landholders in possession, but they had been enemies of Harold and of the house of Godwine, Harold's father. William's first insistence was that he was a true conqueror; all the land of England belonged to him because he had gained it by a conquest title. This was a current legal conception of barbarian origin, but it has remained in our conception that the United States has title to all the Indian land, subject to an Indian right of occupation. Every title to land in England must come from the Conqueror because he had become the owner of it all. This was the cardinal principle, and he and his successors made the claim good by law. The claim met two kinds of opponents: first, the Anglo-Saxon landholders who had not been killed in the Conquest or dispossessed, and who refused to give up their titles; and second, the Norman barons who were conquerors themselves and had dispossessed certain landholders and had carved out their own possessions. They claimed, by as good a title as the Conqueror himself, that they had succeeded to all the rights of the owners whom they had dispossessed. In successive rebellions such Norman claims were destroyed. All the serfs on their holdings were valuable, the free tenant farmers were also valuable. These men went with the land. The actual workers on the land were left undisturbed, but every Norman baron had followers to reward with land and the intermediate Saxon landholders suffered, no doubt, a severe proscription. Little land was left with a Saxon *folcland* title, but even that was held as of the king.

The next principle that the Conqueror tried to insist upon was that all the land of England was held immediately of him as overlord. But this claim he could not make good, except as to the first holder of the land immediately from the king. It was opposed to the whole feudal theory, and it would have rendered impossible a grant by one who held title from the king to a follower of his own, a subvassal of the king. Any one holding his land directly from the king was called a tenant-in-chief. The king theoretically was therefore the chief lord of every fee. The tenant-in-chief would desire to grant to his own vassal a manor to be held by the vassal and his heirs forever. If this subtenant under this subgrant held his land of the king and not from the king's tenant-in-chief, who had made the grant, the king would have the right of escheat, and the estate in that land of the tenant-in-chief would cease. The land might have been granted by the tenant-in-chief upon a military service, such as attending upon the lord in time of war. If this subtenant held of the king he could not at the same time hold of the tenant-in-chief, for he could not render the service. The solution was the rule that all land in England was held either immediately or mediately from the king. Thus came into the law what is called the law of tenure in England. But the feudal law was modified by the Conqueror requiring all vassals and all subvassals to take the oath of fealty directly to himself.

The Normans were a race differing radically in their manners from the Anglo-Saxons. The name of the Normans came, of course, from the Northmen. They were piratical raiders who in former times had come in droves out of Scandinavia seeking plunder and a more temperate climate. They had fallen upon the north coast of France, sailed up the Seine, passed by Paris, and raided the country far up the Marne and the Seine rivers. They raided into the Loire district and sacked Tours. A compromise was attained at last by granting to the Norman Duke that part of France called Normandy, and the Norman Duke acknowledged the King of France as his suzerain. The Normans became the ruling class in Normandy, rapidly coalesced with the French or Gaulish inhabitants, and very rapidly acquired civilization and lost most of their Nordic character.

The result was a remarkable race, with all the Gaulish nimbleness of mind and some of the Northman's strength and determination. Where the Anglo-Saxon was coarse, a gross feeder and heavy swiller of mead, the Norman was temperate and self-restrained. When Lord Eldon, considered a great chancellor, was carried every night to bed, he was a true Anglo-Saxon. His political stupidity put him in the same category. While the Anglo-Saxon was not much better than half civilized, the Norman was highly civilized. The Normans had had peace in their land for many years; schools had multiplied, the great Abbey of Bec furnished scholars for all governmental and Church service. Their lands were highly cultivated. Their buildings were superior. They were a clerkly race, fond of records and of writings. The public business was orderly and carefully recorded in suitable documents. Governmental institutions were well defined. Their discipline in war was so superior, that the Battle of Hastings had been won by much inferior numbers.

The Norman chancery had its writs for all governmental proceedings. From the Roman procedure in Gaul it had obtained the official inquest. The number of men composing the inquest was twelve. Whenever the Norman Duke desired information he held an inquest of twelve men who rendered a verdict as to the fact. The Norman courts were manned by judges learned in the law—ecclesiastics, it is true, following the Roman system passed on to them through the canon law. Above all, the Normans had a language fully developed and expressive, with a rich vocabulary. The terms of the law taken over from the Roman law were suited to a further legal development. The Anglo-Saxons were bound down by a large number of rude and uncouth dialects. Men of different shires could not understand each other, and the poverty of the vocabulary prohibited its use. It was wholly unfit for use by a civilized race. This condition continued for over three hundred years. The only language that could be used was the Norman French. Even to-day the terms of the various professions, the fine arts, of belles-lettres, of governmental administration cannot be found in the English element of our language.

As soon as William was firmly seated on the English throne, he proceeded in the sound Norman way to find out what his English realm contained. He took a census, which not only enumerated almost all of the inhabitants except some of the slaves and serfs but listed their lands and property. It required a number of years to complete this enumeration, but when it was finished the king had what is called the Domesday Book. He could now accurately tell who held particular lands and on what services they were held, what were the lands of the crown and who had claims upon them. The status of the inhabitants was determined with accuracy. How modern it is to picture the king and his clerks thumbing the rolls of the Domesday census, to ascertain where he could screw out a little more revenue or a few more knights and footmen!

There was, of course, no shifting of the inhabitants, but there were very severe regulations as to the royal forests and the game. Since these regulations or laws caused much complaint, a set of forest laws was forged and fathered on the dead King Cnut, who could not defend himself, and in consequence for centuries the Forest Laws of Cnut were accepted as true laws of Cnut. The Norman kings were merely promulgating laws, and putting them forth as already long existing, a process which became active in the reign of the Conqueror's son Henry I, who found it desirable to throw a few legal bones to his Saxon subjects. The bones were rather well coated by Norman polish. No immediate system of laws was put out, but the Kings put their clerks to work to devise various law books, some of them made up of provisions from whatever of the old laws the Normans were willing to accept, modified as they thought best. They were willing to accept the value the Anglo-Saxons put on themselves and their injuries by way of *wer* and *bot*, but the Norman was protected by stringent provisions. Other provisions were importations from Normandy or taken from the English law as revised by the churchmen. The county courts and other local courts were allowed to continue to function, but the Norman kings appointed their own earls and sheriffs to preside therein.

William brought in his train a set of Norman ecclesiastics. Prominent among them was Lanfranc. He is said to have received his education in Roman law at Pavia, which had been stirred into some life by the example of Bologna. He came to the Abbey of Bec in Normandy and was a teacher there. William brought him to England and made him Archbishop of Canterbury, in succession to the Anglo-Saxon Stigand. The first great lawsuit was instituted by Lanfranc to obtain the lands of the see of Canterbury. The county assembly was convened and Lanfranc, having crammed on the Anglo-Saxon terms, discoursed brilliantly on *sac* and *soc, toll* and *team, infangthief* and *utfangthief.*

A more comprehensible and more important case is one between Gundulph, Bishop of Rochester, and Picot, the king's sheriff. It is dated about 1075, only nine years after the Conquest. The Bishop was, of course, an Anglo-Saxon. He claimed lands as belonging to his diocese, but the sheriff had taken possession of them for the king. Probably the situation was that Anglo-Saxon thanes holding lands from the Church had been in Harold's army and naturally the sheriff seized their lands and in doing so ran upon the Church as a landowner. The case shows first that though the king could probably not be sued, the simple device of suing his officer could be used, just as to-day, although one of the states of this Union cannot be sued in a federal court, the device is used of suing the State officer acting under state authority. A bishop of the Church with its power behind him was a very different person from an Anglo-Saxon landowner. The bishop brought an action claiming that the sheriff was deforcing him. The chancery of the king issued a writ commanding that all the men of the county should be assembled and by them it should be proved to whom the land in truth belonged. The writ designated Odo, Bishop of Bayeux, who was then Chief Justiciar of the king, to preside over the court. He was the younger brother of the king.

By the men of the county who were to be assembled as the court, was meant those Anglo-Saxon freemen who, in former days, were assembled as the county court. But this writ imposed a new conception. In Anglo-Saxon days these men were the judges, they as doomsmen spoke the doom, but now they were witnesses to give information to the king's judge, who was the authority to render the judgment. This is a complete revolution and imposed upon England the Roman rule that the judge made the judgment.

The county court was assembled in pursuance of the writ, the Chief Justiciar presiding, but the account says that the men of the county were in fear of the king's sheriff, so they said that the land was the king's. The Bishop of Bayeux presiding did not believe what they said. He directed the county men, if they knew what they said to be true, to select twelve of their number to confirm upon oath what the whole body of the court had said. Here is the first jury of twelve men ever assembled in England to make a conclusive statement of the facts upon which the judge of the court is to act in making his judgment. This is a transplanting of the

Norman inquest of twelve men to become a constituent part of a court in certifying upon oath to the facts.[2] At this time inquests of twelve men were at work all over the realm certifying to the facts of the Domesday survey, but these inquests were not in litigation. The twelve men were selected, they withdrew, but they, too, were greatly terrified by a message from the sheriff and came back and swore that what the men of the county said was true. Thereupon judgment was entered for the king and he had obtained the lands.

Up to this point the case would show certain fundamental changes in procedure, introducing the Norman and Roman proceeding by inquest of twelve men into the court procedure. But the matter went much further. A certain monk now came forward and told the Bishop of Rochester that the verdict was wrong and that one of the twelve knew it, for he held his own lands under the same church title. The Bishop took the monk to the Chief Justiciar, who heard the statement. The account tells of the scene of the Chief Justiciar sending for one of the twelve and of the wrath of the Norman at learning that despite his better judgment he had allowed himself to be imposed upon by a gang of cowardly and perjured Saxon churls. The man in fright threw himself at the Justiciar's feet and confessed that he was a perjurer. Then another of the twelve was called in and he confessed. The Chief Justiciar now convened many of the greater barons. They, both French and English, adjudged the jury to have made a false oath in their verdict.

The question then arose of what to do. There was law in Normandy for convicting an inquest of making a false oath, but there it was unheard of that the judgment based on the false verdict should be set aside and a contrary judgment entered. Nevertheless the Chief Justiciar, without hesitation, did what he could not have done in Normandy. He reversed the judgment and entered a new one for the Bishop of Rochester, awarding him the lands, and the jury were fined three hundred pounds to the king.

2. One should beware of perceiving the jury as solely a Norman transplant. For a discussion of both the Anglo-Saxon and Norman contributions to the shaping of the jury, see Raoul van Caenegem, *The Birth of the English Common Law*, 2d ed. (Cambridge: Cambridge University Press, 1988), pp. 62–84.—C. J. R., Jr.

This proceeding is of the highest importance in English law, for the next we hear of this proceeding is in Glanville's book a hundred years later, but then the proceeding is a settled thing. The point to be noticed here is the original meaning and office of a jury. It is not a body as we know it, which hears the evidence of witnesses and decides from that evidence upon the facts. The original jury was simply twelve men, who are called into court to be the witnesses and the only witnesses as to the facts. They make up their verdict on their own knowledge, and for four hundred and fifty years this was just what an English jury did. The only feasible way in which such a verdict could be set aside was for another better informed body to be called in to say that the former witness jury spoke falsely. Whereupon a new judgment could be entered to the exact contrary of the former judgment. That jury being what it was, this new reversing jury proceeding was an eminently reasonable and proper device. It is much more effective than our method of the judge granting a new trial. A new trial simply wipes out the former verdict, but does not substitute a correct judgment. This procedure gives the new and correct judgment. When we find this procedure again after almost a hundred years of that silence which enshrouds legal matters until Henry II's reign, it is called the process of attainting a jury. It is found to be carried out by a jury of twenty-four knights, following the Bishop of Bayeux's plan of selecting the attainting jury from men of higher standing than that of the jury to be attainted.

It is not often in these early times that we can find the man who invented procedure in the law, but to this Norman is unquestionably to be ascribed, first, the use of a sworn jury of twelve to decide upon the facts in a lawsuit, and second, the procedure of correcting a false finding of the jury. This process of attaint lived long in the law. It was not until about 1650 that a common-law court found that it could grant a new trial. About all that we know of this inventor of the attaint is that in the Conquest he strongly supported his elder brother with men and money. The Bayeux tapestry shows him at the Battle of Hastings on an armored war-horse leading his knights, but he is given a clerical baton instead of an unclerical sword. He was rewarded with great landholdings in Kent and became Chief Justiciar, the highest office in the realm. He afterwards quarreled with the king and was sent back to Normandy. Thence one account says that he was exiled and set out for Rome with a large amount of money to buy the papacy. It was assumed at that time that all that was necessary was to appear at the College of Cardinals and, with the utmost sang-froid, to distribute enough money, and the process of becoming pope, was as easy as becoming a United States Senator in localities where such commodities are for sale. The account says that the good Bishop died at Palermo, the Norman capital of Sicily, before he got a chance to use his funds. Another account says that he enlisted in the first crusade and died at the siege of Antioch. But whether he died as an exile or as a warrior for the tomb of Christ, English law owes to him two procedural institutions that dominated the common law for centuries.

The laws of the Conqueror introduced trial by battle into England. It was extended as a right to all the Norman subjects and an Anglo-Saxon in a contest with a Norman could claim it. The Church was tied down by strict regulation to the effect that no bishop in a bishop's court could implead or excommunicate any of his barons.

When the Conqueror died he was succeeded by his son, another William, who spent his time in quarreling with the Church and wringing money from the Church coffers and lands. The third Norman king was one to whom the English law owes a great deal. He was Henry I, the youngest son of the Conqueror, surnamed Beauclerk, "fine scholar." The Anglo-Saxons were now holding up their heads and complaining, demanding with true popular stupidity the good old laws. Henry had sworn in his coronation oath to observe the old laws, and no doubt decided to tell these Anglo-Saxons what those old laws were. Henry's clerks were put to work to appease the Saxons with older laws, such as the laws of Edward the Confessor, laws of the Anglo-Saxon kings translated with selection and discretion, laws of Cnut, laws of William the Conqueror, and especially the laws of Henry himself, represented to be old laws.

These collections were made up of some little Anglo-Saxon matter, but with a great deal of Canon law and Roman law inserted. The legal historians quote these laws, especially the laws of Henry, to show what the pre-Norman Anglo-Saxon laws were. This is all inadmissible. Those laws simply show what Henry and his clerks desired the old laws to be.

But it is a curious fact that an English historian will go into paroxysms of indignation over the forged Donation of Constantine or the forged Decretals, and yet quote with the greatest equanimity these forged laws of English kings and treat them in all seriousness as proof of the precocity of the pre-Norman law. All this part of the English historical legal writing is without any reliability.

During this long reign of Henry I the king's justices were sent out to make perambulations of the country, to convene the county courts, and to preside in them wherever they came. It is certain that the judgments entered were those of the justices, not those of the men composing the county court. A new court was created called the Exchequer, sitting at Westminster, which heard all matters relating to revenue, and where all the accounts of the king's officers were rendered and settled. The churchmen who were the king's justices decided all the cases of every kind which they found were to be decided. They proved very satisfactorily that if a man desired justice he could obtain a much better justice from the king's clerical justiciars than from the haphazard county tribunals, when no king's judge was present. The Norman population, of course, took their legal matters to the king's justices.

One change made by William the Conqueror was to have lasting results. He, probably at the instance of the churchmen themselves, took the bishop out of the county court and thus created in England the separate ecclesiastical courts of the Church. All the conceded jurisdiction that belonged to the ecclesiastics went to the Church courts. One part of the Church jurisdiction was the trial of any ecclesiastic for any offense. Thus came into the law the procedure of benefit of clergy. This was a right in the defendant to claim that he was an ecclesiastic and, if the fact was established, to be remanded to the bishop and dealt with as an ecclesiastic in the bishop's court. The test was whether the defendant could read or write, and the general result was that for a long time in English law a man who could read and write escaped any punishment for crime, except as the bishop's court might impose it. The change resulting from taking the bishop out of the county court resulted in the contest between the lay courts and the ecclesiastical courts, which continued in England for centuries. One of the first writs devised was the writ of prohibition, still a common-law writ, which prohibited an ecclesiastical court from any further proceeding in a case.

The Conqueror also utilized the Anglo-Saxon institution whereby a rudimentary sort of police organization had been obtained through a certain small number of men becoming sureties for each other's appearing in answer to criminal charges. Under the Norman kings the institution was called the frankpledge, and was applied to the free Anglo-Saxon subjects. The Conqueror also provided a system of taxation whereby all the land was bound to military service and each particular unit of land must produce men for military service. This military service was commuted in many cases for a money payment and finally the tax became a regular tax in money called scutage, the shield tax. The Norman kings did not recognize the claim of the churchmen to the right to tax themselves, and the Church lands were made subject to military service.

Another feature of Norman law was the conception of the king's peace. In Anglo-Saxon times all the holders of jurisdictions had the right to hold that any breach of public order within their jurisdictions was a breach of their peace. The Norman kings took this conception and broadened it always in favor of a greater jurisdiction for the king's judges both in civil and in criminal matters. In actions of trespass the writ issued stated that the trespass was done contrary to the peace of our lord the king. This at once gave the king's judges jurisdiction. All offenses committed in public places were considered as breaches of the king's peace. Every important offense was appropriated as a breach of the peace of the king. The Norman kings did not attempt to do away with wager of law, but they rapidly came to the point where it was allowed before the king's judges only in the matters of actions where it had been applicable. It was not allowed to apply to any new writ, and especially to trespass writs.

After the death of Henry I and the civil war that followed between rival claimants to the throne, the matter was compromised by giving the succession to the grandson of Henry I who is known in history as Henry II. He was a very capable ruler. It s not necessary to consider that he had any wide theoretical views upon the extension of the law and the authority of the king's courts, but he was very vitally interested in the revenues from justice. Not many years after he came upon the throne, certain writs were devised whereby all litigation as to the ownership of land was thrown into the king's court. These different writs were called the assizes of novel disseisin, mort d'ancestor, last presentment, and utrum. The minutiae of law in regard to these writs would not be interesting, but it is sufficient to say that if one man dispossessed another of a freehold estate the other could bring the writ of novel disseisin, or new disseisin. If, upon the death of an owner, a dispute arose between claimants, the writ of "death of ancestor" was used. If a question arose as to who had the right to present a priest to a church, the question was tried upon the writ of last presentment, and if a dispute arose as to whether land belonged to the Church or to a layman, the question was tried on a writ of utrum, whether the land was a lay or an ecclesiastical fee. All these writs were borrowed directly from the Roman law.

The matter of special importance was that in each one of these writs it was stated that the sheriff should call together twelve good and lawful men of the vicinage, and these men should state the fact as to whether on a writ of novel disseisin the defendant had dispossessed the claimant unjustly and without judgment, or on the writ of death of ancestor, whether the ancestor died seised, and the claimant was next heir; and similarly an issue was stated in the other writs. These twelve men were called an assize, and these cases called assizes were tried before the king's judges when they came to the district, although originally the sheriff with his panels of jurors was required to come to the king's court at Westminster with their verdict. It will be seen that this is exactly the procedure to ascertain the fact devised by the Bishop of Bayeux in the Conqueror's reign.

It is plain that by this time the Norman lawyers had worked out the legal conception of seisin as distinct from a good title. Seisin according to them was undisturbed possession for a period. After that period the one who had been in seisin before he had become dispossessed could no longer enter by self-help, he must bring his action. Self-help, however, could not extend to a breach of the peace. Then it was for the assize to say whether the disseisin was rightful. Thus almost every dispute concerning freehold land was brought to the king's judges in the royal courts.

About this time the book called Glanville was written. Its general language is borrowed from the Roman law, but it contains notices of the writs collected in the chancery up to that time, and the growth of the law is easily ascertained up to his date. It is very meager. The newly invented assizes are noticed last in that book, and it is likely that Glanville's treatise followed the writs as they were arranged, one after the other, in the Register of Writs, and that in his time only the writs he noticed were in existence.

There was another writ for trying the title to land called the writ of right, and this writ tried the question as to the highest right to the land. For this writ it was provided that the defendant could put himself on the grand assize or could demand trial by battle. The battle was at first an actual fight. Women could have a champion and afterwards any one could choose a champion. Battle was a defense to crime. In *Ivanhoe* the famous battle issue offered by Rebecca was a strict legal right. If the defendant put himself upon the grand assize, he was given a jury of twenty-four knights. This writ was an invention for the benefit of the Normans, and it came from Normandy.

This situation brings out clearly the power of legislation in the king, sitting in his Great Council. The English Parliament was a gradual growth and was a hundred years away from Henry II's reign. The first actual Parliament with representatives of the commons in it was called together by rebel barons in the middle of the thirteenth century.

By the regulations of Henry II the grand assize was turned into a grand jury, which whenever it was thought desirable, by a presentation called afterwards an indictment, preferred a charge that was a criminal charge. The Anglo-Saxon barbarians' system of compensation was never permitted to apply to these charges. But there at the same time survived the appeal of felony which was a proceeding brought by the injured or if he were dead, his kindred, against the accused. The regulation of the Norman kings permitted the defendant to claim a trial by battle.

There is nothing said in Glanville's book, which dates about 1187, as to any process for setting aside or reversing the verdict either of a grand assize or of the other assize proceedings. Glanville simply says that there is a punishment for false swearing in the grand assize, but he says noth-

ing about any false swearing in the so-called petty assizes of novel disseisin and the others. The only conclusion is that it was already established that a verdict of twelve could be set aside by a verdict of twenty-
four knights. This proceeding to set aside a verdict was one of grace, not
of right. The number of twenty-four would naturally be taken under the
Church's rule of two witnesses against one, and knights were selected as
men of greater standing and importance. There was never any way of attacking the verdict of a grand assize of twenty-four knights. That was a
finality. It is not likely that a jury of Norman knights who could defend
against a crime by battle would submit to be attainted by the verdict of
another twenty-four knights. A jury to attaint a grand assize is said by
Bracton to be impossible. There is a case thirty-six years after the institution of this assize system which shows that at that time a jury could be
attainted. A verdict in an assize of novel disseisin was returned and the
bailiff of the losing party offered the king twenty shillings for a jury of
twenty-four knights to convict the assize of a false oath. The offer was
not accepted, because the bailiff had no sufficient power to bind his
principal, but this case indicates that the attaint was then well known.
The number of the jury and the character of the jurors was fixed for the
attaint, but it indicates that the granting of the writ was discretionary
with the king.

The law went on year after year developing new writs, applicable to
new cases that arose. Every new writ meant a new kind of action. In the
meantime a political quarrel had arisen between the barons and King
John, and the king, by the combined force of the Church and the barons,
was compelled to sign what is called Magna Charta. It contained many
provisions, but the special provision for the general law was the one
which established the doctrine that in England there should be a reign of
law, since the king engaged that he would take no proceedings against
any one except by the judgment of his peers or the law of the land. This
is the classic statement for English law that the government is subject to
the laws; but the provision had also an evil effect. It provided that no one
should be disseised, outlawed, imprisoned, or in any way destroyed, except by the judgment of his peers or the law of the land. This was of effect in driving the common law courts wholly to the use of a jury.

The long minority of John's son, Henry III, enabled the law to be more fully developed. But toward the end of the reign of Henry III, a singularly inept sort of king, there was civil war in England between the king and his barons. It was in this civil war that Bracton's law book was written. The issue in the war was whether the king and the government were bound by the laws. Magna Charta, extorted from King John, merely embodied the prevalent ideas of the age upon law that were in vogue upon the Continent. John of Salisbury, the secretary of Thomas à Becket until that martyr was murdered by the knights of Henry II, had quoted the famous Digna Vox rescript from the Roman Code, mentioned in the preceding chapter, and added that a true king thinks nothing lawful for himself that is contrary to the equality of justice, and he affirmed that a king enfranchised from the bonds of law was really an outlaw. Magna Charta bound the king to govern by the laws. It pledged him that his courts should not deny or delay justice and by its use of the term "the law of the land," afterwards changed to "due process of law," it gave the original statement of a universally used constitutional limitation.

The idea that the community must assent to the law in some way was already in existence. The canon law held that no law was valid unless it was accepted by the custom of those concerned. The canon law affirmed that even the pope was bound by the laws. Beaumanoir, a contemporary of Bracton, stated the law to be that all princes are bound to keep and to cause to be kept the laws, and they are bound by legal custom proved either by the general assent of the whole country or by the judgments of courts, if the custom has been the subject of litigation. It is still the law that a rule of law can be proven by decisions of the courts. Bracton, writing about 1260, adds that laws cannot be changed and destroyed without the common consent of all those by whose advice and consent they were promulgated. He insists that legal customs have the vigor of law. He says that the king has superiors which are God and the law which made him king, and if the king should be without a bridle, a bridle should be put upon him. He lays down the principle that there is no law where power and not right governs, and that the king must attribute to the law what the law gives the king, rule and power, and that the king's power is restrained by the law which is the bridle of power.

There was the practical question as to how the law could be enforced against the king. The lawyers saw the difficulty of the king's writ running against himself. Bracton admits that the king being the fountain of justice cannot be sued, that the remedy is by petition that he correct his act, and if he will not do it, the commonwealth and the baronage ought to correct the act in the court of the king himself, by which he means the Great Council made up of the magnates of the kingdom. Bracton says that in receiving justice the king should be compared to the least of his kingdom. This old law early established is the original of the rule in this country that neither the federal nor state governments can be sued, except as the government may permit.

The law has a long life and a very long memory. At the end of our Civil War the United States government was in effect sued for confiscating without warrant of law the estate of Arlington, where is now the National Cemetery. This land had descended from Washington's stepson to the wife of the rebel commander, General Lee, and to her son, G. W. P. C. Lee. These sentences quoted above from Bracton's treatise were cited by a dissenting judge writing an opinion in that case to justify the claim that the government cannot be sued. It is something momentous in the story of the law that, amidst the bitterness and passions of a great civil war, it could be held that even the government of the people itself could not confiscate property against the law of the land. It reminds us that during our Revolutionary War certain shares of Bank of England stock stood in the name of Washington, who was in arms against the English government, yet all through that war the dividends upon that bank stock were regularly paid to the commander of the army of rebellious Americans. Washington was a rebel in arms against England but the Bank of England was a commercial institution and here as always the honesty instituted by trade is far superior to any other conception of honest conduct. Perhaps this was due to that fine courtesy among cultivated men, so characteristic of the eighteenth century. It is not noticed in our school histories that after the surrender at Yorktown in 1781, Washington gave a dinner to the captured English commander, Lord Cornwallis, and his officers, and to the French allies, Count Rochambeau and his officers. A fine tone of mutual consideration prevailed among the

Americans, English, and French, which ought to be a lesson in manners to some of our present vociferous patriots. Lord Cornwallis in his gallant way proposed the health of Washington and said many true things of that steadfast soul. Not least striking in his toast was his recognition of Washington's fine generalship and fortitude during the dark days of Valley Forge. It is after all much that one should be born a gentleman. Not only are we indebted to England for our laws, but it would be well if we could remember that originally we were indebted to England for those manners of which both Washington and Cornwallis were such splendid examples.

CHAPTER 13
English Law—Righteous and Unrighteous

A SKETCH OF THE DEVELOPMENT of particular rules or doctrines of English law would require too much space for the purposes of this book; but it is necessary in the first place to show those changes in the general form of administration of the law which caused the common law, in the very flower of its development, voluntarily to resign a large part of the field of law to another court. This is in itself an extraordinary fact. The common law of England, which has been the subject of so much laudation, really does not deserve, mainly because of this conspicuous failure, the eulogiums that it has uniformly received from its practitioners. About the year 1300 it became tied down by a number of wholly artificial restrictions which left it confessedly incapable of doing justice in a large number of legal relations, many of them of ordinary occurrence. Another court assumed the abdicated jurisdiction in order to fill the gap and to remedy the admitted inability of the law courts. This other court was the court of the Lord Chancellor and its system of law was called equity. We in America have become so used to this monstrosity in law, that we do not see it in all its absurdity.

For centuries in England was presented the spectacle of one set of courts doing all sorts of injustice that another court might remedy the injustice. All the money spent by England over hundreds of years in foolish dynastic wars to obtain or to preserve territory on the continent of Europe would not equal the incalculable sums that this double system of courts cost English litigants. Both systems professed to emanate from the same king as the fountain of justice, both claimed to exert the same judicial power, both worshiped at the same legal shrine, and both professed to dispense justice in accordance with law. One system enforced in many legal relations rules which the other system pronounced to be unjust and unrighteous, and boldly set at naught. It is apparent that the actual law of England was not administered in those matters by the common law courts, but was in fact determined by the rules of law in that court which had the power to pronounce the common law unrighteous and which enforced that power. The law of England was in those respects most emphatically not the common law.

Some legal writers who are ill informed have undertaken to say that this situation was analogous to the doctrine of Aristotle regarding reasonableness as applied to legal rules, but it is not the case, for the court that was applying the legal rule used the doctrine of reasonableness in its application of the rule. No double system of courts was required. The same legal writers have said that this double system was the same as the Roman law, in its one law for the citizens of Rome and its other pretorian law. Nothing could be further from the truth, and nothing could be more characteristic of the superficial way in which Roman law is considered. Those legal writers have been misled into an error intended to excuse this English system of double courts. The fact is that the Roman law called the *jus civile* was the law which was applied to the Roman citizens in their controversies and legal relations with one another, while the pretorian law was applied to Roman citizens in their disputes or relations with foreigners or in the controversies of foreigners with one another in the courts of the Roman praetor. There was no conflict in the law at Rome as applied to a particular legal relation between particular persons, while in England the exact converse was true. The litigants in an action received one rule of law in the common law courts, but in many cases the same litigants in the same dispute would receive a contrary rule of law in the chancery court.

As a common instance of this description we may take the case of one who had executed a bond (which was, of course, a sealed instrument),

whereby he had agreed to pay to another a certain sum of money, and on
the day fixed for payment the debtor, like an honest man, had paid the
bond in full, but in the stress or hurry of circumstances or perhaps out
of ignorance, the debtor had failed to obtain from the creditor a release
under seal. A dishonest creditor could sue on this paid obligation in the
common law courts and obtain judgment. The common law answered
the swindled debtor who had paid with the words that a sealed instrument could be discharged only by another sealed instrument Thus the
justice of the matter was sacrificed to mere form. A plea of payment
would be held to be insufficient and the dishonest creditor would take
judgment upon the bond although it had in fact been paid. But the defrauded debtor had a refuge in the chancellor, who was considered to
have in his keeping the conscience of the king. He sat in a court of conscience. To such a judge the enforced double payment was abhorrent, for
he had read in the Roman Digest that good faith does not suffer that the
same thing should be twice exacted. The chancellor was, with two exceptions during several centuries, a bishop or an archbishop, a great
prelate of the Church. He knew something of the elevated spirit of the
Roman law in its superiority to mere form and he had none of the rigid
notions of the common law judges.

The complaining debtor, swindled by the law of the law courts, would
present his bill in chancery, piously addressed to his "Dear Fader in
God," telling the circumstances, either that he had been sued and judgment had been given against him or that he was about to be sued upon a
bond that he had paid. The chancellor would issue his writ of subpoena
to the creditor and enforce his attendance and require him to answer
under oath, as to the payment. The creditor would object that the holy
and righteous common law gave no remedy. The chancellor would answer that he sat in a court of conscience and of God, and cared nothing
for the arbitrary rule of the common law which made a payment no payment. The creditor would object that the debtor should not have been
such a fool as to pay without a sealed release. The chancellor would
shortly answer as he did in one case, "God is the protector of fools," and
would force an answer. If the creditor admitted the payment, the chancellor said: "Deliver up your bond and we shall cancel it." If the credi-

tor had a common law judgment, the chancellor issued a writ of injunction forbidding the creditor to proceed further under the judgment.

If the creditor denied the payment, the evidence was taken. Under the Hebrew law, long before imported into the Roman law as the canon law, the payment must be proved by two witnesses. If it were so proved, the same injunctional decree of the chancellor prevented the collection of the bond or forbade suit in the common law court. The common law judges foamed with indignation, but the chancellor said that he did not interfere with them, that he worked upon the party, that his decree required the creditor to do only what equity and good conscience demanded, and that if the party tried to collect a paid bond by using the unrighteous process of the common law court, he would lay this violator of honesty and good conscience by the heels. Thus, what Shakespeare called "old Father Antic, the law," said to the common law court that it could go ahead and do its worst with its unrighteous law and then said to the chancellor that he must remedy the attempted injustice by his righteous law. But is it not plain that the law of England was that payment a second time could not be enforced, and that the law unnecessarily took this expensive, awkward, devious, splay-footed method of arriving at justice?

There was never any sound reason for the common law to descend to such depths of ineptitude. Men of more liberality of mind, of more vision in adjusting law to conditions, of more insight into juristic method, with a keener sense of right and justice, with more knowledge, ability, tact, and skill in handling their legal devices would never have allowed themselves to get into such a position. Some have said that the common law courts were of limited jurisdiction and could not afford a remedy but this is a mistake, for the limitation was not one of jurisdiction. It was one of self-imposed incorrectness. It was thus also in the field of contract. A contract not evidenced by a document under seal, the common law courts would not look at, because of their profound disgust with wager of law and the rascally compurgators, and because they did not see how their courts could decide a question upon such a contract without witnesses. Hence all such contracts went to the local courts like the county courts, where the multitude insisted on their God-given right to adduce perjury by the wager of law.

But a party with such a contract could go to the chancellor, and say that he had a good contract, but that if he went into any of the law courts, he would be met with wager of law. The chancellor would give him justice and would pay no attention to the old wager of law, but would listen to the testimony of witnesses. Thus again the Roman law rescued the law of England from the slough of its common law courts and approached the rule of justice. These are instances of a very ordinary condition. Other instances will be later stated. This result was brought about, as will now be explained, by the adoption of the jury as a necessary part of a law court.

The story of this common law *débâcle* must be preceded by a short description of the common law in its golden age, when it was showing a capacity to redress every civil wrong, and to protect every civil right. If no writ then existed under which an action could be instituted, a new one was invented. It must be kept in mind that the relations of life were comparatively simple; the communities were small and the main object of litigation was land. Land could not pass without livery of seisen, which was a public act, or by a death which was no less public. The neighborhood knew all about such facts. Legal rules and remedies grow as the intricacy of relations of men in society increases. Two hundred years after the Conquest the condition of society was vastly improved over what it had been under the Norman kings or even in the times of the first Plantagenets, but the relations among men were still simple.

Just at this period of two hundred years after the Conquest, about 1260, in the reign of Henry III, a great English law book was written by a priestly judge whom we know as Bracton. His true name was Bratton. By a fortunate discovery, the manuscript which was his collection of cases for writing his book has been identified. Its discovery by the Russian who lived in England for many years and became the greatest English legal scholar of his time, Paul Vinogradoff, deserves to rank with Niebuhr's more famous discovery of the lost Institutes of Gaius. The manuscript, as Bracton's Note Book, has been printed in its Latin form, but has never been translated. Bracton evidently tried to find every kind of case that had arisen and his book and his cases show the common law courts administering every kind of remedy.

Like all the lawyer-priests Bracton had considerable knowledge of the Roman law. He had read the Summa of Azo, at least in one of its parts, but there was no manuscript of the Roman Digest in England, nor probably any manuscript of more than a part of the Code. Printing, of course, was then unknown and manuscripts were rare and costly. With his material of cases taken out of the court rolls, Bracton, using the Roman law and its classification, tried to fit into the field of law the English cases. In his day the priestly judges were passing away and laymen were taking their places. Bracton says that the judges of his time were inferior men. Soon afterwards Edward I made a general fining and discharge of his judges. This fact seems to prove Bracton's statement.

Bracton for his cases goes back to the decisions of two great priestly judges who were on the bench in his early years, Pateshull and Raleigh. It is not necessary to describe the whole field of the recognized law as shown in Bracton's book. It suffices here to say that every kind of case that had yet arisen in England could be disposed of on some writ. About the only objectionable thing in the law was the degraded Anglo-Saxon wager of law, still permitted in the actions of debt and of detinue, which were really two forms of one action called debt.

We may take two cases out of Bracton's Note Book, very far apart in their character, as instances of the widespread jurisdiction of the common law courts. In one case there is a situation that looks like a family scandal in high circles.[1] John de Montacute and Lucy, his wife, were cited into court by the male heir apparent of John to answer why they were bringing up a girl (*garcia*) and representing her as their daughter, when she was not their daughter, to the manifest wrong and prejudice of the demandant, who by the law of England would succeed to John's lands. John kept silent, for he had sold the wardship of the girl as if she were his daughter, but Lucy came, bringing before the court the alleged supposititious daughter Katherine, and asserted that Katherine was her daughter, born on the eve of St. Katherine and therefore named Katherine.

---

1. Zane provides a fuller discussion of this case in his essay, "A Mediaeval Cause Célèbre," *Illinois Law Review* 1 (1906): pp. 363–73.—C. J. R., Jr.

Lucy adduced a string of witnesses, a bishop and barons with great Norman names, one of whom had purchased the wardship and marriage of Katherine from her parents. The witnesses traced the history of Katherine from her early years, and stated by whom she had been brought up. It was proven that both John and Lucy had declared her to be their daughter. The court decided what is still the law, that since Katherine was born while husband and wife were living in wedlock and had been acknowledged by them, the demandant would not be heard to prove the fact to be otherwise and the male heir was amerced for his false claim.

The case looks very much as if Katherine was Lucy's daughter, but not John de Montacute's. But here the law is seen in its flexibility; no jury was necessary nor was one used; witnesses were heard and the case decided on the proposition that the privacies of wedded life would not be inquired into. The peculiar thing is that the heir had no present right, he had no estate in the lands, he might not succeed in any event if he died before John, or if John had a child, even if Katherine was not the daughter of John. The case cannot be a slander of title, for the heir had no title. When John should die, the controversy would arise, and not until then; yet the court entertained the complaint on the principle that it was better to decide the controversy beforehand, and the court settled what would be the rights of the parties upon John's death.

In our day this Montacute case would be called a pure case of declaratory judgment, that settles a controversy by declaring the present status of the right. It will be seen that this is a precocious legal development, anticipating by centuries the present idea of wild legal reformers who think that a party proves that he has a cause of action by stating that he has none at present, but hopes and expects, if he survives, that he will have one in the future. It is no wonder that courts are finding laws authorizing declaratory judgments to be unconstitutional.

Another case is just as extraordinary from the present common law standpoint. A landowner had a mill. Certain persons owed from time out of mind suit and service at the mill, which meant, at least, that they must patronize the mill. In the then language of the law, the mill owner was seized of these services. This, of course, was a valuable right. The mill owner brought a suit to recover the suit and services just as if they were land, saying that they had been withdrawn. It turned out that certain persons, probably in the interest of some other mill, were trying to persuade the peasants owing suit and service to the plaintiff's mill to withdraw their patronage. The court said to the mill owner that he could not recover, for he had shown no suit or service subtracted; but it added that it would give him a writ forbidding any one to interfere with the suitors to his mill. This is a pure case of injunction granted to protect a man in his rights.

All the common law could do in the after days of its supine weakness was to say to the mill owner: "Wait until this outsider has persuaded some one to breach his duty to your mill and then sue the persuader and get a money judgment for your damages. That is all this court of common law can do. But if you wish preventive relief, go to the chancellor; he will issue an injunction and protect your rights." To-day a court with chancery power will enjoin any third party interfering wrongly with the employees' relation to the employer or attempting to bring about any breach of contract on their part or attempting to take away customers by deception, or by persuasion to induce a breach of contract.

The two instances are as far as possible from any common law jurisdiction of later times. The common law from this time forward became tied down to a judgment only for money or to a recovery of specific real or personal property. Even when it gave a judgment in replevin or detinue for personal property, the judgment was in the alternative for the personal property or its value as fixed in the judgment. It could give no other form of judgment. Yet at this period of Henry III the law courts would grant all kinds of specific relief, that is to say relief other than a money judgment. They would cancel a document, they would compel the delivery of deeds, they would compel the delivery of specific personal property, they could grant the specific performance of a contract under seal. They would take and state an account of long involved dealings. They would try questions of freedom. They would restore a serf to his owner, they would liberate a man wrongly held as a serf. A tenant for years had his remedy for eviction. All sorts of remedies were provided as to freehold lands. They were the old petty assizes, the writs of entry, the

actions upon the form of the deed. A widow could obtain the specific relief of having her dower lands measured off to her and of having possession of them. The heir was compelled by a mandatory writ to do this.
If a man was sued for land he could implead the one who sold to him and
make him defend. If this grantor failed to show his title, the one who had
bought the land by poor title, could in the same action have judgment
against his grantor for equivalent lands in lieu of those lost. There was
no reason why the common law by further writs should not develop the
law as new situations arose, had it not been that the law courts became
wedded to a jury.

The courts under the priestly judges had made a procedure where the
judge of the court made the judgment. There was also a method of settling the pleadings borrowed from the Roman law. On the return day of
the writ, the plaintiff's counsel stated orally to the court what his cause
of complaint was. If the court considered it bad in substance, it said so,
and if the plaintiff by additional statements could not make it good to
the court, the plaintiff was amerced for his false claim (*pro falso clamore*)
and the defendant went without day. If the court said that the count or
statement of claim was good, it said to the defendant, "Answer over."
The defendant's counsel thereupon stated his defenses. If he denied the
plaintiff's claim he said, "Ready to deny," and the issue was formed, and
written on the record by the clerks.

But the defendant might have exceptions, as they were called by the
Roman law, to show why the plaintiff should not have a trial. If his first
statement of defense or exception—called later his plea—was not good,
the court told him so and he tried another, until he had exhausted his matters of exception. Then if he was not prepared to deny the plaintiff's
claim by saying that it was untrue, judgment went against him. In his
pleading the defendant might state as an exception some matter admitting
the plaintiff's claim, but avoiding that claim by showing something that
overcame it. If it were so, the court called upon the plaintiff to answer as
to this new matter brought in. If he could not answer it, judgment went
against him. If he could answer it he did so, but at that time it was usually
by denying it, and thus an issue was formed. This pleading was all done
orally and after it was over the clerk of the court wrote up the record.

If an issue had been formed on some question of fact, the court used any method of deciding the facts that it saw fit. In some instances the case went out to the assizes in the proper shire to be tried. If the case were on a writ of assize or the case were of a kind where the jury could pass on the facts, the twelve men were called in to state the facts. In every criminal case the method of trial would be what the court forced the defendant to take. If he refused to agree to a jury trial he was subjected to *peine forte et dure,* which was simply torture. Long afterwards judges boasted that the common law never knew torture, but it was ignorant boasting.

When the case came to an assize or a jury there was never any trial by witnesses or upon evidence. The jury was called in and sworn, it was assumed to know the facts, it was asked for its verdict and it gave it. Magna Charta provided that the king's judges must visit each shire at least once a year to dispose of business. They in fact held a session of what had been the old county court and what remained the old county court, if the king's judges were not present. There was another form of the visit of the king's judges to the shire. It was called an eyre, and by written articles from the king the judges were directed to clean up all the judicial business in the shire. They looked into the whole legal administration. No king's writ ran in the county during the eyre. The judges could and would entertain any kind of complaint and grant any appropriate relief. Some of the cases proposed to them were what afterwards were called equity causes.

In order to show the method of trial then in vogue by a jury, it may be well to describe an actual lawsuit about 1300. It is a case which shows both an original jury trial and a new trial by a larger jury. The question was as to certain land in dispute. Under the then new statute creating estates tail, a controversy had arisen and an assize of novel disseisin had been tried between Frank de Scoland and William de Grandison. The facts were that Frank had had an uncle Geoffrey de Scoland. This uncle Geoffrey had an illegitimate son Richard, who, of course, was not an heir of his father Geoffrey, for by English law a bastard was "no one's son." Geoffrey had granted to his illegitimate son Richard certain land to hold unto Richard and the heirs of his body forever. This created an estate tail in Richard which would cease if and when all descendants of the bastard Richard should cease to exist. When this happened Geoffrey or his heir would take the land. Geoffrey was gathered unto his fathers. His nephew Frank succeeded to all the estate except this land granted to his bastard cousin. Then Richard, the bastard, died without any descendants, and the fee tail in him ceased, and Frank in succession to Geoffrey, who had granted the fee tail and had thus retained the reversion, was entitled as heir, because he had inherited Geoffrey's reversion. Frank took possession.

But now came William de Grandison. He was chief lord of the fee. Of him the land was held by the Scolands. He said that he was entitled to the land by escheat because Geoffrey before he died had released to the bastard Richard the reversion after the fee tail and this reversion merging with the fee tail was the whole estate in the land and gave a fee simple to Richard, and, therefore, when Richard died Frank did not succeed by any reversion, and Richard, being a bastard, could have no collateral heirs. The fee simple thus in Richard, he asserted, had ceased on Richard's death, and he, William de Grandison, had gotten the title by escheat. Acting on this asserted state of facts Grandison ousted Frank. This was a neat case and well put up from Grandison's standpoint, but it was not true. The jury when called in the novel disseisin case brought by Frank could say whether a release had been given. Their statement was final on that point until attainted. The case was tried upon the novel disseisin writ, and the jury (assize) found that the release was made as William de Grandison claimed. William's title by escheat was good if the verdict was true. The verdict was a special verdict, stating only the release, and homage made by Richard to William de Grandison and the damages. Judgment was entered on the verdict for Grandison. Frank tried a new suit on the title and was beaten, and then he obtained from the judges a writ of attaint, upon which a jury of twenty-four knights would be empaneled to say whether the first jury had returned a false verdict. Upon this writ the sheriff summoned Grandison and the jury that had passed on the case. Seven of the jury appeared, three were dead and two defaulted, and the attaint trial came on.

The scene was as picturesque as medieval life. Sitting upon the bench were the king's judges, called justices in eyre. Spigurnel was the chief of

the court, and with him sat other judges, one of whom was named
Harvey de Staunton, called by the irreverent Year Book reporters, Harvey the Hastie, from his tendency to speak too quickly. Each of the
judges was arrayed in his crimson gown or robe edged with spotless
miniver, as they called ermine. The serjeants at law stood before the
bench. They were arrayed in sober parti-colored gowns and had not yet
descended to the deadness of black. Each serjeant wore a white cap or
coif, which he had the privilege of wearing even in the presence of the
king. The serjeants had the sole right of audience, that is of being heard,
in the Common Pleas court, and they were called the Order of the Coif.
French advocates to this day always wear their caps when pleading in the
courts, but if they read from a book or a document they take off the cap.
The rule that is carried out on academic occasions in this country has an
ancient pedigree.

Attending upon the court were the twenty-four knights, wearing their
swords and the rich gowns of the period. Standing as culprits at the bar
were the seven jurors of the jury charged with having rendered a false
verdict. William de Grandison was there, attended by his serjeant.
Thereupon the trial began. Every one who spoke in court used Norman
French and every case reported in the Year Books was in Norman
French. The clerks who were sitting in court to record the proceedings
made their record in Latin and the record continued to be made in Latin
until the middle of the eighteenth century.

Frank de Scoland's serjeant at law stated the particulars wherein the
verdict was false, first, that it falsely found the release; secondly, that it
falsely found that the dead Richard had done homage to Grandison and
held from him; thirdly, that it falsely found the damages. This was
the pleading for the plaintiff which the clerks wrote down. Then began
the oral exceptions for Grandison. First, the point of law was made
that the whole twelve of the jury to be attainted were not present. This
was overruled as a matter of course. The proposition that the death
of any of the jurors destroyed the remedy for a false verdict was as
astonishing as would be a plea by a burglar that his partner in crime was
dead and, therefore, he could not be tried. Next it was objected that the
former judgment, sought to be attainted, was not fully performed. But

Frank's serjeant produced the record, showing that judgment fully satisfied. Next the serjeant of Grandison objected by the plea or exception
that the writ of attaint was not presented at the opening of the eyre, as
required by the articles of the eyre. This was overruled because the justices in eyre could grant writs of attaint and had done so in this case. The
clerks took down none of these pleas since they were bad. Here one of
the counsel for Grandison asked for a bill of exception on this plea. One
of the justices replied: "We will make no exception, you have the testimony of the whole court, so lodge your bill." This was the offered and
rejected plea written out. Vellum cost money in those days and the counsel for Grandison tried to shift the cost on the court. The court neatly
circumvented him by telling him to write it out himself. Finally it was
objected that Grandison's tenant was made a party, and he had not been
a party to the assize in which the verdict was rendered. This was overruled, for the tenant was liable for the damages accruing since William
de Grandison went into possession.

Here, through his counsel, Serjeant Hartlepool, Grandison said to the
court: "By your leave we will imparl [consult] with the accused jurors."
Staunton the Hastie, not waiting for his chief to speak, at once courte-
ously replied: "We pray you to do so." The defendant and the accused
jury went out and consulted and came back and made another objection
which was: "The false oath is assigned to the release, homage, and damages, but not to the whole issue of disseisin." Spigurnel, the chief justice, ruled shortly: "All findings of fact are open to be attainted." The
defendants now having exhausted themselves, the oath was administered
to the twenty-four knights, one by one. Each juryman said: "Hear, ye
Justices, I will speak the truth of this assize and of the freehold of which
I have had the view by command of the king, and of the oath of the
twelve and in naught will I fail." It will be noted that the jury had already
gone to see the land in dispute.

Thereupon Spigurnel stated to the attainting jury of twenty-four the
pleadings at the former trial and the verdict of the twelve, and charged
the twenty-four knights to say whether or not the twelve had made a
false oath in the particulars of the release and the homage and the damages. The twenty-four answered on the spot that the twelve had made a

false oath as to the release, and as to the damages, and as to Richard holding of William de Grandison, but not as to the homage. The judges at
once ruled that the homage was immaterial. Then Spigurnel said:
"Gentlemen, tell us Frank's damages since the assize," that is to say,
since the verdict put him out of possession. The jurymen answered:
"Seven score marks." Thereupon by judgment Frank was given his
seisin, his damages of fifteen marks paid at the first trial, and his amerce-
ment and costs paid on that trial and his further damages of one hundred and forty marks, and his costs in this attaint trial. The mark was
thirteen and a half shillings and money had then twenty times the pur-
chasing power of to-day. William de Grandison paid well for the neat
case which he had concocted.

This actual picture of a trial shows a remarkably businesslike way of
holding court. In this trial, as contrasted with a trial of to-day, the
pleadings are seen to be oral and if disallowed are disregarded. No evidence whatever is offered, no witnesses testify, the jury are the only witnesses and speak from their own knowledge already gained. The lawyers
make no statements or argument to the jury. Plainly such a jury could
be used with advantage only regarding matters of general knowledge.
But there was a reason why this kind of trial should have urged itself
upon the judges. There is a tendency in most men to avoid responsibility. Nothing could be more attractive to the average judge than this ability to shift all responsibility upon the jury as to the facts, the really difficult matter to settle in every lawsuit. Lawyers of the present day have
seen much of this tendency in judges. At any rate the fact is clear that
the common law courts without any statute forced the parties in every
case to a jury trial. No matter what the issue was, the pleading was
forced into such a groove that it could be referred to a jury to decide the
disputed facts.

This natural tendency to rely upon a jury was aided by the apparent
inclination of Magna Charta to insist upon a judgment of "the peers" of
a litigant. When a woman who had lost a suit called the judge by the accurate terms, in her judgment, of "traitor, felon, and robber," the jury
impaneled to try the question and to try her for her accusation, was composed of serjeants at law, considered to be the peers of the judge.

The idea became disseminated that a jury was the best means for ascertaining facts. It was popular with the great mass of people, for it mag-
nified their importance and made them a constituent part of a court.
Originally introduced in a limited way to decide facts as to the seisin of
real property, which were almost certain to be matters of general neighborhood knowledge, the jury became by the insistence of the judges the
means of trial in every law case. Too great a burden was put upon the
jury. In many cases the jury called could not possibly have the requisite
knowledge, but must go out and try to find it. The form of pleadings was
made such that the final pleading of adverse facts on either side was concluded by each party putting himself upon a jury trial. The legal phrase
was that the pleading concluded to the country, i.e., a jury, and the other
party did the like, called the *similiter.*

This tendency to a jury trial was aided by the new creation of a parliament as a law-making device. When the barons under Simon de
Montfort were fighting with King Henry III in the thirteenth century,
Simon, in order to strengthen his position, called together a parliament
made up of the barons as lords and of representatives of the shires and
boroughs as the commons. This was a new kind of assembly in England,
a new adaptation of the representative feature.

Heretofore we have seen that in the history of law before language was
written the laws were wholly customary and knowledge of the customs
belonged to the priests. When written language came into use the customs were written down, and in an uncritical age, their origin not being
known, they were naturally ascribed to God by the priests. Then came
the Greeks with their original belief in a mythical lawgiver who had
molded the older customs, supposed to come from God, to suit later
conditions. The absurdity of amending the divine law of Omniscience
never occurred to any one. At last came Solon at Athens, an actual lawgiver, with laws of his own devising. Then came the assembly at Athens,
where laws could be passed by a town meeting vote. The whole body of
citizens made the law. The Romans followed with the whole body of citizens making the laws, but they compromised by recognizing as law a
resolution of the whole body of citizens or a resolution of the plebs or
for some purposes an ordinance of the Senate. The emperors claimed

that this legislative power of the people was conferred upon them by the people and they alone legislated. Shorn of misleading terms, legislation is simply an act to show acceptance of law by the community, just as this acceptance was formerly shown before legislation by the universal adoption of the custom.

In the Dark Ages, in the matter of conflicting laws, the doctrine was that law to be binding upon the community must have been accepted by the members of the community. This acceptance was shown either by the act of the king and his council or by the decisions of the courts. Now when the English Parliament came into being the fact and the theory was that representatives of boroughs and shires were added to bind the whole body of the people by their acceptance of the enactment as law. It is directly contrary to the truth that law is something imposed by the legislative body upon the people. Acceptance has always been the theory and the fact. No rule of law was ever successful or ever endured unless it received practical general acceptance among the whole body of the people, for the simple reason that universal human experience has demonstrated that a rule of law not accepted by any considerable portion of the people can never be enforced. The history of the law is strewn and will continue to be strewn by just such palpable wrecks of laws not enforced and not enforceable.

Whatever the means by which law is recognized, whether it be by legislative enactments, by decisions of courts, by rescripts of rulers, law is in fact law only when it is cheerfully accepted and gladly obeyed by the great mass of the social body. Acceptance by the community is needed to breathe life into the edict of the harshest despot. As the Roman emperors recognized, the government is the creation of the law. A social community antedates any kind of government. No government ever made law in the sense of creating substantive legal rights and correlative duties. Government may superficially appear to make law as Hobbes and Austin mistakenly supposed, but it is the acceptance of the rules by society that makes laws and government.

But this so-called power of legislation which is in fact the delegated representative power of acceptance, tends to become exclusive. History uniformly shows that a legislative body invariably tends to magnify its own importance, because personal responsibility in such a body can usually be avoided. The tendency is to insist that all changes in the law must be authorized by the legislative body. Parliament grew in power and could insist upon its power, because the king always needed money, for half the time dynastic reasons impelled the English kings to seek a domain on the Continent. Parliament granted money in return for an extension of its own power. The immediate result of Simon de Montfort's parliamentary device, adopted by Edward I, was a great mass of remedial statutes, mainly in the way of making the law by enactment, what it had already become by the medium of court decisions, declaring the law. For our purposes the matter to be noticed is the constant attempts by the legislature to bolster up or to tinker this device of a jury trial, when some discretion should have been exercised regarding the cases to which it was applied.

Before entering upon this matter certain modifying facts should be stated. There had grown up a feeling against priestly judges. It arose from a number of things. The king naturally distrusted judges who looked across the sea to the papal power, although as a matter of fact the priestly judges in the king's court never were wanting in their duty to the secular power. The lay lawyers naturally distrusted judges who were educated in the system of the civil law of which the lay lawyer knew little. The common lawyers were instituting their own schools of instruction in the law. Latin as the language of the courts was gone, although the clerks still wrote the record in Latin. Bracton's great treatise was epitomized in Norman French and forgotten. Norman French was the language of the courts and all the arguments over pleadings were in that tongue. English was never used except possibly to a small extent at the assizes. The fact was that there was no English tongue. There were only barbarous, uncouth dialects. The Northern man could not understand the Southern man and the Middle English was practical Greek to both of the other main dialects. The statutes of Parliament were in Norman French. The poverty of the vocabulary of these English dialects confined their use to the most ignorant people. Steadily, however, among the mass of the people was growing an improved speech compounded of Norman and English.

In the meantime the members of the legal professional class became narrower and narrower in their line of ideas. The Pope forbade any priest to sit in the king's courts and the king forbade the teaching of the civil law in England. England began her legal insularity, from which it took ages for her to recover. The kind of law made by a narrow-minded, hidebound class of lawyers of this kind is sure to be tough and rigid law. Law of all pursuits needs the illumination of general knowledge, but this by their environment was denied to the common lawyers. The Inns of Court, where the law was taught, knew nothing but their own system. While the lawyers were acute and learned in this system, they were ignorant of all others. The scholar Erasmus accurately described them as "a learned class of very ignorant men."

Another matter not much noticed historically was the action of the ecclesiastical courts in creating a prejudice against any court that did not use a jury. To the common ordinary citizen these courts Christian were a great nuisance. They pried into private affairs; they exposed the neighborhood scandals, its fornicators and adulterers, always numerous; they interfered with popular pleasures, all for the purpose of imposing petty fines upon delinquents, or penances that wearied the people. They inspired both fear and irritation in many ways. The priest who intervened to smooth the path of some cowering wretch into the next world, often aroused the animosity of the family by appropriating through a deathbed will some of the goods that the family considered as belonging to them. The great possessions of abbeys, monasteries, and priories, gained from private munificence, aroused the cupidity of both people and rulers. The secular power tried to prohibit such gifts to churches. The priest, secure in his courts and their system of law, could be restrained only by writs of prohibition out of the common law courts. Long before, Glanville had warned the priests: "You priests look only to Rome, and Rome will one day undo you." When any question arose as to a marriage and the legitimacy of a child, the matter was referred to the court Christian. Appeals from the decisions of the church courts went to Rome and they were encouraged. Ecclesiastical lawyers were required to be hired in all courts Christian. A litigant over such questions as marriage to be decided in those Christian courts was thoroughly fleeced.

There is a tale in a case before the King's Council that shows how far the churchmen would go. A great noble, John de Warrenne, Earl of Surrey, had had some irregular connection with a woman out in Norfolk. The facts were such that the Church law held that the woman was the wife of the Earl of Surrey. That troubled him not at all. He married at court a niece of the Queen, wife of Edward II, the "she wolf of France," who afterwards with her paramour Mortimer did to death Edward II. The discarded concubine of John de Warrenne out in Norfolk brought an action in the local Archdeacon's court. That worthy issued his writ commanding the Queen's niece to appear in Norfolk and be fined for living in adultery with John de Warrenne. A shambling, rank-smelling, sandaled priest, the court's summoner, took the writ and made his way to London and into the Palace at Westminster. He managed in some way to get into the royal apartments and served his writ on the Queen's niece in the presence of the Queen. This was not only laughable in its assurance, but a gross breach of all the regalian proprieties. There was a terrific explosion. The Queen shrieked with indignation. The summoner was thoroughly kicked and cuffed and lodged in jail. It is needless to say that nothing came of the Archdeacon's writ, but the case gives an idea of what a priest would undertake with God's power and the Church behind him. If the ecclesiastical court would attempt this sort of proceeding against the Queen's niece and one of the greatest nobles in England, what would it not do to an ordinary citizen? It is nothing to the purpose that the Puritans, when they got into power, were a worse, and the same kind of, nuisance.

Yet at the same time the long roll of the priestly judges who for two hundred years manned the king's courts, steadily maintained the prerogatives of secular government. They were a very capable set of men and sound lawyers. They were as far removed as possible from the clerics in the courts Christian. They made the English common law in the days before it fell from its high estate, and laid its foundations in accordance with the best legal thought of the times. For centuries longer the priestly judges continued in the chancery courts.

Another general idea that helped the growth of the jury was the rooted distrust of witnesses among English lawyers and judges. This distrust was well founded. The barbarian, of course, is not truthful. The idea that he is, is cherished only by the dullest people. The savage tells what he sees; he is not capable of invention, but not so the barbarian. Truth-telling is the result of a long training from generation to generation. Trade, commerce, and business assist in making men truthful, but the simple, raw human being is not truthful any more than the average child is truthful. The spectacle of wager of law had confirmed every lawyer in the opinion that the witnesses a litigant produces are produced because they are ready to commit perjury. Compurgators were always in demand and the supply was equal to the demand. The suit witnesses with which a plaintiff appeared were hardened swearers. It was the way in which they made a living, and "How can a man be wrong in making a living?" is even the modern inquiry of the grafting official. It was supposed in that simple time that a witness produced by a party was bound to prevaricate for him. Witnesses to a document, of course, were different. They had made a record by witnessing a legal act, and forgery was rare, except among those accomplished penmen who forged ancient deeds to support the titles of monasteries, abbeys, or bishops. The idea of the worthlessness of testimony became ingrained in the common lawyers.

Chief Justice Fortescue, writing his Praise of England's Law, points out as one of the advantages of the English jury trial in determining questions of fact over the civil law's method by witnesses, and where two witnesses to a fact are sufficient, that any litigant can find two men who are ready for fear or favor to go counter to the truth in anything. "Who then can live secure in property or person under such law which gives such aid to anyone who would harm him?" He shows that under the civil law justice must often fail for lack of witnesses. Under the English law, he says, the witnesses, the jury, must be twelve, chosen by a duly sworn public official, from among men of property of the vicinage where the controversy arises, men who are indifferent between the parties, subject to challenge and acting under oath. These were the ideas of the profession and they had their effect.

But the fact was and it ought to have been seen, if men are not truthful as witnesses they will not be truthful as witness jurors. This jury was a body finally to pass upon the facts. The names of its members could be ascertained. Any one could get at them, could go to them and talk about the case. Each party would scan the jury, investigate closely who each juryman was, how he could be reached, what persons controlled him, to whom he owed money, from whom he expected favors. Each man on the jury would be subjected to influence or threats or offered inducements or deceived. Barefaced bribery would certainly be used wherever possible. We know now after long experience that such a method of the ascertainment of facts by a jury, wholly uncontrolled, was almost as great a stupidity as wager of law.

These jurors were the only witnesses. They might talk with people out of court in order to gain knowledge of the matter. They might get information out of court as they pleased, and they could not be questioned as to how they came by their knowledge. But the juror must not express his verdict by stating his opinion before the verdict. It is apparent that such a trial was the ascertainment of the general idea of some particular small community where twelve men were selected to give the opinion of the community. This fact explains the insistence on the importance of the venue and of a jury of the vicinage. Theoretically it would be granted that such a body of men, who were even scrupulously honest men, when so acting must be left free to ascertain the truth in their own way, without influence, favor, affection, or any reward or the promise or the hope thereof.

This conception of the jury as mere witnesses was buttressed by a principle which for years prevented the jury from hearing evidence or the offering of evidence in court. One who voluntarily testified to the jury in a case where he was not in privity with a party or related to him or bound to aid him in some way was guilty of the crime of maintenance. If a man was ordered by the court to testify it was justifiable maintenance. But if he came to testify of his own accord it was culpable maintenance. If the jurors came to a man where he lived, seeking information, and he gave it, it was lawfully done, but if he went to the jurors and tried to inform them, he would be punished for maintenance. A party could not obtain nor have compulsory process for witnesses. He could not expect to get witnesses except through fear or money. In trying to comprehend this system one must try to realize that the theory was that the jurors witnessed to a verdict rendered on their own knowledge. There were severe laws against champerty, which was a case of a third party taking a monetary interest in the action, and against embracery, which was a sort of maintaining and supporting a litigant in a lawsuit. It is plain that all this law existed for the purpose of the jury being saved from improper influences. The only way that occurred to this age was to make the party fight his own case by his own exertions, with his lawyer's aid.

Solon at Athens thought that the highest benefit of his laws was the provision that any citizen could be assisted by another citizen in obtaining his rights. But the theory of the common law was the barbaric idea that if one was not himself strong enough to obtain his rights, he was not entitled to them. It was a common thing to give some influential person an interest to gain an advantage or protection. This was a feudal idea. Alice Perrers, the old king's mistress, took an interest in many lawsuits. It is needless to say that the lady whom the king delighted to honor was an influential litigant. She seems to have taken powers of attorney to appear for litigants. Of cases in chancery there is a whole series of appeals to the chancellor to remedy the wrongs done through the juries in courts of law by a notorious maintainer, embracer, and champertist, who rode roughshod over the law, intimidating parties and juries. The obvious solution was to create a better tribunal than a venal and cowardly jury, but in legislation the proper and obvious thing is rarely done. A statute in its preamble recited that "great, fearless and shameless perjury horribly continues and increases daily among the common jurors of the realm." Fresh and stronger statutes against champerty and maintenance were passed. The attainting jury was extended to every kind of lawsuit, but yet the shameless conduct of the jurors continued.

The courts kept on making every case a jury case. In their desire to attain this result, they gave up all the actions based on writs where a jury could not be used. At the same time the judges were trying to get away from wager of law. Parliament, with the dense ignorance characteristic of the ordinary legislative body, kept at work trying to remedy the system of jury trial. Parliament knew that something was wrong, and with some faint idea that it might be the peculiar language used by the

lawyers, passed a statute in 1362 which recited that "the laws, customs
and statutes of this realm are not commonly known in the realm because
they are pleaded, shewed and judged in the French tongue, which is
much unknown in the realm, so that the people which do implead or be
impleaded in the king's courts and in the courts of others, have no
knowledge or understanding of that which is said for them or against
them, by their serjeants or other pleaders." The statute enacted that all
pleas pleaded in the king's courts or in any other courts "shall be
pleaded, shewed, defended, answered, debated and judged in the
English tongue." This statute remained a dead letter. The lawyers
calmly disregarded it. The arguments and opinions continued for more
than a hundred and forty years to be made in the law French. The fact
was that in the crude English dialects the lawyers could not express the
legal terms nor make themselves understood. The statute asked the impossible, just as many another statute has demanded the impossible of
men. Other statutes of various kinds were passed, but without avail.
Litigants were constantly trying to get away from the jury by taking their
cases into the chancery courts.

But after a while the judges of the common law courts were finding
that they were losing business. Fees and emoluments were sacred things.
They touched the pocket. The chancellor's court was taking away a large
part of the ordinary law business. If a man had a contract not in writing
under seal, the common law court would not listen to his case, unless
perchance it was money due for a sale of personal property. If a seller
sued in the common law court, he would bring an action of debt. If the
purchaser sued, he would bring an action of debt alleging the detention
of the personal property sold. In either case the common law court must
listen to the manufactured defense of wager of law. But either party
could go into the chancery court and allege the bargain of sale and say
that he could not get justice in the law court, because the defendant
would be allowed to wage his law. The chancellor would grant relief on
testimony taken.

The common law judges then as now were showing their ignorance of
commercial law. If a foreign merchant had received a promissory note
payable to order or to bearer and had transferred it, the common law

judges knew nothing of the law merchant, which made the note negotiable, and they would allow the defendant to defend, regardless of the rule of the law merchant, with the usual delays from term to term, and a jury of the vicinage or a wager of law. A foreigner was thus practically denied justice. The chancellor, if applied to, would say that the common law did not govern, that the case was under the law of nations, that his court was always open and that continuances could not be given. Imagine a common lawyer looking through his list of writs to find one to suit a transaction like that shown in the Greek lawsuit in a former chapter. In 1287 Thomas Loredano, of the great banking family at Venice, sent to England by Nicoleto Basadona 10,000 pounds of sugar and 1,000 pounds of candy and money, all amounting to 3580 livres. Nicoleto sold the goods in London and then went to St. Botolph's and invested all the money in wool, which he shipped on two sailing vessels to Bruges. Suppose that such a case were submitted to a jury which heard no evidence. Again, if a writing had been made which did not in terms run against the maker of the contract and his heirs and executors, the executors could not be sued in the common law court. If on the other hand the executors of a party desired to sue and the contract did not run to such executors, the common law court gave no remedy. These are but a few instances of the failure of the common law courts which had an effect on the law. Even to-day contracts are drawn between parties and specifically worded to bind the executors and assigns, wholly without any necessity. This shows the age-old tendency of human beings to rely on habit and not on thinking.

In course of time by statute or by change of rule such matters would be remedied, but in the meantime the common law bar saw business transferred to the bar of the chancery courts and the judges saw fees and emoluments lost to them. In their slow, ponderous, and inept way, they began to invent new forms of action using legal fictions by which the action of trespass, where wager of law could not be pleaded, was extended to cover any kind of contract written or unwritten, sealed or unsealed, and to cover almost any kind of wrong. But still the device of a jury remained. Each jury out of its own knowledge, acquired out of court in all sorts of ways, settled the facts.

The common law judges saw the chancery court conducting its proceedings in the English tongue. That language was now developing so
that it could be used by a civilized kind of people. Witnesses, generally
speaking, would have been impossible before a jury until the latter part
of the fifteenth century. But it was no longer the case that the lawyers
could be kept silent before the jury. By 1470 not only the record in the
case was read and explained to the jury, and the counsel for either party
stated to the jury what he desired to bring before them, but the jury, as
Fortescue says, already knew all that the witnesses could tell them, and
they knew all about the credibility and veracity of the witnesses. It must
be remembered that the jury investigated and rendered their verdict at
the peril of being attainted and heavily fined, if a jury of twenty-four
knights said that their verdict was wrong. When we consider that there
was no compulsory process for witnesses, and that the savage laws
against maintenance intimidated possible witnesses, it must be apparent
that the conception of a trial on evidence of witnesses adduced in open
court was not a likely solution to the narrow-minded common lawyers.
So the juries were left to do their worst, for a time, until the pressure to
hear witnesses in court would become irresistible.

The strange spectacle was presented in England that in a criminal
trial the Crown could adduce witnesses, and it long remained the law
that an accused person could not put in evidence to show his innocence.
In the chancery court the only method of trial was by witnesses whose
testimony was written down. Upon it the chancery court acted. The proceedings in the chancery courts were in the English tongue soon after
1435, and the pleadings were in that language. Naturally, litigants sought
a court where they could have some comprehension of what was going
on and where their witnesses would be heard. These influences working
on the common law judges and lawyers at last produced a situation
where the jury could hear in court the evidence of witnesses. As soon as
witnesses began to be heard, the jury would be afraid to find against the
testimony, because an attainting jury hearing the evidence would be sure
to find them guilty of a false verdict and they would be heavily fined.
The thought of fining jurors was pleasant to the king's officers, since
fines swelled the royal exchequer.

But this change threw out of balance the method of correcting a false verdict. The attainting jury to correct a wrong verdict became unmanageable. The trouble was that as soon as evidence was adduced before a jury, it tended to become a judicial body deciding upon the evidence adduced, while its function as a witnessing body out of its own knowledge was no longer being performed. There was no possible compromise. The jury performing a judicial function required strict supervision by the court. Especially it must make no independent, uncontrolled investigations of its own out of court, but confine itself to the evidence adduced in court. Yet the only method of reviewing the verdict was by another attainting jury of twenty-four. The one jury might have correctly acted upon the evidence which it had, while the attainting jury might act upon entirely different evidence.

This became evident even to the common lawyers. The entering wedge was shown by a ruling that a jury could not be attainted for relying upon the witnesses to a supposed deed. Then came a ruling that if in an attaint trial a party gave in a record which had not been shown to the jury being tried, it would be a good defense for the jury on trial for false verdict to say that this record was not shown to it. It is apparent that the jury on trial is no longer being tried to ascertain whether its verdict was in fact false, but is being tried as a judicial body to ascertain whether it acted properly on the evidence before it. The staple of litigation has changed to the minds of men. Life was no longer so simple as before. Commerce and trade, the abolition of villeinage, the growth of towns and cities, had made life more complicated. No longer was litigation concerned with matters that all the neighbors knew, and of which the jury must speak truly at its peril. Yet the neighbors put on the jury must speak truly at their peril in passing upon evidence given to them. It is their mental processes that are now being tried.

The judges could not hold a jury guilty of a false oath when they had seen those jurors listening to evidence and trying in their wooden way to arrive at the truth. The courts soon held that the plaintiff on the attaint trial could not give in evidence any fact that he did not present to the jury on trial. He was not permitted to bring forward additional witnesses, yet the members of the jury defending themselves could offer more evidence than was given to them, and thus show that their verdict was correct, for, perchance, a judge would reason, some of the jury had heard such additional evidence out of court and had acted upon it. The law is generally more practical than logical. Judges were now telling the attainting jury to look to what was the evidence on the first trial given to the jury now on trial, and if that evidence was sufficient, it made no difference what the truth was. But this rule butchered the injured litigant. He had the right to insist that he ought not to be robbed by a verdict manifestly false, and he pointed to the oath administered to the attainting jury that they would find the truth as to the issue. The judges simply said in effect that the oath was immaterial. To them ultimate justice was not the question.

Common sense ought to have suggested that the attainting jury should find, first, was the verdict true or false? Second, if they found it to be false, they should find whether it was arrived at reasonably by the jury. If the attainting jury said that it was false and not arrived at reasonably, the judgment would be reversed and the jury fined, but if it answered that the verdict was false but reasonably arrived at, the judgment would be reversed but the jury would not be fined. Why this obvious solution did not occur to the judges seems inexplicable.

But such a solution as the one suggested did not occur to common law judges, and at last it came about that the gentlemen (the knights) on the attainting jury would not meet "to slander and deface the honest yeomen, their neighbors" on the first jury, and if they did meet more "gladlier" would they confirm the first verdict. An actual trial may show the situation more plainly.

A jury had found a general verdict which in fact disregarded a will of lands. A will of lands was a new thing. It had just been made possible by the Statute of Wills. It was sought to attaint this verdict. The jury had held the will to be invalid. The court ruled that the plaintiff in the attaint trial could not give more in evidence than he adduced before the jury on trial, but that the defendants in the attaint could give more evidence than was given at the former trial. The court observed that it would be wise to have all the evidence written. The judge had learned so much at least from the chancery courts. But, the judge continued, since the evidence is not preserved, the court always, in an attaint case, examines the witnesses upon oath to ascertain whether they gave the same evidence upon the former trial.

The court then stated what the charge was and the evidence and admonished the jury to look to the evidence which had been given to the first jury. He affirmed it as law that if that evidence was full and clear, although false in fact, and although the truth was otherwise, still the attainting jurors ought not to regard that fact, but ought conscientiously to consider what they themselves would have done upon the same good evidence that the first jury had. The justice sagely added in regard to evidence that "men are natural born liars and not angels." Perhaps the judge was thinking of the story centuries old of the Pope who saw on the streets at Rome some fine-looking yellow-haired Anglo-Saxons. He was told that they were Angli (Angles) and replied, "Non Angli, sed angeli" (Not Angles, but angels). In the case above the judge's witticism would have been more in point had he said that witnesses are "non angeli, sed Angli" (not angels, but English).

While these common lawyers were showing themselves so stubborn in clinging to their antiquated system, they were pliable enough when there was a royal demand for particular law. Under Edward I, a statute was passed requiring land to descend according to the form of the deed. If land was deeded to a man and the heirs of his body, that land could never be deeded by any one, as long as heirs of the body of the grantee existed. When those heirs ceased the old deed showed where the land would go. No new deed was necessary or could be made. The judges had evolved this fee tail which, under a deed to a man and the heirs of his body, allowed the man to own land during his life, but he could not alienate it as against the heir in tail and after death the property was in no way responsible for the debts of him who had owned it in life. This was done because of the royal policy of making land practically inalienable so that the king could always be certain of realizing the different taxes upon it. But as time passed on it became the royal policy to make land readily alienable. The Yorkists in the Wars of the Roses were appropriating the lands of the defeated Lancastrians and there was a growing demand that in some way these entailed estates of older days should be made subject to the fines, forfeitures, and exactions laid upon the defeated. The estate tail, if forfeited, merely caused the reversioner or remainder-man after the estate tail to take the land. The judges found no difficulty in devising a form of fictitious lawsuit that would bar the estate tail and the reversion in fee or the remainder in fee as the case might be, without any chance to the reversioner or remainder-man to be heard. This was confiscation of an estate in land and purely confiscation. Land again became alienable in England, by the mere device of a fictitious suit called a common recovery. These judges were resourceful enough when the royal policy of the Yorkist or Tudor sovereigns was in question. To give a simpler method of confiscation the Statute of Fines was passed for the use of a fictitious agreement in court.

In the middle of the fourteenth century a dire pestilence called the Black Death entirely revolutionized the economic condition of England. At that time the condition of serfdom among the laboring population still remained. The reason why serfdom existed and had continued was the simple fact that there was no money to pay laborers; and in return for mere support or for land and its products the laborer gave his services. The various court rolls of manors showed what these services were. The Black Death destroyed more than half these laborers. The demand for labor in the towns was a demand for paid labor. If a serf could reach a town and live there for a year, he would become under the law a free man. His menial services would be at an end. After the Black Death the laborers began leaving their homes to obtain paid wages. The landowners pursued them with writs and lawyers. In about forty years the crisis came to a head. The former serfs rose in insurrection. Out in the country they killed Lord Chief Justice Cavendish. In London the chancellor, Archbishop Sudbury, was murdered. The Inns of Court were rifled and their records destroyed. The cry went up to kill all the lawyers. This insurrection was put down with ruthless cruelty, and a series of drastic statutes began to regulate the relations of employer and employee. Wages were fixed by law. Men could be committed for refusing to work. Serfdom was abolished in form but the fact continued. At last a sort of compromise was agreed upon. Wages must be paid. Employment was to be for not less than a year. Masters could not dismiss their employees, nor could the employees leave service, without good cause. At the same time, drastic laws were passed against combinations of workmen. The chancellor was given by law a jurisdiction that he was already exercising, to repress confederacies and conspiracies to raise wages. The wages of artisans were fixed by justices of the peace. Attempts were made by law to prevent laborers from leaving their parishes, but like all such laws the statutes were failures. The social unrest contributed its part to the civil war in the fifteenth century.[2]

The political development of England, which was proceeding in an orderly way, was interrupted in the fifteenth century by the Wars of the Roses. During these troubled times and their lawlessness, the jury system broke down completely. It is probable that an honest jury verdict in England was rare in those times. There was a time when the law courts were almost deserted, and it looked as if the common law with its sacred institution of the jury was about to pass away. The Court of Star Chamber was devised after the Wars of the Roses to punish the various offenses of parties and juries that were so common in the courts.

But great changes were about this time consummated. First of all the English language came into use in the courts, and the Norman-French Year Book reports ceased. Next a jury trial from causes stated above became a trial before the jurors sitting as a judicial body and hearing evidence. As soon as these results were reached the vocation of the lawyer in the trial of a case as we understand it really began. The whole type of trial changed. The dawning of the Renaissance in England at this time had an effect even upon the lawyers. They became more liberal-minded as they became more liberally educated and as they were released from their bondage to the Anglo-Norman tongue, which had become a barbarous jargon that had lost all pretense of being a genuine language. Naturally lawyers began to look back over the law. Bracton was redis-

2. These legislative efforts were known collectively as the Statutes of Labourers. Still an informative study of these early efforts to regulate wages and working conditions is Bertha H. Putnam, *The Enforcement of the Statutes of Labourers in the First Decade After the Black Death* (1908; reprint, New York: Columbia University Press, 1970).—C. J. R., Jr.

covered. Some knowledge of the Roman and canon law was creeping into the common law bar. The common law took on a new lease of life. The Inns of Court became imbued with new life. The same spirit that was making the spacious age of Elizabeth was rife in the Inns. Gorgeous entertainments and revels, with the production of masques and plays, took away some of the pedantry of the Inns.

The great expansion in national life, increasing trade and commerce, brought the usual results. England began to found her empire of the seas and her colonies. It was impossible that the common lawyers should remain the narrow-minded class that they had been. The new learning of the Renaissance continued to spread. The great Elizabethan age in literature was at hand. The new language compounded of English and French was proving itself capable of complete expression. It was impossible that lawyers should not catch some of the spirit of the times. Judges were now writing elaborate opinions and in an uncritical age such a judge as Catline found no restraint. He is stating the effect of the Statute of Fines as a statute of repose. In Plowden's Reports he is thus reported:

And Catline likened the fine [a concord made and entered as a court record] under this act to Janus, who, he said, was Noah, but the Romans occasionally called him Janus and used to picture him with two faces, one looking backwards, in respect that he had seen the former world which was lost by the flood, and the other looking forwards, in respect that he had begun a new world commencing at the flood, and proceeding from thence forwards, from which they call him Janus *bifrons* (two faced) and they paint him with a key in his hand, signifying by this key his power by his generation to renew the world. So here this act creates a flood, by which all former right before the flood shall be submerged by non-claim, for non-claim is the flood, and the fine produces a new generation, which is the new right, for the fine makes a new right, and is the beginning of a new world which proceeds from the fine forwards.

Thus Catline stunned the court and the serjeants. Where he obtained his Romans who had heard of Noah, we cannot even conjecture; but a small matter like this was nothing to Catline and the hearers believed this monstrous history. On the strength of his own name alone, he claimed as an ancestor Lucius Sergius Catilina, the Roman conspirator, from whom no one who had read Cicero's orations against Catiline ought to desire to be descended. One who reads the prefaces to Coke's Institutes can gain some idea of the Stygian ignorance of the ordinary lawyer of those times as to historical matters, for Coke was rated as preternaturally learned. Imagine a practising barrister who came into the chancery court seeking protection against a prior. He alleged that he had been of counsel against the prior and now the latter was bewitching him to the extent that he had fallen and broken his leg. The chancellor was to enjoin the supernatural.

Sometime between 1500 and 1560 came in another great change in the face of the law. The old system of oral pleading before the court was changed to the present system of putting in written pleading. After the writ was served, the plaintiff now put in his written declaration. The defendant put in his written pleading to answer the declaration. If he desired to object to the declaration as not stating facts sufficient to make in law a good cause of action, he filed the totally new thing called a demurrer which Coke thought had been in use for ages. If he wished to deny the facts pleaded, he put in a written plea. If he pleaded some new matter, the plaintiff replied with a replication. The fact is apparent that this new sort of pleading was due to two causes. The one was the insistence by lawyers that the pleadings should be as they wished them and not as the judges should on oral discussion decide they ought to be, and the lawyers were not prepared to trust the clerks to write out the pleadings as settled upon oral discussion. The other reason was that paper had come into use and the cost of vellum was no longer to be encountered. In some ways paper with its cheapness has been a great curse to the law, but it was and is nothing compared to the incubus of the typewriter and dictation.

This revolution in the method of pleading was brought about quietly. No one can tell the time when it was made. The change was exceedingly unfortunate. The system was of iron. A variance between the declaration and the proof was fatal. The process of stating the case in all possible ways in different counts began. The old rule of only one plea as a defense was continued. The new system had to be tinkered by acts of Parliament, after a great deal of injustice was perpetrated. Several defenses had to be allowed and there began the system of special pleading.

The common law had never cared much about justice and now it cared not at all. Pleadings at law were not required to be verified by oath. Under the science of special pleading, so called, if any truth got into a plea it was by accident, not design. Continual statutes of amendments were required to be passed.

Under the Tudors the religious fight began. The confiscations of the vast church property at the English Reformation made a new distribution of wealth. The religious struggle, as always, let loose the savageries of fanaticism. Men were burned at the stake for beliefs. More, the Lord Chancellor, and Bishop Fisher were beheaded over a mere question of belief. More's was a sad case. He stated that he did not believe that the law could make the king head of the English Church. This was done on the solemn assurance of King Henry that he desired this simply for his own satisfaction. More was immediately tried and brought to the block. Edmund Plowden, the greatest lawyer in England, far more of a man and a much finer lawyer than Coke, never became a serjeant or even more than an apprentice, because he was a Roman Catholic. He was offered the chancellorship if he would abjure. Elizabeth, without any right whatever, caused the next heir to the crown, Mary, Queen of Scots, to be put to death because she would be a Roman Catholic queen. Henry VIII had confiscated the great landed possessions of the religious establishments and distributed the property to make his needy and perfectly receptive adherents sound on the religious question. When Mary, his daughter, a Roman Catholic, came to the throne, Protestant after Protestant was burned at the stake.

It was hard upon the judges, who were required to change their religion as the sovereign changed. One poor man was so troubled at changing his faith that he committed suicide. His death raised a very novel legal question as to when the act of suicide was complete. To commit suicide was to commit a felony. Every felon forfeited his goods, and it was ingeniously argued that the act of suicide was not complete until his death and that hence there was no forfeiture. But the court held otherwise in an opinion that was so absurdly pedantic that it aroused much laughter around the town and some time afterward Shakespeare, who had picked up considerable law somewhere, parodied the discussion

Thomas More (1478–1535), English statesman and
author beheaded by Henry VIII for religious convictions

neatly in the gravediggers scene in the fifth act of *Hamlet*. Dogberry, who so yearned to be writ down an ass, must be a travesty on a certain type of lawyer.

A further important development in English law was the Statute of Wills, noticed above, which gave to every landowner the right to make a will of his lands. As soon as this statute was passed the lawyers began to experiment with it. Prior to this statute, the only way in which the descent of land could be controlled was by a deed, and under that law it was impossible to make an estate in fee simple or fee tail shift by being cut short after it once took effect as a vested estate. But the common lawyers had learned a lesson and in wills they permitted all sorts of conditional limitations under the name of executory devises. As usual a thing good in itself was rapidly run into the ground and a new rule had to be invented to save the alienability of land. The rule devised was that a conditional limitation must take effect within the period of lives in being and twenty-one years thereafter, allowing nine months more for a posthumous child.

In the troubled times in England there had been invented a kind of deed which vested title in one to the use of another. The common lawyers with their imperviousness to ideas, simply refused to recognize these uses. Thereupon the chancery courts zealously seized upon them and protected, and compelled the performance of, the use. The common lawyers, seeing this rich source of litigation lost to them, refused to change their rule of non-recognition, but went to a subservient Parliament and caused the Statute of Uses to be passed. This statute simply turned the estate to the use of another into an actual vested legal estate in that other. The chancery bar, nothing daunted, drove over the common lawyers, by inventing a grant of land upon a trust which was the use in a new form, and brought back the whole subject to the chancery court by means of the trust. The common lawyers could do nothing and the trust has remained unto this day in both real and personal property.

The chancery court at last broke the hearts of the common law bar by inventing a new jurisdiction which was a fell blow to the jury system and the right of the common law courts to do injustice. The attaint had now become unworkable. There was no way to review the verdict of a jury, but the chancellor, when appealed to by a litigant who had lost in the law court by a fraud practised upon him, or as the result of an inadvertence excusable in itself, or by his failure to produce evidence which would show the verdict and judgment to be wrong, and where the failure was not the fault of the losing party, would force a new trial in the law court by the simple device of enjoining the enforcement of the judgment and thus compelling the winning party to agree to a new trial. The chancery court even went further and held that a good equitable defense, which the law courts would not recognize, was a sufficient ground for enjoining a judgment.

The chancellor did not say that the use of perjured evidence in the law court was a fraud sufficient to justify an injunction. That would be simply to say that the chancellor would try the case on the same evidence as had been given and decide it otherwise. The fraud must be some fraud practised by which the losing party was prevented from presenting his case or having a hearing. The newly discovered evidence for a new trial, the chancellor wisely held must be evidence which, if true, would cause a different result in the law trial. Forced in this way, the common law courts first attempted to overrule the chancery court. Coke was the leader of the common lawyers in this movement. When defeated they finally decided that they would now add to the grounds for setting aside a verdict, such as misconduct of the jury, a form of new trial that was already in existence, a further ground of newly discovered evidence. But the chancery courts held to their jurisdiction by holding that a power once in the chancery court could not be taken away by the law court being granted or assuming the same power.

The common law, by the year 1600, had been reorganized. The general distinction between law and equity had been established. The modification of the action of trespass, which had gained practically the wide meaning of any wrongful infringement of another's right, was now developed. A great deal of the old medieval worn-out lumber had been thrown overboard. The system of jury trial had started on its new career, where the jury was a judicial body hearing evidence and making its verdict from the evidence. Those who, like Coke, pretended to know what the old law had been, were making the most palpable mistakes. The language of the law being changed, the Anglo-Norman language was fast being forgotten. As is usual under such circumstances, there was now a demand for a restatement of the law, so that the knowledge of law would be easier of acquirement. The tendency of the human being to shirk hard work is strongly developed in the lawyer. Bacon was proposing the application of the method of the Justinianean compilation to the mass of English law.

But everything was thrown into confusion when the Stuart kings were called upon to expiate the tyrannical sins of the Tudor Henry VIII, Mary, and Elizabeth. Those sovereigns had found the jury system a great help to arbitrary government and Parliament had been pleasantly subservient. But now juries and Parliaments were proving rebellious. The bitterness of religious controversy filled the air. Narrow creeds fanatically held by narrow-minded men are dangerous exactly in proportion to the honesty and sincerity of the believers in them. The Anglicans resented the Puritans and both hated the Presbyterians. The Stuart kings and the Divine Right of Kings people were shocked to find that the conduct of a Henry VIII or Elizabeth would no longer be endured.

The Roman Catholic church which had supported secular government as long as secular government supported it, was now persecuted, and its skilled controversialists were making an absurd spectacle of the kingly divine right to misrule. Parliaments and juries could no longer be trusted. The king's ministers were being called to a bloody reckoning. Coke burrowed into the old law and found the bill of attainder to supplement the impeachment. By the bill of attainder the obnoxious person could be doomed to death without taking any risk with a jury. In each case Parliament made its own law for the case, flouted the idea that an act could not be made a crime after the alleged criminal act had taken place, and simply voted that a man should be executed. The Puritans got into control and Strafford went to the block. A successful Puritan general ruled England, treating with contempt Magna Charta and parliamentary government, acting in a far more arbitrary fashion than any English king had ever dared to attempt. The Stuarts had begun the policy of removing judges. Now the Puritans went much further and supposedly subservient Puritans filled the bench. Cromwell thought that the Lord had given him the power to tell Sir Matthew Hale how to decide a case.

When the Stuarts came back the same course was continued. James II said to his Chief Justice that he intended to find for judges twelve lawyers of his own opinion. The Chief Justice replied that he might find twelve judges of his opinion, but twelve lawyers never. The abortive rebellion of the cowardly Monmouth gave an opportunity for Jeffreys to show what subservient juries could accomplish, but another jury in the case of the Seven Bishops baffled the king's judges and lawyers. The country rose against an arbitrary Roman Catholic king and the Revolution of 1688 brought relief to the law. The net result for the law was a great glorification of the jury system and a fixed tenure for the judges. With this halo of glory around it, the jury system came to America, where it was to be called the bulwark of our liberties.

Some weighty matters in the law during the Tudor and Stuart period ought to be noted. They are chiefly concerned with the absorption by the common law of certain principles of the Roman law. The action of assumpsit called trespass on the case on promises had been developed to the extent that it lay on any kind of contract or contractual undertaking, written or unwritten, sealed or unsealed, for a fixed amount of money or for damages indefinite in amount to be fixed by the evidence, or, as the lawyers say, for unliquidated damages. To this action was applied the Roman law of consideration, for after all that can be said, the English doctrine of the consideration for a contract is the Roman conception. Hence the various categories of consideration in Roman law, the doing of an act for a promise, the giving of one thing for another, and the making of a promise for another promise, came into the English law.

But the stubbornness of the common lawyer and his imperviousness to ideas were again apparent in many matters. One illustrative case is what is called in the old books, accord and satisfaction. If two men had a contract under seal, that contract could be modified or changed only by another contract under seal. As to a sealed contract, no question of consideration could arise, since the seal imported a consideration. If the contract was not under seal, the common law had recognized a debt arising from it, only when one party had parted with something of value to the other party. A mere promise was not recognized and a promise of the one party in consideration for the promise of the other party was then unthinkable. Hence, if one man owed another a debt, a fixed sum of

money, an agreement to pay and to accept a less sum was wholly nugatory. Originally at the common law an action for unliquidated damages
on an unsealed contract would not be entertained. Hence grew up the
law as to accord or agreement to settle a controversy over money. If the
accord was made under seal, an action on the accord could be maintained
by the old action of covenant in the register of writs. Covenant could be
brought either for a fixed amount or for indefinite damages, but it must
be based upon a sealed instrument. Accord, however, was not applied to
that kind of contract. It was applied to an oral or written agreement not
under seal, to settle a pending controversy, and since there was no recognition by the common law of an agreement to pay a sum of money in settlement of some other sum owed, it logically followed that an accord
without satisfaction of the accord by payment was wholly nugatory. The
reason was that if a man agreed, not under seal, to pay a sum of money,
the agreement was not binding upon him. As soon, however, as the sum
was paid and the other accepted it in satisfaction of a claim, there was an
actual agreement fully performed, which was binding as an accord and
satisfaction. The doctrine was stated then in the negative, that an accord
without satisfaction was not binding.

But as soon as the action of assumpsit came into existence, a promise
as a consideration for another's promise became valid. Now a promise
to pay a sum of money in consideration of the other party's agreeing to
accept it, became under the theory of the new rule a binding contract.
Put in another way the party who had promised to accept became
bound because the other party who had agreed to pay became bound.
Under the law as it stood under the new action of assumpsit, two cases
might arise, first, an accord by agreement to pay a less sum than a fixed
amount due on one side and to accept such amount on the other, and
second, an accord by agreement in regard to a claim for unfixed or
unliquidated damages, which agreement was a promise to pay a certain
sum on one side, and a promise to accept that certain sum on the other
side. The common lawyers, however, refused to change their principle.
They could not understand this newfangled Roman promise for a
promise. A judge of some enlightenment decided that since now a
promise for a promise was a good consideration in law, the accord was

binding as an agreement without satisfaction, because such an agreement was binding on both parties. This was answered by the statement of the old and tough common lawyers that an agreement to accept a lesser sum than the sum due by an existing contract was without consideration, and the accord was not binding until the sum agreed to be paid was actually paid and accepted. This was all very well as to a fixed amount due but the reasoning had no application to a claim for unliquidated damages, since the accord settled the amount of those unfixed damages, for the promise to accept as well as the promise to pay were binding. The common law judges, however, kept repeating as to both cases their shibboleth that accord without satisfaction made was not binding. Hence the law was that two parties in dispute as to the amount of unliquidated damages due upon a contract could not make a binding agreement to compromise and settle the dispute and the absurd common lawyers insisted that the parties must have a lawsuit to settle the amount of damages whether they desired a lawsuit or not. But a compromise settlement of a tort claim was good without satisfaction. In this condition of profound contrariety the common law came to this country. Literally hundreds of decisions can be quoted to the effect that an accord without satisfaction is not binding, with various and insufficient grounds given for the decision. In the textbooks on this subject reign "Chaos and old Night." A stupider, blinder following of an inapplicable precedent cannot be found. Thus the dead hand of an obsolete procedure was laid upon the present law by incompetent administrators.

Another illustration of the inherited blind instinct to follow customary ways is found in the wrestling of the common lawyers with such a new problem as a sale of goods not in existence but to be manufactured. The medieval common law was that upon a bargain of sale of goods the property in the goods was immediately in the purchaser and regardless of a delivery, the seller could at once sue in an action of debt for the stipulated price and the purchaser could at once sue in detinue for the goods. So Fortescue laid down the undoubted law. It had never occurred to those lawyers that a man might sell something that remained to be made. So the common law was assumed to be that a sale of a nonexistent thing was simply a nullity, and that it gave no remedy upon such a

sale. Later under the action of assumpsit it was considered that that action gave no remedy for a breach of a contract to sell goods when the
goods were required to be made or to be purchased by the seller. This
was likened to the sale of a specific thing supposed to be in existence but
not so in fact. The bargain was a nullity. One old case was where a man
sold all the wool upon the backs of his sheep. The sale was good, although the wool was growing. So a sale of a growing crop, growing upon
certain land, was held to be a good sale. The reason given was that the
thing was partially in existence. But the ruling covered the case of a crop
not sown, and on a lease of a flock of sheep, a certain portion of the increase to accrue, could be made the property of the lessor. On the other
hand a sale of all the colts which a mare would foal in seven years was
not a bargain of sale according to an old case, but a mere agreement, yet
there was another much later case where a parson sold all his tithes to
accrue for seven years and in Henry VI's time that was agreed to be a
good sale, notwithstanding that the tithes were not in existence at the
time of the contract. It was apparent by this time that the common law
judges were fairly well befogged, and, like Alice in Wonderland, were
seeing strange things.

At last came a case submitted to the great Elizabethan lawyer,
Plowden. It is in Moore's untranslated reports. An "honest yeoman" had
been guilty of most unyeomanlike conduct, fully as bad as that of the
Greek skipper in the Greek lawsuit in a former chapter. The yeoman had
sold for money paid down all the butter which would be made from his
cows for one year; but when he had made the butter, he sold it to a second purchaser. This seems to be a strange tale, for how the butter could
be kept in a merchantable condition for a year seems a mystery. But the
Middle Ages may have considered such ancient butter a delicacy. Let us
hope, however, that the reporter Moore, being merely a common lawyer,
had become entangled between butter and cheese. At any rate the report
says that the butter was sold to the second purchaser, who paid for it, put
his mark upon the "barrels" and confidingly left them in the custody of
the honest yeoman seller. The yeoman generously delivered them to the
first purchaser upon the first sale, and thereupon the second purchaser
brought replevin against the first purchaser, who claimed the property

by reason of the first sale. Thereupon "Monsieur Plowden" was asked to say whether the property was in the first or the second purchaser. Plowden answered that the property was in the second purchaser, for he said, the contract that was first made, which was between the yeoman and the first purchaser, "was only an agreement that the yeoman would sell the butter when it should be made, for before it is in existence it cannot be sold, and before its making it was not in existence; therefore, before the making of it, there was no property in it and so there was no contract for the property." Therefore the second agreement to sell was the alienation of the property and under this award of Plowden the second purchaser took the butter and the first purchaser brought an action against the yeoman for damages.

This case, of course, was wrongly decided by Plowden on the law as it stood. The agreement with the first purchaser was for a sale of *all* the butter to be made by the yeoman, not for a part of it. As soon as the butter was made during the period, it at once became appropriated to that contract without anything more done and the title then passed. The sale to the second purchaser was wholly abortive, because the honest yeoman was selling the property of some one else. Plowden ought to have seen the principle from the parson's sale of all his tithes. If, however, a manufacturer making particular goods must deliver upon a contract some selected part of the goods, then no title passes until the goods are selected and appropriated to the particular contract. The yeoman, as soon as the butter was made, had the right to notify the first purchaser to come and get his butter. If he did not do so, he could store it as the butter of that purchaser, on the ground that title was in that purchaser, and if the price had not been paid, he could sue for that whole price on the ground that the title passed as soon as the butter was made. If Plowden had known the Roman law he would have answered the question correctly, for in that high civilization the problem of selling goods not yet owned or made had been met and answered.

The age of the Tudors and Stuarts was one of hideous cruelty. Rulers had hearts of stone. Henry VIII sent More to the block in a way that would disgrace an Apache Indian. Elizabeth, the "fair vestal," was as merciless as a Domitian. Coke was a compound of brutality, piety, and avarice. The method of prosecution he used toward Sir Walter Raleigh to satisfy the drooling James I, as we shall see in the next chapter, has permanently disgraced the English law. Cromwell and his Puritans were remorseless. Charles I deserted his great minister Strafford in the true Stuart way. Under Charles II, Sir Matthew Hale was trying and executing poor old crazy women for witchcraft, while the Puritans, relying upon the Old Testament for their law as to witches, were doing the like in Massachusetts. The Anglicans were persecuting Dissenters, Presbyterians, Quakers, and Roman Catholics alike. At last came Jeffreys, and his conduct on the bench is the last burning disgrace in the annals of English judges.

In the period of the Stuart kings the one figure that stands out is the great chancellor, Lord Nottingham. One of his first duties was to rectify the abuse of the common law action of assumpsit by which oral contracts of every kind were permitted to be proven, often by the rankest perjury. The common law had gone from the one extreme of no oral contracts to the other extreme of every kind of oral contract, as well as every kind of oral trust. The Statute of Frauds corrected most of the evil by requiring certain contracts and instruments concerning trusts to be in writing. Yet, carefully as that statute was drawn, every word of it has carried the expenditure of a vast sum of money in litigation. The gloss and comment of decisions upon the few sections now fill a large law book. Never yet has there existed a human being capable of drawing a statute of general effect, and doubtless no such human being will ever exist.

Previous to Lord Nottingham's time the different heads of equity jurisdiction were to be found in a great number of unrelated precedents scattered through endless records. Nottingham, having some considerable reading and knowledge of the civil law, and acquaintance with a sound classification, arranged the equity jurisdiction under the various heads of that jurisdiction, both the part which was concurrent with the jurisdiction of the courts of law and the part which was exclusive in the courts of equity. When this was done English equity was found to be a symmetrical system.

It is impossible to imagine what English law would have been without equity; yet it had had a narrow escape. For various not very creditable reasons the Puritans had a violent antipathy to the courts of chancery. While the most of the barristers during the Cromwellian epoch had refused to practise in the courts of law, and the Inns of Court had been closed, the common law courts had kept functioning and the motion for a new trial upon newly discovered evidence or for errors occurring in the course of the trial, had come into vogue. But determined attempts were made to abolish the chancery court and it practically ceased to function. The common lawyers had never understood the chancery system. It is still supposed by ill-informed lawyers that this was a method of discretionary application of the law and of dispensing with law in particular cases, and that it had been misused as a political institution—an idea which is little better than nonsense.

The Puritans mainly disliked equity because they had a dim idea that it was connected in some way with the canon law of the Roman church. This was truer than they supposed. Practically the whole of the chancery procedure and practice was Roman, as were its legal doctrines. But that it had been misused as a political institution, the record does not show. It came back into its own at the Stuart Restoration, and not many years later accomplished lawyers were studying the canon law. A case was being heard in Charles II's reign before Chief Justice Vaughan, sitting with his two associate judges, called in legal phrase his *puisnes*, who had been regular common law barristers. A question arose as to what was the canon law. Both *puisnes* at once with some pride disclaimed all knowledge of that system. Vaughan holding up his hands exclaimed: "In God's name, what crime have I committed, that I must sit here between two judges who openly disclaim all knowledge of the canon law?"

At the Revolution of 1688 the subservient common law judges were removed. New judges were appointed, under the new rule, to hold during good behavior, a rule that has always since obtained in England. In a short time Sir John Holt became Chief Justice. He practically in one case brought into the common law the whole of the Roman law concerning bailments.[3] But the common law yet needed much help from the civil law. The law of corporations, of partnership, of agency, of insurance, all

3. *Coggs v. Bernard,* 92 Eng. Rep. 107 (King's Bench, 1703).—C. J. R., Jr.

the equitable doctrines of the Roman law regarding relations not of contract but of relations analogous to contract, called quasi-contract in the Roman law, remained yet to be absorbed into the law by the work of the greatest of all English judges, Lord Mansfield. Finally after another two hundred years, was to come the triumph of the system of equity borrowed from the Roman law. In 1876 it was at last acknowledged that the righteous law must govern in England by giving courts of common law equitable powers, and by enacting that where the common law rule differed from that of equity, the rule of equity should govern.

The effect of the various political struggles in the seventeenth century was to make the new jury system an impregnable system. Since it had become a judicial body, hearing evidence, the courts were compelled to devise rules of procedure whereby an impartial jury could be impaneled to try the cause, and whereby the production of evidence to the jury should be so controlled by the judge that improper evidence should not be introduced. All evidence was to be subject to cross-examination as a further guaranty of its truth. The primary rule, singularly enough, was the rule enforced by the ancient oath administered to a witness in the earliest period of the common law, that he must testify under oath to what he knew of his own knowledge, not to what some one had told him.

It was at just about this time that the English law was transferred to the American colonies. The extraordinarily rapid development of the colonies, begun before the American Revolution, was hastened after the independence of the states. But independence brought no change in the private law in the various states. Cases in English courts continued to be precedents in the courts of America. Theoretically the law was the same. Even the two conflicting systems of common law and equity were introduced into America, except in the Puritan Commonwealth of Massachusetts and the Quaker state of Pennsylvania. Canada with its millions has for the most part the English law. To-day Australia has the English law. Through the world there are many points of contact between the English and the modern Roman law. In certain English possessions the civil law prevails and appeals from such courts were heard by the King in Council, now by a court called the Judicial Committee of the Privy Council. There no difficulty is found by English judges in deciding upon the rules of the civil law. Since 1701 Scotch appeals have been heard in the English House of Lords. Scotland never had the common law. It always had, generally speaking, the civil law. All this has tended to broaden and liberalize the English lawyers and judges, and assisted in preparing the way for the amalgamation of the common law and equity.

But after all, what the lawyers had gained and what the law had gained was a comprehension of that juristic spirit of the Roman law which looks through form to substance. This was quaintly expressed by Plowden. His work in its Norman-French form was partly printed in 1588 by that great law printer Richard Tottell. It is a beautiful book fully equal to Tottell's edition of the Latin text of Bracton on the Laws and Customs of England. There seems to have been no English translation of Plowden for more than a hundred and fifty years. From the first English translation with its capitalizing is taken the following passage:

> From this Judgment and the cause of it the Reader may observe that it is not the Words of the Law but the internal Sense of it that makes the Law, and our Law (like all others) consists of two Parts, viz: of Body and Soul; the Letter of the Law is the Body of the Law and the Sense and Reason of the Law is the Soul of the Law, because the reason of the Law is the soul of the law. And the Law may be likened to a Nut which has a Shell and within it a Kernel; the Letter of the Law represents the Shell and the Sense of it the Kernel, and as you will be no better for the Nut, if you make use only of the Shell, so you will receive no Benefit by the Law, if you rely only upon the Letter, and as the Fruit and Profit of the Nut lies in the Kernel and not in the Shell, so the Fruit and Profit of the Law consists in the Sense more than in the Letter.

One of the loveliest buildings devoted to law is the Hall of the Middle Temple in London. This we owe to the fine taste of this Elizabethan lawyer. The letter of Queen Elizabeth offering Plowden the chancellorship, if he would desert his religion, was preserved at Plowden Hall until early in the nineteenth century, when it was lost in a fire. Even if the law produced such a man as Coke, it fully atoned for that error by giving us the admirable character of Plowden, who for his book of reports alone must always be numbered among the Children of Light.

Sir Edward Coke (1552–1634)

In one respect the old common law was more capable than our law to-day. When it examined a verdict of a jury and found the verdict to be false, it at once entered the correct judgment as well as fined the jurors who had rendered the perverse verdict. This can no longer be done. If a new trial is granted the whole trial must be gone over again. If the case is appealed and the verdict reversed for lack of evidence, the correct judgment cannot be entered. The whole trial takes place anew. Similarly the judge sitting in a court cannot fine a jury, however perverse its conduct may be in rendering a verdict. The reason for this is an old judgment in Bushell's case which has been called immortal.[4] The reason given in that case is that the jury finds a verdict from its own knowledge as well as from the evidence. This was not true at that time, nor is it true to-day. A verdict could not stand then nor can it stand now, if it be contrary to the evidence, regardless of the fact that a jury may think that it has knowledge of facts contrary to the evidence. Yet such is the persistence of error in repeating the *cantilena* of the law, that the inability of a court to fine a jury for a perverse verdict is based upon such baseless reasoning. The inability of an appellate court or of the trial court to cause to be entered in a jury case, the correct verdict on the evidence greatly prolongs a litigation. The Constitution of the United States and those of most of the States in preserving a jury trial had rendered it impossible for any judgment to be entered upon conflicting evidence at least, except upon a verdict of a jury, if a jury trial is demanded. Thus it happens that the law does not always progress. This is an instance where it has degenerated.

Ages ago a caustic Greek philosopher described what pleading before juries caused the pleader to become. "The pleaders," he said, "are tied down to the point at issue and must talk against a clock. Like slaves they must wheedle their master, the jury, by words and gain its favor by acts. They in consequence are tense and shrewd, but their souls become small and warped. Their life of slavery deprives them of growth, straightforwardness and independence, and their burden of fears and dangers forces them to crooked ways. This burden they cannot bear with uprightness and truth, so they turn at once to deceit. Thus bent and

4. Vaughan 135, 124 Eng. Rep. 1006, 6 Howell's State Trials 999 (1670).—C. J. R., Jr.

stunted, they have no real soundness of mind, although exceedingly clever and wise in their own conceit." Of many lawyers this is true today. Many such men can be found in the baser and more mechanical portion of the profession. But a man who stands on the terrace and enters the courtyard of the Roman Palace of Justice will see statues erected to the memory of great Roman lawyers. He will reflect that these men created a system of law which is still the guide of conduct in vast regions where never flew the Roman eagles. This world-wide system of law still flourishing in undiminished vigor must have been the work of a profession of men of wide and catholic understanding, of pure intentions and of discerning and liberal minds. This is probably the best answer to the strictures of sages or saints or men of literature who have continuously kept alive the tradition of denouncing the lawyers.

Let us turn to another picture to see that these better lawyers have not passed away. In 1869 the bar of England was entertaining at dinner in Middle Temple Hall, Plowden's beautiful structure, the great French advocate Berryer. Lord Brougham, then a very old man, in his speech, maintained a favorite dogma of his that he had been repeating since his part in Queen Caroline's case: "The first and great duty of an advocate is to reckon everything subordinate to the interests of his client." Lord Chief Justice Cockburn, when he responded to the toast to "The Judges" took issue with Lord Brougham and on the spur of the moment amidst the unanimous applause of the bar, uttered those words which will always guide a true lawyer in his duty toward his clients: "The arms which an advocate wields he ought to use as a warrior, not as an assassin. He ought to uphold the interests of his clients *per fas*, not *per nefas*. He ought to know how to reconcile the interests of his clients with the eternal interests of truth and justice." This knowledge must come to every man who is worthy to minister at the altar of justice and to feed its sacred and undying flame.

CHAPTER 14

The Reconciliation of the English Systems of Law

THE EXPULSION OF JAMES II has always been known as the Glorious Revolution of 1688. Its most glorious feature was the establishment of the constitutional rule in England that judges hold their offices during good behavior. To this rule we owe the clause in our Federal Constitution that the justices of the Federal Supreme Court and the circuit and district judges of the United States are protected by the provision that they hold office during good behavior. The original rule in England had been that the judges held at the pleasure of the king, but as a matter of practice they had held by a life tenure, except during the time of the Tudor and Stuart kings. Whatever had been the political changes, the judges preceding that time had not been attacked, at least for political reasons. Edward I's judges, it is true, had been tried and convicted for venality and judicial misconduct. There were, during the reigns of the three Edwards, instances of particular judges being removed. Under Richard II the king's judges were removed and punished by Parliament because Tresilian, the Chief Justice, had caused all the judges except one not punished, to sign an extra-judicial opinion that Parliament had been guilty of high treason. Tresilian, the Chief Justice of the King's Bench, was beheaded, the rest of the judges who signed the paper, and Lokton, the King's Serjeant, were banished to Ireland as a sort of political Botany Bay. All of the judges would have been beheaded in accordance with the cruelty of the times, had it not been for a moving petition from the clergy to the Parliament.

When the Lancastrian Henry IV displaced Richard II there was no change in the judges. In the Wars of the Roses the Yorkists triumphed, but the only judge affected was Chief Justice Fortescue, who had been in the Lancastrian army. When Henry VII defeated the last Yorkist king, Richard III, on the field of Bosworth, there was no change whatever in the judges. When Queen Mary, Henry VIII's daughter, succeeded as a Roman Catholic queen her brother, Edward VI, the judges merely changed their religious allegiance back to the Pope. Elizabeth came in after a few years and the judges very accommodatingly became Protestants again. Under James I, Elizabeth's successor, began the practice of the Crown selling the judgeships for actual cash payments. Cromwell, as Lord Protector, made a clean sweep of the judges in office. Charles II at the Restoration appointed new judges, but kept Sir Matthew Hale. James II twice dismissed his judges. At the Revolution, Jeffreys died before he could be beheaded, but the subservient creatures of James, except one independent judge, were supplanted.

The rule was then established as to the judges that they were not removable, and this rule we inherited in the American colonies, although in many States we have now returned to the worst feature of the Roman system, elective judges. Of all those parts of the world entitled to be called civilized, the States of our Union, except where life tenure has been preserved, are the only places where judges are elected. Generally speaking, the benches of the States would be far better manned if the judges were appointed for life. There are many men who advocate election of judges; but we venture to say that there is not an elective judge who is fit to sit upon the bench, who would not gladly change his tenure to that of the Federal judges. At any rate the advocates of elective judges know little, if anything, of legal history.

The reason for making the judge a permanent officer is that the judge, of all men, is the man who should make no sacrifice for justice. He must pay no price to do justice. Whoever he is, whatever his attainments, he must be left free to be impartial, without any chance of being called to account elsewhere for his conduct as a judge, unless his conduct be crim-

The Court of Wards and Liveries, an administrative tribunal created in 1540
to facilitate the collection of revenue through the exploitation of wardship.
It was abolished in 1645.

inal. The very essence of the administration of the law is uninfluenced impartiality, and the history of the law has proven that men who are put into judicial position, if let alone, generally try to act with an eye single to judicial impartiality. There are many instances of the sacrifice of elective judges to popular clamor. Those who desire to see the judges made subject to influence of any kind, except that of the desire to administer justice in accordance with law, whoever they may be and whatever their motives, and whatever the influence sought to be exerted, whether that influence be of men with good intentions or bad, or of the general pressure of popular opinion, are enemies of good government and without any true sense of civic morality. Therefore it is that the most glorious result of the deposition of the worthless James was the permanent tenure of the English judge. At the same time, England had learned the lesson of the duty of government to compensate its judges with salaries that do not require too great a sacrifice by able men, when the salary is compared with the emoluments of practice.

This judicial reform was a great buttress to the structure of English law. There remained many other reforms not so great. One was the general liberalizing of the common law and its practitioners. Another was the establishing of rules of evidence whereby the jury might become a true judicial body. Another was the reform of methods of pleading so that the actual controversy might be put to the judicial body. But they were of smaller importance than the one that was to be awaited for two hundred years in England, a reform which has been made all over this country, by which the one court of general jurisdiction is given such complete power that it may use whatsoever principle of law may be applicable to the circumstances of the case before the court, and especially the power to be a court either of common law or of chancery, as the case may require.

Here it will be well to survey the law and look back over the long road that had been traveled since the year 1268, when Bracton's eyes were closed in death. By the process of confining itself to the kind of cases whose facts a jury could decide, the common law had narrowed its field, but it had made the jury a judicial body. If narrowness had been of evil effect from some standpoints (those evils have already clearly been pointed out), it had at least left the chancery courts free to develop a parallel system of law, which had been systematized and had been given an interrelation and an interdependence that were calculated to produce judges and a bar that would recall the juristic methods of the Roman jurisconsults.

As to the jury system, it remains to consider its good effects. It brought the average citizen into contact with the law. It made him a constituent part of legal administration. It gave the citizen the sort of training that is needed in a people who are to live under free institutions. It no doubt was due to this jury system that the English began to show political capacity in the people at a time when the rest of Europe was incapable of the least effort toward self-government. The jury system possessed the representative feature, which was applied in the formation of the English Parliament and it will easily be conceded that representative government is, as Montesquieu says, the only actual political invention since Aristotle wrote his Politics. From this standpoint it is to be said that the more intelligent portion of the population received through the jury system a training in the appreciation of, and respect for, law and orderly government which atoned for all its evils.

Nothing has yet been said about the legal profession in any connected way. It is time now to say something of the profession, for when this story comes to the legal profession in this land of ours, it will be necessary to contrast the profession as developed in England with the profession as the peculiar circumstances in this country have transformed it. From an early period of the common law—at least as early as the year 1250—owing to certain historical influences, the legal profession became finally divided into two sharply defined classes: one class consisted of barristers or advocates, who are concerned especially with the work of presenting a cause to the court; and the other class comprised attorneys, who have charge of the work of preparing the case and performing all the greater part of the lawyer's work which does not consist of pleading a cause or of conducting an actual trial, or of performing the consultative work of the barrister. The key to the distinction is that even among our barbarous ancestors one could always have a friend or associate to speak for him in court; but the right to have an attorney who acts for and binds his principal is of much later growth. Originally the barrister's words did not bind the client. In the later days of the Roman empire the advocates had become separated into a distinct class. In England and in France this division of the profession endured. The fact is that the barrister or advocate has always enjoyed a peculiar prestige over the attorney: not only has he enjoyed a higher social standing, but the ranks of the advocates generally have been filled by men enjoying better opportunities in life and coming from a superior social station. In fact, an attorney is defined, in one of the old rules of the Inns of Court, to be "an immaterial person of an inferior character," and for centuries all attorneys have been rigidly excluded from the Inns.

All the literature of the early common law is concerned wholly with the advocate in court. This literature is a priceless heritage in the law, though few now can read it. Arguments of advocates in court are reported from a period as early as 1292. England from that distant time enjoyed a system of law so well developed that the very arguments of the lawyers and the grounds of the decisions of the judges are accurately reported. Careful listeners skilled in the law preserved upon parchment the arguments and in many cases the very words of the English barristers as they pleaded their clients' cases purely on law points in the courts. These collections are known as the Year Books, and reach from the year 1292 until about 1500, with some later fragmentary Year Books. They are all written in Norman French, or, as that artificial tongue became, Anglo-Norman. As the Year Books are closing, the reports such as Dyer, Anderson, and Plowden, which bear more resemblance to our present reports, begin; but the unique value of the Year Books is that they report, with practical accuracy, the debates of the lawyers while the court was ascertaining and getting at the controversy which was to be tried. Here the work of the barrister ended in the early times. The Year Books end when the modern practice of written pleadings begins.

Thus it is plain that of the two parts of the tribunal with which the modern advocate deals, the judges and the jury, the barristers in the early common law dealt only with the judge. Another obvious matter should be noticed, and that is that there was no criminal work for the advocate unless he spoke for the prosecution. In all cases where the Crown prosecuted, the defendant could have no counsel until comparatively late times.

The advocates in 1292 are divided into classes, the serjeants at law and the apprentices (or the seniors and the juniors). Long afterwards were to come the distinctions between serjeants, King's counsel, and utter barristers. At the time we are now considering, an apprentice (or, as we say, a barrister) after years of practice is called to the degree of serjeant. From the serjeants alone are the judges chosen. It is the serjeant whom the judge addresses as brother, not the apprentice. During all these centuries the advocates of the common law practised and argued before judges who had served long years in active practice and, unless they were afflicted with an incurable congenital stupidity, were likely to have become good lawyers.

The advocate at this time is required to be a man of learning. He must know three languages and be able to speak fluently in them all. The oral proceedings in court are all in Norman French. The record of the case is wholly in Latin, but when the barrister talks with his clients he must sometimes know one or more of the barbarous dialects spoken by the middle and lower classes of the English. So far as the Year Books show us, the advocates make no attempt at oratory. Their words are direct, their arguments are very short, and their diction is wholly unadorned. The whole procedure is a sort of informal discussion. As the argument and discussion proceed, new facts are suggested, a new bearing is given to matters already stated, the serjeants and apprentices present who are not engaged in the case intervene with their opinion and advice in a case of any importance, and sometimes the judge sums up the discussion for the benefit of those who are present. The students of the law from the Inns are present listening to the discussion. In one place Bereford, the Chief Justice, says to Serjeant Westcote, who has challenged a point of law laid down by the Chief Justice: "Really I am much obliged to you for your challenge, and that for the sake of the young men here and not for us who sit on the bench. All the same, answer over."

Now and then the bar had the pleasure of hearing one judge impale another. Bereford, this same Chief Justice, tells how he was present in

Parliament when the Countess of Albemarle, who seems to have had quite fixed opinions of her own, was brought in on a writ from the King's Bench court. It was objected to the writ that it did not specify the charges against her. Two of the judges said that the writ was good, but Hengham the Chief Justice, arguing it to be bad, said to one of them: "Yes, you would make such a judgment here as you did at C. where the accessory was hanged, and the principal was afterwards acquitted before you yourself." To the other judge he said: "Before you a man was hanged and afterwards that man's heritage was granted to his heir to repair the injustice, because your judgment was against the law of the land." In Edward III's time Willoughby, J., was laying down the law from the bench. His brother Shareshulle, sitting with him upon the bench said: "That is not law now." Willoughby contemptuously retorted: "One more learned than you are adjudged it."

The advocate sometimes gets a drubbing. A judge says to two learned serjeants arguing against an accounting: "Leave off your noise and deliver yourselves from this account." In another case Howard, J., says to learned counsel: "If you want to cite a case, why don't you cite one in point?" Stonor, C.J., observes as to an apprentice Green who has been lecturing the court: "I am amazed that Green makes himself out to know everything in the world—and he is only a young man."

If we come forward a hundred years to the year 1398, Richard II, the great-great-grandson of Edward I, is on the throne, and we see the same system precisely, the same kind of reports, the same sort of lawyers; but the lawyers have deteriorated. In reading the reports one gets the impression that the lawyers are not open-minded, they seem to have little flexibility of thought, they do not seem to understand or to know how to handle with skill the system of law they administer.

Singularly enough, we have at this very time a serjeant drawn to the life by our first great poet who no doubt knew personally these very lawyers. In the Prologue of the Canterbury Tales, Chaucer has given us a picture of the typical advocate of his time. It will be better to paraphrase and prosaically to amplify Chaucer's obsolete and impracticable English. One can see an authentic picture of the sober, wise-looking, pompous, successful lawyer of his day, whose tribe has by no means passed away after the lapse of more than five hundred years. In that curious collection of people assembled in the Prologue, at the Tabard Inn in Southwark, to wend their way to the shrine of St. Thomas at Canterbury was a serjeant of the law. Wary and wise was he, says Chaucer, and he had served many years at his pillar in the space before St. Paul's. In that glorious time the advocate paid no rent; his office was in the Parvis of St. Paul's, the public space at the columns of the porch of the cathedral, where a pillar or column was assigned to each serjeant. Here he met his clients and took notes upon his parchment roll upon his knee. This serjeant of Chaucer's was a great purchaser of land, "so great a purchaser was nowhere known." But the man seemed busier than he was. He carried with him his parchment book of cases and decisions or dooms gathered from the time of King William the Conqueror, and every statute he could repeat by rote. Chaucer adds to the picture the serjeant's sober medley coat, with a silken sash at the waist. Every one of us can recall at the present day some solemn, pedantic man, looking preternaturally wise and pretending to be busier than he is. Their race has never grown less.

Yet this system produced some very great lawyers and very great men. Such men as Parning, Fortescue, Littleton, and Danby would be great in any age. But we shall not stop to give any particulars regarding them or further to illustrate their styles of argument out of the Year Books, for the procedure as they knew it, has passed away, although the substantive law remains much the same. We will now come forward another hundred years to 1485 and find the barristers after the fierce struggles of Lancastrians and Yorkists in the Wars of the Roses have ended, and Henry VII, the first of the Tudors, is on the throne. The little princes had been killed in the Tower by their uncle, the hunchback Richard III, and Henry VII, who had the title of the red rose of Lancaster, had married the eldest sister of the murdered princes, the White Rose of York, and had gained an undisputed title to the kingship. We have, for about this period, a full description of the English legal system and a detailed account of an advocate's education at the Inns of Court in Chief Justice Fortescue's Latin treatise *De Laudibus Legum Angliae*, or Praise of England's Law, one of the priceless treasures of our legal literature.

The origin of the Inns of Court is lost in antiquity; but it is practically certain that there was a body of law students older than any of the Inns. One set of students in Edward II's reign, or soon thereafter, obtained quarters in the Temple, the confiscated property of the Order of Knights of the Temple, and soon divided into the Middle and the Inner Temple. Another body of students gathered at Lincoln's Inn. Still later another set of students later obtained the mansion of the Lords Grey de Wilton, and became Gray's Inn. Connected with the larger Inns were ten smaller Inns of Chancery, having no connection with the court of chancery, but so called because they were the preparatory schools where the students studied the original writs in lawsuits, which were issued out of the chancery.

But there was, of course, some reason why, on the edge of the old city, just beyond the city wall at what came to be called Temple Bar, all these students should have found lodging places. Fortescue explains that the laws of England cannot be taught at the university, but that they are studied in a much more commodious place, near the king's courts at Westminster, where the laws are daily pleaded and argued and where judgments are rendered by grave judges, of full years, skilled and expert in the laws. The place of study is near an opulent city, but in a spot quiet and retired, where the throng of passers-by does not disturb the students, yet where they can daily attend the courts. The street now called the Strand was then a rural lane. The students walked along it to reach Westminster Hall, where all the courts sat. Even the chancellor sat in the marble chair at the head of this old Norman hall of William Rufus, the Conqueror's son.

These four larger Inns were wholly voluntary institutions. The older and better known barristers of an Inn became the governing body of benchers, and they were self-perpetuating. They alone had and still retain the exclusive privilege of calling to the bar, but upon their refusal to call an appeal lay to the judges. In these four Inns the students studied the cases in the Year Books, the legal treatises called Fleta and Britton, read the statutes, and attended at court in term time. Soon they would be reading Littleton's Tenures and later Coke's crabbed commentary on Littleton.

Instruction was given by arguing moot cases before a bencher and two barristers sitting as judges, and by lectures called readings delivered by some able barrister belonging to the Inn. It was a high honor to be selected as reader, and the expense of the feasts given by the readers at the Inns became very great. After a student had studied seven years (afterwards reduced to five), he was eligible to be called to the bar. The barristers before becoming serjeants were probably called apprentices, although that term was sometimes applied to the students. Whether an examination was required is problematical, but possibly that part of the ceremony of instituting a serjeant, which required the serjeant to plead to a declaration, points to an examination of some perfunctory sort.

Fortescue explains the high cost and expense in keeping a student at the Inns, and artlessly adds that the poorer class and the tradespeople are not willing to pay for such an education, "whence it happens that there is hardly a skilled lawyer who is not a gentleman by birth." Fortescue was himself descended from the Norman who bore the Conqueror's shield at Hastings and his own descendants still enjoy an earldom.

By this time a new set of lawyers was developed in the chancery courts. The chancery bar proper was called barristers, but the mechanical portion of the chancery lawyers was called solicitors. For this bar a study of the common and civil law was necessary. The solicitors were almost invariably graduates of Oxford or Cambridge, and generally were men of more liberalized understanding than the common lawyers; but gradually the chancery bar and the common law bar coalesced to the extent that they indifferently became students at the Inns after they had received a liberal training at the Universities. As a necessary result of their practice and training, the chancery lawyers came to be a superior type of men. The common lawyer in his narrow, slavish way asked merely whether there was a writ to suit the case. If there was no writ and no precedent, no right existed. But the chancery lawyer looked to reason and justice, good faith and fair dealing, and acted accordingly. But since there was more or less of exchange between the two bars, the influence of the chancery tended to broaden the common lawyer.

We shall now move forward another hundred years to 1588, in the reign of Elizabeth. Evidence is now submitted to the jury in open court.

The actions are in the four in contract, the four in tort, and two kinds of ejectment, one of which became the later action of trespass in ejectment. Some of the old actions were retained, but rarely used. The Year Books have ceased and the reports of Keilway, Dyer, Benloe, Dalison, Anderson, Plowden, Moore, and others have begun, to be followed by an unending line. We are now in the period of written pleadings, and the demurrer on point of law has been invented. No longer do we see the free and flexible system of discussing all the proposed facts before the pleadings are settled and written in Latin on the record roll. Now the advocates argue their cases in English even when they are addressing the court. The English language has reached a richness and flexibility that it will retain to our own time. But the reports still are in Norman French—a French, however, that has lost its grammatical form and freely substitutes Latin or English words. The record still is written in Latin, but it too has taken on English words. Fresh force masquerades as the Latin *frisca forcia*.

The ideas of the lawyers of the period can be illustrated by translating from Moore's Anglo-Norman Reports at the Easter term of 24 Elizabeth (1580) a passage from an actual speech of Lord Chancellor Bromley. Dyer, the Chief Justice of the Common Pleas, is just dead. The Queen has appointed Anderson, one of the serjeants, to the vacancy, and the Chancellor sitting upon the Bench says to Anderson, standing at the bar, that the Queen, on account of the opinion which she has conceived of his knowledge, prudence, and integrity, has appointed him Chief Justice;

> at which [says the chancellor] I am greatly pleased, for I have known of your proficiency while you were a student, counsellor, and serjeant, and although I am satisfied of your entire competency I wish to commend to you four things requisite in your office of judge: First, you must have knowledge of the law, as the Holy Spirit in the Psalm exhorts us, "Be learned, ye who judge the earth," and for this you must continue all the time that you can in the study of your books, in order to retain what you have attained. Second, you must observe discretion in your judgments, especially upon demurrers in which there are four requisites for judges to observe, to introduce no general inconvenience in attempting to avoid a private mischief, to open no door for fraud to have passage, to insist not so

much upon form as to neglect the substance, and to prefer the intent before the letter. In trials upon verdicts the judge should, if anything appears doubtful, exhort the jurors to find a special verdict, and in any case to make the evidence plain to the jury without direction one way or the other, and lastly to hear all the proofs of both parties to the fullest extent. The third requisite in justice is impartiality, which is best shown by neither favoring the poor man through pity nor the rich through fear or hope of reward. The fourth thing is diligence, which consists in expediting causes for the avoidance of expense and for the prevention of delays, caused by the death of a party or his decrease of substance, resulting in his loss of profit in that to which he is entitled. It is oftentimes seen that one who pursues his right would rather have a quick judgment against him than a deferred judgment in his favor. These things I advise you to hold in mind, for they tend to the advancement of equity and justice which are the life of the law, and I exhort you to pray continually to the omnipotent God for His direction in this office and function of judge, for you well know that all grace and government proceed from Him.

This was the exhortation of a chancery lawyer to one who had been a common law practitioner.

It is doubtful if better advice could be given to-day, except to add the warning where necessary that arises from a judge being subject to popular election. But the style of the advocate has wholly changed since 1488. Instead of the short, clear, terse remarks of counsel, the arguments have become long and exhaustive, accompanied by an endless citation of cases. Many of them are preserved in the old reports. These lawyers are the contemporaries of Shakespeare, and their language has the richness and metaphorical coloring of the Renaissance.

The greatest change, however, has come from the added duty of the advocate to put in evidence and address the jury, restrained by no rules of evidence. There can be no better instance of the conduct of the advocate, when restrained by no rules of evidence, than the method of Sir Edward Coke on the trial of Sir Walter Raleigh, which took place in 1603. Coke was the most learned lawyer of his time, but at this period he was seeking preferment. He was naturally of a mean and cruel disposition and at heart a savage. His behavior in this case was such that Lord Mansfield, a hundred and fifty years later, said: "I would not have made

Coke's speech in Sir Walter Raleigh's case to gain all Coke's estate and reputation." But Coke's conduct is on a par with all the lawyers' conduct against criminal defendants in Elizabeth's reign, who were prosecuted by government. Hearsay, letters written to a man, accusations without witnesses produced, slander and abuse, were all unscrupulously used. The cases sound like an investigation by a Committee of the United States Senate and show the same reckless abuse of power. This butchery by Coke is remarkable for the gallant fight which Raleigh made for his life.

The charge against Raleigh was high treason committed in the last days of Elizabeth's reign, in trying to fix the succession upon Arabella Stuart instead of upon King James of Scotland, and in trying to bring in the Romish superstition, as it was called. The last charge was, of course, absurd, and advanced simply to prejudice Raleigh, who was a Protestant, a very Protestant of Protestants. The first charge was probably not treason at all.

The curious thing about the trial was that not a word of competent evidence against Raleigh was offered. The judges of the King's Bench, supplemented by several of Raleigh's enemies, were named to try him. A jury was impaneled, and then Coke began a violent and inflammatory speech, winding up by asking Raleigh if he had malice against the King's children.

RALEIGH: To whom speak you this? You tell me news I never heard of.

COKE: Oh, sir, do I ? I will prove you the notoriest traitor that ever came to the bar. After you have taken away the King, you would alter religion.

RALEIGH: Your words cannot condemn me. My innocency is my defence.

COKE: Nay, I will prove all: thou art a monster. Thou hast an English face but a Spanish heart.

RALEIGH: Let me answer for myself.

COKE: Thou shalt not.

RALEIGH: It concerneth my life.

COKE: Oh, do I touch you?

Can any one conceive of the contemptible meanness of Coke in trying to prevent Raleigh from speaking and then turning to the jury with the remark "Oh, do I touch you?" Coke went on to charge Raleigh with negotiating with Lady Arabella Stuart, as to which he was to offer no evidence whatever.

RALEIGH: Did I ever speak with this lady?

Coke did not answer, but made another mass of hearsay charges in the most savage manner.

RALEIGH: I will wash my hands of the indictment and die a true man.
COKE: You are the absolutest traitor that ever was.
RALEIGH: Your words will not prove it.

Coke continued his harangue and wound up by saying: "You, my masters of the jury, respect his cause; if he be guilty, I know you will have care of it, for the preservation of the King, the continuance of the Gospel authorized, and the good of us all."

The most irritating thing about Coke is his bloodthirsty zeal against Raleigh's life while with his sniveling assumption of hypocritical piety he talks of the continuance of the Gospel authorized. The loveliness of the Gospel ideal of mercy and kindliness was as much wasted on Coke as it would have been on a saber-toothed tiger.

Raleigh, refusing to be led off into such a matter as "the continuance of the Gospel authorized," whatever that might mean, stuck to the point of the evidence against him and responded: "I do not hear yet that you have spoken one word of evidence against me. Here is no treason of mine done. If my lord Cobham be a traitor, what is that to me?"

COKE: All that he did was by thy instigation, thou viper; for I *thou* thee, thou traitor.
RALEIGH: It becometh not a man of quality and virtue to call me so. But I take comfort in it, it is all you can do.

Hereupon Chief Justice Popham, a craven example of judicial servility, well knowing that Coke's conduct exceeded all bounds of decency, and that it was the duty of the court to protect the prisoner, since he could have neither counsel nor witnesses, did not reprove Coke, but intervened with this cowardly imbecility: "Sir Walter Raleigh, Mr. Attorney (Coke) speaketh out of the zeal of his duty, for the service of the King and you for your life; be valiant on both sides."

After this opening of Coke where the jury was not warned that Coke was making charges, not offering proof, the evidence began. An examination of Cobham taken privately and *not subscribed by him* was read with not one syllable of evidence in it, yet containing some vague, indefinite statements as to Raleigh, whereupon Raleigh said: "Let me see the accusation. This is absolutely all the evidence can be brought against me. Poor shifts! You, Gentlemen of the Jury, I pray you understand this. This is that which must either condemn or give me life, which must either free me or send my wife and children to beg their bread upon the streets. This must prove me a notorious traitor or a true subject to the King."

Raleigh showed how the deposition had been concocted; and Popham acknowledged that Cobham did not wish to sign it, and that he (Popham) afterwards tried to persuade him to do so, but Cobham would not sign. Coke now made another bitter speech full of railing accusations and seemed to be at the end of what he had to offer. Thereupon Raleigh made the point that two witnesses were necessary against him, which was undoubtedly the law in high treason and afterwards was so held. But Coke denied this to be the law and Popham and the subservient judges held with him. But Coke knew better, for he at once began hunting for some corroborating evidence.

Raleigh demanded the right to be confronted with Cobham, but this was denied him upon the singular ground that Cobham, if brought in, might not stand by his charge. Raleigh, of course, was right in asking that the witness who was available should be called before the court. The right to be confronted by the witness is in our law a constitutional right, except in tribunals or bodies that care nothing for the Constitution. It was ruled in Raleigh's case that the law of England permitted as proof a deposition that the witness had refused to sign and that the prosecution should not call the witness. But Coke knew that the point was good, for another deposition, of no value, was then read and a witness was sworn who said that he heard a man say: "The King shall never be crowned, for Don Raleigh and Don Cobham will cut his throat ere that day come."

RALEIGH: What infer you upon this?
COKE: That your treason hath wings!!

Raleigh then urged that Cobham had afterward denied the accusation fathered upon him, saying: "If truth be constant and constancy be in truth, why hath he forsworn that that he hath said? You have not proved any one thing against me by direct proofs."

COKE: Have you done? The King must have the last.
RALEIGH: Nay, Mr. Attorney, he which speaketh for his life, must speak last. False repetitions and mistakings must not mar my cause. You should speak *secundum allegata et probata*. I appeal to God and the King in this point, whether Cobham's accusation be sufficient to condemn me.
COKE: The King's safety and your clearing cannot agree. I protest before God, I never knew a clearer treason.

This was too much even for Lord Cecil, who had been made a Commissioner because he was an enemy of Raleigh. It is characteristic of the times that Cecil was so degraded as to be willing to sit. Yet even he intervened, saying: "Be not so impatient, good Mr. Attorney, give him leave to speak."

COKE: If I may not be patiently heard, you will encourage traitors and discourage us. I am the King's sworn servant and must speak.

Here Coke sat down angry, "in a chafe," and would speak no more, until the Commissioners and Judges, fearing the King's displeasure, urged and entreated him. Then he made another long speech not any more to the point. Sir Walter Raleigh interrupted him and said: "You do me wrong."

COKE: You are the most vile and execrable traitor that ever lived.
RALEIGH: You speak indiscreetly, barbarously, and uncivilly.
COKE: I want words sufficient to express thy viperous treasons.
RALEIGH: I think you want words, indeed, for you have spoken one thing half a dozen times.

This was a body-blow to Coke, who was no match for Raleigh.

COKE: Thou art an odious fellow, thy name is hateful to all the realm of England for thy pride.

RALEIGH: It will go near to prove a measuring cast between you and me, Mr. Attorney.

COKE: Well, I will now make it appear to the world that there never lived a viler viper upon the face of the earth than thou.

Coke then drew a letter out of his pocket written by Lord Cobham and read it to the jury. Then Raleigh pulled out of his own pocket another letter written by Cobham. In it Cobham protested that Raleigh had never been connected with him, nor did he know of any treason of Raleigh's.

RALEIGH: Now I wonder how many souls this man hath. He damns one in this letter and another in that.

Raleigh had so well withstood the brutal browbeating of Coke that even his enemies were affected, for of the two men first to report the trial to the king, the first said that never any man spoke so well as Raleigh in times past, nor ever would in time to come; the other said that when the trial began he was so led by the common hatred that he would have gone a hundred miles to have seen Raleigh hanged, but he would, ere he parted, have walked a thousand miles to have saved Raleigh's life.

The jury, who must have been a set of hardened ruffians, knowing what was expected of them, without being charged, retired and in fifteen minutes brought in a verdict of guilty and Popham pronounced a sentence of death which was not then carried out. Raleigh lay for years in the Tower a prisoner. It was in that time that he showed his literary genius. Knowledge and scholarship

> brought the wise and brave of ancient days
> To cheer the cell where Raleigh pined alone.

This was probably the best part of his life. Later he was out of prison for a time. But at the end of many years he was brought again before the court and resentenced upon the old verdict, Raleigh saying after the award of execution on the fourteen-year-old judgment: "Here I take

God to be my judge, before whom I shall shortly appear. I was never disloyal to his Majesty, which I will justify where I shall not fear the face of any King on earth."

Thus by the brutality of Coke, who passes as a great lawyer, was done to death one of the bravest and most gallant gentlemen, most richly endowed with wit and ability, that England has ever produced. Yet this was possible because there were no rules of evidence, and because the judges in the face of popular sentiment were utterly craven. Coke received his reward. He became Chief Justice of the Common Pleas and later Chief Justice of the King's Bench. He now changed his habit of servility and was dismissed. He then turned patriot, thus proving the satirical definition that Johnson was later to give in his Dictionary of "patriotism," that it is "the last refuge of the scoundrel."

We turn from this depressing trial and this state of the criminal law to the enlivening one of fees, always to lawyers a sacred word. In this connection it is to be said that money was worth twenty times what it will now buy. A celebrated lawyer of this time was Richard Kingsmill. A letter still extant says: "For Mr. Kingsmill it were well doon that he were with you for his authority and worship, and he will let for no maugre, and yf the enquest passe against you he may showe you sum comfortable remedy, but, sir, his coming will be costly to you." The childlike confidence in the high-priced lawyer is touching. But the fees seem ridiculously small. We know that the Goldsmiths' Company of London paid a retainer of ten shillings. "A breakfast at Westminster spent on our counsel" cost one shilling sixpence. Serjeant Yaxley's retainer from the litigious Plumpton for the next assizes at York, Notts, and Derby, was five pounds, and a fee of forty marks, if the Serjeant attended the assizes.

It is more interesting to one of sound digestion to turn from such fees to a picture of the lawyers in their hours of entertainment and feasting. In social entertainments the Inns shone. Costly feasts, magnificent revels, masks, and plays, where the royal family attended, the splendid celebrations of calls of serjeants, the feasts given by the readers, are all fully described in contemporary annals. We read of "spiced bread, comfits and other goodly conceits, and hippocras," and the bill of supply of one of the feasts, comprising "twenty-four great beefs," "one hundred fat muttons," "fifty-one great veales," "thirty-four porkes," "ninety-one piggs," through endless capons, grouse, pigeons and swans to three hundred and forty dozen larks, gives an idea of the lawyers' carnivorous gormandizing. One might think that these men who had so much time for the Scriptures would have found that incident where at the beginning of the Book of Daniel the Prophet so effectively demonstrated to the Persian King the superiority of vegetarians.

At just this time Coke attempted to destroy the power of the court of chancery to remedy the injustice of the common law courts. Coke was a very narrow-minded man to whom justice was nothing. The chancellor was Lord Ellesmere, who adorned his decisions by frequent and none too apposite quotations from the Scriptures. Coke attempted to use the process of contempt against the injunction of the chancery court. The matter went for decision to King James I. Though not much of a Solomon, James acted upon the advice of Bacon and upheld the chancery court. The chancery bar was strong and took an active part in the fray. The victory of the chancery court was complete. But Coke by his combination of Puritanism and hypocrisy had persuaded the Puritans into an exceeding animosity against the chancery court. Something here might be said of Bacon, who succeeded Lord Ellesmere as Chancellor, but Bacon's career as a judge was not creditable.

The lawyers received little consideration from Cromwell. Passing this period when the Inns of Court were closed, we come to the Restoration in 1660, and find the bar entering upon a new career. At first it is hard to see any improvement over Coke in such a man as Jeffreys, but the bar was steadily growing better. All through the eighteenth century, lawyers were becoming more liberalized. The century began with a great judge, Sir John Holt. He ruled the common law for a long period. The new business of banking and bank notes was to be given its set of rules. Holt was to some extent learned in the Roman law as then taught. He boldly avowed his opinion that practically everything in the English law had come from the civil law. At one stroke the Roman law of bailments was introduced by Holt into English law. He settled the principles of the new law of agency partly from the old law regarding master and servant but mainly from the principles of the Roman law.

Francis Bacon, Viscount St. Alban (1561–1626)

A separate class of lawyers called proctors and advocates had grown up, who practised in the ecclesiastical and the admiralty courts. The advocates corresponding to barristers were called Doctors, and their organization was called Doctors' Commons. The admiralty court, especially as a prize court, was of ever-increasing importance. Divorce cases and matters of probating and executing of wills required more and more legal work. This bar was called that of the canonists and civilians.

England was now in her great career as a trading nation. The law merchant was yet needed to be introduced and a little later the greatest of English judges, Lord Mansfield, became Chief Justice of the King's Bench. He was a Scotchman, who when he was fourteen saw the highroad to England and took it. He never returned to the land of his birth. At last there was on the bench a judge who had knowledge enough to have sat as a Roman judge in the age of Antonines, and to have decided cases in accordance with the Roman law. He introduced into the common law the law pertaining to commercial documents. The law of shipping, insurance, partnership, and of recovery of money on equitable grounds in all the relations covered by the Roman quasi-contract was settled by Lord Mansfield. He tried to liberalize even the English land law.

There was a rule firmly fixed in English law called the Rule in Shelley's Case, which was invented under the Yorkist kings in order to make land more readily alienable, but had in fact come to act in precisely the opposite way. In the case of a will Lord Mansfield held that the plainly expressed intention of the testator should govern and should displace the ordinary result of the Rule in Shelley's Case. In other words, he held that the rule was merely a method of ascertaining intention. If the intention was otherwise plainly expressed, there was no need of invoking the rule. Immediately there was a concerted and unanimous howl from the real property practitioners. Hargrave handed up to Lord Mansfield his own written opinion on that very title given when Mansfield was a barrister. There was a painful scene. Mansfield was extremely disconcerted. He had none of the aplomb of the great Chancellor Lord Westbury. When an opinion of Westbury's as a barrister was handed up to him and he glanced over it and saw that it was to the exact contrary of an opinion he had just delivered as Chancellor, he was not at all abashed.

He merely observed: "I wonder how a man capable of writing such an opinion could ever have attained his present exalted position."

Twelve years after Mansfield reached the bench, one of the greatest cases ever heard before the English House of Lords came on for hearing. The highest appellate jurisdiction in England was that of the Lords. In 1701 had come the Union with Scotland and the English House of Lords became the ultimate court for Scotch appeals. In 1769 was heard the appeal in the Douglas case—a case remarkable for its romantic circumstances, for the great material interests involved, and especially for the eminence of the counsel engaged. It will serve to illustrate the lawyers and the practice in England just before our Revolution, when lawyers in the Colonies were still obtaining their legal education at the Inns of Court in London.[1]

While in form the case was an appeal in a civil case, in essence it was a trial of a dead woman, Lady Jane Douglas, of a descent ancient and illustrious enough to satisfy the cravings of the wildest romancer. The House of Douglas, the noblest in Scotland, had many branches. Its elder line was the Black Douglas, and had the title Earl of Douglas. In ballad and in story there is nothing more stirring than the life of the Black Douglas who fought with Robert the Bruce and at last set out carrying his king's heart to lay it in the Holy Land. The Red Douglas, Earls of Angus, became heads of the house after the ruin of the Black Douglas, and enjoyed the great estates of the lordship of Douglas. They were among the most powerful of Scotch nobles and successively became Marquises of Douglas and of Angus and Dukes of Douglas. The Master of Angus (the eldest son of old Archibald "Bell-the-Cat," Earl of Angus, whom we read of in *Marmion*), with one hundred knights of the Douglas name, each followed by his retainers, died in that devoted ring around King James, on

Flodden's fatal field,
Where shivered was fair Scotland's spear
And broken was her shield!

1. The reader may also wish to consult Lillian de la Torre's *The Heir of Douglas* (New York: Alfred A. Knopf, 1952), a dramatic rendering of this affair.—C. J. R., Jr.

One Earl of Angus was the grandfather of King James VI of Scotland and I of England.

At last, in 1746, the man who was head of the house, Archibald Douglas, Duke and Marquis of Douglas, Marquis and Earl of Angus, the premier peer of Scotland, was a saddened recluse, who had never married and had quarreled with his only sister, Lady Jane, a beautiful but wilful and headstrong woman, with a tendency, irritating to her brother, to encourage the addresses of fascinating and penniless gentlemen, while she rejected every suitor who, in her brother's judgment, was fit to marry his sister. Two duels her brother had fought on her account. In the second duel he had killed a bastard cousin who had presumed to woo his sister. The brand of Cain had driven him into complete retirement. Pressed by her brother to marry, Lady Jane had refused, until they had become completely estranged. She lived most of the time in Paris with the Scotch Jacobites. The two differed even in politics. The Duke stood by the Hanoverian succession, while the sister was a partisan of the exiled house of Stuart. But at last, a woman of forty-eight, she married secretly an old suitor, Colonel Stewart, a ruined and spendthrift Jacobite who had been out in the Forty-five. The couple, without publicly declaring their marriage, had gone to Paris, where the story begins with the birth to Lady Jane of twin sons when she was forty-nine, although it was contended that she was actually fifty-one. The parturition was not impossible, but was, to say the least, very unusual. Before this she had written to her brother disclosing her marriage; he in bitter disgust had not answered but had cut off her allowance; now she wrote again, telling him of her new happiness and that she had named the elder boy Archibald after him, and still the Duke answered not a word.

The next heir after Lady Jane's son was the Duke of Hamilton, a child descended from George Douglas, a younger son of the Angus line, who more than a hundred years before had married Anne, in her own right the Duchess of Hamilton. The members of this family were called the Douglas Hamiltons and they were very powerful through the immense Hamilton patrimony. They seem to have gotten to the Duke of Douglas with whispered accusations that Lady Jane and her adventurer husband were attempting to palm off a supposititious child as the heir of the Douglas lands. He believed them and, highly incensed, made a settlement of his estates on the young Duke of Hamilton. Lady Jane hearing of this came back from France, penniless. Her husband fell into a debtors' prison in London, but she fared on to Scotland; she vainly sought to see her brother, but was turned away from the door of Douglas Castle. Soon the younger twin died, and broken by grief and anxiety, Lady Jane passed away in poverty and actual want. But now the spendthrift husband came into his own, an elder brother died and he became Sir John Stewart and settled 50,000 marks on his son. In explanation of this seeming prodigality in a Scot it should be said that these were Scotch marks, one-tenth the value of the English mark of thirteen and a half shillings. Soon Sir John also died, and both Lady Jane and her husband, knowing the hand of Death to be laid upon them, solemnly asserted that the boy Archibald was their son. It ought to have required exceedingly strong proof to overcome the almost conclusive presumption arising from such evidence.

The Duke of Douglas then married a very distant relative, Miss Margaret Douglas, a *ci-devant* beauty, who took up the child's cause and, in spite of many rebuffs, at last induced her husband to listen to reason and persuaded him to revoke the settlement on the Hamilton heir. In his last illness he acknowledged his nephew as his heir. Ten days later, in 1751, the Duke was dead, and Archibald, the son of Lady Jane, whose sad story had aroused universal compassion, reigned in his stead. But the Hamilton guardians were not idle. They scoffed at what they called a miraculous conception. Their agents went over to France and by a lavish use of money came back with a mass of evidence to show that Archibald was the son of a Parisian glassblower bought by Lady Jane for the occasion of her pretended accouchement. The widowed Duchess of Douglas had had herself appointed the boy Archibald's guardian and money was not wanting. She in her turn went over to Paris and spent her funds still more lavishly to unearth the Hamilton plot.

An action was now begun by the Hamiltons in the Scotch court and the cause was heard in 1767 before the Court of Session, consisting of fifteen judges. Scotland had the Roman procedure. The court, by the original eight to seven decision, held for the Hamilton. There was an immense popular outcry, the mob smashed the prevailing judges' windows, the militia was called out, and it looked almost like a civil war in Scotland between Douglases and Hamiltons.

An appeal was taken to the English House of Lords, and the great Douglas connection rallied round the young heir. First in power came the Duke of Queensberry and Dover, a great personage at court, head of a younger illegitimate Douglas line, also the Earl of Morton, another powerful Douglas, and the Duke of Buccleuch, who in his youth had been a rejected suitor of Lady Jane. But strongest and best of all the Douglas phalanx was the imperious ruler of the great world of fashion, the Duchess of Queensberry, once Catherine Hyde, a reigning toast and noted beauty, great-granddaughter of Lord Chancellor Clarendon and cousin of two Stuart Queens of England, Queen Mary and Queen Anne, the daughters of James II by his first marriage with Clarendon's daughter. She was a great wit with a bitter tongue, in her younger days a patron of letters, the friend of Congreve, Pope, Prior, and Gay. Now in 1767 she was an old woman, faithful to the fashions of her days of beauty, powerful at the court of the young king, George III. There is a vivid description of her Grace of Queensberry, as she was a few years before this time, in the thirty-fourth chapter of Thackeray's *Virginians*, when she dawned on young Henry Warrington's tea and ball. There is pictured a battle royal between the old Duchess and the friend of her youth, that Beatrix Esmond who, in Thackeray's *Esmond*, was the heroine of the finest scene in all historical fiction, where Colonel Warrington broke his sword and renounced all allegiance to the faithless Stuart race.

Both Hamiltons and Douglases began canvassing the House of Lords for votes on the appeal, for in those days all peers voted upon law questions as well as other questions in the House of Lords. In this business the Queensberry Duchess was a past grand mistress. She rapidly disposed of all the proselytizing of the Hamiltons. In the meantime the appeal papers had come up before the Lords, and the Scotch law agents of the Duchess of Douglas came down to London to look over the ground and select their counsel. One evening soon after their arrival they wandered into the celebrated coffee house of Nando's. They sat sipping their wine with true Scotch reserve.

At a near-by table a discussion arose between some gentlemen pre-sumably barristers. One was defending the Scotch decision in the Douglas case. A large man of thirty with a magnificent head and great beetling brows boomed into the discussion, attacking the ruling. This was the redoubtable Edward Thurlow, afterwards Lord Chancellor and the despotic ruler of the House of Lords, then a briefless barrister com-ing into practice, a regular habitué of Nando's and devoted to its excel-lent punch. After pouring forth a flood of argument, the punch becom-ing exhausted, Thurlow rolled home to his chambers. But he had convinced the Scotch agents of his power, for in the morning an im-mense roll of papers was delivered, marked with an astonishing fee, ac-companied by a no less astonishing retainer, and Thurlow was named to prepare the great Douglas case for the appeal in the House of Lords. He was at once presented to her Grace of Queensberry and paid courtly tribute to her fading charms. She was immensely taken with him, pro-nounced his conversation the most charming since Lord Bolingbroke. Her lawyer, she asserted, must not appear in the stuff gown of a junior, so she sought the king, George III. The silk gown of a King's Counsel, which would not have come to him until after years of success at the bar, was granted to the rising barrister at the request of the young King him-self, and Thurlow's fortune was made.

At last the hearing came on before a crowded House of Lords. The Lords had been thoroughly canvassed. The decision depended on Lord Camden, the Chancellor, and Lord Mansfield, the Chief Justice, for the majority of the Lords, while eager to vote for the Douglas claimant, would not disregard the opinion of the two law lords. If the law lords differed the majority would blindly follow Lord Mansfield. Appearing for the Douglas claimant were Thurlow, who had prepared on paper a powerful statement of the case, Sir James Montgomery, the well-known Scotch advocate, and Sir Fletcher Norton. On the other side were Charles Yorke, the Attorney General, the second son of Lord Hard-wicke, the great Chancellor, soon himself to be Chancellor, and Alex-ander Wedderburn, called "Sarcastic Sawney." He afterwards became Lord Loughborough and Chancellor as Earl of Rosslyn, and was just now enjoying an immense reputation for his successful defense of Lord

Clive, the conqueror of India. The actual leader was Dunning, the head of the bar, the man whose great argument before Lord Camden had destroyed general warrants, a man uncouth and ungainly, but with a great genius hidden behind a forbidding exterior. He was a most persuasive speaker, once supposed by many to have been Junius, that "shadow of a mighty name." He was now Solicitor General with a splendid political career before him, which he sacrificed like a true advocate and a brave gentleman by taking the side of the American colonies; yet the American is rare who remembers or even knows of that unselfish act.

Thurlow opened for the appellant and gained immense applause by his wonderful dissection of the evidence. He made a savage attack on the agent of the Hamiltons, who had prepared the Hamilton testimony, accusing him of bribery and subornation of worthless French witnesses. Then came the Scotch Advocate General, thoroughly explaining the evidence and the bearing of the Scotch law. Next came Wedderburn for the Hamiltons; he made the most brilliant speech. Charles James Fox, no mean judge, said that Wedderburn made the best speech that he had ever heard on any subject. Horace Walpole wrote that he spoke with greater applause than was almost ever known. Charles Yorke followed, to the great disgust of the Douglases, for the Duchess of Douglas thought that she had retained him and when she found that he had taken a retainer from the Hamiltons, she said to him: "Then, sir, in the next world, whose will you be, for we have all had you?" This was almost prophetic, for in a short time poor Charles Yorke, become Lord Chancellor in spite of a solemn promise, lay dead, probably a suicide, in utter shame. Then after Dunning the case was closed for the Douglases by Sir Fletcher Norton, once Attorney General, a bold and able pleader noted for his clearness of argument and carelessness as to facts, of whom Lord Mansfield said that it was most difficult to prevent him by his art from misleading a jury. He was known to the political pamphleteers of the time as "Sir Bull-Face Double Fee," which describes accurately both his unabashed front and the large emoluments of his practice.

The throng, many of whom had wagered money on the result, waited for the law lords to give their opinions. Lord Camden, thoroughly primed by Mansfield, spoke giving his opinion for the Douglas claimant.

He was followed by Lord Mansfield (himself belonging to a younger line of the ancient Scotch house of Murray). Lord Mansfield's speech has been criticized, but it is very eloquent, and he knew his audience. He did not discuss the evidence (that had been fully gone over by Lord Camden); but he told in a moving way how Lady Jane in her distress had come to see him when she came from France, the impression of goodness she made upon him, and her pitiful last years of sorrow and suffering. He protested that he could not believe that a lady of her breeding and illustrious descent, a woman of her proud and noble nature, could be guilty of such a heinous fraud. Then the whole House indorsed the opinions of the law lords. The judgment of the Scotch Court for the Hamiltons was reversed with but five dissenting voices, and the Douglas heir had won, but the title of Duke and Marquis of Douglas was extinct, and those of Marquis of Angus and the very ancient earldom of Angus passed by the Scotch law to the Duke of Hamilton. The King at once created the Douglas heir Lord Douglas of Douglas Castle, but the male line has not survived. His descendants are the Douglas Homes, Earls of Home.

But the case was not over. The Scotch agent whom Thurlow had denounced promptly challenged him while the case was being argued. Thurlow at once accepted, to fight when the case was finished. So the next morning after the decision Thurlow proceeded to Hyde Park. On the way he stopped and ate an enormous breakfast; it might be his last. The principals were set at ten paces, they discharged their pistols. Being lawyers both missed, of course. Then they drew their swords and advanced upon each other, when the seconds intervened and stopped the duel. But let us record for the courage of the one combatant and the fairness of the other, that the Scotch agent gallantly acknowledged that "Mr. Thurlow advanced and stood up to him like an elephant."

It has been noted before that the bill of attainder was revived against Lord Strafford. It was supposed to be a judicial proceeding. It had a minor form called a bill of pains and penalties. The difference between the two forms was merely in punishment. Such a proceeding was used by an English king in an attempt to divorce his queen, and it gives another picture of English law in 1820. An interesting volume has been published upon this trial of Queen Caroline, but the best summary of

William Murray, First Earl of Mansfield (1705–93)

the trial is in Atlay's *Victorian Chancellors*, the best of the English books on judges and far more carefully done than Lord Campbell's *Lives of the Lord Chancellors.*[2]

Every one knows the story of how that heartless and profligate dandy, George IV, when Prince of Wales, after his illegal marriage with Mrs. Fitzherbert, was persuaded, in order to get his debts paid, to marry a German princess. In 1795 his cousin, Caroline of Brunswick, was selected for this honor. She was the daughter of that Duke of Brunswick who afterwards fell at the battle of Auerstadt, usually called Jena, and sister of "Brunswick's fated chieftain," who in Byron's lines is at the scene of revelry in Brussels as Napoleon approached for the battle of Waterloo. This Duke rushed from the ball to the field and fell at Quatre-Bras two days before Waterloo.

The Princess was not very prepossessing or refined, and when she was brought to London and the Prince of Wales saw his proposed bride out of the wilds of Brunswick, he hastily called for brandy to enable him to endure the sight; but he managed to get through the wedding ceremony with the help of more copious draughts of brandy. After a daughter had been born to the pair the king developed such a hatred against his wife that he refused to live with her. Even then her indiscretions were the subject of a confidential investigation. When the Prince became Regent she was induced by a liberal allowance to travel in the Mediterranean countries. She dragged in her train a curious retinue of her own choosing. Sad tales of her misdoings came back to England and Sir John Leach, the Vice Chancellor, sent out a commission to investigate. When the old and insane King George III died, the Prince Regent became George IV and Caroline was by right of marriage Queen of England. Their only child, the beloved Princess Charlotte, who had always taken her mother's side, was dead with her newborn child, in the first year of her marriage. Even Byron, who hated royalty, has left a noble elegy on the fair-haired Daughter of the Isles.

2. See also E. A. Smith, *A Queen on Trial: The Affair of Queen Caroline, 1820–1821* (Dover, N.H.: A. Sutton, 1993); and Ruger Fulford, *The Trial of Queen Caroline* (New York: Stein and Day, 1968).—C. J. R., Jr.

In spite of her legal advisers, Queen Caroline came back to England, eagerly welcomed by the mass of the people, and insisted upon taking her place as Queen of England. Her husband's conduct was looked upon as so much worse than hers could possibly be that the great majority of the middle and lower classes were her warm partisans. Curiously enough, the brothers of the King divided upon the question. Two of them tried to argue about the matter in the House of Lords and became so heated as to scandalize the proceedings by an ordinary fist-fight. The King insisted on divorcing the Queen absolutely. He particularly objected to her being prayed for in the church service, although by his own contention she greatly needed the prayers. No court in England had jurisdiction except Parliament. A bill of pains and penalties was proposed in the House of Lords, adjudging her guilty of marital misconduct, depriving her of the title of Queen Consort and absolutely divorcing her from the King. This bill, like any ordinary legislative divorce proceeding in England, was required to be proven by evidence upon a full hearing.

The Queen, as she was entitled, had her own Attorney General and a Solicitor General. First came Brougham, her Attorney General, afterwards leader of the House of Commons and later Lord Chancellor as Lord Brougham, in some ways the most efficient advocate of his time, destined to live far into that century. Next came Denman, of a peculiarly brilliant and unsullied fame. Next came Tindal, afterwards Chief Justice of the Common Pleas, and Wilde, afterwards Chancellor as Lord Truro, an able and determined man. Williams, the law reformer, and the civilian, Dr. Lushington, made up the array of counsel for the Queen. Those who have read the book, *Astarte*, of a scoundrelly grandson, where Lord Lovelace attempts to cover with slime the memory of his grandfather, the great Byron, and those who have read the literature evoked by the book, can be informed of the very questionable conduct of Lushington in that matter of baseless slander.

The counsel for the King were the Attorney General, Sir Robert Gifford, afterwards Chief Justice of the Common Pleas and Master of the Rolls as Lord Gifford, who died at the untimely age of forty-nine. Next him the Solicitor General, Copley, is of peculiar interest, for he is the only English Chancellor who was born in America. In 1772 he first saw the light in Boston; he was the eldest son of the painter John Singleton Copley. His mother was the daughter of that Boston merchant whose cargo of tea the Boston Tea Party dumped into the harbor. The family being Loyalists left for England just prior to the Revolution. The son was educated at Cambridge and studied for the bar. He once came over to Boston to see what he could obtain of his mother's property, which had been confiscated. The United States had never performed the clause of the treaty which required the confiscated property to be returned. It is needless to say that Copley obtained very little from the Bostonians, but Copley Square and the name Copley Plaza for a hotel may be considered a kind of belated expression of a desire to make restitution. Lord Lyndhurst's recollection of his visit never led him to visit Boston again. As a young lawyer Copley came into prominence for his wonderful skill in cross-examination and for an extraordinary clearness of statement in weaving together in one luminous whole the facts and circumstances of an intricate case. He was destined to be four times Lord Chancellor as Lord Lyndhurst, and though born before the Revolution he lived to hear the news of Gettysburg and of the fall of Vicksburg. One of the extraordinary scenes in the House of Lords was Lyndhurst, ninety years old, his eyesight gone but with unspent vigor and memory undimmed, "with a mind unworn, undebased, undecayed," delivering without a note an exhaustive speech, reviewing the complicated diplomatic relations of England with Russia over a long period of years. He was a mental giant.

Another of the counsel for the King was the technical lawyer, afterwards Baron Parke of the Court of the Exchequer, who ruled that court for years and by his technical rulings rendered the Exchequer Reports of his time such a perennial fountain of injustice. He was known as Baron Surrebutter.

The cause was opened in a crowded House of Lords. The approaches to the Parliament Building were barricaded. A regiment of the Guards was posted at Westminster Hall. The Household Cavalry patrolled the streets. The Queen arrived, surrounded by a cheering mob. The foreign witnesses for the King, who had been subjected to rough treatment by the populace when they landed at Dover, were thoroughly washed, newly clothed, and herded together in a separate building under military guard, for around it constantly prowled a mob, inflamed by the usual lower-class hostility toward foreigners, eagerly seeking a chance to maltreat those Italians who had been brought over to testify against the Queen.

Gifford's opening for the prosecution was a failure, but poor as it was the facts he unfolded were so bad that when he sat down the Queen's case seemed lost. Even if she were not guilty of actual misconduct, her behavior had been so reckless as to render her unfit to be Queen. The first witness called was the Italian Majocchi, the Queen's postilion, and when the Queen saw him she further injured her case by flouncing out of the House, the very feathers in her hair fluttering in indignation. The witness told his tale, but on cross-examination by Brougham his stupidity in continuously answering "Non me ricordo" (I do not remember) to any question whatever, broke him down. The cross-examination of the Queen's Swiss waiting maid, Demont, by Williams, along with Coleridge's cross-examination of the Tichborne claimant, remains of classic fame in legal annals. At the close of the prosecution, on account of the powerful cross-examinations, the King's proof was much battered; but then Copley arose and by his consummate skill, his ease, his suavity, and his genius for marshaling testimony, restored the case.

After an adjournment of several weeks Brougham as leader opened for the Queen in the supreme effort of his life; but there was too much oratory and too little attention to the testimony. He savagely assailed some of the witnesses. One paragraph of Brougham's speech described one witness as "that hoary pander, the manner in which he told his story, the haggard look which gave him the appearance of an inhabitant of the infernal regions, and which must have reminded your Lordships of the great Italian poet's description of a broad-faced tailor in Hell peeping and grinning through the eye of a needle." Brougham's recital of the wrongs of the Queen stirred the country to resentment. Especially moving was his description of the deserted wife, hearing for the first time from strangers of the death of her only daughter, long after she should have been informed from England, and before she even knew of the illness. He startled the King and the House of Lords by the threat that he could recriminate with evidence of the King's misdoings. His peroration with his invocation to the Lords has always been admired by those who love florid oratory. It is a remarkable contrast to Burke's famous peroration in the Warren Hastings trial, modeled on Cicero's peroration against Verres, and it is not so good even as that of Thaddeus Stevens in the impeachment of President Johnson.

But when the witnesses were examined for the defense, it was a different story. The Queen's case probably would have been as good if no witnesses had been called. While the Queen's domestic servants supported her, one English officer in her suite admitted damaging facts, and Copley cross-examined another Lieutenant Flynn, who was evidently trying to shield the Queen, until the witness collapsed and was taken out of the court in a fainting condition. Some of the witnesses were too dangerous to call, although they had been unwisely mentioned by name in Brougham's opening speech for the defense. But Brougham fortunately found that one witness for the prosecution had been sent away contrary to a stipulation. He suddenly demanded his presence. The man who had sent him away was asked by Brougham, "Who is your employer?"—striking at the King. Loud cries of "Order" were heard, and then Brougham, whom nothing could intimidate, came back with his famous passage, quoting Milton's *Paradise Lost:*

> Who is the party? I know nothing about this shrouded, this mysterious being, this retiring phantom, this uncertain shape,
>> "If shape it might be called that shape had none
>> Distinguishable in member, joint, or limb;
>
> . . . .
>
>> what seemed his head
>> The likeness of a kingly crown had on."

This cut George IV and added an element of amusement. The Prince was called the First Gentleman of Europe. He was vain of his person, even though he trundled before him a very pendulous and protuberant abdomen. He complained that Brougham might have spared his shape, for everybody allowed, whatever faults he had, that his legs at least were not undistinguishable.

At last the witnesses were finished and Denman arose to sum up the evidence. His speech is wonderful until the very close. There he ruined it by quoting the famous words to the woman taken in adultery: "If no one come forward to condemn thee, neither will I condemn thee. Go and sin no more." In defense of a woman charged with misconduct who was asserting her innocence, this may be called an unpardonable instance of lack of judgment. On the spot some wag invented the epigram, which ran over the city:

> Gracious lady, we implore,
> Go away, and sin no more,
> And if that effort be too great
> Go away at any rate.

Dr. Lushington, who followed Denman, was a divorce practitioner, and he dealt with the evidence. In reply came first the Attorney General Gifford, who now redeemed his failure in opening. That often used device, the comment on the failure to produce witnesses within call who know the facts, was used with crushing effect. Finally Copley closed, ridiculing Denman and Brougham. One of his classical quotations from the thirty-seventh ode of the first book of Horace, describing Cleopatra before the battle of Actium, is noted for its aptness:

> The maddened queen nursing the wildest hopes and drunk with fortune's favors, with her filthy herd of abandoned ruffians, is plotting ruin 'gainst the Capitol and the Empire.

This was a double hit. It struck both the Queen and her attendant mob. Her main supporter, Alderman Wood of London, called "Absolute Wisdom," redeemed himself by being the father of Lord Chancellor Hatherly.

A dispute now arose among the Lords. Certain of them would not agree to convict the Queen and leave her undivorced as Queen of England. Being mainly respectable gentlemen, they balked at a conclusion which left a convicted adulteress Queen of England. But the Bishops who sat in the House of Lords would not agree to an absolute divorce. These impracticable persons took literally, as so many other misguided persons have done, the solemn words in the marriage service: "Whom God hath joined let no man put asunder." So the bill had but nine majority and the ministry abandoned it. Soon "the fickle reek of popular breath" turned from the Queen and the next year she died, asking for her coffin the simple inscription "Caroline, the injured Queen of England."

Ever since 1700, at least, the leading lawyers had taken a prominent part in politics, and their services in the House of Commons as Solicitor General and Attorney General led to high judicial position. Blackstone's famous lectures, called his Commentaries, were rewarded by a seat in the Common Pleas. He wrote the opinion in the appellate court known as the Exchequer Chamber, which reversed Lord Mansfield on the Rule in Shelley's Case. Eminent barristers had an extraordinary field in the great state prosecutions. Wedderburn defended Clive; Law, known best as Lord Ellenborough, defended Warren Hastings. Brougham and Denman we have already seen in the Queen's case, but all the advocates were surpassed by Erskine.[3] In all history he is the greatest advocate that ever argued in court, except the Roman Cicero, who was more than an advocate and one of the greatest men of letters in literature. Later great English lawyers it is not necessary to mention, for the scene now changes with the attempts to reform the legal system. The reforms were, generally speaking, merely in procedure and administration; rarely were they directed to a change in the actual rules of substantive law.

Blackstone's Commentaries are the high-water mark of the English complacency with the legal system. The first dissenting voice was that of Bentham. The reforms were brought about by leading judges and lawyers, but Bentham has received the credit for them. He had tried to be a lawyer and failed, and was thereby made certain that the law needed reforming. He began by criticizing Blackstone's book and by denouncing the English law. For years he was not taken seriously by the English public or by the lawyers. His methods may be criticized. Instead of becom-

3. Thomas Erskine (1750–1823). See Lloyd Paul Stryker, *For the Defense: Thomas Erskine, the Most Enlightened Liberal of His Time* (Garden City, N.Y.: Doubleday, 1947). —C. J. R., Jr.

Sir William Blackstone (1723–80)

ing thoroughly versed in the history not only of the common law but also of the civil law and thus becoming able to understand why the English law was in its then condition, he chose the easier path of an *a priori* theorist. There was no question that the method of pleading in both the common law and chancery needed changes. It was apparent to most enlightened lawyers that the rules which excluded witnesses from testifying had outlived their usefulness. Most of all was required the abolition of the disorderly and expensive system of double courts. Lord Mansfield had done much for the common law, but he was succeeded by narrow-minded practitioners who tried hard to undo his work. In the chancery court Lord Eldon, whose slow and dilatory methods caused most of the complaints against the chancery, opposed himself like a moss-grown promontory to every change. He lasted for a quarter of a century, while his court steadily went from bad to worse, although his opinions, when after long delay he arrived at them, were altogether sound.

It has become customary since Bentham's death to exaggerate his services to legal reform. He was a man of wealth, able to hire secretaries, and he gradually accumulated a great mass of papers upon the subjects of a penal code, of the rationale of evidence and of methods of pleading. He devoted much material to what he called the science of legislation. He tried to formulate a constitution of government which he confidently believed would be suited to the needs of the Khedive of Egypt, to the newly established revolutionary Spanish-Indian republics in South America, and to the wild population of Mexico which is even yet constantly proving its inherent wildness. When Burr was nourishing his scheme of founding a state of his own somewhere in the neighborhood of Texas, Bentham aspired to play the rôle of Tribonian to Burr's Justinian. Time after time Bentham proposed his rather shopworn constitution to those who imagined that something new could be designed in the way of a constitution for newly admitted states of this Union. This farouche sort of reasoning is a true measure of Bentham's hopeless incapacity as a constitutional lawgiver.

It is not disputed that Bentham's ideas on the subject of simplifying procedure and pleading both in the chancery and in the common law courts were mainly sound. His belief that the exclusion of the testimony of interested witnesses was a mistake has become generally accepted, although in most jurisdictions the idea that both sides should be given an equal chance to commit perjury has limited Bentham's rules. It is still the law that if a man be deceased, whether the controversy involve the estate of the deceased or a firm of which he was a party, the living party against the deceased cannot testify to any conversation indicated to be equally within the knowledge of the party and the deceased. The law pronounces its deliberate opinion that under such circumstances the presumption is that the interested party as witness will not tell the truth. This conclusion is no doubt a wise one, but when the legal reformers had made a defendant a competent witness in a criminal case, they forgot to retain this wise and salutary rule, so that it is now the law generally in a murder case that the defendant, having killed the one who could correct his testimony, is left free to concoct in his own exculpation any sort of conversation or transaction with the deceased. Thus the reformers have made the law declare that where one is testifying against a dead man the one who will testify truthfully against the dead is certainly not one who has swindled him, but one who has killed him. A more imbecile conclusion cannot anywhere be found in the law.

The result of the Benthamite idea of evidence has been to remove almost every one of the incapacities of witnesses; but those arising from the marriage relation and from the relation of lawyer and client have been preserved. The other so-called confidential relations of medical treatment and of the confessional have not been recognized, although as an original proposition it seems hard to make any distinction between what a client tells his lawyer in order to be advised as to his legal rights and what he as a patient tells a doctor in order to be advised as to his bodily ailments and what he tells his confessor for the supposed redemption of his immortal soul.[4] But the allowance of witnesses to an accused defendant and of counsel to argue his case not only to the court but to the jury, were not in any way due to Bentham.

4. The incapacity of one spouse to testify against the other has been diminished significantly since Zane wrote. See especially *Trammell v. United States*, 445 U.S. 40 (1980). A broad evidentiary privilege has in recent decades been extended both to the medical profession and to the so-called priest-penitent relationship.—C. J. R., Jr.

In the penal law the improved treatment of prisoners and supposedly improved ideas in the matter of punishment are not due to Bentham but to others. Such things have resulted from an increasing civilization. The tendency of reformers to carry the ideas of criminal reform to impracticable extremes meets us now on every hand. No one disputes that there is such a thing as mental disease which may render a human being so abnormal that he is not responsible for his acts. The plain cases are where the physical manifestations of mental disease or defect are able to be seen. An epileptic with the unreasoning homicidal tendency of the epileptic status is not likely to escape notice. So it is in regard to many other kinds of mental disease. There are on the other hand many departures from normal lawful conduct by human beings which are or result in crimes without any manifestations of mental disease whatever.

There is a class of criminal reformers who seem to have reached the conclusion that there is a standardized human being who acts normally and lawfully and all human beings who depart from this standard are afflicted with mental disease. Since the disease is not shown by any physical affection or modification of the brain itself or its accessories, it can only be detected by conduct, and therefore the test is any departure from the normal, lawful conduct of a human being. The commission of a crime of turpitude at least, is proof positive of mental disease and lack of mental responsibility. It is, however, not questioned that in all civil matters the commission of torts or frauds is no proof of mental disease. None of the penologists is so foolish as to take such ground, but when the wrongful conduct shades off into crimes, then the mere fact of the commission of the crime is proof of lack of mental responsibility. The criminal diagnosticians have gone so far as to give a name to this sort of mental irresponsibility and the wide term used is *dementia praecox*. The term seems to mean that if a man is willing to risk committing a crime to obtain what he desires or covets, he has dementia praecox. Thus if a man goes out upon the street and robs a passer-by to get his money and is detected he has dementia praecox. If he escapes detection he is a mere ordinary person going about his affairs with normal mentality. If the man serves a term in the penitentiary and repeats the offense, the presumption of precocious madness becomes irresistible.

These criminal reformers go further and charge the mental condition of the robber, burglar, or murderer upon society at large. If they
are right in this assertion, they must mean that society has no right to
punish the victim of its processes. But they disclaim any such idea and
say that the law has no right to put the person to death, but must seg-
regate him and imprison him. This seems, then, to be simply the old
argument against the death penalty, which is a purely religious development, founded on some idea of the peculiar sanctity of a criminal's
life while all former law laid stress on the innocent life sacrificed.
These people claim that the criminal is the victim of a mental disease,
generally hereditary, which he is likely to transmit to his progeny. They
assert, so far as their conflicting ideas can be understood, that the victim of dementia praecox will not be cured by segregation and that he
must be prevented from multiplying, for having inherited his condition
he will transmit it.

The only possible answer to this contention is that society would better put its error to death. Why waste time and money on a being who, on
their theory, ought to remain like the mule, without pride of ancestry or
hope of posterity? The general result of the lucubrations of such people
seems to be that they themselves are the persons with dementia praecox.
Their abnormality is to consider a perfectly sane man a precocious de-
mentiac if he goes so far as to commit a crime. They are like the alienist
in Charles Reade's *Hard Cash* who thought almost every one that he saw
was a maniac, and it turned out that he himself was the maniac, for he
progressed in his knowledge so far that the only safe place for him was a
padded cell.

The law and the common sense of mankind have consistently refused
to listen to the confused stammerings of the maudlin penologists that
lead to no reasonable result. The legal test for insanity is the ability in
the human being to comprehend the moral quality of his act. This is a
matter of evidence and is to be decided in each case as it arises. Both law
and morality are founded upon general human conduct, and mainly
upon the tendency in human beings to conform in society to each
other's conduct. If a human being in regard to a crime shows, by his
conduct either before or after his act, that he knows that he is not con-

forming to those human standards, he thereby shows that he comprehends the nature and quality of his act, for the two phrases describe precisely the same thing.

As an instance we may take a case that has excited world-wide comment as a frightful miscarriage of justice.[5] Two young men in easy circumstances, of excellent education, showing by their conduct that they knew that they were doing a wrong and criminal thing, kidnaped a child whom they knew and who knew them, for the sole purpose of extorting money from the parents of the child. They wished the money for the particular purpose of supplementing what would be given them by their own parents for traveling in Europe. Their conduct showed that from the very beginning they contemplated murdering the child after they had obtained the money. They failed to obtain the money, although they attempted to do so both before and after murdering the child. Ingenuity in devising concealing circumstances, both before and after the act, was proven in complete detail. The callous cruelty of their conduct was apparent. Their intelligence and careful premeditation were no less apparent. The death penalty, of course, was the only punishment that could reasonably have been inflicted.

It was strenuously urged that society was in some way responsible for these young men. All that society had to do with it was that the general social conditions were such that their parents were enabled to accumulate property, to bring up these young men in comparative luxury, to educate them at institutions of learning, to furnish them with every incentive against criminal conduct. They, of all people, had no reason to complain of society, yet a stupid and ignorant judge, who never would have reached the bench except under the depraved elective system, for reasons best known to himself, thought that the death penalty would be too harsh a punishment for their young and tender souls and that these precocious criminals, who, of course, were afflicted, in the judgment of penologists, with dementia praecox, should be supported for life at the public expense. The administration of the law was thus thoroughly disgraced.

5. The reference is to the Leopold and Loeb case, a 1924 murder case that received worldwide attention. Clarence Darrow was the attorney for the defense.—C. J. R., Jr.

It is to be said for Bentham that in the domain of responsibility for crime, he was never one of these sappers and miners, trying to subvert the law. Like all reformers he had an exaggerated idea of the value of legislation. He professed to have a formula to determine the test of all legislation. His phrase was the greatest good of the greatest number. His good was determined by a balancing of pleasure and pain to find the utility of an act. Bentham has chapters in his *Principles of Legislation* headed Of the Different Kinds of Pleasure and Pain, and Of the Value of Pleasures and Pains, in which he betrays the most complete ignorance of psychology. To Bentham pleasure and pain are mere conditions of simple sensation, while the psychology of the human social mind shows that the higher pleasures or pains are complicated conceptions of the mind, and the state called happiness is not determined by pleasure or pain as a sensation, but by the individual's realization that he is functioning in the best possible way that he is suited to act as a member of society. Bentham's test is applicable to raw untutored men, not to civilized human beings in a complicated condition of society.

On the other hand social utility as a test of legislation has been acknowledged from the very beginning of legislation to be the reason for legislation and its test. What best subserves the public welfare has always been the goal, not only of legislation but of all law and all morality. But it is equally plain that what best subserves individual welfare will subserve the public welfare. This general social welfare cannot be predicted. It is the result of experience. Bentham's test as he understood it was no test at all and never could be. His balancing of a man's pleasure in killing another against the pain caused by the act is a low, disgusting performance, eminently worthy of Bentham's impractical mind; but as a test of a law against murder it is unthinkable to a man capable of introspection. Murder as a crime is not to be determined by pleasure or pain. It is plain why Bentham had no appreciable effect upon England or English lawyers, nor did his codes appeal to any sound lawyer. But a Frenchman discovered Bentham and was able to introduce some order in his various disorderly manuscripts, and several books by Bentham were published. On the Continent he became a great jurist and has ever since enjoyed a wide reputation. His works came back to England by

Jeremy Bentham (1748–1832)

way of the Continent and they had considerable influence in adding to the sentiment for legal reform. But the English law was reformed by practitioners, not by theorists.

All through the nineteenth century the English Parliament went on improving the law in particulars which it would take too much space to set forth in detail. The system of land law was transformed and a registration of documents affecting lands was devised. The distinction between equity and law courts was abolished in the Judicature Act of 1873, which went into effect in 1876. By it the equitable rule was substituted for the rule of the common law, wherever those rules differed. A new system of county courts had been devised. The practice in chancery cases had been simplified and expedited. The practice in common law cases had also been expedited. The results have been excellent, until today it is, no doubt, true that the best, quickest, and surest enforcement of the criminal law and the most thoroughly enlightened administration of the civil law that exists in the world can be found in that island set in the silver sea, to which we owe practically all our legal conceptions and most of our legal rules.

There is one feature of the law as we look at it to-day, which is not law at all, which yet has an effect upon almost every legal relation. Early in this story it was pointed out that originally all law was pure custom and that the development of law would chiefly be in separating what were merely social customs or morality from those rules of social conduct which would gradually be determined to be of sufficient importance to be enforced as laws, and their violation forbidden by penal or monetary liabilities. One of the great achievements of the Roman jurists was in indicating what part of the social customs should be law and what matters should be left to be enforced as rules of morality or good behavior which have no other warrant than social estimation. The ordinary citizen lives his life without coming into contact with the courts. He manages to live a law-abiding life, because the ordinary and general conduct of a citizen is dictated by received ideas of the ways that are proper, customary, and conventional.

Most human beings have standards of conduct and follow them as readily as they avoid violations of law. Some of these standards have no moral significance whatever. They are as conventional as one's clothes; but the human being is just as careful in his conformity to such standards as he is in his conformity to what he knows to be legal standards. But there are other rules which have a moral significance and they are not a little complicated by religious beliefs. The science of morals will never be an exact science because some men think to be right what other men think to be wrong. Yet in the rough most men at any given time in a particular social organization have the same ideas as to right and wrong. There are certain fundamental simple virtues such as honesty, probity, charity, goodness of heart, mercy, kindliness, compassion, cheerfulness, generosity, sympathy, self-restraint and self-control, and those best virtues of respect for the opinions of others and toleration and indulgence of their ways and ideas and of the expression of ideas differing from one's own, which are traits that most men instinctively respect and admire.

These virtues have an intense social aspect. They render human intercourse genial and kindly. They give one standing, reputation, and character among his fellow men. The individual who has such qualities is so highly civilized that obedience to law is not only a pleasure but a matter of necessary conduct. Rarely does the absence of traits of this kind give rise to claims for legal redress; but they yet form a large part of law in an indirect way. Lawyers know that in the administration of the law a witness or a litigant whose conduct or whose testimony displays a violation of any of the ordinary moral virtues stands partially discredited before a court or a jury. Some particular circumstance of falsehood or double dealing, of cupidity or avarice, of disregard of others or lack of kindly social feeling, of harshness or brutality, or any of the hundred and one things that lawyers look for on the opposite side and dread when they appear on their own—matters, too, which often have no materiality to the legal merits of a controversy—may yet determine a cause before judge or jury. The necessity of appearing well to others, which is at the basis of all primitive law, is still the controlling factor in all social conduct. Those who think that a sharp and fast line can be drawn between law and morals or customary good conduct have had little experience with humanity. They may work out such a hard and fast line in a cloister or a library, but it will not endure for a moment in the light of everyday life. One who thinks that the words of the law or its rules sum up the whole content of law is grossly deceived. In some cases good morals are made a part of the law. As long as the law tells us, for instance, that a contract which is against good morals will not be enforced by the law, it is apparent that from day to day legal rights are to be decided upon the accepted rules of morality. Those who contend that morality concerns only the individual's inner condition of mind, while law concerns one's outward relations with other men, have no true conception of law in its practical bearing upon human conduct. The experienced lawyer knows that underlying the actual words of the law and determining the application of its rules, is a fundamental basis of inherited ideas of religion, morality, sentiment, emotion, and habitual thoughts resulting from general human experience which are mainly instinctive. These factors cannot be expressed in words nor thoroughly prophesied in action by any one however gifted. These things are of the substance of human nature, but the theorists on law and the legal reformers are constantly forgetting them.

Were it not, however, for the rules of law and the tribunals with their juristic methods and for the profession which constantly looks at matters from a legal standpoint, the very factors last spoken of would tend to render legal rights incapable of discernment and expression. It is shown by the history of the law that invariably at some stage of human society, before written language was devised, a particular class was developed which had decisive knowledge of the laws. The method of transmission of such unwritten law was by oral tradition. It is also shown by the history of the law that after written language was devised, there came the demand that the laws should be put into writing so that they would no longer be the possession of this class. When the laws were put into writing, there was developed a legal professional class. Beneath this development is the evidently widespread human experience that special knowledge on a particular point will produce a better conclusion than lack of knowledge. As soon as law becomes rational and the result of reasoning processes, the necessity appears for specially trained minds whose legal knowledge and ability to reason on legal relations are so developed that they are able to an extent to disregard the conflicting moral judgments of ordinary men. Those who ask that the law be made so plain that every man may be his own lawyer, and who ask that the courts be filled with men who know less law and more justice, are simply quarreling with the constitution of the human mind. One might just as well ask that every man be his own engineer or every man his own doctor. In every age comes the demand that the law be certain and sure, as the demand of justice, while at the same time the loudest exponents of this demand are asking that the law be made uncertain by the application of some particular concept of justice or right to each particular case, as it may occur to the judge who is deciding the case.

This conflict between legality and moral judgments can best be illustrated by a case put by a Grecian sage over twenty-four hundred years ago. An importer of grain in the Island of Rhodes has in the harbor a vessel just arrived from Egypt which is loaded with grain. Owing to a scarcity of grain on the Island, the price of grain has risen beyond measure and the importer of grain can ask what he pleases. But he knows what the purchasers do not know, that a half-dozen ships loaded with grain will arrive in a day or two and then the price will fall to normal or below.

Is the importer bound by the law of sales to disclose his private knowledge to the purchasers? One school of Grecian philosophers and Cicero answered the question in the affirmative, but the Stoics answered that the importer was under no obligation to make disclosure. But if many people should be affected by this situation, the case would appeal to the ordinary non-legal mind as a case in which a harsh and grasping wretch was permitted by the law to grind the faces of the poor.

The Roman law in certain relations, at least, imposed this duty of disclosure upon both seller and purchaser. Hence in our law of marine insurance the assured applying for marine insurance is bound to disclose the facts known to him that are relevant to the risk. But before this law of insurance was introduced into the English common law, that law had established the rule that the purchaser buys at his own risk. If he desires protection he must obtain either an express warranty as to the things sold or obtain an implied warranty, but a warranty that the seller or the purchaser knew of no facts that would affect the price would be unheard of, and so indefinite as to afford no legal standard.

A well known case shows that this rule of the common law is still untouched in English law. A man sold in a public market hogs that had been exposed, to his knowledge, to the contagion of a certain disease. The purchaser drove the hogs to his home, they infected his other hogs and he suffered a great loss. The law forbade such a sale in open market, and it was an unlawful sale. The question was whether there was any actionable deception or deceit in this sale. It was contended that on any principles of fair dealing in open market the seller must at least impliedly represent that he was not selling a thing unlawful for him to sell, that every man at least represents that he is acting lawfully, because until proof appears to the contrary, the legal presumption is that every man is acting lawfully. But the courts of England answered this strong contention with the old rule that a purchaser buys at his peril. The common law, of course, would protect a purchaser against the seller's want of title. Most men would probably have the feeling that the law ought not to permit a sale, at least in open public market, of disease-bearing animals.

A system of law which in its administration does not provide in some way for veiling or avoiding a legal judgment that is likely to offend the moral judgment of many people is always in danger. There have been two ways of reaching this result. Popular courts like the Athenian dicasts or the Roman Hundred Courts or the Anglo-Saxon county courts were allowed to make the judgment. If they misstated the rule of law, the violation was veiled in the judgment of many people. But this solution has been long abandoned. The same result was allowed in the old English witness jury. The special value of a jury to-day is that when it violates the rule of law, the law does not bear the burden of an unjust verdict nor does the judge, while if the verdict seems contrary to ordinary ideas of right, the jury bears the odium of the decision. But it is plain that if the moral judgments of men were always to govern in judicial controversies, there would be no general rule of law in any case presenting a strong ethical aspect contrary to the rule of law. The result of such insistence on purely moral judgments is that all men are entitled to equal justice under general rules of law except those who in the opinion of many people are not so entitled. The result of the conflict of ideas in democratic governments is bound to be a compromise, but surely it is best arrived at by smothering under a fog of popular participation in the court the refusal to accord in some peculiar instances the general rule of law. Like all institutions administered by fallible human beings it is probably of more importance that the law should seem to do justice, than that it should arrive at rigidly theoretical just results.

The English common law, as we look back over its history, demonstrated through many centuries that strict and rigid law produced often strict injustice. The law must govern human beings. They cannot be made into logical machines, nor can the law be made into an infallibly logical system without sad results. After all, the vast mass of litigation is over very doubtful cases. The general considerations of justice, the need for human security, the widespread idea of the general public welfare, the respect for law and order, the demand for honesty, good faith, and fair dealing, the general recognition of property rights and the need for keeping contracts, have in the end given sound results in England in later years. Charles Reade's *Hard Cash* is the best of all the legal novels; it is, however, marred by the bad law of using a dying declaration as evidence in a civil case. The Yankee Fullalove in that tale takes his negro man Vespasian into an English court. He tells him that they sell a thing there called justice and they sell it "dear but prime." The price is not so dear as it once was, but the article has lost none of its prime quality in the reduction of the price.

If a competent lawyer compares the English cases on the subject of unfair trade in the common practice of "pirates" trying to appropriate valuable trade names, with the American cases both in Federal and in State courts on that subject, he will see how much more insistent are English judges than American, in trying to secure honest and fair dealing. He will find, too, that the prime sinner in this regard is not among the State courts, though sometimes those judges display an obtuseness to moral considerations of honesty, but is that exalted tribunal, the Supreme Court of the United States.

CHAPTER 15
The Absolute Reign of Law

PRIOR TO THE AMERICAN REVOLUTION the courts in the Colonies were officered by royal judges. As soon as the Colonies reached a stage where there was need of any developed system of law, the whole of the English law was introduced in its system of common law and equity, with exceptions that are not important. In New York when the English took possession of New Amsterdam, no part of the Dutch law was preserved. Royal judges in the Colonies as a matter of necessity administered the only kind of law of which they had any knowledge. The prevalence of English law was fortified by the lawyers, who received their legal education, so far as they received any scholastic legal training, by attending the Inns of Court in London, although for the less fortunate a reading in lawyers' offices furnished some sort of legal education which was sufficient for a highly trained mind. It is no doubt true that those colonials who had been trained at the Inns of Court enjoyed a great deal of prestige among the less fortunate members of the bar in the Colonies. The lack of a system of education for lawyers has had an effect in permanently deciding the form of professional practice in this country.

Edmund Burke in his great speech on America, one of those productions of that extraordinary man which show him at his best as a philosophical statesman, noticed the peculiar fact that there were more copies of Blackstone's Commentaries sold in the American colonies than in

England itself. He did not, however, suggest the real reason for this apparently strange thing—a reason which to us is obvious. In England the form of legal education was fixed. The Inns of Court had their well established method of study. The introduction of a new book like Blackstone was not easy, nor was it considered necessary, but in the Colonies, where there were no schools of law, the Commentaries were hailed as absolutely essential to any legal education and as the only book in which extended legal knowledge could be easily acquired. More and more men in the Colonies were choosing the law as a profession, and most students felt that the mastery of Blackstone was an entirely adequate preparation for the bar. Littleton's Book on Tenures, Coke's huddled annotations of Littleton, Sir Matthew Hale's two treatises, one on the criminal law, the other on the common law, were now supplanted by a book easily read, clear and luminous in its statements and covering apparently the whole field of the law. Every word of it was taken as legal gospel. From that time began the superstitious reverence for Blackstone which could never have found lodgment except in a colonial type of mind. It was to continue through colonial and provincial thought for many years to come. Out in the West Blackstone was far more popular than Kent, because the former was much more condensed and had not so much terrifying Latin and French as Kent presented.

By the time of the American Revolution this lack of educational facilities for lawyers had fixed once for all in this country the form of the profession. In order to maintain the English division of lawyers into barristers and attorneys or solicitors, it was required that there should be not only the aristocratic forms of an old and fixed society and long inherited traditions fully established, but also the apparatus for legal education and for admission to the bar that was furnished by the Inns of Court. It probably would not have been endurable in the Colonies that there should be any social distinction among lawyers who had for the most part pursued the same manner of legal training. It was not possible that the colonists would recognize that any particular portion of the legal profession should have the monopoly of the right to speak or act in court, such as the barristers enjoyed in the English courts. Nor could it be thought of in the Colonies that people would admit the truism that really underlies the British practice in the division of the profession—the conception that the citizen may be considered competent to select an attorney, who can attend to many of his less important legal matters, but when the client comes to decide upon more important and weightier matters of the law, he is not competent but must leave the selection of proper counsel to his attorney, who is supposed to have and doubtless does have far more ability to make a proper selection than the client himself. Later in this chapter the effects of this American method of practising law and many things resulting will be noted. At present the point to observe is that before the Revolution, from entirely natural and controlling causes and from the inadequate provision for legal education, the rule had become fixed once for all that every lawyer in America is potentially and theoretically able to perform all or any part of the duties of a lawyer, whether those duties belong to what are called attorneys and solicitors, or to what are called barristers in England. This is doubtless a profound popular misconception, but it is not likely that it will ever be changed.

At the present time there are so many law schools which are fully competent to designate those who are qualified to enter the profession, that it would be a boon to the profession if the sole right of calling to the bar should be left to such schools. The medical profession is protected from unqualified men in point of instruction, and no sound reason can be suggested for not treating the legal profession in the same way. Individual cases of hardship are wholly immaterial.

The next general subject deserving special comment is the genesis of our constitutional development. This development of a written constitution as binding upon government had its origin in the existence in the Colonies of royal charters under which colonization had taken place. Certain factors of the charters are of importance for the comprehension of the exact struggle between England and the American Colonies and for the creation of constitutional thought. The charters defined the rights and privileges of the colonists. They contained many generous provisions and the custom grew up of appealing to the charters to define colonial rights. The charters were a regularly used form of document. In the long struggle for popular rights in England, the various charters of liberties extorted from the Crown had taken the form of royal grants.

The Great Charter was a grant by King John revised and reissued under his son Henry III, and confirmed by John's grandson, Edward I. The subsequent Petition of Right under Charles I had taken the form of a royal grant. These charters in English history had a peculiar sanctity to the minds of Englishmen. But it had never occurred to the English to define the rights of Englishmen in a form of constitution that would be binding on King and Parliament alike. One reason was that there was no representative machinery and no possibility of any representative machinery, beyond the Lords and the Commons, that could make a constitution. There never was a possibility of conceiving of a Parliament making a constitutional law which some succeeding Parliament could not repeal. The proposition was unthinkable from the times of the earliest Parliament that a Parliament could bind its successors not to change a law enacted by Parliament. Hobbes in his *Leviathan* had gone so far as to say that because a legislative body could not bind its successors, no law was binding on government. Hobbes was guilty of the palpable error of not seeing that the question was whether a law was binding on government, while it stood unrepealed, and whether it could create rights in the individual against the government, while it was in existence. There never, however, had been a time when a constitution binding on the government itself in all its departments, irrevocable and unamendable except according to the method of the Constitution itself, was a possibility in England. The so-called English Constitution could be changed at any time by Parliament.

It is true that in an old Year Book Stonor had laid it down that even an act of Parliament could be unconstitutional. Coke, in the desperation of his battle with the Crown lawyers, had adopted this idea. These lawyers had in mind the same class of thought that caused Bartolus to say that there were certain things that government could not do. His language had been quoted in the former chapter on the Medieval Law. The social contract school of thought would have said that such matters are beyond the original social compact, that certain rights are inalienable by the people, even if common consent be given to their alienation. This conception of a superlaw lies at the basis of the rule against all arbitrary government, whether of the one ruler or of the rule of the many, and has received the sanction of our Supreme Court, even where the Constitution is silent.

But this idea that there are certain acts beyond the power of government never found any lodgment in England. Stonor and Coke found no successors to assert that a law of Parliament could be unconstitutional in this sense or any other. There was once a crisis when the English could have freed themselves from the nothing-without-Parliament idea. When Charles I was beheaded and when the Parliament of King, Lords, and Commons was practically dissolved, and a godly Puritan state was in contemplation, a written constitution was proposed under Cromwell and Englishmen had what they would call a narrow escape from a written constitution; but nothing happened. The old conservative instinct prevailed and England came back to her King, Lords, and Commons with the King to be shorn, not to say shaven, of all power in the combination. After many years the Lords too were to be deposed from an equal partnership.

In the ancient world, at least among the Romans, there was the theory of a fundamental law not written but customary. As an instance may be given the power granted to the consuls by the Senate in times of civil danger that the consuls should "take care that the Commonwealth suffered no harm." This decree of the Senate was supposed to give dictatorial power to the consuls. Yet there was a law to the effect that no Roman citizen could be put to death without an appeal to the whole body of the people. It was contended that the decree of dictatorial power set aside for the occasion the right of appeal to the popular assembly. It was conceded that this was true as to any one openly in arms against the government. Cicero in the year of his consulship, 63 B.C., argued a case brought against a man for killing a Roman citizen under this sort of decree in the year 100 B.C. Cicero himself put to death the Catilinarian conspirators under such a *senatus consultum*. He was banished for it and afterwards brought back in triumph. There was thus a sort of ill-defined unwritten constitutional law in Rome, but it was sometimes regarded and sometimes violated. Among the Athenians when a man was prosecuted for causing the passage of a law, the constitutional standard was anything that the court would make a standard. But the theory of a written constitution was absolutely foreign to Greek and Roman thought. The Athenian constitution was like the English constitution, a mere matter for ordinary legislation.

In early modern times there had been developed a new word in political thought—the term sovereignty. The word was new but the idea was very old. The original Greek and Roman conception of political power was that all political power of every kind—executive, legislative, and judicial—emanated from the body of the people, and the method of its expression was by the voice of the popular assembly. In Rome power to legislate belonged also to the Senate and Council of the Plebs. When the Republic passed away and the Empire began, the powers that were conferred upon Augustus were given him by the vote of the senate and by the people. This grant was made to his successors and the law granting the power was called the *lex regia* or royal law. This grant ceased after a time to be made, but nevertheless in the works of Ulpian it was laid down that the Emperor could make law, because the people had given him the power. This conception was carried into the Roman Digest of Justinian and he, an autocrat in fact, lent his approval to the statement that his autocracy depended upon the will of the people. The doctors of the Bolognese school in commenting on this text asserted that the people, having granted the power, could resume it.

But unfortunately St. Paul had taken in his Epistle to the Romans an excursion into politics and had evolved the proposition that "the powers that be are ordained of God, for there is no power but of God. Therefore he that resisteth the power withstandeth the ordinance of God." Thus the idea came in, as the inspired word of God, higher than all human wisdom, that the Emperor's, or any other ruler's, power came from God, that his authority had been delivered to him from Heaven, not through any human power. Since this power was of sacred origin the priests claimed that they had a part in it and the Pope, as the Vicar of God, inserted himself between God and the ruler as a man ruling men without divine guidance, just as he had inserted himself and his ministers between all men and God.

In the long medieval struggle between the claim of the papacy to control the secular government and the claim of the secular rulers to be independent of the Church, the appeal was made to St. Paul's text as a solid basis for the divine right of kings. Using a new word, the formula of the claim of secular government was summed up in the statement that each national government is sovereign, that is to say, independent of all outside control. This formula overwhelmed the papal claim and it prevailed. But it will be seen that as yet there had been the simple question of what may be called external sovereignty, not any question as to where sovereignty resides within the state itself. All lawyers accepted the conception of the Roman law that sovereignty existed in the body of the people and this popular power was supposed to be the supreme power in the state.

Bodin, a French writer, in his book demonstrated as best he could this idea in order to prove that the Pope had no control over the succession of a Protestant King, Henry IV, to the throne of France.[1] It is true that the French King with the careless statement that the throne was worth a mass ended the discussion; but the idea lies at the basis of all modern international law, to the effect that each national government is, as to all others, a sovereign power. So far the development of sovereignty was impregnable. Bodin went further and ascribed to the sovereign the powers of internal sovereignty.

Thereupon a school of absolutists in government took the position that this power of sovereignty in a government, theretofore considered a freedom from external aggression, must logically require a supreme power, which resides somewhere in each national government, and which must be unaccountable to any other power in the state itself. This is wholly a *non sequitur*. It does not follow at all, because a nation may be sovereign externally and yet internally that power of sovereign control in internal affairs may reside nowhere. Hobbes took up the discussion. He is always a nuisance, because he is always wrong from his fundamental proposition of the natural state of mankind as a war of all against all and of a social contract made to end this war, to his absolutist idea of the divine right of kings. He asserted that a government and its laws were things imposed by a superior upon inferiors. At any rate Hobbes insisted

1. Jean Bodin (1530–96).—C. J. R., Jr.

upon the idea that in every sovereign government the power of uncon-
ditional, uncontrolled sovereignty must reside somewhere. He placed it
in the sovereign, the king. Trained Catholic controversialists like
Molina, Mariana, and Cardinal Bellarmine rapidly made this divine right
of kings wholly ridiculous.[2] At first the Anglican churchmen stood on
this divine right, quoting St. Paul as supporting the turning-the-other-
cheek doctrine of non-resistance and passive obedience to lawless acts of
a king. The Revolution of 1688 vindicated the power of Parliament to
control this so-called sovereign. Then the English took the thought and
reduced it to the proposition that sovereignty in the English government
resides in the Parliament, and from that day to this the English dogma
has been that Parliament is omnipotent. From that time Englishmen
have never escaped from this political dogma.

As a consequence of this dogma the Parliament slowly but surely
usurped control over all the colonies and territorial possessions of Great
Britain. Parliament had had nothing to do with the creation of the
American Colonies, the rights of the colonists were guaranteed by
Crown grants of charters, which were, when accepted and acted upon,
covenants between the Crown and the colonists. Hence, when contentions arose between Colonists and Crown, the colonists appealed to
their rights as written and defined in the charters. Parliament, without
any legal right whatever, assumed that it could annul or revise or redraft
those charter provisions at its pleasure. The Navigation Acts were
passed, violative of the rights of the colonists, in imitation of the ages-
old oppressive laws of the Athenian state striving to make all trading of
the subsidiary states in the Delian League subservient to fostering the
trade of Athens. The colonial lawyers, who knew nothing of and had
never accepted the dogma of parliamentary omnipotence, replied with
the colonial rights given in the charters. Parliament naturally could not
give up its dogma as to its own power and insisted upon its right to do as
it pleased with the Colonies uncontrolled by the charter grants of the
Crown. It could annul any grant of the king in England, so it naturally

2. Luis de Molina (1535–1600), Juan de Mariana (1536–1624), and Robert Bellarmine
(1542–1621).—C. J. R., Jr.

assumed that it could annul any charter grant to the Colonies. This was all assumption of the common lawyers who were incapable of conceiving a royal grant with the Colonies as creating a Crown contract with the Colonies. This argument was never completely worked out by the colonial lawyers but it made impregnable in the colonial mind the idea that there could be a governmental charter or constitution which represented a set of legal rules that were above and beyond, and in control of, the ordinary executive or legislative power.

A discrimination is necessary here. The thought of a charter as a covenant binding upon government, standing by itself, is the precursor of the constitutional doctrine that a corporate charter is a contract, as it was ruled in the Dartmouth College case.[3] But when that doctrine unites with the doctrine of the people, as the ultimate source of political power, resuming for the time its full sovereignty, there results that higher conception of a constitutional supreme rule of law binding on the people itself and all governmental agencies. To complete this full doctrine resort is necessary to the conception of Roman law that all power emanates from the people.

When looked at from the point of view of a governmental compact the Revolutionary struggle was not alone a mere contest over a paltry revenue in taxes; it depended upon deep and fundamental conceptions of the powers of government. The colonists, however, did not meet the issue squarely. They should have laid their troubles at the door of the English Parliament. It is much more grateful to denounce a king than a representative body elected by the people. The colonists should not have foisted that dogma of sovereign control over the Colonies upon the king. He and his ministers no doubt were in the van of the struggle, but his ministers were merely a cabinet representing a ruling committee of the English Lords and Commons. Nothing can be more stupid than the usual historical folly of charging the acts of the cabinet upon the king. Against a word from Parliament to a minister the king was powerless. This idea of parliamentary omnipotence is not at all necessary, because

---

3. *Trustees of Dartmouth College v. Woodward*, 17 U.S. (4 Wheat.) 518 (1819).—
C. J. R., Jr.

during the late war the War Council, which ruled the Empire, had representatives from the Dominions beyond the Seas. To-day the English Crown is the kingly head of Canada, of Australia, and of South Africa, but to not one of those dominions does parliamentary power now extend. At last the American theory has been vindicated, and thus the whirligig of time brings in its revenges.

The fact no one can dispute, that the colonial lawyers were deeply imbued with the idea that there must be an organic instrument of government, that bound government in all its branches and people alike. The colonials added, we repeat, to the theory of governmental law, a revival of the Roman conception that the sovereignty resided in the people itself, in the social community of which the government was the outward expression. This differentiation between the organic social community and the mere form of government and its agencies to which we shall come in a moment, is needed to show our fundamental departure from the English dogma that the government is the actual state or community and no power can exist beyond it. Here it is to be stated that immediately after the Declaration of Independence there began the adoption of state constitutions to supplant the old royal charters. The question was bound to arise and it at once arose: If the state government violates the state constitution, what is the remedy and where is it to be found? The answer came at once. The question is a judicial one; it can be raised by any citizen whose rights are affected and it must be decided by the courts according to the law of the land. The constitution of the state is the supreme law binding alike on government and all its agencies. It is binding on the sovereign people itself, and any law of any governmental agency, any act of any governmental officer, contrary to that supreme law, is simply void. Cases on this basis had been decided before the Constitutional Convention. This is what is meant by the heading of this chapter, the Absolute Reign of Law, which could just as well be stated as the Reign of an Absolute Law, which is the American doctrine of a controlling supreme law emanating from the people and putting limits to the exercise of every governmental power, supplemented by a judicial power to enforce and protect the rule of the supreme law.

This was the situation of American thought when the Federal Constitutional Convention assembled after our Revolutionary War, with the added thought just before mentioned that there had now been developed a deeper and more fundamental conception of the nature of the state. The original thirteen Colonies had developed a social cohesion that had given them the form of a single social community. Long ages before, Cicero, in the thirty-fifth chapter of his treatise on the Commonwealth, which exists now only in fragmentary form, had defined that form of social corporation which is called a state. He said that it is "a union of the people, associated in an agreement of law and a community of interest." Perhaps a better translation would be: "A coming together of a multitude of people associated in an agreement of law for the general advantage." A great Father of the Church, St. Augustine, followed Cicero. This is the true theory of the ancient world that a nation is a greater conception than its mere ruling power. For more than a hundred years Poland was divided into its parts, ruled separately by Russia, Prussia, and Austria, but the undying social community lived on to emerge in happier circumstances as the present state of Poland. The existence of such a social community is a fact. The only test of it is whether it does cohere and whether it continues to cohere. It is no metaphysical question involving a common will expressed in an actual form of governmental contrivances. The state is independent of the form of the government. Generally, however, sooner or later, the social community must attain expression in a governmental form or it will perish.

The best description of such a social organization is Burke's superb phrase that any particular human society "is placed in a just correspondence and symmetry with the order of the world and with the mode of existence decreed to a permanent body composed of transitory parts, wherein, by the disposition of a stupendous wisdom, the whole, at one time, is never old or middle-aged or young, but, in a condition of unchangeable constancy, moves on through the varied tenor of perpetual decay, fall, renovation and progression." Governments may rise and fall, empires may flourish and decay, and the social aggregate, the social community, the state, may remain. This social aggregate considered as the state, when it does attain its particular expression in a form of government, is in all its relations with other governments a unity, a moral person, and our law treats it as a public corporation.

Such a social community existed among the independent American Colonies when the American Constitutional Convention met. Its delegates derived their commission directly from the people of this united social community welding together the people of the states. It makes no difference how that agency to the delegates was granted; it was, and was used as, a delegation of power from the people of the United States who employed for convenience the existing and original divisions of the Colonies in order to select the delegates. When the act of independence had taken place, when the Declaration of Independence was made by the Colonies, it had been the act of the United Colonies.

This conception of the social aggregate as a reversion to the ideas of the ancient Greek and Roman world shows how it is that great and fundamental ideas are rarely entirely lost in the story of law. During the barbarian period and the era of feudalism, any conception of a social community was in fact completely submerged. The sway of a feudal lord and of a king over feudal lords was conceived as merely a personal relation of suzerain and subject. A nation was considered to be a nation not because it was a social community held together by the natural ties of a community of interests in the common bond of law, but because there was a common ruler, to whom were owed by all, the artificial man-created duties of fealty and homage. The Colonies, having grown together in a natural way, were not misled by old feudal ideas, except that when they declared their independence it was a declaration of the dissolution of the tie of allegiance to the British Crown, not to the British Parliament, which in fact was governing the Colonies. The Colonies were historically correct. It was so declared, because the Colonies repudiated any rights over them except those shown by the charters of the English kings. As to other rights, they claimed the general rights of all Englishmen, because those rights defined in the laws which they brought with them, were their common bond of law.

It has always been the doctrine of the Supreme Court of the United States that the nation composed of the people of the United Colonies was in existence before any form of Federal government had been made.

The first Chief Justice stated in an opinion that the Declaration of Independence found the people of the Colonies already united for general purposes and at the same time providing for their more domestic concerns by state governments and other temporary arrangements.[4] The Supreme Court early made the distinction between the social aggregate of the nation and its form of government. The social aggregate, it was asserted by a philosophical jurist in that court, is the complete body of free persons united together for their common benefit, to enjoy peaceably what is their own, to do justice to others, and if necessary to resist aggression. Here, at last, is something new in public law.

The government naturally, in consonance with the English type of thought, has often claimed that it is the social aggregate itself, but the two things are totally distinct. The social union of the Colonies existed before the first form of government (which was the Articles of Confederation) and the present form of government (which is called the Constitution) were ever considered. Time and again our highest tribunal has repeated this doctrine of the cohesive social aggregate antedating the form of government. Another early decision asserted that before the Constitution was adopted this one united political body, existing as a fact, raised armies, conducted military operations, issued bills of credit, borrowed money, received and sent ambassadors and made treaties. The word *state* is used, our Supreme Court tells us, in three senses: it means, first, the political community; secondly, the territory of that community; and thirdly, the government thereof. The difference between the political community and the form of government is emphasized. The Union as a social aggregate, they said, is not an arbitrary and purely artificial relation. It grew out of natural facts of common origin, mutual sympathies, similar interests, and geographical relations. By the Revolutionary War it was confirmed, strengthened, and solidified. By Articles of Confederation it took one arbitrary and purely artificial form of government, and by the Constitution that form was changed. But necessarily the form cannot rise higher than its creator, and that form

4. The Chief Justice is John Jay. The case is *Chisholm v. Georgia*, 2 U.S. (2 Dall.) 419 (1793).—C. J. R., Jr.

was given by the existing consolidated people, who as a people made the form of government.

This is the philosophical theory of this Union of States which was finally settled by our great Civil War. But for many years a certain school of political thought contended that the only genuine social aggregates were the peoples of the various states, and that there was no such thing as a naturally cohesive political community of the whole United States. The state as a social community underlying the government was a new conception in politics and was never understood either in English or in French political circles until years afterwards. After the German Empire was formed, the legal scholars of Bavaria, borrowing from Calhoun's tenets,[5] earnestly contended that there was a political community known as Bavaria and that there was no such natural political community as the people of the German Empire. But a man who is so dull as to deny the natural political community of Germany is as much out of date as many other fossil saurians.

It is necessary at the outset to define this fundamental manner of union, for without it the doctrine of a political community of which the government is the mere creature, cannot be comprehended. Nor can there be any understanding of our political system by one whose mind is befogged by the English theory of the omnipotence of its Parliament constituting the political community with no higher power behind. Those who sigh for an omnipotence of power embodied in our Congress and the President are one hundred and fifty years behind the times. As to the unified political community, no one can say when it came into being. It had a natural growth from natural causes, but as to the form of government it is possible to put a finger on the very time of the artificial agreement and to name the individuals by whom the agreement was made in the Constitutional Convention.

At the time of the adoption of the Constitution the people had resumed for the time all political power whatever and out of the plenitude of its sovereignty was laying down rules that were to be obeyed as the

5. John C. Calhoun (1782–1850), the foremost proponent of states' rights.— C. J. R., Jr.

supreme law of the land, anything in any other law, local or general, "to the contrary notwithstanding." It was assumed that the people, through its delegates to the Constitutional Convention, was exercising all the power of government, whether theretofore resident in the different states or in the whole body of the people. This is the necessary background from which to understand our system.

In the next place the Constitution recognized that there are three powers existing in and issuing out of the social community of the United States and inherent in that body. The delegates, as a part of their commission, were to provide for the exercise of those powers of that general social union. In accordance with the developed legal experience of the ages, and in accordance with a truth recognized since Aristotle, those threefold powers are the legislative, the executive, and the judicial. In accordance with the philosophy of Montesquieu, borrowed from Locke, and extracted from the form of English government, before the dogma of Parliamentary omnipotence had been developed, those three powers must be separate and separately exercised by separate departments. The legislative power is lodged in the legislative department, the executive power in the executive, and the judicial power in the judicial.

The legislative department with its power was given the duty of enacting laws—which, we have seen, is but another form of saying that the legislative enactment of a law is the expression of the nation's acceptance of law. This legislative power looks only to the future. It declares a rule to govern future transactions or acts, not acts or transactions that are past and completed. The legislative department is made up of a Senate and House after the English analogy. The executive department, however, is made a part of the legislative power in this respect: The legislative body, the Congress, is not empowered alone to accept law in the first instance. The executive department, the President, must also accept; but if he refuses to accept the law, a vote of two-thirds of each house is so near a practical approach to unanimity as to show that, in spite of the President's veto, the people with practical unanimity is ready to accept the law.

The executive department is the President, in whom is lodged the executive power. He has the duty of executing the laws. The President cannot make a rule for the future, for that is legislating; he cannot assume to decide a litigated question, for that is a judicial act. The sphere of his domain is strictly in the present, save and except that in the domain of legislation he may by his veto require a more thorough consideration of law and a nearer approach to unanimity.

The judicial power of the United States is by the Constitution vested in a Supreme Court and in inferior courts established by Congress. The judges are to hold their offices during good behavior and each judge is to receive a compensation which cannot be decreased during his continuance in office. This provision embodies, of course, the result of the Revolution of 1688 and the experience of all the ages. Congress cannot legislate a judge out of office by taking away his compensation or diminishing it. The extent of the judicial power given to the government of the United States was considered to be coextensive with the necessities of the Federal government. The Supreme Court, while generally an appellate court, is a court of original jurisdiction in every case where a state is a party and where ambassadors and foreign representatives are affected. It is possible, of course, for Congress to abolish all the jurisdiction of the inferior courts of the United States, but it could not affect the original jurisdiction nor by the best opinion could it prevent the appellate jurisdiction of the Supreme Court from taking effect upon any case within the judicial power of the United States. If this appellate jurisdiction could be abolished, the Supreme Court could be cut down to simply its original jurisdiction. This would in effect leave the Supreme Court without authority to pass upon any constitutional question arising under the Constitution of the United States. It would be possible for Congress to attempt to leave all cases whatsoever to the decision of state courts, except those cases where a state is a party or where foreign representatives are involved; but the Supreme Court has decided that certain jurisdictions of the United States courts are exclusive of the state courts. Owing to the fact that the court has not been entirely consistent in its rulings, it is impossible to say what the law is, but it does seem certain that Congress could not take away the appellate jurisdiction of the Supreme Court. Certainly the Convention never contemplated such a national suicide as being possible. That appellate jurisdiction is subject, of course, to such exceptions as Congress may by law have directed, but the Supreme Court will never make it possible for Congress to ruin the whole scheme of government. By taking away all appellate jurisdiction of the Supreme Court and by abolishing all the inferior Federal courts, every inhibition of the Constitution on the Federal government and on the states would be rendered abortive by leaving all such questions to the state courts, with their varying decisions.

The inhibitions of the original Constitution were of two kinds. One kind is the inhibitions on the Federal Congress itself. Their explanation is found in English history. The inhibition against the passage of a bill of attainder or *ex post facto* law recalls some of the bloodiest pages of English law. Other inhibitions are intended to maintain the equality of the states. No direct tax can be levied except in proportion to the census, nor can Congress by its laws tax exports from one state to another or give any preference of a particular port of one state over those of other states.

When the inhibitions against the states are considered they also contain the provision against passing a bill of attainder or *ex post facto* law as well as against a law impairing the obligation of contracts. The other provisions are against any act that would bring the state into collision with the Federal government. Among them is the provision that no state can join a confederacy of any kind, the provision that was violated by the seceding states in 1861, and was enforced by the armies of the North vindicating the constitutional rule.

As soon as the Constitution was adopted amendments in the way of a Bill of Rights as against the Federal government were adopted. Most of them come out of English history. The inhibition against establishing religion, or preventing its free exercise, or abridging the freedom of speech or of the press, or preventing the right to assemble and petition the government, or against the quartering of soldiers, or against unreasonable searches and seizures, the prohibition of search warrants unless they be granted on probable cause and particularly specify person and place—all find their explanation in English history.

The preservation of a grand jury indictment as a prerequisite to all prosecutions for infamous crimes, the prohibition against putting a defendant twice in jeopardy or compelling him to be a witness against himself, all point to particular abuses under the common law. Magna Charta was kept alive by the provision that no one shall be deprived of life, liberty, or property without due process of law. The old method of purveying is forbidden by the clause against taking private property without just compensation. Nor can the public confiscate property, unless possibly by a constitutional amendment. A defendant in a criminal case is given a certain relief against the old common law in that he must be tried in his district and must be confronted by the witnesses and must have compulsory process for his own witnesses and must be allowed counsel for his defense. These provisions correct the inhumanity of the common law. Excessive bail or fines cannot be exacted nor cruel and unusual punishments inflicted. These provisions recall the history of the Court of Star Chamber and some later trials when tremendous fines were imposed, when ears were cut off and then for a second offense reshaven. Every one will recall old Prynne arraigned a second time before the Star Chamber. His long hair concealed his mutilated ears cut off for a former offense. One inhuman judge exclaimed: "Methinks the gentleman hath ears. Let us see his ears." The hair was pushed back, exposing the stumps of his ears, and he was sentenced to have even the remnants of his ears shaven off. This was the conduct of primordial brutes when Shakespeare was writing of that judicial mercy that falleth as the gentle dew from heaven.

These original amendments as construed affected only the government of the United States. Hence it happened that for many years, while the Federal government could not deprive any person of life, liberty, or property without due process of law, the states could do so, so far as the Federal Constitution was concerned. By the fourteenth amendment, adopted after the Civil War, a state was forbidden by law or otherwise to deprive any person of life, liberty, or property without due process of law or to deny to any one within its jurisdiction the equal protection of the laws, which means the protection of equal laws, an idea that goes back to Cicero. Thus finally the Absolute Law was complete, binding alike on the Federal government and the governments of the states, by a rule enforceable upon all agencies of government by the Federal courts.

Later amendments have permitted income taxes without apportionment or census, in order to enable the poorer states protected in their equal representation in the Senate even against constitutional amendment, to make the richer states pay almost all the expenses of the general government. The direct election of United States senators has been provided—with results that are deplorable. The manufacture or sale, or importation into or exportation from the United States, for beverage purposes of intoxicating liquor has been added as an attempt to improve the general morals. Congress and the states are given concurrent power to enforce this latter provision. A large part of the citizens refuse to obey this prohibition and at present there is a large lawless territory of conduct in the sale of liquor which in some places has developed usages of its own, including private war among those who purvey to the craving for intoxicants.

The final amendment, that the right of citizens to vote shall not be denied or abridged by Congress or by any state on account of sex, places women under the same constitutional protection as colored men formerly were supposed to enjoy; but the provision is not likely to be evaded with the ease with which the color amendment has been evaded. It is not likely that white women will consider colored women entitled to any part of the support of the equal suffragists. Experience has shown that this last amendment will not make any appreciable changes in the general results of voting. Women will vote much as men vote.

The prohibition of intoxicating liquor, however, presents the question whether a law can be enforced which a large part of the citizens refuse to obey. Its enforcement depends upon a gradual forced change in public sentiment, but it must be said that no signs can yet be found of any alteration in public sentiment which has affected the stimulated thirst of many people for ardent spirits. In the end the difficulty will probably be determined by some reasonable compromise. There is too much capacity in this country in adjusting law to social conditions, to permit the present situation to continue. When that adjustment comes about, the artificial condition of lawlessness created by the present legal situation will, of course, pass away. The situation has happened before in various states, but now a wider experience has been gained in regard to the matter, not only in this country but in a number of foreign countries.

It will be seen from this general scheme that the Federal government is a form of government where the various departments are bound down by the supreme law. In certain matters it was intended that there should be no flexibility or compromise. The assertion that the Constitution shall be the supreme law suggests the thought of what shall be the remedy and the recourse if Congress itself or the executive department or some of its officers or the states or their legislatures or officers or agencies should, by passing a law or indulging in other conduct, attempt to overrule or set at naught or violate the supreme law of the land. If such acts can be done and there be no recourse, it follows, of course, that the supreme law has descended to becoming inferior to the law or act that violates it. So much, at least, no reasonable human being who has any respect for his own mind ought to deny.

At the time this Constitution was adopted there had been, as we have seen, a long struggle and controversy to vindicate the chartered rights of the Colonies against the legislative acts of Parliament and the executive acts of its cabinet committee mistakenly called the Crown. As we today look back at the controversy there seems to be no doubt that as a matter of law the Colonies were right and Parliament was wrong. But the point is, as insisted above, that there was imbedded in the colonial mind the thought of a rule of law that transcended legislative and executive power.

After the Declaration of Independence certain of the states adopted new constitutions which became their organic laws. Among them was that of Massachusetts, with its earnest hope that that state should have a government "of laws and not of men." Other states followed. One state made shift to get along for years with its colonial charter. Before the Constitutional Convention produced its new Federal Constitution, there had been decisions on cases in the state courts, as we have seen, that any state legislation in conflict with the state constitution was absolutely void. This conception was well developed in political thought when the Federal Convention met. Probably no one in that Convention had the slightest doubt that it was necessary to have in the Federal government a judicial power that could preserve the Constitution as the supreme law of the land. This necessity was clearly pointed out in the articles of the *Federalist.*

This idea was so firmly imbedded in the minds of all political thinkers, that at once under the new government it was insisted that there should be added by amendments a Bill of Rights, analyzed above, which should define the rights of each and every citizen against the powers of government. Those amendments were adopted without any question, and they contemplated that the rights of citizens thereby guaranteed should be protected against encroachment by any governmental agency. It was not long before a question did arise where a state was sued by citizens of another state, and the Supreme Court by a fine opinion sought to protect helpless Indians against robbery by the State of Georgia, and at once a new amendment was devised and passed to prevent such a contingency again arising; but the amendment was easily avoided by suing state officers.

At last, after the first great political change in party government under the Constitution, it became apparent that the Supreme Court would without question declare a Federal law or an executive act unconstitutional and void, if it, in the judgment of the Court, infringed the Federal Constitution. Politicians, who in their political battles rarely look beyond the moment and are rarely scrupulous as to means selected, decided that something must be done to curb the power of the Supreme Court and to reduce it to subjection to the representatives of the people, as the President and Congress were said to be. The Constitution was surveyed and the indirect method of an impeachment was adopted in order to render the Court subservient to the legislative and executive power. Those two departments combined their forces and moved on the Supreme Court by an impeachment of one of the justices of that court. The victim selected was Samuel Chase of Maryland, a signer of the Declaration of Independence. He had opposed the adoption of the Constitution but had become a Federalist in politics. When made a justice of the Supreme Court he had made himself exceedingly obnoxious to many people by his enforcement of the Alien and Sedition laws, under which it was attempted to put some curb upon the support that was being given to France both by resident aliens and by citizens. Those laws were mildness itself compared with the laws passed during the World

War, but the clamor of the politicians affected was loud, and as usual freedom was in danger, if political rascals were not permitted to prejudice the country.

The precedents of impeachment from English history were not entirely satisfactory. There were many famous impeachment trials, but under the Tudors the impeachment had been deserted by the politicians and the Crown for the more expeditious and bloody proceeding by bill of attainder. No doubt the politicians sighed for the bill of attainder, but a bill of attainder as well as an *ex post facto* law was forbidden by the Federal Constitution. Impeachment, however, had been preserved and it seemed possible by that form of proceeding to escape all judicial restraints.[6]

In 1621 Sir Edward Coke had restored impeachment as a mode of criminal trial. In that very year the Commons heard witnesses, gave judgment, and imposed a punishment, but the House of Lords promptly, on the strength of a precedent in the first year of Henry IV (1399), proved that the Commons were not judges in Parliament and that that jurisdiction belonged to the Lords alone. Then followed, to name a few famous cases, Strafford's impeachment and the speech in his own defense which has become a classic of noble and moving eloquence. Three Lord Chancellors, Clarendon, Somers, and Macclesfield, suffered impeachment, but against Lord Bolingbroke, a prime minister, the more reliable bill of attainder was revived. There is a trial of the impeachment charges against Dr. Sacheverell for the extraordinary offense of preaching two sermons in support of the Tory doctrines of non-resistance and passive obedience. The punishment imposed upon him was to keep silence for three years, which ought to figure as a cruel and unusual punishment against a man so fond of political sermons.

The most interesting of all the English impeachments was that of Warren Hastings, next after Clive, the founder of the English Empire in India, who returned in the splendor of his fame to spend ten years of his life pursued by that towering array of talent, with its extraordinary

6. The reader may also wish to consult Raoul Berger, *Impeachment: The Constitutional Problems* (Cambridge: Harvard University Press, 1973).—C. J. R., Jr.

power of eloquence, Sheridan, Fox, and above all Burke, the ablest
politician, in the noble sense of the word, this world has ever seen. The
advocates of Hastings, headed by Edward Law, afterwards Lord Chief
Justice Ellenborough, broke the force of that impeachment by tying the
great orators down to rules of strict legal procedure and by meeting their
political law and loose testimony with the serried ranks of the rules of
evidence. The superb spectacle in Westminster Hall and the marvelous
efforts of the great statesmen surpassed anything in our history in the
way of an impeachment case.

Of far more political importance than the impeachment of Hastings,
was this impeachment of Samuel Chase, when our Constitution was new
and untried.[7] We had adopted against Federal officers the English
method of impeachment, by giving to the House of Representatives the
sole right to prefer a charge and to the Senate the sole power of trial. In
1804 men who had fought in the Revolution for the independence of a
narrow strip along the Atlantic had lived to see the national domain
stretching to the mouth of the Columbia River in Oregon. In this year
early in our constitutional history the great battle was to be fought between the lawyers and the politicians to determine whether this national
government of ours should be one of laws or merely of men. The trial
of Chase was in fact to determine whether hostile politicians could im-
peach and remove judges of the Supreme Court because of what those
ignorant and prejudiced political gentlemen considered errors of law,
and improper views of the meaning of our Constitution.

Chase was a Federalist in the old and able court headed by Marshall.
His associates were all Federalists, one of them a nephew of Washington.
At the instigation of President Jefferson, working in his devious way, the
House of Representatives had impeached Chase for alleged errors in the
trial of a seditious criminal named Fries, of another named Callender,
and finally for an address to the grand jury on the circuit in which he had
reflected on the dominant party, then called Republican. The real point

7. The impeachment of Samuel Chase has been made the subject of an important
study by the sitting Chief Justice. See William H. Rehnquist, *Grand Inquests: The
Historic Impeachments of Justice Samuel Chase and President Andrew Johnson* (New York:
Morrow, 1992).—C. J. R., Jr.

at issue was whether the legislative power could control the judges by removing them by impeachment on account of their expressed ideas as to constitutional law and then pack the court with their worthless partisans. The situation was acute. Marshall had just informed the administration that the Court would not hesitate in its duty to hold an executive act to be unconstitutional and Jefferson's rage against the sanest man in our history, whom he called "the half-crazy chief judge," was malignant. This impeachment is in its far-reaching results the most important fact in our constitutional history after the adoption of the Constitution.

Yet it is to be said with regret that the men who write our histories with no adequate knowledge of constitutional law, have failed to recognize the overpowering importance of this trial. Two men have very imperfectly essayed the task, but the constitutional histories have missed it altogether. Over thirty years ago students at college, for want of something better, read for their sins, as a textbook on our constitutional history, a work by Von Holst, and in all that voluminous book there is no mention of this impeachment. The wonder is how constitutional history could be written without noticing this trial. Let any man try to conceive what the history of this country would have been if Samuel Chase had been found guilty and removed and if then the politicians, with appetite whetted by the smell of blood, had moved on Chief Justice Marshall and he had been removed by impeachment.

There was long afterwards another important impeachment, that of Andrew Johnson. The charges there were actual violations of a penal statute combined with other charges that were not seriously considered. Owing to the fact that the charges as to violations of the statute failed, no real issue was there presented except the improprieties of the President, and *they* were not matter of impeachment. Johnson's trial, however, is worth reading to see how Evarts, Curtis, and Groesbeck as advocates overthrew the politicians, which is the ordinary outcome of great impeachment trials. It is the victory of the trained and equipped mind over casual and desultory effort. Any one who has pored over those volumes, printed in the miserable type which our government deems worthy of its publications, will remember the detestable vulgarity and pettifogging of Ben Butler, who managed and disgraced the case for the

House, the sophomoric eloquence of Judge Bingham, and the cold, reasoned, cutting logic of old Thad Stevens, unable to stand, carried in a
chair daily from House to Senate, the greatest advocate on either side. If
he could have directed the case Johnson would have been convicted.
Stevens's wit never failed him. One day when he was being carried by
two stalwart attendants, he looked up and said: "Who will carry me,
boys, when you are dead and gone?" Opposed to the House managers in
the Johnson trial were the solemn weight of Curtis's argument, the wit
and adroitness, the suavity and finish of Evarts. These recollections will
remain with any one, who has read the record, as unfading memories of
a great trial. But Johnson's impeachment cannot approach in political
importance this trial of Judge Chase.

It is not necessary to go into the formal statement of the charges
against the Justice. They can be read in the book published in 1805 giving the proceedings. In answer to the charges Judge Chase appeared before the Senate with his counsel, the ablest advocates of that day. The
managers of the impeachment were John Randolph of Roanoke, utterly
ignorant of law, and a number of other men who, among politicians,
passed, no doubt, for lawyers.

Presiding over the Senate was Aaron Burr, fresh from the killing of
Hamilton. Jefferson, formerly Burr's bitter enemy, had lately been con-
ciliating him with offices. Stirred by recollections of the great Hastings
trial, Burr had attempted a pitiful travesty of the pomp of Westminster
Hall in most uncongenial surroundings in the old Senate Chamber,
which is now the Supreme Court Room, in the village that was then the
wretched mudhole of Washington, without houses or streets and with an
unfinished Capitol building. In an amazing riot of color of his own de-
signing, Vice-President Burr performed almost the last act of his official
career. He was just about to cease to be Vice-President and to engage in
the Louisiana venture which aroused again the enmity of Jefferson and
brought him to trial for high treason before Judge Marshall on the circuit. It is to be said for Burr that upon this Chase trial his bearing was a
model of judicial decorum and his part in it could not be a subject of
criticism. As a keen lawyer he must have enjoyed the discomfiture of the
Jeffersonians.

The sole question before the Senate in the Chase trial was on the meaning of the Constitution. In Article II, section 4, it declared that all civil officers of the United States should be removed from office on impeachment for and conviction of treason, bribery, and other high crimes and misdemeanors. Article I, section 3, added that the one convicted should nevertheless be liable and subject to indictment, trial, judgment, and punishment according to law. It is plain that the phrase high crimes and misdemeanors does not mean "high errors," but does mean actual criminal offenses, because that is the meaning the words then bore. This view is strengthened by the collateral consideration that the Constitution evidently supposes that every impeachable offense is indictable and punishable as a crime. Since it was not claimed that Judge Chase had committed any public offense, the articles stated no ground for impeachment.

The attempts of the historians to explain the issues upon this trial are not successful. Historical writers are rarely fortunate in an attempt to explain legal matters. They do not seem to be able to comprehend the terms that are being used. But this is nothing new. Over three hundred years ago Coke, the oracle of the common law, observed: "And for that it is hard for a man to report any part or branch of any art or science justly and truly, which he professeth not, and impossible to make a just and true relation of anything that he understands not, I pray thee beware of chronicle law," or as we say historians' law. In Coke's time there were no histories of England except the jejune chronicles.

Although the law was plain, Campbell, the manager opening the case, contended as had been agreed in Judge Pickering's case just finished, that an impeachable offense need not be indictable. Pickering had been impeached probably for the slimy political reason that thereby a number of Senators could be committed to a particular construction of the words of the Constitution. But these managers were to find that Judge Chase, supported by his court and defended by the flower of the bar, was a very different person from the bibulous and half-demented Judge Pickering of New Hampshire. Impeachment, Randolph vaguely continued the managers' position, was a sort of official inquiry into the conduct of a public officer, more in the nature of a civil investigation than a criminal prosecution. The articles of impeachment, according to Randolph, who did not foresee what he was to meet, charged that Judge Chase had committed errors in his rulings. In other words, the law as decided by a judge of the Supreme Court was, according to the managers, to be passed upon and revised and the legal rulings of the judges were to be submitted to a lot of usually second-rate politicians or indifferent lawyers, filling the senatorial benches, preparatory to removing the judge. This is the original proposition in our history for a judicial referendum. Instead of the manifest imbecility of a *popular* referendum, Randolph and his associates proposed a referendum to the Senate, giving it the final decision upon matters of law, by removing the judges.

But some of the articles of impeachment contradicted this theory; they attempted to charge acts as being criminal offenses, although the acts could not be offenses; others charged mere errors of law, but every act charged, except the address to the grand jury, which was at most a judicial impropriety, not even an error, became on final analysis merely an alleged error of law committed by a judge in the discharge of his judicial duties, and every such error assigned was precluded by the decisions of Marshall and his fellow judges.

Chase's counsel, in their speeches in opening, at once took issue upon this ridiculous legal basis for the impeachment. Thereupon Nicholson, another manager, abandoned this position of the managers. Randolph, who closed the opening speeches, was wholly at sea on the legal points involved, for a Virginia planter, even if he did know a little Latin, could hardly be expected to reply to trained lawyers. After the evidence was in, the managers in closing arguments again attempted to come back to the ground that they were not obliged to prove a criminal offense. They asserted in closing that if they proved violations of law not amounting to crime, the law would impute to every such violation or every breach of duty an evil intent or a corrupt motive. This is tantamount to saying that every time a judge decided a point of law wrongly he committed a high crime or misdemeanor out of evil intent or corrupt motive; yet those deluded partisans knew that appellate courts existed simply for the purpose of correcting errors of law, and the whole theory of appeal is that an error is not a tort or a wrong. The managers without knowing it were going back to Plato's proposition in his *Laws* that for an error the judge appealed from should be tried as for a criminal act. Such was before Bracton's time in an age of barbarism the theory of the common law, but the law had been otherwise for over six hundred years.

One after another Judge Chase's counsel slaughtered the managers' proposition and exposed the ignorance of law shown both in the articles and in the speeches. Luther Martin unsparingly exposed and ridiculed the unfounded assertions as to Maryland and Virginia law for which Randolph was responsible. Nicholson, replying for the managers, again shifted his ground; now he argued that any misbehavior in office amounted to a misdemeanor; otherwise the judges holding during good behavior would be irremovable, and even though a judge became incapable he could not be removed unless he could be impeached. This was the same position as the first, for it depends for its validity upon the proposition not expressed that when a judge commits an error of law he is guilty of a misdemeanor, or if he does something that is not even an error but is a lack of taste or judgment, he is likewise guilty of a misdemeanor. This may sound like a plausible argument to a layman, who does not know the legal term "misdemeanor," or to some lawyer, who believes in the removal of judges by the executive on the address of the legislature, or to those happily few lecturers on civil government and political science who know just enough about constitutional law to be dangerous public nuisances. The answer to Nicholson is that only high crimes or misdemeanors, as the law defined those words, were sufficient for an impeachment, while the removal of a judge for adequate cause of misbehavior could easily be provided for by a constitutional law, since judges by the Constitution hold during good behavior. The Constitution did not make impeachment a remedy for mere misbehavior. The objection of the politicians to passing a law on that subject was that such a law must come sooner or later under the revision of the judiciary for them to say what is good behavior and what is not, and the judges must finally decide what was good or bad behavior in a Federal judge. It was certain that any decision by the Supreme Court on that question would not suit politicians, bent on breaking the Court.

At last came Randolph, in what was supposed to be the effort of his life. He was bewildered and utterly befogged. Knowing nothing of law, he had been intimidated by Luther Martin. He delivered a characteristic harangue, he babbled the drunken nonsense he was accustomed to use in the House, where it passed for eloquence, he became confused, he excused his futility by complaining that he had lost his notes, he broke down and wept, and ending with snuffling sobs left the whole case for the managers in pitiful confusion.

The partisan majority in the Senate rebelled. Chase was triumphantly acquitted. On the one article as to the grand jury address, the poorest of all the charges from the standpoint of constitutional law, the administration mustered its largest vote. Marshall and his fellow judges were left free to lay down the law in a series of great decisions upon which reposed and now reposes the whole fabric of our government. Randolph, cowed and humiliated, came out of the trial cursing what he called the treachery and cowardice of Jefferson in not dragooning his followers into line, and proposing a constitutional amendment that the judges should be removed by the President upon the address of Congress. Such was the effect of this decision that even during the Civil War, when Taney, the Chief Justice, was harassing the government in the courts, no question was made as to the independence of the judiciary. He was merely ignored.

The hero of the Chase impeachment was Luther Martin of Maryland. He was slovenly and unkempt in appearance, generally half drunk and always ready to drink more. Heavy and obese in figure, with a harsh and, when aroused, a screaming voice, he poured forth speeches full of repetitions and redundancies in a great flood of language strung out to interminable length; yet he was a legal genius of vast learning, a most convincing speaker, whose very faults seemed to add to his convincingness. No doubt he was in his day the very head of the American Bar. In the book on the Burr trial can be seen his second complete triumph over Jefferson in the acquittal of Burr.

For thirty years Luther Martin was Attorney General of Maryland. Long after the Chase trial, the story goes, he had so conducted himself while drunk in Judge Chase's court that a warrant was drawn for his commitment. The paper was handed to Judge Chase to sign but he looked at it a moment and threw down his pen saying, "No doubt I owe a duty to the court, but Samuel Chase cannot sign a commitment of Luther Martin." At length, in 1822, Martin was stricken with paralysis and left destitute, but such was his standing and so endeared was he to the bar, that a special tax was imposed upon each lawyer in Maryland for his support and was paid without question. Soon he wandered to New York, where Burr was now practising with success, and we can feel some warmth toward Burr by recalling that he received the old and broken prodigal and took care of him for the rest of his days.

In the meantime the scepter of leadership at the American bar had been held for a time by Pinkney,[8] but when he died in 1820 that leadership had passed to the far greater legal genius of Daniel Webster. The two most extraordinarily statesmanlike intellects in our history were very great lawyers. In sheer mental ability Hamilton was the greater. In rapidity of apprehension and in genius of almost instantly reaching correct conclusions, he no doubt deserved the judgment of Talleyrand, who pronounced Hamilton the ablest man that he had ever known; and Talleyrand had observed closely all the great men of his time. As a reasoner with the power to impress his reasoning on others, Hamilton has never been surpassed in our history. Compared with Hamilton as a lawyer, Luther Martin, of course, is entitled to no consideration. Webster, without the originality of Hamilton, and without his vast constructive genius, had yet a massiveness of mind and a power of massive expression that gave him for thirty years the unquestioned leadership at the bar. No two men in our history have ever had the following of Hamilton and Webster among what may be called the intellectuals of the nation.

In his life Webster made errors, no doubt, but the part of his life that was given to the law had no stains. It is doubtless true that Webster was dependent upon others for much of his material, as in the Dartmouth College case, but it was Webster who put the material in its convincing form. He was always the great lawyer. Had it not been for him Massachusetts might have gone over to the states with elective judges. He,

8. William Pinkney (1764–1822).—C. J. R., Jr.

more than any other lawyer, had a large part in the construction of the edifice of our constitutional law. His oratory was a potent force in producing a national type of thought. His last great speech on the 7th of March, 1850, which was long denounced as a desertion of the cause of the free states, is seen now to have been massively constructed on sure foundations.

It is useless to speculate against the accomplished fact, but if Webster's advice could have been followed and if there could have been less of the unscrupulous state politics in the South, there need never have been a civil war. Slavery would have peaceably gone the way of all things in which the Time Spirit sets his tooth. The fact that one of the last legislative acts of the Southern Confederacy was the abolishment of slavery is a curious epitaph upon that sacred institution. Webster, at least, did his best to avert the struggle, and the men who denounced him, like Seward, were the very first to be ready to sacrifice the Union and the Constitution when the Civil War began. That war at least demonstrated that the original American theory of a social community, bound together so that it could not be disrupted, was a certain fact. The men who made it the accomplished fact were those who accepted the powerful nationalism of Webster. He has come into his own again, and his errors can well be forgotten. There is a stanza in the lovely lines of Oliver Wendell Holmes on the Birthday of Webster, written in 1859, that exactly expresses the final judgment on Webster:

> Death's cold white hand is like the snow
>   Laid softly on the furrowed hill,
> It hides the broken seams below
> And leaves the summit brighter still.

The history of the Supreme Court would be without a flaw could the years from Chief Justice Marshall's death to the Civil War be forgotten. However one may seek to apologize and excuse there are some things in the years from 1848 to 1861 that cannot be forgotten. The glorious years are those of Marshall and Story, the one of powerful mind, the other equipped with a marvelous learning. They kept the Court on an even keel. When Marshall passed away Story did not hesitate to express his

Chief Justice John Marshall (1755–1835)

disgust with the Court as it went from bad to worse. But there is something in the detached, intellectual atmosphere of a court of high jurisdiction that enables a man at many times to rise above what would be
considered his predilections. When the Prize cases were before that
court during the Civil War, the decision was saved by Greer of Pennsylvania and Wayne of Georgia, that stout old Roman who wrote the caustic dissent in the Gaines case. In the days after the Civil War the decisions of the Supreme Court of the United States did much to take away
the bitterness that followed that devastating struggle. All constitutional
law is more or less mixed up with politics. As long as the politics are of
a high grade the mixture is necessary.

The fortunes of the law regulating the private relations among citizens are of more importance to the story of law than are particular questions of constitutional law. A résumé of the general private law is here,
of course, impossible. All our law except unfortunate legislative experiments is a development, by means of the juristic methods of the Roman
jurisconsults, from preceding well settled principles in arriving at either
differentiations or accordances. There are, however, certain conditions
that affect the general form of the law, especially in its administration.
The most important condition for private law is the provision that is
made for the education of the bar.

In the eastern and older states a law school was originally started in
Connecticut soon after the Revolution. After a time the law school of
Harvard College was in large part the work of celebrated judges like
Story and Parsons. Their labors resulted in a series of textbooks that
were of incalculable benefit to law students. Two works especially have
had a noted career. One was the book called *Greenleaf on Evidence,* won-
derfully well written and perfectly lucid. The other was the general work
on the law by James Kent, formerly Chancellor of New York. He was
called upon to supply practically by himself the needs of a law school.
Using Blackstone as a basis, he evolved the book in the form of lectures
that is called *Kent's Commentaries.* It took a much wider range than
Blackstone. Kent was a man of remarkable industry and wide learning
and he levied upon the civilian writers for different phases of Roman law
to illustrate his subject. But up to the time of the Civil War the bulk of

Justice Joseph Story (1779–1845)

legal instruction, at least in the western states, was acquired in law of-fices or by a reading generally inadequate and often desultory.

There is a close connection between the bar and the courts. Generally speaking, inadequately prepared lawyers exercise a very deleterious in-fluence upon the courts. Where the courts are filled with elective judges the result is that bar and court react upon each other to the excessive detriment of both lawyer and judge. It is an old saying that a multitude of the unskilled ruins a court. It is no less true that inadequately equipped judges debase and degrade the bar. When such judges are found in appellate courts they do not discriminate between matters of real substance and matters of form. Being elective judges, except in happy cases, they are bound more or less in communities of the fiercest democracy to cater to the well developed public sentiment.

Certain results from such a situation can be noted: first, an extraordi-nary reverence for the jury trial so conducted that the judge will not take any part in the deliberations of the jury; secondly, the practice of asking written requests for instructions to the jury; thirdly, an excessive techni-cality in appellate courts in passing upon matters of detail; fourthly, a lit-eral use of the rules of evidence so that mere matters of varying ideas of probativeness became important subjects upon appeal. These abuses began in the criminal law and extended to civil cases.

In explanation it may be said generally that the courts were manned with men who in practice had gained the exaggerated notion that, how-ever a jury might be misled, cajoled, or deceived, jury trial was some-thing so sacred that the court not only must tell the jury that they could decide the facts but must not under any circumstances give the jury the slightest intimation of what the judge thought of the testimony or its credibility. Naturally, in rural communities the jury received exagger-ated notions of its own importance. The result was that the judge whose duty it was under the English theory to assist the jury was debarred from being of the slightest assistance.

Since the jury was all-important, an elaborate system of impaneling a jury came into existence, with examinations of jurors on every kind of collateral subject that might seem to give some light as to how a juryman might be affected by the evidence or might be inclined to view the case.

The result became a gross absurdity where in any important criminal trial long periods of time were taken in impaneling a jury, generally with the result that any man intelligent enough to sit would be excluded. The results of this sort of practice have greatly debased the law.

The rule fixed for criminal cases extended at once to civil causes and many of the same evils resulted in those cases. The excessive zeal for jury trial led courts to lay down rules of absurd strictness as to when there was evidence to go to a jury in a civil case. The result was most unfortunate, for the judge finding his function minimized was glad to shirk his duty and to let every case go to a jury. In some states this mistaken practice has been carried so far that it is provided by law that a judge must instruct the jury before the counsel make their arguments to the jury. In this and in many other respects inferior lawyers in state legislatures have been enabled to do their worst to legal administration.

The second evil arising in jury trials was the encouragement of the practice of asking written instructions on every conceivable phase of the case. These instructions must be marked by the judge either held or refused, for the rule was established that a judge need not instruct on a point unless he was requested to do so, and the counterpart of the rule was that if requested he must do so. The old practice of the judge listening to the evidence, sifting it out, and stating it to the jury with pertinent statements as to the law, was lost sight of in the newer states, and the most minute criticisms were applied to these charges given or refused. This part of the law became highly technical, so much so that large volumes of law books were compiled on the subject of instructions to juries. The result was that mere matters of detail of relative unimportance determined a trial and reversals prodigiously increased. The law became so technical that only the most astute could hope to avoid error in a trial.

To all this was added another development. It became an accepted notion that error could be predicted in a trial upon the admission or exclusion of evidence. The rules of evidence were designed to be cautionary rules for the guidance of the judge upon a trial. But unless the point of evidence went to the merits of the whole case, no one would have conceived that the admission or exclusion of evidence was not a matter wholly for the discretion of the judge presiding at the trial. But, first in criminal cases and later in civil cases, the same excessive technicality resulted. Error was predicated upon rulings upon evidence. The question whether the trial had reached a correct result was wholly lost sight of. A trial became a mere game where the question was whether any wrong ruling had been made in regard to the numberless questions asked on the impaneling of a jury, next whether there was any incorrect ruling on the admission or rejection of evidence, and finally whether there was any incorrect ruling on giving or refusing any of the multiplied requests handed up by opposing counsel.

In this connection the exaggerated importance of a jury trial led to the utmost strictness being applied in curtailing the chancery jurisdiction, until many lawyers came to think that the chancery law was a very small and almost useless part of the law. In some way the idea got abroad that before a jury no great equipment of law was needed for success, if the lawyer was possessed of a sort of high-sounding grandiloquent style of speech, that generally lacked any background of convincing thought, while in a hearing before a chancery court no power of clear expression and exposition was necessary, if the lawyer had some knowledge of the outlandish and generally useless learning called equity. Something should here be said about the fortunes of the two systems in this country.

As we have seen, the double system of courts, common law and chancery, came to this country as a part of the English law. When the Constitution of the United States was phrased no doubt had ever entered the minds of its makers that that double system was perfection and should always be preserved. Consequently the provisions of the Constitution, as construed, required both systems of law and that these two jurisdictions should be separately exercised. But while this was true, the same judge sitting in the United States court exercised both jurisdictions, and now the anomaly was presented that the same judge would say to a suitor: "I cannot, sitting in my law court, do anything else than rule against you, but if you will hand up to me sitting in this same place in this same court on this same day a paper setting forth my weakness and inability, so well known to myself, I will enjoin your opponent from applying to myself as a common law judge, and I will thus prevent myself from doing you a great injustice." In this situation the Federal jurisdiction has remained, but the fact that the same court exerts both jurisdictions has taken away a large part of the difficulty. If both jurisdictions are lodged in the same judge the question is merely one of amendment.

Most of the state courts began with this double system of courts, and in some states there was a chancellor as an equity judge separate from the judges of the common law courts. In New York there were two well known lawyers who acted as chancellor. One was the noted lawyer Chancellor Kent. The other was Chancellor Walworth. But New York early began experimenting with its courts. It tried for a time an experiment based on the appellate jurisdiction of the House of Lords. The State Senate was made a court of appeals, and it was probably the worst appellate court that has existed in modern times. The judges in New York became elective. The state adopted a revised procedure amalgamating the two systems of common law and equity. The distinction between them can never be completely abolished, since a jury trial can be asked for in a common law case.

By this time many new western states had been admitted to the Union. They all with one exception adopted the double system of common law and equity, but they all had elective judges, and all except one state had the system of the same judge and same court administering both systems. The State of Louisiana kept the civil law which the French had brought with them. It is a tribute to the essential sameness of the substantive rules of law in both systems that men from other states found no difficulty in adapting themselves to the civil law. In an indirect way this law offered to the states following the two systems of law of England, an easy method of getting rid of some of the technicalities of the English law. The proposals of Edward Livingston arose from his knowledge of the civil law.

The trouble was supposed to be in the pleadings and in the contrast between a bill in chancery and a common law declaration. As a matter of fact the trouble was not there at all, but rather in incompetent administration by incompetent lawyers and judges. This is shown by the fact that in the Federal courts there has never been any actual demand for the abolition of the distinction. Those courts act as if they were using merely two forms of action. If a lawyer mistakes his form, he can easily amend.

The change in the states began with the adoption in various places of the code system of pleading. All the forms of action were abolished and a single form of pleading was provided, and the prescription for it was that the plaintiff should make a plain statement in a concise form of the facts constituting the cause of action. This sounded and seemed simple enough, but it turned out that the common law had in the course of time developed a system of pleading facts by pleading what were called ultimate facts as distinguished from facts that would be considered evidence to prove an ultimate fact. The common law pleading was simple and plain, to the effect that if on such a day at such a place A became indebted to B in a certain sum for goods sold and delivered and A had not paid the bill there was a good pleading. These forms the profession knew and was not prepared to give up. These facts pleaded were ultimate facts. The actual facts were that A had run up a bill at B's store, with nothing said as to price, that B had sent a bill and A had not paid the bill. So it was with most causes of action. In every common law action the one party or the other could claim a jury trial. That distinction was a sacred thing, the palladium of our liberties written in the Constitution of every state. The differences in the forms of an action at law and of a suit in equity could not be abolished. The test then remained to examine the pleadings under the Code, to find out whether the case stated would have been an action at law or a suit in equity, and the answer must be examined to ascertain whether a defense was set up not good at law, but good in equity. If the latter situation existed such a defense could not be submitted to a jury. Even the most hardened jury lover could see this.

But now another source of confusion arose. Many cases belonging to the jurisdiction of the United States court could be brought in the state court in the first instance. A statute provided that under certain circumstances such a case could be removed into the United States court. As soon as the case was removed and the record reached the Federal court the hybrid code pleading paying no regard to the distinction between law and equity must be at once recast, so that the Federal court could, as required by the Federal Constitution, exercise its common law jurisdiction separately from its equity jurisdiction. The state practitioner who had hoped that he could get rid of much necessity for the old learning now found himself afloat on what to him was an uncharted sea. The consequence was that the so-called code lawyer in order to understand his own system was required to have the same knowledge of the common law and equity systems that he would have been required to have were there no system of code pleading, and in addition he was required to be prepared with all the special technical rules that had been introduced by the code and its highly technical and sometimes ill considered language. The lawyer who practised in the Federal courts or in the courts of states like New Jersey or Illinois or Alabama, which had kept the separate systems, looked with pity and contempt upon the code lawyer as a poor creature who was dependent upon a Code of Civil Procedure, which furnished no rule whatever that was capable of intelligent application. To add to the confusion certain states had adopted codes attempting to define the whole field of the private civil law. These codes used the obvious generalizations of the existing law but did not, like the existing law, provide for many exceptional cases. Thus a new element of confusion and uncertainty was added.

But the codes and revised systems of pleading had added a new element of uncertainty in the Federal courts. The double system of pleading being constitutionally preserved in those courts and it being impossible to mingle matter of common law with that of chancery cognizance, an old existing practice in the Federal courts could no longer be followed. The practice in cases at common law in the Federal courts, by a statute of the United States, was made to conform as near as might be to the practice of the courts of the state where the Federal court was sitting. The chancery practice, however, for all the Federal courts is uniform through the country and is fixed by rules of court promulgated by the Federal Supreme Court. State statutes cannot affect this practice in any way. The vast flood of legislation on the practice in the states must be reconciled in some way to the Federal practice by conformity. Where all forms of actions both for law and for equity had been abolished and but one form, whether the case be of chancery or of common law description has been adopted, how was it possible to conform the Federal pleading at law?

In the state itself the abolition of all form had produced the consequence that in a single action matters of common law and equitable cognizance could be mingled in the pleadings both by plaintiff and by way of defense. But the state constitution had preserved a jury trial for law actions and the matters of equitable cognizance must be tried in one way, and other matters of common law cognizance must be tried by a jury, if one was demanded. The change amounted simply to making two kinds of trial in the same case, one without a jury, the other before a jury.

In other of the states without any abolition of the two forms of pleading there has occurred a very great liberalizing of the common law forms, with the distinction between law and equity preserved. Still other states have adhered to the separate jurisdictions of common law and equity, and the equity practice of the state courts differed from the equity practice prescribed in the Federal courts. In Louisiana the civil law has been preserved. Thus there is a very wide variety of practice presented to a lawyer whose activities take him into the courts of more than one state and into the Federal courts.

Fortunately the substantive law that is not the result of statutes is, in almost all the states as to most matters, practically the same. We may take the land law. It is true that there are differences, for instance in the forms and effects of deeds to land, and many common law rules have been discarded; but the practice of registering titles is common and there are no instances of tenure that can properly be so called. Titles in all except the original states with some slight exceptions all come from the government of the United States. In Texas, which is a state that was annexed as a state, the public lands belonged to the state and have been and are being disposed of by the state. In states like California, which was acquired from Mexico, there were old titles originating in Spanish land grants which have produced much litigation. But the general rule is that a land title begins with a land patent from the United States.

There are some kinds of estates in land that are peculiar. The mining laws recognize a title originating by a discovery of mineral and a claim made. This title may be transformed into a title by patent. But if this be not done, the title is recognized as one in fee simple if it is kept good by the doing of a certain amount of work upon the claim each year. This title may be considered as a base fee, a fee that continues as long as the assessment work is done but no longer. It can hardly be called a fee on condition, for no entry is required for condition broken, and on failure to perform work, the land reverts to the public domain.

The estate that is given in mineral land either by a claim properly made and lawfully continued occupancy or by a mineral patent for mineral in place and not in the form of detritus, is a peculiar title in that the title to mineral may and usually does extend below the surface outside of the tract of land as described upon the surface. The original of this law is an old mining custom of England. The shortest way to describe this peculiar estate is to say that the vein is conceived as the filling by mineral of a fissure or separation in the rock. The fissure or separation is conceived as descending with its mineral contents into the earth at an angle from the horizontal. The claim is supposed to be located to cover a distance or length along the edge of the vein exposed at the surface or toward the surface. That length of vein the claimant obtains wherever the vein extends on its descent, whether it extends outside of the space defined by the surface lines or not. The legal rule is that whoever owns a certain length of apex of the vein at the part of the vein nearest the surface owns that particular length of vein wherever it may go upon its descent into the earth. This is a pure case of law made by adoption and acceptance by the mass of the people and afterwards attempted to be put into the form of a statute which has always been inadequate to meet the varying conditions presented in natural formations.

Another development of law arising wholly from adoption and acceptance by the public without a statute is the law of waters which obtains in all the arid portion of this country where irrigation is necessary. By the common law water flowing in a stream was not the subject of exclusive appropriation for a use that consumed the stream. Prescriptive rights, not unreasonable, could be gained by an adverse possession. But in the lands of the older states where irrigation was not used the question of appropriation was not considered. For irrigated lands which will not otherwise produce crops it is necessary to take the water out of the stream in order to use it to any advantage, and the water is thereby consumed. The rule regarding such appropriations is that the one who is first in point of time in appropriation and application to a beneficial use is first in right to the necessary amount of his use. The principle is taken from the Roman law. It came into the western law through the Spaniards, although there are in existence well built ditches of the original Cliff Dwellers which doubtless were used for irrigating purposes, and which had no connection with Spaniards or Mexicans. The doctrine was first applied to the public lands of the United States, and difficult questions arose between appropriators and patentees whose riparian rights antedated the appropriation. Even yet the law is not entirely settled, although all government patents to lands in the arid region have long been made subject to vested or accrued water rights.

The peculiar situation arising from the fact that the states are held to be foreign as to each other, necessitates a vast amount of legal work in regard to corporations. Since most large businesses in the country are carried on under the corporate form, it follows that a great amount of business is done by corporations in states other than the one in which the corporation is formed. Every state has laws requiring a corporation of another state to take out a license in order to carry on business. In many instances, for business or legal reasons, a corporation is incorporated under the laws of a state where it does no business. As long as the business is done from a home office, it may receive protection as interstate commerce, but as against foreign corporations the state governments are constantly striving to derive a revenue from those foreign corporations. As soon as the large interstate corporation finds it necessary to qualify as a foreign corporation to do business in states other than that in which it is incorporated, it becomes instantly an object of attack, if not of pillage, by the state taxing power. In such a business as insurance, which has been held not to be a form of interstate commerce, the exactions of the different states have been enormous, and they have added much to the cost of insurance. Far more than in any other civilized country is it necessary in the United States on account of the multiplicity of laws, for men engaged in business to have the constant advice of lawyers.

But this is not all. It is a common saying that the people in the United States are the most governed people in the world. If it were added that they are in some respects the most and worst governed people in the world the statement would be accurately true. It has been found that in the natural course of events it was necessary to create long ago the Land Department of the United States government, which had under its special control the granting of the public lands. The power of the Federal government to grant patents for inventions and copyrights and trademarks added another large department to the government. These departments performed duties that were more or less judicial in their character, and a large bar was created whose practice was mainly in these departments. Then a department and board for the control of the railroads added the great number of lawyers who devote themselves to practising before the Interstate Commerce Commission, which was specially concerned for years in the task of ruining the railroads. The slow and just processes of the courts were not found satisfactory in regard to matters of trade and commerce and the Federal Trade Commission added its activities. So it has gone on; government board after government board, all with more or less judicial functions, has been created, always adding to the business of lawyers. At last came the income tax amendment, and this vast department rapidly outdistanced all competitors in the magnitude of its work for the legal profession. The living having been taxed to the point of possible depletion, the taxing bodies turned to the property left by the dead. Inheritance taxes, added to other exactions, introduced into business the sudden shifts of property values caused by forced sales to cover the inheritance taxes due upon the estates of the deceased.

The state governments were not to be outdone in this work, and much of the activity of the Federal government was duplicated by every sort of state board, until at present a large business is hardly justified in doing the most ordinary act of corporate business without seeking legal advice in order to ascertain whether there is not some regulatory law that bears upon the matter. If these various governmental boards, both Federal and state, would be satisfied by ordinary voracity, the situation would not be so bad, but through the resources of the government printing office, they are enabled to deluge the land with masses of documents highly laudatory of their activities, and pointing out how further revenue can be obtained. They devote no little time to devising methods by which they can increase their own powers and further circumvent the helpless citizen by amending and reamending the law in the way in which the income tax law and the inheritance tax law are constantly made a still more dangerous morass for the man who carries on business or hopes to die leaving some property to his family. Congress and the state legislatures seem perfectly willing to pass any sort of law that any government board asks for. While every one of substance breathes easier as soon as a legislative body is safely adjourned, there is rarely a session when new burdens have not been imposed upon the responsible public.

This constant flood of legislation is the worst feature of our polity. Laws that regulate minutely the affairs of the citizens are bad enough, but when they are constantly changing, the evil is vastly multiplied. Plato may have had a fantastic idea when he said that children's games ought to be regulated so that they could not be changed, but his reason was this, that when these children were grown up they would not as citizens be constantly changing the laws. His idea was the direct result of the baleful legislative fecundity of Athens. Zaleucus, the lawgiver of the Epizephyrian Locrians, had the provision that the proposer of a law should appear before the assembly with a rope around his neck, and if the law failed of passage the proposer should be instantly hanged. At Athens if a law turned out badly, any citizen could bring a criminal action against the proposer. But under our representative system of government the responsibility for a law cannot be enforced against any one. If in this country proposers of bad laws were indictable the number of courts would need to be doubled.

But on the other hand it is to be said that we are living in a country and in times of unheard-of industrial expansion. Many things take place in business that are indefensible. It is no doubt a very good thing that men can easily rise to great wealth, but when some one has done so by methods that resemble those of the bludgeon, the war club, the tomahawk, and the scalping knife there is a great outcry and demand for a law.

It is the old cry against the barbarian methods of the Middle Ages. But the laws generally are not well conceived, and they accomplish the embarrassment only of those who would never think of using such methods. Administrative boards are multiplied but they seem to do no good. All we can say is that, in general result, the field of action for all kinds of lawyers, good and bad, honest and dishonest, is constantly increased. The profession of law has assumed far more importance in business life than it ever had before.

It must be confessed that many of the evils that exist can be ascribed to this vast mass of men who are supposed in one way or another to be engaged in practising law. Many of them are not qualified either by character or by legal knowledge to be so engaged and there are yet few signs of any improvement. The great mass of responsible legal business, however, is not carried on by such lawyers; yet the profession bears the burden of them, for almost every scheme to circumvent the law originates with some lawyer attempting to further the selfish interests of some clients. Lawyers of sorts fill the legislatures and are influential in passing all descriptions of worthless laws.

If the field of the law is surveyed, it will be seen that the greatest evils in the law result not from the law itself nor from its rules, but from the human elements that enter into the administration of the law. Great judges and a great bar can make even a poor system flexible and adaptable. The very best system with inferior judges and a poor bar is a just cause of complaint. In the field of private law with all the drawbacks to our system the general results of litigation in reaching justice are not a cause for complaint because, generally speaking, the courts of appeal are well constituted.

In the field of criminal law it will readily be admitted that in many parts of the Union the actual enforcement of criminal laws is in a disgraceful condition. This situation is not at all necessary, for the Federal courts generally present the pleasing spectacle of a rigid but just enforcement of criminal statutes. The failure of many state courts is due first of all to the character of the criminal bar. It is not necessary to dilate upon the unpleasing subject, but all know the situation. The judges who sit in the courts are not always competent to meet the situation; but probably the worst evil from the standpoint of the judges is that if a judge tries to improve the administration, he is rebuked by the excessive technicality of the courts of final resort, in insisting upon matters which have little to do with guilt or innocence. Another crying evil is a lack either of intelligence or of character in jurymen. A judge is helpless either to assist the jury in their deliberation or to correct their conduct when it is outrageous.

If one goes into a criminal court of England he is astonished at the contrast. The barristers defend their cases on plain principles of justice. The case is tried with brevity. There is no foolish and prolonged examination of jurymen. The prosecuting counsel are careful in all their conduct and the trial is one of calmness and justice. The defendant's counsel do not descend to unworthy conduct. The men who act in the jury box are men of character in the community. The testimony of the witnesses is put in without any long discussions over its admissibility. Every one seems to be trying to get at the very truth of the case. When the judge instructs the jury he indicates to them with clearness the bearings of the testimony. He states the law to them in connection with the facts and does not read a great mass of written instructions which the ordinary juryman cannot understand. The jury with some promptness agrees upon a verdict and the sentence is given.

In the field of private law it may rightfully be claimed that practically all the difficulties come from the conduct of the bar, and from the inferior character of the jurymen. The contrast between a civil trial in the English courts and in the courts of America is startling, and yet before fairly competent judges, with skilled and experienced lawyers on both sides, a civil trial in America is much like one in England. But this is too often not the case. In some courts in this country a skilled lawyer is often at a positive disadvantage, on account of the inability of the judge to approach the case from a legal standpoint.

The difference between the efficiency of English courts and the inefficiency of many American courts is at bottom certainly due to the respective bars. In England barristers have the sole right of audience, except in the lower and local courts. No attorney or solicitor can try a case in the higher courts of general jurisdiction. It is recognized that men of skill and experience are required as lawyers to conduct cases in court. Other men should not be permitted to waste the time of the public tribunal. The barristers in England must come from the Inns. The Inns have the sole privilege of calling to the bar. Those men who appear in court are selected by the attorneys or solicitors, and the client takes their judgment. The attorneys or solicitors select the barrister solely with reference to their knowledge of his attainments.

But the query will at once come, how is a younger and inexperienced man ever to attain any position at the bar under this system? The answer lies in another unwritten rule of professional usage. The bar is divided between seniors, or leaders, and juniors. A leader cannot take part in a case without the presence of a junior. A junior, of course, can take part without a leader, but until a junior has demonstrated to the attorneys and solicitors his capacity, he is never in court except as he is guided by the experience and skill of his leaders. These matters are self-regulating, and the rules of precedence and conduct are carefully observed. When Lord Westbury was Sir Richard Bethell and a leader at the chancery bar, he and his junior were about to enter the chancery court of appeal. The junior, intensely preoccupied, filled with the case in which he was to speak as junior, grasped the door to pass in ahead of his leader. Sir Richard touched him on the arm, saying in his peculiarly bland but incisive tones: "Softly, softly, my young friend. If we cannot teach these old gentlemen any law, we can at least give them a lesson in manners. I shall precede you."

The English system attains results, and it attains them by recognizing that the conduct of cases in court is the most important part of legal practice and must be in the hands of experts who are not in contact with clients, except through the other branches of the profession. One result of this situation is a hidden one, but it is its best feature. Barristers who alone carry on the litigation and the important consultation work in the practice are, as stated above, never tied to particular clients. They never are employees. They are in a position of absolute independence. Their advice is always impersonal and disinterested. No one can say to a bar-

rister, "You shall do this or that," or "I wish this or that." No attorney
ever is afraid that if he advises or retains a barrister he is jeopardizing his
relation with his client.

This is the rule among *avocats* in France. An *avocat* can accept no employment. He cannot have any business. He cannot be interested in any
business. He cannot be a lawyer regularly employed by a particular
client. A worthy *avocat* who sold the fruits and produce from his farm
in France found that he must reform or leave the bar. No leading barrister in England is ever suspected of representing in his public utterances
any client or clients.

In this country the profession has no division. All lawyers are equally
competent to conduct litigation or to advise. Most of them are afraid, except in rare instances, that the more competent lawyer employed will appropriate the client. Since it is the few who are really competent to be
charged with the conduct of litigation, it necessarily follows that much
of the litigation is poorly conducted. The conduct of litigation in court
has come to be looked upon as much inferior to other activities. Almost
any one may be considered competent to try a cause in court. It is only
in the most important cases that any genuine selection is made with reference to the personality of the lawyer who is to conduct the litigation.
The result has been a steady deterioration in the conduct of litigation.
Such lawyers react upon the courts. A false impression is disseminated
as to the requirements of a judge. Almost any lawyer deems himself fully
competent to sit on the bench. The action of the bar on the courts, assisted by elections of judges, has caused a steady deterioration in judges.
In the courts of a large city like Chicago can be seen the most extraordinary specimens of judicial officers. Some of them almost violate the rule
that the proceedings must be in the English tongue. Elections of judges
are constantly being mixed up with the fortunes of the barons of municipal politics. The societies of lawyers called Bar Associations reflect,
too often, inferior legal thought. The profession has brought most of
this lack of standing upon itself. Leading lawyers have allowed themselves in public places to become representatives of clients. They forgot
that in public place they must be the representatives of the public. The
consequence has been that a leading lawyer in large practice in public

place is looked upon with suspicion, and he seems to be no longer considered available for those public positions which he, if disinterested, could so well fill.

Another result of this general situation in the practice has been the so-called standardization of legal business. The multiplications of a lawyer's duties has led to the creation of very large law offices where legal work is ground out as if it were the standardized production of a factory. Departments and heads of departments consult as to how the business is to be carried on. All the personal relation of a particular lawyer to a particular case ceases. Matters are doled out to employees or clerks without close supervision. The small staff of a great English barrister is impossible in this country even in a modest law office. All the multiplied activities of the extensive contacts centering in a large practice require the use of endless employees. Matters requiring the greatest research must go to these employees. Their work cannot be supervised and directed by long experience and great attainments. The consequence of all these various influences is the legal profession as we see it, no longer a learned profession but simply a business organization conducted by push buttons and call bells.

A so-called reformer would say at once, let us pass a law establishing the English system. But the reformer would have much to learn. The English system is as impossible in this country as would be mastodons roaming the streets. The reasons ought to be apparent to any lawyer or to any intelligent citizen. Let a law be proposed to give a special class of lawyers sole audience in the courts, and one long wail couched in almost all the languages of modern Europe would overwhelm the reformer. The numberless men whose living depends upon the continuance of the present system would furnish an opposition whose weight would be irresistible. It is useless to speculate on changing the present system except, first, by convincing the public that the present system is extraordinarily wasteful, and secondly, by gradually changing the present situation through the long extended process of slowly changing the character of admissions to the bar. The high qualification of a liberal education should be made a positive requirement. Admission committees should be abolished. Only a properly certified school of law with an extended and approved curriculum should be allowed to call to the bar. In the course of time the profession would reform itself. This result is sure to come. The improvement will be slow but it will come in the end and there is no need to take gloomy views of the future of the law or of the profession.

To gain a proper perspective of judgment we must go back hundreds of years. If Aristotle had been told that in the course of time an empire larger than any that he knew, far wider in its sway than the domain of his quondam pupil Alexander, would exist, where there would be no slaves, where every man would be paid for his work, where every citizen from the lowest to the highest would have the right to vote upon all governmental matters, where the head of the government and most of the officers were elected at stated intervals, where millions of people were packed into a single large city, he would have at once pronounced it to be impossible. If a Roman of the days of Augustus, mourning over the loss of the Republic, had been told of such an Empire he would have answered that the body of the people is always unsound and that such an Empire would not last for a year.

If either Aristotle or the Roman had been assured that in that empire there would be such a constitutional polity that any citizen high or low was guaranteed by a written document of government against any infringement of all his ordinary rights, so that the whole body of citizens or the legislative assembly could not take those rights away, the statement would not have been believed. If it had been asserted to either of those men that the courts without command of an army could say to the law-making body, "Your law infringes upon the document of government and it cannot be enforced," and that it would not be enforced; could say to the executive head of the government or to any of his officers, "Your acts, with all the power of government behind you, are not in accordance with the laws, and especially with the supreme law of the land, and we forbid you from further acts of the kind and command you to make redress," the Roman would have said that Cicero in one of his noblest writings had prophesied that such a day would come but that no one believed him. Aristotle would have replied, "That is what I dimly dreamed, but I knew that it was only a dream, for such a nation has a government of laws and not of men." Even Algernon Sydney and Sir Harry Vane, could they have anticipated that their cruel fate should have had its part in bringing about such a reign of law, would have gladly said: "Lord, now lettest Thou Thy servant depart in peace, for mine eyes have seen Thy salvation."

No man knows how manifold are the blessings which he lives with as his common surroundings in a land where every man can, if he has character, work out his own life, express whatever opinion he thinks to be right, and depart with a fair and assured hope. Grant the many evils, corruption in municipal affairs far worse than most men realize, a system of government that is wasteful and extravagant, that offers rewards to many who are incompetent, grant a body of laws and courts that do not always in the first instance attain justice, yet it is true that we have attained that highest and most practical form of justice among men, the equality of all men before the law.

There is a type of political thought in this country that is always insisting that we should be much better governed if our government could approach the English type of legislative omnipotence with a cabinet chosen from the legislative body to be the ruling executive body. This form of government keeps France in a turmoil, while Italy has recovered from it. The fact is that no country but England can make the system work. It is insisted that such a government is more instantly responsive to public opinion. The latter statement is true, and that fact is the greatest objection to it. It is owing to this form of government that so large a part of the English population has always been on the public pay roll, formerly under the Poor Laws and now under some other sort of dole.

Compared with England and her rapid changes, the form of government in this country has been a towering cliff of conservatism. Public opinion has its effect, but time and again a resolute executive by his veto has withstood the demand of preponderating opinion. Years ago we were saved by Grant's veto from the wild fiat paper money heresy. In later times Cleveland withstood the free silver fanatics. Other instances, some of them very late, will readily occur. The fact is that in this country we are preserved in the first place by our great size and diverse interests. It is impossible to get all the foolish people to thinking alike on any particular question. It used to be thought that a Republic could exist only in a small state; now it is seen that it is suited only to a very large one. If, however, the Congressional body does pass some indefensible and dangerous law, it is found that the President has generally a better developed sense of civic responsibility. He can veto and he is impregnable until the end of his term. If he, too, fails the country, the law has yet to pass the scrutiny of the judicial department, and that body has, of all branches of government, as a general rule, the highest sense of civic virtue. The greatest virtue of our form of government is that public opinion must long be tested and winnowed before it can prevail.

The vagaries of public opinion in this country have a double outlet. The various states have their legislatures. There every spurt of the wild effervescence of political thought can be tried out. The states which are most subject to such attacks of popular opinion become hideous and horrible examples. If it were not for the states and their great field of legislative power, which short-sighted people think should be given to the Federal government, our political history would have been and would still be becoming another record of failure in popular government. By the existence of the states as they are, in spite of a very heterogeneous and in many respects mercurial population, this country with universal suffrage remains, without question, from a legal standpoint the most conservative civilized country in the world. Centuries of long and patient effort are needed to construct the fabric of a great body of civilized law, and only a few years of unrestrained public perversity may lay it in the dust. Wild men may lead one state of this Union from folly to folly, the unrestrained nonsense of ignorant men may wreck another state, and even a combination and confederacy may attempt the destruction of the Union, but the great national life flows on, safely contained within the same banks that it received in the Constitutional Convention. Every true lover of his country should hope that a truly conservative nation this country will always remain.

That it has hitherto remained so is the result of the law of the Constitution, preserved by our Supreme Court. There is no more au-

gust spectacle in the world than the Supreme Court of the United
States when it sits to consider a great constitutional question, involving
the interests of many citizens. The very entry of the Court is a model
of impressive dignity. The very atmosphere is one of calm and restraint. The cause has been prepared for hearing carefully, minutely and
thoroughly, with vast research and full attention to detail. The statute
in question or the policy in question has been considered in all the light
that can be obtained from analogous situations. The social aspect of the
question, the social considerations and experience that bear upon the
question, are cited with the fullest detail. The reasons for the enactment, the general public policy involved, the demands of abstract justice, the interference with settled rules, all the reasons for a strict or a
liberal construction, all the different legal rules for interpretation, are
urged, debated, weighed, and tested, and finally the experienced and
trained minds of the judges in their private consultations are brought
to bear. If new grounds develop, a new argument can be had. When an
opinion is reached at last, it is certain that everything of which the
human mind is capable has been used.

The situation is the result of our constitutional system. Anything like
it had never existed before in the history of the law, and this is what renders the Constitution of the United States an epochal document in the
story of law. It represents the contributions of many able minds. Everything in it is an echo of the historical experience of the race and especially of the English race. It is in its fine balance between generality and
particularity a model of sound and enlightened judgment. Without reserve can be commended its dignified and stately form of expression. It
represents the English race at its best, with calmness and self-restraint
composing divergent ideas and wisely compromising hostile tendencies.
It represents a totally new departure in the law, the establishment of a
great empire under the forms of a republic. The fine and just balance between the functions of the federated government and the functions of
the states is the result of what we may call a stupendous wisdom. Every
departure from that true balance between general and local governments, every attempt to modify the just relations of the super-govern-
ment to the states, has been filled with disaster. The tendency among

short-sighted men who think that by laws the conduct of human beings can be forced to an artificial model will always be a source of danger in democratic government. The lawgiver, of all men, should have a sense of historic values.

When one of those who make our laws looks over the world and sees that the future belongs to the great federated commonwealths, when he observes Australia and its federated states, when he considers the constitutional form of government of the Commonwealth of Australia and its Supreme Court, when he ponders the provinces of Canada united under an organic form of government that preserves the balance between general and more local fields of legislation, when he has grasped the extraordinary achievement of the formation of the South African Union with its heterogeneous population, when he realizes that these great social aggregates destined in the future to mold the happiness of uncounted millions of men would have been impossible without the lessons derived from the heritage of American constitutional history, the lawgiver ought to stand in humility and reverence before the noble structure of our constitutional law. Above all, when he follows the historical opinions of the final judicial tribunal established by the Constitution and realizes that in its power, its wisdom, and its calm restraint it has perpetuated the work of the founders of the Republic and has stood between the rights of the citizen and the arbitrary tendencies of legislative or executive power on many a legal battlefield, he may well ask himself, "Who am I, a puny apparition of a day, that I should count my rashness and inexperience higher than the accumulated wisdom of a court, the most august in the world, which will be building still higher the great structure of justice and equality before the law long ages after I am forgotten?" If rash and violent men insist, as they have insisted and will insist in the future, upon the disturbance of the judicial power which has only the interest of preserving a just balance between the public interest and rights of the citizen high or low, weak or powerful, we know that they can never prevail. From Jefferson to Roosevelt popular idols have assaulted that citadel of our government, but they have never made the slightest impression upon its bulwarks. The Court has never fought back, it can make no appeal to popular opinion, it can only rely upon the sober good sense of the average citizen. Yet there is a power in the state which always has supported the duty of the judiciary to declare the law, and that is the power of the professional opinion of the bar. Renegades of no standing have failed to do this, but the great moral force of the bar has never been wanting, for every worthy lawyer knows that this judicial power is the basis of our whole constitutional polity.

CHAPTER 16

International Law

The great lawyer who was chancellor of France, D'Aguesseau, was the first to suggest that the law regarding the relations of states toward each other which by a misapplication of the term had come to be called the law of nations, would much better be described by the phrase "the law between nations." Bentham took this suggestion and translated it into the words "international law," leaving the expression, the law of nations, to revert to its old meaning in the Roman law. It was once commonly supposed that international law was an invention of the modern world, but it is now very well settled that the Greeks by agreements among various of the city-states regulated the rights of the citizens of one city-state in the dominions of another state. They had well-developed laws or customs regarding ambassadors and the making of treaties between states. There was a large body of ancient custom regarding the Amphictyonic Council. In the Amphictyonic League there was an opportunity for a federated league of Greek states, but nothing came of it. The Romans had very strict customs regarding the making and ratifying of treaties. There was a special college of priests which had the care of the approving of all treaties. One custom among the Romans added much to the responsibilities of ambassadors in the negotiating of treaties. If a duly accredited envoy made a treaty which the Roman Senate refused to ratify, it was considered that every obligation was met by the surrender of the ambassador to those with whom he had negotiated. One settled rule with the Romans was that they would never make peace as long as any foreign power had a foothold in Italy. After Rome by her victory over the Carthaginians drove the African power out of Sicily and Spain, she evolved a sort of ancient Monroe Doctrine for Europe. She announced that it was her settled policy that no African or Asiatic power could acquire or hold any territory in Europe. For this principle she began her wars with Mithridates the Great and with the successors of Seleucus in Syria. Another of her propositions was that Rome guaranteed every one of her allies against attack. The opening of Caesar's wars in Gaul was caused by, or at least excused by, the attack of the Helvetians upon tribes in alliance with Rome, and the assault of Ariovistus upon allies of the Roman people. Rome always fought until she made her propositions of international law accomplished facts.

After Rome gained her final supremacy international law was not heard of for hundreds of years, for the simple reason that the whole of the civilized world was under Roman rule and there was no occasion for an international law. All necessary law between states was supplied by the Romans. After the barbarians had overrun the Western Empire and were jeopardizing the remainder of the Roman power in the East, the Pope made constant efforts toward peace, at least among the feudal lords, and the Truce of God was one of these efforts. Rules of international law slowly began to emerge, but with great difficulty. There was a constant desire among better men to reach some basis of peace and the Duc de Sully at the end of the sixteenth century made an effort to restore the Roman peace by a League of Nations.

In the meantime a school of Dutch and French lawyers produced a great development of what is more strictly called international law. The Roman term law of nations meant not the rules between nations, but those general principles of private law which were recognized by all civilized nations to govern the private rights of citizens. This use of the term became lost and the law of nations was applied as a term to describe the law among or between nations. The Dutch jurist De Groodt, whom we call Grotius, did not use the term "law of nations" or "international law." He called his book "The Law of War and Peace" ("De Jure Belli et

Pacis"). He made up from the general principles of the Roman law and from agreements between nations, and from some ancient material governing the law of heralds and ambassadors, a system of principles to govern nations in their conduct toward one another, in a condition of war or of peace. But this kind of law continued to improve with many things well defined until after the Napoleonic wars. Vattel's book, called "The Law of Peoples," summed up the usages to his time.[1] Our Constitution made the treaties of this country with foreign countries a part of the supreme law of the land. Existing international law was expressly recognized in that document. Our Supreme Court in an early decision held that the recognized usages of international law among civilized nations were a part of the law of the land, to which all our courts would give effect. The same result had been reached in England.

Private international law was to receive an unexampled expansion in our own country, by reason of a peculiar construction from the very first put upon our constitutional form of government. It was held, whether wisely or unwisely need not be considered, that although to foreign nations this Union presented the aspect of one single sovereignty, yet, except as the relations of the states toward one another were controlled by the Federal Constitution and the laws thereunder, all of the states were to be considered toward one another as foreign states. The Constitution had provided for records of the state being proven and receiving recognition in all other states and had provided for an extradition of those charged with crime. It had the general provision that the citizens in each state should enjoy the privileges and immunities of citizens of the several states, but the tribunals of the states were at the same time justified in acting as if the rules that controlled them in private law would be the same as those which would be applied between two foreign states. The one great modifying principle was that which arose from the provision in the Federal Constitution which gave the Federal government control of interstate commerce.

It was at first supposed that in all other instances the Federal courts must apply the rules in any state that the state courts would follow.

---

1. Emmerich de Vattel (1714–67). —C. J. R., Jr.

After a while the Supreme Court evolved another rule for Federal tribunals. It was that in rules of general law the Federal courts would not apply the varying law of particular states as to a transaction otherwise governed by the law of a particular state, but would follow their own ideas of what was the proper rule of law.[2] We may take an instance. In Illinois, where the courts held for a long time that a check was a *pro tanto* assignment of a deposit in the bank against which the check was drawn, the Federal courts would not follow such a rule in Illinois, but would follow the general and more intelligent rule, that a check took no effect upon the bank deposit until the check was either accepted or paid by the bank where the deposit was against which the check was drawn. There has thus grown up a large body of transactions in regard to which the Federal courts will not follow the law of the state in which the transaction occurs, unless the rule of that state is considered to be correct. It will be seen that this is a sort of Roman pretorian law.

In another department of law the Federal government treats the states in just the same fashion that the states in Italy subject to the Holy Roman Empire were said to be related to each other. Bartolus in the Middle Ages said that those states in their disputes with each other could not give law unto themselves. So the states of the Union in their disputes with each other cannot insist upon their own laws. The Supreme Court in such cases will use such principles of general law as it deems applicable, and will pay no attention to the laws of the states that are litigating.

It is a dogma of our constitutional law that the various states are sovereign toward each other, but here is an instance where they are compelled to submit to a superstate law imposed upon them by the Supreme Court, although no such law exists by legislation or by any other force than accepted custom, as it is laid down by the Supreme Court. No one would deny that in such cases the rulings of the Supreme Court have the force of law, although the method of using coercive force is problematical. The German Kohler likens the law of federated states to what he calls supernational law, by which he means international law.

2. This was the rule of *Swift v. Tyson*, 41 U.S. (16 Pet.) 1 (1842), since overruled in *Erie Railroad v. Tompkins*, 304 U.S. 64 (1938).—C. J. R., Jr.

There was a court of the United States before the Constitution was adopted. Under the Articles of Confederation a prize court sat at Philadelphia and decided cases which had been reported. This court decided in a case that has been followed by our Supreme Court that no one nation can vary a rule of international law. Doubtless our Supreme Court would take the same view of the ruling regarding the *Appam*, a vessel lying in an American harbor.[3] The German prize court took jurisdiction because the *Appam* could not be brought within the jurisdiction of the court. This amounts to the staggering assertion that a court has jurisdiction because it has not jurisdiction. How incredibly plain such law is!

The development of international law was very marked during the century after the Napoleonic wars. Many matters were supposed to be settled in that department of law until the Great War of 1914. It is noticeable that during our Civil War the Supreme Court of the United States, on the analogy of an older case by Lord Stowell, developed as a part of the international law of blockades the doctrine of ultimate destination. The blockade runners, when the whole coast of the Southern Confederacy was blockaded, attempted to avoid the blockade by landing contraband goods in Mexico to be trans-shipped across the Mexican border. The goods, however, were held to be lawful prize when taken on the high seas before reaching the Mexican port. Similarly, goods ostensibly billed to Nassau were held to be lawful prize, when the fact was that they were designed to be trans-shipped at Nassau to run the Union blockade of southern ports.[4] The diplomatic writing during the Great War emanating from our foreign affairs office regarding these matters of international law is futile in its maladroitness. The doctrine in international law of ultimate destination may now be considered settled.

The operations of Confederate cruisers during our Civil War were destructive of American commerce. Those cruisers were the *Alabama*, the *Florida*, and the *Shenandoah*. It must be said that the American war

3. See *The Appam*, 243 U.S. 124 (1916); see also James Brown Scott, "The Case of *The Appam*," *American Journal of International Law* 10 (1916): 809–31.—C. J. R., Jr.

4. See especially *The Prize Cases*, 66 U.S. (1 Black) 635 (1862); *The Peterhoff*, 68 U.S. (1 Wall.) 28 (1866); and *The Bermuda*, 68 U.S. (1 Wall.) 514 (1868).—C. J. R., Jr.

vessels did not show much capacity for following up those vessels. Toward the end of the war the *Alabama* was destroyed in the English Channel. The fate of the *Florida* was curious. Toward the close of the war she put into a Brazilian port. An American war vessel following her lay outside waiting to sink her; but she did not come out. At last the American vessel steamed into the port and anchored near the *Florida*. The Brazilian authorities appeared with admonitions to keep the peace, but to support their remonstrances they had a wholly inadequate array of little gunboats. The American commander, however, seemed to be in a peaceful frame of mind and there was no sign of hostilities. Most of the crew of the *Florida* went ashore. The American vessel by some occult process seemed to be edging over nearer to the *Florida* and at last without any overt act of hostility a tow line appeared on the *Florida*, attached strangely enough to the American vessel. Soon the American vessel steamed out of the harbor with the *Florida* in tow, until at last the vessels disappeared from the view of the indignant Brazilians.

The Federal government, of course, promptly disavowed the act of the American commander and engaged to return the *Florida* to the Brazilian port. This was the news that greeted the officer with his two vessels when they appeared off the capes at the mouth of Chesapeake Bay. Acting under orders, the vessels turned into the Chesapeake and proceeded up the Bay, but the *Florida* was reported to have sprung a leak. She sank in the middle of the Bay. There she yet reposes. The officer was by a gesture cashiered, but he afterwards unaccountably appeared as a rear admiral. This episode was intensely humorous at the Geneva arbitration, when cited to show the lax ideas entertained by our country on international law.

As soon as the Civil War was over and the French Emperor had been required to withdraw his troops from Mexico, leaving poor Maximilian to his fate, the United States began insistent demands upon England for reparations on account of the depredations of the Confederate cruisers. The English with their incorrigible tendency in American affairs to put their money on the wrong horse and their naïve affection for the South as advocating free trade, had greatly incensed the North by

their conduct during the war. Gladstone, whose judgment was uniformly bad in foreign affairs, had used some very offensive language.
The bitterness felt toward England throughout the North had become
intense, and there was very much reason for it. At last, while Hamilton
Fish was Secretary of State, a treaty was concluded in May, 1871, at
Washington, by which the dispute was to be arbitrated by a tribunal to
assemble at Geneva. The treaty established certain rules, which, with
the rules of international law not inconsistent with them, were to govern the tribunal in its deliberations as to the duty of Great Britain regarding the Confederate cruisers. In December, 1871, in the Hôtel de
Ville at Geneva, the Alabama Arbitration Tribunal assembled. The history of this noted arbitration has never been well understood in this
country.[5]

The United States was represented by William M. Evarts of New
York, then entitled to be called the head of the American Bar. He was
supported by Caleb Cushing of Massachusetts, whom President Grant
afterwards nominated for the Chief Justiceship of the United States.
Before the war Cushing's political career had been anathema to all the
Massachusetts people who looked to Senator Sumner for a guidance almost divine. During the war Cushing had furnished to the administration much legal material of which there was constant need, but of which
Secretary Seward had not the least inkling. Some one, however, produced a letter written by Cushing which was a mere letter of introduction just before the war, but it effectually ruined for the second time his
chance to be Chief Justice. Cushing at Geneva could talk in the language
of the various arbitrators, even in Spanish and Italian. Evarts and
Cushing were supported, but at a long interval, by Morrison R. Waite of
Ohio, whom President Grant after his failure with Cushing successfully
nominated for the Chief Justiceship. Grant seemed to regard the lawyers
in the light of faithful military officers whose success entitled them to
the highest reward in his gift.

5. For further discussion of the significance of the *Alabama* Arbitration Tribunal and
additional bibliographic references, see J. W. H. Verzijl, *International Law in Historical
Perspective*, vol. 10: *The Law of Neutrality* (Leyden: Sijthoff, 1979), pp. 116–20.—
C. J. R., Jr.

The rules formulated in the treaty by worthy English and American gentlemen without any apparent accurate knowledge of international law were that a neutral must use "due diligence" against "the fitting out, arming, or equipping" within its jurisdiction of any vessel which the neutral has "reasonable ground to believe" is intended to cruise or war against a Power with which it is at peace, and to use due diligence to prevent the departure from its jurisdiction of any vessel so intended if that vessel has been specially adapted in whole or in part within its jurisdiction to warlike use. The second rule, as afterwards amended by consent, because its original statement was absurd in the view of both sides to the controversy, forbade a neutral to suffer either belligerent to use its ports or waters as the base of warlike operations against the other or for the recruitment of men.

The first rule is crudely expressed and would have been much clearer if stated by a competent lawyer. As stated above it is inadequate in the phrase "reasonable ground to believe." Does that expression cover the use of due diligence to discover whether a vessel is intended to cruise or make war, or is that phrase satisfied by mere passive waiting for information from the country about to be prejudiced, without active steps being taken to discover information? If the rule had read that a neutral must use reasonable diligence, first, to discover whether a vessel being fitted out, armed, or equipped in its jurisdiction is intended to cruise or war; secondly, to prevent the fitting out, arming, or equipping in its jurisdiction of such a vessel; thirdly, to prevent the departure from its jurisdiction of any vessel so intended, if that vessel has been specially adapted in whole or in part within its jurisdiction to warlike use, the rules would have been comprehensible and stated in ordinary legal terms.

The contention of the United States as to due diligence was that it must be proportioned to circumstances, and as to a reasonable ground of belief the position taken was that the use of reasonable diligence to form a ground of belief was required, while the English contention was that by our own national usage, as well as by international usage, due diligence had been defined in practice as that amount of care which nations ordinarily exercised regarding their own important affairs, and that, as to a reasonable ground of belief, no antecedent diligence was required for the formation of a belief. As the treaty stands, and under former international practice, and especially our own, one is compelled to acknowledge that the English contention was strictly correct.

A second case totally unprovided for in the first rule was this: Suppose a vessel to have been fitted out for war within the neutral jurisdiction and to have gotten away from the neutral's port without any want of due diligence on the neutral's part, is the neutral required by international law to treat such ship as a belligerent man of war after it has been commissioned by the belligerent power, or is it required to deny the ship access to its ports, or, if found within the jurisdiction, to prevent its departure, as if it had just been fitted out there, or does the fact that the ship has fraudulently escaped from the neutral territory and has been commissioned as a regular war vessel, require that it shall be treated by the defrauded neutral in its ports as a regular war vessel? All these inquiries were well known as likely to arise, yet upon the points the oracular treaty was dumb.

Whatever ground is taken it is apparent that these are all questions of fact or bare propositions of international law; motives, feelings, or public utterances in favor of one belligerent or the other can have no possible bearing. The second rule as formulated was so clearly in contravention of international law that it was amended by consent. It did not speak of due diligence, and the question upon the second rule was whether a neutral was an insurer against its ports being used for the recruitment of men, or whether it was sufficient that due diligence was used to prevent such recruitment after information gained. No one can tell what the conference actually decided upon this point.

By the treaty each government was to file at the opening of the tribunal a statement of its case and of its argument in support. The written statement of our case, it will appear, was indefensible. The conduct of the case by our government is not a very pleasant thing to contemplate, and it must be condemned. The condemnation extends not only to conduct during the arbitration but to a painful lack of dignity in choosing our own representative in the tribunal. To condemn one's own country is always an invidious task, but patriotism does not require one to lie for one's country unless one is an ambassador. In fact one may very well tell some truth regarding the arbitration, for very little will be found in the ordinary history as it is written in this country.

The American case was drawn by J. C. Bancroft Davis, who had had some experience in diplomacy but none in advocacy. He died as Reporter of the Supreme Court. If he had any legal talent neither his reports nor this arbitration discloses it. The main question to be settled was as to the *Alabama*, the *Florida*, and the *Shenandoah*, which had operated as Confederate cruisers. Numerous other vessels were spoken of in our statement, but as to some of them there was no evidence whatever, nor the slightest excuse for including them, while as to others England was so clearly not responsible for them that it is amazing to find them referred to at all.

The *Alabama* was built in England, adapted to a warlike use there and allowed to depart from its ports through the accidental sickness of a law officer, but after full warning to the English Government. The *Florida* case stood on different ground. It was built in England, partially adapted for warlike use there, left the English port without negligence on the part of England. It had then entered an English port, the harbor of Nassau. It was there seized by England but exonerated by the English Prize Court on the ground that it was not yet equipped as a vessel of war. It then on a barren island had received its armament, had immediately run through the blockading squadron into Mobile harbor, had there been commissioned as a war vessel, had then run out of the harbor through the blockading squadron a second time and afterwards had been allowed to enter English harbors and to coal as a *bona fide* man of war.

The only evidence of liability as to the *Shenandoah* was that she had enlisted a part of a crew in the English port of Melbourne, Australia, and departed upon her career of devastation among the American whalers.

The English Government could have urged that as to the *Florida* the United States had not performed its duty of keeping down the damages by reasonable care, although the English did contend that after the *Florida* had been allowed to run in and out of Mobile, England was no longer liable for its acts. By its own negligence our country had allowed the *Florida* to run in and out of a supposedly efficiently blockaded harbor, and, in the case of both the *Florida* and the *Alabama*, it had allowed those vessels to pursue their depredations without making any adequate pursuit by a sufficient fleet. One of the most difficult things to comprehend about our Civil War is the insufficient forces used in the pursuit of the cruisers. The *Florida* and the *Alabama* were allowed to sail the seas for over two years, to burn or sink or capture many vessels and to drive almost all of our merchant marine to the protection of the British flag, where our foolish navigation and marine laws have ever since compelled it to remain.

The tribunal was composed of Italy's nominee, Count Sclopis, an Italian jurist of some reading, an urbane, verbose gentleman of polished manners but with rather muddy faculties. He spoke no English. The arbitrator named by Switzerland was Stämpfli; he was not a jurist and he had apparently a very bitter antipathy to England. He is accurately described in a private letter as "as ignorant as a horse and as obstinate as a mule." He also did not speak English. The Brazilian arbitrator was Baron, afterwards Viscount, Itajubà, not a jurist. He was a man of calm and judicial temperament but he knew no English. His attitude, however, as to damages was shown by his statement to the English, "*Vous êtes riches, très riches.*" In other words his attitude was, "You are very rich and therefore should pay heavier damages than would otherwise be awarded." England sent her leading jurist, Chief Justice Cockburn, but we were guilty of the inconceivably bad taste of sending not one of our jurists but Charles Francis Adams. He was the very man who as Minister to England had taken so large a part in these matters and whose mind was fixed upon all the questions to come before the tribunal. There has been a great deal of stupid ignorance printed in regard to the personnel of this board. But these are the facts. There was but one competent jurisconsult on it and that was Cockburn. It is worthy of notice that in the treaty of 1892 providing for the Fur Seal Arbitration, it was required that the arbitrators be jurisconsults of distinguished reputation and acquainted with the English language. It is unfortunate that those provisions were not in the treaty of 1871, but even in 1892 our government went so far as to class Senator Morgan as a distinguished jurisconsult![6]

There were two glaring faults in the American case as stated, let us hope to the best of his ability, by Mr. Davis. The early part of his argument was devoted to an irrelevant but bitter attack upon England, to quoting the hostile words of Gladstone, Lord John Russell, and Palmerston, Liberal statesmen, who had all favored the Confederate cause; to asserting that England, desiring Southern success, had acted in bad faith, in precipitately recognizing the South as a belligerent, in assisting the blockade running, and in conniving at the fitting out of the cruisers. The treaty conceded that only negligence was involved while the argument asserted actual warlike operations. It is much like proving a negligent injury by an assertion of a premeditated assault with intent to commit murder.

The statement was full of bitter hostility and totally unworthy of such an occasion. It is apparent that all this rodomontade as to England's irrelevant conduct in some other matter had nothing to do with the questions purely of fact which were being tried. This was all political buncombe intended solely for home consumption among the Fenians and Anglophobes in the approaching Presidential election of 1872. Any advocate worthy to represent us before an international tribunal should never have stooped to the sort of balderdash which if used in one of our courts in an ordinary negligence case would have at once been suppressed by the judge as prejudicial and clearly outside of the issues to be tried. It would be precisely as if, when Smith was suing Jones for negligence, Smith should complain to the jury that the son of Jones had spoken disrespectfully of Smith's character, and that Jones had loaned money to Smith's enemies.

The English case was drawn by Sir Roundell Palmer, one of England's greatest advocates, afterwards Earl of Selborne and Lord Chancellor. It contained one part that was strongly objected to in the American reply. As bearing upon the questions of what was due diligence and of the ex-

6. Senator John Tyler Morgan (1824–1907), Democrat from Alabama. Senator Morgan's role in the Pribilof Islands negotiations is discussed *infra*, p. 408.—C. J. R., Jr.

istence of a reasonable ground of belief as to the character of a vessel, the English statement cited with particularity and care the practice of our government, first, in regard to the allowing of equipment and departure from our ports of war vessels to prey upon the commerce of Spain and Portugal in 1817 and 1818, with which countries we were then at peace; secondly, in regard to the filibustering expeditions of Walker against Central America and of Lopez against Cuba, which departed from our ports; thirdly, in regard to the Fenian raids on Canada.

The record cited was absolutely shameful. The English case showed beyond all question that the United States had always contended that a foreign government must furnish it with indubitable proof before it would act in detaining an alleged war vessel; and after a vessel had actually gotten away in fraud of our neutrality, that very vessel was permitted even to bring its prizes into our ports; as to the filibustering expeditions, war vessels were allowed to be equipped and men enlisted in our ports to war against a country with which we were at peace, because we insisted on the foreign government furnishing us with absolute proof before we would act; and as to the Fenian expeditions it appeared that men were openly enlisted in our cities and General Sweeney and other loud Fenians openly stated in the public press that the men were being gotten together and armed for a raid on Canada. Certainly this evidence was relevant to show how this country construed the phrase "due diligence" and to that extent it was proper to show that we were not in a position to ask another country to exhibit far greater diligence than we had ever shown in regard to our own ports. But we were anxious to forget the nightmare of our international conduct and earnestly objected. The attitude of the tribunal was shown by the decision early in the arbitration that all this evidence was inadmissible. On what ground the Board against the dissent of the English arbitrator so decided, it is impossible to conjecture. International law is always provable by international practice.

The concluding portion of Mr. Bancroft Davis's statement almost wrecked the arbitration. For our government he put forward enormous claims of more than two billion dollars for indirect damages, so called, arising in a mingled way from the operations of the Confederate cruisers, from the blockade running and shipping of contraband of war, and from the general unfriendly conduct of Great Britain and its early recognition of the belligerency of the Southern States. The claims were stated as loss in the transfer of vessels from the American flag, enhanced payments of insurance on merchant vessels, and the prolongation of the war and delay in the suppression of the rebellion. It was perfectly plain, as Theodore D. Woolsey has pointed out, that such claims were negatived by the treaty, which allowed recovery for direct losses growing out of the operations of the cruisers in capturing, destroying, and burning vessels. It was also plain that the prior negotiations negatived any such indirect damages. No country could afford to submit to arbitration its liability for injuries of this wild and indefinite character or its governmental acts in recognizing belligerents. Every American who was informed knew that such claims were outrageous. President Grant spoke with contempt of the "indirect damage humbug." Both Charles Francis Adams and Secretary Fish knew that the clams had no validity, yet our government did not dare to withdraw them on account of our internal politics.

These ideas had been encouraged for a long time by the folly of Secretary Seward's diplomatic dispatches. He had contended from the first that European countries had no right to recognize the Southern Confederacy as a belligerent! He maintained that the cruisers were pirates and ought to have been treated in all ports as pirates! Yet he knew that we ourselves recognized the Southern Confederacy as a belligerent by blockading its ports and by exchanging prisoners with it. But this sort of statement had been circulated throughout the North until our people were wholly bewildered and had no proper idea of the international situation. If Seward was right, we had no excuse for blockading the South and the whole blockade was illegal. The Supreme Court of the United States decided against Seward's conception; but four dissenting justices, Taney, Nelson, Catron, and Clifford, agreed that the North had no legal right to blockade the South. It was sheer nonsense to contend that a portion of the country with a *de facto* government maintaining large armies in the field was not a belligerent. Perhaps the day will come when some careful writer with the requisite knowledge of international law will properly expose the preposterous character of much of Seward's diplomatic writings during the Civil War, but as it is, our delusions about our own history are such that Seward is looked upon as a great and capable foreign secretary.

The Geneva Conference was left at an impasse created by Mr. Davis's brief. The English refused to proceed. At last it was decided to repudiate Mr. Davis and his claims. But instead of openly withdrawing the claim, Charles Francis Adams, our arbitrator, was driven to propose that the Board should unanimously announce that the indirect claims could not be considered, and this is the best commentary upon the amazing impropriety of Mr. Davis's conduct. When this announcement was made the reply statements had been filed. Sir Roundell Palmer never noticed those parts of the American statement which have been noted as so inexcusable. The arbitration tribunal proceeded to consider and make its decision in regard to the various issues. Having made its decision, it called for further arguments, but this was a mere gesture. The decision was already made, but arguments in writing were delivered from both contestants. Mr. Evarts spoke once, but he was not understood by three members of the Board, for he spoke English.

The award was made holding England responsible for the *Alabama*, and the *Florida*, with their tenders, and for the *Shenandoah*, after she had recruited men at Melbourne. The amount of the award was $15,500,000, but the damages claimed for national pursuit of the cruisers and for prospective earnings of vessels destroyed were disallowed. The sum given was no doubt grossly excessive, although Stämpfli wanted to make it much larger. No persons have yet been found with sufficient damages to exhaust the award, and a large part of it has been devoted to purposes clearly not within the purposes of the award.

The arguments of the different counsel may be read in the four-volume book published by our government, entitled "The Geneva Arbitration." Those of Sir Roundell Palmer will be found models of good English, clear statement, and fair argument. Mr. Evarts was worthy of his great reputation. Caleb Cushing was mediocre, while Mr. Waite was negligible, although his service as counsel paved the way for his selection as Chief Justice of the United States.

The different arbitrators delivered opinions. That of Count Sclopis lays down a rule which every one has condemned. Those of Mr.

Stämpfli and Viscount Itajubà are curious reading, since neither of these gentlemen knew anything about the international law that he was discussing. Mr. Adams's opinion is not that of a jurist and parts of it are not in very good taste.

From the lawyer's standpoint the real legal document in the case is Chief Justice Cockburn's dissenting opinion. Here is something worthy of study. He no doubt felt justified under the circumstances in assuming an advocate's attitude. He had the example of Charles Francis Adams. When at the bar Cockburn was perhaps the most impressive and powerful barrister in England, and at Geneva he fully sustained his great fame. He accomplished only one thing so great as this dissenting opinion, and that was his marvelous summing up of the evidence in the famous prosecution of the Tichborne claimant. He fully argued the whole arbitration. His grasp of the propositions of law, his wide acquaintance with the authorities, his unfailing memory of facts, never missing a document or any evidence bearing upon the particular issue, his enlivening sarcasm, restrained but cutting, upon Mr. Davis's performances, his exposure of the pitiful bid for the favor of the Brazilian, his contemptuous refutation of Stämpfli, make a presentation from the English standpoint that dwarfs every other utterance in the case. He is here the advocate *par excellence*, preëminently the kind of intellect which sees through the innumerable details to the few controlling facts, around which he masses the evidence with the artistic power of a masterly pleader.

He discusses first his strongest position, the *Florida*, and his skill in argument enables him to demolish the contention of the other arbitrators. There he is unanswerable. He proves by international law that when the *Florida* became commissioned as a Confederate cruiser, whatever her prior status had been, she was entitled to recognition as a man of war, and he proves it by an American case. As to the *Alabama* he frankly states his own opinion that England was liable. As to the *Shenandoah* he proves the contention that England was required only to exercise due care in preventing the enlistment of men, and he proves it by the use of American precedents. When a competent historian, in an adequate way, comes to write the story of the Geneva Arbitration, Cockburn's surpassing feat of advocacy will receive its fitting tribute.

It cannot be said that the Geneva Arbitration added much knowledge to the science of international law, beyond the fact that it has ever since rendered this country perfectly scrupulous in its duties as a neutral. One occurrence during the Civil War was of some importance. Commodore Wilkes in command of the *San Jacinto* stopped on the high seas the British steamer *Trent* and took from her the Confederate envoys Mason and Slidell who had escaped through the blockade to Havana. He brought them as prisoners to this country. Secretary Seward, who had a sort of genius for getting on the wrong side of a legal question, took the position that the seizure was entirely justifiable, but President Lincoln, better advised by Caleb Cushing and Lieber,[7] moderated Seward's bellicose attitude. The envoys were surrendered and Seward wrote a letter to appease his wounded feelings, in which he asserted that the English position was precisely that which this country had always supported but which England had constantly denied. There was some truth in the statement, but Seward's information probably came from Cushing and Lieber in the State Department.

One curious arbitration with Great Britain is a matter that most Americans at the present day would be glad to forget. In the War of 1812 a large number of slaves had followed away the British troops. The Treaty of Ghent that closed the War of 1812 provided for an arbitration of this matter. Slavery being involved, the government followed up this matter with almost religious enthusiasm. After many years England paid $1,204,960, rather than return black men, who had once breathed English air, and were therefore free, to slavery in the "land of the free." It was such things as this that made England so skeptical regarding the American attitude toward slavery.

In 1872 the German Emperor arbitrated the war boundary between Vancouver Island and that part of the United States which was the Territory of Washington. In 1877 an award required the United States to pay $5,500,000 to Canada for trespasses by Americans upon Canadian fishing rights. It would seem that those covetous Yankees could have been kept away from the Canadian fishing grounds for less money, espe-

7. Francis Lieber (1800–72). —C. J. R., Jr.

cially when the government was to pay the bill and leave the depredators with their ill-gotten gains.

With Canada we have had a number of arbitrations. Besides the two spoken of, the Alaskan boundary as to the Canadian territory was determined in 1903. The final fisheries arbitration in 1910 ended in another award. But one of the most important from the standpoint of international law was the Fur Seal Arbitration in 1893. There was in this arbitration a splendid display of forensic oratory between James C. Carter for the United States and Sir Charles Russell for the English—or perhaps a better term would be the Canadians, since they have proven themselves a great nation by self-sacrifice and dauntless valor on many a stricken field.

The Pribilof Islands belong to the United States. The seals always resort to those islands to bear their young at a certain season of the year. At another season of the year they seek the mainland. Mr. Carter evolved the novel proposition that these seals, which were wild animals, and in which no individual could have a right of property until capture, as all law, Roman, English, and American, unquestionably decided, were yet the property of the United States as a species of national property. His whole argument was based upon the fact that the herds resorted to the Pribilof Islands to bear their young. If this proposition was sound it followed that the herds remained our national property even when away from the Islands. Hence when they resorted to the mainland the hunters who killed them were trespassing upon our national property. But a purpose on the part of the animals to feed on the mainland was as important as a purpose of production of progeny; both were entirely natural processes and one had no precedence over another. But the whole proposition was entirely unsound, and would instantly become so if it were applied to wild fowl or birds.

Mr. Carter was a great lawyer with much subtlety of analysis, but he had not the robustness of intellect of Sir Charles Russell. Any one with an ordinarily acute mind can detect the flaws and fallacies in the Carter argument. One naturally wonders how any set of sound lawyers could have supposed that other acute minds would accept such a proposition. But it is to be said that this position was taken in default of a better one

408 THE STORY OF LAW

that had been adopted. An unscrupulous Russian had sold to gullible representatives of our government a set of forged Russian documents. They were quoted from at length in the brief of facts filed by us, but just before the hearing it was admitted that the documents never had had any authenticity and were gross frauds. The treaty of 1892 which provided for the arbitration required that the arbitrators should be jurisconsults of distinguished reputation. Our country chose such a jurisconsult as one and Senator Morgan as the other arbitrator. Our jurisconsult, of course, voted against our country, but Senator Morgan found no difficulty in voting for us. He may therefore pass as one who would be called at this day "one hundred per cent American."

This country was really a party to the arbitration of the Venezuela boundary with Great Britain in regard to which President Cleveland startled the country by assuming such a warlike tone. After all the excitement and misleading of the country by a dependence on baseless claims of Venezuela we had the mortification of having Chief Justice Fuller and Justice Brewer, jurisconsults in fact, decide against the unsupportable pretensions. The worst of it was that we had taken the position in defense of a rascally government, which would never have appealed to us if it had not been in the wrong. Canning, the English Foreign Secretary, claimed that he invented the Monroe Doctrine in the grandiloquent phrase: "I called a new world into existence to redress the balance of the old." Perhaps he did so, but John Quincy Adams, our Secretary of State, claimed it as his own invention. If Canning did invent the doctrine the Venezuela case would simply prove the cynical old saw, "Chickens come home to roost." If Canning could have foreseen what the Monroe Doctrine would turn out to be, he certainly would not have been so temerarious in his claim.

Some rules of international law that were supposed until 1914 to have been well settled were rapidly unsettled during the Great War. Until our entry into the war it is plain that our diplomatic writing needed a Caleb Cushing in the background. We may take the case of the *Lusitania's* destruction. It is a good instance of writing first and trying to think afterwards. The sequence of events will show these facts. On February 4, 1915, the German government officially announced to our government, first, that it would sink all enemy merchant vessels in British waters without taking any steps whatever to provide for the safety of passengers or crews, and, second, that it might, or its submarine officers might, by mistake torpedo a neutral vessel. The astounding proposition was the announced readiness and intention to sink a British merchant vessel with American passengers on board without warning and without providing in any way for the safety of the passengers. A possible mistake against an American vessel was a minor matter, practically immaterial under the situation where all Americans crossing the ocean were traveling on British passenger ships.

On February 10, 1915, our government protested against sinking neutral vessels or endangering American lives on *neutral* vessels but said nothing of American lives on British passenger vessels, thereby impliedly admitting the right to sink without warning English passenger liners with Americans on board. This was the "strict accountability note" that was afterwards sought to be considered a protest against the sinking of the *Lusitania* as a British liner with American passengers. It was nothing of the kind. So far as Germany was concerned, she had the right to claim that we in our note conceded that she was acting within her rights in sinking an enemy merchant vessel without warning even if Americans were aboard.

Just prior to this time the captain of the *Lusitania* on a prior voyage, at the request of American passengers to save their own lives supposed to be in imminent danger, had run up the American flag. On February 10, 1915, our country protested to England against the action of the captain of the *Lusitania* in having hoisted the American flag to save Americans at their own request. The State Department showed that it had full knowledge of the contingency of a number of Americans being on a British liner, and for a second reason Germany was entitled to assume that America conceded her monstrous claim. It probably is the fact that our State Department was no better informed, and actually thought that under international law such a massacre of neutrals was justifiable.

But to put the matter fully, Germany on February 16, 1915, reasserted without qualification her intention emphatically expressed for the second time to sink British passenger vessels with Americans on board. This note was not then answered and a second opportunity was lost to put the country right. The *Lusitania* was about to sail from New York with many American passengers. Sometime after April 22, 1915, the German Ambassador, von Bernstorff, drew up and dated April 22, a notice antedated as of April 22, addressed to all Americans traveling to England on an English passenger vessel that they were to be killed on the high seas without warning. Early on May 1, 1915, he published in the daily papers the notice signed "Imperial German Embassy." The *Lusitania* sailed at one o'clock on May 1, and our government, knowing that many Americans were on board and that the German embassy had published a notice that they were to be killed, knowing, too, that the hour of sailing would be wirelessed to submarines lurking in ambush to kill American citizens peacefully and lawfully upon the high seas, sat supinely helpless, failed to call von Bernstorff to account, failed to send an actual warning to Germany, failed to denounce the expressed purpose of Germany. Everything considered, this is the worst failure in our diplomatic history, for a proper protest would have been effective, as the sequel showed.

Then in due course "according to program" on that direful morning of May 7, 1915, came the frightful slaughter of so many Americans, ruthlessly butchered to make a German holiday. At once came the explosion of wrath, horror, and bitter resentment and the government at last discovered in the disgust of the voters that it is contrary to the law of nations for Germany to sink on the high seas an English passenger vessel carrying American passengers, and that it was the duty of the government to protect its citizens on the open main. A protest should have been made in reply to both the German notes of February fourth and February sixteenth. It has not even been noticed that in the meantime our government wholly sacrificed the right to protest the sinking of an English merchantman carrying American goods. On that morning when the *Lusitania* was sinking to her grave Charles Frohman said as he bravely faced his fate: "Why fear death? It is life's most beautiful adventure." He went down with the ship, and he now "in yonder stars mayhap may know" what frightful destruction legally uninformed diplomatic writing may cause.[8]

But the *Lusitania* sinking settled in international law that a merchantman carrying neutral passengers cannot be lawfully sunk except after providing for the safety of passengers and crew. In this rule Germany has concurred. The further point whether neutral goods are protected provided they be not contraband will need some further elucidation.

Events that have occurred in connection with the making of peace after the late war are too recent to give as yet any proper perspective for the purposes of international law. But it may be said here that the claim of a state like China against the justice of extra-territoriality raises the question anew of how it will be possible for business to be transacted by foreigners in China under a system of half-barbarous law which is not sufficiently civilized to furnish rules applicable to the transaction of the business. Japan, of course, was able to achieve the astonishing feat of converting almost overnight a medieval group of laws into a system as thoroughly modern as any on the globe. It has laws to cover the widest ramifications of a modern industrial system in connection with a highly developed trade and commerce. From the standpoint of the history of jurisprudence it may well be doubted that any other country than Japan could have made in a few years a transformation that staggers belief. But China is in a very different case. If it is to carry on trade without granting extra-territorial rights to resident foreigners, if it expects to invite foreigners to do business in China without granting them extra-territorial law, China must transform its laws to suit the conditions of modern business and commerce. No country can enter the number of civilized nations when its population cherishes the hatred of other nations that characterized a barbarian tribe in its feeling toward all other tribes.

The history of the human race and the necessities of a social existence in contact with other nations teaches that among nations the same regard for justice must apply as that which applies in a civilized state among in-

8. Charles Frohman (1860–1915), a leading theater impresario of the late nineteenth and early twentieth centuries.—C. J. R., Jr.

dividuals. The primary notions of freedom and of readiness to grant equality and of respect for the equal rights of others are precisely as binding among nations as they are among individuals. In order that all should be equal before that international law which is the ligament of justice that holds nations together, any particular nation to claim an equality must be ready to concede it to others. It must make its own people respect the rights of other nationals. A country which cannot do this must be denied an equal place with other nations. This is the principle of justice applicable to nations as well as to individuals. The Elizabethan Hooker has put this controlling consideration in the finest way: "For seeing those things which are equal must needs all have one measure, if I cannot but wish to receive all good, even as much at every man's hand as any can wish unto his own soul, how should I look to have any part of my desire herein satisfied, unless myself be careful to satisfy the like desire, which is in other men?"

CHAPTER 17
Conclusion

SOME ONE BY WAY OF A CASUAL REMARK once ventured to say to Lord Chancellor Cottenham that the law was uninteresting. Cottenham replied with the conclusive refutation: "The law uninteresting? I deny it." It is no doubt true that as a subject of conversation by lawyers, except when they are recounting legal anecdotes which as a rule have for at least a hundred years received the full meed of professional approbation, the law is uninteresting to laymen. Nevertheless, the attempt has been made in this book to put the story of legal development in such a way that it may carry interest to the general reader. One who has passed his life in the law is, perhaps, not a good judge of its interest to those who have had with it no direct connection. With very good reason most laymen are anxious to avoid the law as a forbidding and repellent subject. The Bible speaks of the swine who bore a golden jewel in his snout. The great Dramatist with a more refined touch has "the toad, ugly and venomous, that wears a precious jewel in his head." Let us say that the law is like the ugly and sometimes venomous toad, which bears the precious jewel in its head of that spirit of social coöperation which enables us to live in conditions of mutual adjustment. If this be recognized the law need be no more uninteresting than are our fellow men.

The story of law beginning with man as a reasonless animal has been followed from age to age in an attempt to explain, not in any occult way nor by the use of weighty technical terms but on principles of common sense, in a way that any intelligent reader can understand, how much of human life and effort is wrapped up in this science of jurisprudence. But there is an initial mystery in the law. Why is it that man alone of all the animal creation has developed a self-conscious reasoning power? Why is it that man alone has escaped from the fatality of mere animal reactions, so that he can by his purposeful acts alter and overcome to an extent his physical environment? We know that none of the philosophical theories of being and reality can explain this initial mystery. No system of pure idealism like those from Plato or Berkeley or of their later imitators is adequate to solve the mystery. The difficulty is that ideas depend upon and are expressed only in language. Let any man attempt to set forth an idea, and he finds that he must use words. Take away language and idealism cannot exist nor can any systems of metaphysics exist. But before man existed, there was no language and before any opportunity for a system of idealism was presented, before metaphysics had been evolved by human thought, the earth and the universe were what they are now, and they would have continued precisely the same, if man had never created or had never gained his mental power. No creation of the mental power of man can explain the mystery. The pure scientist with his inexorable laws will never fairly meet this mystery that transcends all human thought and experience. Certainly man in himself offers no explanation of why the world is what it is. Men in their inmost souls since they became capable of thought and reflection have known this, and so it is the basic conception of law that the law as created by man, has always had in it a molding and controlling element that transcends all human purpose and design. If we go to the very fundamental conception of the law, we find that all law is, in its ultimate analysis, based upon the conception of what we call "the Moral Government of the Universe," and that on that moral government of the universe has depended the development of reason in man.

Dr. Johnson once said that men of the world were all of one religion and when asked what it was replied: "That, men of the world never tell." But most men will go far enough to say that they have some religion, and if the thought upon religion, that intelligent men of all shades of thought have in common, could be defined, it would probably amount to the statement that all science and all knowledge have put the mystery of life merely a few steps further back, and that behind the Universe looms the thought that the world and its processes and men and their development are the result of this moral governance whose nature we cannot tell. Closely allied with this idea and as a part of it is that idea of the destiny of men, upon which it will be better to quote a great lawyer, not a divine or a philosopher. Webster was arguing in the Supreme Court against the provisions of Stephen Girard's will as being illegal in purpose because in contravention of all religion. Using one of the noblest passages in the Book of Job, he said: "For there is hope of a tree, if it be cut down, that it will sprout again, that the tender branch thereof shall not cease but through the scent of water, it will bud and bring forth boughs like a plant. . . . But if a man die shall he live again? . . . This question nothing but God and the religion of God can answer. Religion does answer it and teaches man that he is to live again and that the duties of this life have reference to the life which is to come."

Thus it is that in the law there is always the controlling thought that colors men's ideas in the law and in its application, that man's moral responsibility is the basis of all law. And in the conception of evolution is after all this divine element of gradually awakening and increasing reasonableness that comes from a better appreciation of what man's moral nature ought to be and what it may become, and that finally the law as reflecting this improving moral nature will gradually grow to be a better and higher system of reason. As we look back on human life we cannot feel much respect for human attempts to formulate and in precise terms to define "the substance of things hoped for, the evidence of things not seen." Ever since man ceased to be the pitiful creature cowering in craven fear before the mysteries of nature and of life, he has substituted his own harsh theology and annexed to it a necessity for belief enforced by a bitter intolerance and cruelty, which are but another name for the poor savage's terrors and attempts to placate an awful deity.

On the other hand religion in its better part with its great emotional appeal has done probably more than all other influences to mold the human race to a reign of law. We have seen that throughout history it is from the priest that the lawyer in all the civilizations that have been examined has received the torch of legal enlightenment. And when the torch was handed to the lawyer the priest still kept the sacred fire burning on the altar by his rites and ceremonies enforcing the moral law. The moral law standing behind and upholding the legal system and improving as religion has improved, has done more for the law than all human statutes. The ordinary man, little of a religionist though he be, unconsciously acts from his long inherited training in the conception of the moral law. The ideals, faith in the things that are good, joy in a well-spent life, hope, mildness, charity and self control, and all things that are of "good report" are yet, though we know it not, the most powerful instinctive emotions to make men just and law-abiding souls. Nowhere has this essential mingling of law and religion been better expressed than by that old lawyer-priest, Bracton, who wrote the first great English law book, and who while his companions slept was toiling upward in the night. "Law," he said, "is called the science of the just and right, whose priests some one has said we are; for justice is our religion and we minister its holy rites." Now and then a noble soul stands forth in the history of the law to tell us that our science is not a low system of chicane, but has truly done much for the progress of humanity and more perhaps than all other sciences put together.

This progress we think has been proven to be a wholly natural process. We have seen that every step forward has been a natural step. Men progressed to the hunting stage and the use of weapons. By association with each other men developed spoken language and thus became capable of reasoning and reflection upon the results of sensation. Then came the domestication of animals assuring to men a more fixed means for the support of life. At last came the cultivation of food plants, and then men could live in still closer relations in villages and towns.

Step by step with this development of the means of living arose all the different human institutions which surround us today. First the notion of a kindred through relationship by means of the mother, then the discovery of that much abused institution, the father, and the formation of the family. Naturally came the progression to the fixed institution of monogamy and the recognition of the headship of the family in the father and his control over all the members of the family.

Along with these various changes came the conception of first the tribal property in which each of the tribe had his share. At the same time as a matter of necessity came the recognition of each one's right to his mere personal belongings and his weapons. As a further necessity came the property of the kindreds when the tribe losing its loose relations began to recognize the tie of kindred, and as the clans or kindreds developed the family, there came by equal necessity the family property, probably in the nomad stage, still retaining the conception of the tribal ownership of the grazing ground. Finally came the aggregations of men for the cultivation of the soil, and at last arose the institution of the family ownership of land with the institution of the inalienable real estate property in the family. As soon as a system of barter developed, this notion of private property became extended to individual property in those kinds of personal property or movables that could be the subject of trade or barter. Real estate where the communities were agricultural would not become the subject of trade or exchange until a higher civilization developed commerce and manufacturers. As soon as the division of labor among men became the rule land itself must become private property, else it could not be sold or conveyed. All these matters and kinds of ownerships require no justification because they could not have been otherwise.

In the course of these various changes it is plain that the human race as a whole never lost any one of these steps that it had gained. But men became divided into civilized men and barbarians. Civilized men dwelt in cities and for hundreds of years waged war upon one another. The barbarian developed a quasi-military organization with kings and leaders in war. Tribes coalesced for the purpose of war. For many centuries went on the continual process of the barbarians descending in overwhelming force upon people of more civilization and property. The better civilized people almost invariably absorbed and elevated the invaders. The great Roman Empire for some hundreds of years held back the barbarians from all the civilized lands. At last the Empire gave way and the half civilized men reduced government and orderly institutions to chaos and wantonly destroyed the larger part of the wealth of the civilized people. Then began the long ascent of the ruined civilization to the modern civilization which we see to-day.

It once was the good fortune of the writer to see brought into sharp contrast the barbarian's idea of law as compared with the higher and more finished product of the civilized man. There was in the year 1890 and is yet a small Mormon town on the Virgin River in southern Utah. Living about twenty miles above this town nearer the headwaters of the Virgin was the remnant of a disorganized Indian tribe. Being under the charge of no Indian Agent, these thirty or forty Indians were amenable to the ordinary laws which governed the citizens. One day there were brought before the Grand Jury in the Territorial District Court some men from the Mormon town who testified that the Indians and especially their leading man, Big Buffalo, had killed a steer belonging to one of the townsmen and a heifer belonging to another, and had divided the carcasses among the whole number of Indians.

The occurrence was a strange thing in itself, for the Indians had always been quiet and peaceful and had never been known to commit any such act before. By means of an interpreter the hidden facts were ascertained. The cattle belonging to people in the town had been left some time before without any herder and had wandered up the canyon of the river until they came in the night to the patch of ground which the Indians were cultivating. The little fields were surrounded by willow fences to keep out the rabbits but such fences presented no obstacle to the cattle, which had literally eaten up the whole crop of the Indians. The next day the Indians had waited upon the Mormon bishop in the town, considered the head man of the white tribe, with a demand for reimbursement in a modest sum. The bishop had paid no attention to the demand. At the end of a week the Indians had come down again, driven off the steer and heifer, and scrupulously divided the carcasses among the families in the little tribe, even to making a division of the hides. They according to their lights had done a perfectly proper act of self-help and reimbursement.

This homely tale shows the barbarian point of view. The supposed kindred of the town owned the cattle that did the damage. The owner without question was liable for the acts of the cattle, and the owner was the tribe of white men in the town. The demand for reimbursement had been made and, no response being made, the lawful course of self-help had been followed and the property taken by distress had been divided among the Indian kindred according to the number of families. The solid obligation of the one kindred or tribe was owing to the other kindred or tribe. This was sound barbarian law, where only kindred ownership was recognized and the kindred was responsible.

On the other hand was the civilized law with its private property laws, where only the owners of the cattle doing the damage could be liable, where the law applicable was that all cattle could be turned out on the open range, and any proprietor who desired to protect his field must erect an adequate fence. As to the Indian law of self-help, there was no such legal remedy recognized. An action must be brought in a court against those individuals liable, where it would be decided that the Indians could not recover at all. In the meantime the Indian, Big Buffalo, such and such cattle, the property of So-and-so, had feloniously stolen, led, and driven away against the peace and dignity, etc., as the unfeeling indictment would sum up his conduct.

It was apparent that the Indians had acted in entire good faith according to their conceptions of law, which unfortunately were several centuries out of date; but at the same time it would be impossible to say that under such circumstances the subject of the larceny had been taken under a claim of right from the standpoint of the law. All that the court could do was to address some admonitory remarks to the stalwart Big Buffalo, which could not be interpreted to him in the Indian language, and to send him home.

Starting from such conceptions as these Indians had, and with tribal and kindred groups, and at last family property, the law begins its progress. Its very first effort among the Babylonians was to reach an exceedingly high expansion in a social condition of wealth accumulated and of large manufacturing and commercial interests with gold and silver and copper as money and above all a written law. This written law is merely a setting down of the important matters of customary usage, but far more is left out of the written law than is inserted, and as in all other systems there is, as there must be, more unwritten than written law. This written law is a divine law delivered from the god of the city to the king, and no way is presented to change it. Among these Babylonians the written language leads to the use of the written document. It at once takes its place as the controlling means of defining legal obligations. This document cannot be attacked or varied. It binds the parties to all the stipulations which they have agreed upon and put into the document. No evidence will be heard against the written document. The cheapness of the writing material permits the clay document to be used in almost every transaction.

This system of law retains all sorts of barbarian primitive survivals, but a court for deciding controversies exists if people wish to use it, and the great majority of documents provide for submitting any dispute arising to the arbitrament of the courts, and early an appellate court is developed to correct mistakes of law in lower courts. But there is as yet no sufficient reflection to ascertain a legislative or a judicial power as anything distinct in the exercise of the general power of the king. This great Babylonian power is ruined by an Assyrian invasion and conquest and the law's story passes to the Jews.

They too have a long history of primitive law preceding a written law, but now all the emphasis is placed on the delivery of the law from God amidst the thunder and lightning from the mountain. Gradually the Hebrew law passes through transformations. Its history is constantly interrupted by invasions and conquests. It has its one brief period of glory under its kings and then disunion destroys the state, which fights long for its existence. This race brings into the law the great doctrines of reasoned moral conduct and the religious element of a personal responsibility of man for his conduct, until at last, the next great gain is attained in the law by the defining of individual responsibility. The dispersion of the Jews through all the great cities of Egypt and the East and their contact with Hellenic civilization bring into the Jewish law the commercial law from Babylon, and bring into Hellenic thought the teachings of the Jewish law.

In the meantime the Greeks, first in the Ionian cities of Asia Minor and then at Athens, bring to the law the acute analysis which lays the foundations in the law of the differentiated powers of government, all emanating from the people. But the forms are crude and unworkable. In all the domains of private law the Greeks develop almost every necessary institution for an enlightened law, including the doctrine of obligations, if their institutions had taken a practical form. Gradually almost every primitive inheritance is weeded out. The doctrine that the state must grant justice to its citizens and must provide courts for that purpose becomes fully developed, but the signal failure of the Greeks is to develop either a competent judicial tribunal or a legislative power, beyond the town meeting. The legal profession has no existence as a separate corps of men devoted to the law. The Greeks never rise above the city-state, and until Rome comes with her dominance imposing peace the history of Greece is a long succession of constant jealousies and wars among the city-states.

At last comes Rome, which gradually rids the state of the old primitive notions, and develops a competent tribunal. The subjugation of the whole of the civilized world makes Rome the center of the world's affairs and of wealth and commerce. A legal profession is developed for the first time in history and this legal profession introduces first the juristic method of attaining law from which the profession has never departed and second the eclectic method of generalizing the legal institutions of all the states subject to the sway of Rome into the one system of the Roman law. The former contributions of the Babylonian, the Hebrew, and the Greek law pass into the Roman law which is finally put into form by the compilers of Justinian.

In the meantime all governmental institutions are destroyed by the German barbarians and the civilized world is reduced to the chaos of the feudal system, out of which emerge the modern states. Feudalism renders real property inalienable and practically destroys all commerce. One of the modern states, England, becomes the chosen home of legal development under the Norman race with its genius for law. It is to make possible the reconciliation of freedom in government with a sound administration of the law. This people, while known as the English, is far back in history the basic race called the Iberian. In their history they produced a cultivation of the soil and a working in the useful metals. The Iberians all over western Europe were overwhelmed by Celtic invaders with a much lower culture. The races amalgamated, and the mixed race had reached almost the former high level of the Iberians when Rome took possession. Rome had introduced a still higher civilization with the finished doctrines of the elevated Roman law. This civilization had been rapidly assimilated but again this race was overwhelmed by hordes of invaders little better than savages. In the course of five hundred years this race recovered some of its ancient culture, but invasions of other barbarians retarded the growth of civilized institutions. At last had come the Normans, then the leading race in Europe, and they came not to ruin but to save; they displayed the same genius for legal institutions that had made the Roman Empire and its law.

Almost at once is developed the separate powers of government. The Norman kings show a method of producing a strong executive, and a competent legislative power. Courts that are competent tribunals are furnished to decide the controversies of citizens in their private relations. The theory that crimes are breaches of the public order to be punished by the public authority is deduced from the dogma of the peace of the king. At last in the exigencies of civil war is produced for the first time in history the representative English Parliament, made up of two houses, representing the different estates of the realm.

From a king in difficulties had already been extorted the Great Charter of Liberties which bound the executive to the rule of law. Immediately followed the Parliamentary power of legislation and the dogma is settled that it is only by the consent of the representatives of the whole nation that taxes can be imposed. At the same time the executive power retains its right to be a constitutive part of the legislative. But finest of all the Norman conceptions of government is the institution of the jury, where the citizen is made a constituent part of the tribunals which pass upon the ordinary rights of citizens. This institution of the jury is of incalculable effect in habituating the citizen to contact with government matters. Supplementing the jury system is the power of the chancery courts to furnish in the field of law relief to the citizen in those cases to which the jury system by its form of judicial administration is wholly incompetent. For centuries this form of judicial administration and of executive and legislative power ruled in England.

The original function of the jury, that of being witnesses and the only witnesses was disorganized by the great burdens laid upon it. The nation was not prepared under any circumstances to give up the jury. The only remedy for its apparent failure was to transform it. In the course of hundreds of years the whole conception of the jury changed. The twelve were made a judicial body to hear evidence and to form their verdict from the evidence. Experience then demonstrated that rules must be devised which would limit the evidence to that which could properly be considered, and thus came into operation the body of law which is called the law of evidence.

It was a wise instinct in the English to cling to the jury and to their common law, whose fortunes were bound up with those of the jury. England in common with other European states passed through a period when the royal power attempted to absorb the legislative power and the judiciary. In that struggle the institutions of the common law and the presence of the jury prevented England from reaching the condition of absolutism from which France was extricated through the bloody processes of the French Revolution. The battles for English freedom, though often apparently lost, were constantly won. This history of legal experience enriched the story of the law with most of those governmental prohibitions and that vast legal experience which can be read in our national Constitution.

Time rolls on and the English hive overflows into the lands inhabited by the barbarian and the savage. Now history is to be reversed all over the world. The barbarian no longer can overwhelm the civilized lands, but the civilized man begins his career of displacement of the uncivilized human being, and every assault of the barbarian in past times is repaid upon him by the cruelty and oppression of the civilized man. Englishmen settled along the coast of North America and founded the American Colonies. The colonists went forth protected by royal charters and carried with them all the rights and laws and traditions that had become the heritage of the English race in its long battles for free institutions. The struggle of the Colonies with the Parliament of England began, and in the struggle was revived the ancient dogma of the Greek and Roman law that power must emanate from the people. A new adaptation of the law was that charters of government create inviolable rights and covenants binding upon rulers and subjects. Upon those ideas of binding and inviolable limitations upon government and of the people as a social community with full power, is based the great charter of our liberties, which is called the Constitution. In it the judicial power with its right to make the supreme law binding upon all departments of the government and upon every governmental officer from the highest to the lowest is securely intrenched. In the Constitution is applied, also, the collected wisdom of all the ages, an application made possible by the fact that a government is being founded in a new land, not tied down and bound by inherited ideas or by fixed divisions among men. That collected wisdom made possible a division of the powers of government among separate and independent departments, a legislative, an executive, and a judicial. With unexampled rapidity the great lands west of the original Colonies were wrested from the savages. Broader and broader extended the national domain until at last men who were children at the adoption of the Constitution were living to see the banners of the Republic dipping "their fringes in the western sea."

In looking back over English legal history it must appear plain that all the different phases through which the law passed were necessary to give that extended experience, whose results are embodied in our national Constitution. It does not take many words to define those prohibitions upon government but each short phrase represents the settled experience of mankind through hundreds of years. That experience determined what principles of government are necessary to be protected against either popular, or legislative or executive power. Above all it had been shown that the only feasible method of restraining such power was a prohibition by a supreme unalterable law enforced by an independent judiciary.

This prophetic vision was correct. In the years from 1787 to 1860 the institutions of our government were solidified and strengthened under the aegis of the judicial power until at last the whole power of the nation, the *posse comitatus* of the whole Republic, was to fight out on many a bloody field the two questions: First, was the constitutional rule imposed by the people upon themselves a binding rule when it made an indestructible union? And second, was the age-old Roman doctrine of Ulpian that by the law of nature and of God all men are created free, to become not alone the heritage of a part of the citizens but the inalienable possession of all the citizens? Those questions were forever settled on the anniversary of our Independence Day when the sound of the guns of the Indestructible Union at Gettysburg was echoed from the surrendered heights at Vicksburg. At last it had been proven that the Reign of Law was an accomplished fact. Since then other great federated Commonwealths have come to convince us that our experiment in government has passed from the stage of experiment to that of unalterable success. We may cherish the belief that in the years to come the decisions of our Supreme Court on constitutional questions may be often illustrated by decisions from the highest courts of the Commonwealths of Australia and of Canada.

One jurist, a figure as commanding as that of Papinian, stands forth. Before the Capitol at Washington is the statue of John Marshall, which was erected by the Bar of the United States. Even the most hardened and unimaginative lawyer cannot pass it without reverence, for there sits in serene and sagacious contemplation the man who more than all others molded our constitutional law, and made possible the beneficent government which brings contentment and happiness to so many millions of men. Great judge and great lawyer as he was, he was even greater in that his character even to his inmost soul was without a stain. The simple virtues of goodness, generosity, and kindliness made him a lovable man. Like all men of that description he had quick sympathies.

It must have been an extraordinary sight to see Webster finishing his speech in the Dartmouth College case. The great orator was giving to his close that touch of emotion without which all oratory is a dull and lifeless thing. The advocate was an impressive man. His great head, dark countenance and deep-sunken, gleaming black eyes aroused even the dyspeptic Carlyle to some enthusiasm in his description of this parliamentary Hercules. Webster after his argument as he came to the end, sunk his deep voice. The justices were bending forward to catch his words. He was speaking as if to Marshall alone. No feature of the clearcut composed countenance of the Chief Justice moved, as Webster in his poignant tone of suppressed feeling, said of his Alma Mater: "It is a small college, but there are those who love it." He hesitated on the

Daniel Webster (1782–1852), Zane's model of great
nineteenth-century lawyers

words, his voice broke, the great eyes filled, while down the granite face of the Chief Justice furrowed by years of thought, started the tears. Then lifting his voice Webster made his magnificent close. The scene shows us that the greatest are the most human.

It is something for a court to have the tradition of such a man as Marshall, but it is a greater thing that the profession reverenced him in life and reveres him in death, for he is the personification to all of us of the just man, not only capable and learned in the law, but also endowed with the statesmanlike vision, that is the very soul of aspiring humanity dreaming on things to come.

The fortunes of the law depend upon the profession. From its ranks come the judges. Harsh things can be said of the lawyers, that are all true. But we have seen that this is always true. We can look back to the very finest days of the Roman law, and read the denouncing words of Pliny the Younger upon the profession in his time. But at that time the legal profession was building the structure of law that still rules the world. And so it is with the law itself. At any period in its history we may see how much it failed to reach perfection. In the days of the greatness of the Roman Republic no man was safe from the attacks of the informer or the demagogue, public law was disgraced, bribery at elections was the rule. In the days of the Antonines when the civilized world enjoyed such perfect peace and repose, when men in point of well-being had little of which to complain, when the private law secured to citizens even-handed distributive justice, the public law made the Empire a despotism, and no man of importance, in the event of a bad ruler, could hope for any safety in life, unless he became a sycophant and a slave. The burning fire of patriotism which had made the Republic was extinct and any man of reflection would have gladly gone back to the days when, with all its evils, Rome was free. All through the Dark Ages men were in the black night of despair. Law, security, hope in life or in death seemed to have departed. For a lover of his kind the eye could find nothing on which to repose. The great Pope Gregory VII summed up the times in his dying words: "I have loved righteousness and hated iniquity, so I am dying in exile." In the fifteenth century of English law, when the jury system had broken down, when nothing in life was safe, when the law seemed a travesty of justice, no one could look forward with any hope. In the next ages savage intolerance left no citizen the right of free speech and for mere beliefs men were burning at the stake. Let one try to conceive how dark seemed the future after our Revolutionary War when it appeared that the Colonies were deliberately committing suicide. In the private law itself the state of the prisons, the institution of imprisonment for debt caused untold human suffering. In the ten years before our Civil War, it seemed that the Union of the States was doomed.

But as we look back for almost a thousand years the law, public and private, has steadily improved. We may praise the good old times, but would any one be willing to go back to them? The blots we see upon the law are all made by human hands and by those hands they can be taken away. The two things of which we can most justly complain, the ineffectiveness of the administration of the criminal law and the corruptions in municipal government, are constantly meeting an awakened public sentiment. The great bulk of the law and the differences in law among the various states are steadily being corrected, while at the present time the disinterested lawyers of the whole country are engaged in the gigantic task of restating in smaller bulk, and in simplifying, the law. There never has been a time upon the earth like the present, when men could look around them not only at their own land, but over the whole civilized world and be so well satisfied with the future of law. This situation is due more to the rule of law than to all other human activities.

The story of the law must teach us that changes are to be made by the innovations of time slowly and by degrees. If suddenly we begin hacking to pieces our aged mother, only evil can result. It must not be true that for some fancied benefit we shall unsettle the landmarks that mark the progress of the ages. Personal desires, the theories of particular men can have little or no effect upon the law, for she must represent the wishes and desires of us all. She must have still the standard that was her standard ages ago, the ordinary reasonable man, not easily moved to action, clinging to his ancestral robe of habits and accustomed ways, yet in the main striving to make this world a better place for his children. The law is like this her favorite son, the average reasonable man. She too must cling to the institutions which she knows and has proven, for she bears upon her shoulders the burdens of humanity. We must not blame her for our many human errors; she gives us the rule, she asks us to apply it reasonably and fairly and when we fail, out of our own want of insight, we turn upon her and bitterly arraign her, but she answers not a word.

> Yes, we arraign her but she,
> The weary Titan with deaf
> Ears and labor-dimmed eyes,
> Regarding neither to right
> Nor left, goes passively by,
> Bearing on shoulders immense,
> Atlantean, the load
> Well-nigh not to be borne
> Of the too vast orb of her fate.

APPENDIX

The Five Ages of the
Bench and Bar of England

THIS ESSAY WAS SOLICITED BY John Wigmore for inclusion in *Select Essays in Anglo-American Legal History,* a three-volume collection of essays, the first volume of which appeared in 1907.[1] Zane's effort would lead Wigmore to describe him to others as "the most learned man in America on the traditions of bench and bar and many other things pertaining to the history of the law."[2]

The "five ages" to which Zane refers is intended as an allusion to classical literature: "The fable of the ancients, which school boys read in Ovid's *Metamorphoses,* divided the history of the world into a golden, a silver, a bronze, and an iron age." But Zane does not follow the classical periodization slavishly; while Ovid's history of the world had four ages and ended in irreversible decay, Zane's account of the English bar con-

---

1. The case for this collection was argued by John Wigmore at the 1905 meeting of the Association of American Law Schools. The essays were collected and edited by a committee of scholars designated for this task by the Association. Such eminent names as Frederic Maitland, Frederick Pollock, Joseph Beale, and William Holdsworth grace its pages. The history of the decision by the AALS to produce this collection and the efforts that were expended in assembling it are reviewed in the *Harvard Law Review*'s book review of *Select Essays.* See *Harvard Law Review* 21 (1908): 640–41.

2. Letter of John H. Wigmore to Robert P. Goldman, December 9, 1920, Wigmore Papers, Northwestern University School of Law.

sists of five ages and closes with the promise of law reform and the
restoration of a bench and bar marked by a renewed sense of profes-
sionalism and integrity.

Zane chose 1066 as the commencement of the golden age of English
law because that year featured the Norman Conquest of England by
William the Conqueror. The Anglo-Saxon regime that William overthrew was, in Zane's estimation, a "barbarous" one, entirely devoid of
lawyers and law.

In advancing this chronology, Zane boldly challenged the deeply cherished status the Anglo-Saxon past held in the minds of generations of
Anglophile historians and political writers. English law and constitutional
order had their roots, according to this older line of thought, in the primitive folk assemblies of the Teutonic peoples who conquered Britain after
the Romans departed. The Norman Conquest subjected this happy warrior culture to a tyrannous yoke, but this oppression eventually resulted
in the forging of a great people and the creation of a great legal system.

Zane implicitly rejected this school of thought when he attributed the
origin of English law to Norman practices and institutions. The monarchy William established was stronger than anything the Anglo-Saxons
experienced, and a series of powerful kings—William himself, Henry II,
Edward I, Edward III—knew how to make use of lawyers and advisers
trained in the law and thereby created a system of law capable of rendering justice.

"Five Ages" is a recounting of the signal events and important per-
sonages in the history of the common law from 1066 down to the
Victorian Age and the enactment of that age's procedural and judicial reforms. It is a story that is told in a lively fashion and with all of the passion of *The Story of Law*. Zane's ability to present always fascinating vi-
gnettes of the personalities involved in the shaping of the law (see, for
example, his account of Lord Eldon) enlivens what would have been, in
lesser hands, a dull recitation of biographical detail. It is a worthy com-
plement to the larger work.

C. J. R., Jr.

The Five Ages of the Bench and Bar of England

BY JOHN MAXCY ZANE [1]

It is a singular fact that but two races in the history of the world have shown what may be called a genius for law. The systems of jurisprudence, which owe their development to those two races, the Roman and the Norman, now occupy the whole of the civilized world. Our common law is peculiarly the work of the Norman element of the English people. There is no English law, nor English lawyer, before the Norman Conquest. Just as the Saxons with their crude weapons and bull-hide shields broke before the Norman knights at Senlac, so their barbarous system of *wer*, *wite*, and *bot*, their ridiculous ordeals in the criminal law, their haphazard judicial tribunals, and their methods of proof, which had no connection with any rational theory of evidence, were certain to yield to the Norman organization, its love of order and of records, its royal inquisition for establishing facts, its King's Court to give uniformity to the law. The Norman Conquest was more than a change of dynasty. It produced a revolution in jurisprudence.

The history of our legal development furnishes ample proof of this. Our huge mass of legal literature is a treasure that no other race possesses. Our records and reports of cases, many of them still imperfectly

Hitherto unpublished, except that the first part appeared in the Illinois Law Review, volume II, p. 1, June, 1907. All five parts were publicly read as lectures, in February and March, 1906, in the Law School of Northwestern University.

1. Lecturer on Legal History and Biography in Northwestern University, 1905–1906. A. B. Michigan University, 1884; admitted to the bar in Salt Lake City, Utah, 1888; Reporter of the Supreme Court of Utah, 1889–1894; Member of the Chicago Bar since 1899; Lecturer on Mining Law in the University of Chicago, since 1902.

Other Publications: Law of Banks and Banking, 1900; Determinable Fees, and other articles in the Harvard Law Review; A Mediaeval Cause Célèbre, Illinois Law Review, 1907.

known, carry our legal history back almost to the Conquest. There the
law can be seen in its growth, taking on new forms to meet new conditions. The genius of the Norman lawyer has developed our legal system
from one precedent to another. Beginning with the barbarous legal ideas
of the Anglo-Saxon, the Norman in the course of two centuries produced a rational coherent system of law, and a procedure capable of indefinite expansion. The growth and changes in our law have followed
Lord Bacon's rule: " It were good, therefore, that men in their innovations would follow the example of time itself; which, indeed, innovateth
greatly, but quietly, and by degrees, scarce to be perceived." The further
fact, that this system of law has been applied by practically but one
court, has rendered the common law uniform. It represents the slow and
patient work of generation after generation of able men. To use a fine
figure of Burke's, our legal system has never been at any one time "old,
or middle-aged, or young. It has preserved the method of nature; in
what has been improved, it was never wholly new; in what it retained, it
was never wholly obsolete." Like some ancient Norman house, "it has its
liberal descent, its pedigree and illustrating ancestors, its bearings and
ensigns armorial, its gallery of portraits, its monumental inscriptions, its
records, evidences, and titles."

The design of these essays is to survey "the gallery of portraits" that
belongs to the English law. It will not be possible to advert to legal doctrines further than may be necessary to illustrate the acts of eminent
lawyers. An attempt will be made to describe the men who have assisted
in the growth and development of our jurisprudence. Unlike France,
England has never had a *noblesse* of the robe. Lawyers have found their
rewards in the same honors that England has given to her admirals and
her generals. The peerage is a fair standard by which to judge of the
honors that have been attained by excellence in the law. While great soldiers are represented in the House of Lords by the Dukes of Marlborough and Wellington, the Marquis of Anglesey, Viscounts Hardinge,
Wolseley and Kitchener, and Lords Napier of Magdala and Raglan,
while great admirals are represented by Earl Nelson, the Earl of
Effingham and Earl Howe, Viscounts Exmouth, St. Vincent, Bridport,
and Torrington, and Lords Rodney and Vernon, the representatives of

lawyers almost fill the benches of the Lords. Lord Thurlow's famous reply to the Duke of Grafton asserted: "The noble duke can not look before him, behind him, or on either side of him, without seeing some noble peer who owes his seat in this House to his successful exertions in the profession to which I belong." The King himself is king of Scotland through his descent from Lord Chief Justice Bruce. The Dukes of Beaufort, Devonshire, Manchester, Newcastle, Norfolk, Portland, Northumberland, Rutland and St. Albans are all descended from English judges. Chief Justice Catlin was an ancestor of the Spencer, who married the Marlborough title. The Marquises of Abergavenny, Ailesbury, Bristol, Camden, Ripon and Townsend, the Earls of Aylesford, Bathurst, Bradford, Buckinghamshire, Cadogan, Cairns, Carlisle, Cottenham, Cowper, Crewe, Eldon, Egerton, Ellesmere, Fortescue, Guildford, Hardwicke, Harrowby, Leicester, Lonsdale, Macclesfield, Mansfield, Sandwich, Selborne, Shrewsbury, Suffolk, Stamford, Verulam, Westmoreland, Nottingham and Winchelsea, and Yarborough, represent names great in English law. Other titles among the barons, such as Abinger, Bolton, Brougham, Erskine, James of Hereford, Le Despencer, Mowbray and Segrave, Northington, Redesdale, Romilly, St. Leonards, Campbell, Tenterden, Walsingham, Thurlow, and many others, were gained by great lawyers.

The fable of the ancients, which school boys read in Ovid's Metamorphoses, divided the history of the world into a golden, a silver, a bronze and an iron age. The golden age *"sine lege fidem et rectum colebat."* This is in a measure true of the common law. Its first age, without statutes, out of its own ample powers, gave a remedy for every wrong. There followed a silver age, *"auro deterior,"* when new remedies could be devised only by statute. Then a bronze or plastic age, by fictions, bent old remedies to suit new conditions. Later, an iron age, harsh and rigid, owing to the jury system, left a large part of jurisprudence to the courts of chancery. The golden age ends with the death of Bracton; the silver age is that of the three Edwards; the bronze age covers the Lancastrian and Yorkist kings to the death of Littleton; the iron age ends with the Revolution of 1688. Then a period of improvement and reform, slowly feeling its way by statutes of jeofails to the great reforms of our century, began; the end of that great effort is now almost attained, and perhaps the golden age is about to return.

I. The Golden Age of the Common Law: From the Norman Conquest to the Death of Bracton[2]

The period of the Norman kings is one of gradual growth. The Norman lawyers, building upon what they found, made no violent changes. The Conqueror, under the wise guidance of Lanfranc, made no attempt to change existing laws and customs. Beyond taking ecclesiastical matters out of the jurisdiction of the county court, and protecting his Norman followers by special laws and tribunals, his reign was occupied in establishing the king as the ultimate owner of the conquered land and in the division of the spoil. But even in that troubled time, one capable man rose to eminence as a lawyer. The Italian Lanfranc, Archbishop of Canterbury, learned in the civil law, by his study of Anglo-Saxon laws prevailed in the one great lawsuit of this reign. The Domesday Survey, which enumerated all the lands in England, and ascertained the status of each subject, and the ownership of the land with its burdens and the rents and the services due from tenants of the land, was probably superintended by this great lawyer.

William Rufus had for his chief minister a man whom the annalist calls *"invictus causidicus,"* an ever successful pleader. This Ranulf Flambard was learned in the civil and the canon law, and is the first of that

---

2. The authorities for this period, beside the well-known works of Pollock and Maitland, Foss, Lord Campbell, Stubbs, Hallam and the other historians, include Bigelow's Placita Anglo-Normannica, Freeman's William Rufus, Burke's Dormant and Extinct Peerages, Dugdale's Baronage, Maitland's Domesday, Pollock's King's Justice (12 Harv. L. Rev.), Pollock's King's Peace (13 Harv. L. Rev.), Foss' Memories of Westminster Hall, Hall's Court Life Under the Plantagenets, Mrs. Green's Henry II., Pulling's Order of the Coif, Beale's Introduction to his edition of Glanville, Maitland's Register of Writs (3 Harv. L. Rev.), Maitland's Introduction to Bracton's Note Book, Maitland's Bracton and Azo, Select Pleas of the Crown (Selden Society), Select Civil Pleas (Selden Society), and numerous sources of general history, such as William of Malmesbury, Matthew Paris, etc.

long line of trained lawyers, whose duty it was to fill the royal treasury. He worked out the legal principles of relief and wardship. Ecclesiastic though he was, he laid his hands upon the broad lands of the church. All church lands held of the king devolved, upon the death of bishop or abbot, according to Ranulf, upon the king as feudal lord. The great revenue to be derived from farming out these lands was an obvious temptation, but Flambard devised a further improvement. Since the bishop or abbot could not be inducted into office without the king's consent and the payment of a relief, the candidate for high clerical honors was compelled to wait a number of years before receiving his office and at the same time was compelled to pay an ample relief before he received investiture of the lands. It is needless to say that the monkish chroniclers have loaded Ranulf's memory with a mass of obloquy.

In Rufus' time an event occurred which every lawyer recalls with peculiar interest. The King contemplated a new palace at Westminster, but only that part of it which constitutes Westminster Hall was built. It is true that the Hall has been twice rebuilt, once in Henry III.'s reign, and again under Richard II., but the Hall itself, saving for its higher roof, its windows, and higher walls, is what it was when finished in 1099. In this Hall the courts of England were held for many centuries. As soon as the Court of Common Pleas was fixed *in certo loco*, it continuously sat there. Later the King's Bench took a portion of it. At one end of the Hall was fixed the marble seat and table of the Chancellor, where his court was held. Thus it happened that for centuries the courts of England were in plain sight of each other. When Sir Thomas More was being inducted as chancellor under Henry VIII., he stopped in his progress to the marble chair and knelt to receive a blessing from his father, a judge sitting in the Common Pleas. There is but one other building in the world that offers such a flood of legal memories. The old Palais de Justice in Paris has been the scene of many a great legal controversy, but Westminster Hall has listened to the judgments of Pateshull and Raleigh and Hengham. Here Gascoigne, Fortescue, Brian, Littleton, Dyer, Coke and Bacon sat. Here Hale and Nottingham, Hardwicke and Mansfield did their work for jurisprudence. The great forensic contests of England, the arguments in the case of Ship-Money, the trial of the Seven Bishops, Erskine's perfect oratory in Hardy's case, and Brougham in the Queen's case, are among the memories that make this solid Norman edifice to lawyers the most interesting spot in England.

In the reign of Henry I., a man splendidly educated for that time, surnamed Beauclerk, the Scholar, we begin to see the growing interest in the law. Wearied of the oppressions of the Conqueror and Rufus, men looked back to the good old times of the Saxon. The King had married a princess of the Saxon royal house. Himself a usurper he looked to his Saxon subjects for support. They won for Stephen the Battle of the Standard against the Scotch, celebrated by Cedric in Ivanhoe. In the Saxon enthusiasm a large crop of Saxon laws appeared, some of them actual translations from old laws, some of them palpable forgeries. The King even promised to restore the old local courts of the Saxons; had he done so, we should have had no common law. It was by this time apparent that the king's court was supplanting the old tribunals. The great lawsuits, being among the magnates, necessarily came before the king's courts. That court was stronger than any other, and suitors instinctively would turn to it. The criminal jurisdiction of the king's court was growing. Its jurisdiction was extended to suitors in civil causes first as a matter of favor. The bishop had been taken out of the county court and given a separate jurisdiction in ecclesiastical matters, among which were numbered the administration of estates of decedents and matters of marriage and divorce. Now under Henry I. began the practice of sending trained lawyers throughout the realm to take pleas of the crown and to hear civil causes. At the same time Roger of Salisbury, who was the legal adviser of Henry I., developed the exchequer portion of the king's court. A group of men, some of them trained lawyers, gathered in the exchequer tribunal. They did incidental justice in civil controversies and traveled the circuit. Indeed, Pulling in his "Order of the Coif" dates his first serjeant at law from 1117; but this must be a printer's error. Otherwise, Pulling's first serjeant is as wild a piece of history as Chief Justice Catlin's descent from Lucius Sergius Catiline.

Besides Roger of Salisbury we know of one very celebrated lawyer in this reign—a man then renowned in the law, named Alberic de Vere. He is described by William of Malmesbury as *causidicus* and *homo causarum varietatibus exercitatus.* Where he gained his legal education is not known. He was a son of one of the Conqueror's chief barons, the Count of Guynes, in Normandy. One of the chiefs of that house marched with Godfrey of Bouillon to the rescue of the Holy Sepulchre. The lists of the men who acted as judges in the king's courts show the names of many well-known Norman families during this reign. The educated lawyers were generally churchmen, yet the Norman barons had a natural taste for litigation. After a hundred years, scions of the great houses were to become the trained lawyers of the profession; but at this time the ecclesiastics did most of the technical legal work. They issued the writs from the chancery; they were needed to keep whatever records were kept. Alberic de Vere was not an ecclesiastic like Roger or Nigel of Salisbury, yet he was high in the confidence of Henry I., who granted to him and his heirs the dignity of Lord Great Chamberlain of England—the only great office of state that by a regular course of inheritance has descended to its present holder.

When Henry I. died, the interregnum caused by the contest between Henry's daughter Matilda and his nephew Stephen covered the land with misgovernment and oppression. Roger of Salisbury's son, euphemistically called his nephew—and it was by no means an uncommon thing for bishops to have sons in those days—became chancellor, but he soon fell under the displeasure of King Stephen, and in consequence the aged Bishop Roger and his family received the harshest treatment. The churchmen complained of the King's conduct, and a great council was called by the Bishop of Winchester to examine into the matter. King Stephen selected Alberic de Vere to represent him at the council. Alberic seems to have successfully defended the King, and either he or his son was rewarded with the earldom of Oxford.

Coke, following a saying of Fortescue, makes the quaint observation that "the blessing of Heaven specially descends upon the posterity of a great lawyer." Certainly the high position of the posterity of Alberic de Vere may be adduced as proof of the saying. Earls of Oxford of the house of Vere were great figures in English history until after the Revolution of 1688. The third earl was one of the barons who extorted Magna Charta from King John. The well-known seal of the Earl of

Oxford is on the charter. The next earl, who had as a younger son been brought up as a lawyer, was head of the Common Bench under Henry III. The seventh earl was in high command at Crecy under Edward III. and at Poitiers under the Black Prince. The ninth earl was a favorite of Richard II. and became Marquis of Dublin and Duke of Ireland. Although his honors were forfeited by Parliament, his uncle, another Alberic (or Aubrey) regained the earldom and the estates under Henry IV. The thirteenth earl was the chief of the party of the Red Rose and during the Yorkist reigns wandered over the continent. Scott's romance, Anne of Geierstein, tells his story while in exile. He came back with Henry VII. and led the Lancastrians at the battle of Bosworth. The seventeenth earl, a courtier and poet, at the court of Elizabeth, did not disdain to introduce gloves and perfumes into England. When the eighteenth earl died without issue, a noted lawsuit ensued over the Oxford peerage; the judgment of Chief Justice Crewe[3] is an oft quoted specimen of judicial eloquence:

"I have laboured to make a covenant with myself, that affection may not press upon judgment; for I suppose there is no man, that hath any apprehension of gentry or nobleness, but his affection stands to the continuance of so noble a name and house, and would take hold of a twig or twine thread to uphold it. And yet, Time hath his revolutions. There must be a period and an end of all temporal things—*finis rerum*—an end of names and dignities and whatsoever is terrene; and why not of De Vere? For, where is Bohun? Where's Mowbray? Where's Mortimer? Nay, which is more, and most of all, where is Plantagenet? They are entombed in the urns and sepulchres of mortality."

But the end of the house was not yet. The nineteenth earl died on the continent while fighting for Protestantism. The twentieth earl, "the noblest subject in England," man of loose morals though he was, was too much a Protestant to follow James II. in his attempt to restore Roman Catholicism. When this twentieth earl died, the male posterity of Aubrey de Vere was extinct; but his daughter and heiress, Diana, was married to Nell Gwynn's son by Charles II., the Duke of St. Albans.

3. W. Jones Rep. 101.

This son had been given the name of Beauclerk, and until recently the name of this family was de Vere Beauclerk. Topham and Lady Di Beauclerk will be remembered as friends of Dr. Johnson. But the present holder of the title seems to wish to forget his name Beauclerk and is well content to be simply de Vere. Heraldry, which is called "the short-hand of history," shows this descent in the coat of arms of the St. Albans family; in the first and fourth quarters are the royal arms, debruised by a baton sinister to show illegitimate descent, while in the second and third quarters is the ancient cognizance of the Earls of Oxford, indicating a marriage with the heiress of the Veres.

Another stout judicial baron of this time is Milo of Gloucester, whose estates enriched in after times the house of Bohun. His exploit in marching to the relief of the widow of Richard de Clare, besieged in her castle by the Welsh after the murder of her husband, may have furnished Sir Walter Scott with his story of "The Betrothed," where he tells of the succor of the Lady Eveline Berenger in the Garde Doloreuse. In fact, if we may judge from Ivanhoe, Scott must have taken many of his names from the judicial barons. Fronteboeuf, Grantmesnil and Malvoisin are names on the rolls of the courts. Segrave, a noted lawyer in Henry III.'s reign, was, like Ivanhoe, a Saxon who attained high position.

In the reign of Henry II., who succeeded Stephen, we begin to get a glimpse of an organized legal profession. This king was a great organizer and lawyer. His statutes of novel disseisin and mort dancester, his assize *utrum* and of last presentment were drawn by lawyers. In his reign the royal inquisition took a great step toward the modern jury. All litigation about land was thrown into the king's courts. Many new writs and forms of action were invented. A fixed court made up of trained lawyers sat at Westminster. At the same time the country was divided into circuits, itinerant justices traveled the circuit and adapted the county court to the regular progresses of the king's judges. The grand jury was now brought into form, and all the important criminal business came before the royal justices.

In the king's court Henry himself often sat. He is surrounded by his council, but every now and then he retires to consult with a special body. The judges take sides and on one occasion the King orders Geoffrey

Ridel, who seems too zealous for one party, from the room. The King peruses the deeds and charters, and when certain charters are produced we hear him swearing that "by God's eyes" they cost him dearly enough. On another occasion two charters of Edward the Confessor, wholly contradictory, are produced. The King, nonplussed, says: "I don't know what to say, except that here is a pitched battle between deeds."

Now began the keeping upon parchment of the records of cases. The best picture of a lawsuit in this reign is the extraordinary litigation of Richard de Anesty. He claimed certain lands as heir of his uncle. An illegitimate daughter of the uncle was in possession. The question was as to her legitimacy and that depended for solution upon the issue of marriage or no marriage. Richard begins by sending to the King in Normandy for a writ of mort dancester. Then the issue of marriage must be directed by writ from the king's court to the ecclesiastical court. The war in France intervenes, and Richard follows the King to France for a writ to order the court Christian to proceed. Three times he appeared in the latter court. Then he appealed from that court to the Pope, and for this he needed the King's license. Finally the Pope decided in his favor. Thereupon Richard came back and followed the King until two justices were sent to hear his case, and at last he had judgment. Everywhere he had lawyers in his pay. His friends and advocates, among them Glanville, appeared for him in the secular court. In the ecclesiastical courts and before the Pope he hired lawyers, who were canonists, some of them learned Italians. After many years he obtained his uncle's lands; but by that time, as he pathetically writes, he had become a bankrupt.

There are noted names among the king's judges in this reign. Richard Lucy, Henry of Essex, William Basset, and Reginald Warenne were among the judges who went the circuit. Roger Bigot and Walter Map, the satirist, were of the itinerant judges. Ranulf Glanville and the three famous clerks, Richard of Ilchester, John of Oxford, and Geoffrey Ridel, sat at Westminster. The zeal with which the Norman barons attended to their judicial duties is amazing. The list of judges is almost an index of the great baronage. Marshalls, Warennes, Bigots, Bohuns, Bassets, Lucys, Laceys, Arundels, Fitz Herveys, Mowbrays, Ardens, Bruces, de Burghs, Beaumonts, Beauchamps, Cantilupes, Cliffords, Clintons,

Cobbehams, de Grays, de Spensers, Fitz Alans, de Clares, Berkeleys, Marmions, de Quinceys, Sackvilles and Zouches are all among the itinerant judges.

The lawyers of this reign include both priests and laymen. Here begin the serjeants at law. Of the thirteen whom Pulling ascribes to this reign, are Geoffrey Ridel and Hugh Murdac, both priests, and such names as Reginald Warenne, William Fitz Stephen, William Basset and Ranulf Glanville, all laymen. It is a matter worthy of notice that the date at which each of the thirteen serjeants received the degrees of the coif is the date at which he began service as a judge. It is probable that the *"status et gradus servientis ad legem,"* in the writ calling a serjeant, was merely a nomination of the man to be a king's justice. The matter is too obscure to admit of positive statement. But there must have been some reason for the rule that obtained for so many centuries, that no man could become a judge until he had been called to the degree of serjeant.

The first name among these lawyers is Glanville's. Whether he wrote our first law book, which is called Glanville, is sharply debated. But he was at any rate a great judge with considerable legal learning. He probably received his legal training in the exchequer. But he was no less a warrior. As sheriff of Yorkshire he gathered an army and defeated the Scottish King and took him prisoner. King Henry entrusted to Glanville the custody of his wife, Elinor, whom he guarded for sixteen years. When in 1179 most of the King's justices were removed, Glanville was continued in office and took his place in the court at Westminster. In the next year he became Chief Justiciar. One slanderous story of his judicial conduct has come down to us, but it is no more than idle gossip. Under Richard the Lion Hearted, Glanville took the vow of a crusader and preceded King Richard to the Holy Land, where he died under the walls of Acre.

It may be that Glanville did not write the book that passes under his name. Perhaps Hubert Walter, his nephew, a learned civil lawyer, who became Archbishop of Canterbury, put it together. It shows traces of the Roman influence, and Glanville was no partisan of Rome. There is on record a writ of prohibition issued by Glanville against the Abbot of Battle. On the hearing Glanville said to the priests: "You monks turn your eyes to Rome alone, and Rome will one day destroy you." The prophecy came true after three hundred years.

Far more noted in this reign is the name of Becket. He was a trained lawyer educated in the canon and the civil law at Paris. He may very well have devised some of Henry's statutes upon legal procedure, while he was chancellor. In the struggle that went on between the warring jurisdictions of courts ecclesiastical and secular courts, he boldly espoused the clerical side. The Chief Justiciar before Glanville, Richard Lucy, drew up the constitutions of Clarendon, which defined the jurisdiction of the king's courts over priests, and brought on the struggle between Henry II. and Becket. Lucy was twice excommunicated by Becket, but he does not appear to have been seriously affected; yet, singularly enough, at the end of his life, he founded an abbey and assuming the cowl of a monk retired to the cloister and passed his remaining years in the works of piety.

The King, astute lawyer that he was, fought the Archbishop with the very best weapons. The chronicler records that Henry II. kept in his pay a gang of "bellowing legists" (ecclesiastical lawyers) whom he "turned loose" whenever he was displeased at an Episcopal election. In his controversy with Becket, Henry used the expert clerks, John of Oxford, Richard of Ilchester, and Geoffrey Ridel. John received as his reward the see of Norwich, Geoffrey was made bishop of Ely. Both of them, priests though they were, admirably served their royal client. They represented the King upon appeals to the Pope. Becket used a weapon against them that would hardly be in the power of a modern chancellor. Both lawyers and judges were excommunicated by the sainted archbishop. But the curse of Heaven and the reprobation of the faithful did not avail. At last, the murder of Becket ended the controversy, and while the victory remained with the King, it gave to Becket the peculiar honor of being one of the only two English chancellors who are numbered as saints in the canon of the church.

When the Conqueror took the bishop out of the county court and established church tribunals for ecclesiastics (a step which was taken at the demand of the priests), it could not have been foreseen what a tremendous influence this regulation would exert upon the history of English law. Yet the struggle which soon began between these warring jurisdictions is probably the real reason why the Roman law exerted so little influence upon the common law or its procedure. At Oxford there was a school of the civil and the canon law. Ecclesiastics educated under that system were constantly filling high judicial positions, yet these men were all faithful to the king's courts and hostile to the ecclesiastical procedure. Practically all the trained lawyers were priests, yet they uniformly upheld the English law. In after times the canon law was to mold the procedure in the chancery courts; but the secular courts were not affected. No doubt the rational conceptions learned by these ecclesiastical lawyers from the civil law had no little effect upon the substance of their decisions; but the Roman law never affected the secular courts' procedure.

An interesting figure among clerical judges is that noted Abbot Samson of St. Edmund's Bury, who was made one of Henry II.'s justices. The priestly chronicler records with pride that a rich suitor cursed a court where neither gold nor silver could confound an adversary. The same chronicler tells us that Osbert Fitz-Hervey, a serjeant at law, the ancestor of the Marquises of Bristol, who was twenty-five years a judge at Westminster, said: "That abbot is a shrewd fellow; if he goes on as he begins, he will cut out every lawyer of us." In a case where the Abbot was a party, Jocelyn says that five of the assize (jury) came to the Abbot to learn how they should decide, meaning to receive money, but the Abbot would promise them nothing, and told them to decide according to their consciences. So they went away in great wrath and found a verdict against the abbey. The juror who regards his place as an opportunity for pecuniary profit seems to be as old as the common law.

The intractability of the academic theorist in the person of Walter Map, the celebrated writer, crops out in his judicial experience. He once went the circuit, but was not called upon the second time, since he insisted on excepting from his oath to do justice to all men, "Jews and white monks," both of which classes he detested. So he went back to his more congenial work of denouncing the whole body of the clergy, from Pope to hedge priest, as all of them busy in the chase for gain. But while that work is forgotten, we still are delighted by his tales of King Arthur and his knights and table round.

Under Richard and John, sons of Henry II., the regular enrolled records of the courts begin. Soon two sets of records are developed, those of the regular tribunal sitting at Westminster and those made in the presence of the king. The first are the records of what became the court of Common Pleas, the second of what became the King's Bench. In John's reign and that of his son Henry III. the learned lay lawyer appears in increasing numbers. First among them is Geoffrey Fitz Peter, who appears in the famous scene in the first act of King John, where the Faulconbridge inheritance is in question. Shakespeare cites the oldest English case on the orthodox rule of the English law, *pater quem nuptiae demonstrant*. Chief Justice Hengham in the next reign cites this case in the Year Book. It is needless to say that if Shakespeare had had the legal knowledge which has been by some lawyers ascribed to him, he could never have made the flagrant errors as to procedure which are found in King John.

Geoffrey Fitz Peter was the son of an itinerant justice of Henry II.'s reign, who had well upheld the dignity of civil justice against the church tribunals. A certain canon of Bedford was convicted of manslaughter in a bishop's court, and was sentenced merely to pay damages to the relatives of the deceased. In open court the judge denounced the canon as a murderer; the priest retorted with insulting words, whereupon the King ordered the priest indicted. Perhaps at this time contempts of court were not punished by the court itself in a summary way. Geoffrey Fitz Peter inherited from his father, the judge, large possessions. With his wife he obtained the title and part of the estates of the Mandeville Earls of Essex. He was a learned lawyer, if we may believe Matthew Paris. He made a ruling which probably had the most far-reaching effect of any judicial decision. The last Mandeville earl, when he found that death was approaching, attempted to atone for a somewhat oragious life by devising a large portion of his lands to the church. Fitz Peter as the husband of one of the co-heiresses was directly interested in the case. Yet he is said to have ruled that a will of lands was invalid. From that day to the passage of the Statute of Wills, a devise of lands was impossible, except by virtue of some local custom. And so it is to-day that the realty devolves upon the heir, the personalty upon the executor. Fitz Peter served as a justice itinerant; he was a serjeant at law and upon John's accession became Chief Justiciar. He held the place of head of the law for fifteen years, and with Hubert Walter, the chancellor, was able to keep King John under some restraint. The King joyfully exclaimed when he heard of his death: "He has gone to join Hubert Walter in hell. Now, by the feet of God, I am, for the first time, king and lord of England." John at once entered upon the course that brought him into conflict with his baronage and ended with Magna Charta.

The long reign of John's son, Henry III., may fairly be claimed as the golden age of the common law. The regular succession of the judges is now settled. John had promised in Magna Charta that he would appoint as judges only those men who knew the law. The judges whom the rolls show as sitting at Westminster establish the character of the court. The judges are promoted in regular order. The head of the court during the first years of this reign was William, Earl of Arundel; then for two years it is Robert de Vere, Earl of Oxford; then for seven years Pateshull, who had been a puisne, was head of the court. He is succeeded by Multon, who served for a long term. Raleigh, the second man in the court, followed Multon. In regular order follow Robert de Lexington, Thurkelby, Henry de Bath, Preston, and Littlebury. Thus it appears that the character of this court, a tribunal filled with trained lawyers, has become fully established.

The Earl of Arundel, who was Henry III.'s Chief Justiciar, belongs to a legal family whose successive marriages with other great legal families form a curious study in history. In the days of Henry I. a certain William de Albini was the son of the king's butler or pincerna. He married Queen Adeliza, the young widow of Henry I., and with her obtained the castle and earldom of Arundel, the only earldom by tenure. The heiress of the de Albinis in the time of Henry II. married the son of John Fitz Alan, a judge in the king's court, and thus the earldom and castle of Arundel passed to the Fitz Alans. Later, in the time of Edward III., the then Earl of Arundel by marriage acquired the title of Earl of Surrey and the estates of the Norman family of Warenne, whose first chief was the companion of the Conqueror and one of his chief justiciars. The great Earl of Arundel, who went to the block in Richard II.'s

time, was the head of this mighty house. Still later the heiress of the
Arundels married the Howard Duke of Norfolk. Singularly enough the
Howards were descended from William Howard, a celebrated English
serjeant at law, who, when the Year Books open, was in large practice in
the courts. He rose to the bench (though he was not, as his tombstone
records, a chief justice). His descendant, Sir Robert Howard, married
the heiress of the Mowbrays, who held the Earl Marshalship of
England hereditary in the Marshals. The sons of the great regent
William Marshal, Earl of Pembroke, dying without male heirs, the dignity passed by marriage to the Bigots, Earls of Norfolk. From them by
a special deed of the lands under the then new statute *De Donis*, these
estates and dignities became vested in Edward I.'s son, Thomas of
Brotherton. His heiress married a Mowbray; the heiress of the Mowbrays married Sir Robert Howard; and when the Howards obtained by
marriage the titles and estates of the Arundel family in the reign of
Elizabeth, all these honors of Warennes, de Albinis, Fitz Alans, Plantagenets, and Mowbrays had become united in the Howards. Perhaps we
may credit this remarkable acquisitiveness through judicious marriages
to the legal strain in the Fitz Alan Howards. Not only the Duke of
Norfolk, premier peer of England, but the Earl of Suffolk and Berk-
shire, the Earl of Effingham, the Earl of Carlisle, and Lords Howard de
Walden and Howard of Glossop, thus represent to-day the serjeant at
law of Edward I.'s reign.

To return to the judges of Henry III.'s reign. Two of them, Pateshull
and Raleigh, have been canonized by Bracton's treatise. Bracton cites
these two judges' decisions almost as his sole authority. Other well-
known judges of the time he notices merely to remark that they committed error—not by any means a failing confined to mediaeval judges.
The greatest of these lawyers, Martin de Pateshull, was a priest—as was
indeed Raleigh also, and Bracton himself. Pateshull's origin was humble,
but he became a justice itinerant in John's reign and for many years he
vigorously performed his duties. One of his brother justices in a letter to
the King plaintively begs to be excused from going the York circuit,
"for," he says, "the said Martin is strong and in his labor so sedulous and
practiced that all his fellows, especially William Raleigh, and the writer,

are overpowered by the work of Pateshull, who labors every day from sunrise until night." The Raleigh just spoken of was Bracton's master. He managed to survive Pateshull, and succeeded him as head of the court. He first served as Pateshull's clerk; his high character is shown by his election over the King's uncle to the rich see of Winchester. Raleigh was ingenious in devising many new writs, and his name is of frequent occurrence in the Register of Writs.

The bravery of these judges in the performance of their duties is shown by a characteristic story. Fawkes de Breauté, a powerful baron and noted swashbuckler of the time, had so oppressed his neighbors that they proceeded against him in the king's court. Three judges, Pateshull, Multon and Braybroc, went up from London to try the cases at Dunstable. Thirty verdicts were found against Fawkes and large fines imposed in all the cases. He was so incensed that he sent his followers under his brother's leadership to seize the judges. He captured and imprisoned one of the court; but this conduct called out the royal power, then wielded by Hubert de Burgh. The brother and thirty of Fawkes' retainers were hanged, but he himself escaped to lifelong exile.

Other judges like Hubert de Burgh, Thomas de Multon, Hugh Bigot, Earl of Norfolk, Humphrey de Bohun, Earl of Hereford, must be passed over. But Robert de Bruce deserves more than a passing mention. The first Robert de Bruce had come over with the Conqueror and had received ninety-four lordships as his share of the spoil. A cadet of the house, a grandson of the first Robert, had gone to the court of the Scottish King and had married the heiress of the lordship of Annandale. The fourth Robert in Scotland was Robert the Noble, lord of Annandale, the husband of a daughter of Prince David (the Knight of the Leopard in Scott's Talisman).

The fifth Robert, a son of the princess, though a Scotch magnate, was educated for the law at Oxford. He practiced in Westminster Hall. He became Chief Justice and held the office until Henry III.'s death. Edward I. passed him by, and he retired in disgust to Scotland. But when the daughter of Alexander III. of Scotland died, the heirs to the throne were the descendants of Prince David's daughters. This Robert, the Chief Justice, preferred his claim. He argued his own case before

Edward I., the referee, but the decision on good legal grounds was given
for John Balliol. But Robert's grandson, another Robert, the national
hero of Scotland, made good his title at Bannockburn.

Other judges of this reign are interesting figures—like the Percy,
whose family is the one so celebrated in ballad and story as the Percys of
Northumberland, or like Gilbert Talbot, who married a Welsh princess,
and whose descendant was the stout warrior John Talbot, the first of the
Earls of Shrewsbury, among whose descendants appeared Lord
Chancellor Talbot in the reign of George II. But the real lawyer of this
reign is the man whom we know as Bracton. His book on the laws and
customs of England is the finest production of the golden age of the
common law. Bracton's father was vicar of the church at Bratton, of
which Raleigh was the rector. The rector took an interest in the boy.
There is a tradition that he put him to school at Oxford. When Raleigh
became a judge, he made Bracton a clerk. In due time Bracton was promoted to a justiceship in eyre, when he became in 1245 a serjeant at law.
From 1245 to 1265 he traveled the circuit, but part of that period he sat
at Westminster with Henry de Bath, Thurkelby and Preston. During
this time he made a large collection of precedents (known as his Note-
Book) out of the decisions of Pateshull and Raleigh. A fortunate inference by Vinogradoff, confirmed by the lamented Maitland, has identified this collection of precedents with a manuscript in the British
Museum, and the work of Bracton, long considered a mere attempt to
apply the civil law to our common law, has been shown to be a careful
statement of the decisions of the notable judges, who preceded him.

That the general conceptions, the arrangement, and the classification
of Bracton's work should have been taken from a writer on the civil law
is not at all strange. There was no other source to consult. The Roman
and the canon law had been taught by Vacarius in England, and he had
written a book for his students. Manuscripts of the Roman law no doubt
were brought to England. The flourishing school *"utriusque juris"* at
Oxford must have had many scholars. Ricardus Anglicus, an
Englishman, gained celebrity in the law in Italy. Italian lawyers came to
England, and the King had in his service the renowned Hostiensis.
Simon Normannus, Odo de Kilkenny, Roger de Cantilupe, and Alex-

ander Saecularis belonged to this band of "Romish footed" legists of the King. English students went to Bologna and studied under Azo, "lord of all the lords of law." Azo's book Bracton had constantly with him as he was writing his "De Legibus et Consuetudinibus Angliae." Yet the substance of Bracton's book is a careful statement of the actual law administered by the courts. A priest himself, he everywhere shows his loyalty to the secular tribunals. Like Henry de Bath, he was dismissed from the king's court on account of his leanings toward the party of the barons; yet he continued a justice in eyre. The barons at one time sent him on a judicial errand to redress grievances. Perhaps Bracton had felt the rough edge of the King's tongue. We are told that to William of York, a distinguished predecessor of Bracton, the King said: "I raised you from the depths, you were the scribbler of my writs, a justice and a hireling." Bracton well knew the great patriot Simon de Montfort, and no doubt sympathized with his cause. We know not what he was doing when the Barons' War was raging, but it is probable that he was quietly attending to his judicial duties.

In Bracton's book we find that the rules of law are fixed and settled. They bind even the king. The sympathies of Bracton with the party of freedom and progress here and there appear. "While the king does justice," says Bracton, "he is the vicegerent of the Eternal King, but when he declines to injustice, he is the minister of the devil." He had a noble ideal of the office of the lawyer and the judge. Using the phrase of the Digest he says of his profession, *namque justitiam colimus et sacra jura ministramus*, "We are the ministers at the altar of justice and feed its sacred flame."[4]

The greatness of Bracton's work is best proven by the reflection that five centuries were to pass away before another English lawyer, in the person of Blackstone, was to appear, competent to write a treatise upon the whole subject of English law. Fortescue's De Laudibus is a panegyric, Littleton's Tenures covers a small field, Coke's Institutes are so poorly arranged and badly written as to be unfit to rank with the clear, precise, and flowing language of Bracton or of Blackstone.

---

4. The above free translation is more than a reminiscence of Coleridge's lines.

The long period from the Conquest in 1066 to Bracton's death in 1267 had been a period of marvelous growth. It began with a varied assortment of local courts lacking settled rules, and ends with a highly organized system of courts administering a settled and rational system of law. It begins with a barbarous procedure, and ends with a rationalized method of ascertaining the facts. In the criminal law it begins with a system where the criminal makes redress to the injured party or his kin, it ends in a direct punishment of crime for the benefit of the whole society. Succeeding ages have merely amplified and glossed the distinctive rules of Bracton. The common law by its very form was made capable of indefinite expansion.

In addition, the general progression of the justices, holding the assizes through the different counties, distributed the royal justice throughout the country. The different local tribunals were subjected to a close scrutiny. In fact, the holding of an eyre was regarded by the inhabitants rather as an oppressive thing. The justices inquired into all the affairs of the counties and into all the acts of the local tribunals, into the enforcement of the criminal law and into the judgments rendered in civil causes. The numerous fines imposed made royal justice the source of an imposing revenue.

About this time the clergy were forbidden by the Pope to study the temporal law, and were inhibited from sitting in lay tribunals. The lawyer ecclesiastics, like Raleigh, Pateshull, William of York, Robert de Lexington, and Bracton, were soon to pass away. While ecclesiastical chancellors remained for centuries, the common law was about to become the heritage of laymen. The lay lawyers are learned men. Fitz Peter, Segrave, Braybroc, Multon and Thurkelby are all cases in point. But the most noticeable thing is that a class of advocates, who practice in the courts, has grown up, and that the judges are uniformly selected from among the profession. The serjeants at law and the apprentices at law now form a distinct body of men, devoting themselves solely to the practice. This separate class needed but schools of law to make it a closed body of men, admission to which required special attainments. This want was soon to be supplied by the Inns of Court, where the common law was taught as at a university. Everywhere the need of retaining good lawyers was felt. This is enforced by the judges. In one of the first Year Books, the reporter makes the Chief Justice say: "B loses his money because he hadn't a good lawyer." A few remarks of this sort from the bench would soon prevent an appearance in court by any one except a trained lawyer.

The division of the profession into barristers and attorneys had already appeared—a distinction that endures to our own day in England.[5] The barrister appears only for a client already present in court by himself or by an attorney. The effect of this division in the profession may be indicated in a later place. At present it is enough to note the influence that is bound to be exerted by the body of professional lawyers. Their judgment upon legal matters is sure to be of controlling importance, and their influence upon the selection of judges has invariably caused in England the promotion to judgeships of men who have proved their ability by the attainment of leadership in the practice. The great advantage of appointive judges over elective is that the influence of professional opinion can be more easily brought to bear upon the appointing power than upon an untutored electorate.

But the growing power of Parliament was making itself felt upon the growth of the law. Perhaps the conservatism of the profession assisted. It was now no longer possible to devise new writs to meet new conditions and to offer new remedies. Parliament was insisting that the grant of new writs and the creation of new remedies was the making of new laws, a power which belonged to the nation's representatives in Parliament. Thus the growth of the law was hindered by the growth of representative government. The English law is now ready to enter upon its second period, which began with the legislative activity of Edward I.'s reign.

The peculiar feature of the development of the common law is that its moving force did not come from the mass of the people, but was imposed upon a population constantly demanding a return to old and bar-

---

5. The origin of this distinction, taking us back to the more primitive Germanic ideas and the contrast between an *attornatus* or *anwalt* and a *vorsprecher, causidicus,* or *conteur,* has been once for all set forth in Professor Heinrich Brunner's essay on *"Die Zulässigkeit der Anwaltschaft im französischen, normannischen, und englischen Rechte des Mittelalters,"* first printed in the *Zeitschrift für vergleichende Rechtswissenschaft,* I, 321, and afterwards abbreviated in § 100 of his *Deutsche Rechtsgeschichte* (1892, vol. II).

barous methods. The universal jurisdiction of the king's courts, the most valuable institution in the history of the law, was looked upon with the greatest jealousy. The extinction of the old ordeals—a measure which began with the sneers of William Rufus and was finished under John— was not demanded by any large portion of the nation. The palladium of our liberties, that jury which grew out of the royal inquisition, was wholly foreign to the English race, and was imposed upon the nation by the Norman and Angevin kings. The grand jury in its inception was to most of the people little better than an engine of royal oppression.

The Norman baronage represents the element of power among the makers of this jurisprudence. In spite of individual exceptions who were cruel and oppressive, the mass of the Normans insisted upon law and order. They demanded men learned in the law for judges, and insisted that the judges should be independent of royal dictation. They asked for their own rights, but in Magna Charta insisted upon the rights of their humblest followers. In the years when the baronage was fighting John or Henry III., when civil war was distracting the land, practically the same judges went on holding court at Westminster, uninfluenced by the varying fortunes of barons or of king. Many a tale has been told to the discredit of the Normans; the *jus primae noctis* superstition is still an article of faith. But the legal historian knows that English liberty and law, even representative government, was the work of the Norman. William, Earl of Pembroke, well answered the king in the spirit of the Norman lawyer: "Nor would it be for the king's honor that I should submit to his will against reason, whereby I should rather do wrong to him and to that justice, which he is bound to administer towards his people; and I should give an ill example to all men in deserting justice and right in compliance with his mistaken will. For this would show that I loved my worldly wealth better than justice." It was not until the Norman baronage was broken by the wars of the Roses that England was ready to submit to the tyranny of the Yorkist and Tudor sovereigns—a tyranny that found its support in the mass of the nation. And when the struggle was resumed against the Stuart kings, the words of Bracton and of William of Pembroke were eagerly cited to prove that the king himself was not above the law of the land.

II. The Silver Age of the Common Law: From the Accession of Edward I. to the Death of Edward III.[6]

The succession of Edward I. in 1272 was practically contemporaneous with Bracton's death in 1268. A dictum of Sir William Herle, Chief Justice under Edward III. (delivered from the bench), asserts that, "he (Edward I.) was the wisest king that ever was." Hale and Blackstone have repeated this language, and have called him the English Justinian. But Edward was no codifier or founder of legal institutions. He simply had the singular good judgment always to keep at hand the best legal advice, and to follow it. He had constantly by his side a very great Italian lawyer, Francis of Accursii. His closest friend was his chancellor, the English lawyer, Robert Burnel.[7] The leading advocates of the bar were kept in his service. Burnel drew the code of laws called the Statute of Wales, which projected the English law over Wales. Chief Justice Hengham (whom Coke calls Ingham) drew the Statute De Donis and the provision that created the bill of exceptions. Other noted advocates like Inge, Lowther, and Cave drew the other well-known statutes, such as Quia Emptores, Coroners, Merchants, etc., which supplied the deficiencies of the existing law and procedure.

During his reign the reports of cases, called Year Books, open. There was for centuries a tradition that the Year Books were official. Plowden guardedly says that he had heard that four reporters were originally appointed by the king. Bacon is somewhat more positive. Coke swallows the tradition entire, and says that "four discreet and learned professors of the law" were appointed by the king. He even asserts that they were

6. General references for this period: The Year Books of Horwood and of Pike; Maitland's Year Books of Edward II, Selden Society; the Liber Assisarum; Maitland's Conveyancer in the Thirteenth Century; Select Pleas in Manorial Courts (Selden Society); Placita de Quo Warranto; Mirror of Magistrates (Selden Society); Thayer's Preliminary Treatise on Evidence; Ames' History of Assumpsit (3 Harv. L. Rev.); Maitland's Register of Writs (3 Harv. L. Rev.); Baldwin's Introduction to his edition of Britton; Fleta; Burke's Dormant and Extinct Peerages; Jenks' Edward I; Pike's History of Crime; the works of Foss, Campbell and Stubbs; Reeves' History of English Law is reliable only in regard to the statute book.

7. The last English Papal bishop who left a family of acknowledged children.

"grave and sad men." Blackstone knows all about them, who they were, how they were paid, and how often the reports were published. But this is simply a growing legal myth. The reports show that they were not official. The reporter chooses among the cases as he pleases. Statements of well-known counsel are inserted as authority. The rulings of the judges are frankly criticized. One decision is said to have been "for the King's profit rather than in accordance with law." In another place the reporter contemptuously says of a judge's dictum: "This is nothing to the purpose." Even the dicta of Chief Justice Hengham are condemned as wrong. Of one ruling the reporter says that the court held the contrary at the Michaelmas term (this practice the courts have continued until the present day). The reporter makes certain judges say that a decision cited was obtained by favor and therefore was not authority. Finally, the reporter nicknames a precipitate judge, Hervey the Hasty. It is, of course, ridiculous to call such reports official, but they are all the more valuable.

The Year Books show us the legal profession in full bloom. The leaders of the bar are the serjeants, but they have not as yet a monopoly of the Common Pleas practice. Other counsel appear in the reports. There is the body of students of law, attending upon the courts; they are sometimes referred to by the judges. The leaders of the bar are few in number, but the weight of professional opinion is apparent. The reporter does not hesitate to say that the opinion of the serjeants against any decision is sure proof that it is erroneous.

The very fact that the Year Books appear shows the influence of professional opinion. The dry Latin records of the cases were sufficient for Bracton, but now there was a demand for the many things which never got on the record—the arguments of counsel, the remarks of the judges during argument, the skilful plea of the one lawyer, the adroit shift of the other, in fact, the whole picture of the lawsuit as it progressed.

These Year Books were written in Norman French, the language of the courts and lawyers. One of the manuscripts shows us what was probably a lawyer's library in the early thirteen hundreds. Besides the reports of cases, it contains a number of statutes of Edward I. and Edward II., Bracton's treatise, another treatise on quashing writs, another on the duties of justices, another on pleas of the crown, Metingham's work on Essoins, and Hengham's treatise called Magnum and Parvum. These works, with Britton and the Register of Writs, would be an ample legal library; and all these books could be tied together in one manuscript volume.

The influence of the profession is apparent in the legislative activity of the opening years of Edward I. The statutes then passed were all remedial. Wherever a case was unprovided for, wherever a remedy was defective, wherever the law seemed insufficient, the existing law was supplemented by statutes. Take the statute creating the bill of exceptions. It enjoined upon the trial judge the duty of sealing a bill of exceptions tendered to any of his rulings, and made the bill a part of the record, which could be examined upon error. We know, without any proof of the fact, that this statute was procured by professional opinion. It brought all rulings to the supreme test of an appellate tribunal. Henceforth there could be but one rule of law for all Englishmen. The fact that these statutes, such as Westminster II. and Westminster III., are still law in almost every state in this Union, is the best proof of the sagacity of those long forgotten lawyers of Edward's reign. Nowhere is better shown the wise conservatism of the true lawyer, whose instinct is not to commit waste upon the inheritance, but to repair the splendid edifice of which he is but the life tenant.

Still another indication of the growing influence of the profession is given by the impeachment of all the judges before Parliament in the year 1289. Some of the judges impeached bore honored names in the profession. Ralph de Hengham, Chief Justice of the King's Bench, upon trivial charges was fined in a small sum, dismissed from office, and not reinstated until ten years had passed. Weyland, Chief Justice of the Common Bench, after a prosperous career as a lawyer and a long service as judge, was found guilty of heinous offenses and abjured the realm. But with lawyer-like skill he had made his wife and children co-foeffees of several of his manors, which were not forfeited. Other judges were fined in large amounts ranging from 4,000 to 2,000 marks—immense sums, when we reflect that a Chief Justice's salary was then but forty pounds. Lovetot, Rochester, and Sadington are not heard of again. Boyland busied himself in building a splendid mansion and left a large fortune. Hopton and Saham returned to the practice. It will be seen that only after a bitter experience did England learn the necessity of paying large salaries to judges.

Two judges were "faithful found among the faithless"—Elias de Beckingham and John de Metingham. The latter was promoted to the headship of the common bench. There he presided for twelve years. His memory is kept alive by the prayer directed to be made at Cambridge *pro animo Domini* John de Metingham, as one of the benefactors of the University. He was a learned and just judge. His treatise on Essoins was a valued law book. He in one of his opinions cites Porphyrius to a definition of surplusage, as something "which may be present or absent without detriment to the subject." Once he ruled against the opinion of all the serjeants, putting his decision on the ground of convenience. In another case he ruled in Mutford's favor, and the gratified counsel burst forth with a quotation from Holy Writ: "Blessed is the womb that bare thee." In another case he patiently listened to many objections to a verdict and then dryly said: "Now it is our turn," and made short work of the objections. A counsel, not a serjeant, who had pleaded badly and lost his client's case, he addresses pityingly as "My poor friend," and explains to him his hopeless error. Metingham in another case thought it no objection to a verdict that the prevailing party had entertained the jury at a tavern. We are reminded that the jury has hardly as yet attained a judicial function.

Hengham came back to the bench as the successor of Metingham. He was also a legal author. His treatise was a work on the method of conducting actions, divided into Magnum and Parvam. His predecessor in the King's Bench, Thornton, had written an abridgment of Bracton. Britton and Fleta belong very close to this period, and it is plain that there was a demand for law books. Hengham is a great authority on writs, and issues instructions to the clerks from the bench. He sometimes delivers long dicta, but the reporter adds in one case that Hengham is wrong. He was firm with the lawyers. In one case he said to Friskeney and his associates: "We forbid you to speak further of that averment on pain of suspension," and, adds the reporter, "they obeyed." Sometimes Hengham lost his judicial poise, as when he says to pertinacious counsel: "Leave off your noise, and deliver yourself from this account." One of his rebukes is on a much higher plane. To a lawyer who offered a plausible but unsound argument Hengham said: "That is a sophistry, and this place is designed for truth."

But the greatest character on the bench is William de Bereford, who succeeded Hengham as Chief Justice of the Common Bench. He served thirty-four years as a judge. We can sit in court and hear Bereford's oaths, "By God" and "By Saint Peter." He says to an absurd plea: "In God's name, now, this is good!" One day he was sitting with Mutford and Stonor, associate judges. Stonor held a lively debate with counsel. Mutford then said: "Some of you have said a good deal that runs counter to what has hitherto been accepted as law." "Yes," interjected Bereford, "that is very true and I won't say who they are." The reporter naively adds, "Some thought he meant Stonor." Bereford is sometimes cutting to counsel: "We wish to know," he once exclaimed, "whether you have anything else to say, for as yet you have done nothing but wrangle and chatter." One day Serjeant Westcote disputed Bereford's law: "Really," Bereford sarcastically rejoined, "I am much obliged to you for the challenge, not for the sake of us who sit on the bench, but for the sake of the young men who are here." He despised the ridiculous Anglo-Saxon wager of law. "Now God forbid," he says from the bench, "that any one should get to his law about a matter of which the jury can take cognizance, so that with a dozen or a half dozen rascals, he could swear an honest man out of his goods." He even corrects in open court statements of his fellow judges as to the law. One day he corrects a ruling of Hervey the Hasty in spite of that judge's protests. He is sharp with the lawyers. To Malberthorpe, counsel in great practice, he says: "You talk at random." To Passeley, a leader of the bar, he says in an action to quiet title: "There are forty fools here who think that, as soon as one has in such case acknowledged, there is nothing more to do, although he claims more than he has. Answer by what title you claim in fee." He sometimes jokes from the bench. The law was that a villein who had gone to a city and remained there for a year became free, but Metingham had ruled that if the villein returned to his villein tenement again he lost his freedom. Bereford illustrates this point by a joke. "I

have heard tell of a man who was taken in a brothel and hanged, and if
he had stayed at home, it would not have happened. So here, if he was
a free citizen, why didn't he remain in the city?" Some of Bereford's
jokes are too broad for quotation. Even if the reporters were "grave and
sad men," as Coke says, they always record Bereford's highly seasoned
anecdotes with apparent zest.

Hervey de Staunton, who is called the Hasty, is quick to answer.
Mutford, a leader of the bar, asserted that a female serf who became free
by marrying a free man, returned to her servile status as soon as her husband died. "That is false," said one judge. "Worse than false, it is a
heresy," added Staunton. In another case a younger lawyer was reproved
by Staunton for a poor plea, and was told to go and seek advice of counsel. Instead of being angry, the lawyer went out and came back with two
eminent counsel, Willoughby and Estrange. But this is the ordinary
thing. Whenever an attorney or a young lawyer attempts to plead without a serjeant, he is quickly detected in an error and told to go out and
get counsel. On the circuit Staunton is reproved by his fellow judges for
making a ruling before he consulted them. The retorts of the judges are
quick enough. "Why," asks Asseby, "did the other side plead that they
were seized?" "Because they are rather foolish," said Hertford, Justice,
shortly, "answer over." Berewick, a judge, says to the great Howard: "If
you wish to cite a case, cite one in point." One almost forgets in reading
this that he is back in the Middle Ages. Sometimes a lawyer is fined for
contempt. Lisle paid a fine of 100 shillings, yet soon afterward was made
a justice of assize.

The most striking phenomenon is the smallness of the bar in active
practice. A few names are constantly recurring. The fees of a leader must
have been enormous. Most of them died rich. The case of William
Howard, from whom flows "all the blood of all the Howards," has been
already instanced in describing the first period. Another great lawyer, a
rival of Howard's, is Hugh de Lowther. He is king's serjeant, and appears in quo warranto proceedings, which Howard often defends. He
was of an ancient family in Westmoreland. His lineal descendant became
Viscount Lonsdale in 1689, and Lowther Castle (where the present Earl
of Lonsdale so magnificently entertained the German Emperor) stands

in the midst of the widespread domain of 35,000 acres which Edward I.'s attorney-general left to his descendants.

The largest fee of that day paid to a lawyer was £133 6s. 8d., paid by Edward II. to Herle, the king's serjeant, and this was supplemented by a seat on the bench. After a long service on the bench Herle was permitted to retire; and it may be of interest to note that the permission spoke of "his approved fidelity, the solidity of his judgment, the gravity of his manner, and his unwearied service in his office."

One of the names that often recurs is that of John Stonor. As a serjeant in large practice, and then as king's serjeant, he no doubt made a fortune. He first served in the Common Pleas, then in the King's Bench, then he was returned to the Common Pleas. Later he was chief Baron of the Exchequer, then Chief Justice of the Common Pleas, superseding Herle; but later Herle was reinstated, and Stonor took second place, but became Chief Justice again. Such is the remarkable record of this judicial maid-of-all-work. The one decision for which he is noted is a holding that an act of Parliament was invalid.

Throughout the Year Books of the three Edwards, it is noticeable that the judges are uniformly selected from the leaders of the bar. If a serjeant appears in large practice, he is almost certain to appear later on the bench. So noticeable is this that there are few great lawyers who do not reach a judicial position. Simon de Trewithosa was evidently a Cornishman. He was in immense practice, was a serjeant at law, but was never a judge. His statements of law are found in the Year Books quoted as of evident value. Another lawyer named Pole did not reach the bench. His practice was very large, and the singular fact is that he was not made even a serjeant at law. But such names as Howard, Lowther, Heyham, Hertford, Inge, Herle, Estrange, Westcote, Warrick, Passeley, Lisle, Touthby, Willoughby, Malberthorpe, Mutford, the two Scropes, Friskeney, Scotre and many others, show that professional eminence found a sure reward in a judgeship. No lawyer is elevated to the higher courts who is not a counsel in large practice.

The judges are no respecters of persons. Magnate and serf are equal before the law. Beauchamp, Earl of Warwick, pleading his own case and showing considerable technical knowledge, is treated like an ordinary counsel. Roger Bigot, Earl of Norfolk and Earl Marshal, son-in-law of the King, receives the same treatment as the humblest suitor. A poor man wrongly seized as a villein is given £100 damages, a verdict equal to ten thousand dollars at the present day. Yet we see the law's delay, for four years elapsed between the awarding of the venire and the verdict.

The judges are skilful, tactful men. In a case where the plaintiffs failed in detinue of a charter on a variance, Berewick, the justice, said to the defendant: "What will this avail you? they can bring a new action and get it, so you may as well give it up," and the charter was surrendered. In another case Howard has reached a difficult place and refuses to plead, but Berewick, the judge, calls up the client, takes him away from his counsel, and questions him so as to get replies which are taken as pleadings. Pleading was at that day a voluntary act. A criminal trial showed one of these judges at his best. Hugh, a man of importance, is arraigned upon an indictment for rape. He asked for counsel. "You ought to know," the Judge replies, "that the king is party here *ex officio*, and you cannot have counsel against him, though if the woman appealed you, you could." The prisoner's counsel were then ordered to withdraw and did so. Hugh was then called upon to plead. Hugh replied that he was a clerk (a priest), and ought not to answer without his bishop. Then he was claimed for the bishop as a clerk. Thus it appears that the bishop had his representative sitting in court ready to claim the trial of any one who said he was a clerk. But the Judge was evidently informed, for he replied: "You have lost your clergy, because you married a widow." Under the statute De Bigamis a priest who had married twice or had married a widow lost his right to be tried in the ecclesiastical court. "Answer," said the Judge, "whether she was a widow or a virgin, and be careful, for I can call upon the jury here to verify your statement." We note that a jury is sitting in court ready to decide, by the knowledge of its members, controverted questions of fact. Hugh replies: "She was a virgin when I married her." The Judge calls upon the jury, who say that she was a widow. Then the Judge rules that he must answer as a layman, and asks him to consent to a jury trial. It is noticeable that the defendant in a criminal case must consent to a jury, a reminiscence of which is the question, and the answer of the prisoner, for centuries to come: "How will you be tried?" "By

God and my country," i.e. by the jury. But the prisoner objected that he was accused by the jury. (It is curious to note that the same jurymen acted as grand and petty jurors.) He further claimed that he was a knight, and the prisoner added: "I ought to be tried by my peers." The Judge gave him a jury of knights, who were called, and the defendant was asked if he had any challenges. But Hugh still refused to consent to a jury trial, and the Judge warned him of close confinement on bread and water, if he did not consent. So Hugh consented, and asked that his challenges be heard. The Justice: "Freely, read them." Then Hugh makes a slip: "I don't know how to read." The Justice: "How is this, you claim the privilege of clergy, and don't know how to read?" Then the prisoner stands much confused; but the Judge calls on a bystander to read the challenges to the prisoner, who speaks them. The challenged jurors are excused. Then the judge states the charge to the jury and the jury say that the woman was ravished by Hugh's men. The Justice: "Did Hugh consent?" The jury: "No." The Justice: "Did the woman consent?" The jury: "She did," and thereupon Hugh was acquitted. But who can say whether he was acquitted because the woman consented, and yet would have been considered liable criminally for the acts of his servants?

The counsel, however eminent, cannot wheedle the judges. In one case, Howard and Lowther on the same side urged a certain form of judgment. To Howard, Berewick replied: "We tell you that you never saw any other judgment under these circumstances, and you will get no other judgment with us." Then Lowther argued with the Court, but Berewick was firm: "You will get no other judgment from us." Again, Howard is on the bench, and Asseby says: "I think you would not give judgment in this wise, if you were in the case," but Howard mildly replies: "I think you are wrong, wherefore answer." But sometimes indulgence is shown. To a count challenged as bad, the Court say: "It would have been formal to have done this, but we will forgive him this time; but let everyone take care in the future, for whoever shall count in this manner, his writ shall abate, for it behooves us to maintain our ancient forms."

In those days the counsel stated the proposed pleadings orally, and if held good by the Court they were reduced to legal form by the clerks. To the present day our pleadings still speak as if the party were in open court stating his pleadings. At this earlier stage of the common law the pleadings were necessarily all true. Whenever counsel in his pleading reaches a point as to which he is not advised, he imparls and seeks his client or the attorney for further information. The advocates show acuteness and ingenuity. The pleading is technically correct. All pleas must follow in their regular order—pleas in abatement before pleas to the merits; there was, however, no such rule as (for example) that the judgment upon a plea in abatement was *quod recuperet*. At this sensible stage of the law there was no need for statutes to allow pleading over. Sometimes counsel get stubborn and refuse to plead further, and then say that they will do so merely to oblige the court. Touthby, a very good lawyer, in one case tries to plead without binding his client, Isolde. "I say for Gilbert de Touthby but not for Isolde," he begins. Whenever the pleadings come to a point where the party whose turn it is to plead cannot deny or avoid, judgment is given at once. The clerks enter up the technical forms of pleadings. The glorious *absque hoc* is present in large numbers. In an action of assault the counsel says orally, in answer to a justification: "He took him of malice and not as he has said, ready, etc." The clerk enters this up as the regular replication *de injuria sua propria absque tali causa*, etc.

In almost every case there are two counsel on each side. In some cases there is a great array. Thus Heyham, Hertford, Howard, and Inge are for the defendant and Lisle and Lowther for the plaintiff. No one seems to lead, but all speak. Sometimes different counsel appear at different terms. In a great case of replevin, Estrange, Scrope, and Westcote are for the defendant and Herle and Hertepol for the plaintiff at one time. At the next term Westcote and Huntingdon are for the defendant and Herle and Hertepol for the plaintiff. At the next term Westcote and Huntingdon are for the defendant, while the plaintiff has Kyngesham, Warrick, and Passeley. The lawyers who are practicing at Westminster are also found on the circuit at the assizes. These men must have kept in mind an enormous amount of procedural rules. There were four hundred and seventy-one different original writs, each showing a different form of action and requiring its own special procedure.

The useful law book was Britton, a sort of epitome of Bracton. Chief Justice Prisot in Henry VI.'s time said that Britton was written under the orders of Edward I., and fixes its date as 1275. It supplanted Bracton, so that judges in after ages would say with singular fatuity that Bracton was never accepted as an authority in English law. Certainly Bracton's Roman law was not understood by his immediate successors; for in Britton the *actio familiae herciscundae* of the Roman law has become an action about the lady of Hertescombe, who probably had estates in Devonshire. Yet Passeley, one of these lawyers, was a civilian, for the judge says to him from the bench: "Passeley, you are a legist, and there is a written law that speaks of this subject," quoting from the Code.

It is noteworthy that no complaints are heard of the practitioners in the higher courts. There is a single case of a lawyer being bribed by the opposing counsel. But the leading lawyers were faithful and zealous. Even against the king they fought well for their clients. Both Edward I. and Edward III. made determined assaults upon the private jurisdictions of various lordships, and in all the cases the defendant's counsel was zealous against the king. But in the lower courts, municipal, local and seigniorial, the legal "shyster" was as brazen and disgraceful as he is to-day. In 1280 the mayor and aldermen of London lamented the ignorance and ill manners of the pleaders and attorneys, who practiced in the city courts. It was ordained that no advocate should be an attorney; and thus it is apparent that the separation of the two branches of the profession, which happily endured in England, was at that early time in full effect. The city fathers were compelled to threaten with suspension the pleader who took money from both sides or reviled his antagonist.

There is an occurrence in the Abbot of Ramsey's court for the fair at St. Ives, which shows the local pettifogger at his worst. William of Bolton is the name of the "shyster." He was lurking around the fair, looking for victims. Simon Blake of Bury was charged with using a false ell for measuring cloth. William, eager for business, rushed in and became surety for Simon's appearance. Then to make certain of his fee he induced Simon's friend John Goldsmith to retain him to defend Simon, and to promise him four shillings as a fee. William agreed to defend, provided Simon would swear that he got the false ell from a merchant of

Rouen. Although Simon did so state and vouched the Rouen merchant to warranty, yet he withdrew his voucher of the Rouen merchant. The scheme, of course, was to fleece the rich foreign merchant; but Simon lost heart or was bought off. Then William had the effrontery to sue John Goldsmith for the four shillings retainer and ten pounds damages because John had induced Simon to withdraw the said voucher of the said merchant of Rouen, "out of whom," William brazenly avers, "the said William had hoped to get a large sum of money." The damages arose because the pettifogger was deprived of an opportunity for levying blackmail. Surely William was thrown away on that early time. He belonged to the "justice shop" of one of our large cities.

The evils of these local courts are manifest. In one case Bereford asks Malberthorpe, "Why did you not plead this exception in the county court?" "Because," replied the counsel, "we thought it would have more chance before you than in that court." In the same year Margery brought a writ of false judgment against the suitors of the court baron of Fulk Fitz Warin, lord of the manor, for failing to record her plea against Fulk in his own court. The suitors appeared in the king's court before Bereford to answer the writ. Bereford, Justice: "Good people, Margery brings her writ, etc. What have you to say?" Heydon, retained for the suitors: "I will tell you all about the business." Bereford: "You shall not say a word about it, but they out of their own mouths shall record it." The suitors then said that they feared to record the woman's plea out of fear of Fulk, who had beaten one of them and overawed them by force, so that they were compelled to come to the king's court under protection. Bereford: "Go aside by yourselves and take a clerk with you and have him write down your record, taking care that Robert Heydon comes not near you." Bereford was determined to get at the exact truth and that the suitors should make their record without the aid of counsel. The record made, Bereford issued a writ against Fulk. The king was far wiser than his subjects when he attempted by his writs of quo warranto to destroy these local courts.

The greatest lawsuit of this reign was not tried in any of the regular courts; for the Kingdom of Scotland was at stake, and the litigants were the claimants of the throne. The contestants referred the matter to the arbitration of Edward I. But Edward at once set his lawyers at work to devise by means of this arbitration some method by which he could extend his sovereignty over Scotland. Burnel, the chancellor, and Roger le Brabazon, a skilled lawyer and one of the puisne judges of the King's Bench, prepared the case. Out of the records and the monkish chronicles, acts of fealty by former Scottish sovereigns were produced, especially that of William the Lion to Henry II. after his capture by Ranulf Glanville. They were careful to suppress Richard Coeur de Lion's cancellation of his rights over Scotland for a large sum of money. Soon a parliament of English and Scotch was convened at Berwick. Brabazon opened the proceedings by a speech in which he adduced his proofs, and required, as a preliminary, that the contestants and all the Scotch swear fealty to Edward as their feudal suzerain. The contestants of course could not offend the court. The Scottish nobles murmured, but after seeing Brabazon's proofs acquiesced. The Scottish commons, however, refused. A trial was then had, and Burnel, for the King, correctly adjudged the throne to Balliol. Then the King tried to extend the jurisdiction of his courts over Scotland. But Wallace, and afterwards Robert the Bruce, kept alive the resistance, until under Edward II. the crushing defeat of the English at Bannockburn ruined Edward I.'s dream of a kingdom of Great Britain. Brabazon, as Chief Justice of the King's Bench, lived to see the fugitives from Bannockburn.

One of the results of the years of warfare was to scatter over England lawless characters called trailbaston men. To suppress these marauders special justices, fearless knights and barons, were sent throughout England. One of these justices in 33 Edward I. was John de Byrun, a lineal descendant of the Norman Ralph de Burun of the Domesday survey. In regular descent from the justice came Sir John Byron, the devoted adherent of Charles I., who was made Lord Byron. His descendant, the sixth Lord Byron, was the poet, who next to Shakespeare has been the greatest intellectual force in English literary history. Byron's friend, the poet Shelley, was descended from William Shelley, a justice of the Common Pleas under Henry VIII. Even Shakespeare belongs on his mother's side to the Norman Ardens, who furnished at least three justices under the Plantagenets; while Francis Beaumont, the collaborator

of Fletcher, was the son and grandson of English judges belonging to
the Norman Beaumonts.

The troubles of Edward II.'s reign had little effect on the courts.
Malberthorpe, Chief Justice of the King's Bench, pronounced sentence
of death on the Earl of Lancaster. When Edward II. was seized by his
wife Isabella and her paramour Roger Mortimer, and put to death,
Malberthorpe was brought to trial for his judgment against the Earl of
Lancaster; but he proved by prelates and peers the fact that he gave that
judgment by command of the King, whom he dared not disobey. Such
is the disgraceful entry upon his pardon. But Malberthorpe was removed and went back to the practice. We pass by the two Scropes;
Bourchier, who founded a distinguished family; and Cantebrig, who
gave most of his property to endow that great institution which is now
Corpus Christi at Cambridge. They were all great lawyers.

The most celebrated lawyer of Edward III.'s reign, however, was
Robert Parning. The Year Books show him to be a man of remarkable
erudition. He came to the Common Pleas as a judge at a rather early age.
In a remarkable case Parning is sitting with Stonor, Shareshulle and
Shardelowe. He takes issue with Shareshulle and a great debate is held
between the judges on the bench, which is accurately reported. In the
end Parning was overruled, but a few months later he became Chief
Justice of the King's Bench and then Chancellor.

This is the first instance of a great common lawyer attaining the marble chair. By reference to the Register, it will be found that in his two
years' service he provided a number of new remedies. Had the chancellors continued to be professors of the common law, there would have
been no separate chancery system. But after Parning's death the chancellorship was again bestowed upon an ecclesiastic. The growing opposition to the church is shown, however, by the Commons' petition to the
king in 1371 that only laymen should be appointed to the higher offices.
Thereupon Robert de Thorpe, Chief Justice of the Common Pleas, was
made chancellor. On his death John Knivet, Chief Justice of the King's
Bench, succeeded to the head of the chancery; but he remained for only
five years, when the office was given to an ecclesiastic. No other layman
held the office until Sir Thomas More. It is interesting to note that

Parning, after he became chancellor, would return to sit in the law courts, and in 1370 there is the following entry in the Year Book: "*Et puis Knivet le chanc. vyent en le place, et le case lui fuit monstre par les justices et il assenty.*"[8]

Some of the happenings of the time give us some light on contemporary manners. Chief Justice Willoughby in 1331 was captured by outlaws and compelled to pay a ransom of ninety marks—more than one year's salary. Seton, a judge under Edward III., sued a woman who called him in his court "traitor, felon and robber." The inference is that he had decided a case against the lady, but had not impressed her with the correctness of his decision. He recovered damages, but he was given a jury of his peers, that is, a jury of lawyers. The quaint simplicity of those times is shown by Thorpe and Green, two judges, going in state to the House of Lords and asking them what was meant by a statute lately passed. It would not occur to our judges to seek for such an explanation of an absurd law. Green once pronounced judgment against the Bishop of Ely for harboring one of the latter's men who had committed arson and murder. For this judgment the Judge was cited before the Pope, and on his refusal to appear he was excommunicated. About this time there was considerable friction between the lawyers, called "gentz de ley," and the churchmen, called "gentz de Sainte Eglise." The "gents of law" probably instigated the petition that only laymen should be chosen to hold such offices as chancellor. But in the next Parliament the "gents of Holy Church" retorted by obtaining a petition from Parliament praying that henceforth "gentz de ley," practicing in the king's courts, who made the Parliament a mere convenience for transacting the affairs of their

8. "And then Knivet the Chancellor came into the court and the case was explained to him by the judges and he concurred."

The words of the last entry show that knowledge of French is passing away. About this time was passed the statute which required all pleadings and judgments in the courts to be couched in English. But the lawyers calmly ignored the statute until the middle of the seventeen hundreds. The reporter of Edward II.'s Year Book was a much better French scholar than the men who reported under Edward III. Serjeant Maynard said that Richard de Winchester reported under Edward II. but he tells us no fact in regard to him, and the name nowhere else appears.

clients, to the neglect of public business, should no longer be eligible as knights of the shire. It is likely that the real ground of hostility to the church was its great possessions. Just as to-day the mass of people look with hatred and envy upon the possessors of great fortunes, so then many people turned to the broad lands of the church for relief against the taxation growing out of the French wars.

But the reign of Edward III. produced a ministerial ecclesiastic worthy to rank with Lanfranc, Flambard, Roger of Salisbury, and Robert Burnel. The career of William of Wykeham is one of the glories of the English church. Of humble birth, educated at Winchester, he attracted the attention of the bishop, who employed Wykeham's truly wonderful architectural talents in the improvements of Winchester cathedral. Here he took the clerical tonsure. A little later he entered the service of the king, and at Windsor, on the site of an old fortress of William the Conqueror, he built the keep and battlemented towers, which are yet the noblest portion of one of the magnificent royal residences of the world. He was rapidly advanced to the bishopric of Winchester and the chancellorship. His declining years were taken up with the foundation of Winchester School, and with the far greater endowment of his college of St. Mary at Oxford, now called New College. Wykeham's foundation still renders it a wealthy institution. After the lapse of five hundred years the buildings remain as they were designed by this greatest of art-loving prelates.[9]

It is sad to turn to the closing years of the king, whose reign began with the triumph of Cressy. He had had a long and in many ways glorious reign. His court had been the most splendid in Europe. The pageantry of knighthood had thrown its glamour over his reign. The

9. New College is equalled by Merton at Oxford, founded by Walter de Merton, Henry III.'s chancellor. Its exquisite chapel and noble hall are the work of that chancellor. Even Christ Church, which was long the most splendid college foundation in the world, is the work of Henry VIII.'s chancellor, Cardinal Wolsey. Magdalen, too, the loveliest of them all, is the work of William of Waynflete, "the right trusty and well beloved clerk and chancellor" of Henry VI. To these may be added Wadham at Oxford, founded from the estate left by a celebrated English judge, and Corpus Christi at Cambridge.

spoil of France had enriched his people. But the ravages of the plague had almost ruined the nation. In the domain of law the prospect was dark. The king's mistress, Alice Perrers, openly intrigued to influence the court's decision. She caused a general ordinance against women attempting the practice of the law. The heavy fees charged for writs in the chancery were the cause of bitter complaint. The royal council was accusing men and trying them without indictment. Justice was delayed by royal writs. The very judges of the land, it was charged, condescended to accept robes and fees from the great lords. One judge was convicted of taking bribes in criminal cases. The inefficacy of appeals was a crying evil, and it was complained that the judges heard appeals against their own decisions. All these various evils were to cause a grim reckoning in the next reign. But here we must close the period which began with the legislation of Edward I. and ended in such ignominy with his grandson's death in 1377.

III. The Bronze Age of the Common Law: From the Death of Edward III. to the Death of Littleton[10]

The period in legal history that reaches from the death of Edward III., in 1377, to the death of Littleton in 1481, may be called the age of bronze, on account of the efforts which the law was making to mold itself to fit new conditions. The amplification of the action of trespass, the

10. The Year Books for this period must be read in the Norman French (so called). Bellewe's Reports are Richard II.'s Year Books so far as printed. Stubbs, Campbell and Foss are, of course, necessary reading. Further general references are: Select Cases in Chancery (Selden Society), Wambaugh's edition of Littleton's Tenures, Plummer's Introduction to Fortescue's Monarchy, Lord Clermont's Fortescue's De Laudibus, Pulling's Order of the Coif, Herbert's Antiquities of the Inns of Court, Pierce's Inns of Court, Douthwaite's Gray's Inn, Loftie's Inns of Court and Chancery, Dillon's Laws and Jurisprudence, Kerly's Equitable Jurisdiction, Ames' History of Assumpsit, Thayer's Preliminary Treatise, Wigmore on Evidence. Ames' Notes to De Laudibus may be read in addition. Reeves now becomes more reliable. Dugdale's Origines Juridiciales has much curious information. Walsingham's Chronicle is valuable. Mr. Holdsworth is to write on The Legal Profession in the 14th and 15th centuries, in the Law Quarterly Review for 1907.

invention of common recoveries, the dawning action of ejectment, were phenomena that characterize this age. The common law was showing little indication of its coming helplessness in the next age, when the developed jury system was to render it incapable of granting any relief but a sum of money or the recovery of specific real or personal property. And in the realm of constitutional law this Lancastrian age reached higher ground than the law was to again occupy for two hundred years.

The reign of Richard II. opens with a frightful tragedy. The effects of the great plague in 1349, the unrest caused by the repressive statutes, the insistence of the landholders upon the villein-services, and the growth of the renting system, resulted in a widening chasm between farmer and laborer, which culminated in Wat Tyler's rebellion. The populace rose over England, and mobs marched on London. The demand was that all serfdom be abolished, and that all vellein services and rentals be commuted for four pence per acre. In London the mob burst into the Tower and murdered the chancellor, Archbishop Sudbury, one of the greatest scholars of his time. But the bitterness was deepest against the lawyers, on account of the parchment records and the actions that had forced many a villein to perform his services. The Temple, the new school of the lawyers, was sacked and its records destroyed. In Shakespeare's Henry VI., Dick the Butcher cries: "The first thing we do, let's kill all the lawyers." Cade: "Nay, that I mean to do. Is not this a lamentable thing, that of the skin of an innocent lamb should be made parchment; that parchment being scribbled o'er should undo a man." It is, perhaps, needless to say that Shakespeare is here completely astray in chronology, for this hatred of lawyers belongs to the revolt of Wat Tyler in 1381, not to Cade's rebellion in 1450.

Out in Suffolk was living the venerable Chief Justice Cavendish. The mob attacked his domain, and finding the Chief Justice, they dragged him forth, gave him a mock trial, and then beheaded him. This fine old lawyer was from the Norman house of De Gernum. Under the name Candish he was in immense practice in the Year Books of Edward III., along with Belknap, Charlton, and Knivet. After serving as a puisne in the Common Pleas he became Chief Justice of the King's Bench. One of his dicta from the bench is a gallant utterance upon the appearance of women: *"Il n'ad nul home en Engleterre,"* he says in barbarous French, *"que puy adjudge a droit deins age ou de plein age, car ascun femes que sont de age xxx ans voilent apperer de age de xviii."*[11] When he was murdered he had just been made Chancellor of the University of Cambridge, after a service on the bench for over ten years, with a great reputation for learning and fair dealing. His descendants in the elder line were Earls of Devonshire, now Dukes of Devonshire. Another descendant in the younger line was the celebrated commander in the Civil War, who became Marquis and Duke of Newcastle; but the estates of this line now belong to the Dukes of Portland, who are Cavendish-Bentincks.

The successor of Chief Justice Cavendish was Robert Tresilian. He had sat as Cavendish's only puisne; and when he held the assizes after Wat Tyler's rebellion, he made a record that was never equaled until Jeffreys held the "Bloody Assizes" after Monmouth's rebellion. Later in the reign of Richard II., Tresilian became involved in the political troubles. Parliament had practically supplanted the King, by appointing eleven commissioners to administer the government. The King at first tried to elect a more favorable parliament. When the election proved unfavorable, Tresilian called the judges together, among them Belknap, Chief Justice of the Common Pleas, Fulthorpe, Burgh, and Holt (Skipwith excused himself), and by violent threats induced the judges to sign a series of prepared answers, holding the act of Parliament invalid. Poor Belknap as he signed the paper said: "Now here lacketh nothing but a rope, that I may receive a reward worthie for my desert." This is an early instance of a practice that became common under the Stuarts, and was put into use as late as 1792 by Lord Eldon; while it has often been used in some of our States. Fulthorpe, one of the judges, at once communicated the matter to Parliament. The judges were appealed of high treason. Tresilian was beheaded, and the other judges were banished. Belknap had been a great advocate and an excellent judge; but he lacked courage, for in 1381 when he went the circuit, the rioters broke up his court and made him swear to hold no more sessions. His banishment

---

11. "There is no man in England who can tell whether she is within age or of full age, for some women who are thirty years old will appear to be only eighteen."

caused a very remarkable ruling. Gascoigne held that Belknap's wife could be sued as a feme sole, although her husband was living. The decision was certainly wrong. Chief Justice Markham at a later time made a rhymed couplet over this decision:

> Ecce modo mirum, quod femina fert breve regis
> Non nominando virum, conjunctum robore legis.[12]

Belknap was allowed to return, the judgment against him was reversed, and his property that had not been alienated was restored.

The year 1388, when the judges were banished, was, of course, marked by a total change in the courts—the first instance in English history when the whole bench was changed for political reasons. Even in 1399, when Henry of Bolingbroke supplanted Richard II. and the reigning king was compelled to sign an abdication, there was no change in the judiciary. The whole proceeding was in strict legal form, for Chief Justice Thirning yielded up the fealty, homage, and allegiance of all the English people, declared the King deposed, and announced Henry IV. to be his successor. The deposition took place in the midst of a splendid pageant in Westminster Hall. The Hall had just been re-modeled in the last two years of the King's reign. The Chancellor's court and the King's Bench, toward the end of Edward III.'s reign, had joined the Common Pleas in the Hall. King Richard, who had a keen appreciation of architectural beauty, had restored and remodeled the Hall after designs by William of Wykeham. The walls were built higher, the pillars in the hall were removed, and the magnificent timber roof, still one of the wonders of architecture, was thrown over the wide hall. Sadly enough, the first use made of the King's structure, after he had rendered it so imposing, was the coronation of his usurping kinsman, Henry IV.

Revolutions or changes in dynasty in England have rarely affected the courts. The two Chief Justices and their colleagues continued to sit in

12.   'Tis a marvel indeed that a wife brings her writ,
                 Not joining her husband, as law maketh fit.
    But the learned Markham was mistaken. The wife did not bring the writ; she was made defendant.

the courts after the new King's accession. One judge, Rickhill, was called upon to answer for a share in the murder of the late King's uncle, the Duke of Gloucester, while in prison at Calais. But Rickhill proved that he had no part in the murder, and was allowed to resume his seat upon the bench. This judge, in attempting to draw his own deed, made some memorable law, which is still common learning. By his deed he attempted to anticipate the law by two centuries, and to settle his lands upon his sons successively in tail, but added a contingent limitation that if any son aliened in fee or in tail, the same lands should go over to the next son in tail. The contingent limitation was held bad as the creation of a remainder, which did not await the natural devolution of the preceding estate, but cut it short by the creation of a freehold beginning *in futuro*. English law was to await the Statute of Uses before such a limitation became good in a deed, and the Statute of Wills before it became possible by will.

Clopton, Chief Justice of the King's Bench, vacated his seat to become a friar of the Minorites, and his successor was the celebrated William Gascoigne, whose surname the ingenious scribes of that day were able to spell in twenty-one different ways. The legend as to his firmness in committing the Prince of Wales for contempt of court is wholly mythical; but it is true that when, in 1405, he was commanded by the king to pronounce sentence of death upon Archbishop Scrope and the Earl Marshal, rebels taken in battle, he resolutely refused, saying: "Neither you, my Lord, nor any of your subjects, can, according to the law of this realm, sentence any prelate to death, and the Earl has a right to be tried by his peers."

Throughout this period the regular succession from eminence at the bar to a judgeship was a constantly recurring process. In the Year Books we notice some interesting interpolations. Thus Hull, a judge, "said secretly," of a decision of Chief Justice Thirning, "that it was never before this day adjudged to be law." Another judge, Hill, passing upon a "stay-out" agreement, where a dyer had bound himself by a bond not to pursue his trade for half a year, ruled that the covenant was against the common law, adding: "And by God, if the plaintiff was here, he should go to prison till he paid a fine to the King." The learned Foss thinks this the only reported oath on the bench, but he is greatly in error. Bereford, Brumpton, Staunton and other judges in the older Year Books frequently invoke the Almighty. Henry II.'s favorite oath while sitting on the bench was, "by God's eyes"; King John swore "by God's feet"; and the Conqueror's favorite oath was "by the splendor of God." Archbishop Arundel, who as Chancellor presided in 1407 over the trial of a Lollard priest, William Thorpe, accused of heresy, swore freely from the marble chair, "by God" and "by St. Peter." The accused priest upon this trial made a most felicitous Biblical quotation in answer to the Archbishop; the latter having said that God had raised him up even as a prophet of old to foretell the utter destruction of the false sect of the priest, the priest retorted with the words of Jeremiah: "When the word that is the prophecy of a prophet is known and fulfilled, then it shall be known that the Lord sent the prophet in truth."[13]

But the most curious circumstance of that age is a performance of Judge Tirwhit, who affords ample proof that no man, not even a judge, can be his own lawyer. Tirwhit had brought an action against the tenants of the manor of Lord de Roos. Both sides were afraid to trust a jury, so the cause was referred to the arbitration of Chief Justice Gascoigne. The Judge thereupon appointed a day, called in the record somewhat cynically, "a loveday," for the parties to come before him with their evidences, limiting the witnesses to a few friends of either party. But Tirwhit assembled four hundred men, who lay in wait for Lord de Roos to do him "harme and dishonure." Lord de Roos avoided the ambuscade, but complained to the king. Tirwhit was arraigned before Parliament and acknowledged that "he hath noght born him as he sholde have doon." The suit, by the award of the Archbishop of Canterbury and Lord de Grey, the Chamberlain, was again referred to Gascoigne, while Tirwhit was required to send two tuns of Gascony wine to Melton Roos, the manor-house of Lord de Roos, and to take there "two fatte oxen, and twelfe fat sheepe to be dispensed in a dyner to hem that there shall be," and Tirwhit was to attend the feast with all "the knights and

13. Our version has it: "When the word of the prophet shall come to pass, then shall the prophet be known, that the Lord hath truly sent him." Jer. 28:9.

esquires and yomen" that had made his forces on the "forsaid loveday." There he was to offer a full speech of apology, which concluded: "forasmuche as I am a justice, that more than a comun man scholde have had me more discreetly and peesfully, I know wele that I have failed and offended yow, my Lord the Roos, whereof I beseke yow of grace and mercy and offer you 500 mark to ben paid at your will." But Lord de Roos was to refuse the 500 marks and forgive the judge and all his party. What happened at the feast, how much of the two hogsheads of heady wine were consumed, whether heated with the good cheer the parties fell to fighting over the legal issue, and how many good men fell (under the table) in the great hall of Melton Roos, history has not told us. But an archbishop who could prescribe a feast and two hogsheads of wine as a peace offering certainly cannot be accused of any prejudice in favor of sobriety.[14]

This was the age of noted lawyers. Such names as Hankford, Markham and Danby, Norton, Prisot, Hody, Moyle, Choke and Brian are great names in the Year Books. Hody, according to Coke, was "one of the famous and expert sages of the law." He and Prisot, a Chief Justice of the Common Pleas, are said to have greatly assisted Littleton in writing his work on Tenures. Hody tried and condemned Roger Bolingbroke, "a gret and konnyng man in astronomye," for attempting "to consume the king's person by way of nygromancie." The unfortunate scientist was sentenced to death and executed. Markham furnishes the first instance, for generations, of the removal of a judge for an unsatisfactory decision. It happened in this wise: Sir Thomas Cooke, lately Lord Mayor of London, was possessed of vast landed wealth. The Yorkists in 1469 brought him to trial for loaning money to Margaret of Anjou, the wife of the deposed king, Henry VI. The cormorants surrounding Edward IV., the hungry relatives of his wife, had condemned Cooke beforehand and considered his estate as their lawful prey. But Markham charged the jury that the act proven was merely misprision of treason, and thus the

---

14. The grandson of a noted lawyer of that time, by name Rede, afterwards endowed Jesus College at Oxford with a fellowship and a brewery. The brewery for the use of undergraduates is a startling commentary on our Puritanical practices.

Lord Mayor was saved from forfeiture of his estate. Markham was immediately superseded as Chief Justice.

Another name celebrated in the Year Books is that of Skrene. He is a favorite with the reporters, for many of his deliverances are noted with the same approval as those of the judges. In later times such men as Coke deemed all statements of law as of equal value, and cited indiscriminately the arguments of counsel and the words of the judges, as entitled to equal credit. Skrene never attained a judicial position, but he left a fine estate called Skrenes which was many years afterwards purchased by Chief Justice Brampston.

Both Brian and Danby are sages of the law often cited by Coke as high authority. Choke, a contemporary, served on the bench for many years. His contribution to the law is composed of two erroneous and troublesome dicta. One asserts that if land be granted to a man and his heirs so long as John A'Down has heirs of his body, and John A'Down dies without heir of his body, the feoffment is determined. John Chipman Gray, with an amplitude of learning that has been wasted on a perverse generation, has demonstrated that Coke and Blackstone are in error in following Choke's deliverance. Not less erroneous is Choke's second dictum as to the reversion of the property of a corporation upon its dissolution, but the courts have long disregarded this latter proposition.

Another judge, Walter Moyle, who sat through the wars of the Roses, is notable as the progenitor of a most distinguished legal family. His granddaughter and heiress married Sir Thomas Finch, descended from an old Norman family. Their son, Henry Finch, was a celebrated serjeant at law. His son, John Finch, was Attorney General, then Chief Justice of the Common Pleas, and later Lord Keeper under Charles I., as Lord Finch of Daventry. Another grandson of the Moyle heiress was Heneage Finch, a celebrated lawyer. His son, another Heneage, was the celebrated chancellor, Lord Nottingham, the Father of Equity and the author of the Statute of Frauds. His son, a third Heneage, became celebrated by his valiant defence of the Seven Bishops and was made Earl of Aylesford. Three earldoms, Winchelsea, Nottingham, and Aylesford, were the rewards of this legal family.

About the middle of the fourteen hundreds, just before the wars of the Roses, it became apparent that the salaries paid to the judges were wholly inadequate. In 1440 William Ascough, who was rapidly advanced, was appointed a justice in the Common Pleas. He petitioned the king representing that "ere he had been two years a serjeant, he was called by your Highness to the bench and made justice, whereby all his earnings, which he would have had, and all the fees that he had in England, were and be ceased and expired to his great impoverishment, for they were the substance of his livelihood." He modestly requested, since he was the poorest of the justices, a life estate in lands of £25 12s. 10d. per year. Even the summons to serjeantcy was sometimes refused, since it might result in an elevation to the bench. It is certain that prior to this time the serjeants had a monopoly of the Common Pleas, for in 1415, William Babington, John Juyn, John Martyn, and William Westbury were called to the degree of the coif. These four with several others declined to qualify and thereupon complaint was made in Parliament that there was an insufficiency of serjeants to carry on the business of the courts. Parliament responded by imposing a large penalty upon any one who refused a summons to become a serjeant. So the persons called assumed the degree, and the four named above afterwards became judges.

A judge who served under Henry VI. in the trying time of Cade's rebellion has served for centuries to add to the gayety of nations. Sir John Fastolf, who held the Kent assizes in 1451, was a gallant soldier and a lover of learning. For some reason Shakespeare pictured him, under the name of Falstaff or Fastolfe, in his Henry VI., as a contemptible coward and craven. Later, in his Henry IV., when he changed the name of the fat knight Oldcastle so as not to offend Puritan prejudices, Shakespeare substituted the name of the character in his older play. In this way the blameless Fastolf has been handed down by the plays of Henry IV. and the Merry Wives of Windsor as the richest comic character in dramatic literature. The real man left a will, of which Judge Yelverton was an executor. It is said in the Paston letters that in a suit over the will Yelverton came down from the bench and pleaded the matter!

But this extraordinary conduct of Yelverton was surpassed by that of Serjeant Fairfax. On one occasion he was employed to prosecute certain defendants; but he declared at the bar that he knew that the men were not guilty, that he would labor their deliverance for alms, not taking a penny, whereupon the prosecutor naturally retained other counsel. It is to be hoped that this professional betrayal was not common at that day, though doubtless the foolish people who prate about the iniquity of a lawyer's advocacy of a bad cause would find in such conduct much to approve. This Fairfax's great-great-grandson was made Lord Fairfax in 1637, and in still later times the then Lord Fairfax, smarting under some court beauty's disdain, buried himself in the Virginia wilderness, and added to history by befriending the young surveyor, George Washington. Washington was sent to survey his friend's vast domain beyond the Blue Ridge, and there gained the knowledge that gave him his first military employment.

The fame of all the Lancastrian and Yorkist lawyers is eclipsed by that of Fortescue and Littleton. Both of them were legal authors and very successful practitioners. Fortescue, the Lancastrian judge, survived Littleton, the Yorkist judge, and will therefore be noticed after him.

Thomas Littleton came of a family that since the days of Henry II. had occupied an estate at South Littleton in Worcestershire. Although he was the eldest son he was bred to the bar at the Inner Temple. He became reader for his Inn, and the subject of his public reading, the Statute *De Donis*, shows the early tendency of his legal studies. He was in practice as early as 1445, for in that year a litigant named Hauteyn petitioned the Lord Chancellor to grant him Littleton as counsel in a case against the widow of Judge Paston, for the reason that none of the men of the court were willing to appear against the widow of a judge and her son, who was an advocate. This would seem to indicate that Littleton's practice lay in the chancery and not in the law courts. In 1452 Littleton received a handsome fee, the grant of a manor for life *pro bono et notabili consilio*. In 1453 he became a serjeant, and in the next year was made king's serjeant. In 1460 he was one of the king's serjeants who successfully evaded an answer to the question asked by Parliament as to whether the Lancastrian King Henry or the Yorkist Duke Richard had the better title to the throne. In fact, from 1455 to 1466 Littleton practiced his profession, refusing to mingle in the political disputes. He even took the lawyer-like precaution in 1461, when Edward IV. supplanted Henry VI., to sue out a general pardon for acts done under the deposed monarch. In 1466 he was made a justice of the Common Pleas, and so remained, even under the short return of Henry VI. He died a judge in 1481. He assisted in fixing the legal landmark of Taltarum's case, which held that a common recovery suffered by a tenant in tail barred not only the issue in tail, but also any remainder limited thereafter, as well as the reversion in fee. His tomb, in the form of an altar of white marble, still remains in Worcester Cathedral. His will, among other curious bequests, gallantly provides for prayers to be said for the good of the soul of his wife's first husband. Gentle sarcasm has little in common with the treatise on Tenures; but it may be that, after an experience with the widow of the deceased, Littleton felt that the unfortunate man deserved the prayers. The will shows Littleton to be a pious soul fully persuaded of the efficacy of prayers to prevent the "long tarying" of the soul in purgatory.

While Littleton's treatise was put into its final form in the latter part of his life, it is probable that the Tenures is an amplification of his reading on *De Donis* and represents the collected work of a lifetime. It is a marvel to find a work on the law into which no apparent error has crept. This book has remained the classic treatise on estates, and its words to-day are cited as the undoubted common law. Following Fortescue's saying that "from the families of judges often descend nobles and great men of the realm," it may be noted that Littleton's eldest son married one of the coheiresses of Edmund Beaufort, Duke of Somerset, and by right of that descent, Littleton's descendants, who are Viscounts Cobham, quarter the royal arms of the house of Lancaster. The descendant of Littleton's second son is Lord Hatherton, while the great-grandson of Littleton's third son was Lord Lyttleton, Lord Keeper under Charles I. Another descendant was a baron of the Exchequer under Charles II.

The traditional portrait of Littleton is unfortunately not authentic. He is shown wearing the collar of SS, still worn by the Lord Chief Justice of England, but absolute discredit is thrown on the portrait by the portcullis of the Tudors, next to the clasp of the collar, which was

not introduced until Henry VII.'s time. The Elizabethan ruff is hardly
the attire we should expect in the Yorkist age. Coke, however, who knew
nothing about it, says that the picture is a very good likeness. But the
monumental effigy of Littleton, possibly authentic, shows a kneeling figure. Out of his mouth issues the motto *ung dieu et ung roy,* and the face
has the smooth look of a Yorkist courtier, but indicating the keenness of
intellect required for the systematizer of the nice discriminations of the
law of real estate.

Littleton was simply a great lawyer and judge, but his greatest contemporary was more than a great lawyer and judge; he was an enlightened statesman, a gallant soldier, a writer of transcendent merit upon
constitutional law, and a scholar whose words upon his profession possess a peculiar charm even for men wholly unacquainted with legal lore.
John Fortescue was a lineal descendant of the knight (Le Fort Escu) who
bore the shield of William the Conqueror at Hastings. Educated at
Exeter College, Oxford, Fortescue was trained for the bar at Lincoln's
Inn, of which he was a governor from 1425 to 1429. In the latter year he
was made a serjeant, and is shown in the Year Books as in immense practice, until in 1442 he became Lord Chief Justice of the King's Bench. His
salary in that office was £120 a year, with an allowance of two robes and
two tuns of Gascony wine per year. His yearly salary was afterwards increased to £160. He served as Chief Justice until 1461. During his term
occurred Cade's rebellion, and one of the charges against Fortescue and
Prisot, the Chief Justices, was that of "falseness." No sooner suppressed
was this rebellion, where Cade took the significant name of Mortimer,
than the Duke of York set up his claim to the throne, as descended
through the Mortimers from the third son of Edward III. The judges,
the king's counsel, the serjeants at law, were all asked for legal opinions
on the title to the throne, but all declined to give an opinion. Both parties took up arms. Chief Justice Fortescue vindicated his descent from a
long line of knightly ancestors by taking the field. He was in almost every
one of the battles; and after Towton, the bloodiest battle in English history, he went into exile with the Lancastrians. He returned and fought at
Tewkesbury, the last battle of the war, and was taken prisoner.

During his exile he had written the work which we call De Laudibus Legum Angliae. The book was written to instil into the young Prince of Wales, Henry VI.'s son, whose education was entrusted to Fortescue, a proper knowledge of English institutions. The book is invaluable as showing not only a profound appreciation of the free and liberal principles of the common law, but also the condition of the English law at that epoch. Fortescue also wrote a tract in support of the Lancastrian title to the throne, which he based upon the solemn declaration of Parliament and the nation's acceptance. When Fortescue found that the Lancastrian cause was ruined, he prayed for a pardon from the Yorkist king. There had been little change in the bar or the courts during Fortescue's exile. Fortescue himself had been succeeded by Markham, and Prisot, another avowed Lancastrian, was displaced by Danby; but all the other judges had remained. The courts had gone on in regular fashion during the fierce wars, and the bar was composed of many of the men who had practiced before Fortescue. Billing, a subservient wretch who had succeeded Markham, although one of the first of a long line of the disgraceful judicial tools of Yorkist, Tudor and Stuart kings, kept up the traditional kindliness of the English bar by intervening strongly for Sir John Fortescue, and obtained for him a pardon with the restoration of his estates. But by a curious whim of Edward IV., Fortescue was required to write, in favor of the Yorkist title, a refutation of his book demonstrating the validity of the Lancastrian title to the throne. The two treatises appear in Fortescue's works, and each of them constitutes the best argument for the respective opposing claims.

If one were asked to name in English law an equal to Fortescue, he could point to but three names—Bacon, Somers and Mansfield. Just as Bacon and Somers were impeached, and Mansfield bitterly denounced, so we find, here and there in the Paston letters, hints that Fortescue was an object of hatred. A correspondent during Cade's rebellion says: "The Chief Justice hath waited to be assaulted all this sevennight nightly in his house, but nothing come as yet, the more pity." It is not uncommon for Fortescue to be represented as more of a politician than a lawyer; but the Year Books of Henry VI. show him to be a consummate master of the

common law, whom even Coke mentions with reverence. One decision of
his, in the case of Thorpe, Speaker of the House of Commons, is written in our Federal and all our State constitutions.

In his books "De Laudibus" and "Monarchy" he shows that he is the
first of England's great constitutional lawyers. He points out to his
young prince that the Roman maxim, *"quidquid principi placuit, habet legis
vigorem,"* has no place in English law; that the king's power is derived
from the people and granted for the preservation of those laws, which
protect the subjects' persons and property; that the king cannot change
the laws without the consent of the three estates of the realm, the baronage, clergy and commons; that the Parliament has power because it is
representative of the whole people; that the king's power of pardon and
the whole domain of equity is the king's for the good of his subjects; that
the limitations upon kingly power are not a humiliation to, but for the
glory of the king; that righteous judgment is his first duty, that the courts
of law are his, but he does not act personally in judgment; that the laws
of England are better than those of France, because they recognize no
torture, because they provide the institution of the jury, carefully regulated courts, a legal profession trained in the great legal university, the
Inns of Court, and because all men's rights are equally protected by law.
Certainly no nobler picture of a constitutional system has ever been put
forth by any English lawyer. It is the precocious development of the three
Henries, a system far ahead of the times; under a strong king like Henry
V., England was the first power in Europe; but a weak king like Henry
VI., kindly, just, temperate, humane, gentle in his methods, pure and upright of life, the best man who ever sat on the English throne, found himself ruined and dethroned. The nation which voluntarily abandoned this
system deserved the Yorkist, Tudor, and Stuart tyranny. And every step
that since was gained in England was obtained by restoring some principle of this theory of government so boldly sketched by Fortescue.

It is a pleasure to know that the manor which the Chief Justice bought
and transmitted to his posterity gave a title to his descendants as
Viscounts Ebrington, and that the head of the family, as Earl Fortescue,
sits in the House of Lords, while three Fortescues since his time have sat
as judges in Westminster Hall.

Here at this period, when modern history is just beginning, when the use of printing was about to multiply books and legal treatises, when the law itself was passing through a great transformation, when the growth of the chancellor's jurisdiction by means of conveyances to uses was to suffer a great expansion, when chancery was to gain its control over common law actions by injunctions, when land was to become again alienable, when the actions of ejectment, of trespass, of trover and of assumpsit were developing and the older actions passing away, when the jury was becoming a body of men which heard evidence only in open court under the control of the judge, when the great advocate with his skill in eliciting evidence and in addressing the jury now first found a place in the practice, and all court proceedings, except formal declarations, were transacted in the English tongue, we have in Fortescue's work a picture of the English legal system. But the most interesting portion of his work is the description of the system of legal education at the Inns.

The origin of the Inns of Court is lost in antiquity; but it is practically certain that there was a body of law students older than any of the Inns. One set of students in Edward II.'s reign, or soon thereafter, obtained quarters in the Temple and soon divided into the Middle and the Inner Temple. Another body of students probably obtained from that ill-starred woman, the heiress of the deLacys, the town-house of the Earls of Lincoln, and became Lincoln's Inn. Still later another body obtained the mansion of the Lords Gray de Wilton, and became Gray's Inn. Connected with the larger Inns were ten smaller Inns of Chancery, having no connection with the court of chancery, but so called because they were the preparatory schools where the students studied the original writs, which were issued out of the chancery.

But there was, of course, some reason why, on the edge of the city, just beyond the city wall, all these students should have found a lodging place. Fortescue explains that the laws of England cannot be taught at the university, but that they are studied in a much more commodious place, near the king's court, where the laws are daily pleaded and argued and where judgments are rendered by grave judges, of full years, skilled and expert in the laws. The place of study is near an opulent city, but in a spot quiet and retired, where the throng of passers-by does not disturb the students, yet where they can daily attend the courts.

In the smaller Inns the nature of writs is studied. The students come there from the universities and grammar schools, and as soon as they have made some progress they pass into the larger Inns. At each of the smaller Inns are about a hundred students, while none of the larger Inns has less than two hundred. These four larger Inns were wholly voluntary institutions. The older and better known barristers of an Inn became the benchers, and they were self-perpetuating. They alone had and still retain the exclusive privilege of calling to the bar, but upon their refusal an appeal lay to the judges. In these four Inns the students studied the cases in the Year Books, the legal treatises called Fleta and Britton, read the statutes, and attended at court in term time.

Instruction was given by arguing moot cases before a bencher and two barristers sitting as judges, and by lectures called readings delivered by some able barrister belonging to the Inn. These readings were often cited as authority. Littleton's was on De Donis, Bacon's was on the Statute of Uses, Dyer's upon the Statute of Wills, Coke's upon the Statute of Fines. It was a high honor to be selected as reader, and the expense of readers' feasts at the Inns became very great. After a student had studied for seven years (afterwards reduced to five), he was eligible to be called to the bar. The barristers before becoming serjeants were probably called apprentices, although that term was sometimes applied to the students. Whether an examination was required is problematical, but possibly that part of the ceremony of instituting a serjeant, which requires the serjeant to plead to a declaration, points to an examination of some perfunctory sort.

While the students were pursuing their studies in the law, they were instructed in various other branches of learning, if we may believe Fortescue. Singing, all kinds of music, dancing, and sports were taught to the students in the same manner as those who were brought up in the king's household were instructed. The revels and masques of the law students became a great feature of court life. On week days the greater part of the students devoted themselves to their legal studies, but on festival days and Sundays after divine service, they read the Holy Scriptures and profane history. In the Inns of Court every virtue is learned and every vice is banished, says Fortescue; the discipline is pleasant, and in every way tends to proficiency. Such is the reputation of these schools that knights, barons, and the higher nobility put their children here, not so much for the purpose of making them lawyers as to form their manners and bring them up with a sound training. The constant harmony among the students, the absence of piques or differences or any bickerings or disturbances, which Fortescue asserts, taxes our credulity. But he claims that an expulsion from an Inn was feared more by the students than punishments are dreaded by criminals.

The high social position of the students, a phenomenon that is always noticeable in the English barrister, is warmly commended by Fortescue. The expense of the residence at an Inn, which is twenty-eight pounds a year (equal to almost twenty times that amount at present money values), restricts the study of the law to the sons of gentle folk. The necessity of a servant doubles this expense, and the poor and common classes are not able to bear so great a cost, while the mercantile people rarely desire to deplete their capital by such an annual burden. "Whence it happens that there is hardly a skilled lawyer who is not a gentleman by birth, and on this account they have a greater regard for their character, their honor and good name."

After a barrister had been called, he generally practised on the circuit. Fortescue himself traveled the western circuit. He narrates how he saw a woman condemned and burned for the murder of her husband, and at the next assizes he heard a servant confess that he had killed the husband and that the wife was entirely innocent. From this occurrence Fortescue draws a justification for the law's delay. "What must we think," he says, "of this precipitate judge's prickings of conscience and remorse, when he reflects that he could have delayed that execution. Often, alas, he has confessed to me that he could never in his whole life cleanse his soul from the stain of this deed." In another place Fortescue makes the remark that has been so often quoted: "Indeed one would much rather that twenty guilty persons should escape the punishment of death, than that one innocent person should be executed."

The barrister after sixteen years' service may be called upon to take the degree of serjeant at law. Then he dons a white silk cap, which a serjeant does not doff even while talking to the king. After much solemn and stately ceremonial and feasting, the new serjeant is assigned his pillar at the Parvis of St. Paul's, where he consults his clients and attorneys. The orthodox rule, which became a custom in England, that it is unprofessional for a barrister to receive his instructions or fee from the client, did not then exist. Even in much later times Wycherly, who had been a law student, sees no incongruity in the client consulting a barrister. In his exceedingly filthy, but witty play, The Plaindealer, the litigious Widow Blackacre is consulting her counsel, Serjeant Ploddon, and says to him: "Go then to your Court of Common Pleas and say one thing over and over again; you do it so naturally, that you will never be suspected for protracting time."

As in after times, the judges were selected only from the serjeants. Fortescue describes the oath which the judges take—to do justice to all men, to delay it to none, even though the king himself command otherwise, that he will take no gift or reward from any man having a cause before him and will take no robes or fees except from the king. Lovingly Fortescue tells of the life of leisure and study of the judges, how the courts sit only in the morning, from eight until eleven. Then the judges go to their dinner. At Serjeants' Inn the judges dined and met the serjeants there. Fortescue himself had chambers in the old Serjeants' Inn.[15] From Clifford's Inn one may now enter the old building where Fortescue lodged, but it is no longer used by the serjeants, for that ancient order is extinct. After their dinner the judges spent the rest of the day in the study of the laws, reading of the Scriptures, and other studies at their pleasure. It is a life rather of contemplation than of action, says Fortescue, free from every care and removed from worldly strife. Proudly he tells his prince that in his time no judge was found that had been corrupted with gifts or bribes.

Fortescue's De Laudibus is the unique production of that age. Here

---

15. The serjeants at law had their lodgings in the Old Serjeants' Inn, which stands in Chancery Lane. But it is likely that the lodgings were occupied only during term time. The Paston Letters tell us how the good wife at home sent up from the country hams, chickens and cheese. But as soon as court adjourned for the long vacation the serjeants and judges hurried to their homes in the country. The arrangement of the terms with the long vacation at harvest time proves the country residence of the judges and lawyers.

we see the legal system set forth, from the day the student enters an Inn of Chancery through his studies in an Inn of Court, his service at the bar, until his elevation and work upon the bench. It is fully described by one of the greatest of common lawyers, "this notable bulwark of our laws," as Sir Walter Raleigh calls Fortescue. But we ought not to part from this great lawyer without remarking his serene and steadfast faith in God's direct government of the world—that wonderful faith of the Middle Ages. Fortescue feels that the good man is blessed. The fact that upright judges leave behind them a posterity is to him one of God's appropriate blessings upon just men. It is a fulfillment of the Prophet's word that the generation of the righteous is blessed, that their children shall be blessed, and that their seed shall endure forever. Perhaps Fortescue, after the fatal field of Tewkesbury, when he lay a prisoner in the Tower, found consolation in the promise of the Psalmist: "The steps of a good man are ordered by the Lord; though he fall, yet shall he not be utterly cast down, for the Lord sustaineth him with his hand." For once at least the promise came true. Fortescue lived his last years in peace and honor. He saw the bloody tyrant, Richard of Gloucester, on Bosworth field, pay the penalty of his many crimes, and when the great Chief Justice passed away, a Lancastrian king was in undisturbed possession of the throne.

IV. The Iron Age of the Common Law: From Henry VII. to the Revolution of 1688[16]

The Yorkist kings had betrayed a tendency to use the courts for the furtherance of tyrannical ends; but Henry VII., who had been trained in the Lancastrian tradition of the independence of the judiciary, made absolutely no change in the judges after his victory at Bosworth. The avarice of this king was, however, so great that we have an instance of a

16. General references for this period: Foss and Campbell now become much fuller in detail. The State Trials are invaluable for the whole period. Besides these may be named: Fitzherbert's Abridgement, New Natura Brevium and Diversity of Courts, Lynwoode's Provinciale, St. Germain's Doctor and Student, Select Cases from the Court of Requests (Selden Society), Select Cases from the Star Chamber (Selden Society),

melancholy practice which became common under the Stuarts. The king sold to Robert Read, a very good lawyer, the chiefship of the Common Pleas, for four thousand marks.

There are no names of great lawyers in this reign. The worthy Fineux, who became Chief Justice, had an immense practice. He was steward to 129 manors and counsel for 16 noblemen. His industry was marvelous, for he left 23 folio volumes of notes of 3,502 cases that he had managed. The growing importance of the mercantile class is shown by the elevation of Frowick, a member of a London family of goldsmiths. He succeeded Brian as Chief Justice of the Common Pleas. Thomas Whittington, a baron of the Exchequer, was a grand nephew of the famous Richard Whittington, who walked to London and who while sitting discouraged at the foot of Highgate Hill heard the prophecy of Bow Bells, and lived to become the banker of kings and the greatest of merchant princes.

Another celebrated lawyer of this time was Richard Kingsmill. A letter still extant says: "For Mr. Kingsmill it were well doon that he were with you for his authority and worship, and he will let for no maugre, and yf the enquest passe against you he may showe you summ comfortable remedy, but, sir, his coming will be costly to you." The childlike confidence in the high-priced lawyer is touching. But the fees seem ridiculously small. We know that the Goldsmiths' Company of London paid a retainer of ten shillings. "A breakfast at Westminster spent on our counsel" cost one shilling sixpence. Serjeant Yaxley's retainer from the litigious Plumpton for the next assizes at York, Notts, and Derby, was five pounds, and a fee of forty marks, if the Serjeant attended the assizes.

Reeves' History of English Law, Spedding's Life of Bacon, Anderson's, Dyer's, Popham's and Plowden's Reports, Pollock's Land Laws, Dugdale's Origines, Staunforde's Pleas of the Crown, Coke upon Littleton, Coke's Institutes, Coke's Reports with the Introductions, Whitelocke's Memorials, Hale's Introduction to Rolle's Abridgement (in Hargrave's Collecteana Juridica), Saunders' Reports, North's Life of Lord Keeper North, Irving's Life of Jeffreys, Roscoe's Lives of Eminent Lawyers. Hale's Pleas of the Crown and History of the Common Law are not critical. For the historical development of the rules of evidence consult Wigmore on Evidence under the particular rule.

Two interesting features of this time are the beginning of our modern law of corporations, as applied to merchant guilds and trading corporations, and the growth of law book printing. Caxton printed no law book; but Wynken de Worde printed Lynwoode's Provinciale, and Lettou and Machlinia, trained under Caxton, printed in 1480 Littleton's Tenures, an edition supposed to have been superintended by the author. This book was most frequently reissued; and two famous printers, Pynson and Redman, got into a savage dispute over the merits of their respective editions. In a few years the demand for law books caused the printing of some of the Year Books, and the publication of the Abridgments or Digests of Statham and Fitzherbert. The New Natura Brevium, St. Germain's Doctor and Student, Fitzherbert's Diversity of Courts, and Perkins' Profitable Book, soon appeared. The Year Books grow more and more scrappy, until under Henry VIII. they pass away. But in these latter years they are sad productions. The reporters have lost their French. Such words as "hue and cry," "shoes," "boots," and "barley," are not turned into French. The law French degenerated until it resembled modern phonetic script. A learned lawyer wrote in this wise: "Richardson, C. J. de C. B., at Assizes at Salisbury in summer 1631, fuit assault per prisoner la condemne pur felony; que puis son condemnation ject un brickbat a le dit justice que narrowly mist. Et pur ceo immediately fuit indictment drawn pur Noy envers le prisoner et son dexter manus ampute et fixe al gibbet sur que luy mesme immediatement hange in presence de court." The matter of reporting, however, was now taken up by well-known lawyers and judges. Anderson, Dyer, Owen, Dalison, Popham, Coke, Plowden, Bendloe, Keilway, and Croke have left valuable reports, all in Norman French.

The evidence all points to a complete breakdown in the jury system at this time. The Star Chamber court merely continued a jurisdiction long existent in the king's council; but some portion of the jurisdiction, such as that over corruptions of sheriffs in making jury panels and in false returns, over the bribery of jurors, and over riots and unlawful assemblies, was now put into statutory form. Yet the court would not allow even Serjeant Plowden to argue that it was confined in its jurisdiction by the words of the statute. The court was at first a most excellent engine for particular cases, and filled a great public necessity, but under the later Tudors and the Stuarts it became an engine of tyranny.

This period was characterized in the criminal law by most shameless oppression in all political cases. The unrestrained rule of Henry VIII. and Elizabeth shows many a cruel instance of judicial sycophancy. Yet it is a fact that both these rulers were always popular among the lawyers. Even to-day, on every state occasion at Gray's Inn, "the glorious, pious, and immortal memory" of Queen Elizabeth is toasted by the benchers, the barristers, and the students rising, three at a time, and taking up the toast in succession. Yet it was Henry VIII. who reduced to an infallible system the art of murder by the forms of law. The judges certified Anne Boleyn to be guilty of high treason, because she was reported to have said the king never had her heart. A jury found the Earl of Surrey guilty of high treason, because he quartered the arms of Edward the Confessor; it is needless to say that Edward never had a coat of arms. The grey-haired, blameless Countess of Salisbury was executed, because her son Reginald Pole had become a Roman cardinal. The king adopted the ingenious methods of Chinese justice, by which, if the offender is not available, his nearest relative suffers in his stead. The judges certified that Catherine Howard, Henry's fifth queen, was guilty of high treason, because she was not a virgin when she espoused the elderly and battered rake. Cromwell, Earl of Essex, committed high treason, because he had not warned Henry that Anne of Cleves, the king's fourth bride, was hideously ugly.

Even torture was resorted to in criminal trials. Fox, in his Book of Martyrs (which is embellished by numberless falsehoods), says that Sir Thomas More tortured a prisoner. Elizabeth ordered Campion the Jesuit to be put upon the rack; and Chief Justice Wray presided over the trial. Throgmorton was convicted on confessions obtained by threats of torture. The evidence, where any was taken, was often worthless hearsay. The trial of Sir Thomas More was a travesty on justice. But the conviction of Fisher, Bishop of Rochester, stamps the judges with infamy. In that trial it appeared that Bishop Fisher, mindful of the act of Parliament which made it high treason to dispute the king's headship of the Church, had steadily refused either to admit or deny the king's supremacy. At last the Attorney General, Richard Rich, who by the most degrading subserviency to the humors of the king had gained preferment, was sent to Fisher in the Tower. He told the Bishop that he came from the King, who desired to know for his own information Fisher's real opinion upon the disputed point. The Bishop spoke of the danger arising from the act of Parliament, but Rich assured him that no advantage would be taken of him and gave him the promise of the King that his answer would never be divulged. Thereupon, the Bishop stated that he thought an act of Parliament could no more declare the King head of the church than it could declare that God was not God. Fisher was at once brought to trial; Rich gave the sole evidence against him; and the judges allowed the Bishop to be convicted and executed. It is said that the judges shed tears when the saintly old man was condemned; but that conduct simply adds to their infamy. Sir Thomas More was convicted and brought to the block upon the very same kind of testimony.

Yet during this whole period the law provided even-handed justice as between one private citizen and another. The reports of Chief Justice Dyer, Chief Justice Anderson, and Serjeant Plowden, during the reign of Elizabeth, abundantly prove the fact. In ordinary criminal trials the law was growing much more lenient. It was only when the government was urging the prosecution that the tyranny of the Tudors and Stuarts left the individual no hope against the Crown. Judicial tenure became dependent upon subserviency to the wishes of the executive. Judicial appointments were given solely to those who pledged themselves to the royal designs. The real history of the law is found in the bloody records of the State Trials. The processes of law are used by the government with almost cynical indecency. The baronage was destroyed, and the great mass of the people, the cities and the country gentry, eagerly supported the royal authority.

Before passing from the reign of Henry VIII. we should notice Lord Chief Justice Montague, who founded a powerful family, and is now represented by the Duke of Manchester, the Earl of Sandwich, and the Earl of Wharncliffe. Another of Henry VIII.'s judges was John Spelman, the grandfather of the celebrated antiquary, Henry Spelman. He is not specially noted for his judicial utterances, but he became by one wife the father of twenty children.

Under Elizabeth, those unfortunate gentlemen upon whom the Queen had showered her favors were in peculiar peril. Anyone of her numerous lovers who had the temerity to take a furlough suffered for high treason. The Earl of Hertford was so misguided as to marry a wife. Although he prudently went abroad, the bride was thrown into the Tower, and when the Earl returned, he also was imprisoned. The Queen had the marriage declared void, and fined the Earl fifteen thousand pounds. The young Earl of Arundel had a similar but more trying experience, when he became reconciled to his wife after having been Elizabeth's favorite. He was condemned to death, but was saved by the Queen's ministers. Hatton, who became chancellor through the graces of his person, had the good sense to remain unmarried; and the Earl of Leicester kept his royal mistress' favor by forgetting his duties as a husband. The Duke of Norfolk was convicted because he was suspected of a desire to marry the Queen of Scots. That Queen was executed after an absurd trial before the judges. The Secretary Davidson, who at the command of Queen Elizabeth had issued the warrant for the execution of the Queen of Scots, was savagely prosecuted and imprisoned for life.

The religious controversies fanned the cruel instincts of the age. Under Henry the faithful Catholics suffered the worst oppressions. The chief tool of Henry VIII. in these matters was Thomas Audley, who was a trained lawyer and succeeded More as Lord Chancellor. He devised those laws which imposed upon every man's conscience the most contradictory oaths. It was a penal offence to acknowledge the Pope, yet it was no less penal to deny a single article of the Romish faith. Whoever was for the Pope was beheaded and whoever was against him was burned. The legislation that plundered the church was Audley's work, and he selected for himself a rich portion of the spoil. The priory of Christ Church in Aldgate became his town house. He claimed the wealthy monastery of Walden, representing that he had sustained great damage and infamy in serving the King. On the ruins of that abbey his grandson Thomas Howard erected the stately Elizabethan mansion of Audley End.

When the Catholics returned to power under Mary, the Protestants in their turn suffered the penalties of heresy. One trial, however, stands out in this reign as the only instance where, under the Tudors, a prosecution for high treason resulted in a verdict of not guilty. Sir Nicholas Throckmorton was prosecuted by the learned Dyer, then Attorney General. The defendant completely outtalked the Attorney General, and made him appear something of a simpleton. He modestly compared himself to the Savior, and pictured Dyer in the character of Pilate. His self-confidence enabled him to interrupt Chief Justice Bromley's charge to the jury. Throckmorton craved "indifferency" from the judge, and helped out the judge's poor memory by his own recital of the facts. The jury that acquitted Throckmorton was imprisoned and heavily fined.

The judges, who were Protestants, on the accession of Mary conveniently became Roman Catholics; one of them, Sir James Hales, had scruples but was induced by his associate, Judge Portman, to recant. This act so worked on Hales' conscience that he drowned himself. The coroner's jury returned a verdict of suicide; and in two cases[17] a number of hair-splitting subtleties were uttered by the court as to the effect of the suicide in forfeiting the Judge's estates. Shakespeare makes the learned gravediggers in Hamlet discourse over Ophelia in words that are almost a literal parody on the arguments of the judges.

Elizabeth's reign produced one very great judge. James Dyer was really appointed to the bench under Mary, but the most of his judicial service was under Elizabeth. He presided in the Common Pleas for twenty-three years. He took no part in the disgraceful political trials of this reign, but directed his court with efficiency and learning. The poet Whetstone has these lines upon Dyer:

> He ruled by law and listened not to art;
> These foes to truth—love, hate, and private gain
> . . . his conscience would not stain.

John Popham offers a remarkable contrast to Dyer. Of high birth, educated at Oxford, he fell into evil ways while at the Middle Temple. He

---

17. Bishop of Chichester v. Webb, 2 Dyer 107; Lady Hales v. Pettit, Plowden 253.

even resorted to the calling of a highwayman to replenish his purse. He reformed, however, and became a consummate lawyer; he was made Solicitor General and Speaker of the House of Commons. In regular order he became Attorney General, and as such took the lead in many state trials. He prosecuted Tilney, and caused Chief Justice Anderson, one of the greatest lawyers of the reign, to charge the jury on wholly insufficient evidence that the defendant was guilty of an attempt upon the Queen's life. He attempted to prosecute Mary Queen of Scots; but Hatton, the Chancellor, took the work out of Popham's hands. Both Elizabeth and Hatton were violently inflamed against the Stuart Queen, on account of the ridicule she had heaped on the love affair of the Virgin Queen and her Chancellor. Even the learned but apologetic Foss is compelled to say that the warmth of Elizabeth's letters to Hatton "would be fatal to the character of a less exalted female." On the trial of Knightley, a Puritan, who in temperate language had published some observations on the due observance of the Sabbath, Popham contended that the defendant, though guilty only of a technical violation of a royal proclamation and for that reason not guilty of an indictable offence, could yet be prosecuted in the Star Chamber. He sagely observed as to the defendant's excuse for publishing his pamphlet: "Methinks he is worthy of greater punishment for giving such a foolish answer as that he did it at his wife's desire." When Popham became Lord Chief Justice he showed his prejudice against his former calling by an unexampled severity against highwaymen. On the trial of Essex he curiously mingled the functions of witness and judge, and in his summing up out of his own knowledge furnished the jury with statements of fact that had not been testified to by any witness. By his exertions at the bar he accumulated an immense estate amounting to ten thousand pounds a year; but it was all squandered by his son, another John Popham.

One court—the Court of Requests—that fulfilled a very important function during this period has long been forgotten. It was a court for civil causes—a companion court to the Star Chamber (which devoted itself to criminal cases). Its duty was to hear the causes of those suitors who were denied justice in the common law courts. Wolsey established one branch of the court at Whitehall, while another branch followed the sovereign. Wolsey's fame as a churchman has wholly obscured his high reputation as a judge. In the court of chancery, in spite of his manifold duties as Prime Minister, he was regular and punctual, and his decrees were invariably sound. He made the Court of Requests emphatically a court to redress the injustice of jury trials. Those who failed before juries on account of the corruption of the panel or the power of their adversaries found themselves protected in the Court of Requests, which followed the chancery practice and was not hampered by a jury. Here the tenants of land appealed for justice against their landlords, here the copyholders sought relief against the enclosures of the commons and waste lands of the manors. The Protector Somerset owed his fall to his active intervention against the landholders; and the strict impartiality of Wolsey's justice and the sternness with which he repressed the lawlessness of powerful nobles aided in his destruction. The Court of Requests was in continual collision with the common law courts. Coke invented certain imaginary judgments in order to destroy it. But the court held on, and in 1627 Henry Montague, a grandson of the Chief Justice, a very able lawyer, came to preside in this court, and gave it such a high reputation that it had almost as many suits and clients as the chancery. Blackstone[18] tells us that this court was abolished in 1640; but he is mistaken, for in 1642, in sixteen days' sittings, the court made 556 orders. It passed away in the turmoils of the civil war.

The jealousy of the common law courts toward the chancery culminated in Henry VIII.'s Statute of Uses, which attempted to convert every use or trust in land into a legal estate in the beneficiary; this was followed by the Statute of Enrollments requiring all conveyances of freehold by bargain and sale to be recorded in a public office. But the chancery judges and lawyers soon "drove a coach and four" through this act of Parliament; and by means of a bargain and sale for a lease, which the statute executed, followed by a release, which did not require recording, they abolished livery of seisin, as well as the recording of deeds. The Statute of Uses also abolished all uses to be declared by the feoffor's will. The uses declared in the will had been sedulously protected by the

18. 3 Com. 50.

chancery court. But when this method of devising lands was abolished by the Statute of Uses, it became necessary to pass the Statute of Wills. Both Coke and Bacon thought that the Statute of Uses abolished all devises except those that would have been good at common law as conveyances. But the statute was construed otherwise, and the chancery lawyers imported into wills all these conveyances to uses, and thus let in the various kinds of executory devises—estates that in wills rendered nugatory all the common law rules as to remainders. All this history shows the futility of attempting to control a natural development, by means of statutes.

In many ways the years of the first two Stuart kings are the saddest in the history of the law. The servility of the judges was no less marked than under the Tudors. As an added evil, judicial offices were openly made the subject of bargain and sale. Henry Montague gave to Buckingham's nominee the clerkship of the court, worth four thousand pounds a year.[19] Coventry paid Coke two thousand angels for his influence in securing a judicial appointment. The chiefship of the Common Pleas cost Richardson seventeen thousand pounds. Sir Charles Caesar paid fifteen thousand pounds for the mastership of the rolls. Henry Yelverton gave the King four thousand pounds for the office of attorney-general—a place for which Ley, afterwards Chief Justice, vainly offered ten thousand pounds. Judge Nichols refused to pay for his place, and James I. always referred to him as "the judge that would give no money." The fifteen serjeants called in 1623 each paid the King five hundred pounds. Under Cromwell, the pious Lord Chief Justice St. John had the granting of all pardons to delinquent lawyers, which netted him forty thousand pounds; nor did he scruple to receive bribes for places under the Protector. Under James II., the young daughters of the leading citizens of Salisbury, who had strewed flowers before the rebel Monmouth, being technically guilty of high treason, obtained pardons by paying money to the Queen's maids of honor, to whom the King had given the pardons.

---

19. Perhaps we ourselves have as yet no right to condemn this, when we still see in some regions masterships in chancery turned over to the successful political party to be filled.

That great and good man William Penn acted as the agent of the needy ladies in collecting the tribute.

The tone of adulation used by lawyers and judges toward the sovereign is almost incredible. Rich compared Henry VIII. "for justice and prudence, to Solomon; for strength and fortitude, to Samson; and for beauty and comeliness, to Absalom." Bacon in a learned treatise felicitates James I. (who was little better than a drooling idiot), upon the deep and broad capacity of his mind, the grasp of his memory, the quickness of his apprehension, the penetration of his judgment, his lucid method of arrangement, and his easy facility of speech. The virtuous Coke claimed that King James was divinely illuminated by the Almighty. But this was the tone of the age. To Shakespeare, Elizabeth was "a fair vestal" and "a most unspotted lily."

The vices of the age are summed up in the rivalry of its two greatest lawyers, Bacon and Coke—the latter, the most learned of lawyers, but narrow, cruel, and unscrupulous; the other, of large insight, capacious intellect, but also little troubled by scruples.

Coke, the elder of the two men, was Solicitor-General, with a large practice and ample fortune, when Bacon, with his great family advantages, tried to gain the office of Attorney-General against him. Coke stood in the line of preferment. He bitterly resented Bacon's nickname of the "Huddler"—not an undeserved name for the author of a book like Coke upon Littleton. Next they became rivals for the hand of the widow of Sir William Hatton, a beautiful woman, only twenty years old, with an immense fortune and great pretensions to fashion. The old and wrinkled Coke, a six months' widower, prevailed. But while the lady was willing to marry Coke, she refused to espouse such an elderly scarecrow at a church wedding. So Coke married her in a private house, and thereby violated the law. His plea when prosecuted was ignorance of the statute. Perhaps this is the real reason for Coke's oft quoted statement as to statute law. But Bacon made a fortunate escape, and had the satisfaction of enjoying Coke's domestic infelicities. Lady Hatton refused, after several quarrels, to live with Coke; she further refused to take his name, which she insisted on spelling "Cook." She refused even to let Coke see the daughter she had borne him, and turned him away from her door.

Then Essex's trial came on. Coke surpassed even himself in brutality, while Bacon deserted his benefactor. The two men soon had a public altercation in the Exchequer Court. To curry favor with the new king, James, Coke prosecuted Raleigh so savagely that even the judges sickened. The remorseless Popham protested, and such a sycophant as Lord Salisbury rebuked Coke. Thereupon Coke sat down in a chafe and sulked, until the judges urged him to go on. Lord Mansfield said long afterwards: "I would not have made Sir Edward Coke's speech against Sir Walter Raleigh to gain all Coke's estate and reputation." When Coke prosecuted the Gunpowder Plot conspirators, he showed to the full his cowardly method of insulting the prisoners. Other trials were no less disgraceful. Yet, all through, worse than Coke's brutality, is his pharisaical self-satisfaction, his pitiable, snivelling, hypocritical piety. The best excuse for Bacon is that he was engaged in a rivalry with such a man.

Coke became Lord Chief Justice of the Common Pleas in 1606, and used his place to humble and coarsely insult Bacon. But Bacon's suppleness was ingratiating him with the King. Coke had become so puffed up that he was growing independent. Bacon induced James to put Coke at the head of the King's Bench. Coke bitterly reproached Bacon, who replied: "Ah, my Lord, you have grown all this while in breadth; you must needs grow in height, or else you would be a monster." Coke on the bench was fully as brutal as at the bar. In one case he told the jury that the defendant, Mrs. Turner, had the seven deadly sins—that she was a whore, a bawd, a sorcerer, a witch, a papist, a felon and a murderer.

At last Coke engaged in his famous controversy with Lord Chancellor Ellesmere, over the power of the Chancery to enjoin proceedings at law, and drew forth the masterly opinion in the famous case of the Earl of Oxford.[20] Coke threatened to imprison everybody concerned; but Bacon persuaded the King that Coke was in the wrong, and the King's Bench submitted. Bacon finally caused Coke to be suspended from office, and to be ordered to correct his book of reports, "wherein be many extravagant and exorbitant opinions set down and published for positive and good law."

20. 2 White and Tudor Lead. Cas. Equity 601.

Bacon now succeeded Ellesmere as Lord Chancellor. But Coke, at the age of sixty-six, was not yet defeated. He had a young and pretty daughter; her he offered as a bride to Sir John Villiers, the brother of Buckingham. Coke's wife fled with her child; but Coke pursued her, tore the child from her mother's arms, and carried her off to London. Bacon was unable to help Lady Hatton. The mother in prison was compelled to submit, and the child, after a splendid marriage, was handed over to Sir John Villiers. The marriage turned out as might have been expected. The young wife eloped with Sir Robert Howard. Her only son was declared illegitimate, and did not receive the name of Villiers.

Coke received no reward for his unexampled baseness. He tried to make his peace with the King by a number of disgraceful judgments in the Star Chamber. But when his efforts met no return, he had himself returned to Parliament as a patriot. Dr. Johnson must have had Coke in mind when he made his famous definition of patriotism as "the last refuge of a scoundrel." Thirsting for revenge on Bacon, Coke caused his impeachment and ruin. Coke lived on to be a very old man. Lady Hatton lent humor to the situation by constantly complaining of her husband's good health. At last he died, watched over by his unfortunate daughter. He made an exceedingly pious end—thus exhibiting his total unconsciousness of his own true character.

Under Charles I., some ably conducted trials took place over the King's attempt to raise a revenue without recourse to Parliament. The bar was independent enough to hold out against the power of the Crown. The judges ruled that a commitment specifying no offense was bad. Another decision prohibited torture of prisoners. The rules of evidence were not yet settled; but in the ordinary criminal trials, a defendant was now held not bound to give evidence against himself. Shakespeare seems to think the rule a bad one, not to be followed in the Court of Heaven; for

> "In the corrupted currents of this world,
> Offence's gilded hand may shove by justice;
> And oft 'tis seen the wicked prize itself
> Buys out the law; but 'tis not so above;
> *There* is no shuffling, there the action lies

In his true nature; and we ourselves compell'd,
Even to the teeth and forehead of our faults,
To give in evidence."

In the famous Ship Money case of Hampden there was a great forensic display. The Solicitor General spoke for three days, the defendant's
leader spoke four days, Oliver St. John for the defense took two days, and
the Attorney General replied in three days. St. John's argument was considered the finest that had ever been heard in Westminster Hall. But this
speech was soon surpassed by the noble and pathetic plea of Strafford in
his own behalf. At last the King himself was put upon trial. The leading
Parliamentary lawyers, Rolle, St. John, and Whitelock, refused to sit in
the court. Bradshaw, an able lawyer, was made Lord President of the illegal tribunal. The King's line of defense was laid out for him by Sir
Matthew Hale. Bradshaw tried to bully the King, but was overwhelmed
by acute reasoning, a royal dignity, and a noble presence, by the King's
liberality of thought and real eloquence. In other trials, such as those of
the Duke of Hamilton, the Earl of Holland, Lord Capel, and Sir John
Owen, the defendants were convicted by conduct as arbitrary as anything under the Tudors. Serjeant Glyn at the trial of the gallant
Penruddock rivalled Coke at Sir Walter Raleigh's trial. The Protector
Cromwell cared little for courts or law. The very men who had declaimed
against ship money saw Cromwell's arbitrary taxation. Chief Justice
Rolle and the judges attempted to try the legality of such a tax; but
Cromwell sent for them and severely reprehended their license, speaking
with ribaldry and contempt of their Magna Charta. He dismissed the
judges, saying that they should not suffer lawyers to prate what it would
not become them to hear. Serjeant Maynard, who had argued against the
tax, was committed to the Tower, while Prynne suffered a fine and imprisonment. Sir Matthew Hale was threatened by Cromwell's government for his strong defense of the Duke of Hamilton and Lord Capel,
but Hale replied that he was pleading in support of the law, was doing
his duty to his clients, and was not to be daunted by threatenings. During
the Cromwellian ascendancy, Hale, at the solicitation of the Royalist
lawyers, accepted a judgeship. On the circuit he tried and condemned
one of Cromwell's soldiers for the murder of a Royalist, and had the

prisoner hanged so quickly that Cromwell could not grant a reprieve. He quashed a panel of jurors when he found that it had been returned at Cromwell's orders. The Protector, on Hale's return to London, soundly berated him, telling him that he was not fit to be a judge.

Many legal reforms were projected during the Commonwealth, but they came to naught at the Restoration. An attempt was made (among others) to substitute the law of Moses for the common law. There was an earnest attempt to abolish the Court of Chancery, but it was frustrated by St. John. An act was passed regulating chancery practice, but it was found to be impracticable. Most of the better class of lawyers were Royalists and ceased court practice. Confiscation and seizures were the order of the day. But the Royalist conveyancers, Orlando Bridgman and Jeffrey Palmer, while they would not appear in court, enjoyed an immense chamber practice and by their new devices of family settlements, superseding entails, preserved many a Royalist estate.

The Inns of Court during the Tudor and earlier Stuart reigns had continued to enjoy great prosperity. From Fortescue's time to Charles I., it is almost impossible to point to a single lawyer of standing who had not been preliminarily educated at Oxford or Cambridge. In the reign of Queen Mary attorneys and solicitors were forever excluded from the Inns. Henceforth only barristers were trained in those institutions, and attorneys became objects of contempt. In fact, in an order in 16 Charles II., an attorney is called "an immaterial person of an inferior character." The instruction in the Inns continued to be the same as in Fortescue's time. The law was now all case-law. Fitzherbert says that the whole Court agreed that Bracton was never taken for an authority in our law. In social entertainments the Inns shone. Costly feasts, magnificent revels, masks, and plays, where the royal family attended, the splendid celebrations of calls of serjeants, the feasts given by the readers, are all fully described in contemporary annals. We read of "spiced bread, comfits and other goodly conceits, and hippocras," and the bill of supply of one of the feasts, comprising "twenty-four great beefs," "one hundred fat muttons," "fifty-one great veales," "thirty-four porkes," "ninety-one piggs," through endless capons, grouse, pigeons and swans to three hundred and forty dozen larks, shows that the vice of the time was gluttony.

It was found necessary during this period to restrain the students. Some of the regulations are curious—the prohibition of beards of over a fortnight's growth, of costly apparel, of the wearing of swords; and the restraints on sports point to unruly members in the Inns. It was found necessary to make attendance at the moots compulsory. The standard of attainment was raised. Ten years' attendance was required before a call to the bar; this was afterwards put back to five years, and then raised to seven; and for three years after his call, a barrister was not permitted to practice before the courts at Westminster.

The Commonwealth time was almost destructive of the Inns, but at the Restoration they started on a new career of splendor. All the old ceremonies and practices were revived. Heneage Finch, afterwards Lord Nottingham, revived the readers' feasts of former days. He saved the Temple walk from being built upon; and his daily consumption of wine offered an admirable example to the deep drinking young blades of the Restoration.

The two great lawyers of Charles II.'s reign were almost exact opposites. Finch, born of an ancient family, of ample fortune, living in magnificent style, princely in his expenditures, a genuine cavalier, was the very antithesis of the Puritanism of Hale. His is one of the noted names on the roll of Christ Church at Oxford. He is the second of our great forensic orators. Ben Jonson has told us of Bacon's impressive and weighty eloquence, but it could not be compared with the silver-tongued oratory and the graceful gestures of the "English Roscius." Finch passed through the grade of Solicitor-General, to the Attorney-General's place, and then became Lord Chancellor, with the title of Lord Nottingham. He was a model of judicial decorum, calm and patient in hearing, prompt in the business of his court, sitting to decide cases while racked with the pain of gout. Careful in the framing of his judgments, and at the same time, a finished man of the world, he stands unrivaled except by Lord Mansfield.

When he came to the marble chair, equity jurisprudence was a confused mass of unrelated precedents. While he invented nothing new, he introduced order into the chaos and settled the great heads of equity in their enduring form.

"Our laws that did a boundless ocean seem,
Were coasted all, and fathomed all by him."

He settled, finally, the restraint upon executory interests, by his great ruling in the Duke of Norfolk's case.[21] It has been forgotten that Nottingham overruled the three chiefs of the common law courts—North, Pemberton and Montague—sitting with him. North, becoming Chancellor, reversed the case, but the House of Lords, at the instance of Lord Jeffreys (as great a lawyer as Nottingham), restored the first ruling, and reëstablished the rule against perpetuities.

Sir Matthew Hale is not such an engaging figure. He was rather a Puritan, and for thirty-six years never missed attendance at church on Sunday. He was Lord Chief Baron after the Restoration, and then Lord Chief Justice. In mere learning he was without a rival. Lord Nottingham has generously spoken of Hale's "indefatigable industry, invincible patience, exemplary integrity, and contempt for worldly things," and Nottingham adds, in his stately way: "He was so absolutely a master of the science of law, and even of the most abstruse and hidden parts of it, that one may truly say of his knowledge in the law what Saint Augustine said of Saint Jerome's knowledge of the divinity—"Quod Hieronymus nescivit, nullus mortalium unquam scivit." Hale's preface to Rolle's Abridgment contains the most helpful words ever addressed to students of law. The criticism, however, was urged against him that he dispatched business too quickly. And it is almost incredible that he believed in witchcraft with the utmost ignorant superstition, and tried and caused to be executed two poor old women, whom a foolish jury under his direction convicted of diabolical possession.[22] It was but a few years later that another woman was tried for witchcraft before Judge Powell, a merry and witty old gentleman. Her offence was that she was able to fly. "Can you fly?" asked the judge. The crazy woman replied that she could. "Well, then," he said, "you may, for there is no law against flying." And so ended the trial.

A character of those times was the learned Prynne, an able lawyer, a great antiquarian authority. He assaulted everything, from long hair and

21. 3 Ch. Cas. 1.
22. 6 State Trials 647.

actresses to bishops. First he lost his ears, then he was disbarred and condemned to the pillory. Again he lost what little of his ears had been left from the first shaving. He attacked the Quakers, then he suffered imprisonment under Cromwell; next he advocated the proceeding against the regicides, even against those who were dead, and at last rounded out his career as keeper of the records in the Tower. Equal to Prynne in fearless constancy was Judge Jenkins, the author of Jenkins' Centuries—a most curious series of reports.

It is customary to represent the succession of judges under James II. to the time of the Revolution of 1688 as a most ignorant, depraved, and worthless set of men. But this picture is badly overdrawn. It is true that the stately and dignified Cavaliers, like Lord Clarendon or Nottingham, were passing away, and that their successors were hardly their equals. Scroggs, the first Chief Justice, owed his elevation to his ability as a forensic orator. Once from the bench he told the listening mob that "the people ought to be pleased with public justice, and not justice seek to please the people. Justice should flow like a mighty stream, and if the rabble, like an unruly wind, blow against it, the stream they made rough will keep its course." And so Scroggs rolled out his periods, making a splendid plea for judicial independence. It is a sign of the times that high prerogative rulings, which seemed perfectly natural under Elizabeth, should arouse such violent public resentment. Scroggs lost all influence with juries; so he was dismissed, and Francis Pemberton took his place. This man, born to a large fortune, had squandered it within a few years after attaining his majority, and awoke one day to find himself imprisoned under a mass of judgments. But in his five years' imprisonment he made himself a consummate lawyer. He obtained a release from prison, and soon acquired eminence and wealth at the bar.

But not long after Pemberton's elevation to the bench, it was determined to forfeit the charters of the City of London, so as to gain control of the panels of jurors, who were selected by a sheriff, elective under the charters. This advice had been given to the King by the noted special pleader, Edmund Saunders. This remarkable man had had a singular career. Born of humble parents, he had run away from home, drifted to London, and found shelter as an errand boy at Clement's Inn. He learned to write, became a copying clerk, and in this way gained an insight into special pleading. The attorneys induced him to enroll himself at an Inn of Court. In due time a barrister, he made himself the greatest master of common law pleading that system has ever known. He had no political opinions, nor did he seek riches or advancement. Witty, genial and gay, he had always around him a crowd of students, with whom he was putting cases, answering objections and debating abstruse points. His physical appearance was repulsive. Brandy was his constant drink, varied by a pot of ale always near him. Drunkenness and gluttony had caused a general decay of his body. Hideous sores and an offensive stench made his presence an affliction. Yet the government had such need of his services that North, the Lord Keeper, actually asked him to dinner. Saunders drew the pleadings in the great Quo Warranto case, and caused the attorneys for the City of London to plead upon a point where they were sure to be defeated. Thereupon Saunders drew up an ingenious replication, to which the city demurred. Just as the cause was about to be argued Pemberton was removed and Saunders was appointed, and (incredible as it may seem) he then heard argument upon his own pleadings. The cause was argued for two terms, but when, at the third term, judgment was delivered, Saunders lay dying in his lodgings. His best memorial is his book of reports, the most perfect specimen of such work in our legal literature.

Saunders was succeeded, after an interval, by the noted Jeffreys, popularly considered the worst judge that ever sat in Westminster Hall. But this popular belief cannot be taken in place of the sober facts. He was of an ancient family in Wales. He received the usual education of his time, and attended at Trinity College, Cambridge. He studied at the Middle Temple, and was admitted to the bar at the age of twenty. He at once leaped to a commanding position. He was made Common Serjeant, and later Recorder of London. This was due to his splendid legal talents. He had one of those rare minds which under great masses of evidence seize upon the real issue. He had a marvelous skill in advocacy, and a flowing, impassioned, magnetic eloquence. Added to this was an overwhelming bitterness of denunciation that sometimes appalled his hearers. We know that Sir Matthew Hale was a good judge of lawyers, and we are told that Jeffreys gained as great an ascendancy over Hale as ever counsel had over a judge.

To his intellectual gifts, Jeffreys added a noble and stately presence. There are three portraits of him; the first represents him when thirty years old, the next is of Jeffreys in his full robes as Lord Chief Justice, the last shows us the man in his robes as Chancellor. It is a very noble, delicate, and refined face that looks out from Kneller's canvas. There is birth, breeding, distinction in every line. He must have been a great lawyer; for to Hale's testimony we may add that of the accomplished judge, a confirmed Whig, Sir Joseph Jekyll; of Speaker Onslow, who bears testimony to his ability and uprightness in private matters; of Roger North, who hated Jeffreys but was forced to admit: "When he was in temper and matters indifferent came before him, he became his seat of justice better than any other I ever saw in his place." But best witnesses of all are his recorded judgments. The incomparable stupidity of Vernon, the reporter, has destroyed the value of Eustace vs. Kildare and of Attorney General vs. Vernon;[23] but his decision in the East India Company's case is admitted by all lawyers to be a marvel of close legal reasoning. In the House of Lords he saved the Duke of Norfolk's case, and even his political enemies after the Revolution did not reverse his cases. A master of the common law, he was yet a great chancellor. He promulgated a set of rules in chancery, the best since Bacon's time. Other of his decisions can be found in the reports of Sir Bartholomew Shower, an excellent lawyer.

No doubt Jeffreys was a hard drinker. So was Lord Eldon, so were many able lawyers in our own country. He was no doubt savage and overbearing at times. He rode roughshod over defendants and their counsel. He hated Puritans and all their works. He was often cruel and remorseless. But even Lord Hale enlivened trials by breaking forth upon witnesses: "Thou art a perjured knave, a very villain! Oh, thou shameless villain!" Jeffreys' "Bloody Assizes" is the greatest stain on his memory; but no innocent person was punished in those trials. The worst that can be said of Jeffreys may be read in Macaulay's History. Much of it is true;

23. 1 Vernon 419, 369.

some of it is untrue; but it all belongs to the spirit of that age of savage disputes and rancorous political hatreds. Yet, after all, Jeffreys was but one of the five judges who sat together on that circuit.

To see Jeffreys at his best, we should see him in the trial of Lord Grey de Werke. Jeffreys' skill and adroitness in putting in the evidence against the great Whig lord, the brazen seducer of his own wife's sixteen-years-old sister; his gentleness and exquisite suavity toward his witnesses, his few words of apology to the court for the tears of the victim's mother, are models of forensic decorum. In his tact, his delicate management, never a word too much, now and then putting a question to bring out some point that had been overlooked, Jeffreys shows throughout the skill of the master.

He prosecuted Lord William Russell and convicted him. His great arts of advocacy simply overwhelmed the defendant; for Russell had a fair trial, and the jury was calmly charged by Pemberton. Jeffreys as judge tried Algernon Sidney, who was convicted upon evidence. Nothing in Jeffreys' career can compare with Coke's conduct at Raleigh's trial, or with Glyn's when he judicially murdered Penruddock. Even in Lady Lisle's case, she was condemned on actual, credible testimony, offered in accordance with the rules of evidence.

When Jeffreys returned from his campaign in the west he was made Lord Chancellor and given a peerage. Wright succeeded as Lord Chief Justice, and before him came on the famous trial of the Seven Bishops. The besotted King attempted to abolish the Test Acts by proclamation. Both dissenters and churchmen united against a declaration which would tolerate Roman Catholics. The bishops remonstrated, and the King, against Jeffreys' advice, caused the bishops to be indicted. The trial came on before the King's Bench. The defense mustered a great array of counsel. Pemberton, a cashiered chief justice, Levinz, another dismissed judge, who had gone the bloody circuit with Jeffreys, Heneage Finch, son of Lord Nottingham, and Somers, afterwards the great Chancellor, appeared for the defense. Such a throng never appeared again at a trial in Westminster Hall, until Warren Hastings came back from India to meet an impeachment. The bishops were acquitted, and Wright and his fellows were disgraced.

The King filled up his court again; and the legality of martial law in the army then came on for trial before Chief Justice Herbert. At that day in England, in case of a desertion or mutiny, the army officers were powerless, unless they called in the sheriff. But Chief Justice Herbert refused to yield to the King's wishes, and held that the army could not be governed by martial law. Again the King cleaned out his court. One of his new tools was Christopher Milton (a brother of the poet). The King called upon his judges to hold that the King by proclamation could dispense with acts of Parliament. Jones, the Chief Justice, refused. He told the King that he was mortified to think that his Majesty thought him capable of a judgment which none but an ignorant or dishonest man could give. The King said that he was determined to have twelve lawyers for judges, all of his way of thinking. Jones replied: "Your Majesty may find twelve judges of your mind, but never twelve lawyers." But the King had now exhausted the public indulgence and he was soon in flight to France.

It would perhaps seem, from the record of this period, that little good could have been accomplished in the development of the law. But this inference would be an error. We have noticed, at the opening of this epoch, a general feeling that jury-trial was worthless. The work accomplished by this age was to improve the methods of jury trials so as to make them promotive of justice. The first thing done in this later period was to make the jury independent, by establishing the rule that they could not be fined or imprisoned for what was conceived to be a false verdict. The second improvement was to give the courts power to grant new trials, and thus to place the verdict under the control of the judge. The final improvement was to establish the rules of evidence. These rules were so framed and moulded as to exclude from the jury all testimony which would improperly influence them, or which did not depend for its credibility upon the veracity of a sworn witness. Above all, the jury was required to proceed solely upon evidence offered in open court, which had been subjected to the test of a cross-examination. It was in the bad times of the Stuarts that these rules were settled. Singularly enough, the first case that is authentic, in excluding hearsay, is a decision by Lord Jeffreys. Although the rules of evidence were amplified by Lord Mansfield, they have not been changed, except by statute, from that day to this. The greatest of forensic orators said in Hardy's case: "The rules of evidence are founded in the charities of religion, in the philosophy of nature, in the truths of history, and in the experience of common life." Surely, a generation of lawyers which created and formulated these rules is entitled to some grateful remembrance, and of that generation, the greatest common lawyer was, undoubtedly, the outlawed Jeffreys.

V. The Period of Reform: From William III. to Victoria[24]

As soon as the judges who had served under James II. had been removed, after the Revolution of 1688, a return was made to the old Lancastrian doctrine that judges hold their office during good behavior, not during the pleasure of the crown. Some of the judges who had refused to obey the mandates of the King, and in consequence had suffered dismissal, were now restored. Since the Revolution there has never been a removal of a judge by the executive power, nor a single known instance of a corrupt decision. The overwhelming importance of the House of Commons has since 1688 given the great prizes of the profession to lawyers who have been useful to their party in Parliament. The regular preferment for an able lawyer has been from a seat in the Commons to the solicitor-generalship, then to the attorney-general's place, and finally to the chiefship of one of the law courts or to the office of Lord Chancellor. But the professional and political preferment has invariably come as the reward, not the cause, of professional eminence. Lord

24. The authorities for this period are too numerous to be named here. Lord Campbell's Lives, both of Chief Justices and of Lord Chancellors, are very full. His lives of Mansfield and Eldon are excellent; but his Brougham and Lyndhurst are pitiable. Foss is reliable. Welsby's Lives of Eminent English Judges, Roscoe's Lives of Eminent Lawyers, Cooksey's Life of Somers, Twiss' Life of Eldon, Brougham's Autobiography, Arnould's Memoir of Denman, Martin's Life of Lyndhurst, Atlay's Victorian Chancellors, and Woolrych's Lives of Eminent Serjeants, may be consulted. A Century of Law Reform summarizes the changes made in the law, while Dicey's Law and Opinion in England shows the spirit underlying the legal changes. There are, of course, endless other authorities for this period, including almost innumerable magazine articles. Bowring's edition of Bentham's works, with his Memoirs prefixed, is valuable.

Somers, Sir John Holt, Lord Talbot, and Lord Hardwicke were very great lawyers before they received any political reward. Later Mansfield, Thurlow, Eldon, Erskine, Loughborough, Melville, and Ellenborough had become leaders of the bar, before they entered upon a parliamentary career. In the last century, Lyndhurst, Brougham, Tenterden, Cottenham, Denman, Campbell, Westbury, Cockburn, Selborne, Cairns, Coleridge, and Russell all gained their professional and judicial preferment by great legal attainments. The office of Master of the Rolls has been considered one of the great professional rewards; but the puisne judges in the various common law courts, and later the vice-chancellors, and still later the lords justices of appeal, have not had any immediate connection with parliamentary life.

The wealth of information which we have in regard to lawyers and judges after the Revolution enables us to see far more clearly than in the case of the older judges the characters of the various great lawyers.[25] But no doubt the same phenomena are noticeable in the preferment of lawyers to the bench that we should find in the earlier centuries if we had more accurate information. The race has not always been to the swift nor the battle to the strong. Often a leather-lunged, heavy-witted mediocrity, distancing brilliant competitors, has gained a seat upon the bench. Among the judges and lawyers, the same traits we notice to-day were prevalent in these former times. The jealousies among lawyers, the favoritism of judges toward some chosen member of the bar, are continually appearing. A mediocre individual, uttering dull wooden platitudes from the bench, has gained the reputation of a great judge, because his mind was on a level with that of a majority of the bar, although to the ablest lawyers his stupidity has been a constant irritation. The celebrated advocate, on the other hand, in certain instances, when he has reached the bench, has known too much law for the ordinary practitioner; he has been too quick, has leaped to conclusions, has taken one side or the other, and, unconscious of partiality, has been practically unfit to properly weigh conflicting evidence or authorities. The laborious lawyer, who

25. No attempt will be made here to do anything more than indicate the attitude of great lawyers toward reforms in the law.

has attained the bench, has often begun a hunt for foolish and irrelevant matters, and has impeded business by a morbid inability to formulate his own conclusions. The haughty, impatient, arbitrary, and overbearing judge, insolent to the bar and savage toward the witnesses, has not been wanting. The judge who has proclaimed his desire for less law and more justice, who has brayed about the people's and the poor man's rights, and has violated settled principles and become a judicial demagogue, has needed the rebuke and correction of higher tribunals. Through all judicial history, it is apparent that the true judicial mind, which hears the whole case before it decides, which is capable of suspending judgment until in possession of every consideration of value, which is absolutely unaffected by mere temporary or irrelevant matters, which looks at every case both from the standpoint of the general, fixed, and settled rules of law, but at the same time with an acute sense for right and a real desire to advance justice, is the rarest type of the human intellect.

But one fact about lawyers is a noticeable one. For centuries the common-law lawyers had been a race of men who took little interest in any science outside the common law itself. Noticing this narrowness of mind joined to acute understanding and wide learning in their own field, the great scholar Erasmus had remarked of the lawyers of Henry VII. and Henry VIII., that they were *"doctissimum genus indoctissimorum hominum."* So far as we can ascertain, few of them knew anything of any other system of law. But a change was beginning to appear. Chief Justice Vaughan in Charles II.'s reign was once sitting in his court between his two puisnes, when a question of canon law arose. Both puisnes with some pride at once disclaimed any knowledge of that learning, but the Chief Justice, holding up his hands, exclaimed: "In God's name, what sin have I committed, that I am condemned to sit here between two men, who openly admit their ignorance of the canon law?" Lord Nottingham had illustrated many of his decisions by references to the civil law. Holt obtained the reputation of enormous learning, by his knowledge of the Roman law. In short, from the Revolution onwards it will be found that the greatest of English lawyers are turning to the Roman jurisprudence and grafting its rules upon the indigenous law. Even Bracton comes into his own again, as the one worthy writer upon our jurisprudence.

As we have noted in preceding essays, the law had hitherto attempted its own reform. Without the aid of statutes, the immense array of common-law actions had been transformed into the few actions which we have in contract, in tort, and for the recovery of specific property. The whole chancery system was a natural, not a legislative growth. Even where statutes had attempted some interference with the law, they had produced little result. A fact that is most difficult for the lay mind, or for the inadequately informed legal mind, to comprehend, but is proven by the history of the law, is that the distinctions between law and equity, the distinctions between forms of action, inhere in the very nature of duties and rights and cannot be obliterated by legislation. While the procedure may be generalized, while the forms of actions may be reduced to one general form, while but one tribunal may be provided for applying to a controversy all the relevant rules furnished by the law, nevertheless we must still talk of contract and tort, of law and equity, of damages and specific relief.

The Revolution produced no changes in the legal procedure, except two. The first gave to persons charged with high treason the benefit of counsel and the right to produce witnesses; but as to all defendants prosecuted for felony the age was content to believe that the government would produce all the witnesses and that the presiding judge would act as counsel for the prisoner. The second was a statute of jeofails proposed by the new Chancellor, Lord Somers. Many of the original provisions of the bill were cut out by amendments, but as it passed it contained some improvements. It required a special demurrer to reach errors of form, but the procedure was practically already in that condition. It saved the statute of limitations from running in favor of persons absent from the realm. It gave the creditor the right to sue upon the bond given to the sheriff for the release of the debtor. It prohibited the issuance of process in chancery until the filing of the bill. This last requirement merely enacted a chancery rule of Lord Jeffreys. But a really important feature of the new law was that a defendant was given the right to plead to the declaration as many pleas as he had defences. Another provision enabled the grantee of land to sue a tenant in possession without proving an attornment. There were other provisions of the law, but the foregoing show its general scope. After its passage the energies of reform were exhausted, and all future changes and improvements, until the Benthamite agitation, were made by the judges themselves.

The new Chief Justice, Sir John Holt, had carefully studied the civil law. He was able to introduce much of the law merchant under the guise of custom. Holt's decisions became a part of the common law, although the form in which the change was made rendered it necessary in many of our States to provide by statute for the rights of the indorsee of negotiable paper. Under other heads of the law, the same judge was able to assist the narrow rules of the common law by the enlightened distinctions of the civil law. In Coggs vs. Bernard[26] the mediaeval law of assumpsit, shown in the opinions of the puisnes, met the civil law in the opinion of Holt, and Bracton was rehabilitated by the Chief Justice as an authority in the English law.

The beginnings of a law of agency are apparent in the decisions upon the new business of banking. During the Middle Ages and up to the Restoration, the strong boxes of the merchants and landowners and their bailiffs provided the only banking facilities; but the practice adopted by goldsmiths of keeping the money of depositors, and the use of orders upon goldsmiths, which are our modern bank checks, came into vogue. The notes of goldsmiths began circulating as money, while the Bank of England, which was founded soon after the Revolution, began to issue its notes. The Childs' banking house, originally a goldsmith's shop, still remains as the oldest banking business in England.

The earlier cases[27] treat all questions of agency in the terms of the law of master and servant. Historically, of course, it is impossible to separate the law of servants from that of agents; yet we now recognize the plain distinction in legal usage that the word "servant" is used only in regard to a liability in tort, while the word "agent" is used as to a liability arising out of a contract or its correlative, deceit. The word "agent," borrowed from the continental jurisprudence, gradually came into common use, but the manner of the development of the law of agency has much

26. Ld. Raym, 909.
27. Ward vs. Evans, 2 Salk. 442; Thorald vs. Smith, 11 Mod. 71, 87; Nickson vs. Brohan, 10 Mod. 109.

to do with the confusion which arises even to-day from the failure to discriminate between an agent and a servant, in the above sense.

In 1733, during the chancellorship of Lord King, the lawyers were finally compelled to use their mother tongue. The record now spoke in
English instead of in Latin, and the declaration and subsequent pleadings entered upon the roll now became literal translations of the old
Latin forms. The advocates of the bill were forced to overcome a strong
opposition from the judges. Lord Chief Justice Raymond on behalf of
all the judges opposed the change. In later times both Blackstone and
Ellenborough regretted the Act. Ellenborough asserted that it had a tendency to make attorneys illiterate; but surely a man must be misguided,
indeed, who considers "law Latin" a literary language.

The influence of the civil law was constantly increasing. Lord Talbot,
the best beloved of all the English chancellors, was learned in the civil
law. Lord Hardwicke studied the Corpus Juris Civilis and the Commentaries of Vinnius and of Voet. Lord Camden pursued the same systematic study of the civil law. Many of Thurlow's judgments are adorned by
illustrations taken from the civil law; though it is said that those portions
of his opinions were supplied by the learned Hargrave, who acted as
Thurlow's "devil" for some years.

Yet none of these men did anything for law reform. Hardwicke, as
great a chancellor as Nottingham or Eldon, never proposed a single reform. Henry Fox, speaking of Hardwicke, said: "Touch but a cobweb of
Westminster Hall, and the old spider of the law is out upon you, with all
his younger vermin at his heels." Lord Camden spent his energies in an
attempt to make the jury judges of both law and fact in prosecutions for
libel. In our helplessness in the presence of unjustifiable libels on every
sort of person, we are to-day much inclined to regret his work and the
subsequent legislation. Camden's insistence upon punitive damages has
made a large figure in the subject of our damage law. Lord Thurlow invented and perfected the equitable doctrine as to the separate estate of
married women, which is the basis of to-day's married-women statutes.
Lord Loughborough's attitude toward law reform is defined by his
undisguised horror of Bentham; while Lord Eldon steadily set his face
against every proposal of reform.

The eighteenth century in Europe was the age of a benevolent autocracy in politics and a cultivated optimism in literature. The latter trait is markedly apparent in England in the legal sphere.

The great mass of the nation and of the lawyers was amply satisfied with the English constitution and its laws. The language used by the worshippers of our own constitution is apparently borrowed from the older worship of the English constitution. Blackstone delivered his famous lectures at Oxford in 1763, and published them from 1765 to 1769. In a broad and comprehensive way, with ample learning, he sketched the whole field of the law. The literary charm of his easily flowing periods made his Commentaries general reading among even laymen. Criticism had not demonstrated any of Blackstone's errors or fallacies. Englishmen, reading the lectures, swelled with pride to hear that "of a constitution, so wisely contrived, so strongly raised, and so highly finished, it is hard to speak with that praise, which is so justly and severely its due." After a description of its solid foundations, its extensive plan, the harmony of its parts, the elegant proportion of the whole, Blackstone with impressive eloquence exhorted his countrymen: "To sustain, to repair, to beautify this noble pile, is a duty which Englishmen owe to themselves, who enjoy it, to their ancestors, who transmitted it, to their posterity, who will claim at their hands this the best birthright and the noblest inheritance of mankind."

But even as Blackstone was writing these sonorous periods, two great reformers were at work. One of them, Lord Mansfield, was working by the slow and careful method of judicial legislation. The other, Jeremy Bentham, was storing up that great supply of reforming material, which was to supply Brougham and Romilly in the next generation. Mansfield's work is not found in the statutes; it is recorded in the law reports. Bentham derided the judge-made law, and maintained that all the law should be written on the statute books. Mansfield followed the traditional practice of the English lawyer; Bentham turned to the continental codifiers. Mansfield extended and transformed old principles, building up whole branches of the law by the expansion of accepted rules. Bentham's idea of a change was to wipe out all existing law, by a set of codes whose words should be the sole rule of decision.

William Murray, the first Earl of Mansfield, was born in 1705. The fates conspired to make him the greatest of lawyers. His family was almost the oldest in Scotland. Compared with these de Moravias or Murrays, the Bourbons, the Hapsburgs, and the Hohenzollerns are things of yesterday; even the house of Savoy is not older. A younger branch of the Murray family had the title of Viscount Stormont, and the Chief Justice was a younger son of that house. Early in life he was sent to England, to be educated, and Dr. Johnson always accounted for his marvellous capacity by saying that "much may be made of a Scotchman, if he is caught young." The youth was carefully educated at Winchester School, and then at Christ Church, Oxford. He was entered at Lincoln's Inn, and while there carefully studied the civil law; he always maintained it to be the foundation of jurisprudence. He studied with no less care the common law, but he had no particular reverence for it. Its oracle, Coke, he disliked; but he took pleasure in Bracton and Littleton. He was thoroughly conversant with the commercial code of France. His knowledge of ancient and modern history was singularly accurate and profound. At the same time he cultivated his literary taste by intimate association with men of letters. His physical constitution became robust and enabled him to sustain great labor. His mental faculties were acute and well-trained, his industry untiring, his memory capacious. When we add to these qualifications a marvellous talent for oratory and a voice of silvery clearness, we have described the best qualified man who ever undertook the profession of law.

Eminence at the bar was assured. He rapidly achieved the highest professional and pecuniary success. He passed from the office of Solicitor General to that of Attorney General, and became leader of his party in the House of Commons. He chose as his reward in 1756 the post of Lord Chief Justice, and held the place until his retirement in 1788. His career upon the bench is common knowledge. The law of shipping, of commerce, and of insurance was molded by him. The common-law action of assumpsit was expanded until it embraced a recovery upon almost every sort of pecuniary obligation. The law of evidence he amplified and illustrated, leaning strongly to the view that objections to testimony went rather to the credibility than to the competency of witnesses. By one decision he created the whole law of *res gestae* in evidence. His broad cultivation gave him a singularly free and open mind. He could not endure the laws against dissenters or Roman Catholics. He would not permit a priest to be convicted of celebrating the mass. In the "no popery riots" his mansion was burned by a Protestant mob. Yet Lord George Gordon, who was tried for high treason in assembling the mob, voluntarily chose to be tried before Lord Mansfield. His calm, colorless charge to the jury, no less than Erskine's defense, caused the prisoner's acquittal.

As a trial judge, his demeanor was blameless. His keenness of mind, his great experience, his firm but courteous manner, his great patience, his impartial treatment of all lawyers, his want of passion and enthusiasm, his power of dispatching business, his absolute freedom from all influence, made him an ideal judge. His decisions, with their fine literary finish, combining the polish of the scholar with the learning of a profound lawyer, make the reports of Burrow and Douglas the great repository of leading cases. In the thirty-three years he served on the bench, no bill of exceptions was ever tendered to one of his rulings; counsel being perfectly satisfied that when the motion for a new trial came before the full bench, the evidence would be fairly stated. Another singular fact is that he had but two judgments reversed, either in the Exchequer Chamber or in the House of Lords. Most rarely, too, did he allow a reargument of a case, and generally his decisions were made upon the conclusion of the arguments.

Lord Mansfield was singularly free from one fault that has characterized some of the greatest judges. He showed neither favoritism nor envy toward any of the leaders of the bar. Sir Matthew Hale had Jeffreys for his favorite, while he hated such men as Scroggs and Wright. Jeffreys, while he had no favorite, displayed violent antipathies. Lord Macclesfield took under his patronage Philip Yorke, afterwards Lord Hardwicke, and made his fortune at the chancery bar. Lord Kenyon had his fortune made by Thurlow, for whom he acted as "devil," and by Dunning, many of whose opinions he signed in Dunning's name. Kenyon while Lord Chief Justice was completely under the sway of Erskine, who induced him to charge the jury in one case that the question of libel or no libel was for the jury. Kenyon hated Law (afterwards Lord Ellenborough), and did whatever he could to oppose and humiliate that most accomplished advocate. Law retorted by sneering at Kenyon's bad Latin, his cheap clothes, his parsimonious habits and general lack of gentlemanly accomplishments. Law delighted in addressing Latin quotations to Kenyon on the bench, and the judge, not understanding the Latin, was always in a quandary, whether to be gratified at the tribute to his learning or to resent the quotation as ridiculing some of his defects. Ellenborough while Lord Chief Justice reserved his most caustic utterances for Campbell; but Campbell revenged himself by writing a life of the judge. Lord Eldon had no favorite, but his kindest demeanor was shown, singularly enough, toward Romilly. Lord Tenterden made Scarlett an especial recipient of his favors, and lost no opportunity to put down Copley (afterwards Lord Lyndhurst). Lyndhurst on the bench was without any partiality or enmity among the lawyers. Brougham, himself never any judge's favorite, hated Sugden, afterwards Lord St. Leonards, and missed no opportunity to sneer at his prosiness.

Had there been a succession of judges like Mansfield, the law would not have needed much statutory reforming. But Mansfield was succeeded by Kenyon, a very narrow-minded lawyer, while in the chancery court Lord Eldon was soon to rule supreme. Both of them were accustomed to talk slightingly of the "late loose notions" that had prevailed in Westminster Hall. Not the least debt the profession owes to Mansfield is his persuasion of Blackstone to deliver his lectures at Oxford. Afterwards Mansfield secured Blackstone a place in the Common Pleas. Yet even Blackstone was the chief factor in the Exchequer Chamber in reversing Mansfield's ruling, where he laid his reforming hand upon the ark of the covenant of the real-estate lawyers, and attempted to make the rule in Shelley's case yield to the clearly expressed intent of the testator.

It was after Mansfield's retirement that the echoes of the French Revolution caused those State prosecutions which furnished the opportunity to Erskine to demonstrate his greatness as a forensic orator. It is a singular fact that the greatest English judge and the greatest English advocate were both Scotchmen of high descent. Erskine was a member of the house of the earls of Mar, the oldest title in Europe which has survived to our times. But he had not the fine training of Mansfield. The poverty of his father, the Earl of Buchan, caused Erskine at an early age to enter the army, and it was not until he was twenty-seven that he turned to the law. Again the profession has Mansfield to thank for his advice to the young subaltern. The uninterrupted career of Erskine at the bar justified Mansfield's judgment. Perhaps the world may see again as perfect a forensic orator, but doubtless up to our time the Roman Cicero is the only advocate who can be found to rank with Erskine.

While Mansfield was on the bench, Jeremy Bentham had been writing his epoch-making works. He was the son and grandson of attorneys, members of the inferior grade of the profession. He was educated at Westminster School and at Queen's College, Oxford. At twenty-five he entered Lincoln's Inn. He attended the court of King's Bench and listened, as he tells us, with rapture to the judgments of Lord Mansfield. He heard Blackstone's lectures at Oxford, but he says that he immediately detected the fallacies underlying those smooth periods. Fortunately, he was the possessor of an ample fortune which gave him leisure for study. Becoming disgusted with the profession, and willing to disappoint the wishes of his father, who had hoped that his son's great talents would at last place him in the marble chair, Bentham voluntarily relinquished all effort to take an active part in life, either as a lawyer or legislator, and devoted himself to the study of the subjects upon which legislation ought to act and the principles upon which it ought to proceed. His ample means to employ secretaries saved him from a life of drudgery. He gathered around him a small but brilliant company; prominent among his circle were Romilly, Mackintosh, and Brougham, the exponents of his views of legal reform.

Bentham's legal reforms were but a small part of his activity. He was a philosopher, who claimed by his one principle to have solved the puzzle of human life and destiny. His utilitarian formula of the greatest happiness of the greatest number is but a restatement of the tenet of a Grecian school of philosophy. The lawyers for centuries had been applying the principle under the form of their maxim, "*salus populi est suprema lex.*" It was this dogma that gave a practical aspect to Bentham's views of law reform. He is one of the few reformers of law who was widely read and instructed in the matter he was trying to reform. He had the capacity of the jurist to grasp legal principles, but with keen logic and inventive mind, he threw a flood of new light upon old stock notions in the law. Having mastered the practical doctrines of the law he took (in Brougham's phrase) "the mighty step of trying the whole provisions of our jurisprudence by the test of expediency." He tested its rules and arrangements by the circumstances of society, the wants of men, and above all by the promotion of human happiness.

Long years of study are contained in Bentham's writings on legislation. In 1776, at the age of thirty-two, he published his Fragment on Government, of which Lord Loughborough said that it formulated a dangerous principle. His Principles of Morals and Legislation came out in 1789. His Art of Packing was published in 1821. His Rationale of Judicial Evidence saw the light in 1827, when he was seventy-nine. These works give but a small part of his labors on the law; bold and hardy indeed is the man who will undertake to read all that Bentham wrote upon the deficiencies of our legal system.

He had little respect for the law as he found it. The separate jurisdictions of law and equity were to him an absurdity. A bill in chancery he characterized as a volume of notorious lies. The technical common law procedure and the occult science of special pleading were relics of barbarism. He assaulted the rules excluding the testimony of parties and interested witnesses. His zeal to moderate the criminal law was a matter of humanity. The jury system did not meet his entire approval. He advocated local courts presided over by a single judge trained to judicial work, without a jury, except when specially demanded, and then only as a security against class feeling, governmental oppression or corruption. At first he was ignored by the profession as a foolish and visionary man, who put his ideas in very bad English. He did manage to secure an act against cruelty to animals, and this was all. Yet when he died in 1832 he was revered as the founder of modern legislation.

His disciples devoted themselves to his practical reforms on the side of the most important part of the law—the means which it provides for the enforcement of rights and the redress of wrongs.[28] Easily accessible courts, a cheapening of legal remedies, and the prevention of delays, were proposed as matters of the first moment. Judicial evidence was to be regulated, so that it would be certain that all the testimony could be heard. Pleadings were to be curtailed and simplified, fictions were to be abolished, sham pleadings made impossible, and all distinctions in forms of actions and in the jurisdiction of courts were to be swept away. For "glittering generalities" Bentham's mind had no tolerance. He dissected with more or less severity the fallacies of our Declaration of Independence. He refuted the so-called self-evident truths that all men are created equal, that they are endowed with certain inalienable rights, among them the right to life, liberty, and the pursuit of happiness.

The struggle for reform had been initiated by Sir Samuel Romilly, in his effort to mitigate the penal code. Year after year Romilly passed his bill through the Commons; but it always failed in the Lords before the opposition of Eldon and Ellenborough. Eventually he must have succeeded, but his wife's death in 1818 plunged him into such profound grief that in a moment of madness he took his own life. His practice at the bar was solely in the chancery court. The favor of Lord Eldon made him the leading chancery barrister. We have preserved to us the substance of his argument in a great leading case.[29] Lord Cottenham, after-

28. One change in the law, which once seemed a very important matter in England, had been made before the reformers set to work. The judges of England had uniformly held that in a prosecution for libel the jury passed upon the facts, the court upon the law. The construction of the written document, whether it was libellous or not, was according to well-settled principles a question for the court. The matters of fact, as to whether the defendant had published the libel and whether its references were to the persons and things stated in the indictment or information, were for the jury. But as long as the jury rendered a general verdict of not guilty, there was presented a chance to the jury to find a verdict of not guilty, upon the ground that, although the publication was found and the innuendoes proven, the document was in fact no libel. The judges had tried to escape this dilemma by putting to the jury the question of publication and of the truth of the innuendoes, but Fox's Libel Act provided, in effect, that the jury should pass upon both fact and law.

29. Hugenin vs. Baselee, 14 Ves. 273.

wards, speaking from the bench[30] of Romilly's celebrated reply, said: "From the hearing of it, I received so much pleasure, that the recollection of it has not been diminished by the lapse of more than thirty years." Romilly's winning personality, his charming manners, his uprightness and love of humanity, his really marvellous eloquence, make him one of the most interesting figures at the English bar. His son Lord Romilly, the well-known Master of the Rolls, has made the name a noted one in the judicial records.

A greater than Romilly now took up the burden of reform. Henry Brougham was, perhaps, at certain times, the most effective orator of the first half of the nineteenth century; but he was never a close and accurate lawyer. He had nothing like the success at the bar of Law, the defender of Warren Hastings, or of Erskine. He had neither steadiness nor application in ordinary practice. But he was the foremost figure in the most celebrated trial of the century. When George IV. attempted to rid himself of his wife, Caroline of Brunswick, by a bill of pains and penalties, she was defended by Brougham, Denman, and Wilde, while John Singleton Copley assisted in the prosecution. All of them attained the highest honors; three of them were chancellors and one a lord chief justice. Both Brougham and Denman on that trial made splendid speeches, but the finest argument from a lawyer's standpoint was Copley's.

Romilly, Brougham, and Mackintosh found the greatest obstacle to their work for law reform to be the presence of Lord Eldon in the House of Lords. Eldon himself had smarted under the attempts to reform his own court of chancery. His long chancellorship had witnessed a great increase in the business of the chancery court. His excessive deliberation clogged the calendar with unheard cases. Many suitors in despair abandoned their cases. Even when a cause had been heard, the decision was long in coming, while the vast expense of chancery proceedings was frightfully oppressive. Regularly, at the opening of each Parliament, Michael Angelo Taylor made his motion for an investigation of Eldon's court. After Taylor gave up the fight, a barrister named John Williams

30. Dent vs. Russell, 4 Myl. & Cr. 277.

took up the annual motion. In the debates the chancery court was roughly handled, although Eldon, as a judge, received every man's praise. Lord Eldon was much annoyed at the complaints, but he resolutely opposed all change in his own court as well as in the common law courts. It perhaps is to his credit that he actually concurred in abolishing trial by battle; but he contested the statute taking away the death penalty for larceny. He opposed all changes in the law of real property. He lamented the bill abolishing fines and common recoveries, and even Sugden, the great authority on real-estate law, pronounced the new plan impossible. The bill abolishing sinecure offices in the chancery and simplifying certain chancery proceedings caused Eldon such anguish that he wrote that he would not go down to Parliament again. Railroads he denounced as dangerous innovations. The abolishment of rotten boroughs was to him a shocking invasion of vested rights. He exclaimed over the Reform bill: " 'Save my country, Heaven,' is my morning and evening prayer, but that it can be saved, cannot be hoped." The proposal to abolish the difference between wills of real and personal property excited Eldon's greatest alarm. He frustrated the efforts of Romilly to mitigate the penal code. He resented reforms in the common law procedure as encroachments upon equity. In the general domain of politics Eldon was the same sort of obstructionist. He bitterly opposed the repeal of the Test Act, and when it was proposed to remove the disabilities of Roman Catholics, he declared in the House of Lords: "If I had a voice that would sound to the remotest corner of the Empire, I would re-echo the principle that, if ever a Roman Catholic is permitted to form part of the legislature of this country, or to hold any of the great executive offices of the government, from that moment the sun of Great Britain is set forever." Such was the attitude toward reform of the man who, if we look alone at the substance of his decisions, must be called the greatest English chancellor.

After Brougham had quarreled with his party, the burden of passing the bills for the promised legal reforms fell upon Sir John Campbell. The ablest opponent of many of these measures was the Conservative leader, Lord Lyndhurst. This great man was born in Boston just before the Revolution. His father was the painter Copley, his mother a daughter of that unfortunate Boston merchant whose cargo of tea was dumped into Boston harbor.[31] Lyndhurst was taken to England, educated at Cambridge, and called to the bar from Lincoln's Inn; he slowly worked his way to the head of the profession. On the Queen's trial he summed up the evidence in a speech which as a piece of legal reasoning far excels Brougham's or Denman's. As a judge he demonstrated that he was gifted with the finest judicial intellect that England can show in the nineteenth century. We are interested here solely in his attitude toward reforms in the law.

When Attorney General he had proposed a bill for reforming the chancery court, which as all parties were compelled to admit, stood in need of reform. In 1826 he made a great speech against allowing counsel for the accused in trials of felony to address the jury; but a few years later he concurred in such a change in the law. It should be remembered that Justice Park threatened to resign if a bill allowing counsel to the accused were passed, and that twelve of the fifteen judges strongly condemned the enactment. Most of the judges opposed the provision allowing defendants in criminal cases to produce witnesses.

In the debates on the Reform Bill there appears a practice in one of the rotten boroughs which throws a curious light on prevalent political morality. Lyndhurst, amidst the laughter of his hearers, read that part of the evidence which showed that Campbell, the eminent reformer, had paid for his election by the Stafford constituency, to five hundred and thirty-one out of five hundred and fifty-six electors, the sum of three pounds ten shillings for a single vote, and six pounds for a plumper. Campbell's defence was that, "this could not properly be called bribery, for he had simply complied with the well-known custom of paying 'head money,' and the voter received the same sum on whichever side he voted." During another debate Lyndhurst condemned the practice of chancery counsel in going from one court to another, and being actually engaged in carrying on causes of importance in two courts at the same time. But this sort of evil was no less marked in the common law courts.

31. This act of larceny is usually described as an outburst of patriotism.

Lyndhurst opposed the original county court bill, which after many changes and improvements has proved of such value in England; yet Lyndhurst appointed both the commission to enquire into the law of real property and another commission to investigate common law procedure. In 1852, when the Common Law Procedure Act was under discussion, both Lyndhurst and Brougham opposed the bill because it did not sweep away all written allegations. As a general rule, Lyndhurst was a friend to reasonable changes in the law, and most of the later reforms had his able advocacy.

Gradually the chancery court was reformed. Its fees and expenses were first reduced. In accordance with the report of a Chancery Commission composed of such lawyers as Lord Romilly, Turner, James, Bethell, and Page-Wood, the masters in chancery were abolished. Later, issues of law were done away with, and the evidence was required to be taken orally before examiners. Finally, examiners were abandoned for a system of evidence given in the form of affidavit for certain proceedings, or given orally before the judge.

As early as 1843 the law of evidence was changed by Lord Denman's act so as to permit interested witnesses to give testimony. In 1851 a party, as well as the husband or wife of a party, became a competent witness in a civil case. All the common law judges and the Chancellor, Lord Truro (better known as the barrister, Wilde, who appeared with Brougham and Denman for Queen Caroline), opposed the bill. Even Lord Campbell, who gave the act its first trial, said: "It has made a very inauspicious start; one party, if not both parties, having hitherto been forsworn in every cause." Finally, in 1898, the defendant in a criminal case was made a competent witness on his trial.

The original changes in the rules of pleading at common law were made under rules formulated by the judges. In 1860 all common law courts were given equity powers as to all questions at issue before them. This bill was violently opposed by Lord St. Leonards, but was supported by all the common law judges. Power was given to all the common law courts to examine witnesses *de bene esse*, to order the discovery of documents, and to compel an examination of a party by his opponent. In this way the whole distinctive auxiliary jurisdiction of equity was swept away.

Finally, the Judicature Commission made its report, and the two great lawyers, Lord Selborne for the Liberals and Lord Cairns for the Conservatives, proposed and carried the Judicature Act of 1873. All the historical courts of England were combined in a single High Court of Justice. It was given a Chancery Division, a King's Bench Division, a Probate, Divorce and Admiralty Division.[32] Above the High Court of Justice was constituted a Court of Appeal, and from the Court of Appeal a further appeal lay to the House of Lords. All branches of the High Court of Justice were given power to administer both legal and equitable relief, and wherever there was any conflict between the rules of equity and the rules of law, equity was to prevail. Power was given to transfer a cause from one division to another, so that Lord Cairns could say:[33] "The court is not now a court of law or a court of equity, but a court of complete jurisdiction." The result of the Act, it was asserted, "has been in the highest degree satisfactory, and has resulted in flexibility, simplicity, uniformity, and economy of judicial time." The final result of the legislation is said by Lord Bowen to be, "that it is not possible in the year 1887 for an honest litigant in her Majesty's Supreme Court to be defeated by any mere technicality, any slip, any mistaken step, in his litigation." It is curious to note that the learned Foss mournfully recorded the Judicature Act. He deplored it as a restoration of the old Norman *Aula Regis*.

Thus we see that practically the whole of the Benthamite series of reforms has been carried out. In the course of a century, step by step, the whole face of the formal portion of the English law has been changed. And yet, as one looks back on the history of the law, he is compelled to admit that at any given time the system of law was fully as good as was merited by the people whom it governed. The highest and best index to the steady progression of the race is the continued improvement in jurisprudence. To the formalism of the old law we owe it that our substantive law is what it is. The growing rigidity of the common law procedure produced that equity system which borrowed so heavily from the Roman

32. The two additional Divisions of the original Act, Common Pleas and Exchequer, were shortly afterwards abolished.

33. 7 App. Cas. 237.

jurisprudence. To the differing jurisdictions of law and equity we are indebted for a progress which was achieved by the careful weighing of the
one system against the other. Even the rules of evidence which excluded
the testimony of interested witnesses and of parties to the litigation have
borne their full fruit in assisting in the growing veracity of our race. The
cruelties of the criminal law did their work in making our criminal law
the most mercifully administered system of public punishment.

It is more than a coincidence that the reorganized procedure should
begin its career in a new home. In 1882 Westminster Hall was finally
abandoned for the new Courts of Justice. The lawyer who loves the traditions of his profession cannot refrain from regret when he parts with
Westminster Hall, or when he sees the extinction of that ancient Order
of the Coif which had endured for seven hundred years. Appropriately
enough the new Courts stand in the midst of the ancient legal university.
To the north rise the towers of Lincoln's Inn, and across the Strand to
the south stand the Middle and Inner Temple. Surrounded by so many
legal memories, dense, indeed, must be the lawyer who is not moved to
be worthy of that science of administering justice which has written the
most glorious pages of English history.

BIBLIOGRAPHY OF THE

WORKS OF JOHN MAXCY ZANE

Books

Bishop on Criminal Law. 9th ed. 2 vols., Edited by John M. Zane and Carl Zollmann. Chicago: T. H. Flood, 1923.

The Grandeur That Was Rome. Chicago: Caxton Club, 1927.

The Law of Banks and Banking, Including Acceptance, Demand and Notice of Dishonor upon Commercial Paper. Chicago: T. H. Flood, 1900.

Lincoln the Constitutional Lawyer. Chicago: Caxton Club, 1932.

Responsibility of the Lawyer. Chicago: The John Marshall Law School, 1914.

The Story of Law. New York: Ives Washburn, 1927.

Articles

"Address on the Occasion of the Presentation of a Portrait of Elisha Baker to the United States Court of Appeals." *Chicago Legal News* 56 (June 12, 1924): 373–75.

"Attaint." *Michigan Law Review* 15 (1916): 1–20; 127–48.

"Bench and Bar in the Golden Age of the Common Law." *Illinois Law Review* 2 (1907): 1–20.

"Bentham." In *Great Jurists of the World*, ed. Sir John McDonnell and Edward Manson, 532–43. Boston: Little, Brown, 1914.

"The Constitution of Utah." *Report of the Third Annual Meeting of the State Bar of Utah*, 1896, 18–39.

"The Cost of a Democratic Bar." *Illinois Law Review* 8 (1914): 539–42.

"Death of the Drawer of a Check." *Harvard Law Review* 17 (1903): 104–18.

"Dedication Papers: The Significance of the Endowment." *Michigan Law Review* 24 (1925): 150–55.

"Determinable Fees in American Jurisprudence." *Harvard Law Review* 17 (1904): 297–316.

"Five Ages of the Bench and Bar of England," In *Select Essays in Anglo-American Legal History*, vol. 1, 625–729. Boston: Little, Brown, 1907.

"The French Advocate." *Illinois Law Review* 14 (1920): 562–80.

"German Legal Philosophy." *Michigan Law Review* 16 (1918): 287–375.

"An Interesting Ancient Document: *Authenticum* of Justinian Presented to the University of Chicago." *Chicago Legal News* 55 (March 29, 1923): 288.

"A Legal Heresy: Immunity of the Government from the Operation of the Laws." *Illinois Law Review* 13 (1918): 431–62. Reprinted as "A Legal Heresy." *American Law Review* 53 (1919): 801–40.

"A Mediaeval Cause Célèbre." *Illinois Law Review* 1 (1906): 363–73.

"Modern Instance of Zenothemis v. Demon." *Michigan Law Review* 23 (1925): 339–61.

"A Pioneer in Comparative Law" (a tribute to John Wigmore). *Illinois Law Review* 29 (1934): 456–59.

"Problem in Mining Law: Walrath v. Champion Mining Company." *Harvard Law Review* 16 (1902): 94–109.

"A Rare Judicial Service: Charles S. Zane." *Journal of the Illinois State Historical Society* 19 (1926): 31–48.

"Renaissance Lawyers." *Illinois Law Review* 10 (1916): 542–66.

"A Roman Lawyer." *Illinois Law Review* 8 (1914): 575–93.

"A Year Book of Richard II." *Michigan Law Review* 13 (1915): 439–65.

Book Reviews

Review of James Montgomery Beck, *Constitution of the United States: Yesterday, Today, Tomorrow? A.B.A. Journal* 10 (1924): 801–2.

Review of Herbert S. Hadley, *Rome and the World Today. Illinois Law Review* 18 (1923): 270–73.

Review of Emmanuel Hertz, *Abraham Lincoln: A New Portrait. A.B.A. Journal* 18 (1932): 483–84.

Review of William S. Holdsworth, *History of English Law*, 3d ed. *Illinois Law Review* 20 (1925): 319–30.

Review of William S. Holdsworth, *Some Lessons from Our Legal History. A.B.A. Journal* 15 (1929): 511–12.

Review of William S. Holdsworth, *Sources and Literature of English Law. Illinois Law Review* 21 (1926): 423–24.

Review of T. F. T. Plucknett, *Year Books of Richard III. A.B.A. Journal* 16 (1930): 813–14.

Review of Paul Vinogradoff, *Custom and Right. Yale Law Journal* 35 (1925): 1026–28.

Review of Charles Warren, *The Supreme Court in United States History. Illinois Law Review* 17 (1923): 466–83.

Review of Percy Winfield, *Chief Sources of English Legal History. A.B.A. Journal* 12 (1926): 72–73.

Review of Percy Winfield, *History of Conspiracy and Abuse of Legal Procedure. Illinois Law Review* 17 (1923): 402–5.

Review of George E. Woodbine, ed., *Bracton, De Legibus et Consuetudinibus Angliae. Yale Law Journal* 32 (1922): 202–8.

SELECTED BIBLIOGRAPHY

ON LEGAL HISTORY

General Works

Allen, Sir Carleton Kemp. *Law in the Making.* 7th ed. Oxford: Oxford University Press, 1964.

Bellomo, Manlio. *The Common Legal Past of Europe, 1000–1800.* Washington, D.C.: Catholic University of America Press, 1995.

Berman, Harold J. *Faith and Order: The Reconciliation of Law and Religion.* Atlanta: Scholars Press, 1993.

———. *Law and Revolution: The Formation of the Western Legal Tradition.* Cambridge: Harvard University Press, 1983.

Bryce, James Viscount. *Studies in History and Jurisprudence.* 2 vols. Oxford: Oxford University Press, 1901.

Cairns, Huntingdon. *Legal Philosophy from Plato to Hegel.* Baltimore: Johns Hopkins University Press, 1949.

Carter, James Coolidge. *Law: Its Origin, Growth, and Function.* New York: G. P. Putnam's Sons, 1907.

Coing, Helmut. *Europäisches Privatrecht.* 2 vols. Munich: C. H. Beck, 1985–89.

———, ed. *Handbuch der Quellen und Literatur der neueren europäischen Privatrechtsgeschichte.* 3 vols. Munich: C. H. Beck, 1973–88.

Dawson, John P. *Oracles of the Law.* Ann Arbor: University of Michigan Law School, 1968.

Dias, R. M. W. *A Bibliography of Jurisprudence.* 3d ed. London: Butterworths, 1979.

Friedrich, Carl J. *The Philosophy of Law in Historical Perspective.* 2d ed. Chicago: University of Chicago Press, 1963.

Hattenhauer, Hans. *Europäische Rechtsgeschichte*. Heidelberg: C. F. Müller, 1992.

Kelly, J. M. *A Short History of Western Legal Theory*. Oxford: Oxford University Press, 1992.

Lee, Guy Carleton. *Historical Jurisprudence: An Introduction to the Systematic Study of the Development of Law*. London: Macmillan, 1900.

McIlwain, C. H. *Constitutionalism: Ancient and Modern*. Ithaca, N.Y.: Cornell University Press, 1947.

Morris, M. F. *An Introduction to the History of the Development of Law*. Washington, D.C.: John Byrne, 1911.

Pollock, Frederick. *Essays in the Law*. London: Macmillan, 1922.

Pound, Roscoe. *Interpretations of Legal History*. New York: Macmillan, 1923.

Robinson, O. F., T. D. Fergus, and W. M. Gordon. *An Introduction to European Legal History*. Abingdon: Professional Books, 1985.

Seagle, William. *The History of Law*. New York: Tudor Publishing, 1946.

Smith, Munroe. *A General View of European Legal History and Other Papers*. New York: Columbia University Press, 1927.

Van Caenegem, R. C. *An Historical Introduction to Private Law*. Cambridge: Cambridge University Press, 1993.

———. *An Historical Introduction to Western Constitutional Law*. Cambridge: Cambridge University Press, 1995.

Wigmore, John Henry. *A Kaleidoscope of Justice: Containing Authentic Accounts of Trial Scenes from All Times and Climes*. Washington, D.C.: Washington Law Book, 1941.

———. *A Panorama of the World's Legal Systems*. 3 vols. St. Paul: West Publishing, 1928.

Primitive Law

Diamond, A. S. *The Evolution of Law and Order*. Westport, Conn.: Greenwood Press, 1973.

———. *Primitive Law*. 2d ed. London: Longmans, Green, 1950.

———. *Primitive Law, Past and Present*. London: Methuen, 1971.

Elias, Taslim Olawale. *The Nature of African Customary Law*. Manchester: Manchester University Press, 1956.

Gluckman, Max. *The Ideas in Barotse Jurisprudence*. New Haven: Yale University Press, 1965.

———. *The Judicial Process Among the Barotse of Northern Rhodesia*. 2d ed. Manchester: Manchester University Press, 1967.

————. *Politics, Law and Ritual in Tribal Society.* Chicago: Aldine, 1965.

Hartland, E. Sidney. *Primitive Law.* London: J. and J. Harper, 1924.

Hocart, A. M. *Kings and Councillors: An Essay in the Comparative Anatomy of Human Society.* Chicago: University of Chicago Press, 1970.

Hoebel, E. Adamson. *The Law of Primitive Man: A Study in Comparative Legal Dynamics.* Cambridge: Harvard University Press, 1954.

Howell, Paul Philip. *A Manual of Nuer Law: Being an Account of Customary Law, Its Evolution, and Development in the Courts Established by the Sudan Government.* Oxford: Oxford University Press, 1954.

Kocourek, Albert, and John H. Wigmore, eds. *Primitive and Ancient Legal Institutions.* Boston: Little, Brown, 1915.

Krader, Lawrence, ed. *Anthropology and Early Law.* New York: Basic Books, 1967.

Llewellyn, Karl N., and E. Adamson Hoebel. *The Cheyenne Way: Conflict and Case Law in Primitive Jurisprudence.* Norman: University of Oklahoma Press, 1941.

Maine, Henry Sumner. *Ancient Law: Its Connection with the Early History of Society, and Its Relation to Modern Ideas.* 1861. Reprint, Tucson: University of Arizona Press, 1986.

————. *Lectures on the Early History of Institutions: A Sequel to Ancient Law.* 1875. Reprint, Buffalo: W. S. Hein, 1987.

Malinowski, Bronislaw. *Crime and Custom in Savage Society.* 1926. Reprint, Totowa, N.J.: Littlefield, Adams, 1982.

Pospisil, Leonard. *Anthropology and Law: A Comparative Theory.* New York: Harper and Row, 1971.

Reid, John Phillip. *A Law of Blood: The Primitive Law of the Cherokee Nation.* New York: New York University Press, 1970.

Ancient Near Eastern Law, Biblical Law, and Post-Biblical Jewish Law

Amram, David Werner. *Leading Cases in the Bible.* Philadelphia: Julius H. Greenstone, 1905.

Boecker, Hans Jochen. *Law and the Administration of Justice in the Old Testament.* Minneapolis: Augsburg Publishing House, 1980.

Carmichael, Calum M. *Law and Narrative in the Bible: The Evidence of the Deuteronomic Laws and the Decalogue.* Ithaca: Cornell University Press, 1985.

————. *The Origins of Biblical Law: The Decalogues and the Book of the Covenant.* Ithaca: Cornell University Press, 1992.

Daube, David. *Studies in Biblical Law*. Cambridge: Cambridge University Press, 1947.

Derrett, J. Duncan M. *Law in the New Testament*. London: Darton, Longman, and Todd, 1970.

Dorff, Elliot N., and Arthur Rosett. *A Living Tree: The Roots and Growth of Jewish Law*. Albany: State University of New York Press, 1988.

Driver, G. R., and John C. Mills. *The Babylonian Laws*. 2 vols. Oxford: Oxford University Press, 1952–55.

Elon, Menachem. *Jewish Law: History, Sources, Principles*. 4 vols. Philadelphia: Jewish Publication Society, 1994.

Golding, Martin P., ed. *Jewish Law and Legal Theory*. New York: New York University Press, 1993.

Karo, Joseph ben Ephraim. *Jewish Code of Jurisprudence: Talmudical Law Decisions, Civil, Criminal, and Social*. 4th ed. Trans. J. L. Kadushin. 3 vols. New Rochelle, N.Y.: Jewish Jurisprudence, 1923.

Kent, Charles Foster. *Israel's Laws and Legal Precedents: From the Days of Moses to the Closing of the Legal Canon*. New York: Charles Scribner's Sons, 1907.

Maimonides, Moses. *The Code of Maimonides*. 14 vols. New Haven: Yale University Press, 1949–80. See also Isadore Twerski, *Introduction to the Code of Maimonides* (New Haven: Yale University Press, 1980).

Schreiber, Aaron M. *Jewish Law and Decision-Making: A Study Through Time*. Philadelphia: Temple University Press, 1979.

Skaist, Aaron Jacob. *The Old Babylonian Loan Contract: Its History and Geography*. Ramat Gan, Israel: Bar-Ilan University Press, 1994.

Watson, Alan. *Jesus and the Jews: The Pharisaic Tradition in John*. Athens: University of Georgia Press, 1995.

———. *Jesus and the Law*. Athens: University of Georgia Press, 1996.

———. *The Trial of Jesus*. Athens: University of Georgia Press, 1995.

Classical Greek and Roman Law

Alexander, Michael C. *Trials in the Late Roman Republic, 149 B.C. to 50 B.C.* Toronto: University of Toronto Press, 1990.

Bonner, Robert Johnson. *Lawyers and Litigants in Ancient Athens: The Genesis of the Legal Profession*. Chicago: University of Chicago Press, 1927.

Bonner, Robert Johnson, and Gertrude Smith. *The Administration of Justice from Homer to Aristotle*. 2 vols. Chicago: University of Chicago Press, 1930.

Buckland, W. W. *A Text-Book of Roman Law from Augustus to Justinian*. 3d ed. Rev. Peter Stein. Cambridge: Cambridge University Press, 1963.

Buckland, W. W., and Arnold D. McNair. *Roman Law and Common Law: A Comparison in Outline.* 2d ed. Rev. F. H. Lawson. Cambridge: Cambridge University Press, 1965.

Cohen, Edward E. *Ancient Athenian Maritime Courts.* Princeton: Princeton University Press, 1973.

Corpus Juris Civilis. The collection of legal texts issued by the Emperor Justinian. The standard edition is the three-volume work edited by Theodor Mommsen, Paul Krueger, Rudolph Schoell, and Wilhelm Kroll, *Corpus Juris Civilis* (Berlin: Weidmann, 1904–11). The entire *Corpus Juris Civilis* has appeared in a translation by Samuel P. Scott, *The Civil Law,* 17 vols. (1932; reprint, New York: AMS Press, 1973). The Scott translation does, however, contain some serious deficiencies. A modern translation of the *Digest* has been produced under the general editorship of Alan Watson. See *The Digest of Justinian,* 4 vols. (Philadelphia: University of Pennsylvania Press, 1985). For an early translation of the *Institutes* published in the United States, see *The Institutes of Justinian, with Notes by Thomas Cooper* (Philadelphia: P. Byrne, 1812). There is also a modern translation of the *Institutes* by Peter Birks and Grant McLeod. See *Justinian's Institutes* (Ithaca: Cornell University Press, 1987).

Daube, David. *Roman Law: Linguistic, Social and Philosophical Aspects.* Edinburgh: Edinburgh University Press, 1969.

Declareuil, J. *Rome the Law-Giver.* 1927. Reprint, Westport, Conn.: Greenwood Press, 1970.

Frier, Bruce W. *A Casebook on the Roman Law of Delict.* Atlanta: Scholars Press, 1989.

————. *Landlords and Tenants in Imperial Rome.* Princeton: Princeton University Press, 1980.

————. *The Rise of the Roman Jurists: Studies in Cicero's Pro Caecina.* Princeton: Princeton University Press, 1985.

Gagarin, Michael. *Early Greek Law.* Berkeley: University of California Press, 1986.

Garner, Richard. *Law and Society in Classical Athens.* London: Croom Helm, 1986.

Greenidge, A. H. J. *A Handbook of Greek Constitutional History.* London: Macmillan, 1896.

————. *The Legal Procedures of Cicero's Time.* 1901. Reprint, South Hackensack, N.J.: Rothman Reprints, 1971.

Harrison, Alick Robin Walsham. *The Law of Athens.* 2 vols. Oxford: Oxford University Press, 1968–71.

Jolowicz, H. F. *Roman Foundations of Modern Law.* 1957. Reprint, Westport, Conn.: Greenwood Press, 1978.

Jones, John Walter. *The Law and Legal Theory of the Greeks: An Introduction.* Oxford: Oxford University Press, 1956.

Kaser, Max. *Das römische Privatrecht.* 2 vols. Munich: C. H. Beck, 1971–75.

————. *Römische Rechtsgeschichte.* Göttingen: Vandenhoeck und Ruprecht, 1950.

————. *Das römische Zivilprozessrecht.* Munich: C. H. Beck, 1966.

Kelly, J.M. *Roman Litigation.* Oxford: Oxford University Press, 1966.

Kunkel, Wolfgang. *An Introduction to Roman Legal and Constitutional History.* 2d ed. Trans. J. M. Kelly. Oxford: Oxford University Press, 1966.

MacDowell, Douglas M. *The Law in Classical Athens.* London: Thames and Hudson, 1978.

Nicholas, Barry. *An Introduction to Roman Law.* Oxford: Oxford University Press, 1962.

Pharr, Clyde. *The Theodosian Code.* Princeton: Princeton University Press, 1952. This code is a compilation of the laws, or decrees, of Rome issued by the emperors from 313, when Constantine consolidated his power in the Western Empire, to 438, in the reign of Theodosius II.

Radin, Max. *Handbook of Roman Law.* St. Paul: West Publishing, 1927.

Schultz, Fritz. *Classical Roman Law.* Oxford: Oxford University Press, 1951.

————. *History of Roman Legal Science.* Oxford: Oxford University Press, 1946.

Treggiari, Susan. *Roman Marriage: Iusti Coniuges from the Time of Cicero to the Time of Ulpian.* Oxford: Oxford University Press, 1991.

Watson, Alan. *Law Making in the Later Roman Republic.* Oxford: Oxford University Press, 1974.

————. *The Law of Obligations in the Later Roman Republic.* Oxford: Oxford University Press, 1965.

————. *The Law of Persons in the Later Roman Republic.* Oxford: Oxford University Press, 1967.

————. *The Law of Property in the Later Roman Republic.* Oxford: Oxford University Press, 1968.

————. *The Law of Succession in the Later Roman Republic.* Oxford: Oxford University Press, 1971.

————. *Roman Private Law Around 200 B.C.* Edinburgh: Edinburgh University Press, 1971.

————. *Rome of the Twelve Tables: Persons and Property.* Princeton: Princeton University Press, 1975.

————. *The Spirit of Roman Law*. Athens: University of Georgia Press, 1995.

————. *Studies in Roman Private Law*. London: Hambledon Press, 1991.

Zulueta, Francis M. de, ed. *The Institutes of Gaius*. 2 vols. Oxford: Oxford University Press, 1946–53. The text was composed in the second century A.D. for Roman law students and was thought to be lost until its rediscovery in the early nineteenth century. This edition, intended for use by modern law students, provides both Latin text and facing English translation. The reader might also wish to consult the new translation by W. M. Gordon and O. F. Robinson, *The Institutes of Gaius* (Ithaca: Cornell University Press, 1988).

Early Medieval and Germanic Law of the Fifth Through Eleventh Centuries

Adams, Henry, ed. *Essays in Anglo-Saxon Law*. Boston: Little, Brown, 1905.

Attenborough, F. L., ed. and trans. *The Laws of the Earliest English Kings*. New York: Russell and Russell, 1963.

Bartlett, Robert. *Trial by Fire and Water: The Medieval Judicial Ordeal*. Oxford: Oxford University Press, 1986.

Binchy, D. A. *Celtic and Anglo-Saxon Kingship*. Oxford: Oxford University Press, 1970.

Davies, Wendy, and Paul Fouracre, eds. *The Settlement of Disputes in Early Medieval Europe*. Cambridge: Cambridge University Press, 1986.

Drew, Katherine Fischer, trans. *The Burgundian Code*. Philadelphia: University of Pennsylvania Press, 1972.

————. *The Laws of the Salian Franks*. Philadelphia: University of Pennsylvania Press, 1991.

————. *The Lombard Laws*. Philadelphia: University of Pennsylvania Press, 1973.

Goebel, Julius, Jr. *Felony and Misdemeanor: A Study in the History of Criminal Law*. Philadelphia: University of Pennsylvania Press, 1976.

Guterman, Simeon L. *The Principle of the Personality of Law in the Germanic Kingdoms of Western Europe from the Fifth to the Eleventh Century*. New York: P. Lang, 1990.

Kern, Fritz. *Kingship and Law in the Middle Ages*. 1948. Reprint, Westport, Conn.: Greenwood Press, 1985.

Levy, Ernst. *West Roman Vulgar Law: The Law of Property*. Philadelphia: American Philosophical Association, 1951.

Miller, William Ian. *Bloodtaking and Peacemaking: Feud, Law, and Society in Saga Iceland*. Chicago: University of Chicago Press, 1990.

Radding, Charles M. *Origins of Medieval Jurisprudence: Pavia and Bologna, 850–1150.* New Haven: Yale University Press, 1988.

Reynolds, Susan. *Fiefs and Vassals: The Medieval Evidence Reinterpreted.* Oxford: Oxford University Press, 1994.

Turk, Milton Haight, ed. *The Legal Code of Alfred the Great.* Boston: Ginn, 1893.

Wallace-Hadrill, J. M. *Early Germanic Kingship in England and on the Continent.* Oxford: Oxford University Press, 1971.

Canon and Civil Law of the Twelfth Through Fifteenth Centuries

Aquinas, Thomas. *On Law, Morality, and Politics.* Indianapolis: Hackett Publishing, 1988.

Blythe, James M., *Ideal Government and the Mixed Constitution in the Middle Ages.* Princeton: Princeton University Press, 1992.

Brett, Annabel S. *Liberty, Right, and Nature: Individual Rights in Later Scholastic Thought.* Cambridge: Cambridge University Press, 1997.

Brundage, James A. *Law, Sex, and Christian Society in Medieval Europe.* Chicago: University of Chicago Press, 1987.

———. *Medieval Canon Law.* London: Longman, 1995.

Corpus Juris Canonici. Assembled in the early sixteenth century, this work collects the most important canon-law texts of the twelfth through fifteenth centuries, including Gratian's *Decretum*, the *Liber Extra* of Pope Gregory IX, the *Liber Sextus* of Pope Boniface VIII, the decretal letters of Pope Clement V, the *Extravagantes* of Pope John XXII, and the *Extravagantes communes.* The leading edition of this collection is Emil Friedberg, *Corpus Juris Canonici*, 2 vols. (Leipzig: B. Tauchnitz, 1879). Most of the *Corpus* remains untranslated, but one should consult Augustine Thompson and James Gordley, trans., *Gratian: The Treatise on Laws with the Ordinary Gloss* (Washington, D.C.: Catholic University of America Press, 1993).

Feenstra, Robert. *Droit romain au moyen âge (1100–1500).* Brussels: Éditions de l'université de Bruxelles, 1979.

Gaudemet, Jean. *Église et cité: Histoire du droit canonique.* Paris: Monchrestien, 1994.

———. *La formation du droit canonique médiéval.* London: Variorum Reprints, 1980.

Helmholz, Richard H. *The Spirit of Classical Canon Law.* Athens: University of Georgia Press, 1996.

Kantorowicz, Hermann Ulrich. *Studies in the Glossators of the Roman Law: Newly Discovered Writings of the Twelfth Century.* Aalen: Scientia Verlag, 1969.

Kuttner, Stephan. *Gratian and the Schools of Canon Law, 1140–1234.* London: Variorum Reprints, 1983.

————. *The History of Ideas and Doctrines of Canon Law in the Middle Ages.* 2d ed. Hampshire, U.K.: Variorum Reprints, 1992.

Le Bras, Gabriel, Charles Lefebvre, and Jacqueline Rambaud. *L'âge classique (1140–1378): Sources et théorie du droit.* Paris: Sirey, 1965.

Ourliac, Paul, and Henri Gilles. *La période post-classique (1378–1500): La problématique de l'époque.* Paris: Sirey, 1974.

Pennington, Kenneth. *The Prince and the Law, 1200–1600: Sovereignty and Rights in the Western Legal Tradition.* Berkeley: University of California Press, 1993.

Post, Gaines. *Studies in Medieval Legal Thought: Public Law and the State, 1100–1322.* Princeton: Princeton University Press, 1964.

Savigny, Friedrich Karl von. *Geschichte des Römischen Rechts im Mittelalter.* 6 vols. Heidelberg: Mohr, 1815–31.

Tierney, Brian. *Church Law and Constitutional Thought in the Middle Ages.* London: Variorum Reprints, 1979.

————. *The Crisis of Church and State, 1050–1300.* Englewood Cliffs, N.J.: Prentice-Hall, 1964.

————. *The Idea of Natural Rights: Studies on Natural Rights, Natural Law, and Church Law, 1150–1625.* Atlanta: Scholars Press, 1997.

————. *Medieval Poor Law: A Sketch of Canonical Theory and Its Application in England.* Berkeley: University of California Press, 1959.

————. *Religion, Law and the Growth of Constitutional Thought, 1150–1650.* Cambridge: Cambridge University Press, 1982.

Ullmann, Walter. *Jurisprudence in the Middle Ages: Collected Studies.* London: Variorum Reprints, 1980.

————. *Law and Politics in the Middle Ages: An Introduction to the Sources of Medieval Political Ideas.* Ithaca: Cornell University Press, 1975.

————. *The Medieval Idea of Law, as Represented by Lucas de Penna: A Study of Fourteenth-Century Legal Scholarship.* London: Methuen, 1946.

Vinogradoff, Paul. *Roman Law in Medieval Europe.* 1909. Reprint, Holmes Beach, Fla.: Wm. W. Gaunt and Sons, 1994.

Zulueta, Francis de, and Peter Stein. *The Teaching of Roman Law in England Around 1200.* London: Selden Society, 1990.

Continental Law Since 1500

GENERAL

Bar, Ludwig von. *A History of Continental Criminal Law.* Boston: Little Brown, 1916.

Engelmann, Arthur. *A History of Continental Civil Procedure.* Boston: Little, Brown, 1927.

Esmein, Adhémar, *A History of Continental Criminal Procedure: With Special Emphasis on France.* 1882. Reprint, Boston: Little, Brown, 1913.

A General Survey of Events, Sources, Persons and Movements in Continental Legal History. Boston: Little, Brown, 1912.

Gierke, Otto von. *Natural Law and the Theory of Society, 1500–1800.* Cambridge: Cambridge University Press, 1934.

Gorla, Gino. *Diritto comparato e diritto comune europeo.* Milan: A. Giuffrè, 1981.

Merryman, John Henry. *The Civil Law Tradition: An Introduction to the Legal System of Western Europe and Latin America.* 2d ed. Stanford, Calif.: Stanford University Press, 1985.

The Progress of Continental Law in the Nineteenth Century. Boston: Little, Brown, 1918.

Savigny, Friedrich Karl von. *System des heutigen römischen Rechts.* 9 vols. Aalen: Scientia Verlag, 1981.

Stein, Peter. *The Character and Influence of the Roman Civil Law: Historical Essays.* London: Hambledon Press, 1988.

Watson, Alan. *The Making of the Civil Law.* Cambridge: Harvard University Press, 1981.

Zimmermann, Reinhard. *The Law of Obligations: Roman Foundations of the Civilian Tradition.* Capetown, South Africa: Juta, 1990.

RENAISSANCE AND HUMANIST JURISPRUDENCE

Kisch, Guido. *Erasmus und die Jurisprudenz seiner Zeit: Studien zum humanistischen Rechtsdenken.* Basel: Helbing und Lichtenhahn, 1960.

———. *Humanismus und Jurisprudenz: Der Kampf zwischen mos italicus und mos gallicus an der Universität Basel.* Basel: Helbing und Lichtenhahn, 1955.

Maclean, Ian. *Interpretation and Meaning in the Renaissance: The Case of Law.* Cambridge: Cambridge University Press, 1992.

Maffei, Domenico. *Gli inizi dell'umanesimo giuridico.* Milan: A. Giuffrè, 1956.

Piano Mortari, Vincenzo. *Diritto, logica, metodo ne secolo XVI.* Naples: Jovene, 1978.

CANON LAW

Bernhard, Jean, Charles Lefebvre, and Francis Rapp. *L'époque de la réforme et du concile de Trente*. Paris: Éditions Cujas, 1989.

Epp, René, Charles Lefebvre, and René Metz. *Le droit et les institutions de l'Église catholique latine de la fin du XVIIIe siècle à 1978: Sources, communauté, chrétienne, et hiérarchie*. Paris: Éditions Cujas, 1981.

Noonan, John. *Power to Dissolve: Lawyers and Marriages in the Courts of the Roman Curia*. Cambridge: Harvard University Press, 1972.

FRENCH LAW

Brissaud, Jean. *History of French Private Law*. Boston: Little, Brown, 1912.

————. *History of French Public Law*. Boston: Little, Brown, 1915.

Olivier-Martin, François. *Histoire du droit français des origines à la Révolution*. Paris: Domat Montchrestien, 1948.

Ourliac, Paul, and J. de Malafosse. *Histoire du droit privé*. 3 vols. Paris: Presses universitaires de France, 1961.

Sagnac, Philippe. *La legislation civile de la révolution Française (1789–1804): essai d'histoire sociale*. Paris: Hachette, 1898.

Schwartz, Bernard, ed. *The Code Napoléon and the Common-Law World*. New York: New York University Press, 1956.

GERMAN LAW

Allgemeines Landrecht für die preussischer Staaten von 1794. 2 vols. Frankfurt am Main: A. Metzner, 1970–73.

Gierke, Otto von. *Das deutsche Genossenschaftsrecht*. 4 vols. Berlin: Weidmann-ische Buchhandlung, 1869.

Huebner, Rodolf. *A History of German Private Law*. Boston: Little, Brown, 1918.

Stinzing, Roderich von. *Geschichte der deutschen Rechtswissenschaft*. 2 vols. Munich: R. Oldenbourg, 1880–84.

Stobbe, Otto. *Geschichte der deutschen Rechtsquellen*. 2 vols. 1860. Reprint, Aalen: Scientia Verlag, 1965.

Whitman, James Q. *The Legacy of Roman Law in the German Romantic Era: Historical Vision and Legal Change*. Princeton: Princeton University Press, 1990.

Wieacker, Franz. *Privatrechtsgeschichte der Neuzeit: Unter besonderer Berück-sichtigung der deutschen Entwicklung*. 2 vols. 2d ed. Göttingen: Vandenhoeck und Ruprecht, 1967.

ITALIAN LAW

Calisse, Carlo. *A History of Italian Law.* Boston: Little, Brown, 1928.

Pertile, Antonio. *Storia del diritto italiano dalla caduta dell'imperio romano codificazione.* 2d ed. 6 vols. Turin: Unione tipografico-editrice, 1892–1902.

THE NETHERLANDS

Lee, R. W. *An Introduction to Roman-Dutch Law.* 4th ed. Oxford: Oxford University Press, 1946.

English Law Since 1066

CONSTITUTIONAL AND LEGAL HISTORY

Adams, George Burton. *Constitutional History of England.* New York: Henry Holt, 1921.

———. *The Origin of the English Constitution.* New Haven: Yale University Press, 1912.

Adams, George Burton, and H. Morse Stephens. *Select Documents of English Constitutional History.* New York: Macmillan, 1924.

Ames, James Barr. *Lectures on Legal History and Miscellaneous Legal Essays.* Cambridge: Harvard University Press, 1913.

Anson, William R. *The Law and Custom of the Constitution.* 2 vols. Oxford: Oxford University Press, 1897.

Baker, John H. *An Introduction to English Legal History.* 3d ed. London: Butterworths, 1990.

———. *The Legal Profession and the Common Law: Historical Essays.* London: Hambledon Press, 1986.

———. *The Order of Serjeants at Law.* London: Selden Society, 1984.

———. *The Third University of England: The Inns of Court and the Common-Law Tradition.* London: Selden Society, 1990.

Beale, Joseph H. *A Bibliography of Early English Law Books.* Cambridge: Harvard University Press, 1926. See also Robert B. Anderson, *A Supplement to Beale's Bibliography of Early English Law Books* (Cambridge: Harvard University Press, 1943).

Beattie, J. M. *Crime and the Courts in England, 1660–1800.* Princeton: Princeton University Press, 1986.

Blatcher, Marjorie. *The Court of King's Bench, 1450–1550: A Study in Self-Help.* London: Athlone Press, 1978.

Bogdanor, Vernon. *The Monarchy and the Constitution.* Oxford: Oxford University Press, 1995.

Brand, Paul. *The Making of the Common Law*. London: Hambledon Press, 1992.

Brooks, C. W. *Pettyfoggers and Vipers of the Commonwealth: The "Lower Branch" of the Legal Profession in Early Modern England*. Cambridge: Cambridge University Press, 1986.

Bryson, W. Hamilton. *The Equity Side of the Exchequer: Its Jurisdiction, Administration, Procedures, and Records*. Cambridge: Cambridge University Press, 1975.

Chrimes, S. B. *English Constitutional Ideas in the Fifteenth Century*. Oxford: Oxford University Press, 1936.

Cowley, J. D. *A Bibliography of Abridgements, Digests, Dictionaries, and Indexes of English Law to the Year 1800*. Abingdon: Professional Books, 1979.

Elton, Geoffrey. *Star Chamber Stories*. London: Methuen, 1958.

Fifoot, C. H. S. *History and Sources of the Common Law: Tort and Contract*. London: Stevens, 1949.

Green, Thomas A. *Verdict According to Conscience: Perspectives on the English Criminal Trial Jury, 1200–1800*. Chicago: University of Chicago Press, 1985.

Hallam, Henry. *The Constitutional History of England*. 3 vols. New York: A. C. Armstrong and Son, 1880.

Hanham, H. J. *The Nineteenth Century Constitution: Documents and Commentary*. Cambridge: Cambridge University Press, 1969.

Harding, Alan. *The Law Courts of Medieval England*. London: George Allen and Unwin, 1973.

———. *A Social History of English Law*. Baltimore: Penguin Books, 1966.

Hastings, Margaret. *The Court of Common Pleas in Fifteenth Century England: A Study of Legal Administration and Procedure*. Ithaca: Cornell University Press, 1947.

Helmholz, Richard H. *Canon Law and the Law of England*. London: Hambledon Press, 1987.

Hogue, Arthur R. *Origins of the Common Law*. Bloomington: Indiana University Press, 1966; Indianapolis: Liberty Fund, 1986.

Holden, J. Milnes. *The History of Negotiable Instruments in English Law*. London: Athlone Press, 1955.

Holdsworth, William S. *Charles Dickens as a Legal Historian*. New York: Haskell House Publishers, 1972.

———. *A History of English Law*. 7th ed rev. 17 vols. London: Methuen, 1956–72.

———. *Some Lessons from Our Legal History*. New York: Macmillan, 1928.

———. *Sources and Literature of English Law*. Oxford: Oxford University Press, 1925.

Holmes, Oliver Wendell. *The Common Law*. 1881. Reprint, Mark DeWolfe Howe, ed. Cambridge: Harvard University Press, 1963.

Holt, J. C. *Magna Carta*. 2d ed. Cambridge: Cambridge University Press, 1991.

Hyams, Paul R. *Kings, Lords, and Peasants in Medieval England: The Common Law of Villeinage in the Twelfth and Thirteenth Centuries*. Oxford: Oxford University Press, 1980.

Jones, Gareth. *History of the Law of Charity, 1532–1827*. Cambridge: Cambridge University Press, 1969.

Jones, W. J. *The Elizabethan Court of Chancery*. Oxford: Oxford University Press, 1967.

Keeton, George W. *The Norman Conquest and the Common Law*. London: Ernest Benn, 1966.

———. *Shakespeare's Legal and Political Background*. London: Sir Isaac Pitman and Sons, 1967.

Keir, David Lindsay. *The Constitutional History of Modern Britain*. 6th ed. Princeton: D. Van Nostrand, 1960.

Langbein, John H. *Prosecuting Crime in the Renaissance: England, Germany, France*. Cambridge: Harvard University Press, 1974.

Lawson, F. H. *The Oxford Law School, 1850–1965*. Oxford: Oxford University Press, 1968.

Lemmings, David. *Gentlemen and Barristers: The Inns of Court and the English Bar, 1680–1730*. Oxford: Oxford University Press, 1990.

Lieberman, David. *The Province of Legislation Determined: Legal Theory in Eighteenth-Century Britain*. Cambridge: Cambridge University Press, 1989.

Lobban, Michael. *The Common Law and English Jurisprudence, 1760–1850*. Oxford: Oxford University Press, 1991.

Lyon, Bryce. *A Constitutional and Legal History of Medieval England*. 2d ed. Toronto: George J. McLeod, 1980.

Maitland, Frederic W. *Canon Law in the Church of England*. London: Methuen, 1898.

———. *The Constitutional History of England: A Course of Lectures Delivered*. London: Cambridge University Press, 1908; Holmes Beach, Fla.: Gaunt, 1993. Maitland's lectures for undergraduates, drawn mainly from Hallam, Stubbs, Dicey, and Anson.

———. *English Law and the Renaissance*. Cambridge: Cambridge University Press, 1901.

———. *The Forms of Action at Common Law: A Course of Lectures*. Cambridge: Cambridge University Press, 1965.

Malden, Henry Elliot, ed. *Magna Carta Commemoration Essays.* London: Royal Historical Society, 1917.

May, Thomas Erskine. *The Constitutional History of England Since the Accession of George III.* 3 vols. London: Longmans, Green, 1912.

McKechnie, William Sharp. *Magna Carta: A Commentary on the Great Charter of King John.* 2d ed. Glasgow: James Maclehose and Sons, 1914.

Milsom, S. F. C. *Historical Foundations of the Common Law.* 2d ed. London: Butterworths, 1981.

———. *The Legal Framework of English Feudalism.* Cambridge: Cambridge University Press, 1976.

———. *Studies in the History of the Common Law.* London: Hambledon Press, 1985.

Nicholls, George. *A History of the English Poor Law in Connection with the State of the Country and the Condition of the People.* 2 vols. London: P. S. King, 1904.

O'Donnell, Bernard. *The Old Bailey and Its Trials.* London: Burke, 1950.

Palmer, Robert C. *English Law in the Age of the Black Death, 1348–1381.* Chapel Hill: University of North Carolina Press, 1993.

Plucknett, T. F. T. *A Concise History of the Common Law.* 5th ed. Boston: Little, Brown, 1956.

———. *Early English Legal Literature.* Cambridge: Cambridge University Press, 1958.

———. *Studies in English Legal History.* London: Hambledon Press, 1983.

Pocock, J. G. A. *The Ancient Constitution and the Feudal Law: A Study of English Historical Thought in the Seventeenth Century.* 2d ed., with a retrospective. Cambridge: Cambridge University Press, 1987.

Pollock, Frederick. *The Expansion of the Common Law.* London: Stevens, 1904.

———. *The Genius of the Common Law.* New York: Columbia University Press, 1912.

Pollock, Frederick, and Frederic W. Maitland. *The History of English Law Before the Time of Edward I.* 2d ed. 2 vols. Cambridge: Cambridge University Press, 1968.

Pound, Roscoe. *The Spirit of the Common Law.* Boston: Marshall Jones, 1921.

Prest, Wilfred R. *The Rise of the Barristers: A Social History of the English Bar, 1590–1640.* Oxford: Oxford University Press, 1986.

Radzinowicz, Leon. *A History of English Criminal Law and Its Administration from 1750.* 5 vols. London: Stevens, 1948–86.

Richardson, H. G., and G. O. Sayles. *Laws and Legislation from Aethelbehrt to Magna Carta.* Edinburgh: Edinburgh University Press, 1966.

Robson, Robert. *The Attorney in Eighteenth-Century England.* Cambridge: Cambridge University Press, 1959.

Roxburgh, Ronald. *The Origins of Lincoln's Inn.* Cambridge: Cambridge University Press, 1963.

Rubin, G. R., and David Sugarman, eds. *Law, Economy, and Society, 1750–1914: Essays in the History of English Law.* Abingdon: Professional Books, 1984.

Russell, Franklin Ferriss. *Outline of Legal History.* New York: Russell, 1929.

Sandoz, Ellis, ed. *The Roots of Liberty: Magna Carta, Ancient Constitution, and the Anglo-American Tradition of Rule of Law.* Columbia: University of Missouri Press, 1993.

Sainty, John. *The Judges of England, 1272–1990.* London: Selden Society, 1993.

Schwoerer, Lois G. *The Declaration of Rights, 1689.* Baltimore: Johns Hopkins University Press, 1981.

Simpson, A. W. B. *Cannibalism and the Common Law: The Story of the Tragic Last Voyage of the Mignonette and the Strange Legal Proceedings to Which It Gave Rise.* Chicago: University of Chicago Press, 1984.

———. *A History of the Common Law of Contract: The Rise of the Action of Assumpsit.* Oxford: Oxford University Press, 1975.

———. *A History of the Land Law.* 2d ed. Oxford: Oxford University Press, 1986.

———. *Leading Cases in the Common Law.* Oxford: Oxford University Press, 1995.

———. *Legal Theory and Legal History: Essays on the Common Law.* London: Hambledon Press, 1987.

Slack, Paul. *The English Poor Law, 1531–1782.* Cambridge: Cambridge University Press, 1995.

Squibb, G. D. *Doctors' Commons: A History of the College of Advocates and Doctors of Law.* Oxford: Oxford University Press, 1977. Doctors' Commons had its origins in a club for clerical lawyers but evolved in the sixteenth and seventeenth centuries into a sort of Inn of Court for lay ecclesiastical and Admiralty lawyers. Squibb traces this institution's history from the fifteenth century to its dissolution in the nineteenth. See also Daniel R. Coquillette, *The Civilian Writers of Doctors' Commons, London: Three Centuries of Juristic Innovation in Comparative, Commercial, and International Law* (Berlin: Duncker and Humblot, 1988).

Stein, Peter. *Legal Evolution: The Story of an Idea.* Cambridge: Cambridge University Press, 1980.

Stenton, Doris M. *English Justice Between the Norman Conquest and the Great Charter, 1066–1215.* Philadelphia: American Philosophical Society, 1964.

Stephen, James Fitzjames. *A History of the Criminal Law of England.* 3 vols. London: Macmillan, 1883.

Stephenson, Carl, and Frederick G. Marcham, eds. and trans. *Sources of English Constitutional History: A Selection of Documents from A.D. 600 to the Present.* New York: Harper and Brothers, 1937.

Stubbs, William. *The Constitutional History of England.* 3d ed. 3 vols. Oxford: Oxford University Press, 1883–87.

————. *Lectures on Early English Legal History.* London: Longmans, Green, 1906.

————. *William Stubbs on the English Constitution.* Ed. Norman Cantor. New York: Thomas Y. Crowell, 1966.

Tanner, J. R. *English Constitutional Conflicts of the Seventeenth Century, 1603–1689.* Cambridge: Cambridge University Press, 1928.

Taswell-Langmead, Thomas Pitt. *English Constitutional History.* Boston: Houghton Mifflin, 1946.

Thorne, Samuel E. *Essays in English Legal History.* London: Hambledon Press, 1985.

Turner, Ralph V. *The English Judiciary in the Age of Glanvill and Bracton, c. 1176–1239.* Cambridge: Cambridge University Press, 1985.

Usher, Roland G. *The Rise and Fall of the High Commission.* Oxford: Oxford University Press, 1913.

Van Caenegem, Raoul. *The Birth of the English Common Law.* 2d ed. Cambridge: Cambridge University Press, 1988.

White, Albert B. *The Making of the English Constitution, 449–1485.* New York: G. P. Putnam's Sons, 1908.

Williams, E. N. *The Eighteenth Century: 1688–1815: Documents and Commentary.* Cambridge: Cambridge University Press, 1960.

Winfield, Percy. *The Chief Sources of English Legal History.* Cambridge: Harvard University Press, 1925.

TREATISES AND TEXTBOOKS

Amos, Sir Maurice. *The English Constitution.* London: Longmans, Green, 1930.

Bagehot, Walter. *The English Constitution.* In *Collected Works.* 1867. Reprint, London: Oxford University Press, 1963.

Blackstone, William. *Commentaries on the Laws of England.* 4 vols. 1765–69. Reprint, Chicago: University of Chicago Press, 1979.

Bracton, Henry de. *On the Laws and Customs of England.* Trans. Samuel E. Thorne. 4 vols. Cambridge: Harvard University Press, 1968–77.

Brazier, Rodney. *Constitutional Practice*. Oxford: Oxford University Press, 1988.

Coke, Sir Edward. *Institutes of the Laws of England*. 4 vols. Buffalo: W. S. Hein, 1986.

De Lolme, Jean Louis. *The Constitution of England*. New York: Arno Press, 1979.

Dicey, Albert Venn. *Introduction to the Study of the Law of the Constitution*. Indianapolis: Liberty Fund, 1982.

Fleta. Ed. and trans. H. G. Richardson and G. O. Sayles. 4 vols. London: Selden Society, 1955–72.

Fortescue, John. *De Laudibus Legum Anglie*. Ed. S. B. Chrimes. Cambridge: Cambridge University Press, 1942.

Glanvill. *The Treatise on the Laws and Customs of England Commonly Called Glanvill*. Ed. and trans. G. D. H. Hall. London: Thomas Nelson, 1965.

Hale, Matthew. *The History of the Common Law of England*. Ed. Charles M. Gray. Chicago: University of Chicago Press, 1971.

Hobbes, Thomas. *A Dialogue Between a Philosopher and a Student of the Common Laws of England*. Ed. Joseph Cropsey. Chicago: University of Chicago Press, 1971. See also William Holdsworth, ed., "Sir Matthew Hale on Hobbes: An Unpublished Manuscript" (*Law Quarterly Review* 37 [1921]: 274–303).

———. *The Elements of Law, Natural and Politic*. Ed. J. C. A. Gaskin. Oxford: Oxford University Press, 1994.

Horne, Andrew. *Mirror of Justices*. Washington, D.C.: John Byrne, 1903.

Jennings, Ivor. *Cabinet Government*. Cambridge: Cambridge University Press, 1959.

Kames, Henry Home, Lord. *Elucidations Respecting the Common and Statute Law of Scotland*. Edinburgh: W. Creech, 1777.

———. *Essays on the Principles of Morality and Natural Religion*. Edinburgh: R. Fleming, 1751.

———. *Historical Law Tracts*. 2 vols. Edinburgh: A. Millar, 1758.

———. *Principles of Equity*. Edinburgh: A. Kincaid and J. Bell, 1760.

Leges Henrici Primi. Ed. and trans. L. J. Downer. Oxford: Oxford University Press, 1972.

Littleton, Thomas. *Littleton's Tenures*. Trans. Eugene Wambaugh. Washington, D.C.: John Byrne, 1903.

Marshall, Geoffrey. *Constitutional Conventions*. Oxford: Oxford University Press, 1984.

Radulphi de Hengham Summa. Ed. William Huse Dunham, Jr. Cambridge: Cambridge University Press, 1932.

St. German, Christopher. *Doctor and Student*. Ed. T. F. T. Plucknett and J. L. Barton. London: Selden Society, 1974.

Selden, John. *Ioannis Seldeni Ad Fletam dissertatio*. Ed. David Ogg. Buffalo: W. S. Hein, 1980.

Smith, Adam. *Lectures on Jurisprudence*. Ed. R. L. Meek, D. D. Raphael, and Peter G. Stein. Oxford: Oxford University Press, 1978; Indianapolis: Liberty Fund, 1982.

Smith, S. A., and Rodney Brazier. *Constitutional and Administrative Law*. 6th ed. London: Penguin, 1989.

Smith, Thomas. *De Republica Anglorum*. Ed. Mary Dewar. Cambridge: Cambridge University Press, 1982.

Wade, E. C. S., and A. W. Bradley. *Constitutional and Administrative Law*. 11th ed. Ed. A. W. Bradley and K. D. Ewing. London: Longman, 1993.

Wood, Thomas. *An Institute of the Laws of England*. New York: Garland Publishing, 1979.

Wooddeson, Richard. *Elements of Jurisprudence*. Dublin: J. Moore, 1792.

――――. *Lectures on the Law of England*. 2d ed. London: Richards, 1834.

――――. *A Systematical View of the Laws of England*. 3 vols. London: T. Payne, 1792–93.

American Law

CONSTITUTIONAL AND LEGAL HISTORY

Arnold, Morris S. *Unequal Laws Unto a Savage Race: European Legal Traditions in Arkansas, 1686–1836*. Fayetteville: University of Arkansas Press, 1985.

Bancroft, George. *History of the Formation of the Constitution of the United States of America*. 2 vols. New York: D. Appleton, 1883.

Bauer, Elizabeth Kelley. *Commentaries on the Constitution, 1790–1860*. New York: Columbia University Press, 1952.

Beard, Charles A. *An Economic Interpretation of the Constitution of the United States*. 1913. Reprint, with an introduction by Forrest McDonald, New York: Free Press, 1986.

Berger, Raoul. *Government by Judiciary*. 2d ed. Indianapolis: Liberty Fund, 1997.

Bickel, Alexander, and Benno C. Schmidt, Jr. *The Judiciary and Responsible Government, 1910–1921*. Vol. 9 of *Oliver Wendell Holmes Devise History of the Supreme Court of the United States*. New York: Macmillan, 1984.

Bloomfield, Maxwell H. *American Lawyers in a Changing Society, 1776–1876*. Cambridge: Harvard University Press, 1976.

Bodenhamer, David J., and James W. Ely, Jr. *Ambivalent Legacy: A Legal History of the South*. Jackson: University of Mississippi Press, 1984.

Bryson, W. Hamilton. *A Bibliography of Virginia Legal History Before 1900*. Charlottesville: University Press of Virginia, 1979.

————. *Census of Law Books in Colonial Virginia*. Charlottesville: University Press of Virginia, 1978.

————. *The Virginia Law Reporters Before 1880*. Charlottesville: University Press of Virginia, 1977.

Chitwood, Oliver P. *Justice in Colonial Virginia*. Baltimore: Johns Hopkins University Press, 1905.

Chroust, Anton-Hermann. *The Rise of the Legal Profession in America*. 2 vols. Norman: University of Oklahoma Press, 1965.

Currie, David P. *The Constitution in the Supreme Court: The First Hundred Years, 1789–1888*. Chicago: University of Chicago Press, 1985.

————. *The Constitution in the Supreme Court: The Second Century, 1888–1986*. Chicago: University of Chicago Press, 1990.

Curtis, George Ticknor. *Constitutional History of the United States*. 2 vols. New York: Harper and Bros., 1896.

Dillon, John Forrest. *The Laws and Jurisprudence of England and America*. Boston: Little, Brown, 1895.

Donahue, William A. *The Politics of the American Civil Liberties Union*. New Brunswick, N.J.: Transaction Books, 1985.

Elliot, Jonathan, ed. *The Debates in the Several State Conventions on the Adoption of the Federal Constitution*. 5 vols. Philadelphia: J. B. Lippincott, 1836.

Ellsworth, Frank L. *Law on the Midway: The Founding of the University of Chicago Law School*. Chicago: University of Chicago Press, 1977.

Fairman, Charles. *Five Justices and the Electoral Commission of 1877*. Supplement to vol. 7 of *Oliver Wendell Holmes Devise History of the Supreme Court of the United States*. New York: Macmillan, 1988.

————. *Reconstruction and Reunion, 1864–1888, Part I and Part II*. Vols. 6 and 7 of *Oliver Wendell Holmes Devise History of the Supreme Court of the United States*. New York: Macmillan, 1971, 1987.

Farrand, Max, ed. *The Records of the Federal Convention of 1787*. 4 vols. New Haven: Yale University Press, 1937. A supplemental fifth volume, edited by James Hutson, was published in 1987.

Fiss, Owen. *Troubled Beginnings of the Modern State, 1888–1910*. Vol. 8 of *Oliver Wendell Holmes Devise History of the Supreme Court of the United States*. New York: Macmillan, 1993.

Flaherty, David H., ed. *Essays in the History of Early American Law*. Chapel Hill: University of North Carolina Press, 1969.

Fleming, Donald, and Bernard Bailyn, eds. *Law in American History*. Perspectives in American History, vol. 6. Cambridge, Mass.: Charles Warren Center for Studies in American History, 1971.

Friedman, Lawrence M. *A History of American Law*. 2d ed. New York: Simon and Schuster, 1985.

Gilmore, Grant. *The Ages of American Law*. New Haven: Yale University Press, 1977.

Ginger, Ann Fagan, and Eugene M. Tobin, eds. *The National Lawyers Guild: From Roosevelt Through Reagan*. Philadelphia: Temple University Press, 1988.

Goebel, Julius, Jr. *Antecedents and Beginnings to 1801*. Vol. 1 of *Oliver Wendell Holmes Devise History of the Supreme Court of the United States*. New York: Macmillan, 1971.

Goebel, Julius, Jr., and Joseph H. Smith. *The Law Practice of Alexander Hamilton*. 5 vols. New York: Columbia University Press, 1964–81.

Goodrich, Herbert F., and Paul A. Wolkin. *The Story of the American Law Institute, 1923–1961*. St. Paul, Minn.: American Law Institute Publishers, 1961.

Haar, Charles M., ed. *The Golden Age of American Law*. New York: George Braziller, 1965.

Haines, Charles Grove. *The Role of the Supreme Court in American Government and Politics, 1789–1835*. Berkeley: University of California Press, 1944.

Haines, Charles Grove, and Foster Sherwood. *The Role of the Supreme Court in American Government and Politics, 1835–1864*. Berkeley: University of California Press, 1957.

Hall, Kermit. *A Comprehensive Bibliography of American Constitutional and Legal History, 1896–1979*. 5 vols. Millwood, N.Y.: Kraus International Publications, 1984.

Hamlin, Paul. *Legal Education in Colonial New York*. New York: New York University, 1939; New York: Da Capo Press, 1970.

Haskins, George Lee. *Law and Authority in Early Massachusetts*. New York: Macmillan, 1960.

Haskins, George Lee, and Herbert A. Johnson. *Foundations of Power: John Marshall, 1801–1815*. Vol. 2 of *Oliver Wendell Holmes Devise History of the Supreme Court of the United States*. New York: Macmillan, 1981.

A History of the School of Law, Columbia University. New York: Columbia University Press, 1955.

Holst, H. von. *The Constitutional and Political History of the United States, 1750–1861.* 8 vols. Chicago: Callaghan, 1889.

Horwitz, Morton J. *The Transformation of American Law, 1780–1860.* Cambridge: Harvard University Press, 1977.

————. *The Transformation of American Law, 1870–1960: The Crisis of Legal Orthodoxy.* New York: Oxford University Press, 1992.

Howard, A. E. Dick. *The Road from Runnymede: Magna Carta and Constitutionalism in America.* Charlottesville: University Press of Virginia, 1968.

Howe, Mark De Wolfe. *The Garden and the Wilderness: Religion and Government in American Constitutional History.* Chicago: University of Chicago Press, 1965.

Hurst, J. Willard. *Law and Economic Growth: The Legal History of the Lumber Industry in Wisconsin, 1836–1915.* Cambridge: Harvard University Press, 1964.

————. *Law and Social Order in the United States.* Ithaca: Cornell University Press, 1977.

————. *Law and the Conditions of Freedom in the Nineteenth-Century United States.* Madison: University of Wisconsin Press, 1956.

————. *The Legitimacy of the Business Corporation in the Law of the United States, 1780–1970.* Charlottesville: University Press of Virginia, 1970.

Irons, Peter. *The New Deal Lawyers.* Princeton: Princeton University Press, 1982.

Johnson, John W. *American Legal Culture, 1908–1940.* Westport, Conn.: Greenwood Press, 1981.

Kalman, Laura. *Legal Realism at Yale, 1927–1960.* Chapel Hill: University of North Carolina Press, 1986.

————. *The Strange Career of Legal Liberalism.* New Haven: Yale University Press, 1996.

Kammen, Michael. *A Machine That Would Go of Itself: The Constitution in American Culture.* New York: Knopf, 1986.

————. *Sovereignty and Liberty: Constitutional Discourse in American Culture.* Madison: University of Wisconsin Press, 1988.

Kelly, Alfred H., Winfred A. Harbison, and Herman Belz. *The American Constitution: Its Origins and Development.* 7th ed. New York: W. W. Norton, 1991.

Kurland, Philip B., and Ralph Lerner, eds. *The Founders' Constitution.* 5 vols. Chicago: University of Chicago Press, 1987.

Lutz, Donald S. *Colonial Origins of the American Constitution: A Documentary History.* Indianapolis: Liberty Fund, 1998.

————. *The Origins of American Constitutionalism.* Baton Rouge: Louisiana State University Press, 1988.

Marcus, Maeva, and James R. Perry, eds. *The Documentary History of the Supreme Court of the United States, 1789–1800.* 5 vols. New York: Columbia University Press, 1985–94.

McDonald, Forrest. *A Constitutional History of the United States.* New York: Franklin Watts, 1982.

————. *Novus Ordo Seclorum: The Intellectual Origins of the Constitution.* Lawrence: University Press of Kansas, 1985.

————. *We the People: The Economic Origins of the Constitution.* Chicago: University of Chicago Press, 1958.

McIlwain, C. H. *Foundations of American Constitutionalism.* New York: New York University Press, 1932.

McLaughlin, Andrew C. *A Constitutional History of the United States.* New York: Appleton-Century-Crofts, 1935.

————. *The Foundations of American Constitutionalism.* 1932. Reprint, Gloucester, Mass.: Peter Smith, 1972.

Miller, Charles A. *The Supreme Court and the Uses of History.* Cambridge: Harvard University Press, 1969.

Miller, Perry, ed. *The Legal Mind in America: From Independence to the Civil War.* Ithaca: Cornell University Press, 1962.

Morris, Richard B. *Studies in the History of American Law: With Special Reference to the Seventeenth and Eighteenth Centuries.* New York: Columbia University Press, 1930.

Nelson, William E. *Americanization of the Common Law: The Impact of Legal Change on Massachusetts Society, 1760–1830.* Cambridge: Harvard University Press, 1975.

————. *Dispute and Conflict Resolution in Plymouth County, Massachusetts, 1725–1825.* Chapel Hill: University of North Carolina Press, 1981.

Nelson, William E., and John Phillip Reid. *The Literature of American Legal History.* New York: Oceana, 1985.

Osgood, Russell K., ed. *The History of the Law in Massachusetts: The Supreme Judicial Court, 1692–1992.* Boston: Supreme Judicial Court Historical Society, 1992.

Pound, Roscoe. *The Formative Era of American Law.* Boston: Little, Brown, 1938.

————. *The Lawyer from Antiquity to Modern Times: With Particular Reference to the Development of Bar Associations in the United States.* St. Paul, Minn.: West Publishing, 1953.

Reid, John Phillip. *Constitutional History of the American Revolution.* 4 vols. Madison: University of Wisconsin Press, 1983–91.

Ritchie, John. *The First Hundred Years: A Short History of the School of Law of the University of Virginia for the Period 1826–1926.* Charlottesville: University Press of Virginia, 1978.

Select Essays in Anglo-American Legal History. 3 vols. Boston: Little, Brown, 1907–9.

Sutherland, Arthur E. *Constitutionalism in America.* New York: Blaisdell Publishing, 1965.

———. *The Law at Harvard: A History of Ideas and Men, 1817–1967.* Cambridge: Harvard University Press, 1967.

Swindler, William. *Court and Constitution in the Twentieth Century.* 3 vols. Indianapolis: Bobbs-Merrill, 1969–74.

Swisher, Carl Brent. *American Constitutional Development.* Boston: Houghton Mifflin, 1954.

———. *The Growth of Constitutional Power in the United States.* Chicago: University of Chicago Press, 1963.

———. *The Taney Period, 1836–1864.* Vol. 5 of *Oliver Wendell Holmes Devise History of the Supreme Court of the United States.* New York: Macmillan, 1974.

Thayer, James Bradley. *Legal Essays.* Boston: Boston Book, 1908.

Thorpe, Francis Newton. *The Constitutional History of the United States, 1765–1895.* 3 vols. Chicago: Callaghan, 1901.

Twiss, Benjamin. *Lawyers and the Constitution.* Princeton: Princeton University Press, 1942.

Vile, M. J. C. *Constitutionalism and the Separation of Powers.* 2d ed. Indianapolis: Liberty Fund, 1998.

Walker, Samuel. *In Defense of American Liberties: A History of the ACLU.* New York, Oxford University Press, 1990.

Warren, Charles. *Congress, the Constitution, and the Supreme Court.* Boston: Little, Brown, 1935.

———. *A History of the American Bar.* Boston: Little, Brown, 1911.

———. *History of the Harvard Law School and of Early Legal Conditions in America.* 3 vols. New York: Lewis Publishing, 1908.

———. *The Making of the Constitution.* Boston: Little, Brown, 1937.

———. *The Supreme Court in United States History.* 2 vols. Boston: Little, Brown, 1926.

White, G. Edward. *Intervention and Detachment: Essays in Legal History and Jurisprudence.* New York: Oxford University Press, 1994.

———. *Patterns of American Legal Thought.* Indianapolis: Bobbs-Merrill, 1978.

————. *Tort Law in America: An Intellectual History*. New York: Oxford University Press, 1980.

White, G. Edward, with the aid of Gerald Gunther. *The Marshall Court and Cultural Change*. Vols. 3 and 4 of *Oliver Wendell Holmes Devise History of the Supreme Court of the United States*. New York: Macmillan, 1988.

Wiecek, William M. *Liberty Under Law: The Supreme Court in American Life*. Baltimore: Johns Hopkins University Press, 1988.

TREATISES AND TEXTBOOKS

Baldwin, Henry. *A General View of the Origin and Nature of the Constitution and Government of the United States*. 1837. Reprint, New York: Da Capo Press, 1970.

Bledsoe, Albert Taylor. *Is Jeff Davis a Traitor: Or Was Secession a Constitutional Right?* Richmond, Va.: Hermitage Press, 1907.

Brownson, Orestes. *The American Republic*. New York: O'Shea, 1865.

Chipman, Nathaniel. *Principles of Government: A Treatise on Free Institutions, Including the Constitution*. Burlington, Vt.: Edward Smith, 1833.

Cooley, Thomas M. *The General Principles of Constitutional Law in the United States of America*. 3d ed. Boston: Little, Brown, 1898.

————. *A Treatise on the Constitutional Limitations Which Rest upon the Legislative Power of the States of the American Union*. Boston: Little, Brown, 1868.

————. *A Treatise on the Law of Torts, or the Wrongs Which Arise Independent of Contract*. Chicago: Callaghan, 1880.

Cooper, Thomas. *Two Essays: 1. On the Foundation of Civil Government; 2. On the Constitution of the United States*. Columbia, S.C.: Faust, 1826.

Corbin, Arthur L. *Corbin on Contracts: A Comprehensive Treatise on the Rules of Contract Law*. 7 vols. St. Paul: West Publishing, 1950–51.

Corwin, Edward S., et al., eds. *The Constitution of the United States: Analysis and Interpretation*. Washington, D.C.: U.S. Government Printing Office, 1973 (and suppls.).

Dane, Nathan. *A General Abridgement and Digest of American Law*. 9 vols. Boston: Cummings, Hilliard, 1823–29.

Duer, William Alexander. *A Course of Lectures on the Constitutional Jurisprudence of the United States*. New York: Harper and Brothers, 1843.

DuPonceau, Peter. *A Brief View of the Constitution of the United States*. Philadelphia: E. G. Dorsey, 1834.

Gray, John Chipman. *The Nature and Sources of the Law*. New York: Columbia University Press, 1909.

Gunther, Gerald. *Cases and Materials on Constitutional Law.* 10th ed. Mineola, N.Y.: Foundation Press, 1980.

Hamilton, Alexander, John Jay and James Madison. *The Federalist.* New York: 1788, with numerous later editions.

Hoffman, David. *A Course of Legal Study, Addressed to Students and the Profession Generally.* 2d ed. 2 vols. in 1. Philadelphia: Thomas, Cowperthwait, 1846. Reprint, Buffalo: W. S. Hein, 1968.

————. *Legal Outlines.* Baltimore: J. Neal, 1836.

Jameson, John Alexander. *A Treatise on Constitutional Conventions.* Chicago: Callaghan, 1887.

Kent, James. *Commentaries on American Law.* 4 vols. 1826. Reprint, Buffalo: W. S. Hein, 1984.

Pomeroy, John Norton. *An Introduction to the Constitutional Law of the United States.* 5th ed., rev. and enl. Boston: Houghton, Osgood, 1880.

————. *Remedies and Remedial Rights by Civil Action.* Boston: Little, Brown, 1876.

Pritchett, C. Herman. *The American Constitution.* New York: McGraw-Hill, 1968.

Rawle, William. *A View of the Constitution of the United States of America.* Philadelphia: Philip Nicklin, 1829.

Stephens, Alexander H. *A Constitutional View of the Late War Between the States.* 2 vols. Philadelphia: National Publishing, 1868.

Story, Joseph. *Commentaries on the Conflict of Laws, Foreign and Domestic.* Boston: Little, Brown, 1834.

————. *Commentaries on the Constitution of the United States.* 3 vols. Boston: Hilliard, Gray, 1833.

————. *Commentaries on Equity Jurisprudence.* 2 vols. Boston: Little, Brown, 1836.

Taylor, John. *Construction Construed, and Constitutions Vindicated.* Richmond, Va.: Shepherd and Pollard, 1820.

————. *An Inquiry into the Principles and Policy of the Government of the United States.* Fredericksburg, Va.: Green and Cady, 1814.

————. *New Views of the Constitution of the United States.* Washington City: Way and Gideon, 1823.

Tribe, Lawrence H. *American Constitutional Law.* 2d ed. Mineola, N.Y.: Foundation Press, 1988.

Tucker, St. George. "View of the Constitution." Appendix to *Blackstone's Commentaries: with Notes of Reference. . . .* 5 vols. Philadelphia: Birch and Small, 1803.

Tucker, John Randolph. *The Constitution of the United States: A Critical Discussion of Its Genesis, Development, and Interpretation.* 2 vols. Chicago: Callaghan, 1899.

Upshur, Abel Parker. *A Brief Enquiry into the Nature and Character of Our Federal Government: Being a Review of Judge Story's "Commentaries on the Constitution."* Petersburg, Va.: Edmund and Julian Ruffin, 1840.

Wigmore, John Henry. *The Principles of Judicial Proof.* Boston: Little, Brown, 1913.

————. *Treatise on the Anglo-American System of Evidence in Trials at Common Law.* 10 vols. Boston: Little, Brown, 1940.

Williston, Samuel A. *The Law Governing Sales of Goods at Common Law and Under the Uniform Sales Act.* Rev. ed. 4 vols. New York: Baker, Voorhis, 1948.

————. *A Treatise on the Law of Contracts.* Rev. ed. 9 vols. New York: Baker, Voorhis, 1936–45.

Autobiographies and Biographies

GENERAL

Macdonnell, John, and Edward Manson. *Great Jurists of the World.* 1914. Reprint, South Hackensack, N.J.: Rothman Reprints, 1968.

Seagle, William. *Men of Law: From Hammurabi to Holmes.* New York: Macmillan, 1947.

CLASSICAL

Cicero: Robert N. Wilken. *Eternal Lawyer: A Legal Biography of Cicero.* New York: Macmillan, 1947; Franz Wieacker, *Cicero als Advokat.* Berlin: Walter de Gruyter, 1965.

Gaius: Anthony M. Honoré. *Gaius.* Oxford: Oxford University Press, 1962.

Justinian: John Barker. *Justinian and the Later Roman Empire.* Madison: University of Wisconsin Press, 1966; John Moorhead. *Justinian.* London: Longman, 1994.

Tribonian: Anthony M. Honoré. *Tribonian.* Ithaca: Cornell University Press, 1978.

Ulpian: Anthony M. Honoré. *Ulpian.* Oxford University Press: 1982.

MEDIEVAL

General: J. A. Clarence Smith. *Medieval Law Teachers and Writers.* Ottawa: University of Ottawa Press, 1975.

Bartolus: C. N. S. Woolf. *Bartolus of Sassoferrato: His Position in the History of Medieval Political Thought.* Cambridge: Cambridge University Press, 1913; Joseph H. Beale, trans. *Bartolus on the Conflict of Laws.* Westport, Conn.: Hyperion Press, 1979.

Huguccio: Wolfgang P. Müller. *Huguccio: The Life, Works, and Thought of a Twelfth-Century Jurist.* Washington, D.C.: Catholic University of America Press, 1994.

Innocent III: Jane E. Sayers. *Innocent III: Leader of Europe, 1198–1216.* London: Longmans, 1994; James M. Powell, ed. *Innocent III: Vicar of Christ or Lord of the World?* 2d, expanded ed. Washington, D.C.: Catholic University of America Press, 1994.

Innocent IV: Alberto Melloni. *Innocenzo IV: la concezione e l'esperienza della cristianità come regimen unius personae.* Genoa: Marietti, 1990.

HUMANIST

General: Robert Feenstra. *Seventeenth-Century Leyden Law Professors and Their Influence on the Development of the Civil Law: A Study of Bronchorst, Vinnius, and Voet.* Amsterdam: North-Holland Publishing, 1975.

Cantiuncula, Claudius: Guido Kisch. *Claudius Cantiuncula: Ein Basler Jurist und Humanist des 16. Jahrhundert.* Basel: Helbing und Lichtenhahn, 1960.

Gentili, Alberico: Gesina H. J. van der Molen. *Alberico Gentili and the Development of International Law: His Life, Work, and Times.* 2d rev. ed. Leyden: A. W. Sijthoff, 1968.

Grotius, Hugo: Edward Dumbauld. *The Life and Legal Writings of Hugo Grotius.* Norman: University of Oklahoma, 1969; Charles S. Edwards. *Hugo Grotius, the Miracle of Holland: A Study in Political and Legal Thought.* Chicago: Nelson-Hall, 1981; R. W. Lee. *Hugo Grotius.* London: H. Milford, 1930; and Hedley Bull, Benedict Kingsbury, and Adam Roberts, eds. *Hugo Grotius and International Relations.* New York: Oxford University Press, 1990.

Zasius, Ulrich: Steven Rowan. *Ulrich Zasius: A Jurist in the German Renaissance, 1461–1535.* Frankfurt am Main: V. Klostermann, 1987; Joseph Neff. *Udalricus Zasius: Ein Beitrag zur Geschichte des Humanismus am Oberrhein.* 2 vols. Freiburg: Lehmann, 1890–91.

ENGLISH

General Biographical References

Campbell, John Lord. *Lives of the Lord Chancellors and Keepers of the Great Seal of England.* 8 vols. London: John Murray, 1846–69.

———. *The Lives of the Chief Justices of England.* 3 vols. London: John Murray, 1849–57.

Fifoot, C. H. S. *Judge and Jurist in the Reign of Victoria.* London: Stevens, 1959.

Holdsworth, William S. *The Historians of Anglo-American Law.* New York: Columbia University Press, 1928.

———. *Some Makers of English Law.* Cambridge: Cambridge University Press, 1938.

Shientag, Bernard L. *Moulders of Legal Thought.* 1943. Reprint, Port Washington, N.Y.: Kennikat Press, 1968.

Simpson, A. W. B. *Biographical Dictionary of the Common Law.* London: Butterworths, 1984.

Biographies of Leading Figures

Bacon, Francis: Catherine Drinker Bowen. *Francis Bacon: The Temper of a Man.* Boston: Little, Brown, 1963; Daniel Coquillette. *Francis Bacon.* Stanford, Calif.: Stanford University Press, 1992.

Bentham, Jeremy: Gerald J. Postema. *Bentham and the Common Law Tradition.* Oxford: Oxford University Press, 1986.

Blackstone, William: David A. Lockmiller. *Sir William Blackstone.* Chapel Hill: University of North Carolina Press, 1938; Lewis C. Warden. *The Life of Blackstone.* Charlottesville, Va.: Michie Company, 1938; and Daniel J. Boorstin. *The Mysterious Science of the Law.* Cambridge: Harvard University Press, 1941.

Brougham, Lord: Robert Stewart. *Henry Brougham, 1778–1868: His Public Career.* London: Bodley Head, 1985.

Coke, Edward: Catherine Drinker Bowen. *The Lion and the Throne: The Life and Times of Sir Edward Coke (1552–1634).* Boston: Little, Brown, 1956; Walter Hastings Lyon. *Edward Coke, Oracle of Law.* Boston: Houghton, Mifflin, 1929; Humphry W. Woolrych. *The Life of the Right Honorable Sir Edward Coke Knt., Lord Chief Justice of the King's Bench.* London: J. and W. T. Clarke, 1826. Reprint, South Hackensack, N.J.: Rothman Reprints, 1972; James Stoner. *Common Law and Liberal Theory: Coke, Hobbes, and the Origins of American Constitutionalism.* Lawrence: University Press of Kansas, 1992; and Steven D. White, *Sir Edward Coke and "The Grievances of the Commonwealth," 1621–1628.* Chapel Hill: University of North Carolina Press, 1979.

Dicey, Albert Venn: Richard A. Cosgrove. *The Rule of Law: Albert Venn Dicey, Victorian Jurist.* Chapel Hill: University of North Carolina Press, 1980.

Eldon, Lord: Horace Twiss. *The Public and Private Life of Lord Chancellor Eldon.* 3 vols. London: John Murray, 1844.

Erskine, Thomas: Lloyd Paul Stryker, *For the Defence: Thomas Erskine, the Most Enlightened Liberal of His Times, 1750–1823.* New York: Doubleday, 1949.

Hale, Matthew: Edmund Heward. *Matthew Hale.* London: Robert Hale, 1972; Alan Cromartie, *Sir Matthew Hale, 1609–1676: Law, Religion, and Natural Philosophy.* Cambridge: Cambridge University Press, 1995; and Gilbert Burnet, *The Life and Death of Sir Matthew Hale, Knt.* 1682. Reprint, South Hackensack, N.J.: Rothman Reprints, 1972.

Hardwicke, Lord: George Harris. *The Life of Lord Chancellor Hardwicke: With Selections from His Correspondence, Diaries, and Speeches.* 3 vols. London: E. Moxon, 1847.

Jeffreys, George: P. J. Helm. *Jeffreys: A New Portrait of England's Hanging Judge.* New York: Thomas Y. Crowell, 1966; H. B. Irving. *The Life of Judge Jeffreys.* London: William Heinemann, 1898.

Kebell, Thomas: E. W. Ives. *The Common Lawyers of Pre-Reformation England: Thomas Kebell, a Case Study.* Cambridge: Cambridge University Press, 1983.

Maine, Henry Sumner: Raymond Cocks. *Sir Henry Maine: A Study in Victorian Jurisprudence.* Cambridge: Cambridge University Press, 1988; Alan Diamond, ed., *The Victorian Achievement of Sir Henry Maine: A Centennial Reappraisal.* Cambridge: Cambridge University Press, 1991.

Maitland, Frederic William: Geoffrey Elton. *F. W. Maitland.* New Haven: Yale University Press, 1985; C. H. S. Fifoot. *Frederic William Maitland: A Life.* Cambridge: Harvard University Press, 1971; James R. Cameron, *Frederic William Maitland and the History of English Law.* Norman: University of Oklahoma Press, 1961; and H. A. L. Fisher. *Frederic William Maitland, Downing Professor of the Laws of England: A Biographical Sketch.* Cambridge: Cambridge University Press, 1910.

Mansfield, Lord: C. H. S. Fifoot. *Lord Mansfield.* 1936. Reprint, Aalen: Scientia Verlag, 1977; James Oldham. *The Mansfield Manuscripts and the Growth of English Law in the Eighteenth Century.* 2 vols. Chapel Hill: University of North Carolina Press, 1992.

More, Thomas: J. A. Guy. *The Public Career of Sir Thomas More.* New Haven: Yale University Press, 1980; Richard Marius. *Thomas More: A Biography.* New York: Knopf, 1984.

Plowden, Edmund: Geoffrey de C. Parmiter. *Edmund Plowden: An Elizabethan Recusant Lawyer.* Southampton, U.K.: Catholic Record Society, 1987.

Romilly, Samuel: Patrick Medd. *Romilly: A Life of Sir Samuel Romilly, Lawyer and Reformer.* London: Collins, 1968; G. C. Oakes. *Sir Samuel Romilly, 1757–1818: "The Friend of the Oppressed."* London: George Allen and Unwin, 1935.

Selden, John: David Sandler Berkowitz, *John Selden's Formative Years: Politics and Society in Early Seventeenth-Century England.* Washington, D.C.: Folger Shakespeare Library, 1988.

Staunton, Harvey de: George W. Keeton. *Harvey the Hasty: A. Mediaeval Chief Justice.* Chichester, England: Rose, 1978.

AMERICAN

General Biographical References

Bryson, W. Hamilton. *Legal Education in Virginia: A Biographical Approach, 1779–1979.* Charlottesville: University Press of Virginia, 1982.

Friedman, Leon, and Fred L. Israel, eds. *The Justices of the United States Supreme Court: Their Lives and Major Opinions.* 5 vols. New York: Chelsea House Publishers, 1995.

Goodhart, Arthur L. *Five Jewish Lawyers of the Common Law.* Oxford: Oxford University Press, 1949.

Lewis, William Draper, ed. *Great American Lawyers.* 8 vols. Philadelphia: John C. Winston, 1907–9.

Noonan, John T. *Persons and Masks of the Law: Cardozo, Holmes, Jefferson, and Wythe as Makers of the Masks.* New York: Farrar, Straus, and Giroux, 1976.

White, G. Edward. *The American Judicial Tradition: Profiles of Leading American Judges.* New York: Oxford University Press, 1988.

Biographies of Leading Figures

Beck, James Montgomery: Morton Keller. *In Defense of Yesterday: James M. Beck and the Politics of Conservatism, 1861–1936.* New York: Coward-McCann, 1958.

Black, Hugo: Roger K. Newman. *Hugo Black: A Biography.* New York: Pantheon Books, 1994; Gerald T. Dunne. *Hugo Black and the Judicial Revolution.* New York: Simon and Schuster, 1977; Hugo Black, Jr. *My Father, A Remembrance.* New York: Random House, 1975; and Howard Ball. *Hugo L. Black: Cold Steel Warrior.* New York: Oxford University Press, 1996.

Brandeis, Louis D.: Stephen W. Baskerville. *Of Laws and Limitations: An Intellectual Portrait of Louis Dembitz Brandeis.* London: Associated University Presses, 1994; Alpheus T. Mason. *Brandeis: A Free Man's Life*. New York: Viking Press, 1946; Lewis J. Paper. *Brandeis*. Englewood Cliffs, N.J.: Prentice Hall, 1983; and Philippa Strum. *Louis D. Brandeis: Justice for the People*. Cambridge: Harvard University Press, 1984.

Cardozo, Benjamin: Beryl Harold Levy. *Cardozo and the Frontiers of Legal Thinking*. Rev. ed. Cleveland: Press of Case Western Reserve University, 1969; George Sidney Hellman. *Benjamin Cardozo, American Judge*. New York: McGraw-Hill, 1940; and Richard A. Posner. *Cardozo: A Study in Reputation*. Chicago: University of Chicago Press, 1990.

Chase, Salmon: Albert Bushnell Hart. *Salmon Portland Chase*. New York: Houghton Mifflin, 1899; John Niven. *Salmon P. Chase: A Biography*. New York: Oxford University Press, 1995; and J. W. Schuckers. *Life and Public Services of Salmon Portland Chase*. New York: D. Appleton, 1874.

Chase, Samuel: James Haw, et al. *Stormy Patriot: The Life of Samuel Chase*. Baltimore: Maryland Historical Society, 1980.

Davis, John W.: William Henry Harbaugh. *Lawyer's Lawyer: The Life of John W. Davis*. New York: Oxford University Press, 1973.

Doe, Charles: John Phillip Reid. *Chief Justice: The Judicial World of Charles Doe*. Cambridge: Harvard University Press, 1967.

Douglas, William O.: William O. Douglas. *Go East Young Man: The Early Years*. New York: Random House, 1974; William O. Douglas. *The Court Years, 1939–1975*. New York: Random House, 1980.

Ellsworth, Oliver: William Garrott Brown. *The Life of Oliver Ellsworth*. New York: Macmillan, 1905.

Field, David Dudley: Daun van Ee. *David Dudley Field and the Reconstruction of the Law*. New York: Garland Publishing, 1986; Henry M. Field. *The Life of David Dudley Field*. New York: Charles Scribner's Sons, 1898.

Field, Stephen: Carl B. Swisher. *Stephen J. Field: Craftsman of the Law*. Chicago: University of Chicago Press, 1930.

Frank, Jerome: Robert Jerome Glennon. *The Iconoclast as Reformer: Jerome Frank's Impact on American Law*. Ithaca: Cornell University Press, 1985; J. Mitchell Rosenberg. *Jerome Frank; Jurist and Philosopher*. New York: Philosophical Library, 1970.

Frankfurter, Felix: H. N. Hirsch. *The Enigma of Felix Frankfurter*. New York: Basic Books, 1981; Philip B. Kurland. *Mr. Justice Frankfurter and the Constitution*. Chicago: University of Chicago Press, 1971; and Liva Baker. *Felix Frankfurter*. New York: Coward-McCann, 1969.

Fuller, Lon L.: Robert S. Summers. *Lon L. Fuller*. Stanford, Calif.: Stanford University Press, 1984.

Fuller, Melville W.: Willard L. King. *Melville Weston Fuller, Chief Justice of the United States, 1888–1910.* New York: Macmillan, 1950; James W. Ely, Jr. *The Chief Justiceship of Melville W. Fuller, 1888–1910.* Columbia: University of South Carolina Press, 1995.

Griswold, Erwin: Erwin Griswold. *Ould Fields, New Corne: The Personal Memoirs of a Twentieth Century Lawyer.* St. Paul, Minn.: West Publishing, 1992.

Hand, Learned: Gerald Gunther. *Learned Hand: The Man and the Judge.* New York: Knopf, 1994.

Harlan, John Marshall (elder): Tinsley E. Yarbrough. *Judicial Enigma: The First Justice Harlan.* New York: Oxford University Press, 1995.

Harlan, John Marshall (younger): Tinsley E. Yarbrough. *John Marshall Harlan: Great Dissenter of the Warren Court.* New York: Oxford University Press, 1992.

Holmes, Oliver Wendell: G. Edward White. *Justice Oliver Wendell Holmes: Law and the Inner Self.* Oxford: Oxford University Press, 1993; Liva Baker. *The Justice from Beacon Hill: The Life and Times of Oliver Wendell Holmes.* New York: HarperCollins, 1991; Sheldon M. Novick. *Honorable Justice: The Life of Oliver Wendell Holmes.* Boston: Little, Brown, 1989; Mark De Wolfe Howe. *Justice Oliver Wendell Holmes.* Cambridge: Harvard University Press, 1957; Catherine Drinker Bowen. *Yankee from Olympus: Justice Holmes and His Family.* Boston: Little, Brown, 1944; David Rosenberg, *The Hidden Holmes: His Theory of Torts in History.* Cambridge: Harvard University Press, 1995; H. L. Pohlman, *Justice Oliver Wendell Holmes and Utilitarian Jurisprudence.* Cambridge: Harvard University Press, 1984; Benjamin Kaplan, Patrick Atiyah, and Jan Vetter. *Holmes and the Common Law: A Century Later: Three Lectures.* Cambridge: Harvard University Press, 1983; James Willard Hurst. *Justice Holmes on Legal History.* New York: Macmillan, 1964; and Felix Frankfurter. *Mr. Justice Holmes and the Supreme Court.* Cambridge: Harvard University Press, 1938.

Hughes, Charles Evans: Merlo J. Pusey. *Charles Evans Hughes.* 2 vols. New York: Macmillan, 1951; Samuel Hendel. *Charles Evans Hughes and the Supreme Court.* New York: King's Crown Press, 1951.

Johnson, William: Donald G. Morgan. *Justice William Johnson, the First Dissenter: The Career and Constitutional Philosophy of a Jeffersonian Judge.* Columbia: University of South Carolina Press, 1954.

Llewyllyn, Karl: William Twining. *Karl Llewyllyn and the Realist Movement.* London: Weidenfeld and Nicolson, 1973.

Marshall, John: Albert J. Beveridge. *The Life of John Marshall.* 4 vols. Boston: Little, Brown, 1919; Leonard Baker, *John Marshall: A Life in Law.* New York: Macmillan, 1974; Charles F. Hobson. *The Great Chief Justice: John Marshall and the Rule of Law.* Lawrence: University Press of Kansas, 1996; Jean Edward Smith. *John Marshall: Definer of a Nation.* New York: Henry Holt, 1996; Frances Howell Rudko. *John Marshall and International Law: Statesman and Chief Justice.* Westport, Conn.: Greenwood Press, 1991; William Finley Swindler. *The Constitution and Chief Justice Marshall.* New York: Dodd, Mead, 1978; Gerald Gunther, ed. *John Marshall's Defense of McCulloch v. Maryland.* Stanford, Calif.: Stanford University Press, 1969; Robert K. Faulkner, *The Jurisprudence of John Marshall.* Princeton: Princeton University Press, 1968; *James Bradley Thayer, Oliver Wendell Holmes, and Felix Frankfurter on John Marshall, with a Contribution by Mark De Wolfe Howe.* Chicago: University of Chicago Press, 1967; Benjamin Munn Ziegler. *The International Law of John Marshall: A Study of First Principles.* Chapel Hill: University of North Carolina Press, 1939; and Edward S. Corwin. *John Marshall and the Constitution: A Chronicle of the Supreme Court.* New Haven: Yale University Press, 1921.

Marshall, Thurgood: Michael D. Davis and Hunter R. Clark. *Thurgood Marshall: Warrior at the Bar, Rebel on the Bench.* New York: Birch Lane Press, 1992; Roger Goldman with David Gallen. *Thurgood Marshall: Justice for All.* New York: Carroll and Graf Publishers, 1992.

Miller, Samuel Freeman: Charles Fairman. *Mr. Justice Miller and the Supreme Court, 1862–1890.* Cambridge: Harvard University Press, 1939.

Murphy, Frank: J. Woodford Howard. *Mr. Justice Murphy.* Princeton: Princeton University Press, 1968.

Parsons, Theophilus: Theophilus Parsons, Jr. *Memoir of Chief Justice Parsons.* Boston: Ticknor and Fields, 1859.

Paterson, William: John E. O'Connor. *William Paterson: Lawyer and Statesman, 1745–1806.* New Brunswick, N.J.: Rutgers University Press, 1979.

Pinkney, William: Robert M. Ireland. *The Legal Career of William Pinkney, 1764–1822.* London: Garland Publishing, 1986.

Pound, Roscoe: Edward B. McLean. *Law and Civilization: The Legal Thought of Roscoe Pound.* Lanham, Md.: University Press of America, 1992.

Powell, Lewis F.: John Calvin Jeffries. *Justice Lewis F. Powell, Jr.* New York: Charles Scribner's Sons, 1994.

Roane, Spencer: Margaret E. Horsnell. *Spencer Roane: Judicial Advocate of Jeffersonian Principles.* New York: Garland Publishing, 1986.

Root, Elihu: Philip C. Jessup, *Elihu Root*. 2 vols. 1938. Reprint, Hamden, Conn.: Archon Books, 1964.

Shaw, Lemuel: Leonard W. Levy. *The Law of the Commonwealth and Chief Justice Shaw*. New York: Oxford University Press, 1957; Frederick Hathaway Chase. *Lemuel Shaw: Chief Justice of the Supreme Judicial Court of Massachusetts, 1830–1860*. Boston: Houghton, Mifflin, 1918.

Stone, Harlan Fiske: Alpheus T. Mason. *Harlan Fiske Stone: Pillar of the Law*. New York: Viking Press, 1953; Samuel J. Konefsky. *Chief Justice Stone and the Supreme Court*. New York: Macmillan, 1946.

Story, Joseph: R. Kent Newmyer. *Supreme Court Justice Joseph Story: Statesman of the Old Republic*. Chapel Hill: University of North Carolina Press, 1985; James McClellan. *Joseph Story and the American Constitution: A Study in Political and Legal Thought*. Norman: University of Oklahoma Press, 1971; and Gerald T. Dunne. *Justice Joseph Story and the Rise of the Supreme Court*. New York: Knopf, 1970.

Sutherland, George: John Francis Paschal. *Mr. Justice Sutherland: A Man Against the State*. Princeton: Princeton University Press, 1951; Hadley Arkes. *The Return of George Sutherland: Restoring a Jurisprudence of Natural Rights*. Princeton: Princeton University Press, 1994.

Taft, William Howard: Alpheus T. Mason. *William Howard Taft: Chief Justice*. New York: Simon and Schuster, 1964.

Taney, Roger: Carl B. Swisher. *Roger B. Taney*. New York: Macmillan, 1935.

Tucker, St. George: Charles T. Cullen. *St. George Tucker and Law in Virginia, 1772–1804*. New York: Garland Publishing, 1987.

Waite, Morrison: C. Peter Magrath. *Morrison R. Waite: The Triumph of Character*. New York: Macmillan, 1963; Bruce R. Trimble. *Chief Justice Waite: Defender of the Public Interest*. Princeton: Princeton University Press, 1938.

Warren, Earl: Bernard Schwartz. *Superchief, Earl Warren and His Supreme Court: A Judicial Biography*. New York: New York University Press, 1983; G. Edward White. *Earl Warren, a Public Life*. New York: Oxford University Press, 1982; and Earl Warren. *The Memoirs of Earl Warren*. Garden City, N.Y.: Doubleday, 1977.

Webster, Daniel: Maurice G. Baxter. *Daniel Webster and the Supreme Court*. Amherst: University of Massachusetts Press, 1966.

White, Edward Douglass: Robert B. Highsaw. *Edward Douglass White: Defender of the Conservative Faith*. Baton Rouge: Louisiana State University Press, 1981.

Wigmore, John Henry: William R. Roalfe. *John Henry Wigmore: Scholar and Reformer*. Evanston, Ill.: Northwestern University Press, 1977.

Williston, Samuel. *Life and Law: An Autobiography.* Boston: Little, Brown, 1940.

Wilson, James: Page Smith. *James Wilson, Founding Father, 1742–1798.* Chapel Hill: University of North Carolina Press, 1956; Robert Green McCloskey, ed. *The Works of James Wilson.* 2 vols. Cambridge: Harvard University Press, 1967.

Wythe, George: Robert B. Kirtland. *George Wythe: Lawyer, Revolutionary, Judge.* New York: Garland Publishing, 1986; Alonzo Thomas Dill. *George Wythe: Teacher of Liberty.* Williamsburg: Virginia Independence Bicentennial Commission, 1979.

Law of Nations

TREATISES

Ayala, Balthazar. *De Jure et Officiis et Disciplina Militari.* Ed. John Westlake. Trans. John Pawley Bate. 2 vols. Washington, D.C.: Carnegie Endowment for World Peace, 1912.

Belch, Stanislaus. *Paulus Vladimiri and His Doctrine Concerning International Law and Politics.* 2 vols. The Hague: Mouton, 1965.

Brierly, J. L. *Law of Nations.* 4th ed. Oxford: Oxford University Press, 1949.

Burlamaqui, Jean Jacques. *The Principles of Natural and Politic Law.* 7th ed. Trans. Thomas Nugent. 2 vols. Philadelphia: P. H. Nicklin and T. Johnson, 1832.

Bynkershoek, Cornelius. *De Domino Maris Dissertatio.* Trans. Ralph van Deman Magoffin. New York: Oxford University Press, 1923. Reprint, Buffalo: William S. Hein, 1995.

Falk, Richard A. *The Role of Domestic Courts in the International Legal Order.* Syracuse, N.Y.: Syracuse University Press, 1964.

———. *The Status of Law in International Society.* Princeton: Princeton University Press, 1970.

Gentili, Alberico. *Hispanicae Advocationis Libri Duo.* Ed. and trans. Frank Frost Abbott. 2 vols. Washington, D.C.: Carnegie Endowment for World Peace, 1921.

———. *De Jure Belli Libri Tres.* Ed. and trans. John C. Rolfe. 2 vols. Oxford: Oxford University Press, 1933.

———. *De Legationibus Libri Tres.* Trans. Gordon J. Laing. Washington, D.C.: Carnegie Endowment for World Peace, 1924.

Grotius, Hugo. *The Rights of War and Peace (De Jure Belli ac Pacis Libri Tres).* Trans. Francis W. Kelsey. Oxford: Oxford University Press, 1925. Reprint (2 vols. in 1), Buffalo: William S. Hein, 1995.

Hall, William E. *International Law*. 8th ed. Ed. Pierce Higgins. Oxford: Oxford University Press, 1880; Aalen: Scientia Verlag, 1979.

Holland, Thomas Erskine. *Studies in International Law*. Oxford: Oxford University Press, 1898.

Jessup, Philip C. *The Birth of Nations*. New York: Columbia University Press, 1974.

———. *A Modern Law of Nations: An Introduction*. 1948. Reprint, Hamden, Conn.: Archon Books, 1968.

———. *Neutrality: Its History, Economics, and Law*. 4 vols. New York: Columbia University Press, 1935–36.

———. *Transnational Law*. New Haven: Yale University Press, 1956.

———. *The Use of International Law: Five Lectures*. Ann Arbor: University of Michigan Press, 1958.

Kelsen, Hans. *Principles of International Law*. 2d ed. New York: Holt, Rinehart, and Winston, 1966.

Legnano, Giovanni da. *Tractatus De Bello, De Represaliis et De Duello*. Ed. and trans. Thomas Erskine Holland. Oxford: Oxford University Press, 1917.

McDougal, Myres S., Harold D. Lasswell, and James C. Miller. *The Interpretation of Agreements and World Public Order*. New Haven: Yale University Press, 1967.

Pufendorf, Samuel. *Elementorum Jurisprudentiae Universalis Libri Duo*. Trans. William Abbott Oldfather. 2 vols. Oxford: Oxford University Press, 1931.

———. *De jure naturae et gentium*. Oxford: Oxford University Press, 1934.

———. *De Officio Hominis et Civis Libri Duo*. Trans. Frank Gardner Moore. 2 vols. Oxford: Oxford University Press, 1927.

Rutherforth, Thomas. *Institutes of Natural Law: Being the Substance of a Course of Lectures on Grotius's "De Jure Belli et Pacis."* 2d American ed. Baltimore: William and Joseph Neal, 1832.

Savigny, Friedrich Karl von. *A Treatise on the Conflict of Laws*. Trans. William Guthrie. Edinburgh: T. and T. Clarke, 1880.

Suárez, Francisco. *Selections from Three Works of Francisco Suárez, S.J.* Trans. Gwladys Williams, Ammi Brown, and John Waldron. 2 vols. Oxford: Oxford University Press, 1944.

Vattel, Emmerich de. *The Law of Nations; or Principles of the Law of Nature*. 5th American ed. Ed. Joseph Chitty. Philadelphia: T. and J. W. Johnson, 1839.

Vitoria, Francisco de. *De indis et de iure belli relectiones*. Ed. Ernest Nys. Washington, D.C.: Carnegie Endowment for World Peace, 1916.

———. *Political Writings*. Ed. and trans. Anthony Pagden and Jeremy Lawrance. Cambridge: Cambridge University Press, 1991.

Wheaton, Henry. *Elements of International Law.* 6th ed. Ed. William Beach Lawrence. Boston: Little, Brown, 1855.

Wolff, Christian. *Jus Gentium Methodo Scientifica Pertractatum.* Trans. Joseph H. Drake. 2 vols. Oxford: Oxford University Press, 1934.

Wright, Quincy. *International Law and the United Nations.* Westport, Conn.: Greenwood Press, 1976.

HISTORY OF THE LAW OF NATIONS

Butler, Geoffrey, and Simon Maccoby. *The Development of International Law.* London: Longmans, Green, 1928.

Kaltenborn, Carl von. *Die Vorläufer des Hugo Grotius auf dem Gebiete des Ius naturae et gentium sowie der Politik im Reformationszeitalter.* Leipzig: Mayer, 1848.

Nussbaum, Arthur. *A Concise History of the Law of Nations.* Rev. ed. New York: Macmillan, 1954.

Russell, Frederick H. *The Just War in the Middle Ages.* Cambridge: Cambridge University Press, 1975.

Vanderpol, Alfred. *La doctrine scolastique du droit de guerre.* Paris: A. Pedone, 1919.

Verzijl, J. H. W. *International Law in Historical Perspective.* 11 vols. Leyden and Dordrecht: A. W. Sijthoff (vols. 1–10); Martinus Nijhoff (vol. 11), 1968–92.

Treatises and Casebooks on Legal History

Berman, Harold J., William Greiner, and Samir N. Saliba. *The Nature and Functions of Law.* 5th ed. Westbury, N.Y.: Foundation Press, 1996.

Goebel, Julius, Jr. *Cases and Materials on the Development of Legal Institutions.* Brattleboro, Vt.: Vermont Printing, 1946.

Hall, Kermit, William Wiecek, and Paul Finkelman, eds. *American Legal History: Cases and Materials.* 2d ed. New York: Oxford University Press, 1996.

Howe, Mark De Wolfe, ed. *Readings in American Legal History.* Cambridge: Harvard University Press, 1949.

Kimball, Spencer L., ed. *Historical Introduction to the Legal System.* St. Paul, Minn.: West Publishing, 1966.

Merryman, John Henry, David S. Clark, and John O. Haley, eds. *The Civil Law Tradition: Europe, Latin America, and East Asia.* Charlottesville, Va.: Michie, 1994.

Plucknett, T. F. T., and Roscoe Pound, eds. *Readings on the History and System of the Common Law.* 3d ed. Holmes Beach, Fla.: William W. Gaunt and Sons, 1993.

Presser, Stephen B., and Jamil S. Zainaldin, eds. *Law and Jurisprudence in American History: Cases and Materials.* St. Paul, Minn.: West Publishing, 1989.

Radin, Max. *Handbook of Anglo-American Legal History.* 1936. Reprint, Holmes Beach, Fla.: William W. Gaunt, 1993.

Smith, Joseph H., ed. *Cases and Materials on the Development of Legal Institutions.* St. Paul, Minn.: West Publishing, 1965.

von Mehren, Arthur Taylor, and James Russell Gordley, eds. *The Civil Law System: An Introduction to the Comparative Study of Law.* 2d ed. Boston: Little, Brown, 1977.

INDEX

This book is set in Ehrhardt, a typeface produced by
Monotype in 1938. Ehrhardt is a Dutch Old Face similar
to Janson. It is based on a type design by Miklós Kis,
a Hungarian who worked in Amsterdam in the late
seventeenth century.

Printed on paper that is acid-free and meets the
requirements of the American National Standard for
Permanence of Paper for Printed Library
Materials, Z39.48-1992. ∞

Book design by Erin Kirk New, Athens, Georgia
Typography by Douglas & Gayle Ltd., Indianapolis, Indiana
Printed and bound by Worzalla Publishing Company,
Stevens Point, Wisconsin

14